Open Internet Law Casebook

Volume II

Michael Risch

Villanova University School of Law

Table of Contents

[1] Note: Each set of readings is designed for a 13 week course, 1.5 credit hours per class, for a total of twenty-six.

Multi-Class Topic: <u>OIL Casebook Topic VI: Copyright Intro</u>

Class 11: 6.1 <u>OIL Casebook: Intro to Copyright</u>

Intellectual Property and the National Information Infrastructure (1995) - Excerpts on Copyright Subject Matter

September 21, 2014 by mrisch

1

INTELLECTUAL PROPERTY

AND THE

NATIONAL INFORMATION INFRASTRUCTURE

THE REPORT OF THE WORKING GROUP ON INTELLECTUAL PROPERTY RIGHTS

BRUCE A. LEHMAN

Assistant Secretary of Commerce and

Commissioner of Patents and Trademarks

CHAIR

INFORMATION INFRASTRUCTURE TASK FORCE

23   *RONALD H. BROWN*

24   *Secretary of Commerce*

25   *CHAIR*

26

27   SEPTEMBER 1995

28

29   http://www.uspto.gov/web/offices/com/doc/ipnii/
30
31   2. Subject Matter and Scope of Protection

32   a. Eligibility for Protection

33   The subject matter eligible for protection under the Copyright Act is set forth in Section 102(a):

34   Copyright protection subsists . . . in original works of authorship fixed in any tangible medium of expression, now known or later developed, from which they can be perceived, reproduced, or otherwise communicated, either directly or with the aid of a machine or device.[1]

35   From this provision, the courts have derived three basic requirements for copyright protection -- originality, creativity and fixation.[2]

36   The requirements of originality and creativity are derived from the statutory qualification that copyright protection extends only to "original works of authorship."[3] To be original, a work merely must be one of independent creation -- *i.e.*, not copied from another. There is no requirement that the work be novel (as in patent law), unique or ingenious. To be creative, there must only be a modicum of creativity. The level required is exceedingly low; "even a slight amount will suffice."[4]

37   The final requirement for copyright protection is fixation in a tangible medium of expression. Protection attaches automatically to an eligible work of authorship the moment the work is sufficiently fixed.[5] A work is fixed "when its embodiment in a copy or phonorecord . . . is sufficiently permanent or stable to permit it to be perceived, reproduced, or otherwise communicated for a period of more than transitory duration."[6]

38   Congress provided considerable room for technological advances in the area of fixation by noting that the method of fixation in copies or phonorecords may be "now known or later developed."[7] The Copyright Act divides the possible media for fixation into "copies" and "phonorecords":

39   "Copies" are material objects, other than phonorecords, in which a work is fixed by any method now known or later developed, and from which the work can be perceived, reproduced, or otherwise communicated, either directly or with the aid of a machine or device.[8]

40   "Phonorecords" are material objects in which sounds, other than those accompanying a motion picture or other audiovisual work, are fixed by any method now known or later developed, and from which the sounds can be perceived, reproduced, or otherwise communicated, either directly or with the aid of a machine or device.[9]

41   According to the House Report accompanying the Copyright Act of 1976, Congress intended the terms "copies" and "phonorecords" to "comprise all of the material objects in which copyrightable works are capable of being fixed."[10]

42   The form of the fixation and the manner, method or medium used are virtually unlimited. A work may be fixed in "words, numbers, notes, sounds, pictures, or any other graphic or symbolic indicia"; may be embodied in a physical object in "written, printed, photographic, sculptural, punched, magnetic, or any other stable form"; and may be capable of perception either "directly or by means of any machine or device 'now known or later developed.'"[11]

43   In digital form, a work is generally recorded (fixed) as a sequence of binary digits (zeros and ones) using media specific encoding. This fits within the House Report's list of permissible manners of fixation.[12] Virtually all works also will be fixed in acceptable material objects -- *i.e.*, copies or phonorecords. For instance, floppy disks, compact discs (CDs), CD-ROMs, optical disks, compact discs-interactive (CD-Is), digital tape, and other digital storage devices are all stable forms in which works may be fixed and from which works may be perceived, reproduced or communicated by means of a machine or device.[13]

44   The question of whether interactive works are fixed (given the user's ability to constantly alter the sequence of the "action") has been resolved by the courts in the context of video games and should not present a new issue in the context of the NII. Such works are generally considered sufficiently fixed to qualify for protection.[14] The sufficiency of the fixation of works transmitted via the NII, however, where no copy or phonorecord has been made prior to the transmission, may not be so clear.

45   A transmission, in and of itself, is not a fixation. While a transmission may result in a fixation, a work is not fixed by virtue of the transmission alone. Therefore, "live" transmissions via the NII will not meet the fixation requirement, and will be unprotected by the Copyright Act, unless the work is being fixed at the same time as it is being transmitted.[15] The Copyright Act provides that a work "consisting of sounds, images, or both, that are being transmitted" meets the fixation requirement "if a fixation of the work is being made simultaneously with its transmission."[16] To obtain protection for a work under this "simultaneous fixation" provision, the simultaneous fixation of the transmitted work must itself qualify as a sufficient fixation.

46   A simultaneous fixation (or any other fixation) meets the requirements if its embodiment in a copy or phonorecord is "sufficiently permanent or stable to permit it to be perceived, reproduced, or otherwise communicated for a period of more than transitory duration." [17] Works are not sufficiently fixed if they are "purely evanescent or transient" in nature, "such as those projected briefly on a screen, shown electronically on a television or cathode ray tube, or captured momentarily in the 'memory' of a computer."[18] Electronic network transmissions from one computer to another, such as e-mail, may only reside on each computer in RAM (random access memory), but that has been found to be sufficient fixation.[19]

47   [...]

56   The Copyright Act provides a definition of "publication" to draw the line between published and unpublished works:

57   "Publication" is the distribution of copies or phonorecords of a work to the public by sale or other transfer of ownership, or by rental, lease, or lending. The offering to distribute copies or phonorecords to a group of persons for purposes of further distribution, public performance, or public display, constitutes publication. A public performance or display of a work does not of itself constitute publication. [29]

58   The definition uses the language of Section 106 describing the exclusive right of distribution, and was intended to make clear that "any form of dissemination in which a material object does not change hands -- performances or displays on television, for example -- is not a publication no matter how many people are exposed to the work."[30] It also makes clear that the distribution must be "to the public." [31] In general, the definition continues principles that had evolved through case law under previous copyright laws,[32] including the doctrine of limited publication.[33] The doctrine was developed by courts to save works from losing copyright protection when copies of the work were only distributed to a restricted number of people and for a restricted purpose without a copyright notice.[34] Those works would not be considered distributed to the public (*i.e.*, published) and, therefore, not subject to the notice requirement. Although the notice requirement has been eliminated, and thus the most critical justification for the doctrine, the few cases dealing with publication since 1989 suggest that courts will continue to apply the doctrine of limited publication.[35]

59   c. Works Not Protected

60   Certain works and subject matter are expressly excluded from protection under the Copyright Act, regardless of their originality, creativity and fixation. Titles, names, short phrases, and slogans generally do not enjoy copyright protection under the Copyright Act.[36] Other material ineligible for copyright protection includes the utilitarian elements of industrial designs;[37] familiar symbols or designs; simple geometrical shapes; mere variations of typographic ornamentation, lettering or coloring; and common works considered public property, such as standard calendars, height and weight charts, and tape measures and rulers.

61   Copyright protection also does not extend to any "idea, procedure, process, system, method of operation, concept, principle, or discovery, regardless of the form in which it is described, explained, illustrated, or embodied" in such work even if it meets the criteria for protection.[38] Thus, although a magazine article on how to tune a car engine is protected by copyright, that protection extends only to the expression of the ideas, facts and procedures in the article, not the ideas, facts and procedures themselves, no matter how creative or original they may be. Anyone may "use" the ideas, facts and procedures in the article to tune an engine -- or to write another article on the same subject. What may not be taken is the expression used by the original author to describe or explain those ideas, facts and procedures.[39]

62   Copyright does not prevent subsequent users from copying from a prior author's work those constituent elements that are not original -- for example . . . facts or materials in the public domain -- as long as such use does not unfairly appropriate the author's original contributions.[40]

63   This idea/expression dichotomy "assures authors the right to their original expression, but encourages others to build freely upon the ideas and information conveyed by a work."[41] Although it "may seem unfair that much of the fruit of the [author's] labor may be used by others without compensation," it is "a constitutional requirement" -- the "means by which copyright advances the progress of science and art."[42]

64   As a matter of law, copyright protection generally is not extended under the Copyright Act to works of the U.S. Government.[43] Therefore, nearly all works of the U.S. Government -- including this Report -- may be reproduced, distributed, adapted, publicly performed and publicly displayed without infringement liability in the United States under its copyright laws.[44] While the Copyright Act leaves most works created by the U.S. Government unprotected under U.S. copyright laws, Congress did not intend for the section to have any effect on the protection of U.S. government works abroad.[45]

65   _____

        [...]

Copyright Act: 17 U.S. Code § 102 - Subject matter of copyright: In general

(a) Copyright protection subsists, in accordance with this title, in original works of authorship fixed in any tangible medium of expression, now known or later developed, from which they can be perceived, reproduced, or otherwise communicated, either directly or with the aid of a machine or device. Works of authorship include the following categories:

(1) literary works;

(2) musical works, including any accompanying words;

(3) dramatic works, including any accompanying music;

(4) pantomimes and choreographic works;

(5) pictorial, graphic, and sculptural works;

(6) motion pictures and other audiovisual works;

(7) sound recordings; and

(8) architectural works.

(b) In no case does copyright protection for an original work of authorship extend to any idea, procedure, process, system, method of operation, concept, principle, or discovery, regardless of the form in which it is described, explained, illustrated, or embodied in such work.

Copyright Act: 17 U.S. Code § 106 - Exclusive rights in copyrighted works

Subject to sections 107 through 122, the owner of copyright under this title has the exclusive rights to do and to authorize any of the following:

(1) to reproduce the copyrighted work in copies or phonorecords;

(2) to prepare derivative works based upon the copyrighted work;

(3) to distribute copies or phonorecords of the copyrighted work to the public by sale or other transfer of ownership, or by rental, lease, or lending;

(4) in the case of literary, musical, dramatic, and choreographic works, pantomimes, and motion pictures and other audiovisual works, to perform the copyrighted work publicly;

(5) in the case of literary, musical, dramatic, and choreographic works, pantomimes, and pictorial, graphic, or sculptural works, including the individual images of a motion picture or other audiovisual work, to display the copyrighted work publicly; and

(6) in the case of sound recordings, to perform the copyrighted work publicly by means of a digital audio transmission.

MAI Systems Corp. v. Peak Computer, Inc.

August 04, 2014 by mrisch

1   991 F.2d 511 (1993)

2   **MAI SYSTEMS CORPORATION, a Delaware corporation, Plaintiff-Appellee,**

v.

PEAK COMPUTER, INC., a California corporation; Vincent Chiechi, an individual; Eric Francis, an individual, Defendants-Appellants.

[...]

4   United States Court of Appeals, Ninth Circuit.

5   [...]

Decided April 7, 1993.

6   [...]

11   **BRUNETTI, Circuit Judge:**

12   [...]

13   **I. FACTS**

14   MAI Systems Corp., until recently, manufactured computers and designed software to run those computers. The company continues to service its computers and the software necessary to operate the computers. MAI software includes operating system software, which is necessary to run any other program on the computer.

15   Peak Computer, Inc. is a company organized in 1990 that maintains computer systems for its clients. Peak maintains MAI computers for more than one hundred clients in Southern California. This accounts for between fifty and seventy percent of Peak's business.

16   Peak's service of MAI computers includes routine maintenance and emergency repairs. Malfunctions often are related to the failure of circuit boards inside the computers, and it may be necessary for a Peak technician to operate the computer and its operating system software in order to service the machine.

17   [...]

28

30

487

39   IV. COPYRIGHT INFRINGEMENT

40   The district court granted summary judgment in favor of MAI on its claims of copyright infringement and issued a permanent injunction against Peak on these claims. The alleged copyright violations include: (1) Peak's running of MAI software licenced to Peak customers [...]

41   A. Peak's running of MAI software licenced to Peak customers

42   To prevail on a claim of copyright infringement, a plaintiff must prove ownership of a copyright and a "`copying' of protectable expression" beyond the scope of a license. [...]

43   MAI software licenses allow MAI customers to use the software for their own internal information processing.[4] This allowed use necessarily includes the loading of the software into the computer's random access memory ("RAM") by a MAI customer. However, MAI software licenses do not allow for the use or copying of MAI software by third parties such as Peak. Therefore, any "copying" done by Peak is "beyond the scope" of the license.

44   It is not disputed that MAI owns the copyright to the software at issue here, however, Peak vigorously disputes the district court's conclusion that a "copying" occurred under the Copyright Act.

45   The Copyright Act defines "copies" as: material objects, other than phonorecords, in which a work is fixed by any method now known or later developed, and from which the work can be perceived, reproduced, or otherwise communicated, either directly or with the aid of a machine or device.

46   17 U.S.C. § 101.

47   The Copyright Act then explains:

48   A work is "fixed" in a tangible medium of expression when its embodiment in a copy or phonorecord, by or under the authority of the author, is sufficiently permanent or stable to permit it to be perceived, reproduced, or otherwise communicated [...] for a period of more than transitory duration.

49   17 U.S.C. § 101.

50   The district court's grant of summary judgment on MAI's claims of copyright infringement reflects its conclusion that a "copying" for purposes of copyright law occurs when a computer program is transferred from a permanent storage device to a computer's RAM. This conclusion is consistent with its finding, in granting the preliminary injunction, that: "the loading of copyrighted computer software from a storage medium (hard disk, floppy disk, or read only memory) into the memory of a central processing unit ("CPU") causes a copy to be made. In the absence of ownership of the copyright or express permission by license, such acts constitute copyright infringement." We find that this conclusion is supported by the record and by the law.

51   Peak concedes that in maintaining its customer's computers, it uses MAI operating software "to the extent that the repair and maintenance process necessarily involves turning on the computer to make sure it is functional and thereby running the operating system." It is also uncontroverted that when the computer is turned on the operating system is loaded into the computer's RAM. As part of diagnosing a computer problem at the customer site, the Peak technician runs the computer's operating system software, allowing the technician to view the systems error log, which is part of the operating system, thereby enabling the technician to diagnose the problem. [5]

52   Peak argues that this loading of copyrighted software does not constitute a copyright violation because the "copy" created in RAM is not "fixed." However, by showing that Peak loads the software into the RAM and is then able to view the system error log and diagnose the

problem with the computer, MAI has adequately shown that the representation created in the RAM is "sufficiently permanent or stable to permit it to be perceived, reproduced, or otherwise communicated for a period of more than transitory duration."

53   After reviewing the record, we find no specific facts (and Peak points to none) which indicate that the copy created in the RAM is not fixed. While Peak argues this issue in its pleadings, mere argument does not establish a genuine issue of material fact to defeat summary judgment. A party opposing a properly supported motion for summary judgment may not rest upon the mere allegations or denials in pleadings, but "must set forth specific facts showing that there is a genuine issue for trial." [...]

54   The law also supports the conclusion that Peak's loading of copyrighted software into RAM creates a "copy" of that software in violation of the Copyright Act. In *Apple Computer, Inc. v. Formula Int'l, Inc.* [...] the district court held that the copying of copyrighted software onto silicon chips and subsequent sale of those chips is not protected by § 117 of the Copyright Act. Section 117 allows "the `owner'[...] of a copy of a computer program to make or authorize the making of another copy" without infringing copyright law, if it "is an essential step in the utilization of the computer program" or if the new copy is "for archival purposes [...] only." 17 U.S.C. § 117 [...] One of the grounds for finding that § 117 did not apply was the court's conclusion that the permanent copying of the software onto the silicon chips was not an "essential step" in the utilization of the software because the software could be used through RAM without making a permanent copy. The court stated:

55   RAM can be simply defined as a computer component in which data and computer programs can be temporarily recorded. Thus, the purchaser of [software] desiring to utilize all of the programs on the diskette could arrange to copy [the software] into RAM. This would only be a temporary fixation. It is a property of RAM that when the computer is turned off, the copy of the program recorded in RAM is lost.

56   [...]

57   While we recognize that this language is not dispositive, it supports the view that the copy made in RAM is "fixed" and qualifies as a copy under the Copyright Act.

58   We have found no case which specifically holds that the copying of software into RAM creates a "copy" under the Copyright Act. However, it is generally accepted that the loading of software into a computer constitutes the creation of a copy under the Copyright Act. *See e.g. Vault Corp. v. Quaid Software Ltd.*, 847 F.2d 255, 260 (5th Cir.1988) ("the act of loading a program from a medium of storage into a computer's memory creates a copy of the program"); 2 *Nimmer on Copyright*, § 8.08 at 8-105 (1983) ("Inputting a computer program entails the preparation of a copy."); *Final Report of the National Commission on the New Technological Uses of Copyrighted Works*, at 13 (1978) ("the placement of a work into a computer is the preparation of a copy"). We recognize that these authorities are somewhat troubling since they do not specify that a copy is created regardless of whether the software is loaded into the RAM, the hard disk or the read only memory ("ROM"). However, since we find that the copy created in the RAM can be "perceived, reproduced, or otherwise communicated," we hold that the loading of software into the RAM creates a copy under the Copyright Act. 17 U.S.C. § 101. We affirm the district court's grant of summary judgment as well as the permanent injunction as it relates to this issue.

59   [...]

685   [4] A representative MAI software license provides in part:

116   4. *Software License.*

(a) *License.*... Customer may use the Software (one version with maximum of two copies permitted — a working and a backup copy) ... solely to fulfill Customer's own internal information processing needs on the particular items of Equipment ... for which the Software is configured and furnished by [MAI]. The provisions of this License ... shall apply to all versions and copies of the Software furnished to Customer pursuant to this Agreement. The term "Software" includes, without limitation, all basic operating system software....

(b) *Customer Prohibited Acts*.... Any possession or use of the Software ... not expressly authorized under this License or any act which might jeopardize [MAI]'s rights or interests in the Software ... is prohibited, including without limitation, examination, disclosure, copying, modification, reconfiguration, augmentation, adaptation, emulation, visual display or reduction to visually perceptible form or tampering....

(c) *Customer Obligations*. Customer acknowledges that the Software is [MAI]'s valuable and exclusive property, trade secret and copyrighted material. Accordingly, Customer shall ... (i) use the Software ... strictly as prescribed under this License, (ii) keep the Software ... confidential and not make [it] available to others....

117   A representative diagnostic license agreement provides in part:

118   6. *Access/Non-Disclosure*.

            Licensee shall not give access nor shall it disclose the Diagnostics (in any form) ... to any person ... without the written permission of [MAI]. Licensee may authorize not more than three (3) of its *bona fide* employees to utilize the Diagnostics ... if, and only if, they agree to be bound by the terms hereof.

119   [...]

17 U.S.C. § 117.—Limitations on exclusive rights: Computer programs

August 30, 2014 by mrisch

This is the edited section 117 after MAI v. Peak. Does it solve all the problems of that case? What if software is licensed rather than owned?

1   (a) **Making of Additional Copy or Adaptation by Owner of Copy.**—Notwithstanding the provisions of section 106, it is not an infringement for the owner of a copy of a computer program to make or authorize the making of another copy or adaptation of that computer program provided:

2   (1) that such a new copy or adaptation is created as an essential step in the utilization of the computer program in conjunction with a machine and that it is used in no other manner, or

3   (2) that such new copy or adaptation is for archival purposes only and that all archival copies are destroyed in the event that continued possession of the computer program should cease to be rightful.

4   [...]

5   (c) **Machine Maintenance or Repair.**—Notwithstanding the provisions of section 106, it is not an infringement for the owner or lessee of a machine to make or authorize the making of a copy of a computer program if such copy is made solely by virtue of the activation of a machine that lawfully contains an authorized copy of the computer program, for purposes only of maintenance or repair of that machine, if—

6   (1) such new copy is used in no other manner and is destroyed immediately after the maintenance or repair is completed; and

7   (2) with respect to any computer program or part thereof that is not necessary for that machine to be activated, such program or part thereof is not accessed or used other than to make such new copy by virtue of the activation of the machine.

8   [...]

491

Cartoon Network LP, LLLP v. CSC Holdings, Inc. - Fixation

June 25, 2014 by mrisch

1   536 F.3d 121

2   ## The CARTOON NETWORK LP, LLLP [...]

v.

CSC HOLDINGS, INC. and Cablevision Systems Corporation[...]

5   United States Court of Appeals, Second Circuit.

6   [...]

7   Decided: August 4, 2008.

8   [...]

19   Before: WALKER, SACK, and LIVINGSTON, Circuit Judges.

20   ## JOHN M. WALKER, JR., Circuit Judge:

21   Defendant-Appellant Cablevision Systems Corporation ("Cablevision") wants to market a new "Remote Storage" Digital Video Recorder system ("RS-DVR"), using a technology akin to both traditional, set-top digital video recorders, like TiVo ("DVRs"), and the video-on-demand ("VOD") services provided by many cable companies. Plaintiffs-Appellees produce copyrighted movies and television programs that they provide to Cablevision pursuant to numerous licensing agreements. They contend that Cablevision, through the operation of its RS-DVR system as proposed, would directly infringe their copyrights both by making unauthorized reproductions, and by engaging in public performances, of their copyrighted works. The material facts are not in dispute. Because we conclude that Cablevision would not directly infringe plaintiffs' rights under the Copyright Act by offering its RS-DVR system to consumers, we reverse the district court's award of summary judgment to plaintiffs, and we vacate its injunction against Cablevision.

22   ## BACKGROUND

23   Today's television viewers increasingly use digital video recorders ("DVRs") instead of video cassette recorders ("VCRs") to record television programs and play them back later at their convenience. DVRs generally store recorded programming on an internal hard drive rather than a cassette. But, as this case demonstrates, the generic term "DVR" actually refers to a growing number of different devices and systems. Companies like TiVo sell a stand-alone DVR device that is typically connected to a user's cable box and television much like a VCR. Many cable companies also lease to their subscribers "set-top storage DVRs," which combine many of the functions of a standard cable box and a stand-alone DVR in a single device.

24   [...] In March 2006, Cablevision, an operator of cable television systems, announced the advent of its new "Remote Storage DVR

System." As designed, the RS-DVR allows Cablevision customers who do not have a stand-alone DVR to record cable programming on central hard drives housed and maintained by Cablevision at a "remote" location. RS-DVR customers may then receive playback of those programs through their home television sets, using only a remote control and a standard cable box equipped with the RS-DVR software. Cablevision notified its content providers, including plaintiffs, of its plans to offer RS-DVR, but it did not seek any license from them to operate or sell the RS-DVR.

25   Plaintiffs, which hold the copyrights to numerous movies and television programs, sued Cablevision for declaratory and injunctive relief. They alleged that Cablevision's proposed operation of the RS-DVR would directly infringe their exclusive rights to both reproduce and publicly perform their copyrighted works. Critically for our analysis here, plaintiffs alleged theories only of direct infringement, not contributory infringement, and defendants waived any defense based on fair use.

26   [...]

27   I. Operation of the RS-DVR System

28   Cable companies like Cablevision aggregate television programming from a wide variety of "content providers"—the various broadcast and cable channels that produce or provide individual programs—and transmit those programs into the homes of their subscribers via coaxial cable. At the outset of the transmission process, Cablevision gathers the content of the various television channels into a single stream of data. Generally, this stream is processed and transmitted to Cablevision's customers in real time. Thus, if a Cartoon Network program is scheduled to air Monday night at 8pm, Cartoon Network transmits that program's data to Cablevision and other cable companies nationwide at that time, and the cable companies immediately re-transmit the data to customers who subscribe to that channel.

29   Under the new RS-DVR, this single stream of data is split into two streams. The first is routed immediately to customers as before. The second stream flows into a device called the Broadband Media Router ("BMR"), [...] which buffers the data stream, reformats it, and sends it to the "Arroyo Server," which consists, in relevant part, of two data buffers and a number of high-capacity hard disks. The entire stream of data moves to the first buffer (the "primary ingest buffer"), at which point the server automatically inquires as to whether any customers want to record any of that programming. If a customer has requested a particular program, the data for that program move from the primary buffer into a secondary buffer, and then onto a portion of one of the hard disks allocated to that customer. As new data flow into the primary buffer, they overwrite a corresponding quantity of data already on the buffer. The primary ingest buffer holds no more than 0.1 seconds of each channel's programming at any moment. Thus, every tenth of a second, the data residing on this buffer are automatically erased and replaced. The [...] data buffer in the BMR holds no more than 1.2 seconds of programming at any time. While buffering occurs at other points in the operation of the RS-DVR, only the BMR buffer and the primary ingest buffer are utilized absent any request from an individual subscriber.

30   As the district court observed, "the RS-DVR is not a single piece of equipment," but rather "a complex system requiring numerous computers, processes, networks of cables, and facilities staffed by personnel twenty-four hours a day and seven days a week." [...] To the customer, however, the processes of recording and playback on the RS-DVR are similar to that of a standard set-top DVR. Using a remote control, the customer can record programming by selecting a program in advance from an on-screen guide, or by pressing the record button while viewing a given program. A customer cannot, however, record the earlier portion of a program once it has begun. To begin playback, the customer selects the show from an on-screen list of previously recorded programs. [...] The principal difference in operation is that, instead of sending signals from the remote to an on-set box, the viewer sends signals from the remote, through the cable, to the Arroyo Server at Cablevision's central facility. *See id.* In this respect, RS-DVR more closely resembles a VOD service, whereby a cable subscriber uses his remote and cable box to request transmission of content, such as a movie, stored on computers at the cable company's facility. [...] But unlike a VOD service, RS-DVR users can only play content that they previously requested to be recorded.

31   Cablevision has some control over the content available for recording: a customer can only record programs on the channels offered by

Cablevision (assuming he subscribes to them). Cablevision can also modify the system to limit the number of channels available and considered doing so during development of the RS-DVR. *[...]*

38 ## DISCUSSION

39 *[...]*

40 "Section 106 of the Copyright Act grants copyright holders a bundle of exclusive rights...." *[...]* This case implicates two of those rights: the right "to reproduce the copyrighted work in copies," and the right "to perform the copyrighted work publicly." 17 U.S.C. § 106(1), (4). As discussed above, the district court found that Cablevision infringed the first right by 1) buffering the data from its programming stream *[...]*

41 ## I. The Buffer Data

42 It is undisputed that Cablevision, not any customer or other entity, takes the content from one stream of programming, after the split, and stores it, one small piece at a time, in the BMR buffer and the primary ingest buffer. As a result, the information is buffered before any customer requests a recording, and would be buffered even if no such request were made. The question is whether, by buffering the data that make up a given work, Cablevision "reproduce[s]" that work "in copies," 17 U.S.C. § 106(1), and thereby infringes the copyright holder's reproduction right.

43 "Copies," as defined in the Copyright Act, "are material objects ... in which a work is fixed by any method ... and from which the work can be ... reproduced." *Id.* § 101. The Act also provides that a work is "'fixed' in a tangible medium of expression when its embodiment ... is sufficiently permanent or stable to permit it to be ... reproduced ... *for a period of more than transitory duration.*" *Id.* (emphasis added). We believe that this language plainly imposes two distinct but related requirements: the work must be embodied in a medium, i.e., placed in a medium such that it can be perceived, reproduced, etc., from that medium (the "embodiment requirement"), and it must remain thus embodied "for a period of more than transitory duration" (the "duration requirement"). *[...]* Unless both requirements are met, the work is not "fixed" in the buffer, and, as a result, the buffer data is not a "copy" of the original work whose data is buffered.

44 The district court mistakenly limited its analysis primarily to the embodiment requirement. As a result of this error, once it determined that the buffer data was "[c]learly ... capable of being reproduced," i.e., that the work was embodied in the buffer, the district court concluded that the work was therefore "fixed" in the buffer, and that a copy had thus been made. *[...]* In doing so, it relied on a line of cases beginning with *MAI Systems Corp. v. Peak Computer Inc.,* 991 F.2d 511 (9th Cir.1993). It also relied on the United States Copyright Office's 2001 report on the Digital Millennium Copyright Act, which states, in essence, that an embodiment is fixed "[u]nless a reproduction manifests itself so fleetingly that *it cannot be copied.*" U.S. Copyright Office, *DMCA Section 104 Report* 111 (Aug.2001) (*"DMCA Report"*) (emphasis added), *available at* http://www.copyright.gov/reports/studies/dmca/sec-104-report-vol-1.pdf.

45 The district court's reliance on cases like *MAI Systems* is misplaced. In general, those cases conclude that an alleged copy is fixed without addressing the duration requirement; it does not follow, however, that those cases assume, much less establish, that such a requirement does not exist. Indeed, the duration requirement, by itself, was not at issue in *MAI Systems* and its progeny. As a result, they do not speak to the issues squarely before us here: If a work is only "embodied" in a medium for a period of transitory duration, can it be "fixed" in that medium, and thus a copy? And what constitutes a period "of more than transitory duration"?

46 In *MAI Systems,* defendant Peak Computer, Inc., performed maintenance and repairs on computers made and sold by MAI Systems. In order to service a customer's computer, a Peak employee had to operate the computer and run the computer's copyrighted operating system software. *[...]* The issue in *MAI Systems* was whether, *[...]* by loading the software into the computer's RAM,[1] the repairman created a "copy" as defined in § 101. *[...]* The resolution of this issue turned on whether the software's embodiment in the computer's RAM was "fixed," within the meaning of the same section. The Ninth Circuit concluded that

47   by showing that Peak loads the software into the RAM and is then able to view the system error log and diagnose the problem with the computer, MAI has adequately shown that the representation created in the RAM is "sufficiently permanent or stable to permit it to be perceived, reproduced, or otherwise communicated for a period of more than transitory duration."

48   *[…]*

49   The *MAI Systems* court referenced the "transitory duration" language but did not discuss or analyze it. The opinion notes that the defendants "vigorously" argued that the program's embodiment in the RAM was not a copy, but it does not specify the arguments defendants made. *[…]* This omission suggests that the parties did not litigate the significance of the "transitory duration" language, and the court therefore had no occasion to address it. This is unsurprising, because it seems fair to assume that in these cases the program was embodied in the RAM for at least several minutes.

50   Accordingly, we construe *MAI Systems* and its progeny as holding that loading a program into a computer's RAM *can* result in copying that program. We do not read *MAI Systems* as holding that, as a matter of law, loading a program into a form of RAM *always* results in copying. Such a holding would read the "transitory duration" language out of the definition, and we do not believe our sister circuit would dismiss this statutory language without even discussing it. It appears the parties in *MAI Systems* simply did not dispute that the duration requirement was satisfied; this line of cases simply concludes that when a program is loaded into RAM, the embodiment requirement is satisfied—an important holding in itself, and one we see no reason to quibble with here.[…]

51   At least one court, relying on *MAI Systems* in a highly similar factual setting, has made this point explicitly. In *Advanced Computer Services of Michigan, Inc. v. MAI Systems Corp.,* the district court expressly noted that the unlicensed user in that case ran copyrighted diagnostic software "for minutes or longer," but that the program's embodiment in the computer's RAM might be too ephemeral to be fixed if the computer had been shut down "within *[…]* seconds or fractions of a second" after loading the copyrighted program. *[…]* We have no quarrel with this reasoning; it merely makes explicit the reasoning that is implicit in the other *MAI Systems* cases. Accordingly, those cases provide no support for the conclusion that the definition of "fixed" does not include a duration requirement. *[…]*

52   Nor does the Copyright Office's 2001 DMCA Report, also relied on by the district court in this case, explicitly suggest that the definition of "fixed" does not contain a duration requirement. However, as noted above, it does suggest that an embodiment is fixed "[u]nless a reproduction manifests itself so fleetingly that it cannot be copied, perceived or communicated." *DMCA Report, supra,* at 111. As we have stated, to determine whether a work is "fixed" in a given medium, the statutory language directs us to ask not only 1) whether a work is "embodied" in that medium, but also 2) whether it is embodied in the medium "for a period of more than transitory duration." According to the Copyright Office, if the work is capable of being copied from that medium *for any amount of time,* the answer to both questions is "yes." The problem with this interpretation is that it reads the "transitory duration" language out of the statute.

53   *[…]*

54   In sum, no case law or other authority dissuades us from concluding that the definition of "fixed" imposes both an embodiment requirement and a duration requirement. *Accord CoStar Group Inc. v. LoopNet, Inc.,* 373 F.3d 544, 551 (4th Cir. 2004) (while temporary reproductions "may be made in this transmission process, they would appear not to be `fixed' in the sense that they are `of more than transitory duration'"). We now turn to whether, in this case, those requirements are met by the buffer data.

55   Cablevision does not seriously dispute that copyrighted works are "embodied" in the buffer. Data in the BMR buffer can be reformatted and transmitted to the other components of the RS-DVR system. Data in the primary ingest buffer can be copied onto the Arroyo hard disks if a user has requested a recording of that data. Thus, a work's "embodiment" in either buffer "is sufficiently permanent or stable to permit it to be perceived, reproduced," (as in the case of the ingest buffer) "or otherwise communicated" (as in the BMR buffer). 17 U.S.C. § 101. The result might be different if only a single second of a much longer work was placed in the buffer in isolation. In such a situation, it might be reasonable to conclude that only a minuscule portion of a work, rather than "a work" was embodied in the buffer. Here,

however, where every second of an entire work is placed, one second at a time, in the buffer, we conclude that the work is embodied in the buffer.

56   Does any such embodiment last "for a period of more than transitory duration"? *Id.* No bit of data remains in any buffer for more than a fleeting 1.2 seconds. And unlike the data in cases like *MAI* [...] *Systems,* which remained embodied in the computer's RAM memory until the user turned the computer off, each bit of data here is rapidly and automatically overwritten as soon as it is processed. While our inquiry is necessarily fact-specific, and other factors not present here may alter the duration analysis significantly, these facts strongly suggest that the works in this case are embodied in the buffer for only a "transitory" period, thus failing the duration requirement.

57   Against this evidence, plaintiffs argue only that the duration is not transitory because the data persist "long enough for Cablevision to make reproductions from them." [...] As we have explained above, however, this reasoning impermissibly reads the duration language out of the statute, and we reject it. Given that the data reside in no buffer for more than 1.2 seconds before being automatically overwritten, and in the absence of compelling arguments to the contrary, we believe that the copyrighted works here are not "embodied" in the buffers for a period of more than transitory duration, and are therefore not "fixed" in the buffers. Accordingly, the acts of buffering in the operation of the RS-DVR do not create copies, as the Copyright Act defines that term. Our resolution of this issue renders it unnecessary for us to determine whether any copies produced by buffering data would be de minimis, and we express no opinion on that question.

58   [...]

001

496

Playboy Enterprises, Inc. v. Frena

August 04, 2014 by mrisch

This case examines what it means to display a work publicly

1   839 F.Supp. 1552 (1993)

2   **PLAYBOY ENTERPRISES, INC., Plaintiff,**

v.

George FRENA, d/b/a Techs Warehouse BBS Systems and Consulting, and Mark Dyess, Defendants.

3   [...]

4   United States District Court, M.D. Florida, Jacksonville Division.

5   December 9, 1993.

6   [...]

8   *ORDER*

9   **SCHLESINGER, District Judge.**

10   This cause is before the Court on Plaintiff's First Motion for Partial Summary Judgment (Copyright Infringement) as to Defendant Frena [..

11   Defendant George Frena operates a subscription computer bulletin board service, Techs Warehouse BBS ("BBS"), that distributed unauthorized copies of Plaintiff Playboy Enterprises, Inc.'s ("PEI") copyrighted photographs. BBS is accessible via telephone modem to customers. For a fee, or to those who purchase certain products from Defendant Frena, anyone with an appropriately equipped computer can log onto BBS. Once logged on subscribers may browse through different BBS directories to look at the pictures and customers may also download[1] the high quality computerized copies of the photographs and then store the copied image from Frena's computer onto their home computer. Many of the images found on BBS include adult subject matter. One hundred and seventy of the images that were available on BBS were copies of photographs taken from PEI's copyrighted materials.

12   Defendant Frena admits that these materials were displayed on his BBS[...] and that each of the accused computer graphic files on BBS is substantially similar to copyrighted PEI photographs[...] Defendant Frena also admits that each of the files in question has been downlc by one of his customers[...]

13   Subscribers can upload[3] material onto the bulletin board so that any other subscriber, by accessing their computer, can see that material. Defendant Frena states in his Affidavit filed August 4, 1993, that he never uploaded any of PEI's photographs onto BBS and that subscribers to BBS uploaded the photographs. *[...]* Defendant Frena states that as soon as he was served with a summons and made aware of this matter, he removed the photographs from BBS and has since that time monitored BBS to prevent additional photographs of PEI from being uploaded. *[...]*

18   I. COPYRIGHT INFRINGEMENT

20   The Copyright Act of 1976 gives copyright owners control over most, if not all, activities of conceivable commercial value. The statute provides that

21   the owner of a copyright ... has the exclusive rights to do and to authorize any of the following: (1) to reproduce the copyrighted work in copies ...; (2) to prepare derivative works based upon the copyrighted work; (3) to distribute copies ... of the copyrighted work to the public ... and (5) in the case of ... pictorial ... works ... to display the copyrighted work publicly.

22   17 U.S.C. § 106. Engaging in or authorizing any of these categories without the copyright owner's permission violates the exclusive [...] rights of the copyright owner and constitutes infringement of the copyright. *See* 17 U.S.C. § 501(a).

23   To establish copyright infringement, PEI must show ownership of the copyright and "copying" by Defendant Frena [...]

24   There is no dispute that PEI owns the copyrights on the photographs in question. PEI owns copyright registrations for each of the 50 issues of Playboy publications that contain the photographs on BBS. [...]

25   Next, PEI must demonstrate copying by Defendant Frena. Since direct evidence of copying is rarely available in a copyright infringement action, copying may be inferentially proven by showing that Defendant Frena had access to the allegedly infringed work, that the allegedly infringing work is substantially similar to the copyrighted work [...] and that one of the rights statutorily guaranteed to copyright owners is implicated by Frena's actions. [...]

26   Access to the copyrighted work is not at issue. Access is essentially undeniable because every month PEI sells over 3.4 million copies of Playboy magazine throughout the United States. [...]

27   Substantial similarity is also a non-issue in this case. Defendant Frena has admitted that every one of the accused images is substantially similar to the PEI copyrighted photograph from which the accused image was produced. [...] Moreover, not only are the accused works substantially similar to the copyrighted work, but the infringing photographs are essentially exact copies. [...] In many cases, the only difference is that PEI's written text appearing on the same page of the photograph has been removed from the infringing copy.

28   The next step is to determine whether Defendant Frena violated one of the rights statutorily guaranteed to copyright owners under 17 U.S.C. § 106. [...]

29   Public distribution of a copyrighted work is a right reserved to the copyright owner, and usurpation of that right constitutes infringement. [PEI's right under 17 U.S.C. § 106(3) to distribute copies to the public has been implicated by Defendant Frena. Section 106(3) grants the copyright owner "the exclusive right to sell, give away, rent or lend any material embodiment of his work." [...] There is no dispute that Defendant Frena supplied a product containing unauthorized copies of a copyrighted work. It does not matter that Defendant Frena claims he did not make the copies itself. *Future revisions to the Copyright Act - the DMCA - might have protected Frena* [...]

30   Furthermore, the "display" rights of PEI have been infringed upon by Defendant Frena. *See* 17 U.S.C. § 106(5). The concept of display is broad. *See* 17 U.S.C. § 101. It covers "the projection of an image on a screen or other surface by any method, the transmission of an image by electronic or other means, and the showing of an image on a cathode ray tube, or similar viewing apparatus connected with any sort of information storage and retrieval system." [...]

31   "Display" covers any showing of a "copy" of the work, "either directly or by means of a film, slide, television image or any other device or process." 17 U.S.C. § 101. However, in order for there to be copyright infringement, the display must be public. A "public display" is a

display "at a place open to the public or ... where a substantial number of persons outside of a normal circle of family and its social acquaintenances is gathered." [...] A place is "open to the public" in this sense even if access is limited to paying customers. [...]

32   Defendant's display of PEI's copyrighted photographs to subscribers was a public display. Though limited to subscribers, the audience consisted of "a substantial number of persons outside of a normal circle of family and its social acquaintenances." [...]

36   The Court finds that the undisputed facts mandate partial summary judgment that Defendant Frena's unauthorized display and distribution of PEI's copyrighted material is copyright infringement under 17 U.S.C. § 501.

48   [...]

88   [1] The process of transferring the image from the bulletin board to one's personal computer is known as downloading.

89   [...]

90   [3] The process of transferring the image from one's personal computer to the bulletin board is known as uploading.

American Broadcasting Companies, Inc. v. Aereo, Inc.

August 05, 2014 by mrisch

This case explores the breadth of the performance right. Is it too broad?

1

134 S.Ct. 2498 (2014)

AMERICAN BROADCASTING COMPANIES, INC., ET AL., PETITIONERS,

v.

AEREO, INC., FKA BAMBOOM LABS, INC.

[...]

2

Supreme Court of the United States.

[...]

Decided June 25, 2014.

3   BREYER, J., delivered the opinion of the Court, in which ROBERTS, C. J., and KENNEDY, GINSBURG, SOTOMAYOR, and KAGAN, JJ., joined. SCALIA, J., filed a dissenting opinion, in which THOMAS and ALITO, JJ., joined.

4   **JUSTICE BREYER, delivered the opinion of the Court.**

5   The Copyright Act of 1976 gives a copyright owner the "exclusive righ[t]" to "perform the copyrighted work publicly." 17 U. S. C. §106(4). The Act's Transmit Clause defines that exclusive right as including the right to

6   "transmit or otherwise communicate a performance. . . of the [copyrighted] work . . . to the public, by means of any device or process, whether the members of the public capable of receiving the performance . . . receive it in the same place or in separate places and at the same time or at different times." §101.

7   We must decide whether respondent Aereo, Inc., infringes this exclusive right by selling its subscribers a technologically complex service that allows them to watch television programs over the Internet at about the same time as the programs are broadcast over the air. We conclude that it does.

8   **I**

9   **A**

10   For a monthly fee, Aereo offers subscribers broadcast television programming over the Internet, virtually as the programming is being broadcast. Much of this program-ming is made up of copyrighted works. Aereo neither owns the copyright in those works nor holds a license from the copyright owners to perform those works publicly.

11   Aereo's system is made up of servers, transcoders, and thousands of dime-sized antennas housed in a central warehouse. It works roughly as follows: First, when a subscriber wants to watch a show that is currently being broadcast, he visits Aereo's website and

500

selects, from a list of the local programming, the show he wishes to see.

12   Second, one of Aereo's servers selects an antenna, which it dedicates to the use of that subscriber (and that subscriber alone) for the duration of the selected show. A server then tunes the antenna to the over-the-air broadcast carrying the show. The antenna begins to receive the broadcast, and an Aereo transcoder translates the signals received into data that can be transmitted over the Internet.

13   Third, rather than directly send the data to the subscriber, a server saves the data in a subscriber-specific folder on Aereo's hard drive. In other words, Aereo's system creates a subscriber-specific copy—that is, a "personal" copy—of the subscriber's program of choice.

14   Fourth, once several seconds of programming have been saved, Aereo's server begins to stream the saved copy of the show to the subscriber over the Internet. (The subscriber may instead direct Aereo to stream the program at a later time, but that aspect of Aereo's service is not before us.) The subscriber can watch the streamed program on the screen of his personal computer, tablet, smart phone, Internet-connected television, or other Internet-connected device. The streaming continues, a mere few seconds behind the over-the-air broadcast, until the subscriber has received the entire show. See A Dictionary of Computing 494 (6th ed. 2008) (defining "streaming" as "[t]he process of providing a steady flow of audio or video data so that an Internet user is able to access it as it is transmitted").

15   Aereo emphasizes that the data that its system streams to each subscriber are the data from his own personal copy, made from the broadcast signals received by the particular antenna allotted to him. Its system does not transmit data saved in one subscriber's folder to any other subscriber. When two subscribers wish to watch the same program, Aereo's system activates two separate antennas and saves two separate copies of the program in two separate folders. It then streams the show to the subscribers through two separate transmissions—each from the subscriber's personal copy.

16   **B**

17   Petitioners are television producers, marketers, distributors, and broadcasters who own the copyrights in many of the programs that Aereo's system streams to its subscribers. They brought suit against Aereo for copyright infringement in Federal District Court. They sought a preliminary injunction, arguing that Aereo was infringing their right to "perform" their works "publicly," as the Transmit Clause defines those terms.

18   [...]

19   **II**

20   This case requires us to answer two questions: First, in operating in the manner described above, does Aereo "perform" at all? And second, if so, does Aereo do so "publicly"? We address these distinct questions in turn.

21   Does Aereo "perform"? See §106(4) ("[T]he owner of [a] copyright . . . has the exclusive righ[t] . . . to *perform* the copyrighted work publicly" (emphasis added)); §101 ("To *perform* . . . a work `publicly' means [among other things] to transmit . . . a performance . . . of the work . . . to the public . . ." (emphasis added)). Phrased another way, does Aereo "transmit . . . a performance" when a subscriber watches a show using Aereo's system, or is it only the subscriber who transmits? In Aereo's view, it does not perform. It does no more than supply equipment that "emulate[s] the operation of a home antenna and [digital video recorder (DVR)]." Brief for Respondent 41. Like a home antenna and DVR, Aereo's equipment simply responds to its subscribers' directives. So it is only the subscribers who "perform" when they use Aereo's equipment to stream television programs to themselves.

22   Considered alone, the language of the Act does not clearly indicate when an entity "perform[s]" (or "transmit[s]") and when it merely supplies equipment that allows others to do so. But when read in light of its purpose, the Act is unmistakable: An entity that engages in activities like Aereo's performs.

23   [...]

30   Aereo is not simply an equipment provider. Rather, Aereo, and not just its subscribers, "perform[s]" (or "transmit[s]"). Aereo's activities are substantially similar to those of the CATV companies that Congress amended the Act to reach. See *id.,* at 89 ("[C]able systems are commercial enterprises whose basic retransmission operations are based on the carriage of copyrighted program material"). Aereo sells a service that allows subscribers to watch television programs, many of which are copyrighted, almost as they are being broadcast. In providing this service, Aereo uses its own equipment, housed in a centralized warehouse, outside of its users' homes. By means of its technology (antennas, transcoders, and servers), Aereo's system "receive[s] programs that have been released to the public and carr[ies] them by private channels to additional viewers." *[...]*

38   Aereo's equipment may serve a "viewer function"; it may enhance the viewer's ability to receive a broadcaster's programs. It may even emulate equipment a viewer could use at home. But the same was true of the equipment that was before the Court, and ultimately before Congress, in *Fortnightly* and *Teleprompter.*

39   We recognize, and Aereo and the dissent emphasize, one particular difference between Aereo's system and the cable systems at issue in *Fortnightly* and *Teleprompter.* The systems in those cases transmitted constantly; they sent continuous programming to each subscriber's television set. In contrast, Aereo's system remains inert until a subscriber indicates that she wants to watch a program. Only at that moment, in automatic response to the subscriber's request, does Aereo's system activate an antenna and begin to transmit the requested program.

40   This is a critical difference, says the dissent. It means that Aereo's subscribers, not Aereo, "selec[t] the copyrighted content" that is "perform[ed]," *[...]* and for that reason they, not Aereo, "transmit" the performance. Aereo is thus like "a copy shop that provides its patrons with a library card." *[...]* A copy shop is not directly liable whenever a patron uses the shop's machines to "reproduce" copyrighted materials found in that library. See §106(1) ("exclusive righ[t] . . . to reproduce the copyrighted work"). And by the same token, Aereo should not be directly liable whenever its patrons use its equipment to "transmit" copyrighted television programs to their screens.

41   In our view, however, the dissent's copy shop argument, in whatever form, makes too much out of too little. Given Aereo's overwhelming likeness to the cable companies targeted by the 1976 amendments, this sole technological difference between Aereo and traditional cable companies does not make a critical difference here. The subscribers of the *Fortnightly* and *Teleprompter* cable systems also selected what programs to display on their receiving sets. Indeed, as we explained in *Fortnightly,* such a subscriber "could choose any of the . . . programs he wished to view by simply turning the knob on his own television set." *[...]* The same is true of an Aereo subscriber. Of course, in *Fortnightly* the television signals, in a sense, lurked behind the screen, ready to emerge when the subscriber turned the knob. Here the signals pursue their ordinary course of travel through the universe until today's "turn of the knob"—a click on a website— activates machinery that intercepts and reroutes them to Aereo's subscribers over the Internet. But this difference means nothing to the subscriber. It means nothing to the broadcaster. We do not see how this single difference, invisible to subscriber and broadcaster alike, could transform a system that is for all practical purposes a traditional cable system into "a copy shop that provides its patrons with a library card."

42   In other cases involving different kinds of service or technology providers, a user's involvement in the operation of the provider's equipment and selection of the content transmitted may well bear on whether the provider performs within the meaning of the Act. But the many similarities between Aereo and cable companies, considered in light of Congress' basic purposes in amending the Copyright Act, convince us that this difference is not critical here. We conclude that Aereo is not just an equipment supplier and that Aereo "perform[s]."

43   **III**

44   Next, we must consider whether Aereo performs petitioners' works "publicly," within the meaning of the Transmit Clause. Under the

Clause, an entity performs a work publicly when it "transmit[s] . . . a performance . . . of the work . . . to the public." §101. Aereo denies that it satisfies this definition. It reasons as follows: First, the "performance" it "transmit[s]" is the performance created by its act of transmitting. And second, because each of these performances is capable of being received by one and only one subscriber, Aereo transmits privately, not publicly. Even assuming Aereo's first argument is correct, its second does not follow.

45   We begin with Aereo's first argument. What performance does Aereo transmit? Under the Act, "[t]o `transmit' a performance . . . is to communicate it by any device or process whereby images or sounds are received beyond the place from which they are sent." *Ibid.* And "[t]o `perform'" an audiovisual work means "to show its images in any sequence or to make the sounds accompanying it audible." *Ibid.*

46   Petitioners say Aereo transmits a *prior* performance of their works. Thus when Aereo retransmits a network's prior broadcast, the underlying broadcast (itself a performance) is the performance that Aereo transmits. Aereo, as discussed above, says the performance it transmits is the *new* performance created by its act of transmitting. That performance comes into existence when Aereo streams the sounds and images of a broadcast program to a subscriber's screen.

47   We assume *arguendo* that Aereo's first argument is correct. Thus, for present purposes, to transmit a performance of (at least) an audiovisual work means to communicate contemporaneously visible images and contemporaneously audible sounds of the work. Cf. *United States v. American Soc. of Composers, Authors and Publishers,* 627 F. 3d 64, 73 (CA2 2010) (holding that a download of a work is not a performance because the data transmitted are not "contemporaneously perceptible"). When an Aereo subscriber selects a program to watch, Aereo streams the program over the Internet to that subscriber. Aereo thereby "communicate[s]" to the subscriber, by means of a "device or process," the work's images and sounds. §101. And those images and sounds are contemporaneously visible and audible on the subscriber's computer (or other Internet-connected device). So under our assumed definition, Aereo transmits a performance whenever its subscribers watch a program.

48   But what about the Clause's further requirement that Aereo transmit a performance "to the public"? As we have said, an Aereo subscriber receives broadcast television signals with an antenna dedicated to him alone. Aereo's system makes from those signals a personal copy of the selected program. It streams the content of the copy to the same subscriber and to no one else. One and only one subscriber has the ability to see and hear each Aereo transmission. The fact that each transmission is to only one subscriber, in Aereo's view, means that it does not transmit a performance "to the public."

49   In terms of the Act's purposes, these differences do not distinguish Aereo's system from cable systems, which do perform "publicly." Viewed in terms of Congress' regulatory objectives, why should any of these technological differences matter? They concern the behind-the-scenes way in which Aereo delivers television programming to its viewers' screens. They do not render Aereo's commercial objective any different from that of cable companies. Nor do they significantly alter the viewing experience of Aereo's subscribers. Why would a subscriber who wishes to watch a television show care much whether images and sounds are delivered to his screen via a large multisubscriber antenna or one small dedicated antenna, whether they arrive instantaneously or after a few seconds' delay, or whether they are transmitted directly or after a personal copy is made? And why, if Aereo is right, could not modern CATV systems simply continue the same commercial and consumer-oriented activities, free of copyright restrictions, provided they substitute such new technologies for old? Congress would as much have intended to protect a copyright holder from the unlicensed activities of Aereo as from those of cable companies.

50   The text of the Clause effectuates Congress' intent. Aereo's argument to the contrary relies on the premise that "to transmit . . . a performance" means to make a single transmission. But the Clause suggests that an entity may transmit a performance through multiple, discrete transmissions. That is because one can "transmit" or "communicate" something through a *set* of actions. Thus one can transmit a message to one's friends, irrespective of whether one sends separate identical e-mails to each friend or a single e-mail to all at once. So can an elected official communicate an idea, slogan, or speech to her constituents, regardless of whether she communicates that idea, slogan, or speech during individual phone calls to each constituent or in a public square.

51   The fact that a singular noun ("a performance") follows the words "to transmit" does not suggest the contrary. One can sing a song to his family, whether he sings the same song one-on-one or in front of all together. Similarly, one's colleagues may watch a performance of a

particular play—say, this season's modern-dress version of "Measure for Measure"—whether they do so at separate or at the same showings. By the same principle, an entity may transmit a performance through one or several transmissions, where the performance is of the same work.

52   The Transmit Clause must permit this interpretation, for it provides that one may transmit a performance to the public "whether the members of the public capable of receiving the performance . . . receive it . . . at the same time or at different times." §101. Were the words "to transmit . . . a performance" limited to a single act of communication, members of the public could not receive the performance communicated "at different times." Therefore, in light of the purpose and text of the Clause, we conclude that when an entity communicates the same contemporaneously perceptible images and sounds to multiple people, it transmits a performance to them regardless of the number of discrete communications it makes.

53   We do not see how the fact that Aereo transmits via personal copies of programs could make a difference. The Act applies to transmissions "by means of any device or process." *Ibid.* And retransmitting a television program using user-specific copies is a "process" of transmitting a performance. A "cop[y]" of a work is simply a "material objec[t] . . . in which a work is fixed . . . and from which the work can be perceived, reproduced, or otherwise communicated." *Ibid.* So whether Aereo transmits from the same or separate copies, it performs the same work; it shows the same images and makes audible the same sounds. Therefore, when Aereo streams the same television program to multiple subscribers, it "transmit[s] . . . a performance" to all of them.

54   Moreover, the subscribers to whom Aereo transmits television programs constitute "the public." Aereo communicates the same contemporaneously perceptible images and sounds to a large number of people who are unrelated and unknown to each other. This matters because, although the Act does not define "the public," it specifies that an entity performs publicly when it performs at "any place where a substantial number of persons outside of a normal circle of a family and its social acquaintances is gathered." *Ibid.* The Act thereby suggests that "the public" consists of a large group of people outside of a family and friends.

55   Neither the record nor Aereo suggests that Aereo's subscribers receive performances in their capacities as owners or possessors of the underlying works. This is relevant because when an entity performs to a set of people, whether they constitute "the public" often depends upon their relationship to the underlying work. When, for example, a valet parking attendant returns cars to their drivers, we would not say that the parking service provides cars "to the public." We would say that it provides the cars to their owners. We would say that a car dealership, on the other hand, does provide cars to the public, for it sells cars to individuals who lack a pre-existing relationship to the cars. Similarly, an entity that transmits a performance to individuals in their capacities as owners or possessors does not perform to "the public," whereas an entity like Aereo that transmits to large numbers of paying subscribers who lack any prior relationship to the works does so perform.

56   Finally, we note that Aereo's subscribers may receive the same programs at different times and locations. This fact does not help Aereo, however, for the Transmit Clause expressly provides that an entity may perform publicly "whether the members of the public capable of receiving the performance . . . receive it in the same place or in separate places and at the same time or at different times." *Ibid.* In other words, "the public" need not be situated together, spatially or temporally. For these reasons, we conclude that Aereo transmits a performance of petitioners' copyrighted works to the public, within the meaning of the Transmit Clause.

57   **IV**

58   Aereo and many of its supporting *amici* argue that to apply the Transmit Clause to Aereo's conduct will impose copyright liability on other technologies, including new technologies, that Congress could not possibly have wanted to reach. We agree that Congress, while intending the Transmit Clause to apply broadly to cable companies and their equivalents, did not intend to discourage or to control the emergence or use of different kinds of technologies. But we do not believe that our limited holding today will have that effect.

59   For one thing, the history of cable broadcast transmissions that led to the enactment of the Transmit Clause informs our conclusion that Aereo "perform[s]," but it does not determine whether different kinds of providers in different contexts also "perform." For another, an entity only transmits a performance when it communicates contemporaneously perceptible images and sounds of a work. See Brief for

Respondent 31 ("[I]f a distributor . . . sells [multiple copies of a digital video disc] by mail to consumers, . . . [its] distribution of the DVDs merely makes it possible for the recipients to perform the work themselves—it is not a `device or process' by which the *distributor* publicly performs the work" (emphasis in original)).

60   Further, we have interpreted the term "the public" to apply to a group of individuals acting as ordinary members of the public who pay primarily to watch broadcast television programs, many of which are copyrighted. We have said that it does not extend to those who act as owners or possessors of the relevant product. And we have not considered whether the public performance right is infringed when the user of a service pays primarily for something other than the transmission of copyrighted works, such as the remote storage of content. See Brief for United States as *Amicus Curiae* 31 (distinguishing cloudbased storage services because they "offer consumers more numerous and convenient means of playing back copies that the consumers have *already* lawfully acquired" (emphasis in original)). In addition, an entity does not transmit to the public if it does not transmit to a substantial number of people outside of a family and its social circle.

61   We also note that courts often apply a statute's highly general language in light of the statute's basic purposes. Finally, the doctrine of "fair use" can help to prevent inappropriate or inequitable applications of the Clause. See *Sony Corp. of America* v. *Universal City Studios, Inc.,* 464 U. S. 417 (1984).

62   We cannot now answer more precisely how the Transmit Clause or other provisions of the Copyright Act will apply to technologies not before us. We agree with the Solicitor General that "[q]uestions involving cloud computing, [remote storage] DVRs, and other novel issues not before the Court, as to which `Congress has not plainly marked [the] course,' should await a case in which they are squarely presented." [...]

64   In sum, having considered the details of Aereo's practices, we find them highly similar to those of the CATV systems in *Fortnightly* and *Teleprompter.* And those are activities that the 1976 amendments sought to bring within the scope of the Copyright Act. Insofar as there are differences, those differences concern not the nature of the service that Aereo provides so much as the technological manner in which it provides the service. We conclude that those differences are not adequate to place Aereo's activities outside the scope of the Act.

65   For these reasons, we conclude that Aereo "perform[s]" petitioners' copyrighted works "publicly," as those terms are defined by the Transmit Clause. We therefore reverse the contrary judgment of the Court of Appeals, and we remand the case for further proceedings consistent with this opinion.

66   *It is so ordered.*

67   [...]

88

London-Sire Records, Inc. v. Doe 1 et al.

August 04, 2014 by mrisch

This case examines what it means to distribute a copyrighted work in the age of electronic file distribution

1   542 F.Supp.2d 153

2   **LONDON-SIRE RECORDS, INC., et al., Plaintiffs,**

v.

DOE 1 et al., Defendants.

3   [...]

4   United States District Court, D. Massachusetts.

5   March 31, 2008.

6   [...]

8   *ORDER ON MOTIONS TO QUASH*

9   **GERTNER, District Judge.**

10   [...]

15   The plaintiffs allege that the defendants used peer-to-peer software to "download and/or distribute to the public certain of the [plaintiffs'] Copyrighted Recordings.... Through his or her continuous and ongoing acts of downloading and/or distributing to the public the Copyrighted Recordings, each Defendant has violated Plaintiffs' exclusive rights of reproduction and distribution." [...]

18   Peer-to-peer software primarily exists to create decentralized networks of individual computer users. The software allows the users to communicate directly with one another, rather than routing their transmissions through a central server — thus the term "peer-to-peer" architecture, as opposed to "client-server." [...]. Each type of architecture has distinct advantages and disadvantages, most of which are not relevant to this case.

19   What is relevant is that users in a peer-to-peer network can remain relatively anonymous or pseudonymous. Because communications between two computers on a peer-to-peer network can take place directly, without passing through a central network server,[4] such transactions are not easily observable by a third party. By the nature of the network and software, then, peer-to-peer users can control what information they display to the world. [...] Moreover, generally speaking, anyone who has the requisite software and internet connection can participate in open peer-to-peer networks, such as the ones the defendants are alleged to have used in this case.

20   [...] However, other files transferred are electronic versions of copyrighted music or video files. Notably, because the files on each user's

506

computer are digital, another computer can make a precise copy of them with no attendant loss in quality. *[...]*

21   In this case, the plaintiffs allege that each of the defendants has taken part in just such a file transfer. To discover potentially infringing transfers, the plaintiffs (acting through their trade association, the Recording Industry Association of America, or "RIAA") have retained a third-party investigator, MediaSentry, Inc. *[...]* MediaSentry essentially functions as an undercover user of the peer-to-peer networks. It connects to the network and searches for the plaintiff record companies' copyrighted files. *[...]* MediaSentry gathers what information it can about the computer from which the files were downloaded (the "sending computer.") Most crucially, that information includes the date and time at which the files were downloaded and the IP number of the sending computer. *[...]*

1. Whether the Plaintiffs Have Asserted a Claim Upon Which Relief Can Be Granted

50   A claim for copyright infringement has two elements. First, the plaintiffs must demonstrate that they hold a valid copyright (an issue the defendants do not contest.) Second, the plaintiff must show that the defendant violated of one of the exclusive rights held by a copyright owner. *[...]* The plaintiffs claim that "each [defendant, without the permission or consent of [p]laintiffs, has ... downloaded] or distribut[ed] to the public" music files to which the plaintiff holds the copyright. *[...]*

51   The movants and the amicus present two broad arguments, each of which requires the Court to consider the scope of a copyright holder's exclusive rights under the statutes quoted above. First, they contend that the copyright laws require an actual dissemination of copyrighted material; merely making copyrighted material available for another person to copy, they argue, is only an attempt at infringement — which is not actionable. *[...]* Second, they contend that the scope of the rights given to copyright owners by § 106 is limited by the definition of "phonorecords" as "material objects" in 17 U.S.C. § 101.[14] In their view, the copyright owner's rights are limited to tangible, physical objects, and purely electronic transmissions over the internet fall outside those rights.[15] *[...]*

a. Whether the Copyright Holder's Right Extends Only to Actual Distributions

53   The first question the Court must address is whether the distribution right under 17 U.S.C. § 106(3) requires an actual dissemination to constitute an infringement.[[...]] It is an important issue, determining in part how to evaluate the proffered evidence in this case. MediaSentry, posing as just another peer-to-peer user, can easily verify that copyrighted material has been made available for download from a certain IP address. Arguably, though, MediaSentry's own downloads are not themselves copyright infringements because it is acting as an agent of the copyright holder, and copyright holders cannot infringe their own rights.[...] If that argument is accepted, MediaSentry's evidence cannot alone demonstrate an infringement.

54   *[...]*

55   The First Circuit has squarely considered and rejected the proposition that copyright liability arises where the defendant authorized an infringement, but no actual infringement occurred. *[...]* It noted that Congress' intent in adding "authorize" to the statute was to "avoid any questions as to the liability of contributory infringers." *[...]*

56   Thus, to constitute a violation of the distribution right under § 106(3), the defendants' actions must do more than "authorize" a distribution; they must actually "do" it. The Court therefore moves to *[...]* the plaintiffs' second argument: Merely making copyrighted works available to the public is enough where, as in this case, the alleged distributor does not need to take any more affirmative steps before an unauthorized copy of the work changes hands. Other courts have split over whether that is a valid reading of the statute. *[...]*

68   "Distribution" is undefined in the copyright statutes. "Publication," however, is defined, and incorporates "distribution" as part of its definition:

64   'Publication' is the distribution of copies or phonorecords of a work to the public by sale or other transfer of ownership, or by rental, lease, or lending. The offering to distribute copies or phonorecords to a group of persons for purposes of further distribution, public performance, or public display, constitutes publication. A public performance or display [169] of a work does not of itself constitute publication.

65   17 U.S.C. § 101. By the plain meaning of the statute, all "distributions ... to the public" are publications. But not all publications are distributions to the public — the statute explicitly creates an additional category of publications that are not themselves distributions. For example, suppose an author has a copy of her (as yet unpublished) novel. If she sells that copy to a member of the public, it constitutes both distribution and publication. If she merely offers to sell it to the same member of the public, that is neither a distribution nor a publication. And if the author offers to sell the manuscript to a publishing house "for purposes of further distribution," but does not actually do so, that is a publication but not a distribution.

66   Plainly, "publication" and "distribution" are not identical. And Congress' decision to use the latter term when defining the copyright holder's rights in 17 U.S.C. § 106(3) must be given consequence. In this context, that means that the defendants cannot be liable for violating the plaintiffs' distribution right unless a "distribution" actually occurred.

67   But that does not mean that the plaintiffs' pleadings and evidence are insufficient. The Court can draw from the Complaint and the current record a reasonable inference in the plaintiffs' favor — that where the defendant has completed all the necessary steps for a public distribution, a reasonable fact-finder may infer that the distribution *actually took place*. [...] The plaintiffs have pled an actual distribution and provided some concrete evidence to support their allegation.

68   ## b. Whether the Distribution Right Is Limited to Physical, Tangible Objects

69   Next, the movants and the EFF contend that the distribution right under 17 U.S.C. § 106(3) is limited to physical, tangible objects. By its terms, the distribution right only extends to distributions of "phonorecords of the copyrighted work to the public by sale or other transfer of ownership, or by rental, lease or lending." In turn, 17 U.S.C. § 101 defined "phonorecords" as "material objects in which sounds ... are fixed." The movants and the EFF focus on the phrase "material object," as well as the meaning of "sale or other transfer," and conclude that purely electronic file sharing does not fall within the scope of the right. If their argument is accepted, it would mean that the plaintiffs' Complaint is legally insufficient to allege a violation of the distribution right protected by§ 106(3).

70   The movants' argument is sweeping, carrying substantial implications for a great deal of internet commerce — any involving computer-to-computer electronic transfers of information. Indeed, this case is an exemplar. The plaintiffs have not [...] alleged a physical distribution. To the contrary, it is clear that their harm comes from the purely electronic copying of music files. [...] After carefully considering the parties' and the EFF's arguments, the Court concludes that § 106(3) confers on copyright owners the right to control purely electronic distributions of their work.

71   As noted above, 17 U.S.C. § 106(3) applies to the distribution of "phonorecords." And "phonorecords" are defined in full as follows:

72   'Phonorecords' are material objects in which sounds, other than those accompanying a motion picture or other audiovisual work, are fixed by any method now known or later developed, and from which the sounds can be perceived, reproduced, or otherwise communicated, either directly or with the aid of a machine or device. The term 'phonorecords' includes the material object in which the sounds are first fixed.

73   17 U.S.C. § 101. The movants and the EFF contend that the electronic distribution, if it occurred, did not involve the "distribution" of a material object "by sale or other transfer of ownership, or by rental, lease or lending," as §§ 106(3) and 101 require. The argument has two closely related prongs-first, that no material object actually changed hands, and second, that even if it did, it was not through one of the methods of transfer enumerated in the statute.

74   Each of those arguments relies on an overly literal definition of "material object," and one that ignores the phrase's purpose in the copyright statutes. Congress intended for the copyright owner to be able to control the public distribution of items that can reproduce the artist's sound recording. It makes no difference that the distribution occurs electronically, or that the items are electronic sequences of data rather than physical objects.

75   [...]

76   (1) Electronic Files Are Material Objects

77   Understanding Congress' use of "material object" requires returning to a fundamental principle of the Copyright Act of 1976 [...] Congress drew "a fundamental distinction between the`original work' which is the product of`authorship' and the multitude of material objects in which it can be embodied. Thus, in the sense of the [Copyright Act], a`book' is not a work of authorship, but is a particular kind of`copy.'" [...]

78   The Copyright Act thus does not use materiality in its most obvious sense — to mean a tangible object with a certain heft, like a book or compact disc. Rather, [...] it refers to materiality as a medium in which a copyrighted work can be "fixed." See 17 U.S.C. § 101 [...]

80   Thus, any object in which a sound recording can be fixed is a "material object." That includes the electronic files at issue here. When a user on a peer-to-peer network downloads a song from another user, he receives into his computer a digital sequence representing the sound recording. That sequence is magnetically encoded on a segment of his hard disk (or likewise written on other media.) With the right hardware and software, the downloader can use the magnetic sequence to reproduce the sound recording. The electronic file (or, perhaps more accurately, the appropriate segment of the hard disk) is therefore a "phonorecord" within the meaning of the statute. [...]

81   With that background, the Court turns to the movants' and the EFF's arguments.

82   (2) The Transmission of an Electronic File Constitutes a "Distribution" Within the Meaning of § 106(3)

83   The movants and the EFF present two reasons why the Court should decline to find that purely electronic transmissions are a violation of the distribution right. First, they note that the distribution right is limited to "phonorecords of the copyrighted work," 17 U.S.C. § 106(3), and that part of the definition of "phonorecords" is that they are "material objects," id. § 101. They focus on the phrase "material objects" to suggest that a copyright owner's distribution right only extends to "tangible" objects. [...]

87   After carefully considering the parties' and the EFF's arguments, the Court concludes that 17 U.S.C. § 106(3) does reach this kind of transaction. First, while the statute requires that distribution be of "material objects," there is no reason to limit "distribution" to processes in which a material object exists throughout the entire transaction — as opposed to a transaction in which a material object is created elsewhere at its finish. Second, while the statute addresses ownership, it is the newly minted ownership rights held by the transferee that concern it, not whether the transferor gives up his own.

88   [...]

92   An electronic file transfer is plainly within the sort of transaction that § 106(3) was intended to reach. Indeed, electronic transfers comprise a growing part of the legitimate market for copyrighted sound recordings. [...] What matters in the marketplace is not whether a material object "changes hands," but whether, when the transaction is completed, the distributee has a material object. The Court therefore concludes that electronic file transfers fit within the definition of "distribution" of a phonorecord. [...]

93   For similar reasons, the Court concludes that an electronic file transfer can constitute a "transfer of ownership" as that term is used in §

106(3). [...]

900   [4] This is a small oversimplification. Many popular peer-to-peer networks use a "supernode" architecture. A supernode is a semicentralized computer that operates only to relay search queries and responses within the peer-to-peer network. Once the desired file is located, however, it may be transferred directly from one computer to another. *[...]*

181   [14] The parties refer to "copies." The statute makes clear that where sound recordings are at issue, "phonorecords" is a more precise term. *See* 17 U.S.C. § 101. The two terms appear to be functionally interchangeable, however, differing only in the nature of the copyrighted work. [...]

182   [15] Strictly speaking, much of the parties' briefing on this issue is directed toward the scope of the distribution right under § 106(3), not the reproduction right under § 106(1). But both refer to "copies or phonorecords," so the arguments implicate both rights, though to different degrees.

183   [...]

Section 106 Hypotheticals Introduction to Intellectual Property

August 30, 2014 by mrisch

Courtesy Professor Post (Temple Law)

1   Identify which of the exclusive rights granted by §106 the copyright holder could plausibly allege have been violated in the following hypotheticals:

2   1. Charlotte turns on the FM radio in her office; it is playing a recording of Bob Dylan's "Tangled Up in Blue"(which you may assume is protected by copyright).

3   2. Daniel goes to an exhibition at the Philadelphia Museum of Art, where he sees a sculpture by Klaus Herring entitled "Abstract #33." [Assume Herring's sculpture is protected by copyright]. His sister is getting married this coming weekend, and as a surprise, Daniel carves an ice sculpture closely resembling the shape and proportions of "Abstract #33."

4   3. Assume that Motion Pictures, Inc. ("MPI") owns the copyright in the recently-released film "There Will Be Blood." Ellen buys a copy of the DVD version at her local video store. Using her computer, she makes a copy of the DVD and sends it to her brother in Canada. She is a high school teacher, and she brings the DVD with her to school one day and shows it to her students.

5   4. Fergus buys fifty copies of Ian McEwan's award winning novel *Atonement*. [Assume it is a copyright protected work] He gives all of the copies (except one) to his friends and relatives at Christmas. As part of his efforts to learn Italian, he translates the fifth and sixth chapters of the book into Italian. He also writes a song –"There will be no Atonement Anymore"–in which he imagines how the lead character from the novel (Briony Tallis) would have reacted had she visited Las Vegas. He performs the song at a local Philadelphia nightclub

6   5. Georgia owns an art gallery specializing in 20th century paintings and photographs. She obtains two large paintings by Jasper Johns and a series of photographs taken by Diane Arbus, hangs them in her gallery, and offers them for sale. [Assume the Johns paintings and Arbus photos are protected by copyright]. She takes photographs of the Johns painting and puts copies of the photograph (a) in her current catalogue (a listing of all art available for sale at the gallery) and (b) on her website.

7   6. Herman, CEO of Multiplex, Inc., buys a copy of "The Best American Poetry of 2008." He is so moved by one of the poems in the collection that he reads it out loud at Multiplex, Inc.'s annual shareholder's meeting.

511

Class 12: 6.2 <u>OIL Casebook: Derivative Works</u>

Midway Mfg. Co. v. Artic Int'l, Inc.

August 08, 2014 by mrisch

This case examines the fixation of video games when the user participates in the creation, and then considers whether speeded up circuit boards are a derivative work

1   704 F.2d 1009 (1983)

2   **MIDWAY MFG. CO., an Illinois corporation, Plaintiff-Appellee,**

v.

ARTIC INTERNATIONAL, INC., a New Jersey corporation, Defendant-Appellant.

3   [...]

4   United States Court of Appeals, Seventh Circuit.

5   [...]
Decided April 11, 1983.

6   [...]

9   **CUMMINGS, Chief Judge.**

10   [...]

11   Plaintiff manufactures video game machines. Inside these machines are printed circuit boards capable of causing images to appear on a television picture screen and sounds to emanate from a speaker when an electric current is passed through them. On the outside of each machine are a picture screen, sound speaker, and a lever or button that allows a person using the machine to alter the images appearing on the machine's picture screen and the sounds emanating from its speaker. Each machine can produce a large number of related images and sounds. These sounds and images are stored on the machine's circuit boards—how the circuits are arranged and connected determines the set of sounds and images the machine is capable of making. When a person touches the control lever or button on the outside of the machine he sends a signal to the circuit boards inside the machine which causes them to retrieve and display one of the sounds and images stored in them. Playing a video game involves manipulating the controls on the machine so that some of the images stored in the machine's circuitry appear on its picture screen and some of its sounds emanate from its speaker.

12   Defendant sells printed circuit boards for use inside video game machines. One of the circuit boards defendant sells speeds up the rate of play—how fast the sounds and images change—of "Galaxian," one of plaintiff's video games, when inserted in place of one of the "Galaxian" machine's circuit boards. Another of defendant's circuit boards stores a set of images and sounds almost identical to that stored in the [...] circuit boards of plaintiff's "Pac-Man" video game machine[1] so that the video game people play on machines containing defendant's circuit board looks and sounds virtually the same as plaintiff's "Pac-Man" game.

13   Plaintiff sued defendant alleging that defendant's sale of these two circuit boards infringes its copyrights in its "Galaxian" and "Pac-Man"

video games. [...]

14   Plaintiff claims that its "Pac-Man" and "Galaxian" video games are "audiovisual works" protected under the 1976 Copyright Act. Section 101 of that Act defines audiovisual works as

15   works that consist of a series of related images which are intrinsically intended to be shown by the use of machines or devices such as projectors, viewers, or electronic equipment, together with accompanying sounds, if any, regardless of the nature of the material objects, such as films or tapes, in which the works are embodied. 17 U.S.C. § 101.

16   It is not immediately obvious that video games fall within this definition. The phrase "series of related images" might be construed to refer only to a set of images displayed in a fixed sequence. Construed that way, video games do not qualify as audiovisual works. Each time a video game is played, a different sequence of images appears on the screen of the video game machine—assuming the game is not played exactly the same way each time. But the phrase might also be construed more broadly to refer to any set of images displayed as some kind of unit. [...] the legislative history of the Copyright Act of 1976 suggests that "Congress probably wanted the courts to interpret the definitional provisions of the new act flexibly, so that it would cover new technologies as they appeared, rather than to interpret those provisions narrowly and so force Congress periodically to update the act." [...]

17   There is a second difficulty that must be overcome if video games are to be classified as audiovisual works. Strictly speaking, the particular sequence of images that appears on the screen of a video game machine when the game is played is not the same work as the set of images stored in the machine's circuit boards. The person playing the game can vary the order in which the stored images appear on the screen by moving the machine's control lever. That makes playing a video game a little like arranging words in a dictionary into sentences or paints on a palette into a painting. The question is whether the creative effort in playing a video game is enough like writing or painting to make each performance of a video game the work of the player and not the game's inventor.

18   We think it is not. Television viewers may vary the order of images transmitted on the same signal but broadcast on different channels by pressing a button that changes the channel on their television. In the *WGN* case, we held that the creative effort required to do that did not make the sequence of images appearing on a viewer's [...] television screen the work of the viewer and not of the television station that transmitted the images. Playing a video game is more like changing channels on a television than it is like writing a novel or painting a picture. The player of a video game does not have control over the sequence of images that appears on the video game screen. He cannot create any sequence he wants out of the images stored on the game's circuit boards. The most he can do is choose one of the limited number of sequences the game allows him to choose. He is unlike a writer or a painter because the video game in effect writes the sentences and paints the painting for him; he merely chooses one of the sentences stored in its memory, one of the paintings stored in its collection.

19   [...]

23   The final argument of defendant's that we address is that selling plaintiff's licensees circuit boards that speed up the rate of play of plaintiff's video games is not an infringement of plaintiff's copyrights. Speeding up the rate of play of a video game is a little like playing at 45 or 78 revolutions per minute ("RPM's") a phonograph record recorded at 33 RPM's. If a discotheque licensee did that, it would probably not be an infringement of the record company's copyright in the record. One might argue by analogy that it is not a copyright infringement for video game licensees to speed up the rate of play of video games, and that it is not a contributory infringement for the defendant to sell licensees circuit boards that enable them to do that.

24   [...]

25   Among a copyright owner's exclusive rights is the right "to prepare derivative works based upon the copyrighted work." 17 U.S.C. § 106(2). If, as we hold, the speeded-up "Galaxian" game that a licensee creates with a circuit board supplied by the defendant is a

derivative work based upon "Galaxian," a licensee who lacks the plaintiff's authorization to create a derivative work is a direct infringer and the defendant is a contributory infringer through its sale of the speeded-up circuit board. *[...]*

26   Section 101 of the 1976 Copyright Act defines a derivative work as "a work based upon one or more preexisting works, such as a translation, musical arrangement, dramatization, fictionalization, motion picture *[...]* version, sound recording, art reproduction, abridgment, condensation, or any other form in which a work may be recast, transformed, or adapted." It is not obvious from this language whether a speeded-up video game is a derivative work. A speeded-up phonograph record probably is not. *[...]* But that is because the additional value to the copyright owner of having the right to market separately the speeded-up version of the recorded performance is too trivial to warrant legal protection for that right. A speeded-up video game is a substantially different product from the original game. As noted, it is more exciting to play and it requires some creative effort to produce. For that reason, the owner of the copyright on the game should be entitled to monopolize it on the same theory that he is entitled to monopolize the derivative works specifically listed in Section 101. The current rage for video games was not anticipated in 1976, and like any new technology the video game does not fit with complete ease the definition of derivative work in Section 101 of the 1976 Act. But the amount by which the language of Section 101 must be stretched to accommodate speeded-up video games is, we believe, within the limits within which Congress wanted the new Act to operate. *[...]*

1-800 CONTACTS, Inc. v. WhenU.com

September 01, 2014 by mrisch

1   309 F.Supp.2d 467 (2003)

2   **1-800 CONTACTS, INC., Plaintiff,**

         v.

         WHENU.COM and Vision Direct, Inc., Defendants.

3   [...]

4   United States District Court, S.D. New York.

5   December 22, 2003.

6   [...]

9   *Opinion*

10   **BATTS, District Judge.**

11   Before the Court is a Motion for a Preliminary Injunction by Plaintiff 1-800 Contacts ("1-800 Contacts" or "Plaintiff") to enjoin Defendants from delivering to computer users competitive "pop-up" Internet advertisements, in violation of federal and state copyright, trademark, and unfair competition laws. [...]

12   **I. BACKGROUND**

13   **A. Procedural Background**

14   On October 9, 2002, Plaintiff filed this action with ten claims for relief.[...] With its Complaint, Plaintiff also filed a Motion for Preliminary Inju

19   **B. Factual Background**

20   [...]

22   Plaintiff 1-800 Contacts, Inc. ("1-800 Contacts") sells and markets replacement contact lenses and related products through its website, located at http://www.1800Contacts.com, and also through telephone and mail orders. [...]

23   Plaintiff is the sole owner of the 1-800Contacts.com website. [...] Plaintiff registered its copyright to the 1-800Contacts.com website with the Copyright Office of the United States Library of Congress on October 2, 2000.[...]

25   Defendant WhenU.com is a software company that has developed and distributes, among other products, the "SaveNow" program, a proprietary software application. [...]

²⁶ ## 2. The Internet and the Windows Operating Environment

²⁷ Since Plaintiff's claims arise from alleged anti-competitive and infringing action by Defendants through the Defendants' use of proprietary software that is distributed to computer users, a brief explanation of the Internet, the computer operating environment and associated terms and definitions is helpful. These facts are not in dispute.

²⁸ [...] With a computer that is connected to the Internet, a computer user can access computer code and information that is stored on the Internet in repositories called "servers." [...] Much of the information stored in servers on the Internet can be viewed by a computer user in the form of "webpages," which are collections of pictures and information, retrieved from the Internet, and assembled on the user's computer screen. [...] "Websites" are collection of webpages that are organized and linked together to allow a computer user to move from webpage to webpage easily. [...] A single website may contain information or pictures that are stored on many different servers. [...]

²⁹ [...]

³¹ Many computer users ("users") access the Internet with computers that use the Microsoft Windows operating system ("Windows"). Windows allows a user to work in numerous software applications simultaneously. [...] In Windows, the background screen is called the "desktop." When a software program is launched, a "window" appears on the desktop, within which the functions of that program are displayed and operate. [...] A user may open multiple windows simultaneously, allowing the user to launch and use more than one software application at the same time. Individual windows may be moved around the desktop, and because the computer screen is two-dimensional, one window may obscure another window, thus appearing to be "in front of" another window. [...]

³³ ## 3. The SaveNow Program

³⁴ The following description of the operation and function of the SaveNow software is not in dispute. The SaveNow program is computer software that only operates in the Microsoft Windows operating system. [...] The SaveNow software, if installed, resides on individual computer users' computer desktops. [...] When a computer user who has installed the SaveNow software (a "SaveNow user") browses the Internet, the SaveNow software scans activity conducted within the SaveNow user's Internet browser, [...] comparing URLs, website addresses, search terms and webpage content accessed by the SaveNow user with a proprietary directory,[17] using algorithms contained in the software. [...]

³⁵ Entering an URL into the browser can "trigger" the SaveNow software to deliver a "pop-up" advertisement.[18] [...] When a user types a search word or URL into the Internet browser, the SaveNow software looks to see what category of products or services the address belongs to. [...] In general, if the SaveNow user's Internet usage "matches" information contained in the SaveNow directory, the SaveNow software will determine that an ad should be shown, will retrieve a pop-up advertisement from a server over the Internet, and will display that pop-up ad in a new window appearing on the user's computer screen. [...] More pertinent to this case, when a user types in "1800contacts.com," the URL for Plaintiff's website, the SaveNow software recognizes that the user is interested in the eye-care category, and retrieves from an Internet server a pop-up advertisement from that category. [...] Mr. Naider described the functioning of the proprietary directory contained in the SaveNow program:

³⁶   [E]ssentially, the program contains a directory of the Internet, and ... has over 40,000 elements in this directory. Elements such as URL's, but many other elements, such as search terms, something we call key-word algorithms. So an example of a keyword algorithm would be, the software processes the content of the page and if I'm reading an article where the word "diabetes" appears four times and the word "type I" or "type II" in conjunction with that, that would be an example of a keyword algorithm. All of those elements, the URL's, the search terms, the key-word algorithms, are processed and compared against this directory of 40,000, and growing, elements. And then a decision is made that says, OK, this user is engaged in activity in a particular category — again, it may be hotel travel or air travel, in this case contact lenses or eye care — and the ad units themselves are basically associated with categories, such that if the software detects, by looking at these elements, activity in a category, it may display an ad that's relevant to that category.

37   [...]

38   Usually there is a "few-second" delay between the moment a user accesses a [...] website, and the point at which a SaveNow pop-up
        advertisement appears on the user's screen. [...]

39   If a SaveNow user who has accessed the 1-800 Contacts website and has received a WhenU.com pop-up advertisement does not want
        to view the advertisement or the advertiser's website, the user can click on the visible portion of the window containing the 1-800
        Contacts website, and the 1-800 Contacts website will move to the front of the screen display, with the pop-up ad moving behind the
        website window. [...] Or, if the user recognizes that a different website has appeared on the screen, the user can close the pop-up
        website by clicking on its "x," or close, button. If the user clicks on the pop-up ad, the main browser window (containing the 1-800
        Contacts website) will be navigated to the website of the advertiser that was featured inside the pop-up advertisement. [...]

42   The SaveNow software generates at least three kinds of ads — an ad may be a small "pop-up" advertisement appearing in the bottom
        right-hand corner of a user's screen; it may be a "pop-under" advertisement that appears behind the webpage the user initially visited; or
        it may be a "panoramic" advertisement that stretches across the bottom of the user's computer screen. [...]

II. DISCUSSION

74   [...]

75   It is well-settled in this Circuit that "a party seeking a preliminary injunction must demonstrate (1) the likelihood of irreparable injury in the
        absence of such an injunction, and (2) either (a) likelihood of success on the merits [...]

B. Copyright Claims

77   To establish a *prima facie* case of copyright infringement, a Plaintiff must show "1) Ownership of valid copyright, and 2) Copying of
        constituent elements of the work that are original." *[...]* *[...]*

78   Plaintiff has filed as an exhibit to its Complaint a certificate of registration with the United States Copyright Office of the "1800 Contacts
        Web site," [...] this serves as *prima facie* evidence of valid ownership of a copyright. 17 U.S.C. § 410(c). This protection extends to both
        the computer code for the website and the screen displays of the website. *[...]*

79   Plaintiff alleges that Defendants have "copied" constituent elements of Plaintiff's website in the "broad sense of invasion of one of the
        exclusive rights secured to copyright owners under the Copyright Act." [...] Plaintiff argues that the 1-800 Contacts website, as
        perceived by a SaveNow user,[37] appears differently than [...] the copyrighted website, and that the website's appearance has therefore
        been "modified and that Defendants' pop-up scheme caused this modification." [...] Specifically, Plaintiff alleges that Defendants have
        invaded Plaintiff's exclusive right to display the 1-800 Contacts website, in violation of 17 U.S.C. § 106(1), and its exclusive right to
        prepare derivative works based on the 1-800 Contacts website, secured to Plaintiff under 17 U.S.C. § 106(2).

1. Display Right, 17 U.S.C. § 106(1)

81   Plaintiff alleges that Defendants have invaded Plaintiff's exclusive right to display the 1-800 Contacts website. 17 U.S.C. § 106(1).
        Plaintiff argues it gives computer users a license to "use and display" its website, but does not give them a license to alter the website or
        change its appearance in any way. Plaintiff argues that, by delivering pop-up advertisements to a SaveNow user's computer while the
        user views Plaintiff's website, Defendants create a new screen display that incorporates Plaintiff's copyrighted work, thereby infringing
        Plaintiff's exclusive right to display its copyrighted work. [...]

82   For this Court to hold that computer users are limited in their use of Plaintiff's website to viewing the website without any obstructing

windows or programs would be to subject countless computer users and software developers to liability for copyright infringement and contributory copyright infringement, since the modern computer environment in which Plaintiff's website exists allows users to obscure, cover, and change the appearance of browser windows containing Plaintiff's website.

83   Without authority or evidence for the claim that users exceed their license to view the copyrighted 1-800 Contacts website when they obscure the website with other browser windows (including pop-up ads generated by the SaveNow program), Plaintiff has little basis for its claim that Defendants have infringed its display right.

84   **2. Derivative Works Right, 17 U.S.C. § 106(2)**

85   Plaintiff also alleges that Defendants have invaded Plaintiff's exclusive right to prepare derivative works based on the 1-800 Contacts website, secured to Plaintiff under 17 U.S.C. § 106(2).

86   Section 106 of the Copyright Act provides that "the owner of copyright under this title has the exclusive right to ... prepare derivative works based upon the copyrighted work." 17 U.S.C. § 106. However, Plaintiff has failed to show that [...] Defendants have created a "derivative work" that infringes Plaintiff's exclusive rights under § 106(2).

87   Plaintiff argues that, by delivering pop-up advertisements to a SaveNow user's computer while the user views Plaintiff's website, Defendants are adding a Vision Direct advertisement to Plaintiff's copyrighted screen display, thus creating a derivative of the Plaintiff's copyrighted screen display, and in the process violating "two fundamental tenets of copyright law — exceeding the license granted and destroying the author's control over the manner in which its work is presented." [...]

88   For the reason set forth above, to the extent Plaintiff's derivative work argument relies on a theory that Defendants cause or contribute to copyright infringement by a SaveNow user when viewing Plaintiff's copyrighted screen display, in excess of the license granted by Plaintiff,[38] this argument fails.

89   Plaintiff's second theory is that Defendants have created a derivative work by adding to or deleting from Plaintiff's copyrighted website, and therefore have transformed or recast the website, in derogation of Plaintiff's exclusive derivative work right. [...] Plaintiff argues that to infringe their derivative work right, Defendants need not have made a copy of the original work in order to create a derivative work,[39] and that to violate its protected right to prepare derivative works, Defendants "need only transform or recast the copyrighted work in some way," as by "adding to or deleting from" Plaintiff's copyrighted website. [...] Plaintiff analogizes the pop-up ads in this case to advertisements added to and interspersed throughout the text of a copyrighted book in *National Bank of Commerce v. Shaklee Corp.*, 503 F.Supp. 533 (W.D.Tex.1980), which were found to be "unauthorized additions" to the book text, in violation of the book author's copyright. [...] Plaintiff's argument fails because Defendants have not created a "derivative work."

90   In order for Plaintiff's derivative work right to have been infringed, the Court must find that the screen display of the 1-800 Contacts website, with Defendant's pop-up ads, is in fact a "derivative work," as defined at 17 U.S.C. § 101.

91   A "derivative work" is:

92   ... a work based upon one or more preexisting works, such as a translation, musical arrangement, dramatization, fictionalization, motion picture version, sound recording, art reproduction, abridgment, condensation, or any other form in which a work may be recast, transformed, or adapted. A work consisting of editorial revisions, annotations, elaborations, or other modifications which, as a whole, *represent an original work of authorship*, is a `derivative work'.

93   17 U.S.C. § 101 (emphasis added).

94   [...]

100 Plaintiff has failed to show that its website, and Defendants' pop-up advertisements are "sufficiently permanent or stable to permit it to be perceived, reproduced or otherwise communicated for a period of more than transitory duration." 17 U.S.C. § 101. Indeed, Defendants' pop-up ad windows may be moved, obscured, or "closed" entirely — thus completely disappearing from perception, with a single click of a mouse. [...]Moreover, to the extent pop-up advertisements fit the description of "transmitted images," they are not "fixed" works, since there is no evidence that a fixation is made "simultaneously with" the pop-up advertisements' "transmission" to the viewer of the website.[40] 17 U.S.C. § 101.

101 Given that the screen display of the 1-800 Contacts website with Defendant's pop-up ads is not "fixed in any medium," it is not sufficiently "original" to qualify as a derivative work under the second sentence of 17 U.S.C. § 101.

102 The first sentence of 17 U.S.C. § 101 also allows "non-original" works to qualify for "derivative" work status. Since the screen display of the 1-800 Contacts website with Defendant's pop-up ads is not a "translation, musical arrangement, dramatization, fictionalization, motion picture version, sound recording, art reproduction, abridgment, condensation," for Plaintiff's to prevail, it must show that Defendants have "recast, transformed, or adapted" the 1-800 Contacts website. None of these three actions seems to describe what is done to Plaintiff's website by Defendants' pop-up ads, since Plaintiff's website remains "intact" on the computer screen. Defendants' pop-up ads may "obscure" or "cover" a portion of Plaintiff's website — but they do not "change" the website, and accordingly do not "recast, transform or adapt" the website. [...] Moreover, if obscuring a browser window containing a copyrighted website with another computer window produces a "derivative work," then *any* action by a computer user that produced a computer window or visual graphic that altered the screen appearance of Plaintiff's website, however slight, would require Plaintiff's permission. A definition of "derivative work" that sweeps within the scope of the copyright law a multi-tasking Internet shopper whose word-processing program [...] obscures the screen display of Plaintiff's website is indeed "jarring," and not supported by the definition set forth at 17 U.S.C. § 101. [...]

103 Since Plaintiff has failed to demonstrate that Defendants have invaded the exclusive rights secured to Plaintiff under the Copyright Act, there is little likelihood that Plaintiff will succeed on the merits of its copyright claims. [...]

104 Accordingly, Plaintiff's motion for a preliminary injunction based on the Defendants' alleged infringement of Plaintiff's copyrights is DENIED.

105 [...]

III. CONCLUSION

231 [...]

234 Plaintiff's Motion for preliminary injunctive relief on its copyright claims is DENIED.

235 [...]

260 [18] "Pop-up" windows are windows containing notifications or advertisements that appear on the screen, usually without any triggering action by the computer user.

262 [...]

268 [37] Plaintiff argues that, under *New York Times Co. v. Tasini*, 533 U.S. 483, 121 S.Ct. 2381, 150 L.Ed.2d 500 (2001), "this Court must view Plaintiff's website as would a PC user surfing the web in order to determine whether Defendant modified Plaintiff's copyrighted works." Plaintiff appears to read *Tasini* too broadly. (Pl. Feb. 28, 2003 at 7). In *Tasini*, the Supreme Court held that the privilege accorded a newspaper, as a collective work copyright owner under § 201(c) of the Copyright Act, to reproduce and distribute parts of a collective work did not shield the newspaper from liability for permitting electronic publishers to include the work of individual authors in electronic

online Databases. *Tasini,* 533 U.S. at 500, 121 S.Ct. 2381. The Court explained that "[i]n determining whether the Articles have been reproduced and distributed `as part of' a `revision' of the collective works in issue, we focus on the Articles as presented to, and perceptible by, the user of the Databases." *Tasini,* 533 U.S. at 499-500, 121 S.Ct. 2381. Although the *Tasini* Court turned to the perceptions of the computer user to determine whether articles had been reproduced and distributed "as part of" a "revision" of collective works for purposes of § 201(c), *Tasini* does not require this Court to "view Plaintiff's website as would a PC user surfing the web in order to determine whether Defendant modified Plaintiff's copyrighted works" in preparing a derivative work in violation of 17 U.S.C. § 106(2).

289   [...]

291   [40] The lack of any "fixation" here explains why Plaintiff errs in its assertion that this case is analogous to *National Bank of Commerce v. Shaklee Corp.,* 503 F.Supp. 533 (W.D.Tex.1980). While in this case any "derivative" work created when a computer user views Plaintiff's copyrighted website as modified by Defendants' pop-up advertisements is not fixed in any tangible medium of expression, the books published with unauthorized interspersed advertisements in *National Bank of Commerce v. Shaklee Corp.,* were clearly "fixed" in print.

292   [...]

306

Lewis Galoob Toys Inc. v. Nintendo of America Inc

August 08, 2014 by mrisch

This short excerpt considers whether modern "speedup" chips are a derivative work

1
964 F.2d 965 (1992)

2

LEWIS GALOOB TOYS, INC., Plaintiff-Appellee,

v.

NINTENDO OF AMERICA, INC., Defendant-Appellant.

[...]

4
United States Court of Appeals, Ninth Circuit.

5

[...]
Decided May 21, 1992.
As Amended August 5, 1992.

6
   [...]

9
[...] FARRIS, Circuit Judge:

10
   [...]

11
FACTS

12
The Nintendo Entertainment System is a home video game system marketed by Nintendo. To use the system, the player inserts a cartridge containing a video game that Nintendo produces or licenses others to produce. By pressing buttons and manipulating a control pad, the player controls one of the game's characters and progresses through the game. The games are protected as audiovisual works under 17 U.S.C. § 102(a)(6).

13
The Game Genie is a device manufactured by Galoob that allows the player to alter up to three features of a Nintendo game. For example, the Game Genie can increase the number of lives of the player's character, increase the speed at which the character moves, and allow the character to float above obstacles. The player controls the changes made by the Game Genie by entering codes provided by the Game Genie Programming Manual and Code Book. The player also can experiment with variations of these codes.

14
The Game Genie functions by blocking the value for a single data byte sent by the game cartridge to the central processing unit in the Nintendo Entertainment System and replacing it with a new value. If that value controls the character's strength, for example, then the character can be made invincible by increasing the value sufficiently. The Game Genie is inserted between a game cartridge and the Nintendo Entertainment System. The Game Genie does not alter the data that is stored in the game cartridge. Its effects are temporary.

15   **DISCUSSION**

16   **1.** *Derivative work*

17   The Copyright Act of 1976 confers upon copyright holders the exclusive right to prepare and authorize others to prepare derivative works based on their copyrighted works. *See* 17 U.S.C. § 106(2). Nintendo argues that the district court erred in concluding that the audiovisual displays created by the Game Genie are not derivative works. The court's conclusions of law are reviewed *de novo. [...]*

18   A derivative work must incorporate a protected work in some concrete or permanent "form." The Copyright Act defines a derivative work as follows:

19   A "derivative work" is a work based upon one or more preexisting works, such as a translation, musical arrangement, dramatization, fictionalization, motion picture version, sound recording, art reproduction, abridgment, condensation, *or any other form in which a work may be recast, transformed, or adapted.* A work consisting of editorial revisions, annotations, elaborations, or other modifications which, as a whole, represent an original work of authorship, is a "derivative work."

20   17 U.S.C. § 101 (emphasis added). The examples of derivative works provided by the Act all physically incorporate the underlying work or works. The Act's legislative history similarly indicates that "the infringing work must incorporate a portion of the copyrighted work in some form." *[...]*

28   Nintendo also argues that our analysis should focus exclusively on the audiovisual displays created by the Game Genie, *i.e.,* that we should compare the altered displays to Nintendo's original displays. Nintendo emphasizes that "`[a]udiovisual works' are works that consist of a series of related images ... *regardless of the nature of the material objects ... in which the works are embodied.*" *[...]* The Copyright Act's definition of "audiovisual works" is inapposite; the *only* question before us is whether the audiovisual displays created by the Game Genie are "derivative works." The Act does not similarly provide that a work can be a derivative work regardless of the nature of the material objects in which the work is embodied. A derivative work must incorporate a protected work in some concrete or permanent form. We cannot ignore the actual source of the Game Genie's display.

29   Nintendo relies heavily on *Midway Mfg. Co. v. Artic Int'l, Inc., [...] Midway* can be distinguished. The defendant in *Midway,* Artic International, marketed a computer chip that could be inserted in Galaxian video games to speed up the rate of play. The Seventh Circuit held that the speeded-up version of Galaxian was a derivative work. *[...].* Artic's chip substantially copied and *replaced* the chip that was originally distributed by Midway. Purchasers of Artic's chip also benefited economically by offering the altered game for use by the general public. The Game Genie does not physically incorporate a portion of a copyrighted work, nor does it supplant demand for a component of that work. The court in *Midway* acknowledged that the Copyright Act's definition of "derivative work" "must be stretched to accommodate speeded-up video games." *[...]* Stretching that definition further would chill innovation and fail to protect "society's competing interest in the free flow of ideas, information, and commerce." *[...]*

30   In holding that the audiovisual displays created by the Game Genie are not derivative works, we recognize that technology often advances by improvement rather than replacement. *[...]* Some time ago, for example, computer companies began marketing spell-checkers that operate within existing word processors by signalling the writer when a word is misspelled. These applications, as well as countless others, could not be produced and marketed if courts were to conclude that the word processor and spell-checker combination is a derivative work based on the word processor alone. The Game Genie is useless by itself, it can only enhance, and cannot duplicate or recaste, a Nintendo game's output. It does not contain or produce a Nintendo game's output in some concrete or permanent form, nor does it supplant demand for Nintendo game cartridges. Such innovations rarely will constitute infringing derivative works under the Copyright Act. *[...]*

⬚⬚   **3.** *Temporary and permanent injunction*

51   Galoob has not violated the Copyright Act. Nintendo therefore is not entitled to a temporary or permanent injunction.

52   AFFIRMED.

53   [...]

Micro Star v. FormGen Inc.

June 22, 2014 by mrisch

1   154 F.3d 1107

2   [...]

3   **MICRO STAR, Plaintiff-Appellant,**
                                              v.
                              FORMGEN INC., a corporation; [...]

5   **United States Court of Appeals,**
                                          Ninth Circuit.

6   [...]
                                   Decided Sept. 11, 1998.

7   [...]

12   Before: KOZINSKI, THOMPSON[*] and TROTT, Circuit Judges.

13   KOZINSKI, Circuit Judge.

14   Duke Nukem routinely vanquishes Octabrain and the Protozoid Slimer. But what about the dreaded Micro Star?

15   I

16   FormGen Inc., GT Interactive Software Corp. and Apogee Software, Ltd. (collectively FormGen) made, distributed and own the rights to
        Duke Nukem 3D (D/N-3D), an immensely popular (and very cool) computer game. D/N-3D is played from the first-person perspective;
        the player assumes the personality and point of view of the title character, who is seen on the screen only as a pair of hands and an
        occasional boot, much as one might see oneself in real life without the aid of a mirror.[1] Players explore a futuristic city infested with evil
        aliens and other hazards. The goal is to zap them before they zap you, while searching for the hidden passage to the next level. The basic

525

game comes with twenty-nine levels, each with a different combination of scenery, aliens, and other challenges. The game also includes a "Build Editor," a utility that enables players to create their own levels. With FormGen's encouragement, players frequently post levels they have created on the Internet where others can download them. Micro Star, a computer software distributor, did just that: It downloaded 300 user-created levels and stamped them onto a CD, which it then sold commercially as Nuke It (N/I). N/I is packaged in a box decorated with numerous "screen shots," pictures of what the new levels look like when played.

17   Micro Star filed suit in district court, seeking a declaratory judgment that N/I did not infringe on any of FormGen's copyrights. FormGen counterclaimed, seeking a preliminary injunction barring further production and distribution of N/I. Relying on Lewis Galoob Toys, Inc. v. Nintendo of Am., Inc., 964 F.2d 965 (9th Cir.1992), the district court held that N/I was not a derivative work and therefore did not infringe FormGen's copyright. The district court did, however, grant a preliminary injunction as to the screen shots, finding that N/I's packaging violated FormGen's copyright by reproducing pictures of D/N-3D characters without a license. The court rejected Micro Star's fair use claims. Both sides appeal their losses.

18   II

19   A party seeking a preliminary injunction must show "either a likelihood of success on the merits and the possibility of irreparable injury, or that serious questions going to the merits were raised and the balance of hardships tips sharply in its favor." […]

20   III

21   To succeed on the merits of its claim that N/I infringes FormGen's copyright, FormGen must show (1) ownership of the copyright to D/N-3D, and (2) copying of protected expression by Micro Star. […] we are satisfied that FormGen has established its ownership of the copyright. We therefore focus on the latter issue.

22   FormGen alleges that its copyright is infringed by Micro Star's unauthorized commercial exploitation of user-created game levels. In order to understand FormGen's claims, one must first understand the way D/N-3D works. The game consists of three separate components: the game engine, the source art library and the MAP files.[2] The game engine is the heart of the computer program; in some sense, it is the program. It tells the computer when to read data, save and load games, play sounds and project images onto the screen. In order to create the audiovisual display for a particular level, the game engine invokes the MAP file that corresponds to that level. Each MAP file contains a series of instructions that tell the game engine (and, through it, the computer) what to put where. For instance, the MAP file might say scuba gear goes at the bottom of the screen. The game engine then goes to the source art library, finds the image of the scuba gear, and puts it in just the right place on the screen.[3] The MAP file describes the level in painstaking detail, but it does not actually contain any of the copyrighted art itself; everything that appears on the screen actually comes from the art library. Think of the game's audiovisual display as a paint-by-numbers kit. The MAP file might tell you to put blue paint in section number 565, but it doesn't contain any blue paint itself; the blue paint comes from your palette, which is the low-tech analog of the art library, while you play the role of the game engine. When the player selects one of the N/I levels, the game engine references the N/I MAP files, but still uses the D/N-3D art library to generate the images that make up that level.

23   FormGen points out that a copyright holder enjoys the exclusive right to prepare derivative works based on D/N-3D. See 17 U.S.C. § 106(2) (1994). According to FormGen, the audiovisual displays generated when D/N-3D is run in conjunction with the N/I CD MAP files are derivative works that infringe this exclusivity. Is FormGen right? The answer is not obvious.

24   The Copyright Act defines a derivative work as

25   a work based upon one or more preexisting works, such as a translation, musical arrangement, dramatization, fictionalization, motion picture version, sound recording, art reproduction, abridgment, condensation, or any other form in which a work may be recast, transformed, or adapted. A work consisting of editorial revisions, annotations, elaborations, or other modifications which, as a whole, represent an original work of authorship, is a "derivative work."

26   Id. § 101. The statutory language is hopelessly overbroad, however, for "[e]very book in literature, science and art, borrows and must necessarily borrow, and use much which was well known and used before." Emerson v. Davies, 8 F. Cas. 615, 619 (C.C.D.Mass.1845) (No. 4436), quoted in 1 Nimmer on Copyright, § 3.01, at 3-2 (1997). To narrow the statute to a manageable level, we have developed certain criteria a work must satisfy in order to qualify as a derivative work. One of these is that a derivative work must exist in a "concrete or permanent form," Galoob, 964 F.2d at 967 (internal quotation marks omitted), and must substantially incorporate protected material from the preexisting work, see Litchfield v. Spielberg, 736 F.2d 1352, 1357 (9th Cir.1984). Micro Star argues that N/I is not a derivative work because the audiovisual displays generated when D/N-3D is run with N/I's MAP files are [...] not incorporated in any concrete or permanent form, and the MAP files do not copy any of D/N-3D's protected expression. It is mistaken on both counts.

27   The requirement that a derivative work must assume a concrete or permanent form was recognized without much discussion in Galoob. There, we noted that all the Copyright Act's examples of derivative works took some definite, physical form and concluded that this was a requirement of the Act. [...] Obviously, N/I's MAP files themselves exist in a concrete or permanent form; they are burned onto a CD-ROM. [...] But what about the audiovisual displays generated when D/N-3D runs the N/I MAP files--i.e., the actual game level as displayed on the screen? Micro Star argues that, because the audiovisual displays in Galoob didn't meet the "concrete or permanent form" requirement, neither do N/I's.

28   In Galoob, we considered audiovisual displays created using a device called the Game Genie, which was sold for use with the Nintendo Entertainment System. The Game Genie allowed players to alter individual features of a game, such as a character's strength or speed, by selectively "blocking the value for a single data byte sent by the game cartridge to the [Nintendo console] and replacing it with a new value." [...] Players chose which data value to replace by entering a code; over a billion different codes were possible. The Game Genie was dumb; it functioned only as a window into the computer program, allowing players to temporarily modify individual aspects of the game. [...]

29   Nintendo sued, claiming that when the Game Genie modified the game system's audiovisual display, it created an infringing derivative work. We rejected this claim because "[a] derivative work must incorporate a protected work in some concrete or permanent form." [...] The audiovisual displays generated by combining the Nintendo System with the Game Genie were not incorporated in any permanent form; when the game was over, they were gone. Of course, they could be reconstructed, but only if the next player chose to reenter the same codes.[4]

30   Micro Star argues that the MAP files on N/I are a more advanced version of the Game Genie, replacing old values (the MAP files in the original game) with new values (N/I's MAP files). But, whereas the audiovisual displays created by Game Genie were never recorded in any permanent form, the audiovisual displays generated by D/N-3D from the N/I MAP files are in the MAP files themselves. In Galoob, the audiovisual display was defined by the original game cartridge, not by the Game Genie; no one could possibly say that the data values inserted by the Game Genie described the audiovisual display. In the present case the audiovisual display that appears on the computer monitor when a N/I level is played is described--in exact detail--by a N/I MAP file.

31   This raises the interesting question whether an exact, down to the last detail, description of an audiovisual display (and--by definition--we know that MAP files do describe audiovisual displays down to the last detail) [...] counts as a permanent or concrete form for purposes of Galoob. We see no reason it shouldn't. What, after all, does sheet music do but describe in precise detail the way a copyrighted melody sounds? [...] To be copyrighted, pantomimes and dances may be "described in sufficient detail to enable the work to be performed from that description." [...] Similarly, the N/I MAP files describe the audiovisual display that is to be generated when the player chooses to play D/N-3D using the N/I levels. Because the audiovisual displays assume a concrete or permanent form in the MAP files, Galoob stands as no bar to finding that they are derivative works.

32   In addition, "[a] work will be considered a derivative work only if it would be considered an infringing work if the material which it has derived from a preexisting work had been taken without the consent of a copyright proprietor of such preexisting work." [...] "To prove infringement, [FormGen] must show that [D/N-3D's and N/I's audiovisual displays] are substantially similar in both ideas and expression."

527

Similarity of ideas may be shown by comparing the objective details of the works: plot, theme, dialogue, mood, setting, characters, etc. See id. Similarity of expression focuses on the response of the ordinary reasonable person, and considers the total concept and feel of the works. See id. at 1356-57. FormGen will doubtless succeed in making these showings since the audiovisual displays generated when the player chooses the N/I levels come entirely out of D/N-3D's source art library. […]

33 Micro Star further argues that the MAP files are not derivative works because they do not, in fact, incorporate any of D/N-3D's protected expression. In particular, Micro Star makes much of the fact that the N/I MAP files reference the source art library, but do not actually contain any art files themselves. Therefore, it claims, nothing of D/N-3D's is reproduced in the MAP files. In making this argument, Micro Star misconstrues the protected work. The work that Micro Star infringes is the D/N-3D story itself--a beefy commando type named Duke who wanders around post-Apocalypse Los Angeles, shooting Pig Cops with a gun, lobbing hand grenades, searching for medkits and steroids, using a jetpack to leap over obstacles, blowing up gas tanks, avoiding radioactive slime. A copyright owner holds the right to create sequels, […] and the stories told in the N/I MAP files are surely sequels, telling new (though somewhat repetitive) tales of Duke's fabulous adventures. A book about Duke Nukem would infringe for the same reason, even if it contained no pictures.[5]

34 […]

37 Micro Star also argues that it is the beneficiary of the implicit license FormGen gave to its customers by authorizing them to create new levels. Section 204 of the Copyright Act requires the transfer of the exclusive rights granted to copyright owners (including the right to prepare derivative works) to be in writing. […] A nonexclusive license may, however, be granted orally or implied by conduct. […] Nothing indicates that FormGen granted Micro Star any written license at all; nor is there evidence of a nonexclusive oral license. The only written license FormGen conceivably granted was to players who designed their own new levels, but that license contains a significant limitation: Any new levels the players create "must be offered [to others] solely for free." The parties dispute whether the license is binding, but it doesn't matter. If the license is valid, it clearly prohibits commercial distribution of levels; if it doesn't, FormGen hasn't granted any written licenses at all.[…]

39   **IV**

40 Because FormGen will likely succeed at trial in proving that Micro Star has infringed its copyright, we reverse the district court's order denying a preliminary injunction and remand for entry of such an injunction. […]

45 [2] So-called because the files all end with the extension ".MAP". Also, no doubt, because they contain the layout for the various levels.

46 [3] Actually, this is all a bit metaphorical. Computer programs don't actually go anywhere or fetch anything. Rather, the game engine receives the player's instruction as to which game level to select and instructs the processor to access the MAP file corresponding to that level. The MAP file, in turn, consists of a series of instructions indicating which art images go where. When the MAP file calls for a particular art image, the game engine tells the processor to access the art library for instructions on how each pixel on the screen must be colored in order to paint that image.

47 [4] A low-tech example might aid understanding. Imagine a product called the Pink Screener, which consists of a big piece of pink cellophane stretched over a frame. When put in front of a television, it makes everything on the screen look pinker. Someone who manages to record the programs with this pink cast (maybe by filming the screen) would have created an infringing derivative work. But the audiovisual display observed by a person watching television through the Pink Screener is not a derivative work because it does not incorporate the modified image in any permanent or concrete form. The Game Genie might be described as a fancy Pink Screener for video games, changing a value of the game as perceived by the current player, but never incorporating the new audiovisual display into a permanent or concrete form.

48 [5] We note that the N/I MAP files can only be used with D/N-3D. If another game could use the MAP files to tell the story of a mousy fellow who travels through a beige maze, killing vicious saltshakers with paper-clips, then the MAP files would not incorporate the

protected expression of D/N-3D because they would not be telling a D/N-3D story.

49   [6] Of course, transformative works have greater recourse to the fair use defense as they "lie at the heart of the fair use doctrine's guarantee of breathing space within the confines of copyright ... and the more transformative the new work, the less will be the significance of other factors, like commercialism, that may weigh against a finding of fair use." Campbell, 510 U.S. at 579, 114 S.Ct. 1164 (citations omitted). N/I can hardly be described as transformative; anything but.

50   [...]

Class 13: 6.3 <u>OIL Casebook: Copyright Fair Use</u>

Authors Guild, Inc. v. HathiTrust

August 17, 2014 by mrisch

This case provides a good introduction to the policies and history of fair use, while also applying the doctrine to the most modern c contexts.

1   755 F.3d 87 (2014)

AUTHORS GUILD, INC., [...] Plaintiffs-Appellants,
v.
HATHITRUST, [...] Defendants-Appellees,[1]
[...]

2   United States Court of Appeals, Second Circuit.

[...]
Decided: June 10, 2014.

3   [...]

23   Before: WALKER, CABRANES, and PARKER, Circuit Judges.

24   **BARRINGTON D. PARKER, Circuit Judge.**

25   Beginning in 2004, several research universities including the University of Michigan, the University of California at Berkeley, Cornell University, and the University of Indiana agreed to allow Google to electronically scan the books in their collections. In October 2008, thirteen universities announced plans to create a repository for the digital copies and founded an organization called HathiTrust to set up and operate the HathiTrust Digital Library (or "HDL"). Colleges, universities, and other nonprofit institutions became members of HathiTrust and made the books in their collections available for inclusion in the HDL. HathiTrust currently has 80 member institutions and the HDL contains digital copies of more than ten million works, published over many centuries, written in a multitude of languages, covering almost every subject imaginable. This appeal requires us to decide whether the HDL's use of copyrighted material is protected against a claim of copyright infringement under the doctrine of fair use. See 18 U.S.C. § 107.

26   **BACKGROUND**

27   **A. The HathiTrust Digital Library**

28   HathiTrust permits three uses of the copyrighted works in the HDL repository. First, HathiTrust allows the general public to search for particular terms across all digital copies in the repository. Unless the copyright holder authorizes broader use, the search results show only the page numbers on which the search term is found within the work and the number of times the term appears on each page. The HDL does not display to the user any text from the underlying copyrighted work (either in "snippet" form or otherwise). Consequently, the user is not able to view either the page on which the term appears or any other portion of the book.

29   [...]

32   Second, the HDL allows member libraries to provide patrons with certified print disabilities access to the full text of copyrighted works. A "print disability" is any disability that prevents a person from effectively reading printed material. Blindness is one example, but print disabilities also include those that prevent a person from physically holding a book or turning pages. To use this service, a patron must obtain certification of his disability from a qualified expert. Through the HDL, a print-disabled user can obtain access to the contents of works in the digital library using adaptive technologies such as software that converts the text into spoken words, or that magnifies the text. Currently, the University of Michigan's library is the only HDL member that permits such access, although other member libraries intend to provide it in the future.

33   [...]

34   The HDL stores digital copies of the works in four different locations. One copy is stored on its primary server in Michigan, one on its secondary server in Indiana, and two on separate backup tapes at the University of Michigan.[3] Each copy contains the full text of the work, in a machine readable format, as well as the *images* of each page in the work as they appear in the print version.

35   **B. The Orphan Works Project**

36   Separate and apart from the HDL, in May 2011, the University of Michigan developed a project known as the Orphan Works Project (or "OWP"). An "orphan work" is an out-of-print work that is still in copyright, but whose copyright holder cannot be readily identified or located. *[...]*

37   The University of Michigan conceived of the OWP in two stages: First, the project would attempt to identify out-of-print works, try to find their copyright holders, and, if no copyright holder could be found, publish a list of orphan works candidates to enable the copyright holders to come forward or be otherwise located. If no copyright holder came forward, the work was to be designated as an orphan work. Second, those works identified as orphan works would be made accessible in digital format to the OWP's library patrons (with simultaneous viewers limited to the number of hard copies owned by the library).

38   The University evidently became concerned that its screening process was not adequately distinguishing between orphan works (which were to be included in the OWP) and in-print works (which were not). As a result, before the OWP was brought online, but after the complaint was filed in this case, the University indefinitely suspended the project. No copyrighted work has been distributed or displayed through the project and it remains suspended as of this writing.

39   [...]

42
40   **DISCUSSION**

50   [...]

54   **I. Fair Use**[...]

55   **A**

56   As the Supreme Court has explained, the overriding purpose of copyright is "`[t]o promote the Progress of Science and useful Arts...'" *[..* This goal has animated copyright law in Anglo-American history, beginning with the first copyright statute, the Statute of Anne of 1709, which declared itself to be "[a]n Act for the Encouragement of Learning, by Vesting the Copies of Printed Books in the Authors ... during the Times therein mentioned." Act for the Encouragement of Learning, 8 Anne, ch. 19. In short, our law recognizes that copyright is "not an inevitable, divine, or natural right that confers on authors the absolute ownership of their creations. It is designed rather to stimulate

activity and progress in the arts for the intellectual enrichment of the public." [...]

57   The Copyright Act furthers this core purpose by granting authors a limited monopoly over (and thus the opportunity to profit from) the
      dissemination of their original works of authorship. [...] The Copyright Act confers upon authors certain enumerated exclusive rights over
      their works during the term of the copyright, including the rights to reproduce the copyrighted work and to distribute those copies to the
      public. [...] The Act also gives authors the exclusive right to prepare certain new works—called "derivative works"—that are based upon
      the copyrighted work. [...] Paradigmatic examples of derivative works include the translation of a novel into another language, the
      adaptation of a novel into a movie or a play, or the recasting of a novel as an e-book or an audiobook. *See id.* § 101. As a general rule, for
      works created after January 1, 1978, copyright protection lasts for the life of the author plus an additional 70 years. *Id.* § 302.

58   At the same time, there are important limits to an author's rights to control original and derivative works. One such limit is the doctrine of
      "fair use," which allows the public to draw upon copyrighted materials without the permission of the copyright holder in certain
      circumstances. *See id.* § 107 ("[T]he fair use of a copyrighted work . . . is not an infringement of copyright."). "From the infancy of
      copyright protection, some opportunity for fair use of copyrighted materials has been thought necessary to fulfill copyright's very
      purpose, `[t]o promote the Progress of Science and useful Arts. . . .'" [...]

59   Under the fair-use doctrine, a book reviewer may, for example, quote from an original work in order to illustrate a point and substantiate
      criticisms, [...] and a biographer may quote from unpublished journals and letters for similar purposes, [...] An artist may employ
      copyrighted photographs in a new work that uses a fundamentally different artistic approach, aesthetic, and character from the original. [
      An internet search engine can display low-resolution versions of copyrighted images in order to direct the user to the website where the
      original could be found. [...] A newspaper can publish a copyrighted photograph (taken for a modeling portfolio) in order to inform and
      entertain the newspaper's readership about a news story. [...] A viewer can create a recording of a broadcast television show in order to
      view it at a later time. [...] And a competitor may create copies of copyrighted software for the purpose of analyzing that software and
      discovering how it functions (a process called "reverse engineering"). [...]

60   The doctrine is generally subject to an important proviso: A fair use must not excessively damage the market for the original by providing
      the public with a substitute for that original work. Thus, a book review may fairly quote a copyrighted book "for the purposes of fair and
      reasonable criticism," [...], but the review may not quote extensively from the "heart" of a forthcoming memoir in a manner that usurps
      the right of first publication and serves as a substitute for purchasing the memoir, [...]

61   In 1976, as part of a wholesale revision of the Copyright Act, Congress codified the judicially created fair-use doctrine at 17 U.S.C. § 107.
      . Section 107 requires a court to consider four nonexclusive factors which are to be weighed together to assess whether a particular use
      is fair:

62   (1) the purpose and character of the use, including whether such use is of a commercial nature or is for nonprofit educational
              purposes;

              (2) the nature of the copyrighted work;

              (3) the amount and substantiality of the portion used in relation to the copyrighted work as a whole; and

              (4) the effect of the use upon the potential market for or value of the copyrighted work.

63   17 U.S.C. § 107.

64   An important focus of the first factor is whether the use is "transformative." A use is transformative if it does something more than
      repackage or republish the original copyrighted work. The inquiry is whether the work "adds something new, with a further purpose or

different character, altering the first with new expression, meaning or message. . . ." *[...]* "[T]he more transformative the new work, the less will be the significance of other factors . . . that may weigh against a finding of fair use." *[...]* Contrary to what the district court implied, a use does not become transformative by making an "invaluable contribution to the progress of science and cultivation of the arts." *[...]*. Added value or utility is not the test: a transformative work is one that serves a new and different function from the original work and is not a substitute for it.

65   The second factor considers whether the copyrighted work is "of the creative or instructive type that the copyright laws value and seek to foster." *[...]* For example, the law of fair use "recognizes a greater need to disseminate factual works than works of fiction or fantasy." *[*

66   The third factor asks whether the secondary use employs more of the copyrighted work than is necessary, and whether the copying was excessive in relation to any valid purposes asserted under the first factor. *[...]*. In weighing this factor, we assess the quantity and value of the materials used and whether the amount copied is reasonable in relation to the purported justifications for the use under the first factor. *[...]*

67   Finally, the fourth factor requires us to assess the impact of the use on the traditional market for the copyrighted work. This is the "single most important element of fair use." *[...]* To defeat a claim of fair use, the copyright holder must point to market harm that results because the secondary use serves as a substitute for the original work. *[...]*

68   **B**

69   As discussed above, the Libraries permit three uses of the digital copies deposited in the HDL. We now consider whether these uses are "fair" within the meaning of our copyright law.

70   **1. Full-Text Search**

71   It is not disputed that, in order to perform a full-text search of books, the Libraries must first create digital copies of the entire books. Importantly, as we have seen, the HDL does not allow users to view any portion of the books they are searching. Consequently, in providing this service, the HDL does not add into circulation any new, human-readable copies of any books. Instead, the HDL simply permits users to "word search"—that is, to locate where specific words or phrases appear in the digitized books. Applying the relevant factors, we conclude that this use is a fair use.

72   **i.**

73   Turning to the first factor, we conclude that the creation of a full-text searchable database is a quintessentially transformative use. *[...]* the result of a word search is different in purpose, character, expression, meaning, and message from the page (and the book) from which it is drawn. Indeed, we can discern little or no resemblance between the original text and the results of the HDL full-text search.

74   There is no evidence that the Authors write with the purpose of enabling text searches of their books. Consequently, the full-text search function does not "supersede[] the objects [or purposes] of the original creation," *[...]* The HDL does not "merely repackage[] or republish[] the original[s]," *[...]* or merely recast "an original work into a new mode of presentation," *[...]* Instead, by enabling full-text search, the HDL adds to the original something new with a different purpose and a different character.

75   *[...]*

76   Cases from other Circuits reinforce this conclusion. In *Perfect 10, Inc.,* the Ninth Circuit held that the use of copyrighted thumbnail images in internet search results was transformative because the thumbnail copies served a different function from the original copyrighted

images. [...] And in *A.V. ex rel. Vanderhye v. iParadigms, LLC*, a company created electronic copies of unaltered student papers for use in connection with a computer program that detects plagiarism. Even though the electronic copies made no "substantive alteration to" the copyrighted student essays, the Fourth Circuit held that plagiarism detection constituted a transformative use of the copyrighted works. [

77   **ii.**

78   The second fair-use factor—the nature of the copyrighted work—is not dispositive. The HDL permits the full-text search of every type of work imaginable. Consequently, there is no dispute that the works at issue are of the type that the copyright laws value and seek to protect. However, "this factor `may be of limited usefulness where,' as here, `the creative work . . . is being used for a transformative purpose." [...] Accordingly, our fair-use analysis hinges on the other three factors.

79   **iii.**

80   The third factor asks whether the copying used more of the copyrighted work than necessary and whether the copying was excessive. As we have noted, "[t]here are no absolute rules as to how much of a copyrighted work may be copied and still be considered a fair use." [...] "[T]he extent of permissible copying varies with the purpose and character of the use." [...] The crux of the inquiry is whether "no more was taken than necessary." [...] For some purposes, it may be necessary to copy the entire copyrighted work, in which case Factor Three does not weigh against a finding of fair use. [...] *Arriba Soft*, 336 F.3d at 821 ("If Arriba only copied part of the image, it would be more difficult to identify it, thereby reducing the usefulness of the visual search engine.").

81   In order to enable the full-text search function, the Libraries, as we have seen, created digital copies of all the books in their collections.[5] Because it was reasonably necessary for the HDL to make use of the entirety of the works in order to enable the full-text search function, we do not believe the copying was excessive.

82   The Authors also contend that the copying is excessive because the HDL creates and maintains copies of the works at four different locations [...] But the record demonstrates that these copies are also reasonably necessary in order to facilitate the HDL's legitimate uses. In particular, the HDL's services are offered to patrons through two servers, one at the University of Michigan (the primary server) and an identical one at the University of Indiana (the "mirror" server). Both servers contain copies of the digital works at issue. According to the HDL executive director, the "existence of a[n] [identical] mirror site allows for balancing the load of user web traffic to avoid overburdening a single site, and each site acts as a back-up of the HDL collection in the event that one site were to cease operation (for example, due to failure caused by a disaster, or even as a result of routine maintenance)." [...] To further guard against the risk of data loss, the HDL stores copies of the works on two encrypted backup tapes, which are disconnected from the internet and are placed in separate secure locations on the University of Michigan campus. [...] The HDL creates these backup tapes so that the data could be restored in "the event of a disaster causing large-scale data loss" to the primary and mirror servers. [...]

83   We have no reason to think that these copies are excessive or unreasonable in relation to the purposes identified by the Libraries and permitted by the law of copyright. In sum, even viewing the evidence in the light most favorable to the Authors, the record demonstrates that these copies are reasonably necessary to facilitate the services HDL provides to the public and to mitigate the risk of disaster or data loss. Accordingly, we conclude that this factor favors the Libraries.

84   **iv.**

85   The fourth factor requires us to consider "the effect of the use upon the potential market for or value of the copyrighted work," 17 U.S.C. § 107(4), and, in particular, whether the secondary use "usurps the market of the original work," [...]

86   The Libraries contend that the full-text-search use poses no harm to any existing or potential traditional market and point to the fact that, in discovery, the Authors admitted that they were unable to identify "any specific, quantifiable past harm, or any documents relating to

any such past harm," resulting from any of the Libraries' uses of their works (including full-text search). [...]

87   At the outset, it is important to recall that the Factor Four analysis is concerned with only one type of economic injury to a copyright holder: the harm that results because the secondary use serves as a substitute for the original work. [...] In other words, under Factor Four, any economic "harm" caused by transformative uses does not count because such uses, by definition, do not serve as substitutes for the original work. [...]

88   To illustrate why this is so, consider how copyright law treats book reviews. Book reviews often contain quotations of copyrighted material to illustrate the reviewer's points and substantiate his criticisms; this is a paradigmatic fair use. And a negative book review can cause a degree of economic injury to the author by dissuading readers from purchasing copies of her book, even when the review does not serve as a substitute for the original. But, obviously, in that case, the author has no cause for complaint under Factor Four: The only market harms that count are the ones that are caused because the secondary use serves as a substitute for the original, not when the secondary use is transformative (as in quotations in a book review). [...]

89   The Authors assert two reasons why the full-text-search function harms their traditional markets. The first is a "lost sale" theory which posits that a market for licensing books for digital search could possibly develop in the future, and the HDL impairs the emergence of such a market because it allows patrons to search books without any need for a license. Thus, according to the Authors, every copy employed by the HDL in generating full-text searches represents a lost opportunity to license the book for search. [...]

90   This theory of market harm does not work under Factor Four, because the full-text search function does not serve as a substitute for the books that are being searched. [...] Thus, it is irrelevant that the Libraries might be willing to purchase licenses in order to engage in this transformative use (if the use were deemed unfair). Lost licensing revenue counts under Factor Four only when the use serves as a substitute for the original and the full-text-search use does not.

91   Next, the Authors assert that the HDL creates the risk of a security breach which might impose irreparable damage on the Authors and their works. In particular, the Authors speculate that, if hackers were able to obtain unauthorized access to the books stored at the HDL, the full text of these tens of millions of books might be distributed worldwide without restriction, "decimat[ing]" the traditional market for those works. [...]

92   The record before us documents the extensive security measures the Libraries have undertaken to safeguard against the risk of a data breach. [...]

93   This showing of the security measures taken by the Libraries is essentially unrebutted. Consequently, we see no basis in the record on which to conclude that a security breach is likely to occur, much less one that would result in the public release of the specific copyrighted works belonging to any of the plaintiffs in this case. [...] Factor Four thus favors a finding of fair use.

96   Without foreclosing a future claim based on circumstances not now predictable, and based on a different record, we hold that the balance of relevant factors in this case favors the Libraries. In sum, we conclude that the doctrine of fair use allows the Libraries to digitize copyrighted works for the purpose of permitting full-text searches.

97   ## 2. Access to the Print-Disabled

98   The HDL also provides print-disabled patrons with versions of all of the works contained in its digital archive in formats accessible to them. In order to obtain access to the works, a patron must submit documentation from a qualified expert verifying that the disability prevents him or her from reading printed materials, and the patron must be affiliated with an HDL member that has opted-into the program. Currently, the University of Michigan is the only HDL member institution that has opted-in. We conclude that this use is also

protected by the doctrine of fair use.

99 **i.**

100 In applying the Factor One analysis, the district court concluded that "[t]he use of digital copies to facilitate access for print-disabled persons is [a] transformative" use. *[...]* This is a misapprehension; providing expanded access to the print disabled is not "transformative."

101 As discussed above, a transformative use adds something new to the copyrighted work and does not merely supersede the purposes of the original creation. *[...]* The Authors state that they "write books to be read (or listened to)." Appellants' Br. 34-35. By making copyrighted works available in formats accessible to the disabled, the HDL enables a larger audience to read those works, but the underlying purpose of the HDL's use is the same as the author's original purpose.

102 Indeed, when the HDL recasts copyrighted works into new formats to be read by the disabled, it appears, at first glance, to be creating derivative works over which the author ordinarily maintains control. *See* 17 U.S.C. § 106(2). As previously noted, paradigmatic examples of derivative works include translations of the original into a different language, or adaptations of the original into different forms or media. *See id.* § 101 (defining "derivative work"). The Authors contend that by converting their works into a different, accessible format, the HDL is simply creating a derivative work.

103 It is true that, oftentimes, the print-disabled audience has no means of obtaining access to the copyrighted works included in the HDL. But, similarly, the non-English-speaking audience cannot gain access to untranslated books written in English and an unauthorized translation is not transformative simply because it enables a new audience to read a work.

104 This observation does not end the analysis. "While a transformative use generally is more likely to qualify as fair use, `transformative use is not absolutely necessary for a finding of fair use.'" *[...]* We conclude that providing access to the print-disabled is still a valid purpose under Factor One even though it is not transformative. We reach that conclusion for several reasons.

105 First, the Supreme Court has already said so. As Justice Stevens wrote for the Court: "Making a copy of a copyrighted work for the convenience of a blind person is expressly identified by the House Committee Report as an example of fair use, with no suggestion that anything more than a purpose to entertain or to inform need motivate the copying." *[...]*

108 **ii.**

109 Through the HDL, the disabled can obtain access to copyrighted works of all kinds, and there is no dispute that those works are of the sort that merit protection under the Copyright Act. As a result, Factor Two weighs against fair use. This does not preclude a finding of fair use, however, given our analysis of the other factors. *[...]*

110 **iii.**

111 Regarding Factor Three, as previously noted, the HDL retains copies as digital image files and as text-only files, which are then stored in four separate locations. The Authors contend that this amount of copying is excessive because the Libraries have not demonstrated their need to retain the digital *image* files in addition to the text files.

112 We are unconvinced. The text files are required for text searching and to create text-to-speech capabilities for the blind and disabled. But the image files will provide an additional and often more useful method by which many disabled patrons, especially students and scholars, can obtain access to these works. These image files contain information, such as pictures, charts, diagrams, and the layout of the text on the printed page that cannot be converted to text or speech. None of this is captured by the HDL's text-only copies. Many legally blind patrons are capable of viewing these images if they are sufficiently magnified or if the color contrasts are increased. And other disabled patrons, whose physical impairments prevent them from turning pages or from holding books, may also be able to use assistive devices

to view all of the content contained in the image files for a book. For those individuals, gaining access to the HDL's image files—in addition to the text-only files—is necessary to perceive the books fully. Consequently, it is reasonable for the Libraries to retain both the text and image copies.[...]

113 **iv.**

114 The fourth factor also weighs in favor of a finding of fair use. It is undisputed that the present-day market for books accessible to the handicapped is so insignificant that "it is common practice in the publishing industry for authors to forgo royalties that are generated through the sale of books manufactured in specialized formats for the blind. . . ." [...] "[T]he number of accessible books currently available to the blind for borrowing is a mere few hundred thousand titles, a minute percentage of the world's books. In contrast, the HDL contains more than ten million accessible volumes." [...] When considering the 1976 Act, Congress was well aware of this problem. The House Committee Report observed that publishers did not "usually ma[ke]" their books available in specialized formats for the blind. [...] That observation remains true today.

115 Weighing the factors together, we conclude that the doctrine of fair use allows the Libraries to provide full digital access to copyrighted works to their print-disabled patrons.[...]

116 **[...]**

120 **CONCLUSION**

128 The judgment of the district court is AFFIRMED, in part, insofar as the district court concluded that [...] the doctrine of "fair use" allows defendants-appellees to create a full-text searchable database of copyrighted works and to provide those works in formats accessible to those with disabilities; [...]

131 [3] Separate from the HDL, one copy is also kept by Google. Google's use of its copy is the subject of a separate lawsuit currently pending in this Court. *[...]*

Los Angeles Times v. Free Republic

August 08, 2014 by mrisch

This case comes out differently on fair use than the book search case, despite the use of new. Why?

1   **LOS ANGELES TIMES, and The Washington Post Company and its wholly owned subsidiary, Washingtonpost.Newsweek Interactive Company, Plaintiffs,**

v.

FREE REPUBLIC, Electronic Orchard, Jim Robinson, and Does 1 Through 10, inclusive, Defendants.

2   [...]

3   United States District Court, C.D. California

4   April 4, 2000.

5   [...]

6   **MARGARET M. MORROW, District Judge.**

7   [...] Plaintiffs Los Angeles Times and The Washington Post Company publish newspapers in print and online versions. Defendant Free Republic is a "bulletin board" website whose members use the site to post news articles to which they add remarks or commentary. Other visitors to the site then read the articles and add their comments. For the most part, Free Republic members post the entire text of articles in which they are interested; among these are verbatim copies of articles from the Los Angeles Times and Washington Post websites. Plaintiffs' complaint alleges that the unauthorized copying and posting of the articles on the Free Republic site constitutes copyright infringement.

8   Defendants have now moved for summary judgment. They assert that the copying of news articles onto their website is protected by the fair use doctrine. Plaintiffs have filed a cross-motion for partial summary judgment, arguing that defendants may not invoke fair use as a defense.

9   The fair use doctrine, codified at 17 U.S.C. § 107, permits the reproduction of copyrighted works for certain purposes. Section 107 sets forth four nonexclusive factors to be considered in determining whether a defendant's copying is fair use: "(1) the purpose and character of the use, including whether such use is of a commercial nature or is for nonprofit educational purposes; (2) the nature of the copyrighted work; (3) the amount and substantiality of the portion used in relation to the copyrighted work as a whole; and (4) the effect of the use upon the potential market for or value of the copyrighted work." 17 U.S.C. § 107. Based on the evidence submitted by the parties, the court concludes that the first, third and fourth factors militate against a finding of fair use in this case. The second factor weighs in defendants' favor. The balance of all factors tips toward plaintiffs, and the court thus finds that defendants are not entitled to assert a fair use defense to the claims of copyright infringement alleged in the complaint.

10   Defendants also allege that the First Amendment protects the posting of plaintiffs' news articles to their website. They contend that, absent wholesale copying, Free Republic visitors will be unable to express their criticism and comments. There are other methods in which the visitors' rights of free expression can be protected, however, and the court cannot conclude that enforcing plaintiffs' rights under the copyright law impermissibly restricts defendants' right to free speech.

11   **I. FACTUAL BACKGROUND**[...]

12   **A. The Parties**

13   Plaintiffs publish the Los Angeles Times and The Washington Post in print and online at "http://www.latimes.com" and "http://www.washingtonpost.com."[2] Their respective websites contain the current edition of the newspaper, which can be viewed free of charge, and archived articles that users must pay to view,[3] The Times charges $1.50 to view an archived article, while the Post charges from $1.50 to $2.95 depending on the time of day.[4] In addition to income generated in this fashion, the websites also produce advertising and licensing revenue for the papers.[5] Because advertising is sold "CPM" (cost per thousand), the revenue generated from this source depends on the volume of traffic the sites experience during a given period.[6] The parties dispute the extent to which being able to access archived articles at a different site for free affects plaintiffs' ability to advertise, license, and sell the archived articles.[7]

14   [...] Defendant Jim Robinson is the owner and operator of [...] Free Republic.[8] [...] Free Republic is a limited liability corporation that operates freerepublic.com.[10] The website, which has been operational since 1996, allows registered visitors to "post" news articles and comments concerning them on the site.[11] Registered members may then post additional comments.[12] Free Republic has approximately 20,000 registered participants. The website receives as many as 100,000 hits per day, and between 25 and 50 million page views each month.[13]

15   Plaintiffs contend that "perfect copies" of news articles appearing in their publications and on their websites are posted to the Free Republic site. Defendants maintain that the posted articles are merely "purported copies" of the original, and assert that one can verify that a posting is an exact copy only by visiting plaintiffs' websites.[14] Defendants nonetheless apparently concede that *some* of the postings are verbatim copies of original articles.[...]

16   [...]

17   The parties dispute whether Free Republic is a for-profit or not-for-profit entity.[...]

19   Defendants concede, however, that Free Republic has facilitated links to web pages run by third-party supporters where donations to Free Republic and/or Robinson are solicited. They also acknowledge that the website carries links to third-party web pages that offer Free Republic-related souvenir items in exchange for donations.[...]

20   [...] The parties also dispute whether the posting of plaintiffs' news articles to the Free Republic site causes an increase or decrease in traffic at the Times and Post websites, whether it diminishes the available market for sale of plaintiffs' news articles, and whether it has a negative impact on plaintiffs' ability to license the works. Defendants assert that plaintiffs' websites actually gain viewers because people go to them after visiting the Free Republic site.[27] Plaintiffs maintain they lose traffic when Internet users read an article posted on freerepublic.com rather than visiting the Times or Post websites. They further assert that their ability to sell copies of the archived articles and their ability to license the works is diminished by having copies made freely available on the Free Republic site.[...]

22   **II. DISCUSSION**

23   **A. Legal Standard Governing Motions For Summary Judgment**

24   A motion for summary judgment must be granted when "the pleadings, depositions, answers to interrogatories, and admissions on file, together with the affidavits, if any, show that there is no genuine issue as to any material fact and that the moving party is entitled to a judgment as a matter of law." [...]

27   **B. Elements Of Copyright Infringement**

28   *[...]*

29   Before proceeding to the substance of the parties' motions, it is important to state what issues are not before the court at this time. Because the parties address the availability of a *defense* to copyright infringement, their motions assume for present purposes that such a claim can be proved. The court expresses no opinion as to whether this is so, given that the "copying" of news articles at issue in this case is to a large extent copying by third-party users of the Free Republic site. The court also makes no determination as to whether plaintiffs have in any manner consented to the copying of their articles.[29]

30   C. The Fair Use Defense

31   *[...]* The fair use defense is a limitation on the exclusive right of a copyright owner "to reproduce the copyrighted work in copies." 17 U.S.C. § 106(1). It is codified at 17 U.S.C. § 107, which provides:

32   "Notwithstanding the provisions of sections 106 and 106A, the fair use of a copyrighted work, including such use by reproduction in copies or phonorecords or by any other means specified by that section, for purposes such as criticism, comment, news reporting, teaching (including multiple copies for classroom use), scholarship, or research, is not an infringement of copyright. In determining whether the use made of a work in any particular case is a fair use the factors to be considered shall include—

(1) the purpose and character of the use, including whether such use is of a commercial nature or is for nonprofit educational purposes;

(2) the nature of the copyrighted work;

(3) the amount and substantiality of the portion used in relation to the copyrighted work as a whole; and

(4) the effect of the use upon the potential market for or value of the copyrighted work.

The fact that a work is unpublished shall not itself bar a finding of fair use if such finding is made upon consideration of all the above factors."

33   Because fair use is an affirmative defense to a claim of infringement, defendants carry the burden of proof on the issue. *[...]*

34   1. The Purpose And Character Of The Use

35   The first factor listed in § 107 is "the purpose and character of the use, including whether such use is of a commercial nature or is for nonprofit educational purposes." 17 U.S.C. § 107. This factor assesses whether "the new work 'merely supersedes the objects' of the original creation, or instead adds something new, with a further purpose or different character, altering the first with new expression, meaning, or message; it asks, in other words, whether and to what extent the new work is 'transformative.' " *[...]* [T]he more transformative the new work, the less will be the significance of other factors, like commercialism, that may weigh against a finding of fair use." *[...]*

36   Inquiry concerning the character and purpose of a challenged use should be guided by the examples provided in the statute—i.e., whether the use was for purposes of "criticism, comment, news reporting, teaching ..., scholarship, or research." 17 U.S.C. § 107; *[...]* The list, however, is not intended to be exhaustive or to single out any particular use as presumptively fair. *[...]* Indeed, the fact that a use falls within one of these categories "is simply one factor in [the] fair use analysis." *[...]* Similarly, while the statute draws a distinction between non-profit and commercial use, not every commercial use of a copyrighted work is presumptively unfair. *[...]*

37   a. The Purpose Of Free Republic's Use And The Extent To Which Its Work Is Transformative

38   [6] There is no dispute that at least some of the items posted on the Free Republic website are exact copies of plaintiffs' articles.[30]While defendants assert there is "no evidence" that *all* of the Times and Post articles that have been posted are verbatim copies,[31]the evidence they have presented reveals that, generally, exact copies of whole or substantial portions of articles[32] are posted.[33]

39   There is little transformative about copying the entirety or large portions of a work verbatim. [...] As the Supreme Court said in *Campbell, supra*:

40   "[W]hether 'a substantial portion of the infringing work was copied verbatim' from the copyrighted work is a relevant question, ... for it may reveal a dearth of transformative character or purpose under the first factor, or a greater likelihood of market harm under the fourth; a work composed primarily of an original, particularly its heart, with little added or changed, is more likely to be a merely superseding use, fulfilling demand for the original." *[...]*

42   [7] Defendants proffer two reasons why their full text copying of plaintiffs' articles is nonetheless transformative. First, they assert that the copies of the articles found on the Free Republic site do not in reality substitute for the originals found on plaintiffs' web pages. Second, they contend they copy no more than necessary to fulfill their purpose of criticizing the manner in which the media covers current events and politics. Each of these contentions will be examined in turn.

43   Defendants' first argument—that the copies of plaintiffs' articles found on the Free Republic site do not substitute for those on plaintiffs' sites—focuses on readers' ability to access and review specific articles in which they are interested. Defendants contend that using the Free Republic site to read current articles would be impractical since there is a delay between the time information is posted to the site and the time it is indexed by third-party search engines. Additionally, they assert that the imprecision of search language makes it difficult to locate archived articles at the site.[34] These arguments overlook the fact that the Free Republic site has its own search engine that apparently has immediate search capability.[35]

44   Even were this not true, the articles posted on the Free Republic site ultimately serve the same purpose as "that [for which] one would normally seek to obtain the original—to have it available ... for ready reference if and when [website visitors adding comments] need[ ] to look at it." *[...]*

45   Defendants' web page acknowledges this. It states, *inter alia,* that the Free Republic site is a place where visitors "can often find breaking news and up to the minute updates."[36] Indeed, it is clear from the content of the representative pages submitted by defendants that visitors can read copies of plaintiffs' current and archived articles at the Free Republic site. For those who visit the site regularly, therefore, the articles posted there serve as substitutes for the originals found on plaintiffs' websites or in their newspapers.

46   Defendants next argue that their use of plaintiffs' works is transformative because registered Free Republic users add comments and criticism concerning the articles following a posting. Copying portions of a copyrighted work for the purpose of criticism or commentary is often considered fair use. [...] The fact that criticism is involved, however, does end the inquiry. [...] Rather, it must be considered in combination with other circumstances to determine if the first factor favors defendants. See *Twin Peaks, supra*, 996 F.2d at 1375–76 (" 'Purpose' in fair use analysis is not an all-or-nothing matter. The issue is not simply whether a challenged work serves one of the non-exclusive purposes identified in section 107, such as comment or criticism, but whether it does so to an insignificant or a substantial extent. The weight ascribed to the 'purpose' factor involves a more refined assessment than the initial, fairly easy decision that a work serves a purpose illustrated by the categories listed in section 107").

47   [8] Since the first posting of an article to the Free Republic site often contains little or no commentary, it does not significantly transform plaintiffs' work. [...]

49   Additionally, even where copying serves the "criticism, comment and news reporting" purposes highlighted in § 107, its extent cannot exceed what is necessary to the purpose. [...] Thus, an individualized assessment of the purpose for which defendants are copying the

works and a comparison of that purpose to the amount copied is required. [...]

50   Here, it seems clear that the primary purpose of the postings to the Free Republic site is to facilitate discussion, criticism and comment by registered visitors. Defendants contend that copying all or parts of articles verbatim is necessary to facilitate this purpose.[40] They argue that full text posting is required because links expire after a week or two, and because unsophisticated Internet users will have difficulty accessing a linked site.[41] Defendants' assertion that links expire after a period of time is presumably a reference to the fact that articles are available on plaintiffs' websites free of charge only for a certain number of days.Thereafter, there is a charge for viewing and/or printing them. That this is so does not make linking plaintiffs' websites to the Free Republic site "impractical." It merely requires that Free Republic visitors pay a fee for viewing plaintiffs' articles just as other members of the public do. Similarly, defendants' suggestion that articles are posted to the Free Republic site long after they are published is not supported by the representative postings they have submitted.[42] These reflect that the vast majority of comments are posted the same day the articles appear or within one to three days afterwards.[43] Finally, defendants' assertion that unsophisticated Internet users would be confused by links is unpersuasive. Linking is familiar to most Internet users, even those who are new to the web.

51   [...]

52   The fact that linking the text of an article as it appears on plaintiffs' websites to the Free Republic site, or summarizing the article's text, is not as easy or convenient for Free Republic users as full text posting does not render the practice a fair use. Rather, the focus of the inquiry must be whether verbatim copying is necessary to defendants' critical purpose. [...]

53   Defendants have not met their burden of demonstrating that verbatim copying of all or a substantial portion of plaintiffs' articles is necessary to achieve their critical purpose. They argue that the purpose of full text posting is to enable Free Republic users to criticize the manner in which the media covers current events.[46] The statement of purpose found on the website, however, is somewhat different. There, defendants state that visitors to the Free Republic site "are encouraged to comment on the news of the day ... and ... to contribute whatever information they may have to help others better understand a particular story."[47] In fact, a review of the representative articles submitted by defendants reveals that visitors' commentary focuses much more on the news of the day than it does on the manner in which the media reports that news.[48] This is significant, since the extent of copying that might be necessary to comment on the nature of the media's coverage of a news event is arguably greater than the amount needed to facilitate comment on the event itself. Commentary on news events requires only recitation of the underlying facts, not verbatim repetition of another's creative expression of those facts in a news article. So too, the fact that a particular media outlet published a given story, or approached that story from a particular angle can be communicated to a large degree without posting a full text copy of the report.[49] For this reason, the court concludes that verbatim posting of plaintiffs' articles is "more than is necessary" to further defendants' critical purpose. [...]

54   For all these reasons, the court concludes that defendants' use of plaintiffs' articles is minimally, if at all, transformative.

55   ## b. Commercial Nature Of The Free Republic Website

56   In addition to examining defendants' purpose in copying plaintiffs' articles, the first fair use factor also directs that the court evaluate the "character" of the use. The mere fact that a use is commercial does not "give rise to a presumption of unfairness." [...] Rather, a defendant's commercial purpose is only "a separate factor that tends to weigh against a finding of fair use." [...] Thus, a court evaluating the first fair use factor "must weigh the extent of any transformation ... against the significance of other factors, including commercialism, that militate against fair use." [...]

57   The parties vigorously dispute whether defendants' operation of the Free Republic website is a profit or non-profit venture as those terms are used in § 107. [...]

62   Section 107(1) does not mandate "a clear-cut choice between two polar characterizations, 'commercial' and 'non-profit.' " *[...]* Here, choosing one of these two extremes does not properly reflect the nature of the Free Republic site, or defendants' activities in operating it. Rather, attempting the "sensitive balancing of interests" required for application of the fair use doctrine *[...]* the court finds that the operation of the Free Republic site is only minimally commercial.

63   *[...]* The relevant inquiry, however, "is not whether the sole motive of the use is monetary gain but whether the user stands to profit from exploitation of the copyrighted material without paying the customary price." *[...]* Here, defendants and registered third-party visitors to the Free Republic site copy and post plaintiffs' news articles, which are then available to others visiting the site free of charge. Since the general purpose of the site is to provide a forum where individuals can discuss current events and media coverage of them, posting copies of plaintiffs' articles assists in attracting viewers to the site.

64   *[...]*

65   Recent Ninth Circuit decisions, for example, assess whether a defendant's copying led directly to the generation of revenue and profit, or whether it merely had an indirect relation to commercial gain. *[...]*

66   the Second Circuit has described the proper analysis as "differentiating between a direct commercial use and [a] more indirect relation to … commercial activity." *[...]*

67   Defendants do not generate revenue or profits from posting plaintiffs' articles on the Free Republic website. At most, they derive indirect economic benefit by enhancing the website's cachet, increasing registrations, and hence increasing donations and other forms of support. Coupled with the fact that Free Republic has many of the attributes of a non-profit organization, this indirect benefit argues against a finding that the use is strictly commercial. Rather, it is more appropriate to conclude that, while defendants do not necessarily "exploit" the articles for commercial gain, their posting to the Free Republic site allows defendants and other visitors to avoid paying the "customary price" charged for the works. *[...]*

68   ## c. Conclusion Regarding First Fair Use Factor

69   *[...]* the court must balance and weigh the various elements of the first fair use factor in deciding whether it favors plaintiffs or defendants. *[...]*

70   Here, the court has found that defendants' copying of plaintiffs' articles is minimally, if at all, transformative. The comments of the individual who posts an article generally add little by way of comment or criticism to its substance. The extent of the copying is more than is necessary to foster the critical purpose it is designed to serve. Because the copying is verbatim, encompasses large numbers of articles, and occurs on an almost daily basis, the evidence supports a finding that defendants (and visitors to the Free Republic page) engage in extensive, systematic copying of plaintiffs' works.

71   Weighed against the essentially non-transformative nature of defendants' use is the fact that they do not directly derive revenue or profit from the posting of plaintiffs' articles, and the fact that their operation of the Free Republic website has many characteristics of a non-profit venture. So too, their use of plaintiffs' articles appears to be intended more for public benefit than for private commercial gain.

72   Since the "central purpose" of the inquiry on the first fair use factor is to determine "whether the new work merely 'supersede[s] the objects' of the original creation, … or instead adds something new" *[...]* the court finds that the nontransformative character of the copying in this case tips the scale in plaintiffs' favor, and outweighs the non-profit/public benefit nature of the purpose for which the copying is performed. This is particularly true since the posting of plaintiffs' articles to the Free Republic site amounts to "systematic … multiplying [of] the available number of copies" of the articles, "thereby serving the same purpose" for which licenses are sold or archive

charges imposed. S[...] The first fair use factor thus favors plaintiffs.

73   ## 2. The Nature Of The Copyrighted Work

74   [...] The second factor identified in § 107 recognizes "that some works are closer to the core of intended copyright protection than
      others, with the consequence that fair use is more difficult to establish when the former works are copied." [...]Thus, "the more creative
      a work, the more protection it should be accorded from copying; correlatively, the more informational or functional the plaintiff's work,
      the broader should be the scope of the fair use defense."[...] Newspaper articles to a large extent gather and report facts. Nonetheless, a
      news reporter must determine which facts are significant and recount them in an interesting and appealing manner. [...]

76   While plaintiffs' news articles certainly contain expressive elements, they are predominantly factual. Consequently, defendants' fair use
      claim is stronger than it would be had the works been purely fictional. S[...] The court concludes that the second factor weighs in favor
      of a finding of fair use of the news articles by defendants in this case.

77   ## 3. The Amount And Substantiality Of The Portion Used In Relation To The Copyrighted Work As A
      Whole

78   [...]Defendants concede that they have copied and posted entire articles published in plaintiffs' newspapers, although they dispute that
      all of plaintiffs' articles posted to the Free Republic site are verbatim copies. As noted earlier, defendants' evidence does not support their
      contention in this regard. In his deposition, defendant Robinson conceded that verbatim copying of entire articles or substantial portions
      thereof is the norm, and the exhibits submitted by defendants bear this out.[54]

79   The fact that exact copies of plaintiffs' article are posted to the Free Republic site weighs strongly against a finding of fair use in this case.

80   Citing the fact that plaintiffs' copyright registration covers their newspapers as a whole, defendants contend that the papers are
      plaintiffs' "works," and not the individual articles that appear in them. Thus, they contend, the copying of a single article constitutes
      reproduction of only a small portion of the work. This proposition is not supported by the case law. See *American Geophysical, supra,* 60
      F.3d at 925–26 (despite the fact that plaintiffs' copyright registration covered their journals as a whole, the court held that copying an
      entire article was equivalent to copying the entire work)[...]

81   [...]Defendants also contend that copying all or a substantial portion of the articles is essential to the critical purpose of the Free
      Republic website. [...]In assessing such an argument, *Campbell* instructs that the court focus on "the persuasiveness of a [copier's]
      justification for the particular copying done," and noted that "the enquiry will harken back to the first of the statutory factors, for ... the
      extent of the permissible copying varies with the purpose and character of the use." [...]

82   As detailed in the court's consideration of the first fair use factor, defendants have not offered a persuasive argument that full-text
      copying is essential to the critical purpose of the Free Republic site. Contrasted with the purpose and character of me use, the wholesale
      copying of plaintiffs' articles weighs against a finding of fair use. [...]

83   ## 4. The Effect Of The Use On The Potential Market For Or Value Of The Copyrighted Work

84   The fourth factor examines "the effect of the use upon the potential market for or value of the copyrighted work." 17 U.S.C. § 107(4). It
      requires evaluating not only the extent of market harm caused by the alleged infringer's use, but also " 'whether unrestricted and
      widespread conduct of the sort engaged in by the defendant ... would result in a substantially adverse impact on the potential market' for
      the original." [...] In this regard, it is significant if widespread use of the type in which the defendant is engaged would "diminish[ ]

potential sales, interfer[e] with marketability, or usurp[ ] the market" for the original. *[...]* Markets for derivative works, i.e., those markets 'that creators of original works would in general develop or license others to develop,' must be considered in addition to the market for the original. *[...]*

85   *[...]* In assessing the fourth factor, courts frequently contrast a use that "suppresses" or "destroys" the market for the original or derivative works with one that "usurps" or "substitutes" for those markets. [...]

86   Applying these principles to the present case, the undisputed evidence shows that the Free Republic website has approximately 20,000 registered users, receives as many as 100,000 hits per day, and attracts between 25 and 50 million page views each month. The evidence also shows that visitors to the site are able to read full text copies of articles from plaintiffs' newspapers and archives without purchasing the papers, visiting plaintiffs' websites or paying the fee plaintiffs charge for retrieving an article from their archives. While defendants argue that the Free Republic site is a "poor substitute" for locating plaintiffs' articles on their websites,[55] the court has found that for those individuals who visit the site, the articles posted to freerepublic.com do substitute for the original works. Given the number of registered visitors, hits and page views Free Republic attracts, the court cannot accept defendants' assertion that the site has only a *de minimis* effect on plaintiffs' ability to control the market for the copyrighted works.[56]

87   [...]

88   This is precisely defendants' argument here—that the Free Republic site is small in comparison to the sites operated by plaintiffs, is not known to the general public, and thus could not divert a substantial amount of business from plaintiffs. As the copyright holders, however, plaintiffs have the "right to control" access to the articles, and defendants' activities affect a market plaintiffs currently seek to exploit.

91   Plaintiffs assert they have lost and will lose revenue because visitors to the Free Republic site can read plaintiffs' archived news articles without paying the fee they would be charged for accessing the articles at plaintiffs' sites. Similarly, plaintiffs contend that defendants' use affects their ability to generate licensing revenue, since the fact that the articles are available for free viewing on Free Republic's web page diminishes their value to licensees. Finally, plaintiffs argue that defendants' copying reduces the number of people visiting their sites, and thus causes them to lose advertising revenue calculated on the number of hits they receive.[58]

92   Defendants respond that plaintiffs have not adduced evidence of lost revenue resulting from operation of the Free Republic site. This, however, is not determinative. See *Sony, supra,* 464 U.S. at 451 ("Actual present harm need not be shown"). [...]

93   [...] Here, plaintiffs have shown that they are attempting to exploit the market for viewing their articles online, for selling copies of archived articles, and for licensing others to display or sell the articles.[59] Defendants' use "substitutes" for the originals, and has the potential of lessening the frequency with which individuals visit plaintiffs' websites, of diminishing the market for the sale of archived articles, and decreasing me interest in licensing the articles. [...]

94   Defendants counter that there is no evidence that people who view me articles on me Free Republic site would ever have visited plaintiffs' websites. It is not necessary, however, to show with certainty that future harm will result. [...] Rather, "[w]hat is necessary is a showing by a preponderance of the evidence that some meaningful likelihood of future harm exists."*Id.* That likelihood is present when articles that would otherwise be available only at sites controlled or licensed by plaintiffs are available at a different site as well. The likelihood only increases when one considers the impact on the market if defendants' practice of full text copying were to become widespread.

95   Defendants also contend that plaintiffs actually benefit from having their articles posted verbatim on the Free Republic site. While they argue that plaintiffs' sites receive "literally tens of thousands, if not hundreds of thousands of hits per month"[60] as a result of referrals from the Free Republic site, this overstates their expert's quantification of the number of referral hits. In his declaration, Richard Stout

states that the Los Angeles Times' website receives approximately 20,000 hits per month from users who visit the Free Republic site before accessing the Times' site. Stout estimates that these referral hits generate approximately $1,000 in revenue for the paper each month.[61] Defendants argue that this information regarding referral hits demonstrates that plaintiffs' advertising revenue is not diminished because of a reduction in the number of hits to their sites. Stout's declaration, however, does not address how many hits are *diverted* from plaintiffs' websites as a consequence of the posting of articles to the Free Republic site, and this is the pertinent inquiry in terms of potential market harm.

96   Defendants assert the evidence regarding referral hits demonstrates that Free Republic is creating a demand for plaintiffs' works. Even if this is the case, it does not mandate a conclusion that the fourth fair use factor favors defendants. Courts have routinely rejected the argument that a use is fair because it increases demand for the plaintiff's copyrighted work. [...]

97   [...] In short, plaintiffs have demonstrated that they are attempting to exploit the market for viewing their articles online, for selling copies of archived articles, and for licensing others to display or sell the articles. They have demonstrated that the availability of verbatim copies of the articles at the Free Republic site has the potential to interfere with these markets, particularly if it becomes a widespread practice. [Defendants, who bear the burden of proof on fair use, have not rebutted this showing by proving "an absence of 'usurpation' harm to" plaintiffs. [...] Accordingly, the fourth factor weighs against a finding of fair use in this case.

98   ## 5. Balancing The Fair Use Factors

99   In sum, three of the four fair use factors weigh in plaintiffs' favor. Moreover, the factor that favors defendants—the nature of the copyrighted work—does not provide strong support for a fair use finding, since defendants copied both the factual *and* the expressive elements of plaintiffs' news articles. Conversely, the amount and substantiality of the copying and the lack of any significant transformation of the articles weigh heavily in favor of plaintiffs on this issue. The court thus finds that defendants may not assert a fair use defense to plaintiffs' copyright infringement claim. [...]

100   ## D. First Amendment Defense

101   Defendants assert, as a separate defense, the fact that the First Amendment protects their posting of copies of plaintiffs' news articles to the Free Republic website.[62] Defendants contend that visitors to the Free Republic site will be unable to express their views concerning the manner in which the media covers current events since the omissions and biases in the articles will be difficult to communicate to readers without the full text of the article available.[...]

102   In *Harper & Row, supra,* Nation magazine reprinted, without authorization, 300 words from the memoirs of President Gerald Ford. 471 U.S. at 542–45. The Court noted that factual information concerning current events contained in news articles is not protected by copyright. It stated, however, that "copyright assures those who write and publish factual narratives ... that they may at least enjoy the right to market the original expression contained therein as just compensation for their investment." [...] It stressed that copyright fosters free expression because it "supplies the economic incentive to create and disseminate ideas" by "establishing a marketable right to the use of one's expression." [...] It noted that copyright also promotes the countervailing First Amendment right to refrain from speech by protecting the owner of a copyrighted work from being forced to publish it. [...] For all these reasons, the Court concluded that "that copyright's idea/expression dichotomy 'strike[s] a definitional balance between the First Amendment and the Copyright Act by permitting free communication of facts while still protecting an author's expression.' " [...] Accordingly, it rejected defendant's First Amendment argument that material could be copied because it was "newsworthy," [...] and "limited its inquiry to 'the traditional equities of fair use,' unexpanded by any free speech concerns." [...] Courts have generally interpreted this discussion in *Harper & Row* to mean that First Amendment considerations are subsumed within the fair use Analysis. [...]

104   defendants have failed to show that copying plaintiffs' news articles verbatim is essential to communication of the opinions and criticisms visitors to the website express. As discussed above in connection with analysis of defendants' fair use defense, visitors' comments more

often concern the underlying news event than they do the manner in which that event was covered by the media. And, even where media coverage is the subject of the critique, the gist of the comments (which concern the fact that a particular media outlet published a story or approached the story from a particular angle) can generally be communicated without full text copying of the article. The availability of alternatives—such as linking and summarizing—further undercuts any claim that First Amendment rights are implicated. While defendants and other users of the Free Republic site may find these options less ideal than copying plaintiffs' articles verbatim, this does not demonstrate that a First Amendment violation will occur if full text posting is prohibited.

105 **III. CONCLUSION**

106 For the foregoing reasons, plaintiffs' motion for summary adjudication with respect to fair use is granted, and defendants' motion is denied.

107 [...]

Clean Flicks of Colorado LLC v. Soderbergh

August 31, 2014 by mrisch

This case tests what transformative means for derivative works and fair use

1   433 F.Supp.2d 1236 (2006)

2   **CLEAN FLICKS OF COLORADO, LLC, Plaintiff** [...]

            Steven SODERBERGH [...]

4   United States District Court, D. Colorado.

5   July 6, 2006.

6   [...]

12 **MEMORANDUM OPINION AND ORDER**

13 **MATSCH, Senior District Judge.**

14   [...] the Motion Picture Studios[1] ("Studios") have moved for a partial summary judgment on their counterclaims of copyright
        infringement against the parties characterized as "Mechanical Editing Parties." An injunction is the relief requested against CleanFlicks,
        LLC, ("CleanFlicks"), Family Flix, U.S.A., L.L.C. ("Family Flix"), as creators and distributors of infringing works and against ASR
        Management Corporation, d/b/a CleanFilms, f/k/a MyCleanFlicks ("CleanFilms") and Play It Clean Video, LLC ("Play It Clean"), as
        distributors of infringing works [...]

15   The applicable law is the Copyright Act, 17 U.S.C. §§ 101-122. The Studios, in the aggregate, have valid copyrights for the motion
        pictures ("movies") identified by name in the filed papers and, therefore, have the exclusive rights granted by § 106 of the Act. They sell
        and otherwise distribute their movies to the consuming public in various ways, including on DVDs and VHS videocassettes for purchase
        and rental. They also sell and otherwise distribute edited versions of their movies for use by airlines, network television and syndicated
        television broadcasters. The Studios' edits are made to conform to such criteria as ratings, content standards and practices, run time,
        formatting and industry standards. The Studios do not now sell or rent copies of edited versions of their movies on home video directly to
        consumers. That is the market reached by the counterclaim defendants' businesses.

16   CleanFlicks is a limited liability company in Utah, owned by Ray and Sharon Lines. It has created and publicly distributed copies of the
        Studios' movies that it altered by deleting "sex, nudity, profanity and gory violence," using its own guidelines. CleanFlicks began editing
        movies on VHS videocassettes in June, 2000, added DVDs at some time and now does only DVDs. The deletions are from both audio and
        visual content of the movies. The editing techniques used include redaction of audio content, replacing the redaction with ambient noise,
        "blending" of audio and visual content to provide transition of edited scenes, cropping, fogging or the use of a black bar to obscure visual
        content.

17   CleanFlicks first obtains an original copy of the movie from its customer or by its own purchase from an authorized retailer. It then makes a digital copy of the entire movie onto the hard drive of a computer, overcoming such technology as a digital content scrambling protection system in the acquired DVD, that is designed to prevent copying. After using software to make the edits, the company downloads from the computer an edited master copy which is then used to create a new recordable DVD-R to be sold to the public, directly or indirectly through a retailer. Thus, the content of the authorized DVD has been changed and the encryption removed. The DVD-R bears the CleanFlicks trademark. CleanFlicks makes direct sales and rentals to consumers online through its web-site requiring the purchaser to buy both the authorized and edited copies. CleanFlicks purchases an authorized copy of each edited copy it rents. CleanFlicks stops selling to any retailer that makes unauthorized copies of an edited movie.

18   Family Flix is an Arizona limited liability company owned by Richard and Sandra Teraci. It also copies authorized versions of movies into a computer and edits them to delete "profanity, nudity, strong graphic violence and sexual content or innuendos." Using methods comparable to CleanFlicks, Family Flix sells or rents its DVD-Rs directly to subscribers and to retailers. The original DVD is disabled and generally mounted inside the case with the DVD-R. The Family Flix logo with a disclaimer sticker is put on the case. There are no technical obstructions to copying the DVD-Rs.

19   [...]

21   The Studios claim that CleanFlicks and Family Flix are infringing their exclusive right to reproduce the copyrighted works under § 106(1); that CleanFlicks and Family Flix are violating the Studios' right to create derivative works under § 106(2); and that all four of the counterclaim defendants are infringing the exclusive right of distribution of copies under § 106(3).

22   Section 106(1) provides that the owner of a copyright has the exclusive right to "reproduce the copyrighted work in copies or phonorecords." Section 101 defines "copies" as "material objects, other than phonorecords, in which a work is fixed by any method now known or later developed, and from which the work can be perceived, reproduced, or otherwise communicated, either directly or with the aid of a machine or device. The term `copies' includes the material object, other than a phonorecord, in which the work is first fixed." The reproduction complained of is the making by CleanFlicks and Family Flix of voluminous fixed copies of the edited master versions of the Studios' movies, i.e., copies of copies, for which their "one-to-one ratio" of edited to original version argument does not preclude a finding of infringement.

23   Section 106(3) gives the owner of a copyright the exclusive right "to distribute copies or phonorecords of the copyrighted work to the public by sale or other transfer of ownership, or by rental, lease, or lending." Here, it is undisputed that all four of the counterclaim defendants distributed, by sale and rental, copies (albeit edited) of the Studios' copyrighted works and are therefore liable for infringement in the absence of any applicable defense.

24   All of the counterclaim defendants assert that they are making "fair use" of the copyrighted works, invoking the limitations on the exclusive rights granted by § 106, as provided in § 107 of the Act. [...]

25   The Supreme Court [...] has instructed that the fair use doctrine must be applied using a case-by-case analysis, considering all four of the statutory factors, no one of which should be considered controlling.

28   Under the purpose and character of use factor, the counterclaim defendants concede that their use of the copyrighted works is for commercial gain, but argue, correctly, that under *Campbell,* that fact is not determinative. They seek to establish a public policy test that they are criticizing the objectionable content commonly found in current movies and that they are providing more socially acceptable alternatives to enable families to view the films together, without exposing children to the presumed harmful effects emanating from the objectionable content.

29   [...]

30   The accused parties make much of their public policy argument and have submitted many communications from viewers expressing their appreciation for the opportunity to view movies in the setting of the family home without concern for any harmful effects on their children. This argument is inconsequential to copyright law and is addressed in the wrong forum. This Court is not free to determine the social value of copyrighted works. What is protected are the creator's rights to protect its creation in the form in which it was created.

31   During the pendency of this case Congress enacted the Family Movie Act of 2005, Pub.L. No. 109-9, 119 Stat. 218, 223-224, amending § 110 to provide an exemption for the editing of motion pictures by a member of a private household if no fixed copy of the altered version of the motion picture is created. That statute eliminated from this case those parties selling technology enabling such private editing. The legislative history shows that the amendment was not intended to exempt actions resulting in fixed copies of altered works which the House Committee believed illegal.[2] Thus, the appropriate branch of government had the opportunity to make the policy choice now urged and rejected it.

32   The Studios contend that the counterclaim defendants are violating the right to create derivative works, being the edited versions of their films. A "derivative work" is defined in § 101 as

33   A "derivative work" is a work based upon one or more preexisting works, such as a translation, musical arrangement, dramatization, fictionalization, motion picture version, sound recording, art reproduction, abridgment, condensation, or any other form in which a work may be recast, transformed, or adapted. A work consisting of editorial revisions, annotations, elaborations, or other modifications which, as a whole, represent an [1241] original work of authorship, is a "derivative work".

34   This raises the question of whether these DVD-Rs are "transformative." That same question arises under the fair use defense. The parties take inconsistent positions on this question. The counterclaim defendants argue that they are making a transformative use of the copyrighted works for purposes of the first factor under § 107(1) — that the purpose and character of their use are for criticism of the objectionable content of the movies, and then deny that their edited versions are derivative works because they are not recasting or revising the copyrighted material in a manner that can be characterized as a work of authorship within the statutory definition. On the other hand, the Studios say that the edited versions meet the definition of derivative works but deny that the character of the use is transformative within the scope of the fair use defense. *This paragraph raises a real conundrum in the law. If Clean Flicks isn't creating a derivative work when it edits, what is it creating?*

35   The transformative nature of the use of copyrighted material requires such a contribution of originality as may be of such public benefit as would serve the underlying purpose of providing copyright protection, as identified in Article 1, § 8 of the Constitution: . . . to Promote the Progress of Science and useful Arts."

36   In *Campbell,* the Supreme Court said that a use is transformative if it "adds something new, with a further purpose or different character, altering the first with new expression, meaning or message." [...] The counterclaim defendants add nothing new to these movies. They delete scenes and dialogue from them.

37   [...]

38   It is undisputed that the edits are a small percentage of most of the films copied and the use *is* clearly for commercial gain. There is nothing transformative about the edited copies. Therefore, the first statutory factor in the fair use defense does not support the infringers.

39   [...]

41   The primary argument on the fair use defense is the fourth statutory factor. The counterclaim defendants contend that there is no

adverse effect from their use of the movies on the value of the copyrighted work to the Studios. They suggest that the Studios benefit because they are selling *The court found that the second and third factors favored the studios.* [...] more copies of their movies as a result of the editing parties' practice of maintaining a one-to-one ratio of the original and edited versions. It is assumed that the consumers of the edited versions would not have themselves purchased the authorized versions because of the objectionable content and the Studios do not compete in this alternative market.

42   The argument has superficial appeal but it ignores the intrinsic value of the right to control the content of the copyrighted work which is the essence of the law of copyright. Whether these films should be edited in a manner that would make them acceptable to more of the public playing them on DVD in a home environment is more than merely a matter of marketing; it is a question of what audience the copyright owner wants to reach.

43   [...]

44   Accepting all of the counterclaim defendants' factual allegations as true, the fair use defense is not applicable to this case. But because the infringing copies of these movies are not used in a transformative manner, they are not derivative works and do not violate § 106(2).

45   [...]

49   Upon the foregoing, it is ORDERED that:

50   1. The Studios' motion for partial summary judgment is granted as to their claim for copyright infringement under 17 U.S.C. § 106(1), the infringement of their right to reproduce their copyrighted works, against counterclaim defendants CleanFlicks, LLC and Family Flix, USA, LLC.

51   2. The Studios' motion for partial summary judgment is denied as to their claim for copyright infringement under 17 U.S.C. § 106(2), the infringement of the right to create derivative works, against counterclaim defendants CleanFlicks, LLC and Family Flix, USA, LLC.

52   3. The Studios' motion for partial summary judgment is granted as to their claim for copyright infringement under 17 U.S.C. § 106(3), the infringement of their right to distribute their copyrighted works, against all counterclaim defendants, CleanFlicks, LLC; ASR Management Corporation d/b/a CleanFilms f/k/a MyCleanFlicks; Family Flix, USA, LLC; and Play It Clean Video, LLC.

53   [...]

Class 14: 6.4 <u>OIL Casebook: Framing and Linking</u>

Perfect 10 v. Amazon.com - server rule

June 29, 2014 by mrisch

1   508 F.3d 1146
2   **PERFECT 10, INC.,** [...]

v.

AMAZON.COM, INC., [...]

Perfect 10, Inc. [...]

v.

Google Inc. [...]

8   United States Court of Appeals, Ninth Circuit.
10   [...]
11   Filed May 16, 2007.
12   Amended December 3, 2007.
13   [...]

22   Before: CYNTHIA HOLCOMB HALL, HAWKINS, and SANDRA S. IKUTA, Circuit Judges.

23   IKUTA, Circuit Judge:

24   In this appeal, we consider a copyright owner's efforts to stop an Internet search engine from facilitating access to infringing images.
        Perfect 10, Inc. sued Google Inc., for infringing Perfect 10's copyrighted photographs of nude models, among other claims. [...] The
        district court preliminarily enjoined Google from creating and publicly displaying thumbnail versions of Perfect 10's images, [...] but did
        not enjoin Google from linking to third-party websites that display infringing full-size versions of Perfect 10's images. Nor did the district
        court preliminarily enjoin Amazon.com from giving users access to information provided by Google. Perfect 10 and Google both appeal
        the district court's order. We have jurisdiction pursuant to *28 U.S.C. § 1292(a)(1).*[[...]

25   district court handled this complex case in a particularly thoughtful and skillful manner. Nonetheless, the district court erred on certain
        issues, as we will further explain below. We affirm in part, reverse in part, and remand.

554

26   I

27   **Background**

28   Google's computers, along with millions of others, are connected to networks known collectively as the "Internet." "The Internet is a world-wide network of networks ... all sharing a common communications technology." [...] Computer owners can provide information stored on their computers to other users connected to the Internet through a medium called a webpage. A webpage consists of text interspersed with instructions written in Hypertext Markup Language ("HTML") that is stored in a computer. No images are stored on a webpage; rather, the HTML instructions on the webpage provide an address for where the images are stored, whether in the webpage publisher's computer or some other computer. In general, webpages are publicly available and can be accessed by computers connected to the Internet through the use of a web browser.

29   Google operates a search engine, a software program that automatically accesses thousands of websites (collections of webpages) and indexes them within a database stored on Google's computers. When a Google user accesses the Google website and types in a search query, Google's software searches its database for websites responsive to that search query. Google then sends relevant information from its index of websites to the user's computer. Google's search engines can provide results in the form of text, images, or videos.

30   The Google search engine that provides responses in the form of images is called "Google Image Search." In response to a search query, Google Image Search identifies text in its database responsive to the query and then communicates to users the images associated with the relevant text. Google's software cannot recognize and index the images themselves. Google Image Search provides search results as a webpage of small images called "thumbnails," which are stored in Google's servers. The thumbnail images are reduced, lower-resolution versions of full-sized images stored on third-party computers.

31   When a user clicks on a thumbnail image, the user's browser program interprets HTML instructions on Google's webpage. These HTML instructions direct the user's browser to cause a rectangular area (a "window") to appear on the user's computer screen. The window has two separate areas of information. The browser fills the top section of the screen with information from the Google webpage, including the thumbnail image and text. The HTML instructions also give the user's browser the address of the website publisher's computer that stores the full-size version of the thumbnail.[2] By following [...] the HTML instructions to access the third-party webpage, the user's browser connects to the website publisher's computer, downloads the full-size image, and makes the image appear at the bottom of the window on the user's screen. Google does not store the images that fill this lower part of the window and does not communicate the images to the user; Google simply provides HTML instructions directing a user's browser to access a third-party website. However, the top part of the window (containing the information from the Google webpage) appears to frame and comment on the bottom part of the window. Thus, the user's window appears to be filled with a single integrated presentation of the full-size image, but it is actually an image from a third-party website framed by information from Google's website. The process by which the webpage directs a user's browser to incorporate content from different computers into a single window is referred to as "in-line linking." [...] The term "framing" refers to the process by which information from one computer appears to frame and annotate the in-line linked content from another computer. [...]

32   Google also stores webpage content in its cache.[3] For each cached webpage, Google's cache contains the text of the webpage as it appeared at the time Google indexed the page, but does not store images from the webpage. [...] Google may provide a link to a cached webpage in response to a user's search query. However, Google's cache version of the webpage is not automatically updated when the webpage is revised by its owner. So if the webpage owner updates its webpage to remove the HTML instructions for finding an infringing image, a browser communicating directly with the webpage would not be able to access that image. However, Google's cache copy of the webpage would still have the old HTML instructions for the infringing image. Unless the owner of the computer changed the HTML address of the infringing image, or otherwise rendered the image unavailable, a browser accessing Google's cache copy of the website could still access the image where it is stored on the website publisher's computer. In other words, Google's cache copy could provide a user's browser with valid directions to an infringing image even though the updated webpage no longer includes that infringing image.

33   [...]

35   Perfect 10 markets and sells copyrighted images of nude models. Among other enterprises, it operates a subscription website on the Internet. Subscribers pay a monthly fee to view Perfect 10 images in a "members' area" of the site. Subscribers must use a password to log into the members' area. Google does not include these password-protected images from the members' area in Google's index or database. Perfect 10 has also licensed Fonestarz Media Limited to sell and distribute Perfect 10's reduced-size copyrighted images for download and use on cell phones.

36   Some website publishers republish Perfect 10's images on the Internet without authorization. Once this occurs, Google's search engine may automatically index the webpages containing these images and provide thumbnail versions of images in response to user inquiries. When a user clicks on the thumbnail image returned by Google's search engine, the user's browser accesses the third-party webpage and in-line links to the full-sized infringing image stored on the website publisher's computer. This image appears, in its original context, on the lower portion of the window on the user's computer screen framed by information from Google's webpage.

37   *[...]*

40   **III**

47   **Direct Infringement**

48   Perfect 10 claims that Google's search engine program directly infringes two exclusive rights granted to copyright holders: its display rights and its distribution rights.[5] "Plaintiffs must satisfy two requirements to present a prima facie case of direct infringement: (1) they must show ownership of the allegedly infringed material and (2) they must demonstrate that the alleged infringers violate at least one exclusive right granted to copyright holders under *17 U.S.C. § 106*." *[...]* Even if a plaintiff satisfies these two requirements and makes a prima facie case of direct infringement, the defendant may avoid liability if it can establish that its use of the images is a "fair use" as set forth in *17 U.S.C. § 107*. *[...]*

49   Perfect 10's ownership of at least some of the images at issue is not disputed. *[...]*

50   The district court held that Perfect 10 was likely to prevail in its claim that Google violated Perfect 10's display right with respect to the infringing thumbnails. *[...]* However, the district court concluded that Perfect 10 was not likely to prevail on its claim that Google violated either Perfect 10's display or distribution right with respect to its full-size infringing images. *[...]* We review these rulings for an abuse of discretion. *[...]*

51   ***A. Display Right***

52   In considering whether Perfect 10 made a prima facie case of violation of its display right, the district court reasoned that a computer owner that stores an image as electronic information and serves that electronic information directly to the user ("i.e., physically sending ones and zeroes over the [I]nternet to the user's browser," *[...]* is displaying the electronic information in violation of a copyright holder's exclusive display right. *[...]* 17 U.S.C. § 106(5). Conversely, the owner of a computer that does not store and serve the electronic information to a user is not displaying that information, even if such owner in-line links to or frames the electronic information. *[...]* The district court referred to this test as the "server test." *[...]*

53   Applying the server test, the district court concluded that Perfect 10 was likely to succeed in its claim that Google's thumbnails constituted direct infringement but was unlikely to succeed in its claim that Google's in-line linking to full-size infringing images constituted a direct infringement. *[...]*. As explained below, because this analysis comports with the language of the Copyright Act, we agree with the district court's resolution of both these issues.

54   We have not previously addressed the question when a computer displays a copyrighted work for purposes of *section 106(5)*. *Section 106(5)* states that a copyright owner has the exclusive right "to display the copyrighted work publicly." The Copyright Act explains that "display" means "to show a copy of it, either directly or by means of a film, slide, television image, or any other device or process...." *17 U.S.C. § 101*. *Section 101* defines "copies" as "material objects, other than phonorecords, in which a work is fixed by any method now known or later developed, and from which the work can be perceived, reproduced, or otherwise communicated, either directly or with the aid of a machine or device." *Id*. Finally, the Copyright Act provides that "[a] work is `fixed' in a tangible medium of expression when its embodiment in a copy or phonorecord, by or under the authority of the author, is sufficiently permanent or stable to permit it to be perceived, reproduced, or otherwise communicated for a period of more than transitory duration." *Id*.

55   We must now apply these definitions to the facts of this case. A photographic image is a work that is "`fixed' in a tangible medium of expression," for purposes of the Copyright Act, when embodied (i.e., stored) in a computer's server (or hard disk, or other storage device). The image stored in the computer is the "copy" of the work for purposes of copyright law. *See MAI Sys. Corp. v. Peak Computer, Inc., 991 F.2d 511, 517-18 (9th Cir.1993)* (a computer makes a "copy" of a software program when it transfers the program from a third party's computer (or other storage device) into its own memory, because the copy of the program recorded in the computer is "fixed" in a manner that is "sufficiently permanent or stable to permit it to be perceived, reproduced, or otherwise communicated for a period of more than transitory duration" (quoting *17 U.S.C. § 101*)). The computer owner shows a copy "by means of a ... device or process" when the owner uses the computer to fill the computer screen with the photographic image stored on that computer, or by communicating the stored image electronically to another person's computer. *17 U.S.C. § 101*. In sum, based on the plain language of the statute, a person displays a photographic image by using a computer to fill a computer screen with a copy of the photographic image fixed in the computer's memory. There is no dispute that Google's computers store thumbnail versions of Perfect 10's copyrighted images and communicate copies of those thumbnails to Google's users.[6] Therefore, Perfect 10 has made a prima facie case that Google's communication of its stored thumbnail images directly infringes Perfect 10's display right.

56   Google does not, however, display a copy of full-size infringing photographic images for purposes of the Copyright Act when Google frames in-line linked images that appear on a user's computer screen. Because Google's computers do not store the photographic images, Google does not have a copy of the images for purposes of the Copyright Act. In other words, Google does not have any "material objects ... in [...] which a work is fixed ... and from which the work can be perceived, reproduced, or otherwise communicated" and thus cannot communicate a copy. *17 U.S.C. § 101*.

57   Instead of communicating a copy of the image, Google provides HTML instructions that direct a user's browser to a website publisher's computer that stores the full-size photographic image. Providing these HTML instructions is not equivalent to showing a copy. First, the HTML instructions are lines of text, not a photographic image. Second, HTML instructions do not themselves cause infringing images to appear on the user's computer screen. The HTML merely gives the address of the image to the user's browser. The browser then interacts with the computer that stores the infringing image. It is this interaction that causes an infringing image to appear on the user's computer screen. Google may facilitate the user's access to infringing images. However, such assistance raises only contributory liability issues, [...] and does not constitute direct infringement of the copyright owner's display rights.

58   Perfect 10 argues that Google displays a copy of the full-size images by framing the full-size images, which gives the impression that Google is showing the image within a single Google webpage. While in-line linking and framing may cause some computer users to believe they are viewing a single Google webpage, the Copyright Act, unlike the Trademark Act, does not protect a copyright holder against acts that cause consumer confusion. *Cf. 15 U.S.C. § 1114(1)* (providing that a person who uses a trademark in a manner likely to cause confusion shall be liable in a civil action to the trademark registrant).[...]

59   [...]

60   Because Google's cache merely stores the text of webpages, our analysis of whether Google's search engine program potentially infringes Perfect 10's display and distribution rights is equally applicable to Google's cache. Perfect 10 is not likely to succeed in showing that a cached webpage that in-line links to full-size infringing images violates such rights. For purposes of this analysis, it is irrelevant

whether cache copies direct a user's browser to third-party images that are no longer available on the third party's website, because it is the website publisher's computer, rather than Google's computer, that stores and displays the infringing image.

61 **B. Distribution Right**

62 The district court also concluded that Perfect 10 would not likely prevail on its claim that Google directly infringed Perfect 10's right to distribute its full-size images. *[...]* The district court reasoned that distribution requires an "actual dissemination" of a copy. *Id.* at 844. Because Google did not communicate the full-size images to the user's computer, Google did not distribute these images. *[...]*

63 Again, the district court's conclusion on this point is consistent with the language of the Copyright Act. *Section 106(3)* provides that the copyright owner has the exclusive right "to distribute copies or phonorecords of the copyrighted work to the public by sale or other transfer of ownership, or by rental, lease, or lending." *17 U.S.C. § 106(3).* As noted, "copies" means "material objects ... in which a work is fixed." *17 U.S.C. § 101.* The Supreme Court has indicated that in the electronic context, copies may be distributed electronically. *See N.Y. Times Co. v. Tasini, 533 U.S. 483, 498, 121 S.Ct. 2381, 150 L.Ed.2d 500 (2001)* (a computer database program distributed copies of newspaper articles stored in its computerized database by selling copies of those articles through its database service). Google's search engine communicates HTML instructions that tell a user's browser where to find full-size images on a website publisher's computer, but Google does not itself distribute copies of the infringing photographs. It is the website publisher's computer that distributes copies of the images by transmitting the photographic image electronically to the user's computer. As in *Tasini,* the user can then obtain copies by downloading the photo or printing it.

64 *[...]*

65 Google does not own a collection of Perfect 10's full-size images and does not communicate these images to the computers of people using Google's search engine. Though Google indexes these images, it does not have a collection of stored full-size images it makes available to the public. *[...]* Accordingly, the district court correctly concluded that Perfect 10 does not have a likelihood of success in proving that Google violates Perfect 10's distribution rights with respect to full-size images.

66 **C. Fair Use Defense**

67 Because Perfect 10 has succeeded in showing it would prevail in its prima facie case that Google's thumbnail images infringe Perfect 10's display rights, the burden shifts to Google to show that it will likely succeed in establishing an affirmative defense. Google contends that its use of thumbnails is a fair use of the images and therefore does not constitute an infringement of Perfect 10's copyright. *See 17 U.S.C. § 107.*

68 The fair use defense permits the use of copyrighted works without the copyright owner's consent under certain situations. The defense encourages and allows the development of new ideas that build on earlier ones, thus providing a necessary counterbalance to the copyright law's goal of protecting creators' work product. "From the infancy of copyright protection, some opportunity for fair use of copyrighted materials has been thought necessary to fulfill copyright's very purpose...." *[...]* "The fair use doctrine thus `permits [and requires] courts to avoid rigid application of the copyright statute when, on occasion, it would stifle the very creativity which that law is designed to foster.'" *[...]*

69 Congress codified the common law of fair use in *17 U.S.C. § 107*, which provides:

70   Notwithstanding the provisions of *sections 106* and *106A,* the fair use of a copyrighted work, including such use by reproduction in copies or phonorecords or by any other means specified by that section, for purposes such as criticism, comment, news reporting, teaching (including multiple copies for classroom use), scholarship, or research, is not an infringement of copyright. In determining whether the use made of a work in any particular case is a fair use the factors to be

considered shall include—

(1) the purpose and character of the use, including whether such use is of a commercial nature or is for nonprofit educational purposes;

(2) the nature of the copyrighted work;

(3) the amount and substantiality of the portion used in relation to the copyrighted work as a whole; and

(4) the effect of the use upon the potential market for or value of the copyrighted work.

The fact that a work is unpublished shall not itself bar a finding of fair use if such finding is made upon consideration of all the above factors.

71   *17 U.S.C. § 107.*

72   We must be flexible in applying a fair use analysis; it "is not to be simplified with bright-line rules, for the statute, like the doctrine it recognizes, calls for case-by-case analysis.... Nor may the four statutory factors be treated in isolation, one from another. All are to be explored, and the results weighed together, in light of the purposes of copyright." *[...]* The purpose of copyright law is "[t]o promote the Progress of Science and useful Arts," U.S. CONST. art. I, § 8, cl. 8, and to serve "`the welfare of the public.'" *[...]*

73   In applying the fair use analysis in this case, we are guided by *Kelly v. Arriba Soft Corp.,* which considered substantially the same use of copyrighted photographic images as is at issue here. *[...]* In *Kelly,* a photographer brought a direct infringement claim against Arriba, the operator of an Internet search engine. The search engine provided thumbnail versions of the photographer's images in response to search queries. *[...].* We held that Arriba's use of thumbnail images was a fair use primarily based on the transformative nature of a search engine and its benefit to the public. *[...]* We also concluded that Arriba's use of the thumbnail images did not harm the photographer's market for his image. *[...]*

74   In this case, the district court determined that Google's use of thumbnails was not a fair use and distinguished *Kelly.* *[...]* We consider these distinctions in the context of the four-factor fair use analysis.

75   *Purpose and character of the use.* The first factor, *17 U.S.C. § 107(1),* requires a court to consider "the purpose and character of the use, including whether such use is of a commercial nature or is for nonprofit educational purposes." The central purpose of this inquiry is to determine whether and to what extent the new work is "transformative." *[...]* A work is "transformative" when the new work does not "merely supersede the objects of the original creation" but rather "adds something new, with a further purpose or different character, altering the first with new expression, meaning, or message." *[...]* Conversely, if the new work "supersede[s] the use of the original," the use is likely not a fair use. *Harper & Row Publishers, Inc. v. Nation Enters., 471 U.S. 539, 550-51, 105 S.Ct. 2218, 85 L.Ed.2d 588 (1985)* (internal quotation omitted) (publishing the "heart" of an unpublished work and thus supplanting the copyright holder's first publication right was not a fair use); *see also Wall Data Inc. v. L.A. County Sheriff's Dep't, 447 F.3d 769, 778-82 (9th Cir.2006)* (using a copy to save the cost of buying additional copies of a computer program was not a fair use).[...]

76   As noted in *Campbell,* a "transformative work" is one that alters the original work *[...]* "with new expression, meaning, or message." *[...]* "A use is considered transformative only where a defendant changes a plaintiff's copyrighted work or uses the plaintiff's copyrighted work in a different context such that the plaintiff's work is transformed into a new creation." *[...]*

77   Google's use of thumbnails is highly transformative. In *Kelly,* we concluded that Arriba's use of thumbnails was transformative because "Arriba's use of the images serve[d] a different function than Kelly's use—improving access to information on the [I]nternet versus artistic

expression." *[...]* Although an image may have been created originally to serve an entertainment, aesthetic, or informative function, a search engine transforms the image into a pointer directing a user to a source of information. Just as a "parody has an obvious claim to transformative value" because "it can provide social benefit, by shedding light on an earlier work, and, in the process, creating a new one," *[...]* a search engine provides social benefit by incorporating an original work into a new work, namely, an electronic reference tool. Indeed, a search engine may be more transformative than a parody because a search engine provides an entirely new use for the original work, while a parody typically has the same entertainment purpose as the original work. *See, e.g., id. at 594-96, 114 S.Ct. 1164* (holding that 2 Live Crew's parody of "Oh, Pretty Woman" using the words "hairy woman" or "bald headed woman" was a transformative work, and thus constituted a fair use); *Mattel, Inc. v. Walking Mountain Prods., 353 F.3d 792, 796-98, 800-06 (9th Cir.2003)* (concluding that photos parodying Barbie by depicting "nude Barbie dolls juxtaposed with vintage kitchen appliances" was a fair use). In other words, a search engine puts images "in a different context" so that they are "transformed into a new creation." *[...]*

78   The fact that Google incorporates the entire Perfect 10 image into the search engine results does not diminish the transformative nature of Google's use. As the district court correctly noted, *[...]* we determined in *Kelly* that even making an exact copy of a work may be transformative so long as the copy serves a different function than the original work, *[...]* For example, the First Circuit has held that the republication of photos taken for a modeling portfolio in a newspaper was transformative because the photos served to inform, as well as entertain. *[...]* In contrast, duplicating a church's religious book for use by a different church was not transformative. *[...]* Nor was a broadcaster's simple retransmission of a radio broadcast over telephone lines transformative, where the original radio shows were given no "new expression, meaning, or message." *[...]* Here, Google uses Perfect 10's images in a new context to serve a different purpose.

79   The district court nevertheless determined that Google's use of thumbnail images was less transformative than Arriba's use of thumbnails in *Kelly* because Google's use of thumbnails superseded Perfect 10's right to sell its reduced-size images for use on cell phones. *[...]* The district court stated that "mobile users can download and save the thumbnails displayed by Google Image Search onto their phones," and concluded "to the extent that users may choose to download free images to their [...] phone rather than purchase [Perfect 10's] reduced-size images, Google's use supersedes [Perfect 10's]." *[...]*

80   Additionally, the district court determined that the commercial nature of Google's use weighed against its transformative nature. *[...]* Although *Kelly* held that the commercial use of the photographer's images by Arriba's search engine was less exploitative than typical commercial use, and thus weighed only slightly against a finding of fair use, *[...]* the district court here distinguished *Kelly* on the ground that some website owners in the AdSense program had infringing Perfect 10 images on their websites, *[...]* The district court held that because Google's thumbnails "lead users to sites that directly benefit Google's bottom line," the AdSense program increased the commercial nature of Google's use of Perfect 10's images. *[...]*

81   In conducting our case-specific analysis of fair use in light of the purposes of copyright, *[...]* we must weigh Google's superseding and commercial uses of thumbnail images against Google's significant transformative use, as well as the extent to which Google's search engine promotes the purposes of copyright and serves the interests of the public. Although the district court acknowledged the "truism that search engines such as Google Image Search provide great value to the public," *[...]* the district court did not expressly consider whether this value outweighed the significance of Google's superseding use or the commercial nature of Google's use. I*[...]*The Supreme Court, however, has directed us to be mindful of the extent to which a use promotes the purposes of copyright and serves the interests of the public. *[...]*

82   We note that the superseding use in this case is not significant at present: the district court did not find that any downloads for mobile phone use had taken place. *See Perfect 10, [...]* Moreover, while Google's use of thumbnails to direct users to AdSense partners containing infringing content adds a commercial dimension that did not exist in *Kelly*, the district court did not determine that this commercial element was significant. *[...]* The district court stated that Google's AdSense programs as a whole contributed "$630 million,

or 46% of total revenues" to Google's bottom line, but noted that this figure did not "break down the much smaller amount attributable to websites that contain infringing content." *I[...]*

83   We conclude that the significantly transformative nature of Google's search engine, particularly in light of its public benefit, outweighs Google's superseding and commercial uses of the thumbnails in this case. In reaching this conclusion, we note the importance of analyzing fair use flexibly in light of new circumstances. *[...]* endorses the purpose and general scope of the judicial doctrine of fair use, but there is no disposition to freeze the doctrine in the statute, especially during a period of rapid technological change.'" *[...]* We are also mindful of the Supreme Court's direction that "the more transformative the new work, the less will be the significance of other factors, like commercialism, that may weigh against a finding of fair use." *[...]*

84   Accordingly, we disagree with the district court's conclusion that because Google's use of the thumbnails could supersede Perfect 10's cell phone download use and because the use was more commercial than Arriba's, this fair use factor weighed "slightly" in favor of Perfect 10 *[...]* Instead, we conclude that the transformative nature of Google's use is more significant than any incidental superseding use or the minor commercial aspects of Google's search engine and website. Therefore, this factor weighs heavily in favor of Google.

85   *The nature of the copyrighted work.* With respect to the second factor, "the nature of the copyrighted work," *17 U.S.C. § 107(2)*, our decision in *Kelly* is directly on point. There we held that the photographer's images were "creative in nature" and thus "closer to the core of intended copyright protection than are more fact-based works." *[...]* However, because the photos appeared on the Internet before Arriba used thumbnail versions in its search engine results, this factor weighed only slightly in favor of the photographer. *[...]*

86   Here, the district court found that Perfect 10's images were creative but also previously published. *[...]* The right of first publication is "the author's right to control the first public appearance of his expression." *[...]* Because this right encompasses "the choices of when, where, and in what form first to publish a work," *id.,* an author exercises and exhausts this one-time right by publishing the work in any medium. *[...]* Once Perfect 10 has exploited this commercially valuable right of first publication by putting its images on the Internet for paid subscribers, Perfect 10 is no longer entitled to the enhanced protection available for an unpublished work. Accordingly the district court did not err in holding that this factor weighed only slightly in favor of Perfect 10.[9] *[...]*

87   *The amount and substantiality of the portion used.* "The third factor asks whether the amount and substantiality of the portion used in relation to the copyrighted work as a whole ... are reasonable in relation to the purpose of the copying." *[...]* In *Kelly,* we held Arriba's use of the entire photographic image was reasonable in light of the purpose of a search engine. *[...]* Specifically, we noted, "[i]t was necessary for Arriba to copy the entire image to allow users to recognize the image and decide whether to pursue more information about the image or the originating [website]. If Arriba only copied part of the image, it would be more difficult to identify it, thereby reducing the usefulness of the visual search engine." *Id.* Accordingly, we concluded that this factor did not weigh in favor of either *[...]* party. *[...]* Because the same analysis applies to Google's use of Perfect 10's image, the district court did not err in finding that this factor favored neither party.

88   *Effect of use on the market.* The fourth factor is "the effect of the use upon the potential market for or value of the copyrighted work." *17 U.S.C. § 107(4).* In *Kelly,* we concluded that Arriba's use of the thumbnail images did not harm the market for the photographer's full-size images. *[...]* We reasoned that because thumbnails were not a substitute for the full-sized images, they did not harm the photographer's ability to sell or license his full-sized images. *[...]* The district court here followed *Kelly's* reasoning, holding that Google's use of thumbnails did not hurt Perfect 10's market for full-size images. *[...]*

89   Perfect 10 argues that the district court erred because the likelihood of market harm may be presumed if the intended use of an image is for commercial gain. However, this presumption does not arise when a work is transformative because "market substitution is at least

less certain, and market harm may not be so readily inferred." *[...]* As previously discussed, Google's use of thumbnails for search engine purposes is highly transformative, and so market harm cannot be presumed.

90   Perfect 10 also has a market for reduced-size images, an issue not considered in *Kelly*. The district court held that "Google's use of thumbnails likely does harm the potential market for the downloading of [Perfect 10's] reduced-size images onto cell phones." *[...]* The district court reasoned that persons who can obtain Perfect 10 images free of charge from Google are less likely to pay for a download, and the availability of Google's thumbnail images would harm Perfect 10's market for cell phone downloads. *[...]* As we discussed above, the district court did not make a finding that Google users have downloaded thumbnail images for cell phone use. This potential harm to Perfect 10's market remains hypothetical. We conclude that this factor favors neither party.

91   Having undertaken a case-specific analysis of all four factors, we now weigh these factors together "in light of the purposes of copyright." *[...]* In this case, Google has put Perfect 10's thumbnail images (along with millions of other thumbnail images) to a use fundamentally different than the use intended by Perfect 10. In doing so, Google has provided a significant benefit to the public. Weighing this significant transformative use against the unproven use of Google's thumbnails for cell phone downloads, and considering the other fair use factors, all in light of the purpose of copyright, we conclude that Google's use of Perfect 10's thumbnails is a fair use. Because the district court here "found facts sufficient to evaluate each of the statutory factors … [we] need not remand for further factfinding." *[...]* We conclude that Google is likely to succeed in proving its fair use defense and, accordingly, we vacate the preliminary injunction regarding Google's use of thumbnail images.

92   *[...]*

900   **VI**

129   We conclude that Google's fair use defense is likely to succeed at trial, and therefore we reverse the district court's determination that Google's thumbnail versions of Perfect 10's images likely constituted a direct infringement. *[...]*

134   [2] The website publisher may not actually store the photographic images used on its webpages in its own computer, but may provide HTML instructions directing the user's browser to some further computer that stores the image. Because this distinction does not affect our analysis, for convenience, we will assume that the website publisher stores all images used on its webpages in the website publisher's own computer.

135   [3] Generally, a "cache" is "a computer memory with very short access time used for storage of frequently or recently used instructions or data." *[...]* There are two types of caches at issue in this case. A user's personal computer has an internal cache that saves copies of webpages and images that the user has recently viewed so that the user can more rapidly revisit these webpages and images. Google's computers also have a cache which serves a variety of purposes. Among other things, Google's cache saves copies of a large number of webpages so that Google's search engine can efficiently organize and index these webpages.

136   *[...]*

137   [5] *17 U.S.C. § 106* states, in pertinent part:

138   Subject to *sections 107* through *122*, the owner of copyright under this title has the exclusive rights to do and to authorize any of the following:

          (1) to reproduce the copyrighted work in copies or phonorecords;

          ....

(3) to distribute copies or phonorecords of the copyrighted work to the public by sale or other transfer of ownership, or by rental, lease, or lending;

....

(5) in the case of literary, musical, dramatic, and choreographic works, pantomimes, and pictorial, graphic, or sculptural works, including the individual images of a motion picture or other audiovisual work, to display the copyrighted work publicly....

139   [6] Because Google initiates and controls the storage and communication of these thumbnail images, we do not address whether an entity that merely passively owns and manages an Internet bulletin board or similar system violates a copyright owner's display and distribution rights when the users of the bulletin board or similar system post infringing works. *[...]*

140   [7] Perfect 10 also argues that Google violates Perfect 10's right to display full-size images because Google's in-line linking meets the Copyright Act's definition of "to perform or display a work `publicly.'" *17 U.S.C. § 101.* This phrase means "to transmit or otherwise communicate a performance or display of the work to ... the public, by means of any device or process, whether the members of the public capable of receiving the performance or display receive it in the same place or in separate places and at the same time or at different times." *Id.* Perfect 10 is mistaken. Google's activities do not meet this definition because Google transmits or communicates only an address which directs a user's browser to the location where a copy of the full-size image is displayed. Google does not communicate a display of the work itself.

141   *[...]*

143   [9] Google contends that Perfect 10's photographic images are less creative and less deserving of protection than the images of the American West in *Kelly* because Perfect 10 boasts of its un-retouched photos showing the natural beauty of its models. Having reviewed the record, we conclude that the district court's finding that Perfect 10's photographs "consistently reflect professional, skillful, and sometimes tasteful artistry" is not clearly erroneous. *[...]* We agree with the district court that there is no basis for concluding that photos of the American West are more deserving of protection than photos of nude models. *[...]*

Ticketmaster Corp. v. Tickets.Com, Inc. - copyright

September 01, 2014 by mrisch

This edited version of the case considers copyright issues. Later versions will consider other issues

1   **TICKETMASTER CORP. et al., Plaintiff**

v.

TICKETS.COM, INC. et al., Defendants.

2   [...]

3   United States District Court, C.D. California.

4   March 7, 2003.

5   [...]

7   **TICKETS.COM'S NOTICE OF MOTION AND MOTION FOR SUMMARY JUDGMENT [...]**

8   **HUPP, J.**

9   **ORDER**

10   [...] This motion by defendant Tickets.com, Inc. (hereafter TX) for summary judgment on plaintiffs Ticketmaster Corporation and Ticket Online–CitySearch, Inc. (hereafter collectively TM), intellectual property issues is [...] granted as to the copyright and trespass to chattels claims, which are dismissed by this minute order.

11   [...]

12   Many of the factual items are not contested, although the legal result of applying the law to the uncontested facts is heavily contested. Among the uncontested facts are the following: Both TM and TX are in the business of selling tickets to all kinds of "events" (sports, concerts, plays, etc.) to the public. They are in heavy competition with one another, but operate in distinctive ways. TM is the largest company in the industry. It sells tickets by the four methods of ticket selling–venue box office, retail outlets, by telephone, and over the internet. Telephone and internet sales require the customer to establish credit with the ticket seller (usually by credit card). Internet sales have been the fastest growing segment of the industry. TX at the time of the events considered in this motion was primarily (but not exclusively) an internet seller. Both TM and TX maintain a web page reachable by anyone with an internet connection. Each of their web pages has many subsidiary (or interior) web pages which describe one event each and provide such basic information as to location, date, time, description of the event, and ticket prices. The TM interior web pages each have a separate electronic address or Uniform Resource Locator ("URL") which, if possessed by the internet user, allows the user to reach the web page for any particular event by by-passing the "home" web page and proceeding past the index to reach the interior web page for the event in question. The TM interior web pages provide telephone numbers for customers or allow the customer to order tickets to the event by interactive computer use. A charge is made for the TM service.

13   TM principally does business by exclusive contracts with the event providers or their producers, and its web pages only list the events for which TM is the exclusive ticket seller. TX also sells tickets to a number of events for which it is the ticket seller. At one point, its web pages attempted to list all events for which tickets were available whether or not TX sold the tickets. Its interior web pages also listed the event, the date, time, ticket prices, and provided for internet purchase if TX could sell the tickets. When TX could not sell the tickets, it listed ticket brokers who sold at premium prices. In early 2000, TX discontinued this practice of listing events with tickets sold by other ticket brokers. Until early 2000, in situations where TM was the only source of tickets, TX provided a "deep link" by which the customer would be transferred to the interior web page of TM's web site, where the customer could purchase the ticket from TM. This process of "deep linking" is the subject of TM's complaint in this action, of which there is now left the contract, copyright, and trespass theories.

14   [...] Starting in 1998 and continuing to July 2001, when it stopped the practice, TX employed an electronic program called a "spider" or "crawler" to review the internal web pages (available to the public) of TM. The "spider" "crawled" through the internal web pages to TM and electronically extracted the electronic information from which the web page is shown on the user's computer. The spider temporarily loaded this electronic information into the Random Access Memory ("RAM") of TX's computers for a period of from 10–15 seconds. TX then extracted the factual information (event, date, time, tickets prices, and URL) and discarded the rest (which consisted of TM identification, logos, ads, and other information which TX did not intend to use; much of this discarded material was protected by copyright). The factual information was then organized in the TX format to be displayed on the TX internal web page. The TX internal web page carried no TM identification and had only the factual information about the event on it which was taken from TM's interior web page but rearranged in TX format plus any information or advertisement added by TX. From March 1998, to early 2000, the TX user was provided the deep linking option described above to go directly from the TX web site to the relevant TM interior web page. This option stopped (or was stopped by TM) in early 2000. For an unknown period afterward, the TX customer was given the option of linking to the TM home page, from which the customer could work his way to the interior web page in which he was interested. (The record does not reveal whether this practice still exists or whether TM objects to it.) Thus, the intellectual property issues in this case appear to be limited to events which occurred between November 1998, when spidering started, and July 2001, when it stopped. The "deep linking" aspect of the case is relevant only from March 1998, to early 2000, when it stopped.

15   [...]

18   [4] The copyright issues are more difficult. They divide into three issues. The first is whether the momentary resting in the TX computers of all of the electronic signals which are used to form the video representation to the viewer of the interior web pages of the TX computer constitutes actionable copyright infringement. The second is whether the URLs, which were copied and used by TX, contain copyrightable material. The third is whether TX's deep-linking caused the unauthorized public display of TM event pages. In examining these questions, we must keep in mind a prime theorem of copyright law–facts, as such, are not subject to copyright protection. What is subject to copyright protection is the manner or mode of expression of those facts. Thus, addresses and telephone numbers contained in a directory do not have copyright protection [...] despite the fact that time, money, and effort went into compiling the information. Similarly, in this case, the existence of the event, its date and time, and its ticket prices, are not subject to copyright. Anyone is free to print (or show on the internet) such information. Thus, if TX had sat down a secretary at the computer screen with instructions manually to go through TM's web sites and pick out and write down purely factual information about the events, and then feed it into the TX web pages (using the TX distinctive format only), no one could complain. The objection is that the same thing was done with an electronic program. However, the difference is that the spider picks up all of the electronic symbols which, if it had been put on a monitor with the right software, would duplicate the TM web page. However, this is not the way it was done. The spider picks up the electronic symbols and loads them momentarily (for 10 to 15 seconds) into the RAM of the TX computers, where a program picks up the factual data (not protected), places same into the TX format for its web pages, and immediately discards the balance, which may consist of TM logos, TM advertisements, TM format for presentation of the material, and other material which is copyrightable. Thus, the actual copying (if it can be called that) is momentary while the non-protected material, all open to the public, is extracted. Is this momentary resting of the electronic symbols from which a TM web page could be (but is not) constructed fair use where the purpose is to obtain non-protected facts? The court thinks the answer is "yes". There is not much law in point. However, there are two Ninth Circuit cases which shed light on the problem. They are *Sony Computer Entertainment* [...] and *Sega* [...]. In each of these cases, the alleged infringer attempted to get at non-protected source code by reverse engineering of the plaintiff's copyrighted software. In doing so, the necessary method was to copy the software and work backwards to derive the unprotected source code. The copied software was then destroyed. In each case, this

was held to be fair use since it was necessary to temporarily copy the software to obtain the non-protected material. There may be a difference with this case, however, at least TM claims so. It asserts in its points and authorities that taking the temporary copy in this case was not the only way to obtain the unprotected information, and that TX was able to, and in actuality did purchase such information from certain third-parties. Both *Sony* and *Sega* stated that the fair use was justified because reverse engineering (including taking a temporary copy) was the only way the unprotected information could be obtained. Although this court recognizes that the holdings of *Sony* and *Sega* were limited to the specific context of "disassembling" copyrighted object code in order to access unprotected elements contained in the source code, this court believes that the "fair use" doctrine can be applied to the current facts.

19   [...] Taking the temporary copy of the electronic information for the limited purpose of extracting unprotected public facts leads to the conclusion that the temporary use of the electronic signals was "fair use" and not actionable. In determining whether a challenged use of copyrighted material is fair, a court must keep in mind the public policy underlying the Copyright Act: to secure a fair return for an author's creative labor and to stimulate artistic creativity for the general good. This court sees no public policy that would be served by restricting TX from using spiders to temporarily download TM's event pages in order to acquire the unprotected, publicly available factual event information. The rest of the event page information (which consisted of TM identification, logos, ads, and other information) was discarded and not used by TX and is not exposed to the public by TX. In temporarily downloading TM's event pages to its RAM through the use of spiders, TX was not exploiting TM's creative labors in any way: its spiders gathered copyrightable and non-copyrightable information alike but then immediately discarded the copyrighted material. It is unlikely that the spiders could have been programmed to take only the factual information from the TM web pages without initially downloading the entire page.

20   Consideration of the fair use factors listed in 17 USC § 106 supports this result. First, TX operates its site for commercial purposes, and this fact tends to weigh against a finding of fair use. [...] TX's use of the data gathered from TM's event pages was only slightly transformative. As for the second factor, the nature of the copyrighted work, the copying that occurred when spiders download the event page, access the source code for each page, and extract the factual data embedded in the code, is analogous to the process of copying that the *Sony* court condoned (however, the Court recognizes that the fair use holding from that decision does not fit perfectly onto the facts at hand). Third, because TX's final product-the TX web site-did not contain any infringing material, the "amount and substantiality of the portion used" is of little weight. [...]. The fourth factor (the effect on the market value of the copyrighted work) is, of course nil, and weighs towards finding fair use. TM's arguments and evidence regarding loss of advertising revenue, as well as the loss of potential business with Volt Delta, are not persuasive.

21   The second copyright problem is whether the URLs (Uniform Resource Locator) are subject to copyright protection. The URLs are copied by TX and, while TX was deep hyper-linking to TM interior web pages, were used by TX to allow the deep-linking (by providing the electronic address of the particular relevant TM interior web page). This electronic address is kept in TX's computer (not provided to the customer) but was used to connect the customer to the TM interior web page when the customer pushed the button to be transferred to the web page of the broker who sells the tickets. In fact, anyone who uses the TM interior web page–TM customer or not–uses the URL to get there, although sometimes through another computer which also has the URL. TM contends that, although the URLs are strictly functional, they are entitled to copyright protection because there are several ways to write the URL, and, thus, original authorship is used. The court disagrees. A URL is simply an address, open to the public, like the street address of a building, which, if known, can enable the user to reach the building. There is nothing sufficiently original to make the URL a copyrightable item, especially the way it is used. [...] There appear to be no cases holding the URLs to be subject to copyright. On principle, they should not be.

22   [...] The third copyright problem is whether TX's deep-linking caused the unauthorized public display of TM event pages in violation of TM's exclusive rights of reproduction and display under 17 U.S.C. § 106. The Ninth Circuit in *Kelly* 9 Cir '02 280 F3d 934, recognized that inline linking and framing of full-sized images of plaintiff's copyrighted photographs within the defendant's web site violated the plaintiff's public display rights. In that case, defendant's web site contained links to plaintiff's photographs (which were on plaintiff's publicly available website). Users were able to view plaintiff's photographs within the context of defendant's site: Plaintiff's images were "framed" by the defendant's window, and were thus surrounded by defendant web page's text and advertising. In one short paragraph in a declaration offered on the preliminary injunction motion, TM alleges that when a user was deep-linked from the TX site to a TM event page, a smaller window was opened. The smaller window was described as containing a page from the TM web site which was "framed" by the larger window. At the time of the preliminary injunction motion, TX stated that whether "framing" occurs or not depends on the

settings on the user's computer, over which TX has no control. Thus, framing occurred on some occasions but not on others. However, TX says that it "did not try to disguise a sale by use of frames occurring on the Tickets.com website." (Reply, p. 10) TX further states that when users were linked to TM web pages, the TM event pages were clearly identified as belonging to TM.

23   However, even if the TM interior web site page was "framed" within the TX web page, this case is distinguishable from *Kelly.* In *Kelly,* the defendant's site would display a variety of "thumbnail" images as a result of the user's search. By clicking on the desired thumbnail image, a user could view the "Images Attributes" page, which displayed the original full-size image, a description of its dimensions, a link to the originating web site, and defendant's banner and advertising. The full-size image was not technically located on defendant's web site, but was taken directly from the originating web site. However, only the image itself, and not any other part of the originating web site, was displayed on the "Images Attributes" page. The Ninth Circuit determined that by importing plaintiff's images into its own web page, and by showing them in the context of its own site, defendant infringed upon plaintiff's exclusive public display right.

24   In this case, a user on the TX site was taken directly to the originating TM site, containing all the elements of that particular TM event page. Each TM event page clearly identified itself as belonging to TM. Moreover, the link on the TX site to the TM event page contained the following notice: "Buy this ticket from another online ticketing company. Click here to buy tickets. These tickets are sold by another ticketing company. Although we can't sell them to you, the link above will take you directly to the other company's web site where you can purchase them." (2d Am.Compl.Ex.I) (emphasis in original) Even if the TM site may have been displayed as a smaller window that was literally "framed" by the larger TX window, it is not clear that, as matter of law, the linking to TX event pages would constitute a showing or public display in violation of 17 U.S.C. § 106(5). Accordingly, summary judgment is granted on the copyright claims of TM and it is eliminated from this action.

Intellectual Reserve, Inc. v. Utah Lighthouse Ministry, Inc.

September 01, 2014 by mrisch

This case serves two purposes. First, it introduces the type of liability that one might face for hyperlinking, even if the content is no hosted on one's own server. Second, in doing so, it introduces the concept of secondary liability, which pervades copyright liability on the internet.

Consider whether this court's view of direct liability by *readers* is consistent with Perfect 10's consideration of thumbnail images.

1   75 F.Supp.2d 1290 (1999)

2   **INTELLECTUAL RESERVE, INC., a Utah corporation, Plaintiff,**

v.

UTAH LIGHTHOUSE MINISTRY, INC., a Utah corporation, et al., Defendants.

3   [...]

4   United States District Court, D. Utah, Central Division.

5   December 6, 1999.

6   [...]

8   **CAMPBELL, District Judge.**

9   This matter is before the court on plaintiff's motion for preliminary injunction. Plaintiff claims that unless a preliminary injunction issues, defendants will directly infringe and contribute to the infringement of its copyright in the *Church Handbook of Instructions* ("Handbook"). Defendants do not oppose a preliminary injunction, but argue that the scope of the injunction should be restricted to only prohibit direct infringement of plaintiff's copyright.

10   Having fully considered the arguments of counsel, the submissions of the parties and applicable legal authorities, the court grants plaintiff's motion for a preliminary injunction. However, the scope of the preliminary injunction is limited.

11   *Discussion*

12   [...] Here, in determining whether plaintiff is now entitled to the injunctive relief, the following factors are to be considered:

13   (1) substantial likelihood that the movant will eventually prevail on the merits: [...]

15   **I.** *Likelihood of Plaintiff Prevailing on the Merits*

16   First, the court considers whether there is a substantial likelihood that plaintiff will eventually prevail on the merits. Plaintiff alleges that the defendants infringed its copyright directly by posting substantial portions of its copyrighted material on defendants' website, and also

contributed to infringement of its copyright by inducing, causing or materially contributing to the infringing conduct of another. To determine the proper scope of the preliminary injunction, the court considers the likelihood that plaintiff will prevail on either or both of its claims.

17   **A.** *Direct Infringement*

18   To prevail on its claim of direct copyright infringement, "[p]laintiff must establish both: (1) that it possesses a valid copyright and (2) that [d]efendants `copied' protectable elements of the copyrighted work." *[...]* Defendants initially conceded in a hearing, for purposes of the temporary restraining order and preliminary injunction, that plaintiff has a valid copyright in the Handbook, and that defendants directly infringed plaintiff's copyright by posting substantial portions of the copyrighted material.[...] Defendants changed their position, in a motion to dismiss, claiming that plaintiff has failed to allege facts necessary to show ownership of a valid copyright. Despite the defendants' newly-raised argument, the court finds, for purpose of this motion, that the plaintiff owns a valid copyright on the material defendants posted on their website. *[...]* Defendants have not advanced any additional affirmative defenses to the claim of direct infringement. Therefore, the court finds that there is a substantial likelihood that plaintiff will prevail on its claim of direct infringement.

19   **B.** *Contributory Infringement*

20   According to plaintiff, after the defendants were ordered to remove the Handbook from their website, the defendants began infringing plaintiff's copyright by inducing, causing, or materially contributing to the infringing conduct of others. It is undisputed that defendants placed a notice on their website that the Handbook was online, and gave three website addresses of websites containing the material defendants were ordered to remove from their website. Defendants also posted emails on their website that encouraged browsing[3] those websites, printing copies of the Handbook and sending the Handbook to others.

21   Although the copyright statute does not expressly impose liability for contributory infringement,

22   [t]he absence of such express language in the copyright statute does not preclude the imposition of liability for copyright infringements on certain parties *[...]* who have not themselves engaged in the infringing activity. For vicarious liability is imposed in virtually all areas of the law, and the concept of contributory infringement is merely a species of the broader problem of identifying the circumstances in which it is just to hold one accountable for the actions of another.

23   *[...]* Even though "'the lines between direct infringement, contributory infringement and vicarious liability are not clearly drawn'" distinctions can be made between them. *[...]* Vicarious liability is grounded in the tort concept of respondeat superior, and contributory infringement is founded in the tort concept of enterprise liability. *[...]* "[B]enefit and control are the signposts of vicarious liability, [whereas] knowledge and participation [are] the touchstones of contributory infringement." *[...]*

24   Liability for contributory infringement is imposed when "one who, with knowledge of the infringing activity, induces, causes or materially contributes to the infringing conduct of another." *[...]* Thus, to prevail on its claim of contributory infringement, plaintiff must first be able to establish that the conduct defendants allegedly aided or encouraged could amount to infringement. *[...]* Defendants argue that they have not contributed to copyright infringement by those who posted the Handbook on websites nor by those who browsed the websites on their computers.

25   *1. Can the Defendants Be Liable Under a Theory of Contributory Infringement for the Actions of Those Who Posted the Handbook on the Three Websites?*

26   *a. Did those who posted the Handbook on the websites infringe plaintiff's copyright?*

27   During a hearing on the motion to vacate the temporary restraining order, defendants accepted plaintiff's proffer that the three websites

contain the material which plaintiff alleges is copyrighted.[4] Therefore, plaintiff at trial is likely to establish that those who have posted the material on the three websites are directly infringing plaintiff's copyright.

28 **b.** *Did the defendants induce, cause or materially contribute to the infringement?*

29 The evidence now before the court indicates that there is no direct relationship between the defendants and the people who operate the three websites. The defendants did not provide the website operators with the plaintiff's copyrighted material, nor are the defendants receiving any kind of compensation from them. The only connection between the defendants and those who operate the three websites appears to be the information defendants have posted on their website concerning the infringing sites. Based on this scant evidence, the court concludes that plaintiff has not shown that defendants contributed to the infringing action of those who operate the infringing websites.

30 **2.** *Can the Defendants Be Liable Under a Theory of Contributory Infringement for the Actions of Those Who Browse the Three Infringing Websites?*

31 Defendants make two arguments in support of their position that the activities [...] of those who browse the three websites do not make them liable under a theory of contributory infringement. First, defendants contend that those who browse the infringing websites are not themselves infringing plaintiff's copyright; and second, even if those who browse the websites are infringers, defendants have not materially contributed to the infringing conduct.

32 **a.** *Do those who browse the websites infringe plaintiff's copyright?*

33 The first question, then, is whether those who browse any of the three infringing websites are infringing plaintiff's copyright. Central to this inquiry is whether the persons browsing are merely viewing the Handbook (which is not a copyright infringement), or whether they are making a copy of the Handbook (which is a copyright infringement). *See* 17 U.S.C. § 106.

34 "Copy" is defined in the Copyright Act as: "material objects ... in which a work is fixed by any method now known or later developed, and from which the work can be perceived, reproduced, or otherwise communicated, either directly or with the aid of a machine or device." 17 U.S.C. § 101. "A work is `fixed' ... when its ... sufficiently permanent or stable to permit it to be perceived, reproduced, or otherwise communicated for a period of more than transitory duration." *Id.*

35 When a person browses a website, and by so doing displays the Handbook, a copy of the Handbook is made in the computer's random access memory (RAM), to permit viewing of the material. And in making a copy, even a temporary one, the person who browsed infringes the copyright.[...] Additionally, a person making a printout or re-posting a copy of the Handbook on another website would infringe plaintiff's copyright.

36 **b.** *Did the defendants induce, cause or materially contribute to the infringement?*

37 The court now considers whether the defendants' actions contributed to the infringement of plaintiff's copyright by those who browse the three websites.

38 The following evidence establishes that defendants have actively encouraged the infringement of plaintiff's copyright[6] After being ordered to remove the Handbook from their website, defendants posted on [...] their website: "Church Handbook of Instructions is back online!" and listed the three website addresses. [...]) Defendants also posted e-mail suggesting that the lawsuit against defendants would be affected by people logging onto one of the websites and downloading the complete handbook. [...] One of the e-mails posted by the defendants mentioned sending a copy of the copyrighted material to the media. [...] In response to an e-mail stating that the sender had unsuccessfully tried to browse a website that contained the Handbook, defendants gave further instruction on how to browse the material. [...] At least one of the three websites encourages the copying and posting of copies of the allegedly infringing material on

other websites. (*See id.,* Ex. 4 ("Please mirror these files.... It will be a LOT quicker for you to download the compressed version ... Needless to say, we need a LOT of mirror sites, as absolutely soon as possible.").)

39   Based on the above, the court finds that the first element necessary for injunctive relief is satisfied.

40   [...]

46   ***Order***

47   Therefore, for the reasons stated, the court orders the following preliminary injunction:

48   1. Defendants, their agents and those under their control, shall remove from and not post on defendants' website the material alleged to infringe plaintiff's copyright;

49   2. Defendants, their agents and those under their control, shall not reproduce or distribute verbatim, in a tangible medium, material alleged to infringe plaintiff's copyright;

50   3. Defendants, their agents and those under their control, shall remove from and not post on defendants' website, addresses to websites that defendants know, or have reason to know, contain the material alleged to infringe plaintiff's copyright;

51   [...]

57   [6] Plaintiff at this point has been unable to specifically identify persons who have infringed its copyright because they were induced or assisted by defendants' conduct, however, there is a substantial likelihood that plaintiff will be able to do so after conducting discovery. There is evidence that at least one of the websites has seen a great increase in "hits" recently. [...] Also, plaintiff does not have to establish that the defendants' actions are the sole cause of another's infringement; rather plaintiff may prevail by establishing that defendants' conduct induces or materially contributes to the infringing conduct of another.

Class 15: 6.5 <u>OIL Casebook: Digital Music Copyright</u>

Digital Millenium Copyright Act: 17 U.S. Code § 114 - Scope of exclusive rights in soun recordings

September 01, 2014 by mrisch

This statute deals with digital broadcasts of sound recordings. It sets up a complex system of licenses required, depending on the interactivity of the service

1   **(a)** The exclusive rights of the owner of copyright in a sound recording are limited to the rights specified by clauses (1), (2), (3) and (6) of section 106, and do not include any right of performance under section 106 (4).

2   **(b)** The exclusive right of the owner of copyright in a sound recording under clause (1) of section 106 is limited to the right to duplicate the sound recording in the form of phonorecords or copies that directly or indirectly recapture the actual sounds fixed in the recording. The exclusive right of the owner of copyright in a sound recording under clause (2) of section 106 is limited to the right to prepare a derivative work in which the actual sounds fixed in the sound recording are rearranged, remixed, or otherwise altered in sequence or quality. The exclusive rights of the owner of copyright in a sound recording under clauses (1) and (2) of section 106 do not extend to the making or duplication of another sound recording that consists entirely of an independent fixation of other sounds, even though such sounds imitate or simulate those in the copyrighted sound recording. The exclusive rights of the owner of copyright in a sound recording under clauses (1), (2), and (3) of section 106 do not apply to sound recordings included in educational television and radio programs (as defined in section 397 of title 47) distributed or transmitted by or through public broadcasting entities (as defined by section 118 (f)): Provided, That copies or phonorecords of said programs are not commercially distributed by or through public broadcasting entities to the general public.

3   **(c)** This section does not limit or impair the exclusive right to perform publicly, by means of a phonorecord, any of the works specified by section 106 (4).

4   **(d) Limitations on Exclusive Right.—** Notwithstanding the provisions of section 106(6)—

   (1) Exempt transmissions and retransmissions.— The performance of a sound recording publicly by means of a digital audio transmission, other than as a part of an interactive service, is not an infringement of section 106 (6) if the performance is part of—

   (A) a nonsubscription broadcast transmission;

   (B) a retransmission of a nonsubscription broadcast transmission: Provided, That, in the case of a retransmission of a radio station's broadcast transmission—

      (i) the radio station's broadcast transmission is not willfully or repeatedly retransmitted more than a radius of 150 miles from the site of the radio broadcast transmitter, however—

      (I) the 150 mile limitation under this clause shall not apply when a nonsubscription broadcast transmission by a radio station licensed by the Federal Communications Commission is retransmitted on a nonsubscription basis by a terrestrial broadcast station, terrestrial translator, or terrestrial repeater licensed by the Federal Communications Commission; and

      (II) in the case of a subscription retransmission of a nonsubscription broadcast retransmission covered by subclause (I), the 150 mile radius shall be measured from the transmitter site of such broadcast retransmitter;

      (ii) the retransmission is of radio station broadcast transmissions that are—

      (I) obtained by the retransmitter over the air;

      (II) not electronically processed by the retransmitter to deliver separate and discrete signals; and

      (III) retransmitted only within the local communities served by the retransmitter;

      (iii) the radio station's broadcast transmission was being retransmitted to cable systems (as defined in section 111 (f)) by a satellite carrier on January 1, 1995, and that retransmission was being retransmitted by cable systems as a separate and discrete signal, and the satellite carrier obtains the radio station's broadcast transmission in an analog format: Provided, That the broadcast transmission being retransmitted may embody the programming of no more than one radio station; or

(iv) the radio station's broadcast transmission is made by a noncommercial educational broadcast station funded on or after January 1, 1995, under section 396(k) of the Communications Act of 1934 (47 U.S.C. 396 (k)), consists solely of noncommercial educational and cultural radio programs, and the retransmission, whether or not simultaneous, is a nonsubscription terrestrial broadcast retransmission; or

(C) a transmission that comes within any of the following categories—

(i) a prior or simultaneous transmission incidental to an exempt transmission, such as a feed received by and then retransmitted by an exempt transmitter: Provided, That such incidental transmissions do not include any subscription transmission directly for reception by members of the public;

(ii) a transmission within a business establishment, confined to its premises or the immediately surrounding vicinity;

(iii) a retransmission by any retransmitter, including a multichannel video programming distributor as defined in section 602(12) [1] of the Communications Act of 1934 (47 U.S.C. 522 (12)), of a transmission by a transmitter licensed to publicly perform the sound recording as a part of that transmission, if the retransmission is simultaneous with the licensed transmission and authorized by the transmitter; or

(iv) a transmission to a business establishment for use in the ordinary course of its business: Provided, That the business recipient does not retransmit the transmission outside of its premises or the immediately surrounding vicinity, and that the transmission does not exceed the sound recording performance complement. Nothing in this clause shall limit the scope of the exemption in clause (ii).

(2) Statutory licensing of certain transmissions.— The performance of a sound recording publicly by means of a subscription digital audio transmission not exempt under paragraph (1), an eligible nonsubscription transmission, or a transmission not exempt under paragraph (1) that is made by a preexisting satellite digital audio radio service shall be subject to statutory licensing, in accordance with subsection (f) if—

(A)

(i) the transmission is not part of an interactive service;

(ii) except in the case of a transmission to a business establishment, the transmitting entity does not automatically and intentionally cause any device receiving the transmission to switch from one program channel to another; and

(iii) except as provided in section 1002 (e), the transmission of the sound recording is accompanied, if technically feasible, by the information encoded in that sound recording, if any, by or under the authority of the copyright owner of that sound recording, that identifies the title of the sound recording, the featured recording artist who performs on the sound recording, and related information, including information concerning the underlying musical work and its writer;

(B) in the case of a subscription transmission not exempt under paragraph (1) that is made by a preexisting subscription service in the same transmission medium used by such service on July 31, 1998, or in the case of a transmission not exempt under paragraph (1) that is made by a preexisting satellite digital audio radio service—

(i) the transmission does not exceed the sound recording performance complement; and

(ii) the transmitting entity does not cause to be published by means of an advance program schedule or prior announcement the titles of the specific sound recordings or phonorecords embodying such sound recordings to be transmitted; and

(C) in the case of an eligible nonsubscription transmission or a subscription transmission not exempt under paragraph (1) that is made by a new subscription service or by a preexisting subscription service other than in the same transmission medium used by such service on July 31, 1998—

(i) the transmission does not exceed the sound recording performance complement, except that this requirement shall not apply in the case of a retransmission of a broadcast transmission if the retransmission is made by a transmitting entity that does not have the right or ability to control the programming of the broadcast station making the broadcast transmission, unless—

(I) the broadcast station makes broadcast transmissions—

(aa) in digital format that regularly exceed the sound recording performance complement; or

(bb) in analog format, a substantial portion of which, on a weekly basis, exceed the sound recording performance complement; and

(II) the sound recording copyright owner or its representative has notified the transmitting entity in writing that broadcast transmissions of the copyright owner's sound recordings exceed the sound recording performance complement as provided in this clause;

(ii) the transmitting entity does not cause to be published, or induce or facilitate the publication, by means of an advance program schedule or prior announcement, the titles of the specific sound recordings to be transmitted, the phonorecords embodying such sound recordings, or, other than for illustrative purposes, the names of the featured recording artists, except that this clause does not disqualify a transmitting entity that makes a prior announcement that a particular artist will be featured within an unspecified future time period, and in the case of a retransmission of a broadcast transmission by a transmitting entity that does not have the right or ability to control the programming of the broadcast transmission, the requirement of this clause shall not apply to a prior oral announcement by the broadcast station, or to an advance program schedule published, induced, or facilitated by the broadcast station, if the transmitting entity does not have actual knowledge and has not received written notice from the copyright owner or its representative that the broadcast station publishes or induces or facilitates the publication of such advance program schedule, or if such advance program schedule is a schedule of classical music programming published by the broadcast station in the same manner as published by that broadcast station on or before September 30, 1998;

(iii) the transmission—

(I) is not part of an archived program of less than 5 hours duration;

(II) is not part of an archived program of 5 hours or greater in duration that is made available for a period exceeding 2 weeks;

(III) is not part of a continuous program which is of less than 3 hours duration; or

(IV) is not part of an identifiable program in which performances of sound recordings are rendered in a predetermined order, other than an archived or continuous program, that is transmitted at—

(aa) more than 3 times in any 2-week period that have been publicly announced in advance, in the case of a program of less than 1 hour in duration, or

(bb) more than 4 times in any 2-week period that have been publicly announced in advance, in the case of a program of 1 hour or more in duration,

except that the requirement of this subclause shall not apply in the case of a retransmission of a broadcast transmission by a transmitting entity that does not have the right or ability to control the programming of the broadcast transmission, unless the transmitting entity is given notice in writing by the copyright owner of the sound recording that the broadcast station makes broadcast transmissions that regularly violate such requirement;

(iv) the transmitting entity does not knowingly perform the sound recording, as part of a service that offers transmissions of visual images contemporaneously with transmissions of sound recordings, in a manner that is likely to cause confusion, to cause mistake, or to deceive, as to the affiliation, connection, or association of the copyright owner or featured recording artist with the transmitting entity or a particular product or service advertised by the transmitting entity, or as to the origin, sponsorship, or approval by the copyright owner or featured recording artist of the activities of the transmitting entity other than the performance of the sound recording itself;

(v) the transmitting entity cooperates to prevent, to the extent feasible without imposing substantial costs or burdens, a transmission recipient or any other person or entity from automatically scanning the transmitting entity's transmissions alone or together with transmissions by other transmitting entities in order to select a particular sound recording to be transmitted to the transmission recipient, except that the requirement of this clause shall not apply to a satellite digital audio service that is in operation, or that is licensed by the Federal Communications Commission, on or before July 31, 1998;

(vi) the transmitting entity takes no affirmative steps to cause or induce the making of a phonorecord by the transmission recipient, and if the technology used by the transmitting entity enables the transmitting entity to limit the making by the transmission recipient of phonorecords of the transmission directly in a digital format, the transmitting entity sets such technology to limit such making of phonorecords to the extent permitted by such technology;

(vii) phonorecords of the sound recording have been distributed to the public under the authority of the copyright owner or the copyright owner authorizes the transmitting entity to transmit the sound recording, and the transmitting entity makes the transmission from a phonorecord lawfully made under the authority of the copyright owner, except that the requirement of this clause shall not apply to a retransmission of a broadcast transmission by a transmitting entity that does not have the right or ability to control the programming of the broadcast transmission, unless the transmitting entity is given notice in writing by the copyright owner of the sound recording that the broadcast station makes broadcast transmissions that regularly violate such requirement;

(viii) the transmitting entity accommodates and does not interfere with the transmission of technical measures that are widely used by sound recording copyright owners to identify or protect copyrighted works, and that are technically feasible of being transmitted by the transmitting entity without imposing substantial costs on the transmitting entity or resulting in perceptible aural or visual degradation of the digital signal, except that the requirement of this clause shall not apply to a satellite digital audio service that is in operation, or that is licensed under the authority of the Federal Communications Commission, on or before July 31, 1998, to the extent that such service has designed, developed, or made commitments to procure equipment or technology that is not compatible with such technical measures before such technical measures are widely adopted by sound recording copyright owners; and

(ix) the transmitting entity identifies in textual data the sound recording during, but not before, the time it is performed, including the title of the sound recording, the title of the phonorecord embodying such sound recording, if any, and the featured recording artist, in a manner to permit it to be displayed to the transmission recipient by the device or technology intended for receiving the service provided by the transmitting entity, except that the obligation in this clause shall not take effect until 1 year after the date of the enactment of the Digital Millennium Copyright Act and shall not apply in the case of a retransmission of a broadcast transmission by a transmitting entity that does not have the right or ability to control the programming of the broadcast transmission, or in the case in which devices or technology intended for receiving the service provided by the transmitting entity that have the capability to display such textual data are not common in the marketplace.

(3) Licenses for transmissions by interactive services.—

(A) No interactive service shall be granted an exclusive license under section 106 (6)for the performance of a sound recording publicly by means of digital audio transmission for a period in excess of 12 months, except that with respect to an exclusive license granted to an interactive service by a licensor that holds the copyright to 1,000 or fewer sound recordings, the period of such license shall not exceed 24 months: Provided, however, That the grantee of such exclusive license shall be ineligible to receive another exclusive license for the performance of that sound recording for a period of 13 months from the expiration of the prior exclusive license.

(B) The limitation set forth in subparagraph (A) of this paragraph shall not apply if—

(i) the licensor has granted and there remain in effect licenses under section 106 (6)for the public performance of sound recordings by means of digital audio transmission by at least 5 different interactive services: Provided, however, That each such license must be for a minimum of 10 percent of the copyrighted sound recordings owned by the licensor that have been licensed to interactive services, but in no event less than 50 sound recordings; or

(ii) the exclusive license is granted to perform publicly up to 45 seconds of a sound recording and the sole purpose of the performance is to promote the distribution or performance of that sound recording.

(C) Notwithstanding the grant of an exclusive or nonexclusive license of the right of public performance under section 106 (6), an interactive service may not publicly perform a sound recording unless a license has been granted for the public performance of any copyrighted musical work contained in the sound recording: Provided, That such license to publicly perform the copyrighted musical work may be granted either by a performing rights society representing the copyright owner or by the copyright owner.

(D) The performance of a sound recording by means of a retransmission of a digital audio transmission is not an infringement of section 106 (6) if—

(i) the retransmission is of a transmission by an interactive service licensed to publicly perform the sound recording to a particular member of the public as part of that transmission; and

(ii) the retransmission is simultaneous with the licensed transmission, authorized by the transmitter, and limited to that particular member of the public intended by the interactive service to be the recipient of the transmission.

(E) For the purposes of this paragraph—

(i) a "licensor" shall include the licensing entity and any other entity under any material degree of common ownership, management, or control that owns copyrights in sound recordings; and

(ii) a "performing rights society" is an association or corporation that licenses the public performance of nondramatic musical works on behalf of the copyright owner, such as the American Society of Composers, Authors and Publishers, Broadcast Music, Inc., and SESAC, Inc.

(4) Rights not otherwise limited.—

(A) Except as expressly provided in this section, this section does not limit or impair the exclusive right to perform a sound recording publicly by means of a digital audio transmission under section 106 (6).

(B) Nothing in this section annuls or limits in any way—

(i) the exclusive right to publicly perform a musical work, including by means of a digital audio transmission, under section 106 (4);

(ii) the exclusive rights in a sound recording or the musical work embodied therein under sections 106 (1), 106 (2) and 106 (3); or

(iii) any other rights under any other clause of section 106, or remedies available under this title, as such rights or remedies exist either before or after the date of enactment of the Digital Performance Right in Sound Recordings Act of 1995.

(C) Any limitations in this section on the exclusive right under section 106 (6) apply only to the exclusive right under section 106 (6) and not to any other exclusive rights under section 106. Nothing in this section shall be construed to annul, limit, impair or otherwise affect in any way the ability of the owner of a copyright in a sound recording to exercise the rights under sections 106 (1), 106 (2) and 106 (3), or to obtain the remedies available under this title pursuant to such rights, as such rights and remedies exist either before or after the date of enactment of the Digital Performance Right in Sound Recordings Act of 1995.

(e) Authority for Negotiations.—

(1) Notwithstanding any provision of the antitrust laws, in negotiating statutory licenses in accordance with subsection (f), any copyright owners of sound recordings and any entities performing sound recordings affected by this section may negotiate and agree upon the royalty rates and license terms and conditions for the performance of such sound recordings and the proportionate division of fees paid among copyright owners, and may designate common agents on a nonexclusive basis to negotiate, agree to, pay, or receive payments.

(2) For licenses granted under section 106 (6), other than statutory licenses, such as for performances by interactive services or performances that exceed the sound recording performance complement—

(A) copyright owners of sound recordings affected by this section may designate common agents to act on their behalf to grant licenses and receive and remit royalty payments: Provided, That each copyright owner shall establish the royalty rates and material license terms and conditions unilaterally, that is, not in agreement, combination, or concert with other copyright owners of sound recordings; and

(B) entities performing sound recordings affected by this section may designate common agents to act on their behalf to obtain licenses and collect and pay royalty fees: Provided, That each entity performing sound recordings shall determine the royalty rates and material license terms and conditions unilaterally, that is, not in agreement, combination, or concert with other entities performing sound recordings.

6   **(f) Licenses for Certain Nonexempt Transmissions.—**

(1)

(A) Proceedings under chapter 8 shall determine reasonable rates and terms of royalty payments for subscription transmissions by preexisting subscription services and transmissions by preexisting satellite digital audio radio services specified by subsection (d)(2) during the 5-year period beginning on January 1 of the second year following the year in which the proceedings are to be commenced, except in the case of a different transitional period provided under section 6(b)(3) of the Copyright Royalty and Distribution Reform Act of 2004, or such other period as the parties may agree. Such terms and rates shall distinguish among the different types of digital audio transmission services then in operation. Any copyright owners of sound recordings, preexisting subscription services, or preexisting satellite digital audio radio services may submit to the Copyright Royalty Judges licenses covering such subscription transmissions with respect to such sound recordings. The parties to each proceeding shall bear their own costs.

(B) The schedule of reasonable rates and terms determined by the Copyright Royalty Judges shall, subject to paragraph (3), be binding on all copyright owners of sound recordings and entities performing sound recordings affected by this paragraph during the 5-year period specified in subparagraph (A), a transitional period provided under section 6(b)(3) of the Copyright Royalty and Distribution Reform Act of 2004, or such other period as the parties may agree. In establishing rates and terms for preexisting subscription services and preexisting satellite digital audio radio services, in addition to the objectives set forth in section 801 (b)(1), the Copyright Royalty Judges may consider the rates and terms for comparable types of subscription digital audio transmission services and comparable circumstances under voluntary license agreements described in subparagraph (A).

(C) The procedures under subparagraphs (A) and (B) also shall be initiated pursuant to a petition filed by any copyright owners of sound recordings, any preexisting subscription services, or any preexisting satellite digital audio radio services indicating that a new type of subscription digital audio transmission service on which sound recordings are performed is or is about to become operational, for the purpose of determining reasonable terms and rates of royalty payments with respect to such new type of transmission service for the period beginning with the inception of such new type of service and ending on the date on which the royalty rates and terms for subscription digital audio transmission services most recently determined under subparagraph (A) or (B) and chapter 8 expire, or such other period as the parties may agree.

(2)

(A) Proceedings under chapter 8 shall determine reasonable rates and terms of royalty payments for public performances of sound recordings by means of eligible nonsubscription transmission services and new subscription services specified by subsection (d)(2) during the 5-year period beginning on January 1 of the second year following the year in which the proceedings are to be commenced, except in the case of a different transitional period provided under section 6(b)(3) of the Copyright Royalty and Distribution Reform Act of 2004, or such other period as the parties may agree. Such rates and terms shall distinguish among the different types of eligible nonsubscription transmission services and new subscription services then in operation and shall include a minimum fee for each such type of service. Any copyright owners of sound recordings or any entities performing sound recordings affected by this paragraph may submit to the Copyright Royalty Judges licenses covering such eligible nonsubscription transmissions and new subscription services with respect to such sound recordings. The parties to each proceeding shall bear their own costs.

(B) The schedule of reasonable rates and terms determined by the Copyright Royalty Judges shall, subject to paragraph (3), be binding on all copyright owners of sound recordings and entities performing sound recordings affected by this paragraph during the 5-year period specified in subparagraph (A), a transitional period provided under section 6(b)(3) of the Copyright Royalty and Distribution [2] Act of 2004, or such other period as the parties may agree. Such rates and terms shall distinguish among the different types of eligible nonsubscription transmission services then in operation and shall include a minimum fee for each such type of service, such differences to be based on criteria including, but not limited to, the quantity and nature of the use of sound recordings and the degree to which use of the service may substitute for or may promote the purchase of phonorecords by consumers. In establishing rates and terms for transmissions by eligible nonsubscription services and new subscription services, the Copyright

Royalty Judges shall establish rates and terms that most clearly represent the rates and terms that would have been negotiated in the marketplace between a willing buyer and a willing seller. In determining such rates and terms, the Copyright Royalty Judges shall base their decision on economic, competitive and programming information presented by the parties, including—

(i) whether use of the service may substitute for or may promote the sales of phonorecords or otherwise may interfere with or may enhance the sound recording copyright owner's other streams of revenue from its sound recordings; and

(ii) the relative roles of the copyright owner and the transmitting entity in the copyrighted work and the service made available to the public with respect to relative creative contribution, technological contribution, capital investment, cost, and risk.

In establishing such rates and terms, the Copyright Royalty Judges may consider the rates and terms for comparable types of digital audio transmission services and comparable circumstances under voluntary license agreements described in subparagraph (A).

(C) The procedures under subparagraphs (A) and (B) shall also be initiated pursuant to a petition filed by any copyright owners of sound recordings or any eligible nonsubscription service or new subscription service indicating that a new type of eligible nonsubscription service or new subscription service on which sound recordings are performed is or is about to become operational, for the purpose of determining reasonable terms and rates of royalty payments with respect to such new type of service for the period beginning with the inception of such new type of service and ending on the date on which the royalty rates and terms for eligible nonsubscription services and new subscription services, as the case may be, most recently determined under subparagraph (A) or (B) and chapter 8 expire, or such other period as the parties may agree.

(3) License agreements voluntarily negotiated at any time between 1 or more copyright owners of sound recordings and 1 or more entities performing sound recordings shall be given effect in lieu of any decision by the Librarian of Congress or determination by the Copyright Royalty Judges.

(4)

(A) The Copyright Royalty Judges shall also establish requirements by which copyright owners may receive reasonable notice of the use of their sound recordings under this section, and under which records of such use shall be kept and made available by entities performing sound recordings. The notice and recordkeeping rules in effect on the day before the effective date of the Copyright Royalty and Distribution Reform Act of 2004 shall remain in effect unless and until new regulations are promulgated by the Copyright Royalty Judges. If new regulations are promulgated under this subparagraph, the Copyright Royalty Judges shall take into account the substance and effect of the rules in effect on the day before the effective date of the Copyright Royalty and Distribution Reform Act of 2004 and shall, to the extent practicable, avoid significant disruption of the functions of any designated agent authorized to collect and distribute royalty fees.

(B) Any person who wishes to perform a sound recording publicly by means of a transmission eligible for statutory licensing under this subsection may do so without infringing the exclusive right of the copyright owner of the sound recording—

(i) by complying with such notice requirements as the Copyright Royalty Judges shall prescribe by regulation and by paying royalty fees in accordance with this subsection; or

(ii) if such royalty fees have not been set, by agreeing to pay such royalty fees as shall be determined in accordance with this subsection.

(C) Any royalty payments in arrears shall be made on or before the twentieth day of the month next succeeding the month in which the royalty fees are set.

(5)

(A) Notwithstanding section 112 (e) and the other provisions of this subsection, the receiving agent may enter into agreements for the reproduction and performance of sound recordings under section 112 (e) and this section by any 1 or more commercial webcasters or noncommercial webcasters for a period of not more than 11 years beginning on January 1, 2005, that, once published in the Federal Register pursuant to subparagraph (B), shall be binding on all copyright owners of sound recordings and other persons entitled to payment under this section, in lieu of any determination by the Copyright Royalty Judges. Any such agreement for commercial webcasters may include provisions for payment of royalties on the basis of a percentage of revenue or expenses, or both, and include a minimum fee. Any such agreement may include other terms and conditions, including requirements by which copyright owners may receive notice of the use of their sound recordings and under which records of such use shall be kept and made available by commercial webcasters or noncommercial webcasters. The receiving agent shall be under no obligation to negotiate any such agreement. The receiving agent shall have no obligation to any copyright owner of sound recordings or any other person entitled to payment under this section in negotiating any such agreement, and no liability to any copyright owner of sound recordings or any other person entitled to payment under this section for having entered into such agreement.

(B) The Copyright Office shall cause to be published in the Federal Register any agreement entered into pursuant to subparagraph (A). Such publication shall include a statement containing the substance of subparagraph (C). Such agreements shall not be included in the Code of Federal Regulations. Thereafter, the terms of such agreement shall be available, as an option, to any commercial webcaster or noncommercial webcaster meeting the eligibility conditions of such agreement.

(C) Neither subparagraph (A) nor any provisions of any agreement entered into pursuant to subparagraph (A), including any rate structure, fees, terms, conditions, or notice and recordkeeping requirements set forth therein, shall be admissible as evidence or otherwise taken into account in any administrative, judicial, or other government proceeding involving the setting or adjustment of the royalties payable for the public performance or reproduction in ephemeral phonorecords or copies of sound recordings, the determination of terms or conditions related thereto, or the establishment of notice or recordkeeping requirements by the Copyright Royalty Judges under paragraph (4) or section 112 (e)(4). It is the intent of Congress that any royalty rates, rate structure, definitions, terms, conditions, or notice and recordkeeping requirements, included in such agreements shall be considered as a compromise motivated by the unique business, economic and political circumstances of webcasters, copyright owners, and performers rather than as matters that would have been negotiated in the marketplace between a willing buyer and a willing seller, or otherwise meet the objectives set forth in section 801 (b). This subparagraph shall not apply to the extent that the receiving agent and a webcaster that is party to an agreement entered into pursuant to subparagraph (A) expressly authorize the submission of the agreement in a proceeding under this subsection.

(D) Nothing in the Webcaster Settlement Act of 2008, the Webcaster Settlement Act of 2009, or any agreement entered into pursuant to subparagraph (A) shall be taken into account by the United States Court of Appeals for the District of Columbia Circuit in its review of the determination by the Copyright Royalty Judges of May 1, 2007, of rates and terms for the digital performance of sound recordings and ephemeral recordings, pursuant to sections 112 and 114.

(E) As used in this paragraph—

  (i) the term "noncommercial webcaster" means a webcaster that—

    (I) is exempt from taxation under section 501 of the Internal Revenue Code of 1986 (26 U.S.C. 501);

    (II) has applied in good faith to the Internal Revenue Service for exemption from taxation under section 501 of the Internal Revenue Code and has a commercially reasonable expectation that such exemption shall be granted; or

    (III) is operated by a State or possession or any governmental entity or subordinate thereof, or by the United States or District of Columbia, for exclusively public purposes;

  (ii) the term "receiving agent" shall have the meaning given that term in section 261.2 of title 37, Code of Federal Regulations, as published in the Federal Register on July 8, 2002; and

  (iii) the term "webcaster" means a person or entity that has obtained a compulsory license under section 112 or 114 and the implementing regulations therefor.

  (F) The authority to make settlements pursuant to subparagraph (A) shall expire at 11:59 p.m. Eastern time on the 30th day after the date of the enactment of the Webcaster Settlement Act of 2009.

7   **(g) Proceeds From Licensing of Transmissions.—**

  (1) Except in the case of a transmission licensed under a statutory license in accordance with subsection (f) of this section—

  (A) a featured recording artist who performs on a sound recording that has been licensed for a transmission shall be entitled to receive payments from the copyright owner of the sound recording in accordance with the terms of the artist's contract; and

(B) a nonfeatured recording artist who performs on a sound recording that has been licensed for a transmission shall be entitled to receive payments from the copyright owner of the sound recording in accordance with the terms of the nonfeatured recording artist's applicable contract or other applicable agreement.

(2) An agent designated to distribute receipts from the licensing of transmissions in accordance with subsection (f) shall distribute such receipts as follows:

(A) 50 percent of the receipts shall be paid to the copyright owner of the exclusive right under section 106 (6) of this title to publicly perform a sound recording by means of a digital audio transmission.

(B) 2 1/2 percent of the receipts shall be deposited in an escrow account managed by an independent administrator jointly appointed by copyright owners of sound recordings and the American Federation of Musicians (or any successor entity) to be distributed to nonfeatured musicians (whether or not members of the American Federation of Musicians) who have performed on sound recordings.

(C) 2 1/2 percent of the receipts shall be deposited in an escrow account managed by an independent administrator jointly appointed by copyright owners of sound recordings and the American Federation of Television and Radio Artists (or any successor entity) to be distributed to nonfeatured vocalists (whether or not members of the American Federation of Television and Radio Artists) who have performed on sound recordings.

(D) 45 percent of the receipts shall be paid, on a per sound recording basis, to the recording artist or artists featured on such sound recording (or the persons conveying rights in the artists' performance in the sound recordings).

(3) A nonprofit agent designated to distribute receipts from the licensing of transmissions in accordance with subsection (f) may deduct from any of its receipts, prior to the distribution of such receipts to any person or entity entitled thereto other than copyright owners and performers who have elected to receive royalties from another designated agent and have notified such nonprofit agent in writing of such election, the reasonable costs of such agent incurred after November 1, 1995, in—

(A) the administration of the collection, distribution, and calculation of the royalties;

(B) the settlement of disputes relating to the collection and calculation of the royalties; and

(C) the licensing and enforcement of rights with respect to the making of ephemeral recordings and performances subject to licensing under section 112 and this section, including those incurred in participating in negotiations or arbitration proceedings under section 112 and this section, except that all costs incurred relating to the section 112 ephemeral recordings right may only be deducted from the royalties received pursuant to section 112.

(4) Notwithstanding paragraph (3), any designated agent designated to distribute receipts from the licensing of transmissions in accordance with subsection (f) may deduct from any of its receipts, prior to the distribution of such receipts, the reasonable costs identified in paragraph (3) of such agent incurred after November 1, 1995, with respect to such copyright owners and performers who have entered with such agent a contractual relationship that specifies that such costs may be deducted from such royalty receipts.

(h) Licensing to Affiliates.—

(1) If the copyright owner of a sound recording licenses an affiliated entity the right to publicly perform a sound recording by means of a digital audio transmission under section 106 (6), the copyright owner shall make the licensed sound recording available under section 106 (6) on no less favorable terms and conditions to all bona fide entities that offer similar services, except that, if there are material differences in the scope of the requested license with respect to the type of service, the particular sound recordings licensed, the frequency of use, the number of subscribers served, or the duration, then the copyright owner may establish different terms and conditions for such other services.

(2) The limitation set forth in paragraph (1) of this subsection shall not apply in the case where the copyright owner of a sound recording licenses—

(A) an interactive service; or

(B) an entity to perform publicly up to 45 seconds of the sound recording and the sole purpose of the performance is to promote the distribution or performance of that sound recording.

9   **(i) No Effect on Royalties for Underlying Works.—** License fees payable for the public performance of sound recordings under section 106 (6) shall not be taken into account in any administrative, judicial, or other governmental proceeding to set or adjust the royalties payable to copyright owners of musical works for the public performance of their works. It is the intent of Congress that royalties payable to copyright owners of musical works for the public performance of their works shall not be diminished in any respect as a result of the rights granted by section 106 (6).

10   **(j) Definitions.—** As used in this section, the following terms have the following meanings:

(1) An "affiliated entity" is an entity engaging in digital audio transmissions covered by section 106 (6), other than an interactive service, in which the licensor has any direct or indirect partnership or any ownership interest amounting to 5 percent or more of the outstanding voting or non-voting stock.

(2) An "archived program" is a predetermined program that is available repeatedly on the demand of the transmission recipient and that is performed in the same order from the beginning, except that an archived program shall not include a recorded event or broadcast transmission that makes no more than an incidental use of sound recordings, as long as such recorded event or broadcast transmission does not contain an entire sound recording or feature a particular sound recording.

(3) A "broadcast" transmission is a transmission made by a terrestrial broadcast station licensed as such by the Federal Communications Commission.

(4) A "continuous program" is a predetermined program that is continuously performed in the same order and that is accessed at a point in the program that is beyond the control of the transmission recipient.

(5) A "digital audio transmission" is a digital transmission as defined in section 101, that embodies the transmission of a sound recording. This term does not include the transmission of any audiovisual work.

(6) An "eligible nonsubscription transmission" is a noninteractive nonsubscription digital audio transmission not exempt under subsection (d)(1) that is made as part of a service that provides audio programming consisting, in whole or in part, of performances of sound recordings, including retransmissions of broadcast transmissions, if the primary purpose of the service is to provide to the public such audio or other entertainment programming, and the primary purpose of the service is not to sell, advertise, or promote particular products or services other than sound recordings, live concerts, or other music-related events.

(7) An "interactive service" is one that enables a member of the public to receive a transmission of a program specially created for the recipient, or on request, a transmission of a particular sound recording, whether or not as part of a program, which is selected by or on behalf of the recipient. The ability of individuals to request that particular sound recordings be performed for reception by the public at large, or in the case of a subscription service, by all subscribers of the service, does not make a service interactive, if the programming on each channel of the service does not substantially consist of sound recordings that are performed within 1 hour of the request or at a time designated by either the transmitting entity or the individual making such request. If an entity offers both interactive and noninteractive services (either concurrently or at different times), the noninteractive component shall not be treated as part of an interactive service.

(8) A "new subscription service" is a service that performs sound recordings by means of noninteractive subscription digital audio transmissions and that is not a preexisting subscription service or a preexisting satellite digital audio radio service.

(9) A "nonsubscription" transmission is any transmission that is not a subscription transmission.

(10) A "preexisting satellite digital audio radio service" is a subscription satellite digital audio radio service provided pursuant to a satellite digital audio radio service license issued by the Federal Communications Commission on or before July 31, 1998, and any renewal of such license to the extent of the scope of the original license, and may include a limited number of sample channels representative of the subscription service that are made available on a nonsubscription basis in order to promote the subscription service.

(11) A "preexisting subscription service" is a service that performs sound recordings by means of noninteractive audio-only subscription digital audio transmissions, which was in existence and was making such transmissions to the public for a fee on or before

July 31, 1998, and may include a limited number of sample channels representative of the subscription service that are made available on a nonsubscription basis in order to promote the subscription service.

(12) A "retransmission" is a further transmission of an initial transmission, and includes any further retransmission of the same transmission. Except as provided in this section, a transmission qualifies as a "retransmission" only if it is simultaneous with the initial transmission. Nothing in this definition shall be construed to exempt a transmission that fails to satisfy a separate element required to qualify for an exemption under section 114 (d)(1).

(13) The "sound recording performance complement" is the transmission during any 3-hour period, on a particular channel used by a transmitting entity, of no more than—

(A) 3 different selections of sound recordings from any one phonorecord lawfully distributed for public performance or sale in the United States, if no more than 2 such selections are transmitted consecutively; or

(B) 4 different selections of sound recordings—

(i) by the same featured recording artist; or

(ii) from any set or compilation of phonorecords lawfully distributed together as a unit for public performance or sale in the United States,

if no more than three such selections are transmitted consecutively:

Provided, That the transmission of selections in excess of the numerical limits provided for in clauses (A) and (B) from multiple phonorecords shall nonetheless qualify as a sound recording performance complement if the programming of the multiple phonorecords was not willfully intended to avoid the numerical limitations prescribed in such clauses.

(14) A "subscription" transmission is a transmission that is controlled and limited to particular recipients, and for which consideration is required to be paid or otherwise given by or on behalf of the recipient to receive the transmission or a package of transmissions including the transmission.

(15) A "transmission" is either an initial transmission or a retransmission.

MY ACCOUNT   EVENTS   BLOG   CONTACT   SEARCH _____

in this section

SHARE THIS PAGE

licensing 101

Please feel free to explore the information below as an educational resource for current and prospective statutory licensees.

NOTE: SoundExchange cannot give legal advice to current or prospective service providers, and all information is presented for educational purposes only. If you have questions regarding your service's eligibility or compliance within statutory licensing, please seek legal counsel.

⊙ What is a statutory license?

The statutory licenses relevant to service providers can be found in sections 112 and 114 of the Copyright Act, 17 U.S.C. §§ 112 and 114. The rates and terms applicable to the statutory licenses for service providers can be found on our website. Currently, SoundExchange is the only entity authorized by Congress to administer the statutory licenses described in sections 112 and 114.

⊙ What kinds of services are covered under the statutory licenses administered by SoundExchange?

The section 114 statutory license covers public performances by four classes of digital music services: eligible nonsubscription services (i.e., noninteractive webcasters and simulcasters that charge no fees), preexisting subscription services (i.e., residential subscription services which began providing music over digital cable or satellite television before July 1998), new subscription services (i.e., noninteractive webcasters and simulcasters that charge a fee, as well as residential subscription services providing music over digital cable or satellite television since July 1998), and preexisting satellite digital audio radio services (i.e., SiriusXM Radio). The section 112 statutory license covers ephemeral reproductions (i.e., temporary server copies) made by all digital music services covered by section 114. Additionally, business establishment services (services streaming background music into bars, restaurants, retail stores, etc.) are exempt from paying public performance royalties under section 114, but must still be otherwise eligible for section 114, as well as operate under section 112.

⊙ How do I know if my service is "noninteractive?"

Non-Waiver of Rights

Important! SoundExchange does not confirm that a service is eligible or compliant with the law by accepting payments, Statements of Account and/or Reports of Use. Also, artists and rights owners do not waive any legal rights by accepting payments from SoundExchange based upon those submissions. Please read on for more detail.

>READ MORE

Licensee Relations:

If you have questions about music licensing and streaming please contact us at:

202-559-0555
email us

Noninteractive services are very generally defined as those in which the user experience mimics a radio broadcast. That is, the users may not choose the specific track or artist they wish to hear, but are provided a pre-programmed or semi-random combination of tracks, the specific selection and order of which remain unknown to the listener (i.e. no pre-published playlist). For services which provide an interactive service or on-demand access to certain tracks or artists (e.g., YouTube), the statutory license does not apply, and a direct license must be obtained from the copyright holder.

How do I obtain a statutory license as described in section 112 or 114?

To obtain a statutory license, you must first notify sound recording copyright owners by filing a Notice of Use of Sound Recordings Under Statutory License ("Notice of Use") with the Copyright Office. All services must file a Notice of Use prior to making the first ephemeral copy or first digital transmission of a sound recording to avoid being subject to liability for copyright infringement. An original Notice of Use with a $40 filing fee should be sent to the Copyright Royalty Board at the U.S. Copyright Office (address located on the form). The Copyright Office will not provide you with any confirmation that it has received your Notice of Use. Once a service files its Notice of Use, it may commence making digital audio transmissions, provided that it complies with all of the terms and conditions of the statutory license, makes all payments, and files all statements of account and reports of use when due. Services providing a Notice of Use are subject to the default rates and terms of the statutory license as set by the Copyright Royalty Board. Services wishing to operate under alternative rates or terms (e.g., pursuant to the Webcaster Settlement Act, etc.) should follow the instructions prescribed in those rates and terms.

How do I qualify for a statutory license?

All statutory licensees must be eligible to operate under section 114, and the specific eligibility requirements are listed there. To be eligible, a service must be (in most cases):

1. a noninteractive service,
2. creating transmissions adherent to the sound recording performance complement,
3. not allowing the listener a reasonable foreknowledge of the transmission of a specific sound recording at a specific date and time (e.g., by the use of a published advanced program, playlist, announcement, etc.),
4. not creating transmissions as part of an "archived program" (a) less than 5 hours in duration, or (b) available for a period exceeding 2 weeks,
5. not creating transmissions as part of a continuous program less than 3 hours in duration,
6. creating audio-only transmissions (i.e. without the use of video imagery synchronized with the audio transmission),
7. reasonably cooperating to prevent certain kinds of

selective transmitting and/or illegal copying of the transmission by the listener,

8. using an ephemeral phonorecord created from a copy of a sound recording that was authorized by the sound recording copyright owner for commercial release,

9. reasonably not interfering with technical copyright protection techniques, and

10. identifying on the receiving device, in textual data, simultaneous to the transmission, the following identifying elements related to the sound recording being transmitted: (a) the name of the featured artist, (b) the title of the sound recording, and, to the extent that one exists, (c) the title of the phonorecord embodying such recording.

◎ What is the "performance complement?"

The performance complement (which limits the amount of times a service may transmit sound recordings from a specific artist or album during a specific period of time) is one qualification to which all webcasters must adhere in order to be eligible under the statutory license. The performance complement may only be violated if the service has received specific waivers from the owner of the sound recording copyright, and unintended violation of these limitations (if corrected) will not cause a service to be ineligible for statutory licensing. The limitations are, specifically:

1. No more than 4 tracks by the same featured artist (or from a compilation album) may be transmitted to the same listener within a 3 hour period (and no more than 3 of those tracks may be transmitted consecutively).

2. No more than 3 tracks from the same album may be transmitted to the same listener within a 3 hour period (and no more than 2 of those tracks may be transmitted consecutively).

◎ How are the rates and terms determined?

The Copyright Royalty and Distribution Reform Act of 2004 created a board of Copyright Royalty Judges (also known as the Copyright Royalty Board) to determine the rates and terms for the statutory license. Under the Copyright Royalty and Distribution Reform Act, "statutory rates" are set through either voluntary negotiations or trial-type hearings before the panel of three Copyright Royalty Judges. In negotiated cases, interested services negotiate rates and terms with SoundExchange and present those to the Copyright Royalty Judges for adoption. If the agreement is adopted by the Judges, it will be available for opt-in by any similarly situated parties. (In fact, the Webcaster Settlement Acts of 2008 and 2009 facilitated the adoption of several such negotiated agreements.) Any parties who have not negotiated agreements may present to the Copyright Royalty Judges, who will conduct a rate setting arbitration to establish royalty rates.

◎ I already pay royalties to ASCAP, BMI, and/or SESAC. Why do I have to pay SoundExchange, too?

Every musical recording embodies two distinct

copyrighted works. The first is the underlying musical composition, comprised of the written notes and lyrics (a "musical work"). The songwriter and/or his or her music publisher usually own the copyright in the musical work. The second copyrighted work is the actual recording itself – the sounds, including the recording artist's interpretation of the musical composition, and the creative efforts of the producer, sound engineers and background musicians (a "sound recording"). A copyright holder, whether a label or an independent musician, owns the copyright or "master" to the sound recording. SoundExchange collects and distributes royalties associated with the sound recordings made by services operating under one of the statutory licenses. By contrast, ASCAP, BMI and SESAC collect and distribute royalties associated with the public performance of musical works. A digital audio transmission of a musical recording will usually require a license for both the sound recording and the underlying musical work.

What happens if it turns out I'm not eligible, but I've been operating anyway?

It is the responsibility of each service provider to be confident about its eligibility and ability to be compliant with rates and terms before beginning operation under statutory licensing. Ultimately, SoundExchange does not confirm such eligibility or compliance: we accept payments, Statements of Account and Reports of Use, and distribute those payments to artists and copyright owners as instructed by those forms and reports, without waiving the rights of anyone we pay, or of anyone whose recordings were transmitted under such intended statutory licensing. Since artists and copyright owners are always free to protect their legal interests, we encourage service providers with any questions in these regards to review our website for more information, and to contact us and/or legal counsel.

UMG Recordings, Inc. v. MP3.Com, Inc.

September 01, 2014 by mrisch

1   92 F.Supp.2d 349

UMG RECORDINGS, INC., Sony Music Entertainment Inc., Warner Bros. Records Inc., Arista Records Inc., Atlantic Recordings Corp., BMG Music d/b/a The RCA Records Label, Capitol Records, Inc., Elektra Entertainment Group, Inc., Interscope Records, and Sire Records Group Inc., Plaintiffs,

v.

MP3.COM, INC., Defendant.

No. 00 Civ. 472(JSR).

United States District Court, S.D. New York.

May 4, 2000.

2   [...]

5   ***OPINION***

6   RAKOFF, District Judge.

7   The complex marvels of cyberspatial communication may create difficult legal issues; but not in this case. Defendant's infringement of plaintiffs' copyrights is clear. Accordingly, on April 28, 2000, the Court granted defendant's motion for partial summary judgment holding defendant liable for copyright infringement. This opinion will state the reasons why.

8   [...]

9   The technology known as "MP3" permits rapid and efficient conversion of compact disc recordings ("CDs") to computer files easily accessed over the Internet. *[...]*Utilizing this technology, defendant MP3.com, on or around January 12, 2000, launched its "My.MP3.com" service, which is advertised as permitting subscribers to store, customize and listen to the recordings contained on their CDs from any place where they have an Internet connection. To make good on this offer, defendant purchased tens of thousands of popular CDs in which plaintiffs held the copyrights, and, without authorization, copied their recordings onto its computer servers so as to be able to replay the recordings for its subscribers.

10   Specifically, in order to first access such a recording, a subscriber to MP3.com must either "prove" that he already owns the CD version of the recording by inserting his copy of the commercial CD into his computer CD-Rom drive for a few seconds (the "Beam-it Service") or must purchase the CD from one of defendant's cooperating online retailers (the "instant Listening Service"). Thereafter, however, the subscriber can access via the Internet from a computer anywhere in the world the copy of plaintiffs' recording made by defendant. Thus, although defendant seeks to portray its service as the "functional equivalent" of storing its subscribers' CDs, in actuality defendant is re-playing for the subscribers converted versions of the recordings it copied, without authorization, from plaintiffs' copyrighted CDs. On its face, this makes out a presumptive case of infringement under the Copyright Act of 1976 ("Copyright Act")[...]

11   Defendant argues, however, that such copying is protected by the affirmative defense of "fair use." *See* 17 U.S.C. § 107. In analyzing
        such a defense, the Copyright Act specifies four factors that must be considered: "(1) the purpose and [351] character of the use,
        including whether such use is of a commercial nature or is for nonprofit educational purposes; (2) the nature of the copyrighted work; (3)
        the amount and substantiality of the portion used in relation to the copyrighted work as a whole; and (4) the effect of the use upon the
        potential market for or value of the copyrighted work." *Id.* Other relevant factors may also be considered, since fair use is an "equitable
        rule of reason" to be applied in light of the overall purposes of the Copyright Act. *Sony Corporation of America v. Universal City Studios, Inc.*

12   Regarding the first factor — "the purpose and character of the use" — defendant does not dispute that its purpose is commercial, for
        while subscribers to My. MP3.com are not currently charged a fee, defendant seeks to attract a sufficiently large subscription base to
        draw advertising and otherwise make a profit. Consideration of the first factor, however, also involves inquiring into whether the new use
        essentially repeats the old or whether, instead, it "transforms" it by infusing it with new meaning, new understandings, or the like. *[...]*
        Here, although defendant recites that My.MP3.com provides a transformative "space shift" by which subscribers can enjoy the sound
        recordings contained on their CDs without lugging around the physical discs themselves, this is simply another way of saying that the
        unauthorized copies are being retransmitted in another medium — an insufficient basis for any legitimate claim of transformation, *See,*
        e.g., Infinity Broadcast Corp. v. Kirkwood, 150 F.3d 104, 108 (2d Cir.1998) (rejecting the fair use defense by operator of a service that
        retransmitted copyrighted radio broadcasts over telephone lines); *Los Angeles News Serv. v. Reuters Television Int'l Ltd.,* 149 F.3d 987
        (9th Cir.1998) (rejecting the fair use defense where television news agencies copied copyrighted news footage and retransmitted it to
        news organizations) *[...]*

13   Here, defendant adds no new "new aesthetics, new insights and understandings" to the original music recordings it copies, *see Castle*
        Rock, 150 F.3d at 142 (internal quotation marks omitted), but simply repackages those recordings to facilitate their transmission through
        another medium. While such services may be innovative, they are not transformative. *You hear this a lot in people who disagree with*
        copyright rulings: it was so innovative! The courts do not always think this is critical. *[...]*

14   Regarding the second factor — "the nature of the copyrighted work" — the creative recordings here being copied are "close[ ] to the core
        of intended copyright protection," *[...]* and, conversely, far removed from the more factual or descriptive work more amenable to "fair use

15   Regarding the third factor — "the amount and substantiality of the portion [of the copyrighted work] used [by the copier] in relation to the
        copyrighted work as a whole" — it is undisputed that defendant copies, and replays, the entirety of the copyrighted works here in issue,
        thus again negating any claim of fair use. *[...]*

16   Regarding the fourth factor — "the effect of the use upon the potential market for or value of the copyrighted work" — defendant's
        activities on their face invade plaintiffs' statutory right to license their copyrighted sound recordings to others for reproduction. *See* 17
        U.S.C. § 106. Defendant, however, argues that, so far as the derivative market here involves is concerned, plaintiffs have not shown that
        such licensing is "traditional, reasonable, or likely to be developed." *[...]* Moreover, defendant argues, its activities can only enhance
        plaintiffs' sales, since subscribers cannot gain access to particular recordings made available by MP3.com unless they have already
        "purchased" (actually or purportedly), or agreed to purchase, their own CD copies of those recordings.

17   Such arguments — though dressed in the garb of an expert's "opinion" (that, on inspection, consists almost entirely of speculative and
        conclusory statements) — are unpersuasive. Any allegedly positive impact of defendant's activities on plaintiffs' prior market in no way
        frees defendant to usurp a further market that directly derives from reproduction of the plaintiffs' copyrighted works. *[...]* This would be
        so even if the copyrightholder had not yet entered the new market in issue, for a copyrighterholder's "exclusive" rights, derived from the
        Constitution and the Copyright Act, include the right, within broad limits, to curb the development of such a derivative market by refusing
        to license a copyrighted work or by doing so only on terms the copyright owner finds acceptable. *[...]* Here, moreover, plaintiffs have
        adduced substantial evidence that they have in fact taken steps to enter that market by entering into various licensing agreements. *[...]*

18   Finally, regarding defendant's purported reliance on other factors, *[...]* this essentially reduces to the claim that My. MP3.com provides a useful service to consumers that, in its absence, will be served by "pirates." Copyright, however, is not designed to afford consumer protection or convenience but, rather, to protect the copyrightholders' property interests. Moreover, as a practical matter, plaintiffs have indicated no objection in principle to licensing their recordings to companies like MP3.com; they simply want to make sure they get the remuneration the law reserves for them as holders of copyrights on creative works. Stripped to its essence, defendant's "consumer protection" argument amounts to nothing more than a bald claim that defendant should be able to misappropriate plaintiffs' property simply because there is a consumer demand for it. This hardly appeals to the conscience of equity.

19   In sum, on any view, defendant's "fair use" defense is indefensible and must be denied as a matter of law. Defendant's *[...]* other affirmative defenses, such as copyright misuse, abandonment, unclean hands, and estoppel, are essentially frivolous and may be disposed of briefly. While defendant contends, under the rubric of copyright misuse, that plaintiffs are misusing their "dominant market position to selectively prosecute only certain online music technology companies," *[...]* the admissible evidence of records shows only that plaintiffs have reasonably exercised their right to determine which infringers to pursue, and in which order to pursue them *[...]* The abandonment defense must also fall since defendant has failed to adduce any competent evidence of an overt act indicating that plaintiffs, who filed suit against MP3.com shortly after MP3.com launched its infringing My.MP3.com service, intentionally abandoned their copyrights. *[...]* Similarly, defendant's estoppel defense must be rejected because defendant has failed to provide any competent evidence that it relied on any action by plaintiffs with respect to defendant's My.MP3.com service. Finally, the Court must reject defendant's unclean hands defense given defendant's failure to come forth with any admissible evidence showing bad faith or misconduct on the part of plaintiffs. *[...]*

21   Accordingly, the Court, for the foregoing reasons, has determined that plaintiffs are entitled to partial summary judgment holding defendant to have infringed plaintiffs' copyrights.

22   *[...]*

A&M Records, Inc. v. Napster, Inc.

September 01, 2014 by mrisch

1   239 F.3d 1004 (2001)

2   **A&M; Records, Inc.** [...]
                                              v.
                                      Napster, Inc. [...]

4   United States Court of Appeals, Ninth Circuit.

5   [...]
                                   Filed February 12, 2001.
                                   As Amended April 3, 2001.

6   [...]

26   Before: MARY M. SCHROEDER, Chief Judge, ROBERT R. BEEZER and RICHARD A. PAEZ, Circuit Judges.

27   [...]

28   **ORDER AND AMENDED OPINION**

29   [...]

33   **BEEZER, Circuit Judge:**

34   Plaintiffs are engaged in the commercial recording, distribution and sale of copyrighted [1011] musical compositions and sound
         recordings. The complaint alleges that Napster, Inc. ("Napster") is a contributory and vicarious copyright infringer. [...]

36   I

37   [...]

38   In 1987, the Moving Picture Experts Group set a standard file format for the storage of audio recordings in a digital format called MPEG-
         3, abbreviated as "MP3." Digital MP3 files are created through a process colloquially called "ripping." Ripping software allows a computer
         owner to copy an audio compact disk ("audio CD") directly onto a computer's hard drive by compressing the audio information on the CD
         into the MP3 format. The MP3's compressed format allows for rapid transmission of digital audio files from one computer to another by
         electronic mail or any other file transfer protocol.

39   Napster facilitates the transmission of MP3 files between and among its users. Through a process commonly called "peer-to-peer" file sharing, Napster allows its users to: (1) make MP3 music files stored on individual computer hard drives available for copying by other Napster users; (2) search for MP3 music files stored on other users' computers; and (3) transfer exact copies of the contents of other users' MP3 files from one computer to another via the Internet. These functions are made possible by Napster's MusicShare software, available free of charge from Napster's Internet site, and Napster's network servers and server-side software. Napster provides technical support for the indexing and searching of MP3 files, as well as for its other functions, including a "chat room," where users can meet to discuss music, and a directory where participating artists can provide information about their music.

40   ## A. Accessing the System

41   In order to copy MP3 files through the Napster system, a user must first access Napster's Internet site and download[1] the MusicShare software to his individual computer. *[...]* Once the software is installed, the user can access the Napster system. A first-time user is required to register with the Napster system by creating a "user name" and password.

42   ## B. Listing Available Files

43   If a registered user wants to list available files stored in his computer's hard drive on Napster for others to access, he *[...]* must first create a "user library" directory on his computer's hard drive. The user then saves his MP3 files in the library directory, using self-designated file names. He next must log into the Napster system using his user name and password. His MusicShare software then searches his user library and verifies that the available files are properly formatted. If in the correct MP3 format, the names of the MP3 files will be uploaded from the user's computer to the Napster servers. The content of the MP3 files remains stored in the user's computer.

44   Once uploaded to the Napster servers, the user's MP3 file names are stored in a server-side "library" under the user's name and become part of a "collective directory" of files available for transfer during the time the user is logged onto the Napster system. The collective directory is fluid; it tracks users who are connected in real time, displaying only file names that are immediately accessible.

45   ## C. Searching For Available Files

46   Napster allows a user to locate other users' MP3 files in two ways: through Napster's search function and through its "hotlist" function.

47   Software located on the Napster servers maintains a "search index" of Napster's collective directory. To search the files available from Napster users currently connected to the network servers, the individual user accesses a form in the MusicShare software stored in his computer and enters either the name of a song or an artist as the object of the search. The form is then transmitted to a Napster server and automatically compared to the MP3 file names listed in the server's search index. Napster's server compiles a list of all MP3 file names pulled from the search index which include the same search terms entered on the search form and transmits the list to the searching user. The Napster server does not search the contents of any MP3 file; rather, the search is limited to "a text search of the file names indexed in a particular cluster. Those file names may contain typographical errors or otherwise inaccurate descriptions of the content of the files since they are designated by other users." *[...]*

48   To use the "hotlist" function, the Napster user creates a list of other users' names from whom he has obtained MP3 files in the past. When logged onto Napster's servers, the system alerts the user if any user on his list (a "hotlisted user") is also logged onto the system. If so, the user can access an index of all MP3 file names in a particular hotlisted user's library and request a file in the library by selecting the file name. The contents of the hotlisted user's MP3 file are not stored on the Napster system.

49   ## D. Transferring Copies of an MP3 file

50   To transfer a copy of the contents of a requested MP3 file, the Napster server software obtains the Internet address of the requesting user and the Internet address of the "host user" (the user with the available files). *[...]* The Napster servers then communicate the host

user's Internet address to the requesting user. The requesting user's computer uses this information to establish a connection with the host user and downloads a copy of the contents of the MP3 file from one computer to the other over the Internet, "peer-to-peer." A downloaded MP3 file can be played directly from the user's hard drive using Napster's MusicShare program or other software. The file may also be transferred back onto an audio CD if the user has access to equipment designed for that purpose. In both cases, the quality of the original sound recording is slightly diminished by transfer to the MP3 format.

51   This architecture is described in some detail to promote an understanding of transmission mechanics as opposed to the content of the transmissions. The content [...] is the subject of our copyright infringement analysis.

52   [...]

56   **III**

57   Plaintiffs claim Napster users are engaged in the wholesale reproduction and distribution of copyrighted works, all constituting direct infringement.[2] The district court agreed. [...]

58   **A. Infringement**

59   Plaintiffs must satisfy two requirements to present a prima facie case of direct infringement: (1) they must show ownership of the allegedly infringed material and (2) they must demonstrate that the alleged infringers violate at least one exclusive right granted to copyright holders under 17 U.S.C. § 106. [...] Plaintiffs have sufficiently demonstrated ownership. The record supports the district court's determination that "as much as eighty-seven percent of the files available on Napster may be copyrighted and more than seventy percent may be owned or administered by plaintiffs." [...]

60   The district court further determined that plaintiffs' exclusive rights under § 106 were violated: "here the evidence establishes [...] that a majority of Napster users use the service to download and upload copyrighted music. . . . And by doing that, it constitutes — the uses constitute direct infringement of plaintiffs' musical compositions, recordings." [...] The district court also noted that "it is pretty much acknowledged . . . by Napster that this is infringement." [...] We agree that plaintiffs have shown that Napster users infringe at least two of the copyright holders' exclusive rights: the rights of reproduction, § 106(1); and distribution, § 106(3). Napster users who upload file names to the search index for others to copy violate plaintiffs' distribution rights. Napster users who download files containing copyrighted music violate plaintiffs' reproduction rights.

61   Napster asserts an affirmative defense to the charge that its users directly infringe plaintiffs' copyrighted musical compositions and sound recordings.

62   **B. Fair Use**

63   Napster contends that its users do not directly infringe plaintiffs' copyrights because the users are engaged in fair use of the material. *See* 17 U.S.C. § 107 ("[T]he fair use of a copyrighted work . . . is not an infringement of copyright."). Napster identifies three specific alleged fair uses: sampling, where users make temporary copies of a work before purchasing; space-shifting, where users access a sound recording through the Napster system that they already own in audio CD format; and permissive distribution of recordings by both new and established artists.

64   The district court considered factors listed in 17 U.S.C. § 107, which guide a court's fair use determination. These factors are: (1) the purpose and character of the use; (2) the nature of the copyrighted work; (3) the "amount and substantiality of the portion used" in relation to the work as a whole; and (4) the effect of the use upon the potential market for the work or the value of the work. *See* 17 U.S.C. § 107. The district court first conducted a general analysis of Napster system uses under § 107, and then applied its reasoning to the alleged fair uses identified by Napster. The district court concluded that Napster users are not fair users.[...] We agree. We first

address the court's overall fair use analysis.

65   1. Purpose and Character of the Use

66   This factor focuses on whether the new work merely replaces the object of the original creation or instead adds a further purpose or different character. In other words, this factor asks "whether and to what extent the new work is `transformative.'" [...]

67   The district court first concluded that downloading MP3 files does not transform the copyrighted work. [...] This conclusion is supportable. Courts have been reluctant to find fair use when an original work is merely retransmitted in a different medium. [...]

68   This "purpose and character" element also requires the district court to determine whether the allegedly infringing use is commercial or noncommercial. [...] A commercial use weighs against a finding of fair use but is not conclusive on the issue. [...] The district court determined that Napster users engage in commercial use of the copyrighted materials largely because (1) "a host user sending a file cannot be said to engage in a personal use when distributing that file to an anonymous requester" and (2) "Napster users get for free something they would ordinarily have to buy." [...]

69   Direct economic benefit is not required to demonstrate a commercial use. Rather, repeated and exploitative copying of copyrighted works, even if the copies are not offered for sale, may constitute a commercial use. *See Worldwide Church of God v. Philadelphia Church of God*, 227 F.3d 1110, 1118 (9th Cir.2000) (stating that church that copied religious text for its members "unquestionably profit[ed]" from the unauthorized "distribution and use of [the text] without having to account to the copyright holder"); *American Geophysical Union v. Texaco, Inc.*, 60 F.3d 913, 922 (2d Cir.1994) (finding that researchers at for-profit laboratory gained indirect economic advantage by photocopying copyrighted scholarly articles). In the record before us, commercial use is demonstrated by a showing that repeated and exploitative unauthorized copies of copyrighted works were made to save the expense of purchasing authorized copies. [...]

70   We also note that the definition of a financially motivated transaction for the purposes of criminal copyright actions includes trading infringing copies of a work for other items, "including the receipt of other copyrighted works." *See* No Electronic Theft Act ("NET Act"), Pub.L. No. 105-147, 18 U.S.C. § 101 (defining "Financial Gain").

71   [...] 2. The Nature of the Use

72   Works that are creative in nature are "closer to the core of intended copyright protection" than are more fact-based works. [...] The district court determined that plaintiffs' "copyrighted musical compositions and sound recordings are creative in nature ... which cuts against a finding of fair use under the second factor." [...]

73   3. The Portion Used

74   "While `wholesale copying does not preclude fair use per se,' copying an entire work `militates against a finding of fair use.'" [...] The district court determined that Napster users engage in "wholesale copying" of copyrighted work because file transfer necessarily "involves copying the entirety of the copyrighted work." [...] We agree. We note, however, that under certain circumstances, a court will conclude that a use is fair even when the protected work is copied in its entirety. *See, e.g., Sony Corp. v. Universal City Studios, Inc.*, 464 U.S. 417, 449-50, 104 S.Ct. 774, 78 L.Ed.2d 574 (1984) (acknowledging that fair use of time-shifting necessarily involved making a full copy of a protected work).

75   4. Effect of Use on Market

76   "Fair use, when properly applied, is limited to copying by others which does not materially impair the marketability of the work which is

copied." *[...]* "[T]he importance of this [fourth] factor will vary, not only with the amount of harm, but also with the relative strength of the showing on the other factors." *[...]* The proof required to demonstrate present or future market harm varies with the purpose and character of the use:

77   A challenge to a noncommercial use of a copyrighted work requires proof either that the particular use is harmful, or that if it should become widespread, it would adversely affect the potential market for the copyrighted work. . . . *If the intended use is for commercial gain, that likelihood [of market harm] may be presumed. But if it is for a noncommercial purpose, the likelihood must be demonstrated.*

78   *Sony [...]*

79   Addressing this factor, the district court concluded that Napster harms the market in "at least" two ways: it reduces audio CD sales among college students and it "raises barriers to plaintiffs' entry into the market for the digital downloading of music." *[...]* The district court relied on evidence plaintiffs submitted to show that Napster use harms the market for their copyrighted musical compositions and sound recordings. In a separate memorandum and order regarding the parties' objections to the expert reports, the district court examined each report, finding some more appropriate and probative than others. *[...]* Notably, plaintiffs' expert, Dr. E. Deborah Jay, conducted a survey (the "Jay Report") using a random sample of college and university students to track their reasons for using Napster and the impact Napster had on their music purchases. *[...]* The court recognized that the Jay Report focused on just one segment of the Napster user population and found "evidence of lost sales attributable to college use to be probative of irreparable harm for purposes of the preliminary injunction motion." *[...]*

80   Plaintiffs also offered a study conducted by Michael Fine, Chief Executive Officer of Soundscan, (the "Fine Report") to determine the effect of online sharing of MP3 *[...]* files in order to show irreparable harm. Fine found that online file sharing had resulted in a loss of "album" sales within college markets. After reviewing defendant's objections to the Fine Report and expressing some concerns regarding the methodology and findings, the district court refused to exclude the Fine Report insofar as plaintiffs offered it to show irreparable harm. *[...]*

81   Plaintiffs' expert Dr. David J. Teece studied several issues ("Teece Report"), including whether plaintiffs had suffered or were likely to suffer harm in their existing and planned businesses due to Napster use. *[...]* Napster objected that the report had not undergone peer review. The district court noted that such reports generally are not subject to such scrutiny and overruled defendant's objections. *[...]*

82   As for defendant's experts, plaintiffs objected to the report of Dr. Peter S. Fader, in which the expert concluded that Napster is *beneficial* to the music industry because MP3 music file-sharing stimulates more audio CD sales than it displaces. *[...]* The district court found problems in Dr. Fader's minimal role in overseeing the administration of the survey and the lack of objective data in his report. The court decided the generality of the report rendered it "of dubious reliability and value." The court did not exclude the report, however, but chose "not to rely on Fader's findings in determining the issues of fair use and irreparable harm." *[...]*

83   The district court cited both the Jay and Fine Reports in support of its finding that Napster use harms the market for plaintiffs' copyrighted musical compositions and sound recordings by reducing CD sales among college students. The district court cited the Teece Report to show the harm Napster use caused in raising barriers to plaintiffs' entry into the market for digital downloading of music. *[...]* The district court's careful consideration of defendant's objections to these reports and decision to rely on the reports for specific issues demonstrates a proper exercise of discretion in addition to a correct application of the fair use doctrine. Defendant has failed to show any basis for disturbing the district court's findings.

84   We, therefore, conclude that the district court made sound findings related to Napster's deleterious effect on the present and future

digital download market. Moreover, lack of harm to an established market cannot deprive the copyright holder of the right to develop alternative markets for the works. *See L.A. Times v. Free Republic,* [...] Here, similar to *L.A. Times* and *UMG Recordings,* the record supports the district court's finding that the "record company plaintiffs have already expended considerable funds and effort to commence Internet sales and licensing for digital downloads." [...] Having digital downloads available for free on the Napster system necessarily harms the copyright holders' attempts to charge for the same downloads.

85   Judge Patel did not abuse her discretion in reaching the above fair use conclusions, nor were the findings of fact with respect to fair use considerations clearly erroneous. We next address Napster's identified uses of sampling and space-shifting.

86   ## 5. Identified Uses

87   Napster maintains that its identified uses of sampling and space-shifting were wrongly excluded as fair uses by the district court.

88   ## [...] a. Sampling

89   Napster contends that its users download MP3 files to "sample" the music in order to decide whether to purchase the recording. Napster argues that the district court: (1) erred in concluding that sampling is a commercial use because it conflated a noncommercial use with a personal use; (2) erred in determining that sampling adversely affects the market for plaintiffs' copyrighted music, a requirement if the use is noncommercial; and (3) erroneously concluded that sampling is not a fair use because it determined that samplers may also engage in other infringing activity.

90   The district court determined that sampling remains a commercial use even if some users eventually purchase the music. We find no error in the district court's determination. Plaintiffs have established that they are likely to succeed in proving that even authorized temporary downloading of individual songs for sampling purposes is commercial in nature. [...] The record supports a finding that free promotional downloads are highly regulated by the record company plaintiffs and that the companies collect royalties for song samples available on retail Internet sites. *Id.* Evidence relied on by the district court demonstrates that the free downloads provided by the record companies consist of thirty-to-sixty second samples or are full songs programmed to "time out," that is, exist only for a short time on the downloader's computer. [...] In comparison, Napster users download a full, free and permanent copy of the recording. [...] The determination by the district court as to the commercial purpose and character of sampling is not clearly erroneous.

91   The district court further found that both the market for audio CDs and market for online distribution are adversely affected by Napster's service. As stated in our discussion of the district court's general fair use analysis: the court did not abuse its discretion when it found that, overall, Napster has an adverse impact on the audio CD and digital download markets. Contrary to Napster's assertion that the district court failed to specifically address the market impact of sampling, the district court determined that "[e]ven if the type of sampling supposedly done on Napster were a non-commercial use, plaintiffs have demonstrated a substantial likelihood that it would adversely affect the potential market for their copyrighted works if it became widespread." [...] The record supports the district court's preliminary determinations that: (1) the more music that sampling users download, the less likely they are to eventually purchase the recordings on audio CD; and (2) even if the audio CD market is not harmed, Napster has adverse effects on the developing digital download market.

92   Napster further argues that the district court erred in rejecting its evidence that the users' downloading of "samples" increases or tends to increase audio CD sales. The district court, however, correctly noted that "any potential enhancement of plaintiffs' sales . . . would not tip the fair use analysis conclusively in favor of defendant." [...] We agree that increased sales of copyrighted material attributable to unauthorized use should not deprive the copyright holder of the right to license the material. *See Campbell,* 510 U.S. at 591 n. 21, 114 S.Ct. 1164 ("Even favorable evidence, without more, is no guarantee of fairness. Judge Leval gives the example of the film producer's appropriation of a composer's previously unknown song that turns the song into a commercial success; the boon to the song does not make the film's simple copying fair.") [...] Nor does positive impact in one market, here the audio CD market, deprive the copyright holder of the right to develop identified alternative markets, here the digital download market. [...]

93   We find no error in the district court's factual findings or abuse of discretion in the court's conclusion that plaintiffs will likely prevail in establishing that sampling does not constitute a fair use.

94   ## b. Space-Shifting

95   Napster also maintains that space-shifting is a fair use. Space-shifting occurs when a Napster user downloads MP3 music files in order to listen to music he already owns on audio CD. *See id.* at 915-16. Napster asserts that we have already held that space-shifting of musical compositions and sound recordings is a fair use. *See Recording Indus. Ass'n of Am. v. Diamond Multimedia Sys., Inc.,* 180 F.3d 1072, 1079 (9th Cir.1999) ("Rio [a portable MP3 player] merely makes copies in order to render portable, or `space-shift,' those files that already reside on a user's hard drive. . . . Such copying is a paradigmatic noncommercial personal use."). *See also generally Sony,* 464 U.S. at 423, 104 S.Ct. 774 (holding that "time-shifting," where a video tape recorder owner records a television show for later viewing, is a fair use).

96   We conclude that the district court did not err when it refused to apply the "shifting" analyses of *Sony* and *Diamond.* Both *Diamond* and *Sony* are inapposite because the methods of shifting in these cases did not also simultaneously involve distribution of the copyrighted material to the general public; the time or space-shifting of copyrighted material exposed the material only to the original user. In *Diamond,* for example, the copyrighted music was transferred from the user's computer hard drive to the user's portable MP3 player. So too *Sony,* where "the majority of VCR purchasers . . . did not distribute taped television broadcasts, but merely enjoyed them at home." *[...]* Conversely, it is obvious that once a user lists a copy of music he already owns on the Napster system in order to access the music from another location, the song becomes "available to millions of other individuals," not just the original CD owner. *See UMG Recordings[...]*

97   ## c. Other Uses

98   Permissive reproduction by either independent or established artists is the final fair use claim made by Napster. The district court noted that plaintiffs did not seek to enjoin this and any other noninfringing use of the Napster system, including: chat rooms, message boards and Napster's New Artist Program. *[...]* Plaintiffs do not challenge these uses on appeal.

99   We find no error in the district court's determination that plaintiffs will likely succeed in establishing that Napster users do not have a fair use defense. *[...]*

100 AFFIRMED IN PART, REVERSED IN PART AND REMANDED.   *The court goes on to consider secondary liability, of Napster for the actions of its users.*

174 *[...]*

175 [2] Secondary liability for copyright infringement does not exist in the absence of direct infringement by a third party. *[...]* It follows that Napster does not facilitate infringement of the copyright laws in the absence of direct infringement by its users.

176 *[...]*

181

Sony BMG Music Entertainment v. Tenenbaum

September 01, 2014 by mrisch

This short note considers copyright statutory damages for music copying

1

[...]

660 F.3d 487

SONY BMG MUSIC ENTERTAINMENT [...]

v.

Joel TENENBAUM [...]

5   Before LYNCH, Chief Judge, TORRUELLA and THOMPSON, Circuit Judges.

6   LYNCH, Chief Judge.

7   Plaintiffs, the recording companies Sony BMG Music Entertainment, Warner Brothers Records Inc., Arista Records LLC, Atlantic Recording Corporation, and UMG Recordings, Inc. (together, "Sony"), brought this action for statutory damages and injunctive relief under the Copyright Act, 17 U.S.C. § 101 *et seq.* Sony argued that the defendant, Joel Tenenbaum, willfully infringed the copyrights of thirty music recordings by using file-sharing software to download and distribute those recordings without authorization from the copyright owners.

8   The district court entered judgment against Tenenbaum as to liability. The jury found that Tenenbaum's infringement of the copyrights at issue was willful and awarded Sony statutory damages of $22,500 for each infringed recording, an award within the statutory range of $750 to $150,000 per infringement that Congress established for willful conduct. *See* 17 U.S.C. § 504(c).

9   [...]

10   Sony brought this action against Tenenbaum in August 2007, seeking statutory damages and injunctive relief pursuant to the Copyright Act. Sony pursued copyright claims against Tenenbaum for only thirty copyrighted works, even though it presented evidence that Tenenbaum illegally downloaded and distributed thousands of copyrighted materials.

18   Sony's complaint elected to seek statutory, not actual damages, pursuant to 17 U.S.C. § 504(c). For each act of infringement, § 504(c) establishes an award range of $750 to $30,000 for non-willful infringements, and a range of $750 to $150,000 for willful infringements.

19   [...]

21   The jury found that Tenenbaum had willfully infringed each of Sony's thirty copyrighted works. The jury returned a damage award, within the statutory range, of $22,500 per infringement, which yielded a total award of $675,000.

22   [...]

23   Regarding the size of the award, the court declined to decide the common law remittitur issue, based on its assumption that Sony would not agree to a reduction of the award and that remittitur would only necessitate a new trial on the issue of damages, and that even after a new trial the same issue of constitutional excessiveness would arise, so, in its view decision on the issue was inevitable. The court itself then found that the award violated due process, over objections that it utilized an impermissible standard, and reduced the award from $22,500 per infringement to $2,250 per infringement for a total award of $67,500.

24   ## B. Factual Background

25   [...]

30   Shortly after peer-to-peer networks first appeared, plaintiffs acknowledged the threat they posed to their industry and initiated a broad campaign to address the illegal infringement of copyrighted materials. They started educating the public that downloading and distributing copyrighted songs over peer-to-peer networks constituted illegal copyright infringement. Plaintiffs also brought legal actions as part of their campaign, and initially targeted the proprietors of peer-to-peer networks, not the individuals who actually used those networks to illegally procure and distribute copyrighted materials. [...] Although these litigation efforts succeeded at shutting down particular networks, individual infringers continued to engage in illegal conduct by finding new peer-to-peer networks through which to download copyrighted songs.

33   Consequently, record companies began to identify and pursue legal actions against individual infringers. The industry identified Internet Protocol (IP) addresses of users known to be engaged in a high volume of downloading and distributing copyrighted materials, and initiated lawsuits against those users. [...] These suits began in 2002 and were widely-publicized.[4]

34   ## 2. Tenenbaum's Conduct

35   Tenenbaum was an early and enthusiastic user of peer-to-peer networks to obtain and distribute copyrighted music recordings. He began downloading and distributing copyrighted works without authorization in 1999. In that year, he installed the Napster peer-to-peer network on his desktop computer at his family's home in Providence, Rhode Island. He used Napster both to download digital versions of copyrighted music recordings from other network users and to distribute to other users digital versions of copyrighted music recordings already saved on his own computer.

36   [...]ks for the same illegal purposes. These networks included AudioGalaxy, iMesh, Morpheus, Kazaa, and Limewire. Tenenbaum shifted to these other networks after Napster's termination despite his knowledge that Napster was forced to close on account of a lawsuit brought against it for copyright infringement.

37   Tenenbaum continued to download and distribute copyrighted materials through at least 2007. During that time span he accessed a panoply of peer-to-peer networks for these illegal purposes from several computers. From 1999 until 2002, he primarily downloaded and distributed copyrighted works to and from his desktop computer at his family's home in Providence. He left home to attend Goucher College in Baltimore, Maryland, in 2002, at which point he began using a laptop to download and distribute copyrighted works. Following his graduation from Goucher in 2006, he began using a second laptop for these purposes in tandem with his other computers. Over the duration of Tenenbaum's conduct, he intentionally downloaded thousands of songs to his own computers from other network users. He also purposefully made thousands of songs available to other network users. He did this in the period after lawsuits were brought, and publicized, against individuals who downloaded and distributed music without authorization. At one point in time in 2004 alone,

Tenenbaum had 1153 songs on his "shared-directory" on the Kazaa network. [...] Any of those files within Tenenbaum's shared directory could be easily downloaded by other Kazaa users. Although there was no way to determine the exact number of times other users had downloaded files from Tenenbaum's shared directory, it was frequent. Most of the networks Tenenbaum used had a "traffic tab" that informed him of the frequency with which other users were downloading his shared files. Tenenbaum regularly looked at the traffic tab, and he admitted it "definitely wasn't uncommon" for other users to be downloading materials from his computer.

38   Tenenbaum knew that his conduct, both his downloading and distribution, was illegal and received warnings the industry had started legal proceedings against individuals. He received several warnings regarding the potential liability his actions carried with them. While Tenenbaum was at Goucher College in 2002, his father, Dr. Arthur Tenenbaum, called him to warn him that his use of peer-to-peer networks to obtain and distribute music recordings was unlawful. Dr. Tenenbaum knew that his son was illegally downloading music because, prior to leaving for college, Tenenbaum had showed his father the array of songs that could be downloaded from the Kazaa network. After Dr. Tenenbaum became aware that lawsuits were being brought against individuals who used file-sharing programs to download and distribute music, he instructed Tenenbaum not to continue to engage in such conduct. Dr. Tenenbaum testified that, during their conversation, Tenenbaum did not appear [...] concerned about the consequences of his actions. Despite his father's request, Tenenbaum continued his illegal activity.

39   Tenenbaum also received direct warnings from Goucher College. Each year Tenenbaum received a Goucher student handbook warning that using the college's network to download and distribute copyrighted materials was illegal, but he did so anyway. The handbook also warned that illegally downloading and distributing music files could subject the copyright infringer to up to $150,000 of liability per infringement, alerting Tenenbaum to his potential exposure for violating the law. [...]

44   In a September 2005 letter, plaintiffs themselves informed Tenenbaum that he had been detected infringing copyrighted materials and notified him that his conduct was illegal. The letter stated: "We are writing in advance of filing suit against you in the event that you have an interest in resolving these claims."[6] The letter urged Tenenbaum to consult with an attorney immediately, and explained that the recording companies were prepared to initiate a legal action against Tenenbaum [...]

46   The letter also instructed Tenenbaum to preserve any relevant evidence including "the entire library of recordings that you have made available for distribution as well as any recordings you have downloaded...."[7]

47   [...]

48   Despite these warnings and his knowledge that he was and had been engaging in illegal activity which could subject him to liability of up to $150,000 per infringement, Tenenbaum continued the illegal downloading and distribution of copyrighted materials until at least 2007 —a full two years after receiving the letter from Sony. He stopped his activity only after this lawsuit was filed against him.

49   [...]

53   II.

54   **Tenenbaum's Challenges to the Constitutionality and Applicability of the Copyright Act**

55   [...]

88   ## C. Statutory Damages under 17 U.S.C. § 504 and Actual Harm

88   Tenenbaum next argues that the statutory damages provision is nonetheless inapplicable because, in his view, as a matter of law there can be no statutory damages where "harm caused by a particular defendant has not been proved." Again, he is wrong both as a matter of

law and on the facts of record.

89   The district court properly rejected Tenenbaum's proffered interpretation of § 504. Section 504 clearly sets forth two alternative damage calculations a plaintiff can elect: actual damages and statutory damages. *See* 17 U.S.C. § 504(a) $[...]$

90   Under § 504(b), a plaintiff may elect to receive "the actual damages suffered by him or her as a result of the infringement, and any profits of the infringer that are attributable to the infringement and are not taken into account in computing the actual damages."

91   Alternatively, under § 504(c), "the copyright owner may elect, at any time before final judgment is rendered, to recover, *instead of actual damages and profits,* an award of statutory damages for all infringements involved in the action, with respect to any one work." $[...]$ The statute makes clear that statutory damages are an independent and alternative remedy that a plaintiff may elect "instead of actual damages."

92      $[...]$ The Supreme Court explained that before statutory damages were available, plaintiffs, "though proving infringement," would often be able to recover only nominal damages and the "ineffectiveness of the remedy encouraged willful and deliberate infringement." $[...]$ The Supreme Court has since reaffirmed that "[e]ven for uninjurious and unprofitable invasions of copyright the court may, if it deems it just, impose a liability within statutory limits to sanction and vindicate the statutory policy." $[...]$

989

IV.

130

The District Court's Bypassing of Common Law Remittitur and Reducing the Award on Disputed Constitutional Grounds

131   After handling the trial with great skill, the district court committed reversible error when, after the jury awarded statutory damages, it bypassed the issue of common law remittitur, and instead resolved a disputed question of whether the jury's award of $22,500 per infringement violated due process, and decided itself to reduce the award. The court declined to adhere to the doctrine of constitutional avoidance on the ground that it felt resolution of a constitutional due process question was inevitable in the case before it. A decision on a constitutional due process question was not necessary, was not inevitable, had considerable impermissible consequences, and contravened the rule of constitutional avoidance. That rule had more than its usual import in this case because there were a number of difficult constitutional issues which should have been avoided but were engaged.

132   Facing the constitutional question of whether the award violated due process was not inevitable. The district court should first have considered the non-constitutional issue of remittitur, which may have obviated any constitutional due process issue and attendant issues. Had the court ordered remittitur of a particular amount, Sony would have then had a choice. It could have accepted the reduced award. Or, it could have rejected the remittitur, in which case a new trial would have ensued. $[...]$

133   In reaching and deciding that due process constitutional question, the district court also unnecessarily decided several related constitutional issues. The court determined that the statutory damage award was effectively a punitive damage award for due process purposes and applied the factors set forth in *BMW v. Gore,* 517 U.S. 559, 116 S.Ct. 1589, 134 L.Ed.2d 809 (1996), to assess its constitutionality. The court declined to apply the *Williams* standard the Supreme Court had previously applied to statutory damage awards. $[...]$ The district court's tack also led to unnecessary resolution of Seventh Amendment issues. The decision to reduce the jury's award without offering Sony a new trial implicitly presupposed that, in reducing a statutory damage award issued by a jury, a court need not offer plaintiffs the option of a new jury trial in order to comport with the Seventh Amendment.

134     $[...]$

168   This was a difficult and contentious case and the parties received a fair trial from an admirably patient and able district judge.

170   We affirm the finding of liability against Tenenbaum and in favor of plaintiffs. We affirm the injunctive relief. [...]

171   We vacate the district court's due process damages ruling and reverse the reduction of the jury's statutory damages award. We reinstate the jury's award of damages and remand for consideration of defendant's motion for common law remittitur based on excessiveness.[28]

172   If, on remand, the court allows any reduction through remittitur, then plaintiffs must be given the choice of a new trial or acceptance of remittitur.

173   So ordered.

174   [...]

178   [4] We are aware of only one other action against an individual that has proceeded to trial. *See Capitol Records, Inc. v. Thomas-Rasset,* [...

179   [...]

180   [6] Tenenbaum contacted Sony as a result of the letter. While there were some settlement discussions, the parties were unable to resolve the matter.

181   [7] After receiving this letter, Tenenbaum nonetheless took his laptop computer for repairs and had its operating system reinstalled and its hard drive reformatted. At trial, Tenenbaum maintained that he only had work done on the computer because "the thing wouldn't run," and that he instructed the computer repairman not to tamper with the music files stored on his computer.

182   [...]

Note on Tenenbaum and constitutional challenge to statutory damages

In Sony BMG Entertainment v. Tenenbaum, 719 F.3d 67 (1st Cir. 2013), the court considered another appeal. On remand from the prior case, the district court held that:

1. Remittitur was not proper in this case, and

2. Copyright statutory damages did not violate constitutional due process.

Tenenbaum did not appeal the remittitur, but did appeal on constitutional grounds. The appeals court agreed with the district court (as it had hinted it would in its prior opinion) that statutory damages did not violate due process.

Copyright Act: 17 U.S. Code § 109 - Limitations on exclusive rights: Effect of transfer o particular copy or phonorecord

September 01, 2014 by mrisch

1   **(a)** Notwithstanding the provisions of section 106 (3), the owner of a particular copy or phonorecord lawfully made under this title, or any person authorized by such owner, is entitled, without the authority of the copyright owner, to sell or otherwise dispose of the possession of that copy or phonorecord. Notwithstanding the preceding sentence, copies or phonorecords of works subject to restored copyright under section 104A that are manufactured before the date of restoration of copyright or, with respect to reliance parties, before publication or service of notice under section 104A (e), may be sold or otherwise disposed of without the authorization of the owner of the restored copyright for purposes of direct or indirect commercial advantage only during the 12-month period beginning on—

   (1) the date of the publication in the Federal Register of the notice of intent filed with the Copyright Office under section 104A (d)(2) (A), or

   (2) the date of the receipt of actual notice served under section 104A (d)(2)(B),

whichever occurs first.

2   **(b)**

   (1)

   (A) Notwithstanding the provisions of subsection (a), unless authorized by the owners of copyright in the sound recording or the owner of copyright in a computer program (including any tape, disk, or other medium embodying such program), and in the case of a sound recording in the musical works embodied therein, neither the owner of a particular phonorecord nor any person in possession of a particular copy of a computer program (including any tape, disk, or other medium embodying such program), may, for the purposes of direct or indirect commercial advantage, dispose of, or authorize the disposal of, the possession of that phonorecord or computer program (including any tape, disk, or other medium embodying such program) by rental, lease, or lending, or by any other act or practice in the nature of rental, lease, or lending. Nothing in the preceding sentence shall apply to the rental, lease, or lending of a phonorecord for nonprofit purposes by a nonprofit library or nonprofit educational institution. The transfer of possession of a lawfully made copy of a computer program by a nonprofit educational institution to another nonprofit educational institution or to faculty, staff, and students does not constitute rental, lease, or lending for direct or indirect commercial purposes under this subsection.

   (B) This subsection does not apply to—

   (i) a computer program which is embodied in a machine or product and which cannot be copied during the ordinary operation or use of the machine or product; or

   (ii) a computer program embodied in or used in conjunction with a limited purpose computer that is designed for playing video games and may be designed for other purposes.

   (C) Nothing in this subsection affects any provision of chapter 9 of this title.

   (2)

   (A) Nothing in this subsection shall apply to the lending of a computer program for nonprofit purposes by a nonprofit library, if each copy of a computer program which is lent by such library has affixed to the packaging containing the program a warning of copyright in accordance with requirements that the Register of Copyrights shall prescribe by regulation.

   (B) Not later than three years after the date of the enactment of the Computer Software Rental Amendments Act of 1990, and at such times thereafter as the Register of Copyrights considers appropriate, the Register of Copyrights, after consultation with representatives of copyright owners and librarians, shall submit to the Congress a report stating whether this paragraph has achieved its intended purpose of maintaining the integrity of the copyright system while providing nonprofit libraries the capability to fulfill their function. Such report shall advise the Congress as to any information or recommendations that the Register of Copyrights considers necessary to carry out the purposes of this subsection.

(3) Nothing in this subsection shall affect any provision of the antitrust laws. For purposes of the preceding sentence, "antitrust laws" has the meaning given that term in the first section of the Clayton Act and includes section 5 of the Federal Trade Commission Act to the extent that section relates to unfair methods of competition.

(4) Any person who distributes a phonorecord or a copy of a computer program (including any tape, disk, or other medium embodying such program) in violation of paragraph (1) is an infringer of copyright under section 501 of this title and is subject to the remedies set forth in sections 502, 503, 504, and 505. Such violation shall not be a criminal offense under section 506 or cause such person to be subject to the criminal penalties set forth in section 2319 of title 18.

3   **(c)** Notwithstanding the provisions of section 106 (5), the owner of a particular copy lawfully made under this title, or any person authorized by such owner, is entitled, without the authority of the copyright owner, to display that copy publicly, either directly or by the projection of no more than one image at a time, to viewers present at the place where the copy is located.

4   **(d)** The privileges prescribed by subsections (a) and (c) do not, unless authorized by the copyright owner, extend to any person who has acquired possession of the copy or phonorecord from the copyright owner, by rental, lease, loan, or otherwise, without acquiring ownership of it.

5   **(e)** Notwithstanding the provisions of sections 106 (4) and 106 (5), in the case of an electronic audiovisual game intended for use in coin-operated equipment, the owner of a particular copy of such a game lawfully made under this title, is entitled, without the authority of the copyright owner of the game, to publicly perform or display that game in coin-operated equipment, except that this subsection shall not apply to any work of authorship embodied in the audiovisual game if the copyright owner of the electronic audiovisual game is not also the copyright owner of the work of authorship.

Capitol Records, LLC v. ReDigi Inc.

September 01, 2014 by mrisch

This case shows the uphill battle companies face in the digital music market

1   934 F.Supp.2d 640

2   **CAPITOL RECORDS, LLC, Plaintiff,**

v.

ReDIGI INC., Defendant.

3   [...]

4   United States District Court,
S.D. New York.

5   March 30, 2013.

6   [...]

8   **Memorandum and Order**

9   **RICHARD J. SULLIVAN, District Judge.**

10   Capitol Records, LLC (Capitol), the recording label for such classic vinyls as [...] Frank Sinatra's Come Fly With Me and The Beatles' Yellow Submarine, brings this action against ReDigi Inc. (ReDigi), a twenty-first century technology company that touts itself as a virtual marketplace for pre-owned digital music. What has ensued in a fundamental clash over culture, policy, and copyright law, with Capitol alleging that ReDigi's web-based service amounts to copyright infringement in violation of the Copyright Act of 1976 (the Copyright Act), 17 U.S.C. 101 *et seq.* Now before the Court are Capitol's motion for partial summary judgment and ReDigi's motion for summary judgment, both filed pursuant to Federal Rule of Civil Procedure 56. Because this is a court of law and not a congressional subcommittee or technology blog, the issues are narrow, technical, and purely legal. Thus, for the reasons that follow, Capitol's motion is granted and ReDigi's motion is denied.

11   **I. Background**

12   **A. Facts**

13   ReDigi markets itself as the world's first and only online marketplace for digital used music. [...] Launched on October 13, 2011, ReDigi's website invites users to sell their legally acquired digital music files, and buy used digital music from others at a fraction of the price currently available on iTunes. [...] Thus, much like used record stores, ReDigi permits its users to recoup value on their unwanted music. Unlike used record stores, however, ReDigi's sales take place entirely in the digital domain. [...]

14   To sell music on ReDigi's website, a user must first download ReDigi's Media Manager to his computer. [...] Once installed, Media Manager analyzes the user's computer to build a list of digital music files eligible for sale. [...] A file is eligible only if it was purchased on

iTunes or from another ReDigi user; music downloaded from a CD or other file-sharing website is ineligible for sale. [...] After this validation process, Media Manager continually runs on the user's computer and attached devices to ensure that the user has not retained music that has been sold or uploaded for sale. [...] However, Media Manager cannot detect copies stored in other locations. [...] If a copy is detected, Media Manager prompts the user to delete the file. [...] The file is not deleted automatically or involuntarily, though ReDigi's policy is to suspend the accounts of users who refuse to comply. [...]

15   After the list is built, a user may upload any of his eligible files to ReDigi's Cloud Locker, an ethereal moniker for what is, in fact, merely a remote server in Arizona. [...] ReDigi's upload process is a source of contention between the parties. [...] ReDigi asserts that the process involves migrating a user's file, packet by packetanalogous to a trainfrom the user's computer to the Cloud Locker so that data does not exist in two places at any one time.[...] Capitol asserts [...] that, semantics aside, ReDigi's upload process necessarily involves copying a file from the user's computer to the Cloud Locker. [...] Regardless, at the end of the process, the digital music file is located in the Cloud Locker and not on the user's computer. [...] Moreover, Media Manager deletes any additional copies of the file on the user's computer and connected devices. [...]

16   Once uploaded, a digital music file undergoes a second analysis to verify eligibility. [...] If ReDigi determines that the file has not been tampered with or offered for sale by another user, the file is stored in the Cloud Locker, and the user is given the option of simply storing and streaming the file for personal use or offering it for sale in ReDigi's marketplace. [...] If a user chooses to sell his digital music file, his access to the file is terminated and transferred to the new owner at the time of purchase. [...] Thereafter, the new owner can store the file in the Cloud Locker, stream it, sell it, or download it to her computer and other devices. [...] No money changes hands in these transactions. [...] Instead, users buy music with credits they either purchased from ReDigi or acquired from other sales. [...] ReDigi credits, once acquired, cannot be exchanged for money. [...] Instead, they can only be used to purchase additional music. [...]

18   Finally, ReDigi earns a fee for every transaction. [...] ReDigi's website prices digital music files at fifty-nine to seventy-nine cents each. [...] When users purchase a file, with credits, 20% of the sale price is allocated to the seller, 20% goes to an escrow fund for the artist, and 60% is retained by ReDigi.[3] [...]

19   [...]

[648] III. Discussion

26   Section 106 of the Copyright Act grants the owner of copyright under this title certain exclusive rights, including the right to reproduce the copyrighted work in copies or phonorecords, to distribute copies or phonorecords of the copyrighted work to the public by sale or other transfer of ownership, and to publicly perform and display certain copyrighted works. 17 U.S.C. 106(1), (3)-(5). However, these exclusive rights are limited by several subsequent sections of the statute. Pertinently, Section 109 sets forth the first sale doctrine, which provides that the owner of a particular copy or phonorecord lawfully made under this title, or any person authorized by such owner, is entitled, without the authority of the copyright owner, to sell or otherwise dispose of the possession of that copy or phonorecord. *Id.* 109(a). The novel question presented in this action is whether a digital music file, lawfully made and purchased, may be resold by its owner through ReDigi under the first sale doctrine. The Court determines that it cannot.

A. Infringement of Capitol's Copyrights

28   To state a claim for copyright infringement, a plaintiff must establish that it owns a valid copyright in the work at issue and that the defendant violated one of the exclusive rights the plaintiff holds in the work. [...] It is undisputed that Capitol owns copyrights in a number of the recordings sold on ReDigi's website. [...]

29   **1. Reproduction Rights**

30   Courts have consistently held that the unauthorized duplication of digital music files over the Internet infringes a copyright owner's exclusive right to reproduce. *[...]* However, courts have not previously addressed whether the unauthorized transfer of a digital music file over the Internetwhere only one file exists before and after the transferconstitutes reproduction within the meaning of the Copyright Act. The Court holds that it does.

31   The Copyright Act provides that a copyright owner has the exclusive right to reproduce the copyrighted work *in ... phonorecords.* 17 U.S.C. 106(1) (emphasis added). Copyrighted works are defined to include, *inter alia,* sound recordings, which are works that result from the fixation of a series of musical, spoken, or other sounds. *Id.* 101. Such works are distinguished from their material embodiments. These include phonorecords, which are the *material objects* in which sounds ... are fixed by any method now known or later developed, and from which the sounds can be perceived, reproduced, or otherwise communicated, either directly or with the aid of a machine or device. *Id.* 101 (emphasis added). Thus, the plain text of the Copyright Act makes clear that reproduction occurs when a copyrighted work is fixed in a new *material object.* *[...]*

33   Put differently, the reproduction right is the exclusive right to embody, and to prevent others from embodying, the copyrighted work (or sound recording) in a new material object (or phonorecord). *[...]*

35   Courts that have dealt with infringement on peer-to-peer (P2P) file-sharing systems provide valuable guidance on the application of this right in the digital domain. For instance, in *LondonSire Records, Inc. v. John Doe 1,* the court addressed whether users of P2P software violated copyright owners' distribution rights. *[...]* Citing the material object requirement, the court expressly differentiated between the copyrighted workor digital music fileand the phonorecordor appropriate segment of the hard disk that the file would be embodied in following its transfer. *[...]* Specifically,

36   [w]hen a user on a [P2P] network downloads a song from another user, he receives into his computer a digital sequence representing the sound recording. That sequence is magnetically encoded on a segment of his hard disk (or likewise written on other media). With the right hardware and software, the downloader can use the magnetic sequence to *reproduce* the sound recording. The electronic file (or, perhaps more accurately, the appropriate segment of the hard disk) is therefore a phonorecord within the meaning of the statute.

37   *Id.* (emphasis added). Accordingly, when a user downloads a digital music file or digital sequence to his hard disk, the file is reproduce[d] on a new phonorecord within the meaning of the Copyright Act. *Id.*

38   This understanding is, of course, confirmed by the laws of physics. It is simply impossible that the same material object can be transferred over the Internet. Thus, logically, the court in *LondonSire* noted that the Internet transfer of a file results in a material object being created elsewhere at its finish. *[...]* Because the reproduction right is necessarily implicated when a copyrighted work is embodied in a new material object, and because digital music files must be embodied in a new material object following their transfer over the Internet, the Court determines that the embodiment of a digital music file on a new hard disk is a reproduction *[...]* within the meaning of the Copyright Act.

39   *[...]*

40   Given this finding, the Court concludes that ReDigi's service infringes Capitol's reproduction rights under any description of the technology. ReDigi stresses that it migrates a file from a user's computer to its Cloud Locker, so that the same file is transferred to the ReDigi server and no copying occurs.[5] However, even if that were the case, the fact that a file has moved from one material objectthe user's computerto anotherthe ReDigi servermeans that a reproduction has occurred. Similarly, when a ReDigi user downloads a new purchase from the ReDigi website to her computer, yet another reproduction is created. It is beside the point that the original

phonorecord no longer exists. It matters only that a new phonorecord has been created.

41   [...] ReDigi argues that [...] its users must purchase a song on iTunes in order to sell a song on ReDigi. [...] Therefore, no duplication
      occurs. [...] ReDigi's argument is unavailing. [...] ReDigi's service by necessity creates a new material object when a digital music file is
      either uploaded to or downloaded from the Cloud Locker.   *Note that this follows directly from UMG.*

42   ReDigi also argues that the Court's conclusion would lead to irrational outcomes, as it would render illegal any movement of copyrighted
      files on a hard drive, including relocating files between directories and defragmenting. [...] However, this argument is nothing more than a
      red herring. As Capitol has conceded, such reproduction is almost certainly protected under other doctrines or defenses, and is not
      relevant to the instant motion. [...]

43   Accordingly, the Court finds that, absent the existence of an affirmative defense, the sale of digital music files on ReDigi's website
      infringes Capitol's exclusive right of reproduction.

44   [...]

45   In addition to the reproduction right, a copyright owner also has the exclusive right to distribute copies or phonorecords of the
      copyrighted work to the public by sale or other transfer of ownership. 17 U.S.C. 106(3). Like the court in *LondonSire,* the Court agrees
      that [a]n electronic file transfer is plainly within the sort of transaction that 106(3) was intended to reach [and] ... fit[s] within the
      definition of distribution of a phonorecord. [...] For that reason, courts have not hesitated to find copyright infringement by distribution in
      cases of file-sharing or electronic transmission of copyrighted works. [...]

46   There is no dispute that sales occurred on ReDigi's website. Capitol has established that it was able to buy more than one-hundred of its
      own recordings on ReDigi's webite, and ReDigi itself compiled a list of its completed sales of Capitol's recordings. [...]

47   Accordingly, the Court concludes that, absent the existence of an affirmative defense, the sale of digital music files on ReDigi's website
      infringes Capitol's exclusive right of distribution.[6]

48   [...]

52   ## B. Affirmative Defenses

53   Having concluded that sales on ReDigi's website infringe Capitol's exclusive rights of reproduction and distribution, the Court turns to
      whether the fair use or first sale defenses excuse that infringement. For the reasons set forth below, the Court determines that they do
      not.

54   ### 1. Fair Use

55   The ultimate test of fair use ... is whether the copyright law's goal of promot[ing] the Progress of Science and useful Arts' would be better
      served by allowing [...] the use than by preventing it. [...] Accordingly, fair use permits reproduction of copyrighted work without the
      copyright owner's consent for purposes such as criticism, comment, news reporting, teaching (including multiple copies for classroom
      use), scholarship, or research. 17 U.S.C. 107. The list is not exhaustive but merely illustrates the types of copying typically embraced by
      fair use. [...]

58   On the record before it, the Court has little difficulty concluding that ReDigi's reproduction and distribution of Capitol's copyrighted
      works falls well outside the fair use defense. ReDigi obliquely argues that uploading to and downloading from the Cloud Locker for

storage and personal use are protected fair use.[7] [...] Significantly, Capitol does not contest that claim. [...] Instead, Capitol asserts only that uploading to and downloading from the Cloud Locker *incident to sale* fall outside the ambit of fair use. The Court agrees. *See Arista Records, LLC v. Doe 3*, 604 F.3d 110, 124 (2d Cir.2010) (rejecting application of fair use to user uploads and downloads on P2P file-sharing network).

59   Each of the statutory factors counsels against a finding of fair use. The first factor requires the Court to determine whether ReDigi's use transforms the copyrighted work and whether it is commercial. *[...]* Both inquiries disfavor ReDigi's claim. Plainly, the upload, sale, and download of digital music files on ReDigi's website does nothing to add [ ] something new, with a further purpose or different character to the copyrighted works. *[...]* ReDigi's use is also undoubtedly commercial. ReDigi and the uploading user directly profit from the sale of a digital music file, and the downloading user saves significantly on the price of the song in the primary market. *[...]* ReDigi asserts that downloads for personal, and not public or commercial, use must be characterized as ... noncommercial, nonprofit activity. [...] However, ReDigi twists the law to fit its facts. When a user downloads purchased files from the Cloud Locker, the resultant reproduction is an essential component of ReDigi's commercial enterprise. Thus, ReDigi's argument is unavailing.

60   The second factor—the nature of the copyrighted work—also weighs against application of the fair use defense, as creative works like sound recordings are close to the core of the intended copyright protection and far removed from the ... factual or descriptive work more amenable to fair use. *[...]* The third factor—the portion of the work copied—suggests a similar outcome because ReDigi transmits the works in their entirety, negating any claim of fair use. *[...]* Finally, ReDigi's sales are likely to undercut the market for or value of the copyrighted work and, accordingly, the fourth factor cuts against a finding of fair use. *[...]* The product sold in ReDigi's secondary market is indistinguishable from that sold in the legitimate primary market save for its lower price. The clear inference is that ReDigi will divert buyers away from that primary market. ReDigi incredibly argues that Capitol is preempted from making a market-based argument because Capitol itself condones downloading of its works on iTunes. [...] Of course, Capitol, as copyright owner, does not forfeit its right to claim copyright infringement merely because it permits certain uses of its works. This argument, too, is therefore unavailing.

61   In sum, ReDigi facilitates and profits from the sale of copyrighted commercial recordings, transferred in their entirety, with a likely detrimental impact on the primary market for these goods. Accordingly, the Court concludes that the fair use defense does not permit ReDigi's users to upload and download files to and from the Cloud Locker incident to sale.

62   ## 2. First Sale

63   The first sale defense, a common law principle recognized in *Bobbs–Merrill Co. v. Straus,* 210 U.S. 339, 350, 28 S.Ct. 722, 52 L.Ed. 1086 (1908) and now codified at Section 109(a) of the Copyright Act, provides that:

64   Notwithstanding the provisions of section 106(3), the owner of a particular copy or phonorecord lawfully made under this title, or any person authorized by such owner, is entitled, without the authority of the copyright owner, to sell or otherwise dispose of the possession of that copy or phonorecord.

65   17 U.S.C. 109. Under the first sale defense, once the copyright owner places a copyrighted item [here, a phonorecord] in the stream of commerce by selling it, he has exhausted his exclusive statutory right to control its distribution. *[...]*

66   ReDigi asserts that its service, which involves the resale of digital music files lawfully purchased on iTunes, is protected by the first sale defense. *[...]* The Court disagrees.

67   As an initial matter, it should be noted that the fair use defense is, by its own terms, limited to assertions of the *distribution right.* 17 U.S.C. 109 (referencing Section 106(3)) *[...]* Because the Court has concluded that ReDigi's service violates Capitol's reproduction right, the first sale defense does not apply to ReDigi's infringement of those rights. *[...]*

68   In addition, the first sale doctrine does not protect ReDigi's distribution of Capitol's copyrighted works. This is because, as an unlawful reproduction, a digital music file sold on ReDigi is not lawfully made under this title. 17 U.S.C. 109(a). Moreover, the statute protects only distribution by the owner of a *particular* copy or phonorecord ... of *that* copy or phonorecord. *Id.* Here, a ReDigi user owns the phonorecord that was created when she purchased and downloaded a song from iTunes to her hard disk. But to sell that song on ReDigi, she must produce a new phonorecord on the ReDigi server. Because it is therefore impossible for the user to sell her particular phonorecord on ReDigi, the first sale statute cannot provide a defense. Put another way, the first sale defense is limited to material items, like records, that the copyright owner put into the stream of commerce. Here, ReDigi is not distributing such material items; rather, it is distributing *reproductions* of the copyrighted code embedded in new material objects, namely, the ReDigi server in Arizona and its users' hard drives. The first sale defense does not cover this any more than it covered the sale of cassette recordings of vinyl records in a bygone era.

69   Rejecting such a conclusion, ReDigi argues that, because technological change has rendered its literal terms ambiguous, the Copyright Act must be construed in light of [its] basic purpose, namely, to incentivize creative work for the ultimate[ ] ... cause of promoting broad public availability of literature, music, and the other arts. *[...]* Thus, ReDigi asserts that refusal to apply the first sale doctrine to its service would grant Capitol a Court sanctioned extension of rights under the [C]opyright [A]ct ... which is against policy, and should not be endorsed by this Court. *[...]*

70   The Court disagrees. ReDigi effectively requests that the Court amend the statute to achieve ReDigi's broader policy goalsgoals that happen to advance ReDigi's economic interests. However, ReDigi's argument fails for two reasons. First, while technological change may have rendered Section 109(a) unsatisfactory to many contemporary observers and consumers, it has not rendered it ambiguous. The statute plainly applies to the lawful owner's particular phonorecord, a phonorecord that by definition cannot be uploaded and sold on ReDigi's website. Second, amendment of the Copyright Act in line with ReDigi's proposal is a legislative prerogative that courts are unauthorized and ill suited to attempt.

71   Nor are the policy arguments as straightforward or uncontested as ReDigi suggests. Indeed, when confronting this precise subject in its report on the Digital Millenium Copyright Act, 17 U.S.C. 512, the United States Copyright Office (the USCO) rejected extension of the first *[...]* sale doctrine to the distribution of digital works, noting that the justifications for the first sale doctrine in the physical world could not be imported into the digital domain. *[...]* For instance, the USCO stated that the impact of the [first sale] doctrine on copyright owners [is] limited in the off-line world by a number of factors, including geography and the gradual degradation of books and analog works. DMCA Report at xi. Specifically,

72   [p]hysical copies of works degrade with time and use, making used copies less desirable than new ones. Digital information does not degrade, and can be reproduced perfectly on a recipient's computer. The used copy is just as desirable as (in fact, is indistinguishable from) a new copy of the same work. Time, space, effort and cost no longer act as barriers to the movement of copies, since digital copies can be transmitted nearly instantaneously anywhere in the world with minimal effort and negligible cost. The need to transport physical copies of works, which acts as a natural brake on the effect of resales on the copyright owner's market, no longer exists in the realm of digital transmissions. The ability of such used copies to compete for market share with new copies is thus far greater in the digital world.

73   *[...]* Thus, while ReDigi mounts attractive policy arguments, they are not as one-sided as it contends.

74   Finally, ReDigi feebly argues that the Court's reading of Section 109(a) would in effect exclude digital works from the meaning of the statute. *[...]* That is not the case. Section 109(a) still protects a lawful owner's sale of her particular phonorecord, be it a computer hard disk, iPod, or other memory device onto which the file was originally downloaded. While this limitation clearly presents obstacles to resale that are different from, and perhaps even more onerous than, those involved in the resale of CDs and cassettes, the limitation is hardly absurdthe first sale doctrine was enacted in a world where the ease and speed of data transfer could not have been imagined. There are many reasons, some discussed herein, for why such physical limitations may be desirable. It is left to Congress, and not this Court, to

deem them outmoded.

75   Accordingly, the Court concludes that the first sale defense does not permit sales of digital music files on ReDigi's website.

76   [...]

88   **IV. Conclusion**

95   At base, ReDigi seeks judicial amendment of the Copyright Act to reach its desired policy outcome. However, [s]ound policy, as well as history, supports [the Court's] consistent deference to Congress when major technological innovations alter the market for copyrighted materials. Congress has the constitutional authority and the institutional ability to accommodate fully the varied permutations of competing interests that are inevitably implicated by such new technology. *[...]* Such defence often counsels for a limited interpretation of copyright protection. However, here, the Court cannot of its own accord condone the wholesale application of the first sale defense to the digital sphere, particularly when Congress itself has declined to take that step. Accordingly, and for the reasons stated above, the Court GRANTS Capitol's motion for summary judgment on its claims for ReDigi's direct, [...] contributory, and vicarious infringement of its distribution and reproduction rights. The Court also DENIES ReDigi's motion in its entirety.

96   [...]

98   SO ORDERED.

99   [...]

101   [3] On June 11, 2012, ReDigi launched ReDigi 2.0, new software that, when installed on a user's computer, purportedly directs the user's new iTunes purchases to upload from iTunes directly to the Cloud Locker. [...] Accordingly, while access may transfer from user to user upon resale, the file is never moved from its initial location in the Cloud Locker. [...] However, because ReDigi 2.0 launched after Capitol filed the Complaint and more days before the close of discovery, the Court will not consider it in this action. [...]

104   [6] Capitol argues that ReDigi also violated its distribution rights simply by making Capitol's recordings available for sale to the public, regardless of whether a sale occurred. (*See* Cap. Mem. 11 n. 8 (citing *Hotaling v. Church of Jesus Christ of LatterDay Saints,* 118 F.3d 199, 201 (4th Cir.1997))). However, a number of courts, including one in this district, have cast significant doubt on this make available theory of distribution. *[...]* In any event, because the Court concludes that actual sales on ReDigi's website infringed Capitol's distribution right, it does not reach this additional theory of liability.

105   [7] ReDigi's argument is, perhaps, a relic of the argument it previously levied that copying to the Cloud Locker is protected as space shifting under the fair use doctrine. [...]

Class 16: 6.6 <u>OIL Casebook: Copyright Secondary Liability I</u>

(For Villanova Students:

Supplemental: read Pinterest article on Blackboard)

Religious Technology Center v. Netcom On-line Communication Services, Inc.

September 01, 2014 by mrisch

This is a foundational case in secondary liability

1   907 F.Supp. 1361 (1995)

2   ## RELIGIOUS TECHNOLOGY CENTER [...]
        v.
        ## NETCOM ON-LINE COMMUNICATION SERVICES, INC. [...]

4   United States District Court, N.D. California.

5   November 21, 1995.

6   [...]

10   ## ORDER DENYING DEFENDANT NETCOM'S MOTION FOR SUMMARY JUDGMENT; DENYING DEFENDANT KLEMESRUD'S MOTION FOR JUDGMENT ON THE PLEADINGS; AND DENYING PLAINTIFFS' MOTION FOR PRELIMINARY INJUNCTION AGAINST NETCOM AND KLEMESRUD

11   **WHYTE, District Judge.**

12   This case concerns an issue of first impression regarding intellectual property rights in cyberspace.[1] Specifically, this order addresses whether the operator of a computer bulletin board service ("BBS"), and the large Internet[2] access provider that allows that BBS to reach the Internet, should be liable for copyright infringement committed by a subscriber of the BBS.

13   Plaintiffs Religious Technology Center ("RTC") and Bridge Publications, Inc. ("BPI") hold copyrights in the unpublished and published works of L. Ron Hubbard, the late founder of the Church of Scientology ("the Church"). Defendant Dennis Erlich ("Erlich")[3] is a former minister of Scientology turned vocal critic of the Church, whose pulpit is now the Usenet newsgroup[4] alt.religion.scientology ("a.r.s."), an on-line forum for discussion and criticism of Scientology. Plaintiffs maintain that Erlich infringed their copyrights when he posted portions of their [...] works on a.r.s. Erlich gained his access to the Internet through defendant Thomas Klemesrud's ("Klemesrud's") BBS "support.com." Klemesrud is the operator of the BBS, which is run out of his home and has approximately 500 paying users. Klemesrud's BBS is not directly linked to the Internet, but gains its connection through the facilities of defendant Netcom On-Line Communications, Inc. ("Netcom"), one of the largest providers of Internet access in the United States.

14   After failing to convince Erlich to stop his postings, plaintiffs contacted defendants Klemesrud and Netcom. Klemesrud responded to plaintiffs' demands that Erlich be kept off his system by asking plaintiffs to prove that they owned the copyrights to the works posted by Erlich. However, plaintiffs refused Klemesrud's request as unreasonable. Netcom similarly refused plaintiffs' request that Erlich not be allowed to gain access to the Internet through its system. Netcom contended that it would be impossible to prescreen Erlich's postings and that to kick Erlich off the Internet meant kicking off the hundreds of users of Klemesrud's BBS. Consequently, plaintiffs named Klemesrud and Netcom in their suit against Erlich, although only on the copyright infringement claims.[...]

16   **I. NETCOM'S MOTION FOR SUMMARY JUDGMENT OF NONINFRINGEMENT**

17   [...]

18   Because the court is looking beyond the pleadings in examining this motion, it will be treated as a motion for summary judgment rather than a motion to dismiss. [...] Summary judgment is proper when "the pleadings, depositions, answers to interrogatories, and admissions on file, together with the affidavits, if any, show that there is no genuine issue as to any material fact and that the moving party is entitled to judgment as a matter of law." [...] There is a "genuine" issue of material fact only when there is sufficient evidence such that a reasonable juror could find for the party opposing the motion. [...]

19   **B. Copyright Infringement**

20   To establish a claim of copyright infringement, a plaintiff must demonstrate (1) ownership of a valid copyright and (2) "copying"[7] [...] of protectable expression by the defendant. [...] Infringement occurs when a defendant violates one of the exclusive rights of the copyright holder. 17 U.S.C. § 501(a). These rights include the right to reproduce the copyrighted work, the right to prepare derivative works, the right to distribute copies to the public, and the right to publicly display the work. 17 U.S.C. §§ 106(1)-(3) & (5). The court has already determined that plaintiffs have established that they own the copyrights to all of the Exhibit A and B works, [...] The court also found plaintiffs likely to succeed on their claim that defendant Erlich copied the Exhibit A and B works and was not entitled to a fair use defense. Plaintiffs argue that, although Netcom was not itself the source of any of the infringing materials on its system, it nonetheless should be liable for infringement, either directly, contributorily, or vicariously.[9] Netcom disputes these theories of infringement and further argues that it is entitled to its own fair use defense.

21   **1. Direct Infringement**

22   Infringement consists of the unauthorized exercise of one of the exclusive rights of the copyright holder delineated in section 106. 17 U.S.C. § 501. Direct infringement does not require intent or any particular state of mind,[10] although willfulness is relevant to the award of statutory damages. 17 U.S.C. § 504(c).

23   Many of the facts pertaining to this motion are undisputed. The court will address the relevant facts to determine whether a theory of direct infringement can be supported based on Netcom's alleged reproduction of plaintiffs' works. [...] The court will additionally examine whether Netcom is liable for infringing plaintiffs' exclusive rights to publicly distribute and display their works.

24   **a.** *Undisputed Facts*

25   The parties do not dispute the basic processes that occur when Erlich posts his allegedly infringing messages to a.r.s. Erlich connects to Klemesrud's BBS using a telephone and a modem. Erlich then transmits his messages to Klemesrud's computer, where they are automatically briefly stored. According to a prearranged pattern established by Netcom's software, Erlich's initial act of posting a message to the Usenet results in the automatic copying of Erlich's message from Klemesrud's computer onto Netcom's computer and onto other computers on the Usenet. In order to ease transmission and for the convenience of Usenet users, Usenet servers maintain postings from newsgroups for a short period of time — eleven days for Netcom's system and three days for Klemesrud's system. Once on Netcom's computers, messages are available to Netcom's customers and Usenet neighbors, who may then download the messages to their [...] own computers. Netcom's local server makes available its postings to a group of Usenet servers, which do the same for other servers until all Usenet sites worldwide have obtained access to the postings, which takes a matter of hours. [...]

26   Unlike some other large on-line service providers, such as CompuServe, America Online, and Prodigy, Netcom does not create or control the content of the information available to its subscribers. It also does not monitor messages as they are posted. It has, however, suspended the accounts of subscribers who violated its terms and conditions, such as where they had commercial software in their posted files. Netcom admits that, although not currently configured to do this, it may be possible to reprogram its system to screen postings containing particular words or coming from particular individuals. Netcom, however, took no action after it was told by plaintiffs

that Erlich had posted messages through Netcom's system that violated plaintiffs' copyrights, instead claiming that it could not shut out Erlich without shutting out all of the users of Klemesrud's BBS.

27   **b.** *Creation of Fixed Copies*

28   The Ninth Circuit addressed the question of what constitutes infringement in the context of storage of digital information in a computer's random access memory ("RAM"). *MAI Systems Corp. v. Peak Computer, Inc.* *[...]* In *MAI,* the Ninth Circuit upheld a finding of copyright infringement where a repair person, who was not authorized to use the computer owner's licensed operating system software, turned on the computer, thus loading the operating system into RAM for long enough to check an "error log." *[...]* Copyright protection subsists in original works of authorship "*fixed* in any tangible medium of expression, now known or later developed, from which they can be perceived, reproduced, or otherwise communicated, either directly or with the aid of a machine or device." *[...]* A work is "fixed" when its "embodiment in a copy … is sufficiently permanent or stable to permit it to be perceived, reproduced, or otherwise communicated for a period of more than transitory duration." *Id.* § 101. *MAI* established that the loading of data from a storage device into RAM constitutes copying because that data stays in RAM long enough for it to be perceived. *MAI Systems* *[...]*

29   In the present case, there is no question after *MAI* that "copies" were created, as Erlich's act of sending a message to a.r.s. caused reproductions of portions of plaintiffs' works on both Klemesrud's and Netcom's storage devices. Even though the messages remained on their systems for at most eleven days, they were sufficiently "fixed" to constitute recognizable copies under the Copyright Act. *[...]*

30   **c.** *Is Netcom Directly Liable for Making the Copies?*

31   Accepting that copies were made, Netcom argues that Erlich, and not Netcom, is directly liable for the copying. *MAI* did not address the question raised in this case: whether possessors of computers are liable for incidental copies automatically made on their computers using their software as part of a process initiated by a third party. Netcom correctly distinguishes *MAI* on the ground that Netcom did not take any affirmative action that directly resulted in copying plaintiffs' works other than by installing and maintaining a system whereby software automatically forwards messages received from subscribers onto the Usenet, and temporarily stores copies on its system. Netcom's actions, to the extent that they created a copy of plaintiffs' works, were necessary to having a working system for transmitting Usenet postings to and from the Internet. Unlike the defendants in *MAI,* neither Netcom nor Klemesrud initiated the copying. The defendants in *MAI* turned on their customers' computers thereby creating temporary copies of the operating system, whereas Netcom's and Klemesrud's systems can operate without any human intervention. Thus, unlike *MAI,* the mere fact that Netcom's system incidentally makes temporary copies *[...]* of plaintiffs' works does not mean Netcom has caused the copying.[11] The court believes that Netcom's act of designing or implementing a system that automatically and uniformly creates temporary copies of all data sent through it is not unlike that of the owner of a copying machine who lets the public make copies with it.[12] Although some of the people using the machine may directly infringe copyrights, courts analyze the machine owner's liability under the rubric of contributory infringement, not direct infringement. *[...]* Plaintiffs' theory would create many separate acts of infringement and, carried to its natural extreme, would lead to unreasonable liability. It is not difficult to conclude that Erlich infringes by copying a protected work onto his computer and by posting a message to a newsgroup. However, plaintiffs' theory further implicates a Usenet server that carries Erlich's message to other servers regardless of whether that server acts without any human intervention beyond the initial setting up of the system. It would also result in liability for every single Usenet server in the worldwide link of computers transmitting Erlich's message to every other computer. These parties, who are liable under plaintiffs' theory, do no more *[...]* than operate or implement a system that is essential if Usenet messages are to be widely distributed. There is no need to construe the Act to make all of these parties infringers. Although copyright is a strict liability statute, there should still be some element of volition or causation which is lacking where a defendant's system is merely used to create a copy by a third party.

32   Plaintiffs point out that the infringing copies resided for eleven days on Netcom's computer and were sent out from it onto the "Information Superhighway." However, under plaintiffs' theory, any storage of a copy that occurs in the process of sending a message to the Usenet is an infringement. While it is possible that less "damage" would have been done if Netcom had heeded plaintiffs' warnings and acted to prevent Erlich's message from being forwarded,[13] this is not relevant to its *direct* liability for copying. The same argument is

true of Klemesrud and any Usenet server. Whether a defendant makes a direct copy that constitutes infringement cannot depend on whether it received a warning to delete the message. *[...]* This distinction may be relevant to contributory infringement, however, where knowledge is an element. *[...]*

33   The court will now consider two district court opinions that have addressed the liability of BBS operators for infringing files uploaded by subscribers.

34   **d.** *Playboy Case*

35   *Playboy Enterprises, Inc. v. Frena* involved a suit against the operator of a small BBS whose system contained files of erotic pictures. *[...]* A subscriber of the defendant's BBS had uploaded files containing digitized pictures copied from the plaintiff's copyrighted magazine, which files remained on the BBS for other subscribers to download. *Id.* The court did not conclude, as plaintiffs suggest in this case, that the BBS is itself liable for the unauthorized *reproduction* of plaintiffs' work; instead, the court concluded that the BBS operator was liable for violating the plaintiff's right to publicly *distribute and display* copies of its work. *[...]*

36   In support of their argument that Netcom is directly liable for copying plaintiffs' works, plaintiffs cite to the court's conclusion that "[t]here is no dispute that [the BBS operator] supplied a product containing unauthorized copies of a copyrighted work. It does not matter that [the BBS operator] claims he did not make the copies [him]self." *[...]* It is clear from the context of this discussion[14] that the *Playboy* court was looking only at the exclusive right to distribute copies to the public, where liability exists regardless of whether the defendant makes copies. Here, however, plaintiffs do not argue that Netcom is liable for its public distribution of copies. Instead, they claim that Netcom is liable because its computers in fact made copies. Therefore, the above-quoted language has no bearing on the issue of direct liability for unauthorized reproductions. Notwithstanding *Playboy*'s holding that a BBS operator may be directly liable for *distributing or displaying* to the public copies of protected works,[15] this court holds *[...]* that the storage on a defendant's system of infringing copies and retransmission to other servers is not a direct infringement by the BBS operator of the exclusive right to *reproduce* the work where such copies are uploaded by an infringing user. *Playboy* does not hold otherwise.[16]

37   **e.** *Sega Case*

38   A court in this district addressed the issue of whether a BBS operator is liable for copyright infringement where it solicited subscribers to upload files containing copyrighted materials to the BBS that were available for others to download. *Sega Enterprises Ltd. v. MAPHIA, [...]* The defendant's "MAPHIA" BBS contained copies of plaintiff Sega's video game programs that were uploaded by users. *[...]* The court found that copies were made by unknown users of the BBS when files were uploaded and downloaded. *[...]* Further, the court found that the defendant's knowledge of the infringing activities, encouragement, direction and provision of the facilities through his operation of the BBS constituted contributory infringement, even though the defendant did not know exactly when files were uploaded or downloaded. *[...]*

39   This court is not convinced that *Sega* provides support for a finding of direct infringement where copies are made on a defendant's BBS by users who upload files. Although there is some language in *Sega* regarding *direct* infringement, it is entirely conclusory:

40   *[...]*. Sega has established that unauthorized copies of its games *are made* when such games are uploaded to the MAPHIA bulletin board, here with the knowledge of Defendant Scherman. *[...]*

41   The court's reference to the "knowledge of Defendant" indicates that the court was focusing on contributory infringement, as knowledge is not an element of direct infringement. Perhaps, *Sega*'s references to direct infringement and that "copies ... are made" are to the direct liability of the "unknown users," as there can be no contributory infringement by a defendant without direct infringement by another. *[...]* Thus, the court finds that neither *Playboy* nor *Sega* requires finding Netcom liable for direct infringement of plaintiffs' exclusive right to

reproduce their works.[17]

42   **f.** *Public Distribution and Display?*

43   Plaintiffs allege that Netcom is directly liable for making *copies* of their works. [...] They also allege that Netcom violated their exclusive rights to publicly display copies of their works. [....] There are no allegations that Netcom violated plaintiffs' exclusive right to publicly distribute their works. However, in their discussion of direct infringement, plaintiffs insist that Netcom is liable for "maintain[ing] copies of [Erlich's] messages on its server for eleven days for access by its subscribers and `USENET neighbors'" and they compare this case to the *Playboy* case, which discussed [...] the right of public distribution. [....] Because this could be an attempt to argue that Netcom has infringed plaintiffs' rights of public distribution and display, the court will address these arguments.

44   *Playboy* concluded that the defendant infringed the plaintiff's exclusive rights to publicly distribute and display copies of its works. [...] The court is not entirely convinced that the mere possession of a digital copy on a BBS that is accessible to some members of the public constitutes direct infringement by the BBS operator. Such a holding suffers from the same problem of causation as the reproduction argument. Only the subscriber should be liable for causing the distribution of plaintiffs' work, as the contributing actions of the BBS provider are automatic and indiscriminate. Erlich could have posted his messages through countless access providers and the outcome would be the same: anyone with access to Usenet newsgroups would be able to read his messages. There is no logical reason to draw a line around Netcom and Klemesrud and say that they are uniquely responsible for distributing Erlich's messages. Netcom is not even the first link in the chain of distribution — Erlich had no direct relationship with Netcom but dealt solely with Klemesrud's BBS, which used Netcom to gain its Internet access. Every Usenet server has a role in the distribution, so plaintiffs' argument would create unreasonable liability. Where the BBS merely stores and passes along all messages sent by its subscribers and others, the BBS should not be seen as causing these works to be publicly distributed or displayed. *Does this analysis survive Aereo?*

45   Even accepting the *Playboy* court's holding, the case is factually distinguishable. Unlike the BBS in that case, Netcom does not maintain an archive of files for its users. Thus, it cannot be said to be "suppl[ying] a product." In contrast to some of its larger competitors, Netcom does not create or control the content of the information available to its subscribers; it merely provides *access* to the Internet, whose content is controlled by no single entity. Although the Internet consists of many different computers networked together, some of which may contain infringing files, it does not make sense to hold the operator of each computer liable as an infringer merely because his or her computer is linked to a computer with an infringing file. It would be especially inappropriate to hold liable a service that acts more like a conduit, in other words, one that does not itself keep an archive of files for more than a short duration. Finding such a service liable would involve an unreasonably broad construction of public distribution and display rights. No purpose would be served by holding liable those who have no ability to control the information to which their subscribers have access, even though they might be in some sense helping to achieve the Internet's automatic "public distribution" and the users' "public" display of files.

46   **g.** *Conclusion*

47   The court is not persuaded by plaintiffs' argument that Netcom is directly liable for the copies that are made and stored on its computer. Where the infringing subscriber is clearly directly liable for the same act, it does not make sense to adopt a rule that could lead to the liability of countless parties whose role in the infringement is nothing more than setting up and operating a system that is necessary for the functioning of the Internet. Such a result is unnecessary as there is already a party directly liable for causing the copies to be made. Plaintiffs occasionally claim that they only seek to hold liable a party that refuses to delete infringing files after they have been warned. However, such liability cannot be based on a theory of direct infringement, where knowledge is irrelevant. The court does not find workable a theory of infringement that would hold the entire Internet liable for activities that cannot reasonably be deterred. Billions of bits of data flow through the Internet and are necessarily stored on servers throughout the network and it is thus practically impossible [... to screen out infringing bits from noninfringing bits. Because the court cannot see any meaningful distinction (without regard to knowledge) between what Netcom did and what every other Usenet server does, the court finds that Netcom cannot be held liable for direct infringement. [...]

48   ## 2. Contributory Infringement

49   Netcom is not free from liability just because it did not directly infringe plaintiffs' works; it may still be liable as a contributory infringer. Although there is no statutory rule of liability for infringement committed by others,

50   > [t]he absence of such express language in the copyright statute does not preclude the imposition of liability for copyright infringement on certain parties who have not themselves engaged in the infringing activity. For vicarious liability is imposed in virtually all areas of the law, and the concept of contributory infringement is merely a species of the broader problem of identifying the circumstances in which it is just to hold one individual accountable for the actions of another.

51   *Sony Corp. v. Universal City Studios, Inc.,* 4[...] Liability for participation in the infringement will be established where the defendant, "with knowledge of the infringing activity, induces, causes or materially contributes to the infringing conduct of another." [...]

52   **a. *Knowledge of Infringing Activity***

53   Plaintiffs insist that Netcom knew that Erlich was infringing their copyrights at least after receiving notice from plaintiffs' counsel indicating that Erlich had posted copies of their works onto a.r.s. through Netcom's system. Despite this knowledge, Netcom continued to allow Erlich to post messages to a.r.s. and left the allegedly infringing messages on its system so that Netcom's subscribers and other Usenet servers could access them. Netcom argues that it did not possess the necessary type of knowledge because (1) it did not know of Erlich's planned infringing activities when it agreed to lease its facilities to Klemesrud, (2) it did not know that Erlich would infringe prior to any of his postings, (3) it is unable to screen out infringing postings before they are made, and (4) its knowledge of the infringing nature of Erlich's postings was too equivocal given the difficulty in assessing whether the registrations were valid and whether Erlich's use was fair. The court will address these arguments in turn.

54   Netcom cites cases holding that there is no contributory infringement by the lessors of premises that are later used for infringement unless the lessor had knowledge of the intended use at the time of the signing of the lease. [...] The contribution to the infringement by the defendant in *Deutsch* was merely to lease use of the premises to the infringer. Here, Netcom not only leases space but also serves as an access provider, which includes the storage and transmission of information necessary to facilitate [...] Erlich's postings to a.r.s. Unlike a landlord, Netcom retains some control over the use of its system. [...] Thus, the relevant time frame for knowledge is not when Netcom entered into an agreement with Klemesrud. It should be when Netcom provided its services to allow Erlich to infringe plaintiffs' copyrights. [...] It is undisputed that Netcom did not know that Erlich was infringing before it received notice from plaintiffs. Netcom points out that the alleged instances of infringement occurring on Netcom's system all happened prior to December 29, 1994, the date on which Netcom first received notice of plaintiffs' infringement claim against Erlich. [...] Thus, there is no question of fact as to whether Netcom knew or should have known of Erlich's infringing activities that occurred more than 11 days before receipt of the December 28, 1994 letter.

55   However, the evidence reveals a question of fact as to whether Netcom knew or should have known that Erlich had infringed plaintiffs' copyrights following receipt of plaintiffs' letter. Because Netcom was arguably participating in Erlich's public distribution of plaintiffs' works, there is a genuine issue as to whether Netcom knew of any infringement by Erlich before it was too late to do anything about it. If plaintiffs can prove the knowledge element, Netcom will be liable for contributory infringement since its failure to simply cancel Erlich's infringing message and thereby stop an infringing copy from being distributed worldwide constitutes substantial participation in Erlich's public distribution of the message. [...]

56   Netcom argues that its knowledge after receiving notice of Erlich's alleged infringing activities was too equivocal given the difficulty in assessing whether registrations are valid and whether use is fair. Although a mere unsupported allegation of infringement by a copyright owner may not automatically put a defendant on notice of infringing activity, Netcom's position that liability must be unequivocal is unsupportable. While perhaps the typical infringing activities of BBSs will involve copying software, where BBS operators are better equipped to judge infringement, the fact that this involves written works should not distinguish it. Where works contain copyright notices

within them, as here, it is difficult to argue that a defendant did not know that the works were copyrighted. To require proof of valid registrations would be impractical and would perhaps take too long to verify, making it impossible for a copyright holder to protect his or her works in some cases, as works are automatically deleted less than two weeks after they are posted. The court is more persuaded by the argument that it is beyond the ability of a BBS operator to quickly and fairly determine when a use is not infringement where there is at least a colorable claim of fair use. Where a BBS operator cannot reasonably verify a claim of infringement, either because of a possible fair use defense, the lack of copyright notices on the copies, or the copyright holder's failure to provide the necessary documentation to show that there is a likely infringement, the operator's lack of knowledge will be found reasonable and there will be no liability for contributory infringement for allowing the continued distribution of the works on its system.

57   Since Netcom was given notice of an infringement claim before Erlich had completed his infringing activity, there may be a question of fact as to whether Netcom knew or should have known that such activities were infringing. Given the context of a dispute between a former minister and a church he is criticizing, Netcom may be able to show that its lack of knowledge that Erlich was infringing was reasonable. However, Netcom admits that it did not even look at the postings once given notice and that had it looked at the copyright notice and statements [...] regarding authorship, it would have triggered an investigation into whether there was infringement. [...] These facts are sufficient to raise a question as to Netcom's knowledge once it received a letter from plaintiffs on December 29, 1994. [21]

58   **b.** *Substantial Participation*

59   Where a defendant has knowledge of the primary infringer's infringing activities, it will be liable if it "induces, causes or materially contributes to the infringing conduct of" the primary infringer. *[...]* Such participation must be substantial. *[...]*

60   Providing a service that allows for the automatic distribution of all Usenet postings, infringing and noninfringing, goes well beyond renting a premises to an infringer. *See Fonovisa, Inc. v. Cherry Auction, Inc.,* 847 F.Supp. 1492, 1496 (E.D.Cal.1994) (finding that renting space at swap meet to known bootleggers not "substantial participation" in the infringers' activities). It is more akin to the radio stations that were found liable for rebroadcasting an infringing broadcast. *[...]* Netcom allows Erlich's infringing messages to remain on its system and be further distributed to other Usenet servers worldwide. It does not completely relinquish control over how its system is used, unlike a landlord. Thus, it is fair, assuming Netcom is able to take simple measures to prevent further damage to plaintiffs' copyrighted works, to hold Netcom liable for contributory infringement where Netcom has knowledge of Erlich's infringing postings yet continues to aid in the accomplishment of Erlich's purpose of publicly distributing the postings. Accordingly, plaintiffs do raise a genuine issue of material fact as to their theory of contributory infringement as to the postings made after Netcom was on notice of plaintiffs' infringement claim.

61   ## 3. Vicarious Liability

62   Even if plaintiffs cannot prove that Netcom is contributorily liable for its participation in the infringing activity, it may still seek to prove vicarious infringement based on Netcom's relationship to Erlich. A defendant is liable for vicarious liability for the actions of a primary infringer where the defendant (1) has the right and ability to control the infringer's acts and (2) receives a direct financial benefit from the infringement. *[...]* Unlike contributory infringement, knowledge is not an element of vicarious liability. *[...]*

63   **a.** *Right and Ability To Control*

64   The first element of vicarious liability will be met if plaintiffs can show that Netcom has the right and ability to supervise the conduct of its subscribers. Netcom argues that it does not have the right to control its users' postings before they occur. Plaintiffs dispute this and argue that Netcom's terms and conditions, to which its subscribers[22] must agree, specify that Netcom reserves the right to take remedial action against subscribers. *[...]* Plaintiffs argue that under "netiquette," the informal rules and customs that have developed on the Internet, violation of copyrights by a user is unacceptable and the access provider has a duty take measures to prevent this; where the immediate service [...] provider fails, the next service provider up the transmission stream must act. *[...]* Further evidence of Netcom's right to restrict infringing activity is its prohibition of copyright infringement and its requirement that its subscribers indemnify it for any damage to third parties. *[...]* Plaintiffs have thus raised a question of fact as to Netcom's right to control Erlich's use of its services.

65   Netcom argues that it could not possibly screen messages before they are posted given the speed and volume of the data that goes through its system. Netcom further argues that it has never exercised control over the content of its users' postings. Plaintiffs' expert opines otherwise, stating that with an easy software modification Netcom could identify postings that contain particular words or come from particular individuals. [...] Plaintiffs further dispute Netcom's claim that it could not limit Erlich's access to Usenet without kicking off all 500 subscribers of Klemesrud's BBS. As evidence that Netcom has in fact exercised its ability to police its users' conduct, plaintiffs cite evidence that Netcom has acted to suspend subscribers' accounts on over one thousand occasions. [...] Further evidence shows that Netcom can delete specific postings. [...] Whether such sanctions occurred before or after the abusive conduct is not material to whether Netcom can exercise control. The court thus finds that plaintiffs have raised a genuine issue of fact as to whether Netcom has the right and ability to exercise control over the activities of its subscribers, and of Erlich in particular.

66   **b.** *Direct Financial Benefit*

67   Plaintiffs must further prove that Netcom receives a direct financial benefit from the infringing activities of its users. For example, a landlord who has the right and ability to supervise the tenant's activities is vicariously liable for the infringements of the tenant where the rental amount is proportional to the proceeds of the tenant's sales. [...] However, where a defendant rents space or services on a fixed rental fee that does not depend on the nature of the activity of the lessee, courts usually find no vicarious liability because there is no direct financial benefit from the infringement. [...]

68   [...] Plaintiffs cannot provide any evidence of a direct financial benefit received by Netcom from Erlich's infringing postings. Unlike *Shapiro, Bernstein*, and like *Fonovisa*, Netcom receives a fixed fee. There is no evidence that infringement by Erlich, or any other user of Netcom's services, in any way enhances the value of Netcom's services to subscribers or attracts new subscribers. Plaintiffs argue, however, that Netcom somehow derives a benefit from its purported "policy of refusing to take enforcement actions against its subscribers and others who transmit infringing messages over its computer networks." [...] Plaintiffs point to Netcom's advertisements that, compared to competitors like CompuServe and America Online, Netcom provides easy, regulation-free Internet access. Plaintiffs assert that Netcom's policy attracts copyright infringers to its system, resulting in a direct financial benefit. The court is not convinced that such an argument, if true, would constitute a direct financial benefit to Netcom from *Erlich's* infringing activities. [...]

69   Because plaintiffs have failed to raise a question of fact on this vital element, their claim of vicarious liability fails. [...]

71   ## 4. First Amendment Argument

72   Netcom argues that plaintiffs' theory of liability contravenes the first amendment, as it would chill the use of the Internet because every access provider or user would be subject to liability when a user posts an infringing work to a Usenet newsgroup. While the court agrees that an overbroad *injunction* might implicate the First Amendment, [...] imposing *liability* for infringement where it is otherwise appropriate does not necessarily raise a First Amendment issue. The copyright concepts of the idea/expression dichotomy and the fair use defense balance the important First Amendment rights with the constitutional authority for "promot[ing] the progress of science and useful arts," [...] Netcom argues that liability here would force Usenet servers to perform the impossible — screening all the information that comes through their systems. However, the court is not convinced that Usenet servers are directly liable for causing a copy to be made, and absent evidence of knowledge and participation or control and direct profit, they will not be contributorily or vicariously liable. If Usenet servers were responsible for screening all messages coming through their systems, this could have a serious chilling effect on what some say may turn out to be the best public forum for free speech yet [...] devised. [...] Finally, Netcom admits that its First Amendment argument is merely a consideration in the fair use argument, which the court will now address. [...]

73   ## 5. Fair Use Defense

74   Assuming plaintiffs can prove a violation of one of the exclusive rights guaranteed in section 106, there is no infringement if the

defendant's use is fair under section 108. The proper focus here is on whether Netcom's actions qualify as fair use, not on whether Erlich himself engaged in fair use; the court has already found that Erlich was not likely entitled to his own fair use defense, as his postings contained large portions of plaintiffs' published and unpublished works quoted verbatim with little added commentary.

75   [...]

88   Netcom argues that there is no evidence that making accessible plaintiffs' works, which consist of religious scriptures and policy letters, will harm the market for these works by preventing someone from participating in the Scientology religion because they can view the works on the Internet instead. Further, Netcom notes that the relevant question is whether the postings fulfill the demand of an individual who seeks to follow the religion's teachings, and not whether they suppress the desire of an individual who is affected by the criticism posted by Erlich. Netcom argues that the court must focus on the "normal market" for the copyrighted work, which in this case is through a Scientology-based organization. Plaintiffs respond that the Internet's extremely widespread distribution — where more than 25 million people worldwide have access — multiplies the effects of market substitution. In support of its motion for a preliminary injunction against Erlich, plaintiffs submitted declarations regarding the potential effect of making the Church's secret scriptures available over the Internet. Plaintiffs point out that, although the Church currently faces no competition, groups in the past have used stolen copies of the Church's scriptures in charging for Scientology-like religious training. *[...]* This evidence raises a genuine issue as to the possibility that Erlich's postings, made available over the Internet by Netcom, could hurt the market for plaintiffs' works.

88   **e.** *Equitable Balancing*

89   In balancing the various factors, the court finds that there is a question of fact as to whether there is a valid fair use defense. Netcom has not justified its copying plaintiffs' works to the extent necessary to establish entitlement to summary judgment in light of evidence that it knew that Erlich's use was infringing and had the ability to prevent its further distribution. While copying all or most of a work will often preclude fair use, courts have recognized the fair use defense where the purpose of the use is beneficial to society, complete copying is necessary given the type of use, the purpose of the use is completely different than the purpose of the original, and there is no evidence that the use will significantly harm the market for the original. This case is distinguishable from those cases recognizing fair use *[...]* despite total copying. In *Sony,* the home viewers' use was not commercial and the viewers were allowed to watch the entire shows for free. In *Sega v. Accolade,* the complete copying was necessitated to access the unprotectable idea in the original. Here, plaintiffs never gave either Erlich or Netcom permission to view or copy their works. Netcom's use has some commercial aspects. Further, Netcom's copying is not for the purpose of getting to the unprotected idea behind plaintiffs' works. Although plaintiffs may ultimately lose on their infringement claims if, among other things, they cannot prove that posting their copyrighted works will harm the market for these works, [fair use presents a factual question on which plaintiffs have at least raised a genuine issue of fact. Accordingly, the court does not find that Netcom's use was fair as a matter of law.

90   # C. Conclusion

91   The court finds that plaintiffs have raised a genuine issue of fact regarding whether Netcom should have known that Erlich was infringing their copyrights after receiving a letter from plaintiffs, whether Netcom substantially participated in the infringement, and whether Netcom has a valid fair use defense. Accordingly, Netcom is not entitled to summary judgment on plaintiffs' claim of contributory copyright infringement. However, plaintiffs' claims of direct and vicarious infringement fail.

92   [...]

129   [7] In this context, "copying" is "shorthand for the infringing of any of the copyright owner's five exclusive rights." *[...]*

131   [9] Plaintiffs have argued at times during this litigation that Netcom should only be required to respond after being given notice, which is only relevant to contributory infringement. Nevertheless, the court will address all three theories of infringement liability.

132   [...]

134   [12] Netcom compares itself to a common carrier that merely acts as a passive conduit for information. In a sense, a Usenet server that forwards all messages acts like a common carrier, passively retransmitting every message that gets sent through it. Netcom would seem no more liable than the phone company for carrying an infringing facsimile transmission or storing an infringing audio recording on its voice mail. As Netcom's counsel argued, holding such a server liable would be like holding the owner of the highway, or at least the operator of a toll booth, liable for the criminal activities that occur on its roads. Since other similar carriers of information are not liable for infringement, there is some basis for exempting Internet access providers from liability for infringement by their users. The IITF Report concluded that "[i]f an entity provided only the wires and conduits — such as the telephone company, it would have a good argument for an exemption if it was truly in the same position as a common carrier and could not control who or what was on its system." IITF Report at 122. Here, perhaps, the analogy is not completely appropriate as Netcom does more than just "provide the wire and conduits." Further, Internet providers are not natural monopolies that are bound to carry all the traffic that one wishes to pass through them, as with the usual common carrier. [...] However, the carrier must not have any direct or indirect control over the content or selection of the primary transmission. [...] In any event, common carriers are granted statutory exemptions for liability that might otherwise exist. Here, Netcom does not fall under this statutory exemption, and thus faces the usual strict liability scheme that exists for copyright. Whether a new exemption should be carved out for online service providers is to be resolved by Congress, not the courts. [...]

137   [15] Given the ambiguity in plaintiffs' reference to a violation of the right to "publish" and to *Playboy,* it is possible that plaintiffs are also claiming that Netcom infringed their exclusive right to publicly distribute their works. The court will address this argument *infra.*

138   [16] The court further notes that *Playboy* has been much criticized. [...] The finding of direct infringement was perhaps influenced by the fact that there was some evidence that defendants in fact knew of the infringing nature of the works, which were digitized photographs labeled "Playboy" and "Playmate."

139   [17] To the extent that *Sega* holds that BBS operators are directly liable for copyright infringement when users upload infringing works to their systems, this court respectfully disagrees with the court's holding for the reasons discussed above. Further, such a holding was dicta, as there was evidence that the defendant knew of the infringing uploads by users and, in fact, actively encouraged such activity, thus supporting the contributory infringement theory. [...]

144   [22] In this case, Netcom is even further removed from Erlich's activities. Erlich was in a contractual relationship only with Klemesrud. Netcom thus dealt directly only with Klemesrud. However, it is not crucial that Erlich does not obtain access directly through Netcom. The issue is Netcom's right and ability to control the use of its system, which it can do indirectly by controlling Klemesrud's use.

145   [...]

Digital Millenium Copyright Act: 17 U.S. Code § 512 - Limitations on liability relating to material online

September 02, 2014 by mrisch

1   **(a) Transitory Digital Network Communications.—** A service provider shall not be liable for monetary relief, or, except as provided in subsection (j), for injunctive or other equitable relief, for infringement of copyright by reason of the provider's transmitting, routing, or providing connections for, material through a system or network controlled or operated by or for the service provider, or by reason of the intermediate and transient storage of that material in the course of such transmitting, routing, or providing connections, if—

> **(1)** the transmission of the material was initiated by or at the direction of a person other than the service provider;

> **(2)** the transmission, routing, provision of connections, or storage is carried out through an automatic technical process without selection of the material by the service provider;

> **(3)** the service provider does not select the recipients of the material except as an automatic response to the request of another person;

> **(4)** no copy of the material made by the service provider in the course of such intermediate or transient storage is maintained on the system or network in a manner ordinarily accessible to anyone other than anticipated recipients, and no such copy is maintained on the system or network in a manner ordinarily accessible to such anticipated recipients for a longer period than is reasonably necessary for the transmission, routing, or provision of connections; and

> **(5)** the material is transmitted through the system or network without modification of its content.

2   **(b) System Caching.—**

> **(1) Limitation on liability.—** A service provider shall not be liable for monetary relief, or, except as provided in subsection (j), for injunctive or other equitable relief, for infringement of copyright by reason of the intermediate and temporary storage of material on a system or network controlled or operated by or for the service provider in a case in which—

> > **(A)** the material is made available online by a person other than the service provider;

> > **(B)** the material is transmitted from the person described in subparagraph (A) through the system or network to a person other than the person described in subparagraph (A) at the direction of that other person; and

> > **(C)** the storage is carried out through an automatic technical process for the purpose of making the material available to users of the system or network who, after the material is transmitted as described in subparagraph (B), request access to the material from the person described in subparagraph (A),

> if the conditions set forth in paragraph (2) are met.

> > [...]

3   **(c) Information Residing on Systems or Networks At Direction of Users.—**

(1) In general.— A service provider shall not be liable for monetary relief, or, except as provided in subsection (j), for injunctive or other equitable relief, for infringement of copyright by reason of the storage at the direction of a user of material that resides on a system or network controlled or operated by or for the service provider, if the service provider—

(A)

(i) does not have actual knowledge that the material or an activity using the material on the system or network is infringing;

(ii) in the absence of such actual knowledge, is not aware of facts or circumstances from which infringing activity is apparent; or

(iii) upon obtaining such knowledge or awareness, acts expeditiously to remove, or disable access to, the material;

(B) does not receive a financial benefit directly attributable to the infringing activity, in a case in which the service provider has the right and ability to control such activity; and

(C) upon notification of claimed infringement as described in paragraph (3), responds expeditiously to remove, or disable access to, the material that is claimed to be infringing or to be the subject of infringing activity.

(2) Designated agent.— The limitations on liability established in this subsection apply to a service provider only if the service provider has designated an agent to receive notifications of claimed infringement described in paragraph (3), by making available through its service, including on its website in a location accessible to the public, and by providing to the Copyright Office, substantially the following information:

(A) the name, address, phone number, and electronic mail address of the agent.

(B) other contact information which the Register of Copyrights may deem appropriate.

The Register of Copyrights shall maintain a current directory of agents available to the public for inspection, including through the Internet, and may require payment of a fee by service providers to cover the costs of maintaining the directory.

(3) Elements of notification.—

(A) To be effective under this subsection, a notification of claimed infringement must be a written communication provided to the designated agent of a service provider that includes substantially the following:

(i) A physical or electronic signature of a person authorized to act on behalf of the owner of an exclusive right that is allegedly infringed.

(ii) Identification of the copyrighted work claimed to have been infringed, or, if multiple copyrighted works at a single online site are covered by a single notification, a representative list of such works at that site.

(iii) Identification of the material that is claimed to be infringing or to be the subject of infringing activity and that is to be removed or access to which is to be disabled, and information reasonably sufficient to permit the service provider to locate the material.

(iv) Information reasonably sufficient to permit the service provider to contact the complaining party, such as an address, telephone number, and, if available, an electronic mail address at which the complaining party may be contacted.

(v) A statement that the complaining party has a good faith belief that use of the material in the manner complained of is not authorized by the copyright owner, its agent, or the law.

(vi) A statement that the information in the notification is accurate, and under penalty of perjury, that the complaining party is authorized to act on behalf of the owner of an exclusive right that is allegedly infringed.

(B)

(i) Subject to clause (ii), a notification from a copyright owner or from a person authorized to act on behalf of the copyright owner that fails to comply substantially with the provisions of subparagraph (A) shall not be considered under paragraph (1)(A) in determining whether a service provider has actual knowledge or is aware of facts or circumstances from which infringing activity is apparent.

(ii) In a case in which the notification that is provided to the service provider's designated agent fails to comply substantially with all the provisions of subparagraph (A) but substantially complies with clauses (ii), (iii), and (iv) of subparagraph (A), clause (i) of this subparagraph applies only if the service provider promptly attempts to contact the person making the notification or takes other reasonable steps to assist in the receipt of notification that substantially complies with all the provisions of subparagraph (A).

4 **(d) Information Location Tools.—** A service provider shall not be liable for monetary relief, or, except as provided in subsection (j), for injunctive or other equitable relief, for infringement of copyright by reason of the provider referring or linking users to an online location containing infringing material or infringing activity, by using information location tools, including a directory, index, reference, pointer, or hypertext link, if the service provider—

(1)

(A) does not have actual knowledge that the material or activity is infringing;

(B) in the absence of such actual knowledge, is not aware of facts or circumstances from which infringing activity is apparent; or

(C) upon obtaining such knowledge or awareness, acts expeditiously to remove, or disable access to, the material;

(2) does not receive a financial benefit directly attributable to the infringing activity, in a case in which the service provider has the right and ability to control such activity; and

(3) upon notification of claimed infringement as described in subsection (c)(3), responds expeditiously to remove, or disable access to, the material that is claimed to be infringing or to be the subject of infringing activity, except that, for purposes of this paragraph, the information described in subsection (c)(3)(A)(iii) shall be identification of the reference or link, to material or activity claimed to be infringing, that is to be removed or access to which is to be disabled, and information reasonably sufficient to permit the service provider to locate that reference or link.

5 [...]

6 **(f) Misrepresentations.—** Any person who knowingly materially misrepresents under this section—

(1) that material or activity is infringing, or

(2) that material or activity was removed or disabled by mistake or misidentification,

shall be liable for any damages, including costs and attorneys' fees, incurred by the alleged infringer, by any copyright owner or copyright owner's authorized licensee, or by a service provider, who is injured by such misrepresentation, as the result of the service provider relying upon such misrepresentation in removing or disabling access to the material or activity claimed to be infringing, or in replacing the removed material or ceasing to disable access to it.

7 **(g) Replacement of Removed or Disabled Material and Limitation on Other Liability.—**

(1) No liability for taking down generally.— Subject to paragraph (2), a service provider shall not be liable to any person for any claim based on the service provider's good faith disabling of access to, or removal of, material or activity claimed to be infringing or based on facts or circumstances from which infringing activity is apparent, regardless of whether the material or activity is ultimately determined to be infringing.

[...]

8

9   **(i) Conditions for Eligibility.—**

(1) Accommodation of technology.— The limitations on liability established by this section shall apply to a service provider only if the service provider—

(A) has adopted and reasonably implemented, and informs subscribers and account holders of the service provider's system or network of, a policy that provides for the termination in appropriate circumstances of subscribers and account holders of the service provider's system or network who are repeat infringers; and

(B) accommodates and does not interfere with standard technical measures.

[...]

10

11   **(k) Definitions.—**

    (1) Service provider.—

    (A) As used in subsection (a), the term "service provider" means an entity offering the transmission, routing, or providing of connections for digital online communications, between or among points specified by a user, of material of the user's choosing, without modification to the content of the material as sent or received.

    (B) As used in this section, other than subsection (a), the term "service provider" means a provider of online services or network access, or the operator of facilities therefor, and includes an entity described in subparagraph (A).

    [...]

12   **(l) Other Defenses Not Affected.—** The failure of a service provider's conduct to qualify for limitation of liability under this section shall not bear adversely upon the consideration of a defense by the service provider that the service provider's conduct is not infringing under this title or any other defense.

13   [...]

14   **(n) Construction.—** Subsections (a), (b), (c), and (d) describe separate and distinct functions for purposes of applying this section. Whether a service provider qualifies for the limitation on liability in any one of those subsections shall be based solely on the criteria in that subsection, and shall not affect a determination of whether that service provider qualifies for the limitations on liability under any other such subsection.

Ellison v. Robertson

September 02, 2014 by mrisch

This case applies Section 512 to a system similar to that at issue in Netcom. How does the DMCA change the analysis?

1	357 F.3d 1072 (2004)

2	**Harlan ELLISON, Plaintiff-Appellant,**

v.

Stephen ROBERTSON [...] and
America Online Inc., a Corporation, Defendant-Appellee.

3	[...]

4	United States Court of Appeals, Ninth Circuit.

5	[...]
Filed February 10, 2004.

6	[...]

13	Before PREGERSON, THOMAS, Circuit Judges, and OBERDORFER,[1] Senior District Judge.

14	**PREGERSON, Circuit Judge:**

15	Harlan Ellison appeals the district court's summary judgment dismissal of his copyright infringement action against America Online, Inc. (AOL). The copyright infringement action arose when, without Ellison's authorization, Stephen Robertson posted copies of some of Ellison's copyrighted short stories on a peer-to-peer file sharing network, the USENET.[2] Because AOL provides its subscribers access to the USENET news-group[3] at issue, Ellison brought claims for vicarious and contributory copyright infringement against AOL. AOL moved for summary judgment. It asserted defenses to Ellison's infringement claims and alternatively argued that it qualified for one of the four safe harbor limitations of liability under Title II of the Digital Millennium Copyright Act (DMCA).[4] The district court concluded that AOL was not liable for vicarious infringement. Although the court found there to be triable issues of material fact concerning Ellison's contributory infringement claim, it nonetheless granted summary judgment because it held that AOL qualified for the DMCA safe harbor limitation of liability under 17 U.S.C. § 512(a).

16	We hold that the district court erred in granting AOL's motion for summary judgment. We affirm the district court's holdings as to vicarious and contributory infringement, but we reverse the district court's application of the safe harbor limitation from liability. There are triable issues of material fact concerning whether AOL meets the threshold requirements, set forth in § 512(i), to assert the safe harbor limitations of liability of §§ 512(a-d). If after remand a jury finds AOL to be eligible under § 512(i) to assert the safe harbor limitations of §§ 512(a-d), the parties need not relitigate whether AOL qualifies for the limitation of liability provided by § 512(a); the district court's resolution of that issue at the summary judgment stage is sound. We affirm in part, reverse in part, and remand.

17 **Facts and Procedural Background**

18   Harlan Ellison is the author of numerous science fiction novels and short stories, [...] and he owns valid copyrights to those works. In the spring of 2000, Stephen Robertson electronically scanned and copied a number of Ellison's fictional works to convert them to digital files. Robertson subsequently uploaded the files onto the USENET news-group "alt.binaries.e-book." Robertson accessed the Internet through his local Internet service provider, Tehama County Online, and his USENET service was provided by RemarQ Communities, Inc. The USENET news-group at issue in this case was used primarily to exchange unauthorized digital copies of works by famous authors, including Ellison.

19   After Robertson made the infringing copies of Ellison's works accessible to the news-group, the works were forwarded and copied throughout the USENET to servers all over the world, including those belonging to AOL. As a result, AOL's subscribers had access to the news-group containing the infringing copies of Ellison's works. At the time Robertson posted the infringing copies of Ellison's works, AOL's policy was to store and retain files attached to USENET postings on the company's servers for fourteen days.

20   On or about April 13, 2000, Ellison learned of the infringing activity and contacted legal counsel. On April 17, 2000, in compliance with the notification procedures the DMCA requires, Ellison's counsel sent an e-mail message to agents of Tehama County Online and AOL to notify the service providers of the infringing activity. Ellison received an acknowledgment of receipt from Tehama County Online but received nothing from AOL, which claims never to have received the e-mail.

21   On April 24, 2000, Ellison filed an action against AOL and others in the United States District Court for the Central District of California. Upon receipt of Ellison's complaint, AOL blocked its subscribers' access to the news-group at issue. AOL thereafter moved for summary judgment, arguing that the undisputed facts did not prove Ellison's copyright infringement claims. AOL alternatively asserted the safe harbor limitations to liability under Title II of the DMCA. [...]

22 **Discussion**

23   [...]

25 **II. The Law of Copyright Infringement and the DMCA**

26   Ellison alleges that AOL infringed his copyrighted works. As a threshold question, a plaintiff who claims copyright infringement must show: (1) ownership of a valid copyright; and (2) that the defendant violated the copyright owner's exclusive rights under the Copyright Act. 17 U.S.C. § 501(a) [...] We recognize three doctrines of copyright liability: direct copyright infringement, contributory copyright infringement, and vicarious copyright infringement. To prove a claim of direct copyright infringement, a plaintiff must show that he owns the copyright and that the defendant himself violated one or more of the plaintiff's exclusive rights under the Copyright Act.[...] "One who, with knowledge of the infringing activity, induces, causes or materially contributes to the infringing conduct *of another* may be liable as a `contributory' [copyright] infringer." [...] We have interpreted the knowledge requirement for contributory copyright infringement to include both those with *actual knowledge* and those who *have reason to know* of direct infringement. [...] A defendant is vicariously liable for copyright infringement if he enjoys a direct financial benefit from *another's* infringing activity and "has the right and ability to supervise" the infringing activity. [...]

27   Congress enacted the DMCA in 1998 to comply with international copyright treaties and to update domestic copyright law for the online world. [...] Difficult and controversial questions of copyright liability in the online world prompted Congress to enact Title II of the DMCA, the Online Copyright Infringement Liability Limitation Act (OCILLA). 17 U.S.C. § 512 (2003). OCILLA endeavors to facilitate cooperation among Internet service providers and copyright owners "to detect and deal with copyright infringements that take place in the digital networked environment." [...] Congress hoped to provide "greater certainty to service providers concerning their legal exposure for infringements that may occur in the course of their activities." [...]

28   But "[r]ather than embarking on a wholesale clarification of" the various doctrines of copyright liability, Congress opted "to leave current law in its evolving state and, instead, to create a series of `safe harbors,' for certain common activities of service providers." [...] Under OCILLA's four safe harbors, service providers may limit their liability for claims of copyright infringement. 17 U.S.C. § 512(a-d). These safe [...] harbors provide protection from liability for: (1) transitory digital network communications;[6] (2) system caching;[7] (3) information residing on systems or networks at the direction of users;[8] and (4) information location tools.[9] Far short of adopting enhanced or wholly new standards to evaluate claims of copyright infringement against online service providers, Congress provided that OCILLA's "limitations of liability apply if the provider is found to be liable *under existing principles of law*." [...]

29   We thus agree with the district court that "[t]he DMCA did not simply rewrite copyright law for the on-line world." [...] Congress would have done so if it so desired. Claims against service providers for direct, contributory, or vicarious copyright infringement, therefore, are generally evaluated just as they would be in the non-online world.

30   ## III. Ellison's Claims Against AOL

31   ## A. Contributory Copyright Infringement

32   Ellison alleged in his complaint that AOL was contributorily liable for copyright infringement. To substantiate his claim, he must show that AOL knew or had reason to know of the infringing activity taking place on its USENET servers and that AOL materially contributed to the infringing activity.

33   ### 1. Knowledge

34   We first consider whether AOL knew or had reason to know of the infringing activity. The district court found that AOL did not have actual knowledge of the infringement before Ellison filed his copyright infringement action, but concluded that "a reasonable trier of fact could certainly find that AOL had reason to know that infringing copies of Ellison's works were stored on their Usenet servers." [...] We agree.

35   AOL changed its contact e-mail address from "copyright@aol.com" to "aolcopyright@aol.com" in the fall of 1999, but waited until April 2000 to register the change with the U.S. Copyright Office. Moreover, AOL failed to configure the old e-mail address so that it would either forward messages to the new address or return new messages to their senders. In the meantime, complaints such as Ellison's went unheeded, and complainants were not notified that their messages had not been delivered. Furthermore, there is evidence in the record suggesting that a phone call from AOL subscriber John J. Miller to AOL should have put AOL on notice of the infringing activity on the particular USENET group at issue in this case, "alt.binaries.e-book." Miller contacted AOL to report the existence of unauthorized copies of works by various authors. Because there is evidence indicating that AOL changed its e-mail address in an unreasonable manner and that AOL should have been on notice of infringing activity we conclude that a reasonable trier of fact could find that AOL had reason to know of potentially infringing activity occurring within its USENET network.

36   ### 2. Material Contribution

37   The second element a plaintiff must prove to succeed on a claim of contributory copyright infringement is that the defendant materially contributed to another's infringement. [...] The district court found that Ellison demonstrated a triable issue regarding [...] whether AOL materially contributed to the copyright infringement:

38   T [...]

39   In *Netcom,* the copyright holders of certain works of L. Ron Hubbard sued the operator of a news-group and a large Internet service provider, Netcom, for copyright infringement. The *Netcom* court held that the fact that the USENET service allowed Netcom's subscribers access to copyrighted works was sufficient to raise a triable issue regarding material contribution. [...] We conclude that this reasoning

applies to Ellison's claim of contributory copyright infringement. Because a reasonable trier of fact could conclude that AOL materially contributed to the copyright infringement by storing infringing copies of Ellison's works on its USENET groups and providing the groups' users with access to those copies, we agree with the district court's finding that this constituted a triable issue.

40   **B. Vicarious Copyright Infringement**

41   [...]

46   We recognize, of course, that there is usually substantial overlap between aspects of goods or services that customers value and aspects of goods or services that ultimately draw the customers. There are, however, cases in which customers value a service that does not "act as a draw." Accordingly, Congress cautions courts that "receiving a one-time set-up fee and flat periodic payments for service ... [ordinarily] would not constitute receiving a `financial benefit directly attributable to the infringing activity.'" [...] But "where the value of the service lies in providing access to infringing material," courts might find such "one-time set-up and flat periodic" fees to constitute a direct financial benefit. [...] Thus, the central question of the "direct financial benefit" inquiry in this case is whether the infringing activity constitutes a draw for subscribers, not just an added benefit.

47   The record lacks evidence that AOL attracted or retained subscriptions because of the infringement or lost subscriptions because of AOL's eventual obstruction of the infringement. Accordingly, no jury could reasonably conclude that AOL received a direct financial benefit from providing access to the infringing material. Therefore, Ellison's claim of vicarious copyright infringement fails.[11]

48   **[...] IV. AOL and the Safe Harbors from Liability Under the DMCA**

49   **A. Threshold Eligibility Under § 512(i) for OCILLA's Safe Harbors**

50   To be eligible for any of the four safe harbor limitations of liability, a service provider must meet the conditions for eligibility set forth in OCILLA. 17 U.S.C. § 512(i). The safe harbor limitations of liability only apply to a service provider that:

51   (A) has adopted and reasonably implemented, and informs subscribers and account holders of the service provider's system or network of, a policy that provides for the termination in appropriate circumstances of subscribers and account holders of the service provider's system or network who are repeat infringers; and

(B) accommodates and does not interfere with standard technical measures.[12]

52   17 U.S.C. § 512(i)(1). If a service provider does not meet these threshold requirements, it is not entitled to invoke OCILLA's safe harbor limitations on liability. 17 U.S.C. § 512(i)(1).

53   We hold that the district court erred in concluding on summary judgment that AOL satisfied the requirements of § 512(i). There is at least a triable issue of material fact regarding AOL's eligibility for the safe harbor limitations of liability in this case. Section 512(i)(1)(A) requires service providers to: (1) adopt a policy that provides for the termination of service access for repeat copyright infringers in appropriate circumstances; (2) implement that policy in a reasonable manner; and (3) inform its subscribers of the policy. It is difficult to conclude as a matter of law, as the district court did, that AOL had "reasonably implemented" a policy against repeat infringers. There is ample evidence in the record that suggests that AOL did not have an effective notification procedure in place at the time the alleged infringing activities were taking place. Although AOL did notify the Copyright Office of its correct e-mail address before Ellison's attorney attempted to contact AOL and did post its correct e-mail address on the AOL website with a brief summary of its policy as to repeat infringers, AOL also: (1) changed the e-mail address to which infringement notifications were supposed to have been sent; and (2) failed to provide for forwarding of messages sent to the old address or notification that the e-mail address was inactive. [...] AOL should have closed the old e-mail account or forwarded the e-mails sent to the old account to the new one. Instead, AOL allowed notices of potential copyright infringement to fall into a vacuum and to go unheeded; that fact is sufficient for a reasonable jury to conclude that AOL had not reasonably implemented its policy against repeat infringers.

54 ## B. AOL and the Limitation of Liability Under § 512(a)

55 If after remand a jury finds AOL eligible under § 512(i) to assert OCILLA's safe harbor limitations of liability, the court need not revisit whether AOL qualifies for the limitation of liability provided by § 512(a).

56 The first safe harbor in OCILLA pertains to "transitory digital network communications." [...] 17 U.S.C. § 512(a). Under this section, a service provider would not be liable for copyright infringement:

57 by reason of the provider's transmitting, routing, or providing connections for, material through a system or network controlled or operated by or for the service provider, or by reason of the intermediate and transient storage of that material in the course of such transmitting, routing, or providing connections, if —

(1) the transmission of the material was initiated by or at the direction of a person other than the service provider;

(2) the transmission, routing, provision of connections, or storage is carried out through an automatic technical process without selection of the material by the service provider;

(3) the service provider does not select the recipients of the material except as an automatic response to the request of another person;

(4) no copy of the material made by the service provider in the course of such intermediate or transient storage is maintained on the system or network in a manner ordinarily accessible to anyone other than anticipated recipients, and no such copy is maintained on the system or network in a manner ordinarily accessible to such anticipated recipients for a longer period than is reasonably necessary for the transmission, routing, or provision of connections; and

(5) the material is transmitted through the system or network without modification of its content.

58 *Id.* The definition of "service provider" for the purposes of the § 512(a) safe harbor limitation of liability is "an entity offering the transmission, routing, or providing of connections for digital online communications, between or among points specified by a user, of material of the user's choosing, without modification to the content of the material as sent or received." 17 U.S.C. § 512(k)(1)(A).

59 Whether AOL functioned as a conduit service provider in this case presents pure questions of law: was the fourteen day period during which AOL stored and retained the infringing material "transient" and "intermediate" within the meaning of § 512(a)?; was "no ... copy ... maintained on the system or network ... for a longer period than is reasonably necessary for the transmission, routing, or provision of connections?" The district court appropriately answered these questions in the affirmative. In doing so, the court relied upon on the legislative history indicating that Congress intended the relevant language of § 512(a) to codify the result of *Netcom,* 907 F.Supp. at 1361 (provider that stored Usenet messages for 11 days not liable for direct infringement merely for "installing and maintaining a system whereby software automatically forwards messages received from subscribers onto the Usenet, and temporarily stores copies on its system"), and to extend it to claims for secondary liability. We affirm the district court's ruling that AOL is eligible for the safe harbor limitation of liability of § 512(a). [...]

60 # Conclusion

61 We conclude that the district court correctly identified triable issues of fact with respect to Ellison's claim against AOL for contributory copyright infringement. We also agree with the district court that Ellison's claim for vicarious copyright infringement fails; Ellison did not offer sufficient evidence that AOL received a direct [1082] financial benefit from the infringement to survive summary judgment. Further, because we conclude that the district court failed to discern triable issues of fact concerning AOL's threshold eligibility under § 512(i) for the DMCA's safe harbor limitations of liability, we reverse the district court's judgment on this matter. If a jury determines that AOL is eligible for the DMCA's safe harbor limitations of liability under § 512(i), the parties do not need to relitigate whether AOL satisfies the requirements of § 512(a) in this case; we agree with the district court that it does.

62   In sum, we AFFIRM in part and REVERSE in part the district court's summary judgment in favor of AOL. We REMAND for trial on Ellison's claim of contributory copyright liability, and, if necessary, on AOL's eligibility under § 512(i) to assert the DMCA's safe harbor limitations of liability. Each party to bear its own costs.

63   AFFIRMED in part, REVERSED in part, and REMANDED.

64   [...]

65   [2] USENET is an abbreviation of "user network." This term refers to an international collection of organizations and individuals (known as "peers") whose computers connect to one another and exchange messages posted by USENET users. *[...]*

Ellison v. Robertson - district court

September 07, 2014 by mrisch

This district court case examines the usenet posting discussed in the appellate case

1   189 F.Supp.2d 1051 (2002)

2   **Harlan ELLISON**[...]

                                                       v.

                                          Stephen ROBERTSON[...]

3

6   **ORDER GRANTING DEFENDANT AOL'S MOTION FOR SUMMARY JUDGMENT**

7   **COOPER, District Judge.**

8   [...]

    B. DMCA Limitations on Liability

78   AOL claims to qualify for two of the DMCA's "safe-harbor" provisions, subsection (a), Transitory digital network communications, and subsection (c), Information residing on systems or networks at direction of users. *See* 17 U.S.C. § 512(a), (c). These safe harbors do not confer absolute immunity upon ISPs, but do drastically limit their potential liability based on specific functions they perform (e.g. user-directed information storage). *See generally* 17 U.S.C. § 512. [...]

    2. Section 512's limitations on liability (a) through (d)

96   Section 512(n) explicitly provides that each of the four limitation-on-liability safe [1067] harbors found in subsections (a) through (d) "describe separate and distinct functions for purposes of applying this section." *Id.* As a result, "[w]hether a service provider qualifies for the limitation of liability in any one of the subsections shall be based solely on the criteria in that subsection, and shall not affect a determination of whether the service provider qualifies for the limitations on liability under any other such subsection." *Id.* The DMCA's legislative history provides the following instructional example:

97   Section 512's limitations on liability are based on functions, and each limitation is intended to describe a separate and distinct function. Consider, for example, a service provider that provides a hyperlink to a site containing infringing material which it then caches on its system in order to facilitate access to it by its users. This service provider is engaging in at least three functions that may be subject to the limitation on liability: transitory digital network communications under subsection (a), system caching under subsection (b), and information locating tools under subsection (d).

98   H.R. Rep. 105-551(II), at p. 65 (July 22, 1998). In this example, if the service provider met the threshold requirements of subsection (i), "then for its acts of system caching it is eligible for that limitation on liability with corresponding narrow injunctive relief. But if the same company is committing an infringement by using information locating tools to link its users to infringing material, then its fulfillment of the requirements to claim the system caching liability limitation does not affect whether it qualifies for the liability limitation for information

location tools." 3 NIMMER ON COPYRIGHT § 12B.06[A], at 12B-53, 54.

99   Although AOL performs many Internet-service-provider-related functions, Plaintiff's claims against AOL are based solely on its storage of USENET messages on its servers and provision of access to those USENET messages to AOL users and others accessing the AOL system from outside.

100   AOL claims that it is eligible under both subsections (a) and (c) for a limitation on liability regarding Plaintiff's claims against it.

101   *3. Subsection (a)'s limitation on liability*

102   AOL contends that it meets all the criteria for the limitation-on-liability safe harbor found in subsection (a), which provides:

103   (a) Transitory digital network communications.—A service provider shall not be liable for monetary relief, or, except as provided in subsection (j), for injunctive or other equitable relief, for the infringement of copyright by reason of the provider's transmitting, routing, or providing connections for, material through a system or network controlled or operated by or for the service provider, or by reason of the intermediate and transient storage of that material in the course of transmitting, routing, or providing connections, if -

            (1) the transmission of the material was initiated by or at the direction of a person other than the service provider;

            (2) the transmission, routing, provision of connections, or storage is carried out through an automatic technical process without selection of the material by the service provider;

            (3) the service provider does not select the recipients of the material except as an automatic response to the request of another person;

            (4) no copy of the material made by the service provider in the course of such intermediate or transient storage is maintained on the system or network in a manner ordinarily accessible to anyone [1068] other than anticipated recipients, and no such copy is maintained on the system or network in a manner ordinarily accessible to such anticipated recipients for a longer period than is reasonably necessary for the transmission, routing, or provision of connections; and

            (5) the material is transmitted through the system without modification of its content.

104   Subsection (a) does not require ISPs to remove or block access to infringing materials upon receiving notification of infringement, as is the case with subsections (c) and (d).

105   On the other hand, the term "service provider" is defined more restrictively for subsection (a) than it is throughout the rest of section 512. *See* 17 U.S.C. § 512(k). "As used in subsection (a), the term `service provider' means an entity offering the transmission, routing, or providing of connections for digital online communication, between or among points specified by a user, of material of the user's choosing, without modification to the content of the material as sent or received."[16] *Id.* In effect, this definition merely restates a number of the requirements that are already set forth in subsection (a). Therefore, Plaintiff's contention that AOL does not meet the restrictive definition of a "service provider" as subsection (k) defines that term for subsection (a) does not need to be addressed separately from Plaintiff's arguments that AOL cannot satisfy the requirements of subsection (a). The Court addresses each of those requirements in turn.

106   Plaintiff argues that AOL's USENET servers do not engage in "intermediate and transient storage" of USENET messages such as the one posted by Robertson. Instead, AOL stores USENET messages containing binary files on its servers for up to fourteen days.[17] AOL, however, claims that the USENET message copies are "intermediate." AOL's role is as an intermediary between the original USENET user who posts a message, such as Robertson, and the recipient USENET users who later choose to view the message.

107   By itself, the term "intermediate and transient storage" is rather ambiguous. And it is unclear from reading the DMCA whether AOL's

636

storage of USENET messages containing binary files on its servers for fourteen days in order to make those messages accessible to AOL users constitutes "intermediate and transient storage." Certain functions such as the provision of e-mail service or Internet connectivity clearly fall under the purview of subsection (a); other functions such as hosting a web site or chatroom fall under the scope of subsection (c). The question presented by this case is which subsection applies to the function performed by AOL when it stores USENET messages in order to provide USENET access to users. Faced with the ambiguous language in the statute itself, the Court looks to the DMCA's legislative history for guidance in interpretation. The only real guidance is provided in the House Judiciary Committee Report. *See* H.R. Rep. 105-551 (May 22, 1998).

108   [...] The Court is mindful that reliance on the Report issued by the House Judiciary Committee, "the body that traditionally vets copyright legislation",[18] is somewhat problematic. The Report's section-by-section analysis was based on an early version of the DMCA which differs in a number of ways from the final version that was eventually enacted by Congress. And the Court recognizes that "even if the language of a given feature [in the earlier version of the bill] does ultimately follow through to the Digital Millennium Copyright Act, the meaning may be different in the context of a law containing vastly more provisions than the [earlier version]." 3 NIMMER ON COPYRIGHT § 12B.01[C], at 12B-19. Nonetheless, the Court believes that the analysis in the House Judiciary Committee Report provides the clearest guidance concerning Congress' intent.

109   At the time the first House Report was issued, the Committee was considering a version of the bill that differs in many ways from the final version that was eventually enacted into law as the DMCA. However, the previous version's language regarding "the intermediate storage and transmission of material" is very similar to the "intermediate and transient storage of that material" language that is found in the final version of the DMCA. Moreover, the portion of subsection (a) in the previous version, having to do with maintaining material on the system, is also extremely similar to the corresponding language found in the enacted version of the DMCA at 512(a)(4).[19] Although other aspects of the bill changed substantially before the final version was enacted into law, the language dealing with the "intermediate storage" did not. Accordingly, the section-by-section analysis found in the First House Report is relevant to interpreting whether AOL's storage of USENET messages in order to provide USENET access to AOL users constitutes (1) "intermediate and transient storage" of (2) copies that are not "maintained on the system or network ... for a longer period than is reasonably necessary for the transmission, routing, or provision of connections." 17 U.S.C. § 512(a), (a)(4).

110   The First House Report answers both of those questions with a resounding yes:

111   The exempted storage and transmissions are those carried out through an automatic technological process that is indiscriminate—i.e., the provider takes no part in the selection of the particular material transmitted—where the copies are retained no longer than necessary for the purpose of carrying out the transmission. This conduct would ordinarily include forwarding of customers' Usenet postings to other Internet sites [...] in accordance with configuration settings that apply to all such postings...

              This exemption codifies the result of *Religious Technology Center v. Netcom On-Line Communication Services, Inc.*, 907 F.Supp. 1361 (N.D.Cal.1995) ("Netcom"), with respect to liability of providers for direct copyright infrigement.[20] See *id.* at 1368-70. In Netcom the court held that a provider is not liable for direct infringement where it takes no `affirmative action that [directly results] in copying ... works other than by installing and maintaining a system whereby software automatically forwards messages received from subscribers ... and temporarily stores copies on its system.' *By referring to temporary storage of copies, Netcom recognizes implicitly that intermediate copies may be retained without liability for only a limited period of time. The requirement in 512(a)(1) that "no copy be maintained on the system or network ... for a longer period than reasonably necessary for the transmission" is drawn from the facts of the Netcom case, and is intended to codify this implicit limitation in the Netcom holding.*

112   H.R. Rep. 105-551(I), at p. 24. (emphasis added).

113   In *Netcom*, infringing USENET postings were stored on Netcom's servers for up to *eleven days*, during which those postings were accessible to Netcom users. *See Netcom*, 907 F.Supp. at 1368. In AOL's case, messages containing binary files, such as the message

posted by Robertson, were stored on AOL's servers for up to *fourteen days*. While "intermediate copies may be retained without liability for only a limited period of time," the three-day difference between AOL's USENET storage and that of Netcom is insufficient to distinguish the two cases.

114   Accordingly, the Court finds that AOL's storage of Robertson's posts on its USENET servers constitutes "intermediate and transient storage" that was not "maintained on the system or network ... for a longer period than is reasonably necessary for the transmission, routing, or provision of connections."

115   While this issue presented the central disagreement regarding AOL's qualifications for subsection(a)'s limitation-onliability safe harbor, the parties also dispute whether AOL satisfies other requirements set forth in subsection (a).

116   [...] *(1) the transmission of the material was initiated by or at the direction of a person other than the service provider*

117   It is clear that the transmission of Robertson's newsgroup message was not initiated by or at the direction of AOL. In fact, Plaintiff does not appear to even dispute this conclusion. (Plaintiff's Separate Statement of Genuine Issues at II(3), 6/4/2001 Motion for summary judgment).

118   *(2) the transmission, routing, provision of connections, or storage is carried out through an automatic technical process without selection of the material by the service provider*

119   Plaintiff claims that AOL selects the material that is transmitted, routed, and stored in its USENET groups. Namely, AOL decides which newsgroups its subscribers may access through its newsgroup service.

120   AOL did not select the individual postings on the alt.binaries.e-book newsgroup, let alone the handful of infringing Robertson posts. 512(a)(2) is concerned with "selection of the material," meaning the allegedly infringing material, not material generally. By focusing on AOL's decision to not carry every single newsgroup conceivably available, Plaintiff is attempting to slip from the specific to the general, despite the fact that subsection (a) is concerned with the specific material giving rise to the Plaintiff's claims against AOL.

121   Even if Plaintiff were right, and AOL's treatment of USENET messages in general was the relevant inquiry, AOL's failure to carry every newsgroup available would not disqualify it from subsection (a)(2). Although this would present a closer call, the Court thinks that an ISP would need to take a greater editorial role than merely choosing not to carry certain newsgroups. Although the legislative history states that "subsection (a)(2) means the editorial function of determining what material to send, or the specific sources of material to place on-line," H.R. Rep. 105-551(II) (July 22, 1998), the better interpretation of (a)(2) is that the ISP would have to choose specific postings, or perhaps block messages sent by users expressing opinions with which the ISP disagrees. If an ISP forfeits its ability to qualify for subsection (a)'s safe harbor by deciding not to carry every USENET newsgroup or web site possible, then the DMCA would have the odd effect of punishing ISPs that choose not to carry, for example, newsgroups devoted to child pornography and prostitution, or web sites devoted to ritual torture.[21] Given the concern Congress has shown in other bills for children's access to obscene materials online, it would be absurd to conclude that Congress intended such a result with regard to the DMCA.

122   *(3) the service provider does not select the recipients of the material except as an automatic response to the request of another person*

123   Plaintiff argues that AOL selects the recipients of the material because it chooses to engage in USENET peering agreements with some entities but not with others. First, as with (a)(2), Plaintiff's argument fails because section 512(a) is concerned with AOL's selection of the recipients of the material in question in this lawsuit, i.e. Robertson's infringing posts. It is clear that AOL did not select certain recipients for that material. Rather, it was accessible to any AOL user through AOL's USENET newsgroup server. Second, and also analogous to (a)(2), the better interpretation is that AOL would have to direct material to certain recipients (e.g. all AOL members whose names start with "G") but not others. If [...] AOL were to lose its ability to qualify for subsection(a)'s safe harbor because it has peer agreements with some entities but not with others, then the DMCA would appear to place an affirmative obligation on AOL to enter into peering

arrangements with every conceivable peering entity in the world. This could not have been what Congress' intent.

124 **(5) the material is transmitted through the system without modification of its content**

125 Plaintiff does not seriously contest that AOL does not modify the content of newsgroup messages stored on its servers and transmitted through its system. Moreover, Plaintiff has presented no evidence that AOL in any way modified the content of Robertson's infringing posts.

126 The Court hereby finds that AOL qualifies for the limitation-on-liability provided under subsection 512(a).[22]

127 [...]

145 [16] By contrast, for the purposes of the rest of section 512, the term `service provider' is defined more broadly as "a provider of online services or network access, or the operator of facilities therefor." 17 U.S.C. § 512(k)(2)

146 [17] Plaintiff has presented evidence suggesting that despite AOL's 14-day storage protocol, certain USENET messages containing binary files might have resided on AOL's servers for up to thirty-one days, but he makes no claim that such was the case with the messages containing infringing copies of his works (nor with any other infringing messages in the alt.binaries.e-book newsgroup). When deciding whether AOL qualifies for subsection (a)'s limitations on liability, the Court considers only the allegedly infringing postings.

147 [...]

150 [20] Any argument that this codification of *Netcom*'s facts regarding intermediate storage was only meant to apply to direct infringement, and not to vicarious or contributory infringement, is forestalled by subsection (2) of the version of the bill then under consideration by the Judiciary Committee. [...]

152 [22] Accordingly, we need not reach the arguments presented by the parties regarding AOL's satisfaction of the requirements of subsection 512(c).

A&M Records, Inc. v. Napster, Inc. - district court

September 07, 2014 by mrisch

Recall that Napster's peer-to-peer file sharing system involved a database managed by Napster that each user could connect to in order to search music and other file names. This excerpt considers a DMCA defense for such a system.

1   54 U.S.P.Q.2d 1746 (2000)

2   **A & M RECORDS, INC.** [...]

           NAPSTER, INC. [...]

3

4   United States District Court, N.D. California.

5   May 12, 2000.

6   **PATEL, Chief J.**

7   [...] Now before this court is defendant's motion for summary adjudication of the applicability of a safe harbor provision of the Digital Millennium Copyright Act ("DMCA"), 17 U.S.C. section 512(a), to its business activities. Defendant argues that the entire Napster system falls within the safe harbor and, hence, that plaintiffs may not obtain monetary damages or injunctive relief, except as narrowly specified by subparagraph 512(j)(1)(B). In the alternative, Napster asks the court to find subsection 512(a) applicable to its role in downloading MP3 music files,[1] as opposed to searching for or indexing such files. Having considered the parties' arguments and for the reasons set forth below, the court enters the following memorandum and order.

8   *[...]*

20   Napster claims that its business activities fall within the safe harbor provided by subsection 512(a). This subsection limits liability "for infringement of copyright by reason of the [service] provider's transmitting, routing, or providing connections for, material through a system or network controlled or operated by or for the service provider, or by reason of the intermediate and transient storage of that material in the course of such transmitting, routing, or providing connections," if five conditions are satisfied:

22   [...]

24   Citing the "definitions" subsection of the statute, Napster argues that it is a "service provider" for the purposes of the 512(a) safe harbor. *See* 17 U.S.C. § 512(k)(1)(A).[4] First, it claims to offer the "transmission, routing, or providing of connections for digital online communications" by enabling the connection of users' hard-drives and the transmission of MP3 files "directly from the Host hard drive and Napster browser through the Internet to the user's Napster browser and hard drive." [...] Second, Napster states that users choose the online communication points and the MP3 files to be transmitted with no direction from Napster. Finally, the Napster system does not modify the content of the transferred files. Defendant contends that, because it meets the definition of "service provider,"[5] it need only satisfy the five remaining requirements of the safe harbor to prevail in its motion for summary adjudication.

25   Defendant then seeks to show compliance with these requirements by arguing: (1) a Napster user, and never Napster itself, initiates the

transmission of MP3 files; (2) the transmission occurs through an automatic, technical process without any editorial input from Napster; (3) Napster does not choose the recipients of the MP3 files; (4) Napster does not make a copy of the material during transmission; and (5) the content of the material is not modified during transmission. Napster maintains that the 512(a) safe harbor thus protects its core function– "transmitting, routing and providing connections for sharing of the files its users choose." $[...]$

29   **I. *Independent Analysis of Functions***

30   Subsection 512(n) of the DMCA states:

31   Subsections (a), (b), (c), and (d) describe separate and distinct functions for purposes of applying this section. Whether a service provider qualifies for the limitation on liability in any one of those subsections shall be based solely on the criteria in that subsection and shall not affect a determination of whether that service provider qualifies for the limitations on liability under any other such subsections.

32   Citing subsection 512(n), plaintiffs argue that the 512(a) safe harbor does not offer blanket protection to Napster's entire system. Plaintiffs consider the focus of the litigation to be Napster's function as an information location tool–eligible for protection, if at all, under the more rigorous subsection 512(d). They contend that the system does not operate as a passive conduit within the meaning subsection 512(a). In this view, Napster's only possible safe harbor is subsection 512(d), which applies to service providers "referring or linking users to an online location containing infringing material or infringing activity, by using information location tools, including a directory, index, reference, pointer, or hypertext link...." Subsection 512(d) imposes more demanding eligibility requirements because it covers active assistance to users.

33   Defendant responds in two ways. First, it argues that subsection 512(a), rather than 512(d), applies because the information location tools it provides are incidental to its core function of automatically transmitting, routing, or providing connections for the MP3 files users select. In the alternative, defendant maintains that, even if the court decides to analyze the information location functions under 512(d), it should hold that the 512(a) safe harbor protects other aspects of the Napster service.

34   Napster undisputedly performs some information location functions. The Napster server stores a transient list of the files that each user currently logged-on to that server wants to share. $[...]$ If a user wants to find a particular song or recording artist, she enters a search, and Napster looks for the search terms in the index. $[...]$

37   Because the parties dispute material issues regarding the operation of Napster's index, directory, and search engine, the court declines to hold that these functions are peripheral to the alleged infringement, or that they should not be analyzed separately under subsection 512(d).[6] Indeed, despite its contention that its search engine and indexing functions are incidental to the provision of connections and transmission of MP3 files, Napster has advertised the ease with which its users can locate "millions of songs" online without "wading through page after page of unknown artists." $[...]$ Such statements by Napster to promote its service are tantamount to an admission that its search and indexing functions are essential to its marketability. Some of these essential functions–including but not limited to the search engine and index–should be analyzed under subsection 512(d).

38   However, the potential applicability of subsection 512(d) does not completely foreclose use of the 512(a) safe harbor as an affirmative defense. *See* 17 U.S.C. § 512(n). The court will now turn to Napster's eligibility for protection under subsection 512(a). It notes at the outset, though, that a ruling that subsection 512(a) applies to a given function would not mean that the DMCA affords the service provider blanket protection.

39   **II. *Subsection 512(a)***

40    $[...]$ As defendant correctly notes, the words "conduit" or "passive conduit" appear nowhere in 512(a), but are found only in the legislative history and summaries of the DMCA. The court must look first to the plain language of the statute, "construing the provisions of the entire law, including its object and policy, to ascertain the intent of Congress." $[...]$ The language of subsection 512(a) makes the safe harbor

applicable, as a threshold matter, to service providers "transmitting, routing or providing connections for, material *through a system or network* controlled or operated by or for the service provider...." 17 U.S.C. § 512(a) (emphasis added). According to plaintiffs, the use of the word "conduit" in the legislative history explains the meaning of "through a system."

41   Napster has expressly denied that the transmission of MP3 files ever passes through its servers. *[...]*. Indeed, Kessler declared that "files reside on the computers of Napster users, and are transmitted directly between those computers." *[...]* MP3 files are transmitted "from the Host user's hard drive and Napster browser, *through the Internet* to the recipient's Napster browser and hard drive." *[...]* The Internet cannot be considered "a system or network controlled or operated by or for the service provider," however. 17 U.S.C. § 512(a). To get around this problem, Napster avers (and plaintiffs seem willing to concede) that "Napster's servers and Napster's MusicShare browsers on its users' computers are all part of Napster's overall system." *[...]*

42   Even assuming that the system includes the browser on each user's computer, the MP3 files are not transmitted "through" the system within the meaning of subsection 512(a). Napster emphasizes the passivity of its role–stating that "[a]ll files transfer directly from the computer of one Napster user *through the Internet* to the computer of the requesting user." *[...]* This means that, even if each user's Napster browser is part of the system, the transmission goes *from* one part of the system to another, or *between* parts of the system, but not "through" the system. The court finds that subsection 512(a) does not protect the transmission of MP3 files.

43   The prefatory language of subsection 512(a) is disjunctive, however. The subsection applies to "infringement of copyright by reason of the provider's transmitting, routing, *or* providing connections through a system or network controlled or operated by or for the service provider." 17 U.S.C. § 512(a) (emphasis added). The court's finding that transmission does not occur "through" the system or network does not foreclose the possibility that subsection 512(a) applies to "routing" or "providing connections." Rather, each of these functions must be analyzed independently.

44   Napster contends that providing connections between users' addresses "constitutes the value of the system to the users and the public." This connection cannot be established without the provision of the host's address to the Napster browser software installed on the requesting user's computer. *[...]* The central Napster server delivers the host's address. *[...]* While plaintiffs contend that the infringing material is not *transmitted* through the Napster system, they provide no evidence to rebut the assertion that Napster supplies the requesting user's computer with information necessary to facilitate a connection with the host.

45   Nevertheless, the court finds that Napster does not provide connections "through" its system. Although the Napster server conveys address information to establish a connection between the requesting and host users, the connection itself occurs through the Internet. The legislative history of section 512 demonstrates that Congress intended the 512(a) safe harbor to apply only to activities "in which a service provider plays the role of a "conduit" for the communications of others." *[...]* Drawing inferences in the light most favorable to the non-moving party, this court cannot say that Napster serves as a conduit for the connection itself, as opposed to the address information that makes the connection possible. Napster enables or facilitates the initiation of connections, but these connections do not pass through the system within the meaning of subsection 512(a).

46   Neither party has adequately briefed the meaning of "routing" in subsection 512(a), nor does the legislative history shed light on this issue. Defendant tries to make "routing" and "providing connections" appear synonymous–stating, for example, that "the central Napster server *routes* the transmission by providing the Host's address to the Napster browser that is installed on and in use by Userl's computer." However, the court doubts that Congress would have used the terms "routing" and "providing connections" disjunctively if they had the same meaning.[7] It is clear from both parties' submissions that the route of the allegedly infringing material goes through the Internet from the host to the requesting user, not through the Napster server. *[...]* The court holds that routing does not occur through the Napster system.

47   Because Napster does not transmit, route, or provide connections through its system, it has failed to demonstrate that it qualifies for the 512(a) safe harbor. The court thus declines to grant summary adjudication in its favor.

48   [...]

60   [4] Subparagraph 512(k)(1)(A) provides:

64   As used in subsection (a), the term "service provider" means an entity offering the transmission, routing, or providing of
            connections for digital online communications, between or among points specified by a user, of material of the user's choosing,
            without modification to the content of the material sent or received.

65   [...]

68   [6] The court need not rule on the applicability of subsection 512(d) to the functions plaintiffs characterize as information location tools
       because defendant does not rely on subsection 512(d) as grounds for its motion for summary adjudication.

69   [...]

Class 17: 6.7 <u>OIL Casebook: Copyright Secondary Liability II</u>

Viacom Intern., Inc. v. YouTube, Inc.

June 25, 2014 by mrisch

1
[...]

676 F.3d 19

VIACOM INTERNATIONAL, INC., [...], Plaintiffs–Appellants,

v.

YOUTUBE, INC., [...]
[...]
Defendants–Appellees.

[...]

United States Court of Appeals, Second Circuit.

Argued: Oct. 18, 2011. Decided: April 5, 2012.

2
[...]

6
Before: CABRANES and LIVINGSTON, Circuit Judges.[...]

7
JOSÉ A. CABRANES, Circuit Judge:

8
This appeal requires us to clarify the contours of the "safe harbor" provision of the Digital Millennium Copyright Act (DMCA) that limits the liability of online service providers for copyright infringement that occurs "by reason of the storage at the direction of a user of material that resides on a system or network controlled or operated by or for the service provider." 17 U.S.C. § 512(c).[...]

9
The plaintiffs-appellants in these related actions—Viacom International, Inc. ("Viacom"), The Football Association Premier League Ltd. ("Premier League"), and various film studios, television networks, music publishers, and sports leagues (jointly [...] —appeal from an August 10, 2010 judgment of the United States District Court for the Southern District of New York (Louis L. Stanton, Judge), which granted summary judgment to defendants-appellees YouTube, Inc., YouTube, LLC, and Google Inc. (jointly, "YouTube" or the "defendants"). The plaintiffs alleged direct and secondary copyright infringement based on the public performance, display, and reproduction of approximately 79,000 audiovisual "clips" that appeared on the YouTube website between 2005 and 2008. They demanded, inter alia, statutory damages pursuant to 17 U.S.C. § 504(c) or, in the alternative, actual damages from the alleged infringement, as well as declaratory and injunctive relief.[...]

10
In a June 23, 2010 Opinion and Order (the "June 23 Opinion"), the District Court held that the defendants were entitled to DMCA safe harbor protection primarily because they had insufficient notice of the particular infringements in suit. [...] In construing the statutory

645

safe harbor, the District Court concluded that the "actual knowledge" or "aware[ness] of facts or circumstances" that would disqualify an online service provider from safe harbor protection under § 512(c)(1)(A) refer to "knowledge of specific and identifiable infringements." [..] The District Court further held that item-specific knowledge of infringing activity is required for a service provider to have the "right and ability to control" infringing activity under § 512(c)(1)(B). Id. at 527. Finally, the District Court held that the replication, transmittal, and display of videos on YouTube constituted activity "by reason of the storage at the direction of a user" within the meaning of § 512(c)(1). [.

11   These related cases present a series of significant questions of statutory construction. We conclude that the District Court correctly held that the § 512(c) safe harbor requires knowledge or awareness of specific infringing activity, but we vacate the order granting summary judgment because a reasonable jury could find that YouTube had actual knowledge or awareness of specific infringing activity on its website. We further hold that the District Court erred by interpreting the "right and ability to control" provision to require "item-specific" knowledge. Finally, we affirm the District Court's holding that three of the challenged YouTube software functions fall within the safe harbor for infringement that occurs "by reason of" user storage; we remand for further fact-finding with respect to a fourth software function.

12   ## BACKGROUND

13   ### A. The DMCA Safe Harbors

14   "The DMCA was enacted in 1998 to implement the World Intellectual Property Organization Copyright Treaty," [...], and to update domestic copyright law for the digital age, [...]. Title II of the DMCA, separately titled the "Online Copyright Infringement Liability Limitation Act" (OCILLA), was designed to "clarif[y] the liability faced by service providers who transmit potentially infringing material over their networks." S.Rep. No. 105–190 at 2 (1998). But "[r]ather than embarking upon a wholesale clarification" of various copyright doctrines, Congress elected "to leave current law in its evolving state and, instead, to create a series of 'safe harbors[ ]' for certain common activities of service providers." [...] To that end, OCILLA established a series of four "safe harbors" that allow qualifying service providers to limit their liability for claims of copyright infringement based on (a) "transitory digital network communications," (b) "system caching," (c) "information residing on systems or networks at [the] direction of users," and (d) "information location tools." 17 U.S.C. § 512(a)-(d).

15   To qualify for protection under any of the safe harbors, a party must meet a set of threshold criteria. First, the party must in fact be a "service provider," defined, in pertinent part, as "a provider of online services or network access, or the operator of facilities therefor." 17 U.S.C. § 512(k)(1)(B). A party that qualifies as a service provider must also satisfy certain "conditions of eligibility," including the adoption and reasonable implementation of a "repeat infringer" policy that "provides for the termination in appropriate circumstances of subscribers and account holders of the service provider's system or network." Id. § 512(i)(1)(A). In addition, a qualifying service provider must accommodate "standard technical measures" that are "used by copyright owners to identify or protect copyrighted works." Id. § 512(i)(1)(B), (i)(2).

16   Beyond the threshold criteria, a service provider must satisfy the requirements of a particular safe harbor. In this case, the safe harbor at issue is § 512(c), which covers infringement claims that arise "by reason of the storage at the direction of a user of material that resides on a system or network controlled or operated by or for the service provider." Id. § 512(c)(1). The § 512(c) safe harbor will apply only if the service provider:

17   (A) (i) does not have actual knowledge that the material or an activity using the material on the system or network is infringing;

             (ii) in the absence of such actual knowledge, is not aware of facts or circumstances from which infringing activity is apparent; or

             (iii) upon obtaining such knowledge or awareness, acts expeditiously to remove, or disable access to, the material;

             (B) does not receive a financial benefit directly attributable to the infringing activity, in a case in which the service provider has the right and ability to control such activity; and

(C) upon notification of claimed infringement as described in paragraph (3), responds expeditiously to remove, or disable access to, the material that is claimed to be infringing or to be the subject of infringing activity.

18   Id. § 512(c)(1)(A)-(C). Section 512(c) also sets forth a detailed notification scheme that requires service providers to "designate[ ] an agent to receive notifications of claimed infringement," id. § 512(c)(2), and specifies the components of a proper notification, commonly known as a "takedown notice," to that agent, see id. § 512(c)(3). Thus, actual knowledge of infringing material, awareness of facts or circumstances that make infringing activity apparent, or [...] receipt of a takedown notice will each trigger an obligation to expeditiously remove the infringing material.

19   With the statutory context in mind, we now turn to the facts of this case.

20   **B. Factual Background**

21   YouTube was founded in February 2005 by Chad Hurley ("Hurley"), Steve Chen ("Chen"), and Jawed Karim ("Karim"), three former employees of the internet company Paypal. When YouTube announced the "official launch" of the website in December 2005, a press release described YouTube as a "consumer media company" that "allows people to watch, upload, and share personal video clips at www. You Tube. com." Under the slogan "Broadcast yourself," YouTube achieved rapid prominence and profitability, eclipsing competitors such as Google Video and Yahoo Video by wide margins. In November 2006, Google acquired YouTube in a stock-for-stock transaction valued at $1.65 billion. By March 2010, at the time of summary judgment briefing in this litigation, site traffic on YouTube had soared to more than 1 billion daily video views, with more than 24 hours of new video uploaded to the site every minute.

22   The basic function of the YouTube website permits users to "upload" and view video clips free of charge. Before uploading a video to YouTube, a user must register and create an account with the website. The registration process requires the user to accept YouTube's Terms of Use agreement, which provides, inter alia, that the user "will not submit material that is copyrighted ... unless [he is] the owner of such rights or ha[s] permission from their rightful owner to post the material and to grant YouTube all of the license rights granted herein." When the registration process is complete, the user can sign in to his account, select a video to upload from the user's personal computer, mobile phone, or other device, and instruct the YouTube system to upload the video by clicking on a virtual upload "button."

23   Uploading a video to the YouTube website triggers a series of automated software functions. During the upload process, YouTube makes one or more exact copies of the video in its original file format. YouTube also makes one or more additional copies of the video in "Flash" format,[4] a process known as "transcoding." The transcoding process ensures that YouTube videos are available for viewing by most users at their request. The YouTube system allows users to gain access to video content by "streaming" the video to the user's computer in response to a playback request. YouTube uses a computer algorithm to identify clips that are "related" to a video the user watches and display links to the "related" clips.

24   **C. Procedural History**

25   [...]

27   In the dual-captioned June 23 Opinion, the District Court denied the plaintiffs' motions and granted summary judgment to the defendants, finding that YouTube qualified for DMCA safe harbor protection with respect to all claims of direct and secondary copyright infringement. the District Court identified the crux of the inquiry with respect to YouTube's copyright liability as follows:

28   [T]he critical question is whether the statutory phrases "actual knowledge that the material or an activity using the material on the system or network is infringing," and "facts or circumstances from which infringing activity is apparent" in § 512(c)(1)(A)(i) and (ii) mean a general awareness that there are infringements (here, claimed to be widespread and common), or rather mean actual or constructive knowledge of specific and identifiable infringements of individual items.

29   [...] After quoting at length from the legislative history of the DMCA, the District Court held that "the phrases 'actual knowledge that the

material or an activity' is infringing, and 'facts or circumstances' indicating infringing activity, describe knowledge of specific and identifiable infringements of particular individual items." [...] "Mere knowledge of [the] prevalence of such activity in general," the District Court concluded, "is not enough." [...]

30   In a final section labeled "Other Points," the District Court rejected two additional claims. First, it rejected the plaintiffs' argument that the replication, transmittal and display of YouTube videos are functions that fall outside the protection § 512(c)(1) affords for "infringement of copyright by reason of ... storage at the direction of the user." [...] Second, it rejected the plaintiffs' argument [...] that YouTube was ineligible for safe harbor protection under the control provision, holding that the "right and ability to control" infringing activity under § 512(c)(1)(B) requires "item-specific" knowledge thereof, because "the provider must know of the particular case before he can control it." [...]

32   **DISCUSSION**

33   [...]

34   **A. Actual and "Red Flag" Knowledge: § 512(c)(1)(A)**

35   The first and most important question on appeal is whether the DMCA safe harbor at issue requires "actual knowledge" or "aware[ness]" of facts or circumstances indicating "specific and identifiable infringements," [...] consider first the scope of the statutory provision and then its application to the record in this case.

36   **1. The Specificity Requirement**

37   "As in all statutory construction cases, we begin with the language of the statute," [...]. Under § 512(c)(1)(A), safe harbor protection is available only if the service provider:

38   (i) does not have actual knowledge that the material or an activity using the material on the system or network is infringing;

(ii) in the absence of such actual knowledge, is not aware of facts or circumstances from which infringing activity is apparent; or

(iii) upon obtaining such knowledge or awareness, acts expeditiously to remove, or disable access to, the material....

39   17 U.S.C. § 512(c)(1)(A). As previously noted, the District Court held that the statutory phrases "actual knowledge that the material ... is infringing" and "facts or circumstances from which infringing activity is apparent" refer to "knowledge of specific and identifiable infringements." [...]

40   Although the parties marshal a battery of other arguments on appeal, it is the text of the statute that compels our conclusion. In particular, we are persuaded that the basic operation of § 512(c) requires knowledge or awareness of specific infringing activity. Under § 512(c)(1)(A), knowledge or awareness alone does not disqualify the service provider; rather, the provider that gains knowledge or awareness of infringing activity retains safe-harbor protection if it "acts expeditiously to remove, or disable access to, the material." 17 U.S.C. § 512(c)(1)(A)(iii). Thus, the nature of the removal obligation itself contemplates knowledge or awareness of specific infringing material, because expeditious removal is possible only if the service provider knows with particularity which items to remove. Indeed, to require expeditious removal in the absence of specific knowledge [...] or awareness would be to mandate an amorphous obligation to "take commercially reasonable steps" in response to a generalized awareness of infringement. Viacom Br. 33. Such a view cannot be reconciled with the language of the statute, which requires "expeditious[ ]" action to remove or disable " the material " at issue. 17 U.S.C. § 512(c)(1)(A)(iii) (emphasis added).

41   On appeal, the plaintiffs dispute this conclusion by drawing our attention to § 512(c)(1)(A)(ii), the so-called "red flag" knowledge

provision. See id. § 512(c)(1)(A)(ii) (limiting liability where, "in the absence of such actual knowledge, [the service provider] is not aware of facts or circumstances from which infringing activity is apparent"). In their view, the use of the phrase "facts or circumstances" demonstrates that Congress did not intend to limit the red flag provision to a particular type of knowledge. The plaintiffs contend that requiring awareness of specific infringements in order to establish "aware[ness] of facts or circumstances from which infringing activity is apparent," 17 U.S.C. § 512(c)(1)(A)(ii), renders the red flag provision superfluous, because that provision would be satisfied only when the "actual knowledge" provision is also satisfied. For that reason, the plaintiffs urge the Court to hold that the red flag provision "requires less specificity" than the actual knowledge provision. [...]

42   This argument misconstrues the relationship between "actual" knowledge and "red flag" knowledge. It is true that "we are required to 'disfavor interpretations of statutes that render language superfluous.' " [...] But contrary to the plaintiffs' assertions, construing § 512(c)(1)(A) to require actual knowledge or awareness of specific instances of infringement does not render the red flag provision superfluous. The phrase "actual knowledge," which appears in § 512(c)(1)(A)(i), is frequently used to denote subjective belief. [...] By contrast, courts often invoke the language of "facts or circumstances," which appears in § 512(c)(1)(A)(ii), in discussing an objective reasonableness standard. [...]

43   The difference between actual and red flag knowledge is thus not between specific and generalized knowledge, but instead between a subjective and an objective standard. In other words, the actual knowledge provision turns on whether the provider actually or "subjectively" knew of specific infringement, while the red flag provision turns on whether the provider was subjectively aware of facts that would have made the specific infringement "objectively" obvious to a reasonable person. The red flag provision, because it incorporates an objective standard, is not swallowed up by the actual knowledge provision under our construction of the § 512(c) safe harbor. Both provisions do independent work, and both apply only to specific instances of infringement.

44   [...]

45   [...] we note that no court has embraced the contrary proposition—urged by the plaintiffs—that the red flag provision "requires less specificity" than the actual knowledge provision.

46   Based on the text of § 512(c)(1)(A), as well as the limited case law on point, we affirm the District Court's holding that actual knowledge or awareness of facts or circumstances that indicate specific and identifiable instances of infringement will disqualify a service provider from the safe harbor.

47   **2. The Grant of Summary Judgment**

48   The corollary question on appeal is whether, under the foregoing construction of § 512(c)(1)(A), the District Court erred in granting summary judgment to YouTube on the record presented. For the reasons that follow, we hold that although the District Court correctly interpreted § 512(c)(1)(A), summary judgment for the defendants was premature.

49   **i. Specific Knowledge or Awareness**

50   The plaintiffs argue that, even under the District Court's construction of the safe harbor, the record raises material issues of fact regarding YouTube's actual knowledge or "red flag" awareness of specific instances of infringement. To that end, the plaintiffs draw our attention to various estimates regarding the percentage of infringing content on the YouTube website. For example, Viacom cites evidence [...] that YouTube employees conducted website surveys and estimated that 75–80% of all YouTube streams contained copyrighted material. The class plaintiffs similarly claim that Credit Suisse, acting as financial advisor to Google, estimated that more than 60% of YouTube's content was "premium" copyrighted content—and that only 10% of the premium content was authorized. These approximations suggest that the defendants were conscious that significant quantities of material on the YouTube website were infringing. See Viacom Int'l, 718 F.Supp.2d at 518 ("[A] jury could find that the defendants not only were generally aware of, but welcomed, copyright-infringing material being placed on their website."). But such estimates are insufficient, standing alone, to create a

triable issue of fact as to whether YouTube actually knew, or was aware of facts or circumstances that would indicate, the existence of particular instances of infringement.

51   Beyond the survey results, the plaintiffs rely upon internal YouTube communications that do refer to particular clips or groups of clips. The class plaintiffs argue that YouTube was aware of specific infringing material because, inter alia, YouTube attempted to search for specific Premier League videos on the site in order to gauge their "value based on video usage." In particular, the class plaintiffs cite a February 7, 2007 e-mail from Patrick Walker, director of video partnerships for Google and YouTube, requesting that his colleagues calculate the number of daily searches for the terms "soccer," "football," and "Premier League" in preparation for a bid on the global rights to Premier League content. On another occasion, Walker requested that any "clearly infringing, official broadcast footage" from a list of top Premier League clubs—including Liverpool Football Club, Chelsea Football Club, Manchester United Football Club, and Arsenal Football Club—be taken down in advance of a meeting with the heads of "several major sports teams and leagues." YouTube ultimately decided not to make a bid for the Premier League rights—but the infringing content allegedly remained on the website.

52   The record in the Viacom action includes additional examples. For instance, YouTube founder Jawed Karim prepared a report in March 2006 which stated that, "[a]s of today[,] episodes and clips of the following well-known shows can still be found [on YouTube]: Family Guy, South Park, MTV Cribs, Daily Show, Reno 911, [and] Dave Chapelle [sic]." Karim further opined that, "although YouTube is not legally required to monitor content ... and complies with DMCA takedown requests, we would benefit from preemptively removing content that is blatantly illegal and likely to attract criticism." He also noted that "a more thorough analysis" of the issue would be required. At least some of the TV shows to which Karim referred are owned by Viacom. A reasonable juror could conclude from the March 2006 report that Karim knew of the presence of Viacom-owned material on YouTube, since he presumably located specific clips of the shows in question before he could announce that YouTube hosted the content "[a]s of today." A reasonable juror could also conclude that Karim believed the clips he located to be infringing (since he refers to them as "blatantly illegal"), and that YouTube did not remove the content from the website until conducting "a more thorough analysis," thus exposing the company to liability in the interim.

53   Furthermore, in a July 4, 2005 e-mail exchange, YouTube founder Chad Hurley sent an e-mail to his co-founders with the subject line "budlight commercials," and stated, "we need to reject these too." Steve Chen responded, "can we please [...] leave these in a bit longer? another week or two can't hurt." Karim also replied, indicating that he "added back in all 28 bud videos." Similarly, in an August 9, 2005 e-mail exchange, Hurley urged his colleagues "to start being diligent about rejecting copyrighted / inappropriate content," noting that "there is a cnn clip of the shuttle clip on the site today, if the boys from Turner would come to the site, they might be pissed?" Again, Chen resisted:

54   but we should just keep that stuff on the site. i really don't see what will happen. what? someone from cnn sees it? he happens to be someone with power? he happens to want to take it down right away. he gets in touch with cnn legal. 2 weeks later, we get a cease & desist letter. we take the video down.

          And again, Karim agreed, indicating that "the CNN space shuttle clip, I like. we can remove it once we're bigger and better known, but for now that clip is fine."

55   Upon a review of the record, we are persuaded that the plaintiffs may have raised a material issue of fact regarding YouTube's knowledge or awareness of specific instances of infringement. The foregoing Premier League e-mails request the identification and removal of "clearly infringing, official broadcast footage." The March 2006 report indicates Karim's awareness of specific clips that he perceived to be "blatantly illegal." Similarly, the Bud Light and space shuttle e-mails refer to particular clips in the context of correspondence about whether to remove infringing material from the website. On these facts, a reasonable juror could conclude that YouTube had actual knowledge of specific infringing activity, or was at least aware of facts or circumstances from which specific infringing activity was apparent. See § 512(c)(1)(A)(i)-(ii). Accordingly, we hold that summary judgment to YouTube on all clips-in-suit, especially in the absence of any detailed examination of the extensive record on summary judgment, was premature. [...]

56   We hasten to note, however, that although the foregoing e-mails were annexed as exhibits to the summary judgment papers, it is unclear whether the clips referenced therein are among the current clips-in-suit. By definition, only the current clips-in-suit are at issue in this litigation. Accordingly, we vacate the order granting summary judgment and instruct the District Court to determine on remand whether any specific infringements of which YouTube had knowledge or awareness correspond to the clips-in-suit in these actions.

57   **ii. "Willful Blindness"**

58   The plaintiffs further argue that the District Court erred in granting summary judgment to the defendants despite evidence that YouTube was "willfully blind" to specific infringing activity. On this issue of first impression, we consider the application of the common law willful blindness doctrine in the DMCA context.

59   "The principle that willful blindness is tantamount to knowledge is hardly novel." [...] A person is "willfully blind" or engages in "conscious avoidance" amounting to knowledge where the person " 'was aware of a high probability of the fact in dispute and consciously avoided confirming that fact.' " [...] Writing in the trademark infringement context, we have held that "[a] service provider is not ... permitted willful blindness. When it has reason to suspect that users of its service are infringing a protected mark, it may not shield itself from learning of the particular infringing transactions by looking the other way." [...]

60   The DMCA does not mention willful blindness. As a general matter, we interpret a statute to abrogate a common law principle only if the statute "speak[s] directly to the question addressed by the common law." [...] The relevant question, therefore, is whether the DMCA "speak[s] directly" to the principle of willful blindness. [...] The DMCA provision most relevant to the abrogation inquiry is § 512(m), which provides that safe harbor protection shall not be conditioned on "a service provider monitoring its service or affirmatively seeking facts indicating infringing activity, except to the extent consistent with a standard technical measure complying with the provisions of subsection (i)." 17 U.S.C. § 512(m)(1). Section 512(m) is explicit: DMCA safe harbor protection cannot be conditioned on affirmative monitoring by a service provider. For that reason, § 512(m) is incompatible with a broad common law duty to monitor or otherwise seek out infringing activity based on general awareness that infringement may be occurring. That fact does not, however, dispose of the abrogation inquiry; as previously noted, willful blindness cannot be defined as an affirmative duty to monitor. [...] Because the statute does not "speak[ ] directly" to the willful blindness doctrine, § 512(m) limits—but does not abrogate—the doctrine. Accordingly, we hold that the willful blindness doctrine may be applied, in appropriate circumstances, to demonstrate knowledge or awareness of specific instances of infringement under the DMCA.

61   The District Court cited § 512(m) for the proposition that safe harbor protection does not require affirmative monitoring, [...] but did not expressly address the principle of willful blindness or its relationship to the DMCA safe harbors. As a result, whether the defendants made a "deliberate effort to avoid guilty knowledge," [...] remains a fact question for the District Court to consider in the first instance on remand [...]

62   **B. Control and Benefit: § 512(c)(1)(B)**

63   Apart from the foregoing knowledge provisions, the § 512(c) safe harbor provides that an eligible service provider must "not receive a financial benefit directly attributable to the infringing activity, in a case in which the service provider has the right and ability to control such activity." 17 U.S.C. § 512(c)(1)(B). The District Court addressed this issue in a single paragraph, quoting from § 512(c)(1)(B), the so-called "control and benefit" provision, and concluding that "[t]he 'right and ability to control' the activity requires knowledge of it, which must be item-specific." [...] For the reasons that follow, we hold that the District Court erred by importing a specific knowledge requirement into the control and benefit provision, and we therefore remand for further fact-finding on the issue of control.

64   **1. "Right and Ability to Control" Infringing Activity**

65   On appeal, the parties advocate two competing constructions of the "right and ability to control" infringing activity. 17 U.S.C. § 512(c)(1)(B). Because each is fatally flawed, we reject both proposed constructions in favor of a fact-based inquiry to be conducted in the first instance by the District Court.

66   The first construction, pressed by the defendants, is the one adopted by the District Court, which held that "the provider must know of the particular case before he can control it." Viacom, 718 F.Supp.2d at 527. The Ninth Circuit recently agreed, holding that "until [the

service provider] becomes aware of specific unauthorized material, it cannot exercise its 'power or authority' over the specific infringing item. In practical terms, it does not have the kind of ability to control infringing activity the statute contemplates." [...] The trouble with this construction is that importing a specific knowledge requirement into § 512(c)(1)(B) renders the control provision duplicative of § 512(c)(1)(A). Any service provider that has item-specific knowledge of infringing activity and thereby obtains financial benefit would already be excluded from the safe harbor under § 512(c)(1)(A) for having specific knowledge of infringing material and failing to effect expeditious removal. No additional service provider would be excluded by § 512(c)(1)(B) that was not already excluded by § 512(c)(1)(A). Because statutory interpretations that render language superfluous are disfavored, [...] we reject the District Court's interpretation of the control provision.

67   The second construction, urged by the plaintiffs, is that the control provision codifies the common law doctrine of vicarious copyright liability. The common law imposes liability for vicarious copyright infringement "[w]hen the right and ability to supervise coalesce with an obvious and direct financial interest in the exploitation of copyrighted materials—even in the absence of actual knowledge that the copyright mono [poly] is being impaired." [...] To support their codification argument, the plaintiffs rely [...] on a House Report relating to a preliminary version of the DMCA: "The 'right and ability to control' language ... codifies the second element of vicarious liability.... Subparagraph (B) is intended to preserve existing case law that examines all relevant aspects of the relationship between the primary and secondary infringer." [...] In response, YouTube notes that the codification reference was omitted from the committee reports describing the final legislation, and that Congress ultimately abandoned any attempt to "embark[ ] upon a wholesale clarification" of vicarious liability, electing instead "to create a series of 'safe harbors' for certain common activities of service providers." [...]

68   Happily, the future of digital copyright law does not turn on the confused legislative history of the control provision. The general rule with respect to common law codification is that when "Congress uses terms that have accumulated settled meaning under the common law, a court must infer, unless the statute otherwise dictates, that Congress means to incorporate the established meaning of those terms." [...] Under the common law vicarious liability standard, " '[t]he ability to block infringers' access to a particular environment for any reason whatsoever is evidence of the right and ability to supervise.' " [...] To adopt that principle in the DMCA context, however, would render the statute internally inconsistent. Section 512(c) actually presumes that service providers have the ability to "block ... access" to infringing material. [...] Indeed, a service provider who has knowledge or awareness of infringing material or who receives a takedown notice from a copyright holder is required to "remove, or disable access to, the material" in order to claim the benefit of the safe harbor. 17 U.S.C. § 512(c)(1)(A)(iii) & (C). But in taking such action, the service provider would—in the plaintiffs' analysis—be admitting the "right and ability to control" the infringing material. Thus, the prerequisite to safe harbor protection under § 512(c)(1)(A)(iii) & (C) would at the same time be a disqualifier under § 512(c)(1)(B).

69   Moreover, if Congress had intended § 512(c)(1)(B) to be coextensive with vicarious liability, "the statute could have accomplished that result in a more direct manner." [...]

70   It is conceivable that Congress ... intended that [service providers] which receive a financial benefit directly attributable to the infringing activity would not, under any circumstances, be able to qualify for the subsection (c) safe harbor. But if that was indeed their intention, it would have been far simpler and much more straightforward to simply say as much. [...]

71   In any event, the foregoing tension—elsewhere described as a "predicament"[...] and a "catch22"[...]—is sufficient to establish that the control provision "dictates" [...] a departure from the common law vicarious liability standard [...]. Accordingly, we conclude that the "right and ability to control" infringing activity under § 512(c)(1)(B) "requires something more than the ability to remove or block access to materials posted on a service provider's website." [...] The remaining—and more difficult—question is how to define the "something more" that is required.

72   To date, only one court has found that a service provider had the right and ability to control infringing activity under § 512(c)(1)(B).[13] In Perfect 10, Inc. v. Cybernet Ventures, Inc., 213 F.Supp.2d 1146 (C.D.Cal.2002), the court found control where the service provider instituted a monitoring program by which user websites received "detailed instructions regard[ing] issues of layout, appearance, and

content." [...] The service provider also forbade certain types of content and refused access to users who failed to comply with its instructions. [...] Similarly, inducement of copyright infringement under Metro–Goldwyn–Mayer Studios Inc. v. Grokster, Ltd., 545 U.S. 913 which "premises liability on purposeful, culpable expression and conduct," id. at 937, 125 S.Ct. 2764, might also rise to the level of control under § 512(c)(1)(B). Both of these examples involve a service provider exerting substantial influence on the activities of users, without necessarily—or even frequently—acquiring knowledge of specific infringing activity.

73   In light of our holding that § 512(c)(1)(B) does not include a specific knowledge requirement, we think it prudent to remand to the District Court to consider in the first instance whether the plaintiffs have adduced sufficient evidence to allow a reasonable jury to conclude that YouTube had the right and ability to control the infringing activity and received a financial benefit directly attributable to that activity.

74   **C. "By Reason of" Storage: § 512(c)(1)**

75   The § 512(c) safe harbor is only available when the infringement occurs "by reason of the storage at the direction of a user of material that resides on a system or network controlled or operated by or for the service provider." 17 U.S.C. § 512(c)(1). In this case, the District Court held that YouTube's software functions fell within the safe harbor for infringements that occur "by reason of" user storage. Viacom, 718 F.Supp.2d at 526 (noting that a contrary holding would "confine[ ] the word 'storage' too narrowly to meet the statute's purpose"). For the reasons that follow, we affirm that holding [...] with respect to three of the challenged software functions—the conversion (or "transcoding") of videos into a standard display format, the playback of videos on "watch" pages, and the "related videos" function. We remand for further fact-finding with respect to a fourth software function, involving the third-party syndication of videos uploaded to YouTube.

76   As a preliminary matter, we note that "the structure and language of OCILLA indicate that service providers seeking safe harbor under [§] 512(c) are not limited to merely storing material." [...] The structure of the statute distinguishes between so-called "conduit only" functions under § 512(a) and the functions addressed by § 512(c) and the other subsections. See 17 U.S.C. § 512(n) ("Subsections (a), (b), (c), and (d) describe separate and distinct functions for purposes of applying this section."). Most notably, OCILLA contains two definitions of "service provider." 17 U.S.C. § 512(k)(1)(A)-(B). The narrower definition, which applies only to service providers falling under § 512(a), is limited to entities that "offer[ ] the transmission, routing or providing of connections for digital online communications, between or among points specified by a user, of material of the user's choosing, without modification to the content of the material as sent or received." Id. § 512(k)(1)(A) (emphasis added). No such limitation appears in the broader definition, which applies to service providers—including YouTube—falling under § 512(c). Under the broader definition, "the term 'service provider' means a provider of online services or network access, or the operator of facilities therefor, and includes an entity described in subparagraph (A)." Id. § 512(k)(1)(B). In the absence of a parallel limitation on the ability of a service provider to modify user-submitted material, we conclude that § 512(c) "is clearly meant to cover more than mere electronic storage lockers." [...]

77   The relevant case law makes clear that the § 512(c) safe harbor extends to software functions performed "for the purpose of facilitating access to user-stored material." [...] Two of the software functions challenged here—transcoding and playback—were expressly considered by our sister Circuit in Shelter Capital, which held that liability arising from these functions occurred "by reason of the storage at the direction of a user." [...] Transcoding involves "[m]aking copies of a video in a different encoding scheme" in order to render the video "viewable over the Internet to most users." [...] The playback process involves "deliver[ing] copies of YouTube videos to a user's browser cache" in response to a user request. [...] The District Court correctly found that to exclude these automated functions from the safe harbor would eviscerate the protection afforded to service providers by § 512(c). [...]

78   A similar analysis applies to the "related videos" function, by which a YouTube computer algorithm identifies and displays "thumbnails" of clips that are "related" to the video selected by the user. The plaintiffs claim that this practice constitutes content promotion, not "access" to stored content, and therefore falls beyond the scope of the safe harbor. Citing similar language in the Racketeer Influenced and Corrupt Organizations Act ("RICO"), 18 U.S.C. §§ 1961–68, and the Clayton [676 F.3d 40] Act, 15 U.S.C. §§ 12 et seq., the plaintiffs argue that the statutory phrase "by reason of" requires a finding of proximate causation between the act of storage and the infringing

activity. [...] But even if the plaintiffs are correct that § 512(c) incorporates a principle of proximate causation—a question we need not resolve here—the indexing and display of related videos retain a sufficient causal link to the prior storage of those videos. The record makes clear that the related videos algorithm "is fully automated and operates solely in response to user input without the active involvement of YouTube employees." [...] Furthermore, the related videos function serves to help YouTube users locate and gain access to material stored at the direction of other users. Because the algorithm "is closely related to, and follows from, the storage itself," and is "narrowly directed toward providing access to material stored at the direction of users," [...] we conclude that the related videos function is also protected by the § 512(c) safe harbor.

79   The final software function at issue here—third-party syndication—is the closest case. In or around March 2007, YouTube transcoded a select number of videos into a format compatible with mobile devices and "syndicated" or licensed the videos to Verizon Wireless and other companies. The plaintiffs argue—with some force—that business transactions do not occur at the "direction of a user" within the meaning of § 512(c)(1) when they involve the manual selection of copyrighted material for licensing to a third party. The parties do not dispute, however, that none of the clips-in-suit were among the approximately 2,000 videos provided to Verizon Wireless. In order to avoid rendering an advisory opinion on the outer boundaries of the storage provision, we remand for fact-finding on the question of whether any of the clips-in-suit were in fact syndicated to any other third party.

80   [...]

81   **CONCLUSION**

88   To summarize, we hold that:

89   (1) The District Court correctly held that 17 U.S.C. § 512(c)(1)(A) requires knowledge or awareness of facts or circumstances that indicate specific and identifiable instances of infringement;

(2) However, the June 23, 2010 order granting summary judgment to YouTube is **VACATED** because a reasonable jury could conclude that YouTube had knowledge or awareness under § 512(c)(1)(A) at least with respect to a handful of specific clips; the cause is **REMANDED** for the District Court to determine whether YouTube had knowledge or awareness of any specific instances of infringement corresponding to the clips-in-suit;

(3) The willful blindness doctrine may be applied, in appropriate circumstances, to demonstrate knowledge or awareness of specific instances of infringement under § 512(c)(1)(A); the cause is **REMANDED** for the [...] District Court to consider the application of the willful blindness doctrine in the first instance;

(4) The District Court erred by requiring "item-specific" knowledge of infringement in its interpretation of the "right and ability to control" infringing activity under 17 U.S.C. § 512(c)(1)(B), and the judgment is **REVERSED** insofar as it rests on that erroneous construction of the statute; the cause is **REMANDED** for further fact-finding by the District Court on the issues of control and financial benefit;

(5) The District Court correctly held that three of the challenged YouTube software functions—replication, playback, and the related videos feature—occur "by reason of the storage at the direction of a user" within the meaning of 17 U.S.C. § 512(c)(1), and the judgment is **AFFIRMED** insofar as it so held; the cause is **REMANDED** for further fact-finding regarding a fourth software function, involving the syndication of YouTube videos to third parties.

On remand, the District Court shall allow the parties to brief the following issues, with a view to permitting renewed motions for summary judgment as soon as practicable:

(A) Whether, on the current record, YouTube had knowledge or awareness of any specific infringements (including any clips-in-suit not expressly noted in this opinion);

(B) Whether, on the current record, YouTube willfully blinded itself to specific infringements;

(C) Whether YouTube had the "right and ability to control" infringing activity within the meaning of § 512(c)(1)(B); and

[...]

90   [...]

92   [4] The "Flash" format "is a highly compressed streaming format that begins to play instantly. Unlike other delivery methods, it does not require the viewer to download the entire video file before viewing." [...]

102   [9] We express no opinion as to whether the evidence discussed above will prove sufficient to withstand a renewed motion for summary judgment by YouTube on remand. In particular, we note that there is at least some evidence that the search requested by Walker in his February 7, 2007 e-mail was never carried out. See Joint App'x III:256. We also note that the class plaintiffs have failed to identify evidence indicating that any infringing content discovered as a result of Walker's request in fact remained on the YouTube website. The class plaintiffs, drawing on the voluminous record in this case, may be able to remedy these deficiencies in their briefing to the District Court on remand.

103   [...]

Perfect 10, Inc. v. CCBILL, LLC

September 02, 2014 by mrisch

This case is an example of the safe harbor under Section 512(d) for linking

1   340 F.Supp.2d 1077 (2004)

2   **PERFECT 10, INC., Plaintiff,**

                                           v.

                       CCBILL, LLC, et al., Defendants.

3   [...]

4   United States District Court, C.D. California.

5   June 22, 2004.

6   [...]

10   **BAIRD, District Judge.**

12   **I. INTRODUCTION**

13   [...]

14   **II. FACTUAL AND PROCEDURAL HISTORY**

15   **A.** *Factual History*

16   The facts are undisputed unless otherwise noted.

17   **1.** *Perfect 10*

18   Perfect 10 is the publisher of the adult entertainment magazine Perfect 10 and the owner of the website perfect10.com. *[...]* Perfect 10 has created approximately 5,000 photographic images for display in its magazine and on its website. *[...]* Perfect 10 holds registered U.S. copyrights for these images. *[...]*

19   **3.** *Internet Key*

22   *[...]* Internet Key is an age verification system for adult content websites. *[...]* Starting in 1997, Internet Key has provided adult verification services, including providing links, to third-party adult content websites. *[...]* Currently, Internet Key verifies age and provides a link to approximately 30,000 third-party adult content websites that participate in the SexKey system ("Affiliated Websites"). *[...]* A

656

user (consumer) cannot access an Affiliated Website without proving he or she is of legal age. [...] Internet Key provides each Affiliated Website with a site ID and an HTML code to place on their site. [...] When a new user clicks onto an Affiliated Website, a link that tracks the site ID automatically directs the user to sexkey.com for age verification. *Id.* The user is directed to Internet Key's registration page, which contains Internet Key's User Agreement. [...] Internet Key does not store the content of the Affiliated Websites on its computer system. [...] It only stores information related to the Affiliated Websites' URLs, site descriptions and webmaster information. [...]

23   [...]

24   Internet Key also acts as a search engine (similar to Yahoo or Google) for free adult content on the Internet. I [...] Sometimes, when an Affiliated Website is accessed through SexKey, the words "sexkey.com" appear in the URL. [...] Internet Key did not adopt a DMCA policy until August 21, 2002. [...]

2. *Internet Key's Motion for Summary Judgment on Perfect 10's Copyright Claim*

81   Internet Key contends that it is entitled to summary judgment on Perfect 10's Claim 1 for copyright infringement because the claim falls within the safe harbor provided by the DMCA under § 512(d). [...]

c. Safe Harbor Under §§ 512(d) [...]

106   Section 512(d) states:

107   (d) Information location tools. A service provider shall not be liable for monetary relief, or, except as provided in subsection (j), for injunctive or other equitable relief, for infringement of copyright by reason of the provider referring or linking users to an online location containing infringing material or infringing activity, by using information location tools, including a directory, index, reference, pointer, or hypertext link, if the service provider—

                (1) (A) does not have actual knowledge that the material or activity is infringing;

                (B) in the absence of such actual knowledge, is not aware of facts or circumstances from which infringing activity is apparent; or

                (C) upon obtaining such knowledge or awareness, acts expeditiously to remove, or disable access to, the material;

                (2) does not receive a financial benefit directly attributable to the infringing activity, in a case in which the service provider has the right and ability to control such activity; and

                (3) upon notification of claimed infringement as described in subsection (c)(3), responds expeditiously to remove, or disable access to, the material that is claimed to be infringing or to be the subject of infringing activity, except that, for purposes of this paragraph, the information described in subsection (c)(3)(A)(iii) shall be identification of the reference or link, to material or activity claimed to be infringing, that is to be removed or access to which is to be disabled, and information reasonably sufficient to permit the service provider to locate that reference or link.

108   17 U.S.C. § 512(d).

109   Perfect 10 contends that Internet Key does not fall within the safe harbor provided by § 512(d) because Internet Key (1) does not use an information location tool, (2) has actual knowledge of infringements, (2) is aware of facts or circumstances from which infringing activity is apparent.

110   Perfect 10 argues that Internet Key does not use an information location tool as defined in § 512(d) because Internet Key is not like
       Yahoo! or Google which provide links to millions of websites with whom it has no relationship. Perfect 10 reasons that because Internet
       Key merely links to a relatively small universe of websites with whom it has in place contractual relationships and established review
       procedures, it is not entitled to protection under [...] § 512(d). Section 512(d) does not state that the safe harbor is limited to internet
       service providers that provide links to millions of websites. Nor does § 512(d) state that the use of an information location tool is limited
       to internet service providers that do not have contractual relationships with their affiliate websites. Therefore, these arguments are
       without merit.

111   Section 512(d) refers to service providers who refer or link users to an online location containing infringing material or infringing activity,
       by using information location tools, including a directory, index, reference, pointer, or hypertext link. § 512(d). Internet Key's sexkey.com
       website provides that function and is therefore covered by § 512(d).

112   Pursuant to § 512(d), the internet service provider must also (1) not be aware of facts or circumstances from which infringing activity is
       apparent and (2) not receive a financial benefit directly attributable to the infringing activity, in a case in which the service provider has
       the right and ability to control such activity. Perfect 10 argues that Internet Key fails both of these requirements. Perfect 10 argues that
       Internet Key should have known there were copyright infringements on its clients' websites because of the disclaimers on some of those
       websites. The disclaimers generally claim that the copyrighted images are in the public domain or that the webmaster is posting the
       images for newsworthy purposes. [...] These disclaimers are not sufficient to raise a red flag of copyright infringement. Therefore, Perfect
       10 has not demonstrated that Internet Key was aware of facts or circumstances from which infringing was apparent.

113   The second requirement is that the internet service provider not receive a direct financial benefit directly attributable to the infringing
       activity when it has the right and ability to control such activity. A right and ability to control infringing activity, "as the concept is used in
       the DMCA, cannot simply mean the ability of a service provider to remove or block access to materials posted on its website or stored in
       its system." [...] Internet Key's right and ability to control infringing activity is limited to disconnecting the webmasters' access to Internet
       Key's service. That type of control is not sufficient, under the DMCA, to demonstrate a "right and ability to control" the infringing activity.
       As recognized in *Perfect 10 v. Cybernet Ventures, Inc.* [...] "closing the safe harbor based on the mere ability to exclude users from the
       system is inconsistent with the statutory scheme." [...] Since Internet Key does not have a right and ability to control the infringing
       activity, the Court need not address whether Internet Key receives a direct financial benefit from the infringing conduct.

114   [...]

115   The Court finds that there is no genuine issue of material fact that Internet Key is entitled to the safe harbors [...] Based on the
       foregoing, Internet Key's motion for summary judgment for infringements after August 21, 2002 based on the safe harbors under §
       512(d) and § 512(a) is granted. However, Internet Key's motion for summary judgment on Perfect 10's copyright infringement claim for
       infringements before August 21, 2002 is denied.

118   [...]

120

Metro-Goldwyn-Mayer, Inc. v. Grokster

June 30, 2014 by mrisch

1   545 U.S. 913
                                                          [...]

METRO-GOLDWYN-MAYER STUDIOS INC. ET AL.
v.
GROKSTER, LTD., ET AL.

[...]
Supreme Court of United States.
[...]
Decided June 27, 2005.

2   [...]

11   [...]

12   SOUTER, J., delivered the opinion for a unanimous Court. [...]

17   JUSTICE SOUTER delivered the opinion of the Court.

18   The question is under what circumstances the distributor of a product capable of both lawful and unlawful use is liable [...] for acts of
copyright infringement by third parties using the product. We hold that one who distributes a device with the object of promoting its use
to infringe copyright, as shown by clear expression or other affirmative steps taken to foster infringement, is liable for the resulting acts of
infringement by third parties.

19   I

20   A

21   Respondents, Grokster, Ltd., and StreamCast Networks, Inc., defendants in the trial court, distribute free software products that allow
computer users to share electronic files through peer-to-peer networks, so called because users' computers communicate directly with
each other, not through [...] central servers. The advantage of peer-to-peer networks over information networks of other types shows up
in their substantial and growing popularity. Because they need no central computer server to mediate the exchange of information or files
among users, the high-bandwidth communications capacity for a server may be dispensed with, and the need for costly server storage
space is eliminated. Since copies of a file (particularly a popular one) are available on many users' computers, file requests and retrievals
may be faster than on other types of networks, and since file exchanges do not travel through a server, communications can take place
between any computers that remain connected to the network without risk that a glitch in the server will disable the network in its
entirety. Given these benefits in security, cost, and efficiency, peer-to-peer networks are employed to store and distribute electronic files
by universities, government agencies, corporations, and libraries, among others.[1]

22   Other users of peer-to-peer networks include individual recipients of Grokster's and StreamCast's software, and although the networks that they enjoy through using the software can be used to share any type of digital file, they have prominently employed those networks in sharing copyrighted music and video files without authorization. A group of copyright holders (MGM for short, but including motion picture studios, recording companies, songwriters, and music publishers) sued Grokster and StreamCast for their users' copyright infringements, alleging that they [...] knowingly and intentionally distributed their software to enable users to reproduce and distribute the copyrighted works in violation of the Copyright Act, 17 U. S. C. § 101 *et seq.* [...] MGM sought damages and an injunction.

23   Discovery during the litigation revealed the way the software worked, the business aims of each defendant company, and the predilections of the users. Grokster's eponymous software employs what is known as FastTrack technology, a protocol developed by others and licensed to Grokster. StreamCast distributes a very similar product except that its software, called Morpheus, relies on what is known as Gnutella technology.[3] A user who downloads and installs either software possesses the protocol to send requests for files directly to the computers of others using software compatible with FastTrack or Gnutella. On the FastTrack network opened by the Grokster software, the user's request goes to a computer given an indexing capacity by the software and designated a supernode, or to some other computer with comparable power and capacity to collect temporary indexes of the files available on the computers of users connected to it. The supernode (or indexing computer) searches its own index and may communicate the search request to other supernodes. If the file is found, the supernode discloses its location to the computer requesting it, and the requesting user can download the file directly from the computer located. The copied file is placed in a designated sharing folder on the requesting user's computer, where it is available for other users to download in turn, along with any other file in that folder.[[...]] In the Gnutella network made available by Morpheus, the process is mostly the same, except that in some versions of the Gnutella protocol there are no supernodes. In these versions, peer computers using the protocol communicate directly with each other. When a user enters a search request into the Morpheus software, it sends the request to computers connected with it, which in turn pass the request along to other connected peers. The search results are communicated to the requesting computer, and the user can download desired files directly from peers' computers. As this description indicates, Grokster and StreamCast use no servers to intercept the content of the search requests or to mediate the file transfers conducted by users of the software, there being no central point through which the substance of the communications passes in either direction.[...]

24   Although Grokster and StreamCast do not therefore know when particular files are copied, a few searches using their software would show what is available on the networks the software reaches. MGM commissioned a statistician to conduct a systematic search, and his study showed that nearly 90% of the files available for download on the FastTrack system were copyrighted works.[5] Grokster and StreamCast dispute this figure, raising methodological problems and arguing that free copying even of copyrighted works may be authorized by the rightholders. They also argue that potential noninfringing uses of their software are significant in kind, even if infrequent in practice. Some musical performers, for example, have gained new audiences by distributing [...] their copyrighted works for free across peer-to-peer networks, and some distributors of unprotected content have used peer-to-peer networks to disseminate files, Shakespeare being an example. Indeed, StreamCast has given Morpheus users the opportunity to download the briefs in this very case, though their popularity has not been quantified.

25   As for quantification, the parties' anecdotal and statistical evidence entered thus far to show the content available on the FastTrack and Gnutella networks does not say much about which files are actually downloaded by users, and no one can say how often the software is used to obtain copies of unprotected material. But MGM's evidence gives reason to think that the vast majority of users' downloads are acts of infringement, and because well over 100 million copies of the software in question are known to have been downloaded, and billions of files are shared across the FastTrack and Gnutella networks each month, the probable scope of copyright infringement is staggering.

26   Grokster and StreamCast concede the infringement in most downloads, [...] and it is uncontested that they are aware that users employ their software primarily to download copyrighted files, even if the decentralized FastTrack and Gnutella networks fail to reveal which files are being copied, and when. From time to time, moreover, the companies have learned about their users' infringement directly, as from users who have sent e-mail to each company with questions about playing copyrighted movies they had downloaded, to whom the companies have responded with guidance.[...] And MGM notified the companies of 8 million copyrighted files that could be obtained using their software.

27   Grokster and StreamCast are not, however, merely passive recipients of information about infringing use. The record is replete with evidence that from the moment Grokster [...] and StreamCast began to distribute their free software, each one clearly voiced the objective that recipients use it to download copyrighted works, and each took active steps to encourage infringement.

28   After the notorious file-sharing service, Napster, was sued by copyright holders for facilitation of copyright infringement, [...] StreamCast gave away a software program of a kind known as OpenNap, designed as compatible with the Napster program and open to Napster users for downloading files from other Napster and OpenNap users' computers. Evidence indicates that "[i]t was always [StreamCast's] intent to use [its OpenNap network] to be able to capture email addresses of [its] initial target market so that [it] could promote [its] StreamCast Morpheus interface to them," App. 861; indeed, the OpenNap program was engineered "'to leverage Napster's 50 million user base,'" [...]

29   StreamCast monitored both the number of users downloading its OpenNap program and the number of music files they downloaded. [...] It also used the resulting OpenNap network to distribute copies of the Morpheus software and to encourage users to adopt it. I[...] Internal company documents indicate that StreamCast hoped to attract large numbers of former Napster users if that company was shut down by court order or otherwise, and that StreamCast planned to be the next Napster. [...]. A kit developed by StreamCast to be delivered to advertisers, for example, contained press articles about StreamCast's potential to capture former Napster users, [...] and it introduced itself to some potential advertisers as a company "which is similar to what Napster was," [...] It broadcast banner advertisements to users of other Napster-compatible software, urging them to adopt its OpenNap. [...] An internal e-mail from a company executive stated: "'We have put this network in [545 U.S. 925] place so that when Napster pulls the plug on their free service . . . or if the Court orders them shut down prior to that . . . we will be positioned to capture the flood of their 32 million users that will be actively looking for an alternative.'" [...]

30   Thus, StreamCast developed promotional materials to market its service as the best Napster alternative. One proposed advertisement read: "Napster Inc. has announced that it will soon begin charging you a fee. That's if the courts don't order it shut down first. What will you do to get around it?" [...] Another proposed ad touted StreamCast's software as the "#1 alternative to Napster" and asked "[w]hen the lights went off at Napster . . . where did the users go?" Id., at 836 (ellipsis in original).[7] StreamCast even planned to flaunt the illegal uses of its software; when it launched the OpenNap network, the chief technology officer of the company averred that "[t]he goal is to get in trouble with the law and get sued. It's the best way to get in the new[s]." Id., [...]

31   The evidence that Grokster sought to capture the market of former Napster users is sparser but revealing, for Grokster launched its own OpenNap system called Swaptor and inserted digital codes into its Web site so that computer users using Web search engines to look for "Napster" or "[f]ree file sharing" would be directed to the Grokster Web site, where they could download the Grokster software. [...] And Grokster's name is an apparent derivative of Napster.

32   StreamCast's executives monitored the number of songs by certain commercial artists available on their networks, and an internal communication indicates they aimed to have a larger number of copyrighted songs available on their networks [...] than other file-sharing networks. Id., at 868. The point, of course, would be to attract users of a mind to infringe, just as it would be with their promotional materials developed showing copyrighted songs as examples of the kinds of files available through Morpheus. [...] Morpheus in fact allowed users to search specifically for "Top 40" songs, [...] which were inevitably copyrighted. Similarly, Grokster sent users a newsletter promoting its ability to provide particular, popular copyrighted materials. [...]

33   In addition to this evidence of express promotion, marketing, and intent to promote further, the business models employed by Grokster and StreamCast confirm that their principal object was use of their software to download copyrighted works. Grokster and StreamCast receive no revenue from users, who obtain the software itself for nothing. Instead, both companies generate income by selling advertising

space, and they stream the advertising to Grokster and Morpheus users while they are employing the programs. As the number of users of each program increases, advertising opportunities become worth more. […] While there is doubtless some demand for free Shakespeare, the evidence shows that substantive volume is a function of free access to copyrighted work. Users seeking Top 40 songs, for example, or the latest release by Modest Mouse, are certain to be far more numerous than those seeking a free Decameron, and Grokster and StreamCast translated that demand into dollars.

34   Finally, there is no evidence that either company made an effort to filter copyrighted material from users' downloads or otherwise impede the sharing of copyrighted files. Although Grokster appears to have sent e-mails warning users about infringing content when it received threatening notice from the copyright holders, it never blocked anyone from continuing to use its software to share copyrighted files. [[…] StreamCast not only rejected another company's offer of help to monitor infringement, *[…]* but blocked the Internet Protocol addresses of entities it believed were trying to engage in such monitoring on its networks, *id.,* […]

35   **B**

36   […] The District Court held that those who used the Grokster and Morpheus software to download copyrighted media files directly infringed MGM's copyrights, a conclusion not contested on appeal, but the court nonetheless granted summary judgment in favor of Grokster and StreamCast as to any liability arising from distribution of the then-current versions of their software. Distributing that software gave rise to no liability in the court's view, because its use did not provide the distributors with actual knowledge of specific acts of infringement. […]

37   The Court of Appeals affirmed. […] In the court's analysis, a defendant was liable as a contributory infringer when it had knowledge of direct infringement and materially contributed to the infringement. But the court read *Sony Corp. of America* v. *Universal City Studios, Inc.,* 464 U. S. 417 (1984), as holding that distribution of a commercial product capable of substantial noninfringing uses could not give rise to contributory liability for infringement unless the distributor had actual knowledge of specific instances of infringement and failed to act on that knowledge. The fact that the software was capable of substantial noninfringing uses in the Ninth Circuit's view meant […] that Grokster and StreamCast were not liable, because they had no such actual knowledge, owing to the decentralized architecture of their software. The court also held that Grokster and StreamCast did not materially contribute to their users' infringement because it was the users themselves who searched for, retrieved, and stored the infringing files, with no involvement by the defendants beyond providing the software in the first place.

38   […] We granted certiorari. […]

39   **II**

40   **A**

41   MGM and many of the *amici* fault the Court of Appeals's holding for upsetting a sound balance between the respective values of supporting creative pursuits through copyright protection and promoting innovation in new communication technologies by limiting the incidence of liability for copyright infringement. The more artistic protection is favored, the more technological innovation may be discouraged; the administration of copyright law is an exercise in managing the tradeoff. […]

42   The tension between the two values is the subject of this case, with its claim that digital distribution of copyrighted material threatens copyright holders as never before, because every copy is identical to the original, copying is easy, […] and many people (especially the young) use file-sharing software to download copyrighted works. This very breadth of the software's use may well draw the public directly into the debate over copyright policy, […] and the indications are that the ease of copying songs or movies using software like Grokster's and Napster's is fostering disdain for copyright protection, […] As the case has been presented to us, these fears are said to be offset by the different concern that imposing liability, not only on infringers but on distributors of software based on its potential for

662

unlawful use, could limit further development of beneficial technologies. [...]

43   The argument for imposing indirect liability in this case is, however, a powerful one, given the number of infringing downloads that occur every day using StreamCast's and Grokster's software. When a widely shared service or product is used to commit infringement, it may be impossible to [...] enforce rights in the protected work effectively against all direct infringers, the only practical alternative being to go against the distributor of the copying device for secondary liability on a theory of contributory or vicarious infringement. [...]

44   One infringes contributorily by intentionally inducing or encouraging direct infringement, [...] and infringes vicariously by profiting from direct infringement while declining to exercise a right to stop or limit it, [...] [9] Although "[t]he Copyright Act does not expressly render anyone liable for infringement committed by another," [...] these doctrines of secondary liability emerged from common law principles and are well established in the law, [...]

45   **B**

46   Despite the currency of these principles of secondary liability, this Court has dealt with secondary copyright infringement in only one recent case, and because MGM has tailored its principal claim to our opinion there, a look at our earlier holding is in order. In *Sony Corp.* v. *Universal City Studios, supra,* this Court addressed a claim that secondary liability for infringement can arise from the very distribution of a commercial product. There, the product, novel at the time, was what we know today as the videocassette recorder or VCR. Copyright holders sued Sony as the manufacturer, claiming it was contributorily liable for infringement that occurred when VCR owners taped copyrighted programs because it supplied the means used to infringe, and it had constructive knowledge that infringement would occur. At the trial on the merits, the evidence showed that the principal use of the VCR was for "`time-shifting,'" or taping a program for later viewing at a more convenient time, which the Court found to be a fair, not an infringing, use. [...] There was no evidence that Sony had expressed an object of bringing about taping in violation of copyright or had taken active steps to increase its profits from unlawful taping. [...] Although Sony's advertisements urged consumers to buy the VCR to "`record favorite shows'" or "`build a library'" of recorded programs, [...] neither of these uses was necessarily infringing, [...]

47   On those facts, with no evidence of stated or indicated intent to promote infringing uses, the only conceivable basis for imposing liability was on a theory of contributory infringement arising from its sale of VCRs to consumers with knowledge that some would use them to infringe. [...] But because the VCR was "capable of commercially significant noninfringing uses," we held the manufacturer [...] could not be faulted solely on the basis of its distribution. *Id.,* [...]

48   This analysis reflected patent law's traditional staple article of commerce doctrine, now codified, that distribution of a component of a patented device will not violate the patent if it is suitable for use in other ways. 35 U. S. C. § 271(c); [...] The doctrine was devised to identify instances in which it may be presumed from distribution of an article in commerce that the distributor intended the article to be used to infringe another's patent, and so may justly be held liable for that infringement. "One who makes and sells articles which are only adapted to be used in a patented combination will be presumed to intend the natural consequences of his acts; he will be presumed to intend that they shall be used in the combination of the patent." [...]

49   In sum, where an article is "good for nothing else" but infringement, [...] at 489, there is no legitimate public interest in its unlicensed availability, and there is no injustice in presuming or imputing an intent to infringe, [...] Conversely, the doctrine absolves the equivocal conduct of selling an item with substantial lawful as well as unlawful uses, and limits liability to instances of more acute [...] fault than the mere understanding that some of one's products will be misused. It leaves breathing room for innovation and a vigorous commerce. [...]

50   The parties and many of the *amici* in this case think the key to resolving it is the *Sony* rule and, in particular, what it means for a product to

be "capable of commercially significant noninfringing uses." *[...]* MGM advances the argument that granting summary judgment to Grokster and StreamCast as to their current activities gave too much weight to the value of innovative technology, and too little to the copyrights infringed by users of their software, given that 90% of works available on one of the networks was shown to be copyrighted. Assuming the remaining 10% to be its noninfringing use, MGM says this should not qualify as "substantial," and the Court should quantify *Sony* to the extent of holding that a product used "principally" for infringement does not qualify. *[...]* As mentioned before, Grokster and StreamCast reply by citing evidence that their software can be used to reproduce public domain works, and they point to copyright holders who actually encourage copying. Even if infringement is the principal practice with their software today, they argue, the noninfringing uses are significant and will grow.

51   We agree with MGM that the Court of Appeals misapplied *Sony,* which it read as limiting secondary liability quite beyond the circumstances to which the case applied. *Sony* barred secondary liability based on presuming or imputing intent to cause infringement solely from the design or distribution of a product capable of substantial lawful use, which the distributor knows is in fact used for infringement. The *[...]* Ninth Circuit has read *Sony's* limitation to mean that whenever a product is capable of substantial lawful use, the producer can never be held contributorily liable for third parties' infringing use of it; it read the rule as being this broad, even when an actual purpose to cause infringing use is shown by evidence independent of design and distribution of the product, unless the distributors had "specific knowledge of infringement at a time at which they contributed to the infringement, and failed to act upon that information." *[* Because the Circuit found the StreamCast and Grokster software capable of substantial lawful use, it concluded on the basis of its reading of *Sony* that neither company could be held liable, since there was no showing that their software, being without any central server, afforded them knowledge of specific unlawful uses.

52   This view of *Sony,* however, was error, converting the case from one about liability resting on imputed intent to one about liability on any theory. Because *Sony* did not displace other theories of secondary liability, and because we find below that it was error to grant summary judgment to the companies on MGM's inducement claim, we do not revisit *Sony* further, as MGM requests, to add a more quantified description of the point of balance between protection and commerce when liability rests solely on distribution with knowledge that unlawful use will occur. It is enough to note that the Ninth Circuit's judgment rested on an erroneous understanding of *Sony* and to leave further consideration of the *Sony* rule for a day when that may be required.

53   **C**

54   *Sony's* rule limits imputing culpable intent as a matter of law from the characteristics or uses of a distributed product. But nothing in *Sony* requires courts to ignore evidence of intent if there is such evidence, and the case was never meant to foreclose rules of fault-based liability derived from *[...]* the common law.[10] *Sony Corp.* v. *Universal City Studios, supra,* at 439 ("If vicarious liability is to be imposed on Sony in this case, it must rest on the fact that it has sold equipment with constructive knowledge" of the potential for infringement). Thus, where evidence goes beyond a product's characteristics or the knowledge that it may be put to infringing uses, and shows statements or actions directed to promoting infringement, *Sony's* staple-article rule will not preclude liability.

55   The classic case of direct evidence of unlawful purpose occurs when one induces commission of infringement by another, or "entic[es] or persuad[es] another" to infringe, Black's Law Dictionary 790 (8th ed. 2004), as by advertising. Thus at common law a copyright or patent defendant who "not only expected but invoked [infringing use] by advertisement" was liable for infringement "on principles recognized in every part of the law." *Kalem Co.* v. *Harper Brothers,* 222 U. S., at 62-63 (copyright infringement). See also *Henry* v. *A. B. Dick Co.,* 224 U. S., at 48-49 (contributory liability for patent infringement may be found where a good's "most conspicuous use is one which will coöperate in an infringement when sale to such user is invoked by advertisement" of the infringing use); *Thomson-Houston Electric Co.* v. *Kelsey Electric R. Specialty Co.,* 75 F. 1005, 1007-1008 (CA2 1896) (relying on advertisements and displays to find defendant's "willingness . . . to aid other persons in any attempts which they may be disposed to make towards [patent] infringement"); *Rumford Chemical Works* v. *Hecker,* 20 F. Cas. 1342, 1346 (No. 12,133) (CC NJ 1876) (demonstrations of infringing activity along with "avowals of the [infringing] purpose and use for which it was made" supported liability for patent infringement).

56   *[...]* The rule on inducement of infringement as developed in the early cases is no different today.[11] Evidence of "active steps . . . taken to encourage direct infringement," *[...]* such as advertising an infringing use or instructing how to engage in an infringing use, show an

affirmative intent that the product be used to infringe, and a showing that infringement was encouraged overcomes the law's reluctance to find liability when a defendant merely sells a commercial product suitable for some lawful use, [...]

57   For the same reasons that *Sony* took the staple-article doctrine of patent law as a model for its copyright safe-harbor rule, the inducement rule, too, is a sensible one for copyright. We adopt it here, holding that one who distributes a device with the object of promoting its use to infringe copyright, as [...] shown by clear expression or other affirmative steps taken to foster infringement, is liable for the resulting acts of infringement by third parties. We are, of course, mindful of the need to keep from trenching on regular commerce or discouraging the development of technologies with lawful and unlawful potential. Accordingly, just as *Sony* did not find intentional inducement despite the knowledge of the VCR manufacturer that its device could be used to infringe, [...] mere knowledge of infringing potential or of actual infringing uses would not be enough here to subject a distributor to liability. Nor would ordinary acts incident to product distribution, such as offering customers technical support or product updates, support liability in themselves. The inducement rule, instead, premises liability on purposeful, culpable expression and conduct, and thus does nothing to compromise legitimate commerce or discourage innovation having a lawful promise.

58   **III**

59   **A**

60   The only apparent question about treating MGM's evidence as sufficient to withstand summary judgment under the theory of inducement goes to the need on MGM's part to adduce evidence that StreamCast and Grokster communicated an inducing message to their software users. The classic instance of inducement is by advertisement or solicitation that broadcasts a message designed to stimulate others to commit violations. MGM claims that such a message is shown here. It is undisputed that StreamCast beamed onto the computer screens of users of Napster-compatible programs ads urging the adoption of its OpenNap program, which was designed, as its name implied, to invite the custom of patrons of Napster, then under attack in the courts for facilitating massive infringement. Those who accepted StreamCast's OpenNap program were offered software to perform the same services, which a factfinder could conclude [...] would readily have been understood in the Napster market as the ability to download copyrighted music files. Grokster distributed an electronic newsletter containing links to articles promoting its software's ability to access popular copyrighted music. And anyone whose Napster or free file-sharing searches turned up a link to Grokster would have understood Grokster to be offering the same file-sharing ability as Napster, and to the same people who probably used Napster for infringing downloads; that would also have been the understanding of anyone offered Grokster's suggestively named Swaptor software, its version of OpenNap. And both companies communicated a clear message by responding affirmatively to requests for help in locating and playing copyrighted materials.

61   In StreamCast's case, of course, the evidence just described was supplemented by other unequivocal indications of unlawful purpose in the internal communications and advertising designs aimed at Napster users ("When the lights went off at Napster . . . where did the users go?" [...] Whether the messages were communicated is not to the point on this record. The function of the message in the theory of inducement is to prove by a defendant's own statements that his unlawful purpose disqualifies him from claiming protection (and incidentally to point to actual violators likely to be found among those who hear or read the message). [...] Proving that a message was sent out, then, is the preeminent but not exclusive way of showing that active steps were taken with the purpose of bringing about infringing acts, and of showing that infringing acts took place by using the device distributed. Here, the summary judgment record is replete with other evidence that Grokster and StreamCast, unlike the manufacturer and distributor in *Sony,* acted with a purpose to cause copyright violations by use of software suitable for illegal use. [...]

62   Three features of this evidence of intent are particularly notable. First, each company showed itself to be aiming to satisfy a known source of demand for copyright infringement, the market comprising former Napster users. StreamCast's internal documents made constant reference to Napster, it initially distributed its Morpheus software through an OpenNap program compatible with Napster, it advertised its OpenNap program to Napster users, and its Morpheus software functions as Napster did except that it could be used to distribute more kinds of files, including copyrighted movies and software programs. Grokster's name is apparently derived from Napster, it too initially offered an OpenNap program, its software's function is likewise comparable to Napster's, and it attempted to divert queries for Napster onto its own Web site. Grokster and StreamCast's efforts to supply services to former Napster users, deprived of a

mechanism to copy and distribute what were overwhelmingly infringing files, indicate a principal, if not exclusive, intent on the part of each to bring about infringement.

63   Second, this evidence of unlawful objective is given added significance by MGM's showing that neither company attempted to develop filtering tools or other mechanisms to diminish the infringing activity using their software. While the Ninth Circuit treated the defendants' failure to develop such tools as irrelevant because they lacked an independent duty to monitor their users' activity, we think this evidence underscores Grokster's and StreamCast's intentional facilitation of their users' infringement.[12]

64   Third, there is a further complement to the direct evidence of unlawful objective. It is useful to recall that StreamCast [...] and Grokster make money by selling advertising space, by directing ads to the screens of computers employing their software. As the record shows, the more the software is used, the more ads are sent out and the greater the advertising revenue becomes. Since the extent of the software's use determines the gain to the distributors, the commercial sense of their enterprise turns on high-volume use, which the record shows is infringing.[13] This evidence alone would not justify an inference of unlawful intent, but viewed in the context of the entire record its import is clear.

65   The unlawful objective is unmistakable.

66   **B**

67   In addition to intent to bring about infringement and distribution of a device suitable for infringing use, the inducement theory of course requires evidence of actual infringement by recipients of the device, the software in this case. As the account of the facts indicates, there is evidence of infringement on a gigantic scale, and there is no serious issue of the adequacy of MGM's showing on this point in order to survive the companies' summary judgment requests. Although [...] an exact calculation of infringing use, as a basis for a claim of damages, is subject to dispute, there is no question that the summary judgment evidence is at least adequate to entitle MGM to go forward with claims for damages and equitable relief.

68   [...]

69   In sum, this case is significantly different from *Sony* and reliance on that case to rule in favor of StreamCast and Grokster was error. *Sony* dealt with a claim of liability based solely on distributing a product with alternative lawful and unlawful uses, with knowledge that some users would follow the unlawful course. The case struck a balance between the interests of protection and innovation by holding that the product's capability of substantial lawful employment should bar the imputation of fault and consequent secondary liability for the unlawful acts of others.

70   MGM's evidence in this case most obviously addresses a different basis of liability for distributing a product open to alternative uses. Here, evidence of the distributors' words and deeds going beyond distribution as such shows a purpose to cause and profit from third-party acts of copyright infringement. If liability for inducing infringement is ultimately found, it will not be on the basis of presuming or imputing fault, but from inferring a patently illegal objective from statements and actions showing what that objective was.

71   There is substantial evidence in MGM's favor on all elements of inducement, and summary judgment in favor of Grokster and StreamCast was error. On remand, reconsideration of MGM's motion for summary judgment will be in order.

72   The judgment of the Court of Appeals is vacated, and the case is remanded for further proceedings consistent with this opinion.

73   *It is so ordered.*

74   [...] JUSTICE GINSBURG, with whom THE CHIEF JUSTICE and JUSTICE KENNEDY join, concurring.

75   I concur in the Court's decision, which vacates in full the judgment of the Court of Appeals for the Ninth Circuit, [...] and write separately
        to clarify why I conclude that the Court of Appeals misperceived, and hence misapplied, our holding in *Sony Corp. of America* v. *Universal
        City Studios, Inc.*, 464 U. S. 417 (1984). There is here at least a "genuine issue as to [a] material fact," Fed. Rule Civ. Proc. 56(c), on the
        liability of Grokster or StreamCast, not only for actively inducing copyright infringement, but also, or alternatively, based on the
        distribution of their software products, for contributory copyright infringement. On neither score was summary judgment for Grokster
        and StreamCast warranted.

76   [...]

77   In *Sony*, 464 U. S. 417, the Court considered Sony's liability for selling the Betamax videocassette recorder. It did so enlightened by a full
        trial record. Drawing an analogy to the staple article of commerce doctrine from patent law, [...] the *Sony* Court observed that the "sale
        of an article . . . adapted to [a patent] infringing use" does not suffice "to make the seller a contributory infringer" if the article "is also
        adapted to other and lawful uses." [...]

78   "The staple article of commerce doctrine" applied to copyright, the Court stated, "must strike a balance between a copyright holder's
        legitimate demand for effective—not merely symbolic—protection of the statutory monopoly, and the rights of others freely to engage in
        substantially unrelated areas of commerce." [...] "Accordingly," the Court held, "the sale of copying equipment, like the sale of other
        articles of commerce, does not constitute contributory infringement if the product is widely used for legitimate, unobjectionable
        purposes. Indeed, it need merely be capable of substantial noninfringing uses." [...] Thus, to resolve the *Sony* case, the Court explained, it
        had to determine "whether the Betamax is capable of commercially significant noninfringing uses." [...]

81   This case differs markedly from *Sony*. [...] Here, there has been no finding of any fair use and little beyond anecdotal evidence of
        noninfringing uses. In finding the Grokster and StreamCast software products capable of substantial noninfringing uses, the District
        Court and the Court of Appeals appear to have relied largely on declarations submitted by the defendants. [...]

83   Even if the absolute number of noninfringing files copied using the Grokster and StreamCast software is large, it does not follow that the
        products are therefore put to substantial noninfringing uses and are thus immune from liability. The number of noninfringing copies may
        be reflective of, and dwarfed by, the huge total volume of files shared. Further, the District Court and the Court of Appeals did not sharply
        distinguish between uses of Grokster's and StreamCast's software products (which this case is about) and uses of peer-to-peer
        technology generally (which this case is not about).

84   [...]

87   JUSTICE BREYER, with whom JUSTICE STEVENS and JUSTICE O'CONNOR join, concurring.

88   I agree with the Court that the distributor of a dual-use technology may be liable for the infringing activities of third parties where he or
        she actively seeks to advance the infringement. [...] I further agree that, in light of our holding today, we need not now "revisit" *Sony Corp.
        of America* v. *Universal City Studios, Inc.*, 464 U. S. 417 (1984). [...]

88   When measured against *Sony*'s underlying evidence and analysis, the evidence now before us shows that Grokster passes *Sony*'s test—
        that is, whether the company's product is capable of substantial or commercially significant noninfringing uses. [...]. For one thing,
        petitioners' (hereinafter MGM) own expert declared that 75% of current files available on Grokster are infringing and 15% are "likely

infringing." [...] That leaves some number of files near 10% that apparently are noninfringing, a figure very similar to the 9% or so of authorized time-shifting uses of the VCR that the Court faced in *Sony.*

99   [...]

104   The nature of these and other lawfully swapped files is such that it is reasonable to infer quantities of current lawful use roughly approximate to those at issue in *Sony.* At least, MGM has offered no evidence sufficient to survive summary judgment that could plausibly demonstrate a significant quantitative difference. [...] To be sure, in quantitative terms these uses account for only a small percentage of the total number of uses of Grokster's product. But the same was true in *Sony,* which characterized the relatively limited authorized copying market as "substantial." (The Court made clear as well in *Sony* that the amount of material then presently available for lawful copying—if not actually copied— was significant, see 464 U. S., at 444, and the same is certainly true in this case.)

105   [...] *Sony* also used the word "capable," asking whether the product is *"capable of"* substantial noninfringing uses. Its language and analysis suggest that a figure like 10%, if fixed for all time, might well prove insufficient, but that such a figure serves as an adequate foundation where there is a reasonable prospect of expanded legitimate uses over time. See *ibid.* (noting a "significant potential for future authorized copying"). And its language also indicates [...] the appropriateness of looking to potential future uses of the product to determine its "capability."

106   [...]

120   [1] Peer-to-peer networks have disadvantages as well. Searches on peer-to-peer networks may not reach and uncover all available files because search requests may not be transmitted to every computer on the network. There may be redundant copies of popular files. The creator of the software has no incentive to minimize storage or bandwidth consumption, the costs of which are borne by every user of the network. Most relevant here, it is more difficult to control the content of files available for retrieval and the behavior of users.

146   [...]

149   [5] By comparison, evidence introduced by the plaintiffs in *A&M Records, Inc.* v. *Napster, Inc.,* 239 F. 3d 1004 (CA9 2001), showed that 87% of files available on the Napster file-sharing network were copyrighted, *id.,* at 1013.

150   [...]

151   [7] The record makes clear that StreamCast developed these promotional materials but not whether it released them to the public. Even if these advertisements were not released to the public and do not show encouragement to infringe, they illuminate StreamCast's purposes.

152   [...]

153   [9] We stated in *Sony Corp. of America* v. *Universal City Studios, Inc.,* 464 U. S. 417 (1984), that "`the lines between direct infringement, contributory infringement and vicarious liability are not clearly drawn' . . . . [R]easoned analysis of [the *Sony* plaintiffs' contributory infringement claim] necessarily entails consideration of arguments and case law which may also be forwarded under the other labels, and indeed the parties . . . rely upon such arguments and authority in support of their respective positions on the issue of contributory infringement," [...] In the present case MGM has argued a vicarious liability theory, which allows imposition of liability when the defendant profits directly from the infringement and has a right and ability to supervise the direct infringer, even if the defendant initially lacks knowledge of the infringement. [...] Because we resolve the case based on an inducement theory, there is no need to analyze

separately MGM's vicarious liability theory.

154   [10] Nor does the Patent Act's exemption from liability for those who distribute a staple article of commerce, 35 U. S. C. § 271(c), extend
to those who induce patent infringement, § 271(b).

155   [...]

156   [12] Of course, in the absence of other evidence of intent, a court would be unable to find contributory infringement liability merely based
on a failure to take affirmative steps to prevent infringement, if the device otherwise was capable of substantial noninfringing uses. Such
a holding would tread too close to the *Sony* safe harbor.

157   [13] Grokster and StreamCast contend that any theory of liability based on their conduct is not properly before this Court because the
rulings in the trial and appellate courts dealt only with the present versions of their software, not "past acts . . . that allegedly encouraged
infringement or assisted . . . known acts of infringement." Brief for Respondents 14; see also *id.,* at 34. This contention misapprehends the
basis for their potential liability. It is not only that encouraging a particular consumer to infringe a copyright can give rise to secondary
liability for the infringement that results. Inducement liability goes beyond that, and the distribution of a product can itself give rise to
liability where evidence shows that the distributor intended and encouraged the product to be used to infringe. In such a case, the
culpable act is not merely the encouragement of infringement but also the distribution of the tool intended for infringing use. [...]

Perfect 10, Inc. v. Visa Int'l Service Ass'n

September 02, 2014 by mrisch

1   494 F.3d 788 (2007)

2   **PERFECT 10, INC.** [...]

v.

VISA INTERNATIONAL SERVICE, ASSOCIATION [...]

4   United States Court of Appeals, Ninth Circuit.

5   [...]
Filed July 3, 2007.

6   [...]

14   ## MILAN D. SMITH, JR., Circuit Judge:

15   Perfect 10, Inc. (Perfect 10) sued Visa International Service Association, Master-Card International Inc., and several affiliated banks and data processing services (collectively, the Defendants), alleging secondary liability under federal copyright and trademark law and liability under California statutory and common law. It sued because Defendants continue to process credit card payments to websites that infringe Perfect 10's intellectual property rights after being notified by Perfect 10 of infringement by those websites. The district court dismissed all causes of action under Federal Rule of Civil Procedure 12(b)(6) for failure to state a claim upon [...] which relief can be granted. We affirm the decision of the district court.

16   ## FACTS AND PRIOR PROCEEDINGS

17   Perfect 10 publishes the magazine "PERFECT10" and operates the subscription website www.perfect10.com., both of which "feature tasteful copyrighted images of the world's most beautiful natural models." [...]. Perfect 10 alleges that numerous websites based in several countries have stolen its proprietary images, altered them, and illegally offered them for sale online.

18   Instead of suing the direct infringers in this case, Perfect 10 sued Defendants, financial institutions that process certain credit card payments to the allegedly infringing websites. The Visa and Master-Card entities are associations of member banks that issue credit cards to consumers, automatically process payments to merchants authorized to accept their cards, and provide information to the interested parties necessary to settle the resulting debits and credits. Defendants collect fees for their services in these transactions. Perfect 10 alleges that it sent Defendants repeated notices specifically identifying infringing websites and informing Defendants that some of their consumers use their payment cards to purchase infringing images. Defendants admit receiving some of these notices, but they took no action in response to the notices after receiving them.

19   [...]

20   Perfect 10 filed suit against Defendants on January 28, 2004 alleging contributory and vicarious copyright and trademark infringement

670

[...]

27 **DISCUSSION**

28 [...]

29 **A. Secondary Liability for Copyright Infringement**

30 Perfect 10 alleges that numerous websites based in several countries—and their paying customers—have directly infringed its rights under the Copyright Act, 17 U.S.C. § 101, *et seq.*[1] In the present suit, however, Perfect 10 has sued Defendants, not the direct infringers, claiming contributory and vicarious copyright infringement because Defendants process credit card charges incurred by customers to acquire the infringing images.

31 We evaluate Perfect 10's claims with an awareness that credit cards serve as the primary engine of electronic commerce and that Congress has determined it to be the "policy of the United States—(1) to promote the continued development of the Internet and other interactive computer services and other interactive media [and] (2) to preserve the vibrant and competitive free market that presently exists for the Internet and other interactive computer services, unfettered by Federal or State regulation." 47 U.S.C. §§ 230(b)(1), (2).[2]

32 **1. Contributory Copyright Infringement**

33 Contributory copyright infringement is a form of secondary liability with [795] roots in the tort-law concepts of enterprise liability and imputed intent. *[...]* This court and the United States Supreme Court (Supreme Court) have announced various formulations of the same basic test for such liability. We have found that a defendant is a contributory infringer if it (1) has knowledge of a third party's infringing activity, and (2) "induces, causes, or materially contributes to the infringing conduct." *[...]* Most recently, in a case also brought by Perfect 10, we found that "an actor may be contributorily liable [under *Grokster*] for intentionally encouraging direct infringement if the actor knowingly takes steps that are substantially certain to result in such direct infringement." *[...]*

34 We understand these several criteria to be non-contradictory variations on the same basic test, i.e., that one contributorily infringes when he (1) has knowledge of another's infringement and (2) either (a) materially contributes to or (b) induces that infringement. Viewed in isolation, the language of the tests described is quite broad, but when one reviews the details of the actual "cases and controversies" before the relevant court in each of the testdefining cases and the actual holdings in those cases, it is clear that the factual circumstances in this case are not analogous. To find that Defendants' activities fall within the scope of such tests would require a radical and inappropriate expansion of existing principles of secondary liability and would violate the public policy of the United States.

35 **a. Knowledge of the Infringing Activity**

36 Because we find that Perfect 10 has not pled facts sufficient to establish that Defendants induce or materially contribute to the infringing activity, Perfect 10's contributory copyright infringement claim fails and we need not address the Defendants' knowledge of the infringing activity.[4]

37 [...] **b. Material Contribution, Inducement, or Causation**

38 To state a claim of contributory infringement, Perfect 10 must allege facts showing that Defendants induce, cause, or materially contribute to the infringing conduct. *[...]* Three key cases found defendants contributorily liable under this standard: *Fonovisa,* 76 F.3d 259; *Napster,* 239 F.3d 1004; and *Grokster,* 545 U.S. 913, 125 S.Ct. 2764, 162 L.Ed.2d 781. In *Fonovisa,* we held a swap meet operator contributorily liable for the sale of pirated works at the swap meet. In *Napster,* we held the operator of an electronic file sharing system liable when users of that system employed it to exchange massive quantities of copyrighted music. In *Grokster,* the Supreme Court found liability for the substantially similar act of distributing software that enabled exchange of copyrighted music on a peer-to-peer, rather than a centralized basis.[5] Perfect 10 argues that by continuing to process credit card payments to the infringing websites despite

having knowledge of ongoing infringement, Defendants induce, enable and contribute to the infringing activity in the same way the defendants did in *Fonovisa, Napster* and *Grokster.* We disagree.

39 **1. Material Contribution**

40   The credit card companies cannot be said to materially contribute to the infringement in this case because they have no direct connection to that infringement. Here, the infringement rests on the reproduction, alteration, display and distribution of Perfect 10's images over the Internet. Perfect 10 has not alleged that any infringing material passes over Defendants' payment networks or through their payment processing systems, or that Defendants' systems are used to alter or display the infringing images. In *Fonovisa,* the infringing material was physically located in and traded at the defendant's market. Here, it is not. Nor are Defendants' systems used to locate the infringing images. The search engines in *Amazon.com* provided links to specific infringing images, and the services in *Napster* and *Grokster* allowed users to locate and obtain infringing material. Here, in contrast, the services provided by the credit card companies do not help locate and are not used to distribute the infringing images. While Perfect 10 has alleged that Defendants make it easier for websites to profit from this infringing activity, the issue here is reproduction, alteration, display and distribution, which can occur without payment. Even if infringing images were not paid for, there would still be infringement. *[...]*

41   Our analysis is fully consistent with this court's recent decision in *Perfect 10 v. Amazon.com,* where we found that "Google could be held contributorily liable if it had knowledge that infringing Perfect 10 images were available using its search engine, could take simple measures to prevent further damage to Perfect 10's copyrighted works, and failed to take such steps." *[...]* The dissent claims this statement applies squarely to Defendants if we just substitute "payment systems" for "search engine." *[...]* But this is only true if search engines and payment systems are equivalents for these purposes, and they are not. The salient distinction is that Google's search engine itself assists in the distribution of infringing content to Internet users, while Defendants' payment systems do not. The *Amazon.com* court noted that "Google substantially assists websites to distribute their infringing copies to a worldwide market and assists a worldwide audience of users to access infringing materials." *[...]* Defendants do not provide such a service. They in no way assist or enable Internet users to locate infringing material, and they do not distribute it. They do, as alleged, make infringement more profitable, and people are generally more inclined to engage in an activity when it is financially profitable. However, there is an additional step in the causal chain: Google may materially contribute to infringement by making it fast and easy for third parties to locate and distribute infringing material, whereas Defendants make it easier for infringement to be *profitable,* which tends to increase financial incentives to infringe, which in turn tends to increase infringement.[6]

42   The dissent disagrees with our reading of *Amazon.com* and charges us with wishful thinking, dissent at 811, and with "draw[ing] a series of ephemeral distinctions," dissent at 825. We respectfully disagree and assert that our construction of the relevant statutes and case law is completely consistent with existing federal law, is firmly grounded in both commercial and technical reality and conforms to the public policy of the United States. Helping users to locate an image might substantially assist users to download infringing images, but processing payments does not. If users couldn't pay for images with credit cards, infringement could continue on a large scale because other viable funding mechanisms are available. For example, a website might decide to allow users to download some images for free and to make its profits from advertising, or it might develop other payment mechanisms that do not depend on the credit card companies.[7] In either case, the unlicensed use of Perfect 10's copyrighted images would still be infringement.[8] We acknowledge that Defendants' *[...* payment systems make it easier for such an infringement to be profitable, and that they therefore have the effect of increasing such infringement, but because infringement of Perfect 10's copyrights can occur without using Defendants' payment system, we hold that payment processing by the Defendants as alleged in Perfect 10's First Amended Complaint does not constitute a "material contribution" under the test for contributory infringement of copyrights.[9]

43   *[...]*

48   Unlike the *Napster* (and *Grokster*) defendants, they do not provide users the tools to locate infringing material, nor does any infringing material ever reside on or pass through any network or computer Defendants operate.[11] Defendants merely provide a method of payment, not a "site" or "facility" of infringement. Any conception of "site and facilities" that encompasses Defendants would also include

a number of peripherally-involved third parties, such as computer display companies, storage device companies, and software companies that make the software necessary to alter and view the pictures and even utility companies that provide electricity to the Internet.

49   Perfect 10 seeks to side-step this reality by alleging that Defendants are still contributory infringers because they could refuse to process payments to the infringing websites and thereby undermine their commercial viability.[12] Even though we must take this factual allegation as true, that Defendants have the power to undermine the commercial viability of infringement does not demonstrate that the Defendants materially contribute to that infringement. As previously noted, the direct infringement here is the reproduction, alteration, display and distribution of Perfect 10's images over the Internet. Perfect 10 has not alleged that any infringing material passes over Defendants' payment networks or through their payment processing systems, or that Defendants designed or promoted their payment systems as a means to infringe. While Perfect 10 has alleged that Defendants make it easier for websites to profit from this infringing activity, the infringement stems from the failure to obtain a license to distribute, not the processing of payments.

50   ## 2. Inducement

51   In *Grokster,* the Supreme Court applied the patent law concept of "inducement" to a claim of contributory infringement against a file-sharing program. *[...]* The court found that "one who distributes a device with the object of promoting its use to infringe copyright, as shown by clear expression or other affirmative steps taken to foster infringement, is liable for the resulting acts of infringement by third parties." *[...]* Perfect 10 claims that *Grokster* is analogous because Defendants induce customers to use their cards to purchase goods and services, and are therefore guilty of specifically inducing infringement if the cards are used to purchase images from sites that have content stolen from Perfect 10. This is mistaken. Because Perfect 10 alleges no "affirmative steps taken to foster infringement" and no facts suggesting that Defendants promoted their payment system as a means to infringe, its claim is premised on a fundamental misreading of *[...]* *Grokster* that would render the concept of "inducement" virtually meaningless.

52   The *Grokster* court announced that the standard for inducement liability is providing a service "with the object of promoting its use to infringe copyright." *Id.* "[M]ere knowledge of infringing potential or actual infringing uses would not be enough here to subject [a defendant] to liability." *[...]* Instead, inducement "premises liability on purposeful, culpable expression and conduct, and thus does nothing to compromise legitimate commerce or discourage innovation having a lawful promise." *[...]* Moreover, to establish inducement liability, it is crucial to establish that the distributors "communicated an inducing message to their . . . users," the classic example of which is an "advertisement or solicitation that broadcasts a message designed to stimulate others to commit violations." *[...]*

55   Perfect 10 has not alleged that any of these standards are met or that any of these considerations are present here. Defendants do, of course, market their credit cards as a means to pay for goods and services, online and elsewhere. But it does not follow that Defendants affirmatively promote each product that their cards are used to purchase. The software systems in *Napster* and *Grokster* were engineered, disseminated, and promoted explicitly for the purpose of facilitating piracy of copyrighted music and reducing legitimate sales of such music to that extent. Most Napster and Grokster users understood this and primarily used those systems to purloin copyrighted music. Further, the Grokster operators explicitly targeted then-current users of the Napster program by sending them ads for its OpenNap program. *[...]* In contrast, Perfect 10 does not allege that Defendants created or promote their payment systems as a means to break laws. Perfect 10 simply alleges that Defendants generally promote their cards and payment systems but points to no "clear expression" or "affirmative acts" with any specific intent to foster infringement.

56   The *Amazon.com* court recognized this distinction and applied it in a matter fully consistent with our analysis in this case. While the *Amazon.com* court did not bifurcate its analysis of contributory liability into "material contribution" liability and "inducement" liability, it did recognize that contributory liability "may be predicated on actively encouraging (or inducing) infringement through specific acts." *[...]* It also found that Google could be held contributorily liable if it has "actual knowledge that specific infringing material is available using its system, and can take simple measures to prevent further damage," but does not. *[...]* As discussed above, Perfect 10 has not alleged any "specific acts" intended to encourage or induce infringement. And moreover, Defendants are distinguishable under the *Amazon.com* test because, unlike Google, infringing material is not "available using [their] system" of payment processing. *[...]*

58   ## 2. Vicarious Copyright Infringement

59   Vicarious infringement is a concept related to, but distinct from, contributory infringement. Whereas contributory infringement is based on tort-law principles of enterprise liability and imputed intent, vicarious infringement's roots lie in the agency principles of *respondeat superior. [...]* To state a claim for vicarious copyright infringement, a plaintiff must allege that the defendant has (1) the right and ability to supervise[13] the infringing conduct and (2) a direct financial interest in the infringing activity. *[...]* The Supreme Court has recently offered (in dictum) an alternate formulation of the test: "One . . . infringes vicariously by profiting from direct infringement while declining to exercise a right to stop or limit it." *Grokster [...]* Perfect 10 alleges that Defendants have the right and ability to control the content of the infringing websites by refusing to process credit card payments to the websites, enforcing their own rules and regulations, or both. We hold that Defendants' conduct alleged in Perfect 10's first amended complaint fails to state a claim for vicarious copyright infringement.

60   ## a. Right and Ability to Supervise the Infringing Activity

61   In order to join a Defendant's payment network, merchants and member banks must agree to follow that Defendant's rules and regulations. These rules, among other things, prohibit member banks from providing services to merchants engaging in certain illegal activities and require the members and member banks to investigate merchants suspected of engaging in such illegal activity and to terminate their participation in the payment network if certain illegal activity is *[...]* found. Perfect 10 has alleged that certain websites are infringing Perfect 10's copyrights and that Perfect 10 sent notices of this alleged infringement to Defendants. Accordingly, Perfect 10 has adequately pled that (1) infringement of Perfect 10's copyrights was occurring, (2) Defendants were aware of the infringement, and (3) on this basis, Defendants could have stopped processing credit card payments to the infringing websites. These allegations are not, however, sufficient to establish vicarious liability because even with all reasonable inferences drawn in Perfect 10's favor, Perfect 10's allegations of fact cannot support a finding that Defendants have the right and ability to control the infringing activity.

62   In reasoning closely analogous to the present case, the *Amazon.com* court held that Google was not vicariously liable for third-party infringement that its search engine facilitates. In so holding, the court found that Google's ability to control its own index, search results, and webpages does not give Google the right to control the infringing acts of third parties even though that ability would allow Google to affect those infringing acts to some degree. *[...]* Moreover, and even more importantly, the *Amazon.com* court rejected a vicarious liability claim based on Google's policies with sponsored advertisers, which state that it reserves "the right to monitor and terminate partnerships with entities that violate others' copyright[s]." *[...]*

63   *Id.* This reasoning is equally applicable to the Defendants in this case. Just like Google, Defendants could likely take certain steps that may have the indirect effect of reducing infringing activity on the Internet at large. However, neither Google nor Defendants has any ability to directly control that activity, and the mere ability to withdraw a financial "carrot" does not create the "stick" of "right and ability to control" that vicarious infringement requires. A finding of vicarious liability here, under the theories advocated by the dissent, would also require a finding that Google is vicariously liable for infringement—a conflict we need not create, and radical step we do not take.

65   [...]

69   Perfect 10 also argues that were infringing websites barred from accepting the Defendants' credit cards, it would be impossible for an online website selling adult images to compete and operate at a profit.[18] While we must take this allegation as *[...]* true, it still fails to state a claim because it conflates the power to stop profiteering with the right and ability to control infringement. Perfect 10's allegations do not establish that Defendants have the authority to prevent theft or alteration of the copyrighted images, remove infringing material from these websites or prevent its distribution over the Internet. Rather, they merely state that this infringing activity could not be *profitable* without access to Defendants' credit card payment systems. The alleged infringement does not turn on the payment; it turns on the reproduction, alteration and distribution of the images, which Defendants do not do, and which occurs over networks Defendants do not control.

70   The Supreme Court's recent decision in *Grokster* does not undermine the validity of this distinction. As we held in *Amazon.com[...]* *Grokster* does not stand for the proposition that just because the services provided by a company help an infringing enterprise generate revenue, that company is necessarily vicariously liable for that infringement. Numerous services are required for the third party infringers referred to by Perfect 10 to operate. In addition to the necessity of creating and maintaining a website, numerous hardware manufacturers must produce the computer on which the website physically sits; a software engineer must create the program that copies and alters the stolen images; technical support companies must fix any hardware and software problems; utility companies must provide the electricity that makes all these different related operations run, etc. All these services are essential to make the businesses described viable, they all profit to some degree from those businesses, and by withholding their services, they could impair—perhaps even destroy—the commercial viability of those business. But that does not mean, and *Grokster* by no means holds, that they are all potentially liable as vicarious infringers. Even though they have the "right" to refuse their services, and hence the literal power to "stop or limit" the infringement, they, like Defendants, do not exercise sufficient control over the actual infringing activity for vicarious liability to attach.

71   ## b. Obvious and Direct Financial Interest in the Infringing Activity

72   Because Perfect 10 has failed to show that Defendants have the right and ability to control the alleged infringing conduct, it has not pled a viable claim of vicarious liability. Accordingly, we need not reach the issue of direct financial interest.

73   [...]

88   # CONCLUSION

95   We decline to create any of the radical new theories of liability advocated by Perfect 10 and the dissent and we affirm the district court's dismissal with prejudice of all causes of action in Perfect 10's complaint for failure to state a claim upon which relief can be granted.

96   AFFIRMED.

97   [...]

100   [1] While Perfect 10's complaint does not clearly specify which of Perfect 10's rights are being infringed, it appears that at least four such rights are potentially at issue: reproduction (17 U.S.C. § 106(1)); derivative works (17 U.S.C. § 106(2)); distribution of copies (17 U.S.C. § 106(3)); and public display (17 U.S.C. § 106(5)).

149   [2] Congress expressed similar sentiments when it enacted the Digital Millennium Copyright Act (DMCA), 17 U.S.C. § 512, one of the stated purposes of which was to "facilitate the robust development and worldwide expansion of electronic commerce, communications, research, development, and education in the digital age." [...]

151   [4] We note that an anomaly exists regarding the concept of notice in secondary copyright infringement cases outside a FRCP 12(b)(6) context. Congress addressed the issue of notice in the DMCA, which grants a safe harbor against liability to certain Internet service providers, even those with actual knowledge of infringement, if they have not received statutorily-compliant notice. [...] Because Defendants are not "service providers" within the scope of the DMCA, they are not eligible for these safe harbors. The result, under Perfect 10's theories, would therefore be that a service provider with actual knowledge of infringement and the actual ability to remove the infringing material, but which has not received a statutorily compliant notice, is entitled to a safe harbor from liability, while credit card companies with actual knowledge but *without* the actual ability to remove infringing material, would benefit from no safe harbor. We recognize that the DMCA was not intended to displace the development of secondary liability in the courts; rather, we simply take note of the anomalous result Perfect 10 seeks.

152   [5] Because the *Grokster* court focused primarily on an "inducement" theory rather than a "material contribution" theory, our primary discussion of *Grokster* is located below in the "inducement" section of this opinion.

153   [...]

181

Copyright Statutes

Copyright Act: 17 U.S. Code § 101 - Definitions

Except as otherwise provided in this title, as used in this title, the following terms and their variant forms mean the following:

An "anonymous work" is a work on the copies or phonorecords of which no natural person is identified as author.

An "architectural work" is the design of a building as embodied in any tangible medium of expression, including a building, architectural plans, or drawings. The work includes the overall form as well as the arrangement and composition of spaces and elements in the design, but does not include individual standard features.

"Audiovisual works" are works that consist of a series of related images which are intrinsically intended to be shown by the use of machines, or devices such as projectors, viewers, or electronic equipment, together with accompanying sounds, if any, regardless of the nature of the material objects, such as films or tapes, in which the works are embodied.

The "Berne Convention" is the Convention for the Protection of Literary and Artistic Works, signed at Berne, Switzerland, on September 9, 1886, and all acts, protocols, and revisions thereto.

The "best edition" of a work is the edition, published in the United States at any time before the date of deposit, that the Library of Congress determines to be most suitable for its purposes.

A person's "children" are that person's immediate offspring, whether legitimate or not, and any children legally adopted by that person.

A "collective work" is a work, such as a periodical issue, anthology, or encyclopedia, in which a number of contributions, constituting separate and independent works in themselves, are assembled into a collective whole.

A "compilation" is a work formed by the collection and assembling of preexisting materials or of data that are selected, coordinated, or arranged in such a way that the resulting work as a whole constitutes an original work of authorship. The term "compilation" includes collective works.

A "computer program" is a set of statements or instructions to be used directly or indirectly in a computer in order to bring about a certain result.

"Copies" are material objects, other than phonorecords, in which a work is fixed by any method now known or later developed, and from which the work can be perceived, reproduced, or otherwise communicated, either directly or with the aid of a machine or device. The term "copies" includes the material object, other than a phonorecord, in which the work is first fixed.

"Copyright owner", with respect to any one of the exclusive rights comprised in a copyright, refers to the owner of that particular right.

A "Copyright Royalty Judge" is a Copyright Royalty Judge appointed under section 802 of this title, and includes any individual serving as an interim Copyright Royalty Judge under such section.

A work is "created" when it is fixed in a copy or phonorecord for the first time; where a work is prepared over a period of time, the portion of it that has been fixed at any particular time constitutes the work as of that time, and where the work has been prepared in different versions, each version constitutes a separate work.

A "derivative work" is a work based upon one or more preexisting works, such as a translation, musical arrangement, dramatization, fictionalization, motion picture version, sound recording, art reproduction, abridgment, condensation, or any other form in which a work may be recast, transformed, or adapted. A work consisting of editorial revisions, annotations, elaborations, or other modifications which, as a whole, represent an original work of authorship, is a "derivative work".

A "device", "machine", or "process" is one now known or later developed.

A "digital transmission" is a transmission in whole or in part in a digital or other non-analog format.

To "display" a work means to show a copy of it, either directly or by means of a film, slide, television image, or any other device or process or, in the case of a motion picture or other audiovisual work, to show individual images nonsequentially.

An "establishment" is a store, shop, or any similar place of business open to the general public for the primary purpose of selling goods or services in which the majority of the gross square feet of space that is nonresidential is used for that purpose, and in which nondramatic musical works are performed publicly.

The term "financial gain" includes receipt, or expectation of receipt, of anything of value, including the receipt of other copyrighted works.

A work is "fixed" in a tangible medium of expression when its embodiment in a copy or phonorecord, by or under the authority of the author, is sufficiently permanent or stable to permit it to be perceived, reproduced, or otherwise communicated for a period of more than transitory duration. A work consisting of sounds, images, or both, that are being transmitted, is "fixed" for purposes of this title if a fixation of the work is being made simultaneously with its transmission.

A "food service or drinking establishment" is a restaurant, inn, bar, tavern, or any other similar place of business in which the public or patrons assemble for the primary purpose of being served food or drink, in which the majority of the gross square feet of space that is nonresidential is used for that purpose, and in which nondramatic musical works are performed publicly.

The "Geneva Phonograms Convention" is the Convention for the Protection of Producers of Phonograms Against Unauthorized Duplication of Their Phonograms, concluded at Geneva, Switzerland, on October 29, 1971.

The "gross square feet of space" of an establishment means the entire interior space of that establishment, and any adjoining outdoor space used to serve patrons, whether on a seasonal basis or otherwise.

The terms "including" and "such as" are illustrative and not limitative.

An "international agreement" is—

(1) the Universal Copyright Convention;

(2) the Geneva Phonograms Convention;

(3) the Berne Convention;

(4) the WTO Agreement;

(5) the WIPO Copyright Treaty;

(6) the WIPO Performances and Phonograms Treaty; and

(7) any other copyright treaty to which the United States is a party.

A "joint work" is a work prepared by two or more authors with the intention that their contributions be merged into inseparable or interdependent parts of a unitary whole.

"Literary works" are works, other than audiovisual works, expressed in words, numbers, or other verbal or numerical symbols or indicia, regardless of the nature of the material objects, such as books, periodicals, manuscripts, phonorecords, film, tapes, disks, or cards, in which they are embodied.

The term "motion picture exhibition facility" means a movie theater, screening room, or other venue that is being used primarily for the exhibition of a copyrighted motion picture, if such exhibition is open to the public or is made to an assembled group of viewers outside of a normal circle of a family and its social acquaintances.

"Motion pictures" are audiovisual works consisting of a series of related images which, when shown in succession, impart an impression of motion, together with accompanying sounds, if any.

To "perform" a work means to recite, render, play, dance, or act it, either directly or by means of any device or process or, in the case of a motion picture or other audiovisual work, to show its images in any sequence or to make the sounds accompanying it audible.

A "performing rights society" is an association, corporation, or other entity that licenses the public performance of nondramatic musical works on behalf of copyright owners of such works, such as the American Society of Composers, Authors and Publishers (ASCAP), Broadcast Music, Inc. (BMI), and SESAC, Inc.

"Phonorecords" are material objects in which sounds, other than those accompanying a motion picture or other audiovisual work, are fixed by any method now known or later developed, and from which the sounds can be perceived, reproduced, or otherwise communicated, either directly or with the aid of a machine or device. The term "phonorecords" includes the material object in which the sounds are first fixed.

"Pictorial, graphic, and sculptural works" include two-dimensional and three-dimensional works of fine, graphic, and applied art, photographs, prints and art reproductions, maps, globes, charts, diagrams, models, and technical drawings, including architectural plans. Such works shall include works of artistic craftsmanship insofar as their form but not their mechanical or utilitarian aspects are concerned; the design of a useful article, as defined in this section, shall be considered a pictorial, graphic, or sculptural work only if, and only to the extent that, such design incorporates pictorial, graphic, or sculptural features that can be identified separately from, and are capable of existing independently of, the utilitarian aspects of the article.

For purposes of section 513, a "proprietor" is an individual, corporation, partnership, or other entity, as the case may be, that owns an establishment or a food service or drinking establishment, except that no owner or operator of a radio or television station licensed by the Federal Communications Commission, cable system or satellite carrier, cable or satellite carrier service or programmer, provider of online services or network access or the operator of facilities therefor, telecommunications company, or any other such audio or audiovisual service or programmer now known or as may be developed in the future, commercial subscription music service, or owner or operator of any other transmission service, shall under any circumstances be deemed to be a proprietor.

A "pseudonymous work" is a work on the copies or phonorecords of which the author is identified under a fictitious name.

"Publication" is the distribution of copies or phonorecords of a work to the public by sale or other transfer of ownership, or by rental, lease, or lending. The offering to distribute copies or phonorecords to a group of persons for purposes of further distribution, public performance, or public display, constitutes publication. A public performance or display of a work does not of itself constitute publication.

To perform or display a work "publicly" means—

(1) to perform or display it at a place open to the public or at any place where a substantial number of persons outside of a normal circle of a family and its social acquaintances is gathered; or

(2) to transmit or otherwise communicate a performance or display of the work to a place specified by clause (1) or to the public, by means of any device or process, whether the members of the public capable of receiving the performance or display receive it in the same place or in separate places and at the same time or at different times.

"Registration", for purposes of sections 205 (c)(2), 405, 406, 410 (d), 411, 412, and 506(e), means a registration of a claim in the original or the renewed and extended term of copyright.

"Sound recordings" are works that result from the fixation of a series of musical, spoken, or other sounds, but not including the sounds accompanying a motion picture or other audiovisual work, regardless of the nature of the material objects, such as disks, tapes, or other phonorecords, in which they are embodied.

"State" includes the District of Columbia and the Commonwealth of Puerto Rico, and any territories to which this title is made applicable by an Act of Congress.

A "transfer of copyright ownership" is an assignment, mortgage, exclusive license, or any other conveyance, alienation, or hypothecation of a copyright or of any of the exclusive rights comprised in a copyright, whether or not it is limited in time or place of effect, but not including a nonexclusive license.

A "transmission program" is a body of material that, as an aggregate, has been produced for the sole purpose of transmission to the public in sequence and as a unit.

To "transmit" a performance or display is to communicate it by any device or process whereby images or sounds are received beyond the place from which they are sent.

A "treaty party" is a country or intergovernmental organization other than the United States that is a party to an international agreement.

The "United States", when used in a geographical sense, comprises the several States, the District of Columbia and the Commonwealth of Puerto Rico, and the organized territories under the jurisdiction of the United States Government.

For purposes of section 411, a work is a "United States work" only if—

(1) in the case of a published work, the work is first published—

    (A) in the United States;

    (B) simultaneously in the United States and another treaty party or parties, whose law grants a term of copyright protection that is the same as or longer than the term provided in the United States;

    (C) simultaneously in the United States and a foreign nation that is not a treaty party; or

    (D) in a foreign nation that is not a treaty party, and all of the authors of the work are nationals, domiciliaries, or habitual residents of, or in the case of an audiovisual work legal entities with headquarters in, the United States;

(2) in the case of an unpublished work, all the authors of the work are nationals, domiciliaries, or habitual residents of the United States, or, in the case of an unpublished audiovisual work, all the authors are legal entities with headquarters in the United States; or

(3) in the case of a pictorial, graphic, or sculptural work incorporated in a building or structure, the building or structure is located in the United States.

A "useful article" is an article having an intrinsic utilitarian function that is not merely to portray the appearance of the article or to convey information. An article that is normally a part of a useful article is considered a "useful article".

The author's "widow" or "widower" is the author's surviving spouse under the law of the author's domicile at the time of his or her death, whether or not the spouse has later remarried.

The "WIPO Copyright Treaty" is the WIPO Copyright Treaty concluded at Geneva, Switzerland, on December 20, 1996.

The "WIPO Performances and Phonograms Treaty" is the WIPO Performances and Phonograms Treaty concluded at Geneva, Switzerland, on December 20, 1996.

A "work of visual art" is—

(1) a painting, drawing, print, or sculpture, existing in a single copy, in a limited edition of 200 copies or fewer that are signed and consecutively numbered by the author, or, in the case of a sculpture, in multiple cast, carved, or fabricated sculptures of 200 or fewer that are consecutively numbered by the author and bear the signature or other identifying mark of the author; or

(2) a still photographic image produced for exhibition purposes only, existing in a single copy that is signed by the author, or in a limited edition of 200 copies or fewer that are signed and consecutively numbered by the author.

, work of visual art does not include—

(A)

(i) any poster, map, globe, chart, technical drawing, diagram, model, applied art, motion picture or other audiovisual work, book, magazine, newspaper, periodical, data base, electronic information service, electronic publication, or similar publication;

(ii) any merchandising item or advertising, promotional, descriptive, covering, or packaging material or container;

(iii) any portion or part of any item described in clause (i) or (ii);

(B) any work made for hire; or

(C) any work not subject to copyright protection under this title.

A "work of the United States Government" is a work prepared by an officer or employee of the United States Government as part of that person's official duties.

A "work made for hire" is—

(1) a work prepared by an employee within the scope of his or her employment; or

(2) a work specially ordered or commissioned for use as a contribution to a collective work, as a part of a motion picture or other audiovisual work, as a translation, as a supplementary work, as a compilation, as an instructional text, as a test, as answer material for a test, or as an atlas, if the parties expressly agree in a written instrument signed by them that the work shall be considered a work made for hire. For the purpose of the foregoing sentence, a "supplementary work" is a work prepared for publication as a secondary adjunct to a work by another author for the purpose of introducing, concluding, illustrating, explaining, revising, commenting upon, or assisting in the use of the other work, such as forewords, afterwords, pictorial illustrations, maps, charts, tables, editorial notes, musical arrangements, answer material for tests, bibliographies, appendixes, and indexes, and an "instructional text" is a literary, pictorial, or graphic work prepared for publication and with the purpose of use in systematic instructional activities.

ı determining whether any work is eligible to be considered a work made for hire under paragraph (2), neither the amendment contained ı section 1011(d) of the Intellectual Property and Communications Omnibus Reform Act of 1999, as enacted by section 1000(a)(9) fPublic Law 106–113, nor the deletion of the words added by that amendment—

(A) shall be considered or otherwise given any legal significance, or

(B) shall be interpreted to indicate congressional approval or disapproval of, or acquiescence in, any judicial determination,

by the courts or the Copyright Office. Paragraph (2) shall be interpreted as if both section 2(a)(1) of the Work Made For Hire and Copyright Corrections Act of 2000 and section 1011(d) of the Intellectual Property and Communications Omnibus Reform Act of 1999, as enacted by section 1000(a)(9) ofPublic Law 106–113, were never enacted, and without regard to any inaction or awareness by the Congress at any time of any judicial determinations.

The terms "WTO Agreement" and "WTO member country" have the meanings given those terms in paragraphs (9) and (10), respectively, of section 2 of the Uruguay Round Agreements Act.

Copyright Act: 17 U.S. Code § 102 - Subject matter of copyright: In general

(a) Copyright protection subsists, in accordance with this title, in original works of authorship fixed in any tangible medium of expression, now known or later developed, from which they can be perceived, reproduced, or otherwise communicated, either directly or with the aid of a machine or device. Works of authorship include the following categories:

(1) literary works;

(2) musical works, including any accompanying words;

(3) dramatic works, including any accompanying music;

(4) pantomimes and choreographic works;

(5) pictorial, graphic, and sculptural works;

(6) motion pictures and other audiovisual works;

(7) sound recordings; and

(8) architectural works.

(b) In no case does copyright protection for an original work of authorship extend to any idea, procedure, process, system, method of operation, concept, principle, or discovery, regardless of the form in which it is described, explained, illustrated, or embodied in such work.

Copyright Act: 17 U.S. Code § 103 - Subject matter of copyright: Compilations and derivative works

(a) The subject matter of copyright as specified by section 102 includes compilations and derivative works, but protection for a work employing preexisting material in which copyright subsists does not extend to any part of the work in which such material has been used unlawfully.

(b) The copyright in a compilation or derivative work extends only to the material contributed by the author of such work, as distinguished from the preexisting material employed in the work, and does not imply any exclusive right in the preexisting material. The copyright in such work is independent of, and does not affect or enlarge the scope, duration, ownership, or subsistence of, any copyright protection in the preexisting material.

Copyright Act: 17 U.S. Code § 106 - Exclusive rights in copyrighted works

Subject to sections 107 through 122, the owner of copyright under this title has the exclusive rights to do and to authorize any of the following:

(1) to reproduce the copyrighted work in copies or phonorecords;

(2) to prepare derivative works based upon the copyrighted work;

(3) to distribute copies or phonorecords of the copyrighted work to the public by sale or other transfer of ownership, or by rental, lease, or lending;

(4) in the case of literary, musical, dramatic, and choreographic works, pantomimes, and motion pictures and other audiovisual works, to perform the copyrighted work publicly;

(5) in the case of literary, musical, dramatic, and choreographic works, pantomimes, and pictorial, graphic, or sculptural works, including the individual images of a motion picture or other audiovisual work, to display the copyrighted work publicly; and

(6) in the case of sound recordings, to perform the copyrighted work publicly by means of a digital audio transmission.

Copyright Act: 17 U.S. Code § 107 - Limitations on exclusive rights: Fair use

Notwithstanding the provisions of sections 106 and 106A, the fair use of a copyrighted work, including such use by reproduction in copies or phonorecords or by any other means specified by that section, for purposes such as criticism, comment, news reporting, teaching (including multiple copies for classroom use), scholarship, or research, is not an infringement of copyright. In determining whether the use made of a work in any particular case is a fair use the factors to be considered shall include—

(1) the purpose and character of the use, including whether such use is of a commercial nature or is for nonprofit educational purposes;

(2) the nature of the copyrighted work;

(3) the amount and substantiality of the portion used in relation to the copyrighted work as a whole; and

(4) the effect of the use upon the potential market for or value of the copyrighted work.

he fact that a work is unpublished shall not itself bar a finding of fair use if such finding is made upon consideration of all the above factors.

Copyright Act: 17 U.S. Code § 109 - Limitations on exclusive rights: Effect of transfer of particular copy or phonorecord

(a) Notwithstanding the provisions of section 106 (3), the owner of a particular copy or phonorecord lawfully made under this title, or any person authorized by such owner, is entitled, without the authority of the copyright owner, to sell or otherwise dispose of the possession of that copy or phonorecord. Notwithstanding the preceding sentence, copies or phonorecords of works subject to restored copyright under section 104A that are manufactured before the date of restoration of copyright or, with respect to reliance parties, before publication or service of notice under section 104A (e), may be sold or otherwise disposed of without the authorization of the owner of the restored copyright for purposes of direct or indirect commercial advantage only during the 12-month period beginning on—

    (1) the date of the publication in the Federal Register of the notice of intent filed with the Copyright Office under section 104A (d)(2)(A), or

    (2) the date of the receipt of actual notice served under section 104A (d)(2)(B),

whichever occurs first.

(b)

    (1)

        (A) Notwithstanding the provisions of subsection (a), unless authorized by the owners of copyright in the sound recording or the owner of copyright in a computer program (including any tape, disk, or other medium embodying such program), and in the case of a sound recording in the musical works embodied therein, neither the owner of a particular phonorecord nor any person in possession of a particular copy of a computer program (including any tape, disk, or other medium embodying such program), may, for the purposes of direct or indirect commercial advantage, dispose of, or authorize the disposal of, the possession of that phonorecord or computer program (including any tape, disk, or other medium embodying such program) by rental, lease, or lending, or by any other act or practice in the nature of rental, lease, or lending. Nothing in the preceding sentence shall apply to the rental, lease, or lending of a phonorecord for nonprofit purposes by a nonprofit library or nonprofit educational institution. The transfer of possession of a lawfully made copy of a computer program by a nonprofit educational institution to another nonprofit educational institution or to faculty, staff, and students does not constitute rental, lease, or lending for direct or indirect commercial purposes under this subsection.

        (B) This subsection does not apply to—

            (i) a computer program which is embodied in a machine or product and which cannot be copied during the ordinary operation or use of the machine or product; or

            (ii) a computer program embodied in or used in conjunction with a limited purpose computer that is designed for playing video games and may be designed for other purposes.

        (C) Nothing in this subsection affects any provision of chapter 9 of this title.

    (2)

        (A) Nothing in this subsection shall apply to the lending of a computer program for nonprofit purposes by a nonprofit library, if each copy of a computer program which is lent by such library has affixed to the packaging containing the program a warning of copyright in accordance with requirements that the Register of Copyrights shall prescribe by regulation.

        (B) Not later than three years after the date of the enactment of the Computer Software Rental Amendments Act of 1990, and at such times thereafter as the Register of Copyrights considers appropriate, the Register of Copyrights, after consultation with representatives of copyright owners and librarians, shall submit to the Congress a report stating whether this paragraph has achieved its intended purpose of maintaining the integrity of the copyright system while providing nonprofit libraries the capability to fulfill their function. Such report shall advise the Congress as to any information or recommendations that the Register of Copyrights considers necessary to carry out the purposes of this subsection.

(3) Nothing in this subsection shall affect any provision of the antitrust laws. For purposes of the preceding sentence, "antitrust laws" has the meaning given that term in the first section of the Clayton Act and includes section 5 of the Federal Trade Commission Act to the extent that section relates to unfair methods of competition.

(4) Any person who distributes a phonorecord or a copy of a computer program (including any tape, disk, or other medium embodying such program) in violation of paragraph (1) is an infringer of copyright under section 501 of this title and is subject to the remedies set forth in sections 502, 503, 504, and 505. Such violation shall not be a criminal offense under section 506 or cause such person to be subject to the criminal penalties set forth in section 2319 of title 18.

(c) Notwithstanding the provisions of section 106 (5), the owner of a particular copy lawfully made under this title, or any person authorized by such owner, is entitled, without the authority of the copyright owner, to display that copy publicly, either directly or by the projection of no more than one image at a time, to viewers present at the place where the copy is located.

(d) The privileges prescribed by subsections (a) and (c) do not, unless authorized by the copyright owner, extend to any person who has acquired possession of the copy or phonorecord from the copyright owner, by rental, lease, loan, or otherwise, without acquiring ownership of it.

(e) Notwithstanding the provisions of sections 106 (4) and 106 (5), in the case of an electronic audiovisual game intended for use in coin-operated equipment, the owner of a particular copy of such a game lawfully made under this title, is entitled, without the authority of the copyright owner of the game, to publicly perform or display that game in coin-operated equipment, except that this subsection shall not apply to any work of authorship embodied in the audiovisual game if the copyright owner of the electronic audiovisual game is not also the copyright owner of the work of authorship.

Copyright Act: 17 U.S. Code § 110 - Limitations on exclusive rights: Exemption of certain performances and displays

Notwithstanding the provisions of section 106, the following are not infringements of copyright:

(1) performance or display of a work by instructors or pupils in the course of face-to-face teaching activities of a nonprofit educational institution, in a classroom or similar place devoted to instruction, unless, in the case of a motion picture or other audiovisual work, the performance, or the display of individual images, is given by means of a copy that was not lawfully made under this title, and that the person responsible for the performance knew or had reason to believe was not lawfully made;

(2) except with respect to a work produced or marketed primarily for performance or display as part of mediated instructional activities transmitted via digital networks, or a performance or display that is given by means of a copy or phonorecord that is not lawfully made and acquired under this title, and the transmitting government body or accredited nonprofit educational institution knew or had reason to believe was not lawfully made and acquired, the performance of a nondramatic literary or musical work or reasonable and limited portions of any other work, or display of a work in an amount comparable to that which is typically displayed in the course of a live classroom session, by or in the course of a transmission, if—

  (A) the performance or display is made by, at the direction of, or under the actual supervision of an instructor as an integral part of a class session offered as a regular part of the systematic mediated instructional activities of a governmental body or an accredited nonprofit educational institution;

  (B) the performance or display is directly related and of material assistance to the teaching content of the transmission;

  (C) the transmission is made solely for, and, to the extent technologically feasible, the reception of such transmission is limited to—

    (i) students officially enrolled in the course for which the transmission is made; or

    (ii) officers or employees of governmental bodies as a part of their official duties or employment; and

  (D) the transmitting body or institution—

    (i) institutes policies regarding copyright, provides informational materials to faculty, students, and relevant staff members that accurately describe, and promote compliance with, the laws of the United States relating to copyright, and provides notice to students that materials used in connection with the course may be subject to copyright protection; and

    (ii) in the case of digital transmissions—

      (I) applies technological measures that reasonably prevent—

        (aa) retention of the work in accessible form by recipients of the transmission from the transmitting body or institution for longer than the class session; and

        (bb) unauthorized further dissemination of the work in accessible form by such recipients to others; and

      (II) does not engage in conduct that could reasonably be expected to interfere with technological measures used by copyright owners to prevent such retention or unauthorized further dissemination;

(3) performance of a nondramatic literary or musical work or of a dramatico-musical work of a religious nature, or display of a work, in the course of services at a place of worship or other religious assembly;

(4) performance of a nondramatic literary or musical work otherwise than in a transmission to the public, without any purpose of direct or indirect commercial advantage and without payment of any fee or other compensation for the performance to any of its performers, promoters, or organizers, if—

(A) there is no direct or indirect admission charge; or

(B) the proceeds, after deducting the reasonable costs of producing the performance, are used exclusively for educational, religious, or charitable purposes and not for private financial gain, except where the copyright owner has served notice of objection to the performance under the following conditions:

  (i) the notice shall be in writing and signed by the copyright owner or such owner's duly authorized agent; and

  (ii) the notice shall be served on the person responsible for the performance at least seven days before the date of the performance, and shall state the reasons for the objection; and

  (iii) the notice shall comply, in form, content, and manner of service, with requirements that the Register of Copyrights shall prescribe by regulation;

(5)

  (A) except as provided in subparagraph (B), communication of a transmission embodying a performance or display of a work by the public reception of the transmission on a single receiving apparatus of a kind commonly used in private homes, unless—

   (i) a direct charge is made to see or hear the transmission; or

   (ii) the transmission thus received is further transmitted to the public;

  (B) communication by an establishment of a transmission or retransmission embodying a performance or display of a nondramatic musical work intended to be received by the general public, originated by a radio or television broadcast station licensed as such by the Federal Communications Commission, or, if an audiovisual transmission, by a cable system or satellite carrier, if—

   (i) in the case of an establishment other than a food service or drinking establishment, either the establishment in which the communication occurs has less than 2,000 gross square feet of space (excluding space used for customer parking and for no other purpose), or the establishment in which the communication occurs has 2,000 or more gross square feet of space (excluding space used for customer parking and for no other purpose) and—

    (I) if the performance is by audio means only, the performance is communicated by means of a total of not more than 6 loudspeakers, of which not more than 4 loudspeakers are located in any 1 room or adjoining outdoor space; or

    (II) if the performance or display is by audiovisual means, any visual portion of the performance or display is communicated by means of a total of not more than 4 audiovisual devices, of which not more than 1 audiovisual device is located in any 1 room, and no such audiovisual device has a diagonal screen size greater than 55 inches, and any audio portion of the performance or display is communicated by means of a total of not more than 6 loudspeakers, of which not more than 4 loudspeakers are located in any 1 room or adjoining outdoor space;

   (ii) in the case of a food service or drinking establishment, either the establishment in which the communication occurs has less than 3,750 gross square feet of space (excluding space used for customer parking and for no other purpose), or the establishment in which the communication occurs has 3,750 gross square feet of space or more (excluding space used for customer parking and for no other purpose) and—

    (I) if the performance is by audio means only, the performance is communicated by means of a total of not more than 6 loudspeakers, of which not more than 4 loudspeakers are located in any 1 room or adjoining outdoor space; or

    (II) if the performance or display is by audiovisual means, any visual portion of the performance or display is communicated by means of a total of not more than 4 audiovisual devices, of which not more than one audiovisual device is located in any 1 room, and no such audiovisual device has a diagonal screen size greater than 55 inches, and any audio portion of the performance or display is communicated by means of a total of not more than 6 loudspeakers, of which not more than 4 loudspeakers are located in any 1 room or adjoining outdoor space;

   (iii) no direct charge is made to see or hear the transmission or retransmission;

(iv) the transmission or retransmission is not further transmitted beyond the establishment where it is received; and

(v) the transmission or retransmission is licensed by the copyright owner of the work so publicly performed or displayed;

(6) performance of a nondramatic musical work by a governmental body or a nonprofit agricultural or horticultural organization, in the course of an annual agricultural or horticultural fair or exhibition conducted by such body or organization; the exemption provided by this clause shall extend to any liability for copyright infringement that would otherwise be imposed on such body or organization, under doctrines of vicarious liability or related infringement, for a performance by a concessionnaire, [1] business establishment, or other person at such fair or exhibition, but shall not excuse any such person from liability for the performance;

(7) performance of a nondramatic musical work by a vending establishment open to the public at large without any direct or indirect admission charge, where the sole purpose of the performance is to promote the retail sale of copies or phonorecords of the work, or of the audiovisual or other devices utilized in such performance, and the performance is not transmitted beyond the place where the establishment is located and is within the immediate area where the sale is occurring;

(8) performance of a nondramatic literary work, by or in the course of a transmission specifically designed for and primarily directed to blind or other handicapped persons who are unable to read normal printed material as a result of their handicap, or deaf or other handicapped persons who are unable to hear the aural signals accompanying a transmission of visual signals, if the performance is made without any purpose of direct or indirect commercial advantage and its transmission is made through the facilities of:

(i) a governmental body; or

(ii) a noncommercial educational broadcast station (as defined in section 397 of title47); or

(iii) a radio subcarrier authorization (as defined in 47 CFR 73.293–73.295 and 73.593–73.595); or

(iv) a cable system (as defined in section 111 (f));

(9) performance on a single occasion of a dramatic literary work published at least ten years before the date of the performance, by or in the course of a transmission specifically designed for and primarily directed to blind or other handicapped persons who are unable to read normal printed material as a result of their handicap, if the performance is made without any purpose of direct or indirect commercial advantage and its transmission is made through the facilities of a radio subcarrier authorization referred to in clause (8)(iii), Provided, That the provisions of this clause shall not be applicable to more than one performance of the same work by the same performers or under the auspices of the same organization;

(10) notwithstanding paragraph (4), the following is not an infringement of copyright: performance of a nondramatic literary or musical work in the course of a social function which is organized and promoted by a nonprofit veterans' organization or a nonprofit fraternal organization to which the general public is not invited, but not including the invitees of the organizations, if the proceeds from the performance, after deducting the reasonable costs of producing the performance, are used exclusively for charitable purposes and not for financial gain. For purposes of this section the social functions of any college or university fraternity or sorority shall not be included unless the social function is held solely to raise funds for a specific charitable purpose; and

(11) the making imperceptible, by or at the direction of a member of a private household, of limited portions of audio or video content of a motion picture, during a performance in or transmitted to that household for private home viewing, from an authorized copy of the motion picture, or the creation or provision of a computer program or other technology that enables such making imperceptible and that is designed and marketed to be used, at the direction of a member of a private household, for such making imperceptible, if no fixed copy of the altered version of the motion picture is created by such computer program or other technology.

he exemptions provided under paragraph (5) shall not be taken into account in any administrative, judicial, or other governmental roceeding to set or adjust the royalties payable to copyright owners for the public performance or display of their works. Royalties ayable to copyright owners for any public performance or display of their works other than such performances or displays as are xempted under paragraph (5) shall not be diminished in any respect as a result of such exemption.

In paragraph (2), the term "mediated instructional activities" with respect to the performance or display of a work by digital transmission under this section refers to activities that use such work as an integral part of the class experience, controlled by or under the actual supervision of the instructor and analogous to the type of performance or display that would take place in a live classroom setting. The term does not refer to activities that use, in 1 or more class sessions of a single course, such works as textbooks, course packs, or other material in any media, copies or phonorecords of which are typically purchased or acquired by the students in higher education for their independent use and retention or are typically purchased or acquired for elementary and secondary students for their possession and independent use.

For purposes of paragraph (2), accreditation—

(A) with respect to an institution providing post-secondary education, shall be as determined by a regional or national accrediting agency recognized by the Council on Higher Education Accreditation or the United States Department of Education; and

(B) with respect to an institution providing elementary or secondary education, shall be as recognized by the applicable state certification or licensing procedures.

For purposes of paragraph (2), no governmental body or accredited nonprofit educational institution shall be liable for infringement by reason of the transient or temporary storage of material carried out through the automatic technical process of a digital transmission of the performance or display of that material as authorized under paragraph (2). No such material stored on the system or network controlled or operated by the transmitting body or institution under this paragraph shall be maintained on such system or network in a manner ordinarily accessible to anyone other than anticipated recipients. No such copy shall be maintained on the system or network in a manner ordinarily accessible to such anticipated recipients for a longer period than is reasonably necessary to facilitate the transmissions for which it was made.

For purposes of paragraph (11), the term "making imperceptible" does not include the addition of audio or video content that is performed or displayed over or in place of existing content in a motion picture.

Nothing in paragraph (11) shall be construed to imply further rights under section 106 of this title, or to have any effect on defenses or limitations on rights granted under any other section of this title or under any other paragraph of this section.

Digital Millenium Copyright Act: 17 U.S. Code § 114 - Scope of exclusive rights in sound recordings

(a) The exclusive rights of the owner of copyright in a sound recording are limited to the rights specified by clauses (1), (2), (3) and (6) of section 106, and do not include any right of performance under section 106 (4).

(b) The exclusive right of the owner of copyright in a sound recording under clause (1) of section 106 is limited to the right to duplicate the sound recording in the form of phonorecords or copies that directly or indirectly recapture the actual sounds fixed in the recording. The exclusive right of the owner of copyright in a sound recording under clause (2) of section 106 is limited to the right to prepare a derivative work in which the actual sounds fixed in the sound recording are rearranged, remixed, or otherwise altered in sequence or quality. The exclusive rights of the owner of copyright in a sound recording under clauses (1) and (2) of section 106 do not extend to the making or duplication of another sound recording that consists entirely of an independent fixation of other sounds, even though such sounds imitate or simulate those in the copyrighted sound recording. The exclusive rights of the owner of copyright in a sound recording under clauses (1), (2), and (3) of section 106 do not apply to sound recordings included in educational television and radio programs (as defined in section 397 of title 47) distributed or transmitted by or through public broadcasting entities (as defined by section 118 (f)): Provided, That copies or phonorecords of said programs are not commercially distributed by or through public broadcasting entities to the general public.

(c) This section does not limit or impair the exclusive right to perform publicly, by means of a phonorecord, any of the works specified by section 106 (4).

(d) Limitations on Exclusive Right.— Notwithstanding the provisions of section 106(6)—

(1) Exempt transmissions and retransmissions.— The performance of a sound recording publicly by means of a digital audio transmission, other than as a part of an interactive service, is not an infringement of section 106 (6) if the performance is part of—

(A) a nonsubscription broadcast transmission;

(B) a retransmission of a nonsubscription broadcast transmission: Provided, That, in the case of a retransmission of a radio station's broadcast transmission—

(i) the radio station's broadcast transmission is not willfully or repeatedly retransmitted more than a radius of 150 miles from the site of the radio broadcast transmitter, however—

(I) the 150 mile limitation under this clause shall not apply when a nonsubscription broadcast transmission by a radio station licensed by the Federal Communications Commission is retransmitted on a nonsubscription basis by a terrestrial broadcast station, terrestrial translator, or terrestrial repeater licensed by the Federal Communications Commission; and

(II) in the case of a subscription retransmission of a nonsubscription broadcast retransmission covered by subclause (I), the 150 mile radius shall be measured from the transmitter site of such broadcast retransmitter;

(ii) the retransmission is of radio station broadcast transmissions that are—

(I) obtained by the retransmitter over the air;

(II) not electronically processed by the retransmitter to deliver separate and discrete signals; and

(III) retransmitted only within the local communities served by the retransmitter;

(iii) the radio station's broadcast transmission was being retransmitted to cable systems (as defined in section 111 (f)) by a satellite carrier on January 1, 1995, and that retransmission was being retransmitted by cable systems as a separate and discrete signal, and the satellite carrier obtains the radio station's broadcast transmission in an analog format: Provided, That the broadcast transmission being retransmitted may embody the programming of no more than one radio station; or

(iv) the radio station's broadcast transmission is made by a noncommercial educational broadcast station funded on or after January 1, 1995, under section 396(k) of the Communications Act of 1934 (47 U.S.C. 396 (k)), consists solely of noncommercial educational and cultural radio programs, and the retransmission, whether or not simultaneous, is a nonsubscription terrestrial broadcast retransmission; or

(C) a transmission that comes within any of the following categories—

(i) a prior or simultaneous transmission incidental to an exempt transmission, such as a feed received by and then retransmitted by an exempt transmitter: Provided, That such incidental transmissions do not include any subscription transmission directly for reception by members of the public;

(ii) a transmission within a business establishment, confined to its premises or the immediately surrounding vicinity;

(iii) a retransmission by any retransmitter, including a multichannel video programming distributor as defined in section 602(12) [1] of the Communications Act of 1934 (47 U.S.C. 522 (12)), of a transmission by a transmitter licensed to publicly perform the sound recording as a part of that transmission, if the retransmission is simultaneous with the licensed transmission and authorized by the transmitter; or

(iv) a transmission to a business establishment for use in the ordinary course of its business: Provided, That the business recipient does not retransmit the transmission outside of its premises or the immediately surrounding vicinity, and that the transmission does not exceed the sound recording performance complement. Nothing in this clause shall limit the scope of the exemption in clause (ii).

(2) Statutory licensing of certain transmissions.— The performance of a sound recording publicly by means of a subscription digital audio transmission not exempt under paragraph (1), an eligible nonsubscription transmission, or a transmission not exempt under paragraph (1) that is made by a preexisting satellite digital audio radio service shall be subject to statutory licensing, in accordance with subsection (f) if—

(A)

(i) the transmission is not part of an interactive service;

(ii) except in the case of a transmission to a business establishment, the transmitting entity does not automatically and intentionally cause any device receiving the transmission to switch from one program channel to another; and

(iii) except as provided in section 1002 (e), the transmission of the sound recording is accompanied, if technically feasible, by the information encoded in that sound recording, if any, by or under the authority of the copyright owner of that sound recording, that identifies the title of the sound recording, the featured recording artist who performs on the sound recording, and related information, including information concerning the underlying musical work and its writer;

(B) in the case of a subscription transmission not exempt under paragraph (1) that is made by a preexisting subscription service in the same transmission medium used by such service on July 31, 1998, or in the case of a transmission not exempt under paragraph (1) that is made by a preexisting satellite digital audio radio service—

(i) the transmission does not exceed the sound recording performance complement; and

(ii) the transmitting entity does not cause to be published by means of an advance program schedule or prior announcement the titles of the specific sound recordings or phonorecords embodying such sound recordings to be transmitted; and

(C) in the case of an eligible nonsubscription transmission or a subscription transmission not exempt under paragraph (1) that is made by a new subscription service or by a preexisting subscription service other than in the same transmission medium used by such service on July 31, 1998—

(i) the transmission does not exceed the sound recording performance complement, except that this requirement shall not apply in the case of a retransmission of a broadcast transmission if the retransmission is made by a transmitting entity that does not have the right or ability to control the programming of the broadcast station making the broadcast transmission, unless—

(I) the broadcast station makes broadcast transmissions—

  (aa) in digital format that regularly exceed the sound recording performance complement; or

  (bb) in analog format, a substantial portion of which, on a weekly basis, exceed the sound recording performance complement; and

  (II) the sound recording copyright owner or its representative has notified the transmitting entity in writing that broadcast transmissions of the copyright owner's sound recordings exceed the sound recording performance complement as provided in this clause;

(ii) the transmitting entity does not cause to be published, or induce or facilitate the publication, by means of an advance program schedule or prior announcement, the titles of the specific sound recordings to be transmitted, the phonorecords embodying such sound recordings, or, other than for illustrative purposes, the names of the featured recording artists, except that this clause does not disqualify a transmitting entity that makes a prior announcement that a particular artist will be featured within an unspecified future time period, and in the case of a retransmission of a broadcast transmission by a transmitting entity that does not have the right or ability to control the programming of the broadcast transmission, the requirement of this clause shall not apply to a prior oral announcement by the broadcast station, or to an advance program schedule published, induced, or facilitated by the broadcast station, if the transmitting entity does not have actual knowledge and has not received written notice from the copyright owner or its representative that the broadcast station publishes or induces or facilitates the publication of such advance program schedule, or if such advance program schedule is a schedule of classical music programming published by the broadcast station in the same manner as published by that broadcast station on or before September 30, 1998;

(iii) the transmission—

  (I) is not part of an archived program of less than 5 hours duration;

  (II) is not part of an archived program of 5 hours or greater in duration that is made available for a period exceeding 2 weeks;

  (III) is not part of a continuous program which is of less than 3 hours duration; or

  (IV) is not part of an identifiable program in which performances of sound recordings are rendered in a predetermined order, other than an archived or continuous program, that is transmitted at—

  (aa) more than 3 times in any 2-week period that have been publicly announced in advance, in the case of a program of less than 1 hour in duration, or

  (bb) more than 4 times in any 2-week period that have been publicly announced in advance, in the case of a program of 1 hour or more in duration,

  except that the requirement of this subclause shall not apply in the case of a retransmission of a broadcast transmission by a transmitting entity that does not have the right or ability to control the programming of the broadcast transmission, unless the transmitting entity is given notice in writing by the copyright owner of the sound recording that the broadcast station makes broadcast transmissions that regularly violate such requirement;

(iv) the transmitting entity does not knowingly perform the sound recording, as part of a service that offers transmissions of visual images contemporaneously with transmissions of sound recordings, in a manner that is likely to cause confusion, to cause mistake, or to deceive, as to the affiliation, connection, or association of the copyright owner or featured recording artist with the transmitting entity or a particular product or service advertised by the transmitting entity, or as to the origin, sponsorship, or approval by the copyright owner or featured recording artist of the activities of the transmitting entity other than the performance of the sound recording itself;

(v) the transmitting entity cooperates to prevent, to the extent feasible without imposing substantial costs or burdens, a transmission recipient or any other person or entity from automatically scanning the transmitting entity's transmissions alone or together with transmissions by other transmitting entities in order to select a particular sound recording to be transmitted to the transmission recipient, except that the requirement of this clause shall not apply to a satellite digital audio service that is in operation, or that is licensed by the Federal Communications Commission, on or before July 31, 1998;

(vi) the transmitting entity takes no affirmative steps to cause or induce the making of a phonorecord by the transmission recipient, and if the technology used by the transmitting entity enables the transmitting entity to limit the making by the transmission recipient of phonorecords of the transmission directly in a digital format, the transmitting entity sets such technology to limit such making of phonorecords to the extent permitted by such technology;

(vii) phonorecords of the sound recording have been distributed to the public under the authority of the copyright owner or the copyright owner authorizes the transmitting entity to transmit the sound recording, and the transmitting entity makes the transmission from a phonorecord lawfully made under the authority of the copyright owner, except that the requirement of this clause shall not apply to a retransmission of a broadcast transmission by a transmitting entity that does not have the right or ability to control the programming of the broadcast transmission, unless the transmitting entity is given notice in writing by the copyright owner of the sound recording that the broadcast station makes broadcast transmissions that regularly violate such requirement;

(viii) the transmitting entity accommodates and does not interfere with the transmission of technical measures that are widely used by sound recording copyright owners to identify or protect copyrighted works, and that are technically feasible of being transmitted by the transmitting entity without imposing substantial costs on the transmitting entity or resulting in perceptible aural or visual degradation of the digital signal, except that the requirement of this clause shall not apply to a satellite digital audio service that is in operation, or that is licensed under the authority of the Federal Communications Commission, on or before July 31, 1998, to the extent that such service has designed, developed, or made commitments to procure equipment or technology that is not compatible with such technical measures before such technical measures are widely adopted by sound recording copyright owners; and

(ix) the transmitting entity identifies in textual data the sound recording during, but not before, the time it is performed, including the title of the sound recording, the title of the phonorecord embodying such sound recording, if any, and the featured recording artist, in a manner to permit it to be displayed to the transmission recipient by the device or technology intended for receiving the service provided by the transmitting entity, except that the obligation in this clause shall not take effect until 1 year after the date of the enactment of the Digital Millennium Copyright Act and shall not apply in the case of a retransmission of a broadcast transmission by a transmitting entity that does not have the right or ability to control the programming of the broadcast transmission, or in the case in which devices or technology intended for receiving the service provided by the transmitting entity that have the capability to display such textual data are not common in the marketplace.

(3) Licenses for transmissions by interactive services.—

(A) No interactive service shall be granted an exclusive license under section 106 (6)for the performance of a sound recording publicly by means of digital audio transmission for a period in excess of 12 months, except that with respect to an exclusive license granted to an interactive service by a licensor that holds the copyright to 1,000 or fewer sound recordings, the period of such license shall not exceed 24 months: Provided, however, That the grantee of such exclusive license shall be ineligible to receive another exclusive license for the performance of that sound recording for a period of 13 months from the expiration of the prior exclusive license.

(B) The limitation set forth in subparagraph (A) of this paragraph shall not apply if—

(i) the licensor has granted and there remain in effect licenses under section 106 (6)for the public performance of sound recordings by means of digital audio transmission by at least 5 different interactive services: Provided, however, That each such license must be for a minimum of 10 percent of the copyrighted sound recordings owned by the licensor that have been licensed to interactive services, but in no event less than 50 sound recordings; or

(ii) the exclusive license is granted to perform publicly up to 45 seconds of a sound recording and the sole purpose of the performance is to promote the distribution or performance of that sound recording.

(C) Notwithstanding the grant of an exclusive or nonexclusive license of the right of public performance under section 106 (6), an interactive service may not publicly perform a sound recording unless a license has been granted for the public performance of any copyrighted musical work contained in the sound recording: Provided, That such license to publicly perform the copyrighted musical work may be granted either by a performing rights society representing the copyright owner or by the copyright owner.

(D) The performance of a sound recording by means of a retransmission of a digital audio transmission is not an infringement of section 106 (6) if—

(i) the retransmission is of a transmission by an interactive service licensed to publicly perform the sound recording to a particular member of the public as part of that transmission; and

(ii) the retransmission is simultaneous with the licensed transmission, authorized by the transmitter, and limited to that particular member of the public intended by the interactive service to be the recipient of the transmission.

(E) For the purposes of this paragraph—

(i) a "licensor" shall include the licensing entity and any other entity under any material degree of common ownership, management, or control that owns copyrights in sound recordings; and

(ii) a "performing rights society" is an association or corporation that licenses the public performance of nondramatic musical works on behalf of the copyright owner, such as the American Society of Composers, Authors and Publishers, Broadcast Music, Inc., and SESAC, Inc.

(4) Rights not otherwise limited.—

(A) Except as expressly provided in this section, this section does not limit or impair the exclusive right to perform a sound recording publicly by means of a digital audio transmission under section 106 (6).

(B) Nothing in this section annuls or limits in any way—

(i) the exclusive right to publicly perform a musical work, including by means of a digital audio transmission, under section 106 (4);

(ii) the exclusive rights in a sound recording or the musical work embodied therein under sections 106 (1), 106 (2) and 106 (3); or

(iii) any other rights under any other clause of section 106, or remedies available under this title, as such rights or remedies exist either before or after the date of enactment of the Digital Performance Right in Sound Recordings Act of 1995.

(C) Any limitations in this section on the exclusive right under section 106 (6) apply only to the exclusive right under section 106 (6) and not to any other exclusive rights under section 106. Nothing in this section shall be construed to annul, limit, impair or otherwise affect in any way the ability of the owner of a copyright in a sound recording to exercise the rights under sections 106 (1), 106 (2) and 106 (3), or to obtain the remedies available under this title pursuant to such rights, as such rights and remedies exist either before or after the date of enactment of the Digital Performance Right in Sound Recordings Act of 1995.

(e) Authority for Negotiations.—

(1) Notwithstanding any provision of the antitrust laws, in negotiating statutory licenses in accordance with subsection (f), any copyright owners of sound recordings and any entities performing sound recordings affected by this section may negotiate and agree upon the royalty rates and license terms and conditions for the performance of such sound recordings and the proportionate division of fees paid among copyright owners, and may designate common agents on a nonexclusive basis to negotiate, agree to, pay, or receive payments.

(2) For licenses granted under section 106 (6), other than statutory licenses, such as for performances by interactive services or performances that exceed the sound recording performance complement—

(A) copyright owners of sound recordings affected by this section may designate common agents to act on their behalf to grant licenses and receive and remit royalty payments: Provided, That each copyright owner shall establish the royalty rates and material license terms and conditions unilaterally, that is, not in agreement, combination, or concert with other copyright owners of sound recordings; and

(B) entities performing sound recordings affected by this section may designate common agents to act on their behalf to obtain licenses and collect and pay royalty fees: Provided, That each entity performing sound recordings shall determine the royalty rates and material license terms and conditions unilaterally, that is, not in agreement, combination, or concert with other entities performing sound recordings.

(f) Licenses for Certain Nonexempt Transmissions.—

(1)

(A) Proceedings under chapter 8 shall determine reasonable rates and terms of royalty payments for subscription transmissions by preexisting subscription services and transmissions by preexisting satellite digital audio radio services specified by subsection (d)(2) during the 5-year period beginning on January 1 of the second year following the year in which the proceedings are to be commenced, except in the case of a different transitional period provided under section 6(b)(3) of the Copyright Royalty and Distribution Reform Act of 2004, or such other period as the parties may agree. Such terms and rates shall distinguish among the different types of digital audio transmission services then in operation. Any copyright owners of sound recordings, preexisting subscription services, or preexisting satellite digital audio radio services may submit to the Copyright Royalty Judges licenses covering such subscription transmissions with respect to such sound recordings. The parties to each proceeding shall bear their own costs.

(B) The schedule of reasonable rates and terms determined by the Copyright Royalty Judges shall, subject to paragraph (3), be binding on all copyright owners of sound recordings and entities performing sound recordings affected by this paragraph during the 5-year period specified in subparagraph (A), a transitional period provided under section 6(b)(3) of the Copyright Royalty and Distribution Reform Act of 2004, or such other period as the parties may agree. In establishing rates and terms for preexisting subscription services and preexisting satellite digital audio radio services, in addition to the objectives set forth in section 801 (b)(1), the Copyright Royalty Judges may consider the rates and terms for comparable types of subscription digital audio transmission services and comparable circumstances under voluntary license agreements described in subparagraph (A).

(C) The procedures under subparagraphs (A) and (B) also shall be initiated pursuant to a petition filed by any copyright owners of sound recordings, any preexisting subscription services, or any preexisting satellite digital audio radio services indicating that a new type of subscription digital audio transmission service on which sound recordings are performed is or is about to become operational, for the purpose of determining reasonable terms and rates of royalty payments with respect to such new type of transmission service for the period beginning with the inception of such new type of service and ending on the date on which the royalty rates and terms for subscription digital audio transmission services most recently determined under subparagraph (A) or (B) and chapter 8 expire, or such other period as the parties may agree.

(2)

(A) Proceedings under chapter 8 shall determine reasonable rates and terms of royalty payments for public performances of sound recordings by means of eligible nonsubscription transmission services and new subscription services specified by subsection (d)(2) during the 5-year period beginning on January 1 of the second year following the year in which the proceedings are to be commenced, except in the case of a different transitional period provided under section 6(b)(3) of the Copyright Royalty and Distribution Reform Act of 2004, or such other period as the parties may agree. Such rates and terms shall distinguish among the different types of eligible nonsubscription transmission services and new subscription services then in operation and shall include a minimum fee for each such type of service. Any copyright owners of sound recordings or any entities performing sound recordings affected by this paragraph may submit to the Copyright Royalty Judges licenses covering such eligible nonsubscription transmissions and new subscription services with respect to such sound recordings. The parties to each proceeding shall bear their own costs.

(B) The schedule of reasonable rates and terms determined by the Copyright Royalty Judges shall, subject to paragraph (3), be binding on all copyright owners of sound recordings and entities performing sound recordings affected by this paragraph during the 5-year period specified in subparagraph (A), a transitional period provided under section 6(b)(3) of the Copyright Royalty and Distribution [2] Act of 2004, or such other period as the parties may agree. Such rates and terms shall distinguish among the different types of eligible nonsubscription transmission services then in operation and shall include a minimum fee for each such type of service, such differences to be based on criteria including, but not limited to, the quantity and nature of the use of sound recordings and the degree to which use of the service may substitute for or may promote the purchase of phonorecords by consumers. In establishing rates and terms for transmissions by eligible nonsubscription services and new subscription services, the Copyright Royalty Judges shall establish rates and terms that most clearly represent the rates and terms that would have been negotiated in the marketplace between a willing buyer and a willing seller. In determining such rates and terms, the Copyright Royalty Judges shall base their decision on economic, competitive and programming information presented by the parties, including—

    (i) whether use of the service may substitute for or may promote the sales of phonorecords or otherwise may interfere with or may enhance the sound recording copyright owner's other streams of revenue from its sound recordings; and

    (ii) the relative roles of the copyright owner and the transmitting entity in the copyrighted work and the service made available to the public with respect to relative creative contribution, technological contribution, capital investment, cost, and risk.

In establishing such rates and terms, the Copyright Royalty Judges may consider the rates and terms for comparable types of digital audio transmission services and comparable circumstances under voluntary license agreements described in subparagraph (A).

(C) The procedures under subparagraphs (A) and (B) shall also be initiated pursuant to a petition filed by any copyright owners of sound recordings or any eligible nonsubscription service or new subscription service indicating that a new type of eligible nonsubscription service or new subscription service on which sound recordings are performed is or is about to become operational, for the purpose of determining reasonable terms and rates of royalty payments with respect to such new type of service for the period beginning with the inception of such new type of service and ending on the date on which the royalty rates and terms for eligible nonsubscription services and new subscription services, as the case may be, most recently determined under subparagraph (A) or (B) and chapter 8 expire, or such other period as the parties may agree.

(3) License agreements voluntarily negotiated at any time between 1 or more copyright owners of sound recordings and 1 or more entities performing sound recordings shall be given effect in lieu of any decision by the Librarian of Congress or determination by the Copyright Royalty Judges.

(4)

(A) The Copyright Royalty Judges shall also establish requirements by which copyright owners may receive reasonable notice of the use of their sound recordings under this section, and under which records of such use shall be kept and made available by entities performing sound recordings. The notice and recordkeeping rules in effect on the day before the effective date of the Copyright Royalty and Distribution Reform Act of 2004 shall remain in effect unless and until new regulations are promulgated by the Copyright Royalty Judges. If new regulations are promulgated under this subparagraph, the Copyright Royalty Judges shall take into account the substance and effect of the rules in effect on the day before the effective date of the Copyright Royalty and Distribution Reform Act of 2004 and shall, to the extent practicable, avoid significant disruption of the functions of any designated agent authorized to collect and distribute royalty fees.

(B) Any person who wishes to perform a sound recording publicly by means of a transmission eligible for statutory licensing under this subsection may do so without infringing the exclusive right of the copyright owner of the sound recording—

    (i) by complying with such notice requirements as the Copyright Royalty Judges shall prescribe by regulation and by paying royalty fees in accordance with this subsection; or

    (ii) if such royalty fees have not been set, by agreeing to pay such royalty fees as shall be determined in accordance with this subsection.

(C) Any royalty payments in arrears shall be made on or before the twentieth day of the month next succeeding the month in which the royalty fees are set.

(5)

(A) Notwithstanding section 112 (e) and the other provisions of this subsection, the receiving agent may enter into agreements for the reproduction and performance of sound recordings under section 112 (e) and this section by any 1 or more commercial webcasters or noncommercial webcasters for a period of not more than 11 years beginning on January 1, 2005, that, once published in the Federal Register pursuant to subparagraph (B), shall be binding on all copyright owners of sound recordings and other persons entitled to payment under this section, in lieu of any determination by the Copyright Royalty Judges. Any such agreement for commercial webcasters may include provisions for payment of royalties on the basis of a percentage of revenue or expenses, or both, and include a minimum fee. Any such agreement may include other terms and conditions, including requirements by which copyright owners may receive notice of the use of their sound recordings and under which records of such use shall be kept and made available by commercial webcasters or noncommercial webcasters. The receiving agent shall be under no obligation to negotiate any such agreement. The receiving agent shall have no obligation to any copyright owner of sound recordings or any other person entitled to payment under this section in negotiating any such agreement, and no liability to any copyright owner of sound recordings or any other person entitled to payment under this section for having entered into such agreement.

(B) The Copyright Office shall cause to be published in the Federal Register any agreement entered into pursuant to subparagraph (A). Such publication shall include a statement containing the substance of subparagraph (C). Such agreements shall not be included in the Code of Federal Regulations. Thereafter, the terms of such agreement shall be available, as an option, to any commercial webcaster or noncommercial webcaster meeting the eligibility conditions of such agreement.

(C) Neither subparagraph (A) nor any provisions of any agreement entered into pursuant to subparagraph (A), including any rate structure, fees, terms, conditions, or notice and recordkeeping requirements set forth therein, shall be admissible as evidence or otherwise taken into account in any administrative, judicial, or other government proceeding involving the setting or adjustment of the royalties payable for the public performance or reproduction in ephemeral phonorecords or copies of sound recordings, the determination of terms or conditions related thereto, or the establishment of notice or recordkeeping requirements by the Copyright Royalty Judges under paragraph (4) or section 112 (e)(4). It is the intent of Congress that any royalty rates, rate structure, definitions, terms, conditions, or notice and recordkeeping requirements, included in such agreements shall be considered as a compromise motivated by the unique business, economic and political circumstances of webcasters, copyright owners, and performers rather than as matters that would have been negotiated in the marketplace between a willing buyer and a willing seller, or otherwise meet the objectives set forth in section 801 (b). This subparagraph shall not apply to the extent that the receiving agent and a webcaster that is party to an agreement entered into pursuant to subparagraph (A) expressly authorize the submission of the agreement in a proceeding under this subsection.

(D) Nothing in the Webcaster Settlement Act of 2008, the Webcaster Settlement Act of 2009, or any agreement entered into pursuant to subparagraph (A) shall be taken into account by the United States Court of Appeals for the District of Columbia Circuit in its review of the determination by the Copyright Royalty Judges of May 1, 2007, of rates and terms for the digital performance of sound recordings and ephemeral recordings, pursuant to sections 112 and 114.

(E) As used in this paragraph—

(i) the term "noncommercial webcaster" means a webcaster that—

(I) is exempt from taxation under section 501 of the Internal Revenue Code of 1986 (26 U.S.C. 501);

(II) has applied in good faith to the Internal Revenue Service for exemption from taxation under section 501 of the Internal Revenue Code and has a commercially reasonable expectation that such exemption shall be granted; or

(III) is operated by a State or possession or any governmental entity or subordinate thereof, or by the United States or District of Columbia, for exclusively public purposes;

(ii) the term "receiving agent" shall have the meaning given that term in section 261.2 of title 37, Code of Federal Regulations, as published in the Federal Register on July 8, 2002; and

(iii) the term "webcaster" means a person or entity that has obtained a compulsory license under section 112 or 114 and the implementing regulations therefor.

(F) The authority to make settlements pursuant to subparagraph (A) shall expire at 11:59 p.m. Eastern time on the 30th day after the date of the enactment of the Webcaster Settlement Act of 2009.

(g) Proceeds From Licensing of Transmissions.—

(1) Except in the case of a transmission licensed under a statutory license in accordance with subsection (f) of this section—

(A) a featured recording artist who performs on a sound recording that has been licensed for a transmission shall be entitled to receive payments from the copyright owner of the sound recording in accordance with the terms of the artist's contract; and

(B) a nonfeatured recording artist who performs on a sound recording that has been licensed for a transmission shall be entitled to receive payments from the copyright owner of the sound recording in accordance with the terms of the nonfeatured recording artist's applicable contract or other applicable agreement.

(2) An agent designated to distribute receipts from the licensing of transmissions in accordance with subsection (f) shall distribute such receipts as follows:

(A) 50 percent of the receipts shall be paid to the copyright owner of the exclusive right under section 106 (6) of this title to publicly perform a sound recording by means of a digital audio transmission.

(B) 21/2 percent of the receipts shall be deposited in an escrow account managed by an independent administrator jointly appointed by copyright owners of sound recordings and the American Federation of Musicians (or any successor entity) to be distributed to nonfeatured musicians (whether or not members of the American Federation of Musicians) who have performed on sound recordings.

(C) 21/2 percent of the receipts shall be deposited in an escrow account managed by an independent administrator jointly appointed by copyright owners of sound recordings and the American Federation of Television and Radio Artists (or any successor entity) to be distributed to nonfeatured vocalists (whether or not members of the American Federation of Television and Radio Artists) who have performed on sound recordings.

(D) 45 percent of the receipts shall be paid, on a per sound recording basis, to the recording artist or artists featured on such sound recording (or the persons conveying rights in the artists' performance in the sound recordings).

(3) A nonprofit agent designated to distribute receipts from the licensing of transmissions in accordance with subsection (f) may deduct from any of its receipts, prior to the distribution of such receipts to any person or entity entitled thereto other than copyright owners and performers who have elected to receive royalties from another designated agent and have notified such nonprofit agent in writing of such election, the reasonable costs of such agent incurred after November 1, 1995, in—

(A) the administration of the collection, distribution, and calculation of the royalties;

(B) the settlement of disputes relating to the collection and calculation of the royalties; and

(C) the licensing and enforcement of rights with respect to the making of ephemeral recordings and performances subject to licensing under section 112 and this section, including those incurred in participating in negotiations or arbitration proceedings under section 112 and this section, except that all costs incurred relating to the section 112 ephemeral recordings right may only be deducted from the royalties received pursuant to section 112.

(4) Notwithstanding paragraph (3), any designated agent designated to distribute receipts from the licensing of transmissions in accordance with subsection (f) may deduct from any of its receipts, prior to the distribution of such receipts, the reasonable costs

identified in paragraph (3) of such agent incurred after November 1, 1995, with respect to such copyright owners and performers who have entered with such agent a contractual relationship that specifies that such costs may be deducted from such royalty receipts.

(h) Licensing to Affiliates.—

(1) If the copyright owner of a sound recording licenses an affiliated entity the right to publicly perform a sound recording by means of a digital audio transmission under section 106 (6), the copyright owner shall make the licensed sound recording available under section 106 (6) on no less favorable terms and conditions to all bona fide entities that offer similar services, except that, if there are material differences in the scope of the requested license with respect to the type of service, the particular sound recordings licensed, the frequency of use, the number of subscribers served, or the duration, then the copyright owner may establish different terms and conditions for such other services.

(2) The limitation set forth in paragraph (1) of this subsection shall not apply in the case where the copyright owner of a sound recording licenses—

(A) an interactive service; or

(B) an entity to perform publicly up to 45 seconds of the sound recording and the sole purpose of the performance is to promote the distribution or performance of that sound recording.

(i) No Effect on Royalties for Underlying Works.— License fees payable for the public performance of sound recordings under section 106 (6) shall not be taken into account in any administrative, judicial, or other governmental proceeding to set or adjust the royalties payable to copyright owners of musical works for the public performance of their works. It is the intent of Congress that royalties payable to copyright owners of musical works for the public performance of their works shall not be diminished in any respect as a result of the rights granted by section 106 (6).

(j) Definitions.— As used in this section, the following terms have the following meanings:

(1) An "affiliated entity" is an entity engaging in digital audio transmissions covered by section 106 (6), other than an interactive service, in which the licensor has any direct or indirect partnership or any ownership interest amounting to 5 percent or more of the outstanding voting or non-voting stock.

(2) An "archived program" is a predetermined program that is available repeatedly on the demand of the transmission recipient and that is performed in the same order from the beginning, except that an archived program shall not include a recorded event or broadcast transmission that makes no more than an incidental use of sound recordings, as long as such recorded event or broadcast transmission does not contain an entire sound recording or feature a particular sound recording.

(3) A "broadcast" transmission is a transmission made by a terrestrial broadcast station licensed as such by the Federal Communications Commission.

(4) A "continuous program" is a predetermined program that is continuously performed in the same order and that is accessed at a point in the program that is beyond the control of the transmission recipient.

(5) A "digital audio transmission" is a digital transmission as defined in section 101, that embodies the transmission of a sound recording. This term does not include the transmission of any audiovisual work.

(6) An "eligible nonsubscription transmission" is a noninteractive nonsubscription digital audio transmission not exempt under subsection (d)(1) that is made as part of a service that provides audio programming consisting, in whole or in part, of performances of sound recordings, including retransmissions of broadcast transmissions, if the primary purpose of the service is to provide to the public such audio or other entertainment programming, and the primary purpose of the service is not to sell, advertise, or promote particular products or services other than sound recordings, live concerts, or other music-related events.

(7) An "interactive service" is one that enables a member of the public to receive a transmission of a program specially created for the recipient, or on request, a transmission of a particular sound recording, whether or not as part of a program, which is selected by or on behalf of the recipient. The ability of individuals to request that particular sound recordings be performed for reception by the public at large, or in the case of a subscription service, by all subscribers of the service, does not make a service interactive, if the programming on each channel of the service does not substantially consist of sound recordings that are performed within 1 hour of the request or at a time designated by either the transmitting entity or the individual making such request. If an entity offers both interactive and noninteractive services (either concurrently or at different times), the noninteractive component shall not be treated as part of an interactive service.

(8) A "new subscription service" is a service that performs sound recordings by means of noninteractive subscription digital audio transmissions and that is not a preexisting subscription service or a preexisting satellite digital audio radio service.

(9) A "nonsubscription" transmission is any transmission that is not a subscription transmission.

(10) A "preexisting satellite digital audio radio service" is a subscription satellite digital audio radio service provided pursuant to a satellite digital audio radio service license issued by the Federal Communications Commission on or before July 31, 1998, and any renewal of such license to the extent of the scope of the original license, and may include a limited number of sample channels representative of the subscription service that are made available on a nonsubscription basis in order to promote the subscription service.

(11) A "preexisting subscription service" is a service that performs sound recordings by means of noninteractive audio-only subscription digital audio transmissions, which was in existence and was making such transmissions to the public for a fee on or before July 31, 1998, and may include a limited number of sample channels representative of the subscription service that are made available on a nonsubscription basis in order to promote the subscription service.

(12) A "retransmission" is a further transmission of an initial transmission, and includes any further retransmission of the same transmission. Except as provided in this section, a transmission qualifies as a "retransmission" only if it is simultaneous with the initial transmission. Nothing in this definition shall be construed to exempt a transmission that fails to satisfy a separate element required to qualify for an exemption under section 114 (d)(1).

(13) The "sound recording performance complement" is the transmission during any 3-hour period, on a particular channel used by a transmitting entity, of no more than—

(A) 3 different selections of sound recordings from any one phonorecord lawfully distributed for public performance or sale in the United States, if no more than 2 such selections are transmitted consecutively; or

(B) 4 different selections of sound recordings—

(i) by the same featured recording artist; or

(ii) from any set or compilation of phonorecords lawfully distributed together as a unit for public performance or sale in the United States,

if no more than three such selections are transmitted consecutively:

Provided, That the transmission of selections in excess of the numerical limits provided for in clauses (A) and (B) from multiple phonorecords shall nonetheless qualify as a sound recording performance complement if the programming of the multiple phonorecords was not willfully intended to avoid the numerical limitations prescribed in such clauses.

(14) A "subscription" transmission is a transmission that is controlled and limited to particular recipients, and for which consideration is required to be paid or otherwise given by or on behalf of the recipient to receive the transmission or a package of transmissions including the transmission.

(15) A "transmission" is either an initial transmission or a retransmission.

Digital Millenium Copyright Act: 17 U.S. Code § 512 - Limitations on liability relating to material online

(a) Transitory Digital Network Communications.— A service provider shall not be liable for monetary relief, or, except as provided in subsection (j), for injunctive or other equitable relief, for infringement of copyright by reason of the provider's transmitting, routing, or providing connections for, material through a system or network controlled or operated by or for the service provider, or by reason of the intermediate and transient storage of that material in the course of such transmitting, routing, or providing connections, if—

(1) the transmission of the material was initiated by or at the direction of a person other than the service provider;

(2) the transmission, routing, provision of connections, or storage is carried out through an automatic technical process without selection of the material by the service provider;

(3) the service provider does not select the recipients of the material except as an automatic response to the request of another person;

(4) no copy of the material made by the service provider in the course of such intermediate or transient storage is maintained on the system or network in a manner ordinarily accessible to anyone other than anticipated recipients, and no such copy is maintained on the system or network in a manner ordinarily accessible to such anticipated recipients for a longer period than is reasonably necessary for the transmission, routing, or provision of connections; and

(5) the material is transmitted through the system or network without modification of its content.

(b) System Caching.—

(1) Limitation on liability.— A service provider shall not be liable for monetary relief, or, except as provided in subsection (j), for injunctive or other equitable relief, for infringement of copyright by reason of the intermediate and temporary storage of material on a system or network controlled or operated by or for the service provider in a case in which—

(A) the material is made available online by a person other than the service provider;

(B) the material is transmitted from the person described in subparagraph (A) through the system or network to a person other than the person described in subparagraph (A) at the direction of that other person; and

(C) the storage is carried out through an automatic technical process for the purpose of making the material available to users of the system or network who, after the material is transmitted as described in subparagraph (B), request access to the material from the person described in subparagraph (A),

if the conditions set forth in paragraph (2) are met.

(2) Conditions.— The conditions referred to in paragraph (1) are that—

(A) the material described in paragraph (1) is transmitted to the subsequent users described in paragraph (1)(C) without modification to its content from the manner in which the material was transmitted from the person described in paragraph (1)(A);

(B) the service provider described in paragraph (1) complies with rules concerning the refreshing, reloading, or other updating of the material when specified by the person making the material available online in accordance with a generally accepted industry standard data communications protocol for the system or network through which that person makes the material available, except that this subparagraph applies only if those rules are not used by the person described in paragraph (1)(A) to prevent or unreasonably impair the intermediate storage to which this subsection applies;

(C) the service provider does not interfere with the ability of technology associated with the material to return to the person described in paragraph (1)(A) the information that would have been available to that person if the material had been obtained by the subsequent users described in paragraph (1)(C) directly from that person, except that this subparagraph applies only if that technology—

(i) does not significantly interfere with the performance of the provider's system or network or with the intermediate storage of the material;

(ii) is consistent with generally accepted industry standard communications protocols; and

(iii) does not extract information from the provider's system or network other than the information that would have been available to the person described in paragraph (1)(A) if the subsequent users had gained access to the material directly from that person;

(D) if the person described in paragraph (1)(A) has in effect a condition that a person must meet prior to having access to the material, such as a condition based on payment of a fee or provision of a password or other information, the service provider permits access to the stored material in significant part only to users of its system or network that have met those conditions and only in accordance with those conditions; and

(E) if the person described in paragraph (1)(A) makes that material available online without the authorization of the copyright owner of the material, the service provider responds expeditiously to remove, or disable access to, the material that is claimed to be infringing upon notification of claimed infringement as described in subsection (c)(3), except that this subparagraph applies only if—

(i) the material has previously been removed from the originating site or access to it has been disabled, or a court has ordered that the material be removed from the originating site or that access to the material on the originating site be disabled; and

(ii) the party giving the notification includes in the notification a statement confirming that the material has been removed from the originating site or access to it has been disabled or that a court has ordered that the material be removed from the originating site or that access to the material on the originating site be disabled.

(c) Information Residing on Systems or Networks At Direction of Users.—

(1) In general.— A service provider shall not be liable for monetary relief, or, except as provided in subsection (j), for injunctive or other equitable relief, for infringement of copyright by reason of the storage at the direction of a user of material that resides on a system or network controlled or operated by or for the service provider, if the service provider—

(A)

(i) does not have actual knowledge that the material or an activity using the material on the system or network is infringing;

(ii) in the absence of such actual knowledge, is not aware of facts or circumstances from which infringing activity is apparent; or

(iii) upon obtaining such knowledge or awareness, acts expeditiously to remove, or disable access to, the material;

(B) does not receive a financial benefit directly attributable to the infringing activity, in a case in which the service provider has the right and ability to control such activity; and

(C) upon notification of claimed infringement as described in paragraph (3), responds expeditiously to remove, or disable access to, the material that is claimed to be infringing or to be the subject of infringing activity.

(2) Designated agent.— The limitations on liability established in this subsection apply to a service provider only if the service provider has designated an agent to receive notifications of claimed infringement described in paragraph (3), by making available through its service, including on its website in a location accessible to the public, and by providing to the Copyright Office, substantially the following information:

(A) the name, address, phone number, and electronic mail address of the agent.

(B) other contact information which the Register of Copyrights may deem appropriate.

The Register of Copyrights shall maintain a current directory of agents available to the public for inspection, including through the Internet, and may require payment of a fee by service providers to cover the costs of maintaining the directory.

(3) Elements of notification.—

(A) To be effective under this subsection, a notification of claimed infringement must be a written communication provided to the designated agent of a service provider that includes substantially the following:

(i) A physical or electronic signature of a person authorized to act on behalf of the owner of an exclusive right that is allegedly infringed.

(ii) Identification of the copyrighted work claimed to have been infringed, or, if multiple copyrighted works at a single online site are covered by a single notification, a representative list of such works at that site.

(iii) Identification of the material that is claimed to be infringing or to be the subject of infringing activity and that is to be removed or access to which is to be disabled, and information reasonably sufficient to permit the service provider to locate the material.

(iv) Information reasonably sufficient to permit the service provider to contact the complaining party, such as an address, telephone number, and, if available, an electronic mail address at which the complaining party may be contacted.

(v) A statement that the complaining party has a good faith belief that use of the material in the manner complained of is not authorized by the copyright owner, its agent, or the law.

(vi) A statement that the information in the notification is accurate, and under penalty of perjury, that the complaining party is authorized to act on behalf of the owner of an exclusive right that is allegedly infringed.

(B)

(i) Subject to clause (ii), a notification from a copyright owner or from a person authorized to act on behalf of the copyright owner that fails to comply substantially with the provisions of subparagraph (A) shall not be considered under paragraph (1)(A) in determining whether a service provider has actual knowledge or is aware of facts or circumstances from which infringing activity is apparent.

(ii) In a case in which the notification that is provided to the service provider's designated agent fails to comply substantially with all the provisions of subparagraph (A) but substantially complies with clauses (ii), (iii), and (iv) of subparagraph (A), clause (i) of this subparagraph applies only if the service provider promptly attempts to contact the person making the notification or takes other reasonable steps to assist in the receipt of notification that substantially complies with all the provisions of subparagraph (A).

(d) Information Location Tools.— A service provider shall not be liable for monetary relief, or, except as provided in subsection (j), for injunctive or other equitable relief, for infringement of copyright by reason of the provider referring or linking users to an online location containing infringing material or infringing activity, by using information location tools, including a directory, index, reference, pointer, or hypertext link, if the service provider—

(1)

(A) does not have actual knowledge that the material or activity is infringing;

(B) in the absence of such actual knowledge, is not aware of facts or circumstances from which infringing activity is apparent; or

(C) upon obtaining such knowledge or awareness, acts expeditiously to remove, or disable access to, the material;

(2) does not receive a financial benefit directly attributable to the infringing activity, in a case in which the service provider has the right and ability to control such activity; and

(3) upon notification of claimed infringement as described in subsection (c)(3), responds expeditiously to remove, or disable access to, the material that is claimed to be infringing or to be the subject of infringing activity, except that, for purposes of this paragraph, the information described in subsection (c)(3)(A)(iii) shall be identification of the reference or link, to material or activity claimed to be infringing, that is to be removed or access to which is to be disabled, and information reasonably sufficient to permit the service provider to locate that reference or link.

(e) Limitation on Liability of Nonprofit Educational Institutions.—

(1) When a public or other nonprofit institution of higher education is a service provider, and when a faculty member or graduate student who is an employee of such institution is performing a teaching or research function, for the purposes of subsections (a) and (b) such faculty member or graduate student shall be considered to be a person other than the institution, and for the purposes of subsections (c) and (d) such faculty member's or graduate student's knowledge or awareness of his or her infringing activities shall not be attributed to the institution, if—

(A) such faculty member's or graduate student's infringing activities do not involve the provision of online access to instructional materials that are or were required or recommended, within the preceding 3-year period, for a course taught at the institution by such faculty member or graduate student;

(B) the institution has not, within the preceding 3-year period, received more than two notifications described in subsection (c)(3) of claimed infringement by such faculty member or graduate student, and such notifications of claimed infringement were not actionable under subsection (f); and

(C) the institution provides to all users of its system or network informational materials that accurately describe, and promote compliance with, the laws of the United States relating to copyright.

(2) For the purposes of this subsection, the limitations on injunctive relief contained in subsections (j)(2) and (j)(3), but not those in (j)(1), shall apply.

(f) Misrepresentations.— Any person who knowingly materially misrepresents under this section—

(1) that material or activity is infringing, or

(2) that material or activity was removed or disabled by mistake or misidentification,

hall be liable for any damages, including costs and attorneys' fees, incurred by the alleged infringer, by any copyright owner or copyright wner's authorized licensee, or by a service provider, who is injured by such misrepresentation, as the result of the service provider relying pon such misrepresentation in removing or disabling access to the material or activity claimed to be infringing, or in replacing the ɛmoved material or ceasing to disable access to it.

(g) Replacement of Removed or Disabled Material and Limitation on Other Liability.—

(1) No liability for taking down generally.— Subject to paragraph (2), a service provider shall not be liable to any person for any claim based on the service provider's good faith disabling of access to, or removal of, material or activity claimed to be infringing or based on facts or circumstances from which infringing activity is apparent, regardless of whether the material or activity is ultimately determined to be infringing.

(2) Exception.— Paragraph (1) shall not apply with respect to material residing at the direction of a subscriber of the service provider on a system or network controlled or operated by or for the service provider that is removed, or to which access is disabled by the service provider, pursuant to a notice provided under subsection (c)(1)(C), unless the service provider—

(A) takes reasonable steps promptly to notify the subscriber that it has removed or disabled access to the material;

(B) upon receipt of a counter notification described in paragraph (3), promptly provides the person who provided the notification under subsection (c)(1)(C) with a copy of the counter notification, and informs that person that it will replace the removed material or cease disabling access to it in 10 business days; and

(C) replaces the removed material and ceases disabling access to it not less than 10, nor more than 14, business days following receipt of the counter notice, unless its designated agent first receives notice from the person who submitted the notification under subsection (c)(1)(C) that such person has filed an action seeking a court order to restrain the subscriber from engaging in infringing activity relating to the material on the service provider's system or network.

(3) Contents of counter notification.— To be effective under this subsection, a counter notification must be a written communication provided to the service provider's designated agent that includes substantially the following:

(A) A physical or electronic signature of the subscriber.

(B) Identification of the material that has been removed or to which access has been disabled and the location at which the material appeared before it was removed or access to it was disabled.

(C) A statement under penalty of perjury that the subscriber has a good faith belief that the material was removed or disabled as a result of mistake or misidentification of the material to be removed or disabled.

(D) The subscriber's name, address, and telephone number, and a statement that the subscriber consents to the jurisdiction of Federal District Court for the judicial district in which the address is located, or if the subscriber's address is outside of the United States, for any judicial district in which the service provider may be found, and that the subscriber will accept service of process from the person who provided notification under subsection (c)(1)(C) or an agent of such person.

(4) Limitation on other liability.— A service provider's compliance with paragraph (2) shall not subject the service provider to liability for copyright infringement with respect to the material identified in the notice provided under subsection (c)(1)(C).

(h) Subpoena To Identify Infringer.—

(1) Request.— A copyright owner or a person authorized to act on the owner's behalf may request the clerk of any United States district court to issue a subpoena to a service provider for identification of an alleged infringer in accordance with this subsection.

(2) Contents of request.— The request may be made by filing with the clerk—

(A) a copy of a notification described in subsection (c)(3)(A);

(B) a proposed subpoena; and

(C) a sworn declaration to the effect that the purpose for which the subpoena is sought is to obtain the identity of an alleged infringer and that such information will only be used for the purpose of protecting rights under this title.

(3) Contents of subpoena.— The subpoena shall authorize and order the service provider receiving the notification and the subpoena to expeditiously disclose to the copyright owner or person authorized by the copyright owner information sufficient to identify the alleged infringer of the material described in the notification to the extent such information is available to the service provider.

(4) Basis for granting subpoena.— If the notification filed satisfies the provisions of subsection (c)(3)(A), the proposed subpoena is in proper form, and the accompanying declaration is properly executed, the clerk shall expeditiously issue and sign the proposed subpoena and return it to the requester for delivery to the service provider.

(5) Actions of service provider receiving subpoena.— Upon receipt of the issued subpoena, either accompanying or subsequent to the receipt of a notification described in subsection (c)(3)(A), the service provider shall expeditiously disclose to the copyright owner or person authorized by the copyright owner the information required by the subpoena, notwithstanding any other provision of law and regardless of whether the service provider responds to the notification.

(6) Rules applicable to subpoena.— Unless otherwise provided by this section or by applicable rules of the court, the procedure for issuance and delivery of the subpoena, and the remedies for noncompliance with the subpoena, shall be governed to the greatest extent practicable by those provisions of the Federal Rules of Civil Procedure governing the issuance, service, and enforcement of a subpoena duces tecum.

(i) Conditions for Eligibility.—

(1) Accommodation of technology.— The limitations on liability established by this section shall apply to a service provider only if the service provider—

(A) has adopted and reasonably implemented, and informs subscribers and account holders of the service provider's system or network of, a policy that provides for the termination in appropriate circumstances of subscribers and account holders of the service provider's system or network who are repeat infringers; and

(B) accommodates and does not interfere with standard technical measures.

(2) Definition.— As used in this subsection, the term "standard technical measures" means technical measures that are used by copyright owners to identify or protect copyrighted works and—

(A) have been developed pursuant to a broad consensus of copyright owners and service providers in an open, fair, voluntary, multi-industry standards process;

(B) are available to any person on reasonable and nondiscriminatory terms; and

(C) do not impose substantial costs on service providers or substantial burdens on their systems or networks.

(j) Injunctions.— The following rules shall apply in the case of any application for an injunction under section 502 against a service provider that is not subject to monetary remedies under this section:

(1) Scope of relief.—

(A) With respect to conduct other than that which qualifies for the limitation on remedies set forth in subsection (a), the court may grant injunctive relief with respect to a service provider only in one or more of the following forms:

(i) An order restraining the service provider from providing access to infringing material or activity residing at a particular online site on the provider's system or network.

(ii) An order restraining the service provider from providing access to a subscriber or account holder of the service provider's system or network who is engaging in infringing activity and is identified in the order, by terminating the accounts of the subscriber or account holder that are specified in the order.

(iii) Such other injunctive relief as the court may consider necessary to prevent or restrain infringement of copyrighted material specified in the order of the court at a particular online location, if such relief is the least burdensome to the service provider among the forms of relief comparably effective for that purpose.

(B) If the service provider qualifies for the limitation on remedies described in subsection (a), the court may only grant injunctive relief in one or both of the following forms:

(i) An order restraining the service provider from providing access to a subscriber or account holder of the service provider's system or network who is using the provider's service to engage in infringing activity and is identified in the order, by terminating the accounts of the subscriber or account holder that are specified in the order.

(ii) An order restraining the service provider from providing access, by taking reasonable steps specified in the order to block access, to a specific, identified, online location outside the United States.

(2) Considerations.— The court, in considering the relevant criteria for injunctive relief under applicable law, shall consider—

(A) whether such an injunction, either alone or in combination with other such injunctions issued against the same service provider under this subsection, would significantly burden either the provider or the operation of the provider's system or network;

(B) the magnitude of the harm likely to be suffered by the copyright owner in the digital network environment if steps are not taken to prevent or restrain the infringement;

(C) whether implementation of such an injunction would be technically feasible and effective, and would not interfere with access to noninfringing material at other online locations; and

(D) whether other less burdensome and comparably effective means of preventing or restraining access to the infringing material are available.

(3) Notice and ex parte orders.— Injunctive relief under this subsection shall be available only after notice to the service provider and an opportunity for the service provider to appear are provided, except for orders ensuring the preservation of evidence or other orders having no material adverse effect on the operation of the service provider's communications network.

(k) Definitions.—

(1) Service provider.—

(A) As used in subsection (a), the term "service provider" means an entity offering the transmission, routing, or providing of connections for digital online communications, between or among points specified by a user, of material of the user's choosing, without modification to the content of the material as sent or received.

(B) As used in this section, other than subsection (a), the term "service provider" means a provider of online services or network access, or the operator of facilities therefor, and includes an entity described in subparagraph (A).

(2) Monetary relief.— As used in this section, the term "monetary relief" means damages, costs, attorneys' fees, and any other form of monetary payment.

(l) Other Defenses Not Affected.— The failure of a service provider's conduct to qualify for limitation of liability under this section shall not bear adversely upon the consideration of a defense by the service provider that the service provider's conduct is not infringing under this title or any other defense.

(m) Protection of Privacy.— Nothing in this section shall be construed to condition the applicability of subsections (a) through (d) on—

(1) a service provider monitoring its service or affirmatively seeking facts indicating infringing activity, except to the extent consistent with a standard technical measure complying with the provisions of subsection (i); or

(2) a service provider gaining access to, removing, or disabling access to material in cases in which such conduct is prohibited by law.

(n) Construction.— Subsections (a), (b), (c), and (d) describe separate and distinct functions for purposes of applying this section. Whether a service provider qualifies for the limitation on liability in any one of those subsections shall be based solely on the criteria in that subsection, and shall not affect a determination of whether that service provider qualifies for the limitations on liability under any other such subsection.

Class 18: 7 <u>OIL Casebook Topic VII: Section 230: Non-IP Secondary Liability</u>

Communications Decency Act: 47 U.S. Code § 230 - Protection for private blocking an screening of offensive material

July 09, 2015 by mrisch

Communications Decency Act: 47 U.S. Code § 230 – Protection for private blocking and screening of offensive material

1   **(a) Findings**

The Congress finds the following:

(1) The rapidly developing array of Internet and other interactive computer services available to individual Americans represent an extraordinary advance in the availability of educational and informational resources to our citizens.

(2) These services offer users a great degree of control over the information that they receive, as well as the potential for even greater control in the future as technology develops.

(3) The Internet and other interactive computer services offer a forum for a true diversity of political discourse, unique opportunities for cultural development, and myriad avenues for intellectual activity.

(4) The Internet and other interactive computer services have flourished, to the benefit of all Americans, with a minimum of government regulation.

(5) Increasingly Americans are relying on interactive media for a variety of political, educational, cultural, and entertainment services.

2   **(b) Policy**

It is the policy of the United States—

(1) to promote the continued development of the Internet and other interactive computer services and other interactive media;

(2) to preserve the vibrant and competitive free market that presently exists for the Internet and other interactive computer services, unfettered by Federal or State regulation;

(3) to encourage the development of technologies which maximize user control over what information is received by individuals, families, and schools who use the Internet and other interactive computer services;

(4) to remove disincentives for the development and utilization of blocking and filtering technologies that empower parents to restrict their children's access to objectionable or inappropriate online material; and

(5) to ensure vigorous enforcement of Federal criminal laws to deter and punish trafficking in obscenity, stalking, and harassment by means of computer.

3   **(c) Protection for "Good Samaritan" blocking and screening of offensive material**

(1) Treatment of publisher or speaker

No provider or user of an interactive computer service shall be treated as the publisher or speaker of any information provided by another information content provider.

(2) Civil liability

No provider or user of an interactive computer service shall be held liable on account of—

(A) any action voluntarily taken in good faith to restrict access to or availability of material that the provider or user considers to be obscene, lewd, lascivious, filthy, excessively violent, harassing, or otherwise objectionable, whether or not such material is constitutionally protected; or

(B) any action taken to enable or make available to information content providers or others the technical means to restrict access to material described in paragraph (1). [1]

4   **(d) Obligations of interactive computer service**

A provider of interactive computer service shall, at the time of entering an agreement with a customer for the provision of interactive computer service and in a manner deemed appropriate by the provider, notify such customer that parental control protections (such as computer hardware, software, or filtering services) are commercially available that may assist the customer in limiting access to material that is harmful to minors. Such notice shall identify, or provide the customer with access to information identifying, current providers of such protections.

5   **(e) Effect on other laws**

(1) No effect on criminal law

Nothing in this section shall be construed to impair the enforcement of section 223 or231 of this title, chapter 71 (relating to obscenity) or 110 (relating to sexual exploitation of children) of title 18, or any other Federal criminal statute.

(2) No effect on intellectual property law

Nothing in this section shall be construed to limit or expand any law pertaining to intellectual property.

(3) State law

Nothing in this section shall be construed to prevent any State from enforcing any State law that is consistent with this section. No cause of action may be brought and no liability may be imposed under any State or local law that is inconsistent with this section.

(4) No effect on communications privacy law

Nothing in this section shall be construed to limit the application of the Electronic Communications Privacy Act of 1986 or any of the amendments made by such Act, or any similar State law.

6   **(f) Definitions**

As used in this section:

(1) Internet

The term "Internet" means the international computer network of both Federal and non-Federal interoperable packet switched data networks.

(2) Interactive computer service

The term "interactive computer service" means any information service, system, or access software provider that provides or enables computer access by multiple users to a computer server, including specifically a service or system that provides access to the Internet and such systems operated or services offered by libraries or educational institutions.

(3) Information content provider

The term "information content provider" means any person or entity that is responsible, in whole or in part, for the creation or development of information provided through the Internet or any other interactive computer service.

(4) Access software provider

The term "access software provider" means a provider of software (including client or server software), or enabling tools that do any one or more of the following:

(A) filter, screen, allow, or disallow content;

(B) pick, choose, analyze, or digest content; or

(C) transmit, receive, display, forward, cache, search, subset, organize, reorganize, or translate content.

7

[1] So in original. Probably should be "subparagraph (A)."

Zeran v. American Online Inc.

September 14, 2014 by mrisch

Zeran is widely viewed as the first case to interpret Section 230, and it is followed in virtually every case since.

1   [...]

2   129 F.3d 327

3   [...]

4   Kenneth M. ZERAN, Plaintiff-Appellant,
                                      v.
                  AMERICA ONLINE, INCORPORATED, Defendant-Appellee.

5   [...]

6   United States Court of Appeals,
                           Fourth Circuit.

7   [...]
                        Decided Nov. 12, 1997.

8   [...]

12   OPINION

13   WILKINSON, Chief Judge:

14   Kenneth Zeran brought this action against America Online, Inc. ("AOL"), arguing that AOL unreasonably delayed in removing defamatory messages posted by an unidentified third party, refused to post retractions of those messages, and failed to screen for similar postings thereafter. The district court granted judgment for AOL on the grounds that the Communications Decency Act of 1996 ("CDA")--47 U.S.C. § 230--bars Zeran's claims. Zeran appeals, arguing that § 230 leaves intact liability for interactive computer service providers who possess notice of defamatory material posted through their services. He also contends that § 230 does not apply here because his claims arise from AOL's alleged negligence prior to the CDA's enactment. Section 230, however, plainly immunizes computer service providers like AOL from liability for information that originates with third parties. Furthermore, Congress clearly expressed its intent that § 230 apply to lawsuits, like Zeran's, instituted after the CDA's enactment. Accordingly, we affirm the judgment of the district court.

15   I.

16   "The Internet is an international network of interconnected computers," currently used by approximately 40 million people

worldwide. [...] One of the many means by which individuals access the Internet is through an interactive computer service. These services offer not only a connection to the Internet as a whole,

17   [...]

18   The instant case comes before us on a motion for judgment on the pleadings, see Fed.R.Civ.P. 12(c), so we accept the facts alleged in the complaint as true. [...] On April 25, 1995, an unidentified person posted a message on an AOL bulletin board advertising "Naughty Oklahoma T-Shirts." The posting described the sale of shirts featuring offensive and tasteless slogans related to the April 19, 1995, bombing of the Alfred P. Murrah Federal Building in Oklahoma City. Those interested in purchasing the shirts were instructed to call "Ken" at Zeran's home phone number in Seattle, Washington. As a result of this anonymously perpetrated prank, Zeran received a high volume of calls, comprised primarily of angry and derogatory messages, but also including death threats. Zeran could not change his phone number because he relied on its availability to the public in running his business out of his home. Later that day, Zeran called AOL and informed a company representative of his predicament. The employee assured Zeran that the posting would be removed from AOL's bulletin board but explained that as a matter of policy AOL would not post a retraction. The parties dispute the date that AOL removed this original posting from its bulletin board.

19   On April 26, the next day, an unknown person posted another message advertising additional shirts with new tasteless slogans related to the Oklahoma City bombing. Again, interested buyers were told to call Zeran's phone number, to ask for "Ken," and to "please call back if busy" due to high demand. The angry, threatening phone calls intensified. Over the next four days, an unidentified party continued to post messages on AOL's bulletin board, advertising additional items including bumper stickers and key chains with still more offensive slogans. During this time period, Zeran called AOL repeatedly and was told by company representatives that the individual account from which the messages were posted would soon be closed. Zeran also reported his case to Seattle FBI agents. By April 30, Zeran was receiving an abusive phone call approximately every two minutes.

20   Meanwhile, an announcer for Oklahoma City radio station KRXO received a copy of the first AOL posting. On May 1, the announcer related the message's contents on the air, attributed them to "Ken" at Zeran's phone number, and urged the listening audience to call the number. After this radio broadcast, Zeran was inundated with death threats and other violent calls from Oklahoma City residents. Over the next few days, Zeran talked to both KRXO and AOL representatives. He also spoke to his local police, who subsequently surveilled his home to protect his safety. By May 14, after an Oklahoma City newspaper published a story exposing the shirt advertisements as a hoax and after KRXO made an on-air apology, the number of calls to Zeran's residence finally subsided to fifteen per day.

21   Zeran first filed suit on January 4, 1996, against radio station KRXO in the United States District Court for the Western District of Oklahoma. On April 23, 1996, he filed this separate suit against AOL in the same court. Zeran did not bring any action against the party who posted the offensive messages. [1] [...]

23   II.

24   A.

25   Because § 230 was successfully advanced by AOL in the district court as a defense to Zeran's claims, we shall briefly examine its operation here. Zeran seeks to hold AOL liable for defamatory speech initiated by a third party. He argued to the district court that once he notified AOL of the unidentified third party's hoax, AOL had a duty to remove the defamatory posting promptly, to notify its subscribers of the message's false nature, and to effectively screen future defamatory material. Section 230 entered this litigation as an affirmative defense pled by AOL. The company claimed that Congress immunized interactive computer service providers from claims based on information posted by a third party.

26   The relevant portion of § 230 states: "No provider or user of an interactive computer service shall be treated as the publisher or

speaker of any information provided by another information content provider." 47 U.S.C. § 230(c)(1). [2] By its plain language, § 230 creates a federal immunity to any cause of action that would make service providers liable for information originating with a third-party user of the service. Specifically, § 230 precludes courts from entertaining claims that would place a computer service provider in a publisher's role. Thus, lawsuits seeking to hold a service provider liable for its exercise of a publisher's traditional editorial functions--such as deciding whether to publish, withdraw, postpone or alter content--are barred.

27   The purpose of this statutory immunity is not difficult to discern. Congress recognized the threat that tort-based lawsuits pose to freedom of speech in the new and burgeoning Internet medium. The imposition of tort liability on service providers for the communications of others represented, for Congress, simply another form of intrusive government regulation of speech. Section 230 was enacted, in part, to maintain the robust nature of Internet communication and, accordingly, to keep government interference in the medium to a minimum. In specific statutory findings, Congress recognized the Internet and interactive computer services as offering "a forum for a true diversity of political discourse, unique opportunities for cultural development, and myriad avenues for intellectual activity." Id. § 230(a)(3). It also found that the Internet and interactive computer services "have flourished, to the benefit of all Americans, with a minimum of government regulation." Id. § 230(a)(4) (emphasis added). Congress further stated that it is "the policy of the United States ... to preserve the vibrant and competitive free market that presently exists for the Internet and other interactive computer services, unfettered by Federal or State regulation." Id. § 230(b)(2) (emphasis added).

28   None of this means, of course, that the original culpable party who posts defamatory messages would escape accountability. While Congress acted to keep government regulation of the Internet to a minimum, it also found it to be the policy of the United States "to ensure vigorous enforcement of Federal criminal laws to deter and punish trafficking in obscenity, stalking, and harassment by means of computer." Id. § 230(b)(5). Congress made a policy choice, however, not to deter harmful online speech through the separate route of imposing tort liability on companies that serve as intermediaries

29   [...]

30   Congress' purpose in providing the § 230 immunity was thus evident. [...] The specter of tort liability in an area of such prolific speech would have an obvious chilling effect. It would be impossible for service providers to screen each of their millions of postings for possible problems. Faced with potential liability for each message republished by their services, interactive computer service providers might choose to severely restrict the number and type of messages posted. Congress considered the weight of the speech interests implicated and chose to immunize service providers to avoid any such restrictive effect.

31   Another important purpose of § 230 was to encourage service providers to self-regulate the dissemination of offensive material over their services. In this respect, § 230 responded to a New York state court decision, [...] There, the plaintiffs sued Prodigy--an interactive computer service like AOL--for defamatory comments made by an unidentified party on one of Prodigy's bulletin boards. The court held Prodigy to the strict liability standard normally applied to original publishers of defamatory statements, rejecting Prodigy's claims that it should be held only to the lower "knowledge" standard usually reserved for distributors. The court reasoned that Prodigy acted more like an original publisher than a distributor both because it advertised its practice of controlling content on its service and because it actively screened and edited messages posted on its bulletin boards.

32   Congress enacted § 230 to remove the disincentives to selfregulation created by the Stratton Oakmont decision. Under that court's holding, computer service providers who regulated the dissemination of offensive material on their services risked subjecting themselves to liability, because such regulation cast the service provider in the role of a publisher. Fearing that the specter of liability would therefore deter service providers from blocking and screening offensive material, Congress enacted § 230's broad immunity "to remove disincentives for the development and utilization of blocking and filtering technologies that empower parents to restrict their children's access to objectionable or inappropriate online material." 47 U.S.C. § 230(b)(4). In line with this purpose, § 230 forbids the imposition of publisher liability on a service provider for the exercise of its editorial and self-regulatory functions.

33   B.

34   Zeran argues, however, that the § 230 immunity eliminates only publisher liability, leaving distributor liability intact. Publishers can be held liable for defamatory statements contained in their works even absent proof that they had specific knowledge of the statement's inclusion. [...] According to Zeran, interactive computer service providers like AOL are normally considered instead to be distributors, like traditional news vendors or book sellers. Distributors cannot be held liable for defamatory statements contained in the materials they distribute unless it is proven at a minimum that they have actual knowledge of the defamatory statements upon which liability is predicated. [...] Zeran contends that he provided AOL with sufficient notice of the defamatory statements appearing on the company's bulletin board. This notice is significant, says Zeran, because AOL could be held liable as a distributor only if it acquired knowledge of the defamatory statements' existence.

35   Because of the difference between these two forms of liability, Zeran contends that the term "distributor" carries a legally distinct meaning from the term "publisher."

36   [...]

37   The terms "publisher" and "distributor" derive their legal significance from the context of defamation law. Although Zeran attempts to artfully plead his claims as ones of negligence, they are indistinguishable from a garden variety defamation action. Because the publication of a statement is a necessary element in a defamation action, only one who publishes can be subject to this form of tort liability. [...] Publication does not only describe the choice by an author to include certain information. In addition, both the negligent communication of a defamatory statement and the failure to remove such a statement when first communicated by another party--each alleged by Zeran here under a negligence label--constitute publication. [...] In fact, every repetition of a defamatory statement is considered a publication. [...]

38   In this case, AOL is legally considered to be a publisher. "[E]very one who takes part in the publication ... is charged with publication." Id. Even distributors are considered to be publishers for purposes of defamation law:

39   Those who are in the business of making their facilities available to disseminate the writings composed, the speeches made, and the information gathered by others may also be regarded as participating to such an extent in making the books, newspapers, magazines, and information available to others as to be regarded as publishers. They are intentionally making the contents available to others, sometimes without knowing all of the contents--including the defamatory content--and sometimes without any opportunity to ascertain, in advance, that any defamatory matter was to be included in the matter published.

40   [...] AOL falls squarely within this traditional definition of a publisher and, therefore, is clearly protected by § 230's immunity.

41   Zeran contends that decisions like Stratton Oakmont and Cubby, Inc. v. CompuServe Inc., [...] recognize a legal distinction between publishers and distributors. He misapprehends, however, the significance of that distinction for the legal issue we consider here. It is undoubtedly true that mere conduits, or distributors, are subject to a different standard of liability. As explained above, distributors must at a minimum have knowledge of the existence of a defamatory statement as a prerequisite to liability. But this distinction signifies only that different standards of liability may be applied within the larger publisher category, depending on the specific type of publisher concerned. [...] To the extent that decisions like Stratton and Cubby utilize the terms "publisher" and "distributor" separately, the decisions correctly describe two different standards of liability. Stratton and Cubby do not, however, suggest that distributors are not also a type of publisher for purposes of defamation law.

42   Zeran simply attaches too much importance to the presence of the distinct notice element in distributor liability. The simple fact of notice surely cannot transform one from an original publisher to a distributor in the eyes of the law. To the contrary, once a computer service provider receives notice of a potentially defamatory posting, it is thrust into the role of a traditional publisher. The computer

service provider must decide whether to publish, edit, or withdraw the posting. In this respect, Zeran seeks to impose liability on AOL [...]

44   Our view that Zeran's complaint treats AOL as a publisher is reinforced because AOL is cast in the same position as the party who originally posted the offensive messages. According to Zeran's logic, AOL is legally at fault because it communicated to third parties an allegedly defamatory statement. This is precisely the theory under which the original poster of the offensive messages would be found liable. If the original party is considered a publisher of the offensive messages, Zeran certainly cannot attach liability to AOL under the same theory without conceding that AOL too must be treated as a publisher of the statements.

45   Zeran next contends that interpreting § 230 to impose liability on service providers with knowledge of defamatory content on their services is consistent with the statutory purposes outlined in Part IIA. Zeran fails, however, to understand the practical implications of notice liability in the interactive computer service context. Liability upon notice would defeat the dual purposes advanced by § 230 of the CDA. Like the strict liability imposed by the Stratton Oakmont court, liability upon notice reinforces service providers' incentives to restrict speech and abstain from self-regulation.

46   If computer service providers were subject to distributor liability, they would face potential liability each time they receive notice of a potentially defamatory statement--from any party, concerning any message. Each notification would require a careful yet rapid investigation of the circumstances surrounding the posted information, a legal judgment concerning the information's defamatory character, and an on-the-spot editorial decision whether to risk liability by allowing the continued publication of that information. Although this might be feasible for the traditional print publisher, the sheer number of postings on interactive computer services would create an impossible burden in the Internet context. [...] Because service providers would be subject to liability only for the publication of information, and not for its removal, they would have a natural incentive simply to remove messages upon notification, whether the contents were defamatory or not. [...] Thus, like strict liability, liability upon notice has a chilling effect on the freedom of Internet speech.

47   Similarly, notice-based liability would deter service providers from regulating the dissemination of offensive material over their own services. Any efforts by a service provider to investigate and screen material posted on its service would only lead to notice of potentially defamatory material more frequently and thereby create a stronger basis for liability. Instead of subjecting themselves to further possible lawsuits, service providers would likely eschew any attempts at self-regulation.

48   More generally, notice-based liability for interactive computer service providers would provide third parties with a no-cost means to create the basis for future lawsuits. Whenever one was displeased with the speech of another party conducted over an interactive computer service, the offended party could simply "notify" the relevant service provider, claiming the information to be legally defamatory. In light of the vast amount of speech communicated through interactive computer services, these notices could produce an impossible burden for service providers, who would be faced with ceaseless choices of suppressing controversial speech or sustaining prohibitive liability. Because the probable effects of distributor liability on the vigor of Internet speech and on service provider self-regulation are directly contrary to § 230's statutory purposes, we will not assume that Congress intended to leave liability upon notice intact.

49   [...]

61   For the foregoing reasons, we affirm the judgment of the district court.

62   AFFIRMED.

63   [...]

68   1 Zeran maintains that AOL made it impossible to identify the original party by failing to maintain adequate records of its users. The issue

of AOL's record keeping practices, however, is not presented by this appeal.

66   2 Section 230 defines "interactive computer service" as "any information service, system, or access software provider that provides or
      enables computer access by multiple users to a computer server, including specifically a service or system that provides access to the
      Internet and such systems operated or services offered by libraries or educational institutions." 47 U.S.C. § 230(e)(2). The
      term"information content provider" is defined as "any person or entity that is responsible, in whole or in part, for the creation or
      development of information provided through the Internet or any other interactive computer service." Id. § 230(e)(3). The parties do not
      dispute that AOL falls within the CDA's "interactive computer service" definition and that the unidentified third party who posted the
      offensive messages here fits the definition of an "information content provider."

Blumenthal v. Drudge

July 18, 2014 by mrisch

This case considers whether immunity applies when a party pays for content from another source

1   992 F.Supp. 44 (1998)

2   **Sidney BLUMENTHAL** [...]

                                             v.

                     Matt DRUDGE and America Online, Inc. [...]

4   United States District Court, District of Columbia.

5   April 22, 1998.

6   [...]

9   *OPINION*

10   **PAUL L. FRIEDMAN, District Judge.**

11   This is a defamation case revolving around a statement published on the Internet by defendant Matt Drudge. On August 10, 1997, the following was available to all having access to the Internet:

12   The DRUDGE REPORT has learned that top GOP operatives who feel there is a double-standard of only reporting republican shame believe they are holding an ace card: New White House recruit Sidney Blumenthal has a spousal abuse past that has been effectively covered up.

         The accusations are explosive.

         There are court records of Blumenthal's violence against his wife, one influential republican, who demanded anonymity, tells the DRUDGE REPORT.

         If they begin to use [Don] Sipple and his problems against us, against the Republican Party ... to show hypocrisy, Blumenthal would become fair game. Wasn't it Clinton who signed the Violence Against Women Act?

         [There goes the budget deal honeymoon.] One White House source, also requesting anonymity, says the Blumenthal wife-beating allegation is a pure fiction that has been created by Clinton enemies. [The First Lady] would not have brought him in if he had this in his background, assures the wellplaced staffer. This story about Blumenthal has been in circulation for years.

         Last month President Clinton named Sidney Blumenthal an Assistant to the President as part of the Communications Team. He's brought in to work on communications strategy, special projects themeing — a newly created position.

         Every attempt to reach Blumenthal proved unsuccessful.

13   [...]

14   Currently before this Court are a motion for summary judgment filed by defendant America Online, Inc. ("AOL") and a motion to dismiss or transfer for lack of personal jurisdiction filed by defendant Matt Drudge. Upon consideration of the papers filed by the parties and the oral arguments of counsel, the Court concludes that AOL's motion should be granted and Drudge's motion should be denied.

15   I. BACKGROUND

16   [...] Sidney Blumenthal works in the White House as an Assistant to the President of the United States. His first day of work as Assistant to the President was Monday, August 11, 1997, the day after the publication of the alleged defamatory statement. Jacqueline Jordan Blumenthal, Sidney Blumenthal's wife, also works in the White House as Director of the President's Commission On White House Fellowships. [...]

17   Defendant Matt Drudge, a Takoma Park, Maryland native, is a resident of the State of California, where he has lived continuously since 199 In early 1995, defendant Drudge created an electronic publication called the Drudge Report, a gossip column focusing on gossip from Hollywood and Washington, [...]

18   Access to defendant Drudge's world wide web site is available at no cost to anyone who has access to the Internet at the Internet address of "www.drudgereport.com." [...] Drudge had developed a list of regular readers or subscribers to whom he e-mailed each new edition of the Drudge Report. [...]

20   In late May or early June of 1997 [...] defendant Drudge entered into a written license agreement with AOL.[3] The agreement made the Drudge Report available to all members of AOL's service for a period of one year. In exchange, defendant Drudge received a flat monthly "royalty payment" of $3,000 from AOL. During the time relevant to this case, defendant Drudge has had no other source of income. [...] Under the licensing agreement, Drudge is to create, edit, update and "otherwise manage" the content of the Drudge Report, and AOL may "remove content that AOL reasonably determine[s] to violate AOL's then standard terms of service." [...] Drudge transmits new editions of the Drudge Report by e-mailing them to AOL. AOL then posts the new editions on the AOL service. [...] Drudge also has continued to distribute each new edition of the Drudge Report via e-mail and his own web site. [...]

21   Late at night on the evening of Sunday, August 10, 1997 (Pacific Daylight Time), defendant Drudge wrote and transmitted the edition of the Drudge Report that contained the alleged defamatory statement about the Blumenthals. Drudge transmitted the report from Los Angeles, California by e-mail to his direct subscribers and by posting both a headline and the full text of the Blumenthal story on his world wide web site. He then [...] transmitted the text but not the headline to AOL, which in turn made it available to AOL subscribers. [...]

22   After receiving a letter from plaintiffs' counsel on Monday, August 11, 1997, Complaint, Ex. 6, defendant Drudge retracted the story through a special edition of the Drudge Report posted on his web site and e-mailed to his subscribers. [...] At approximately 2:00 a.m. on Tuesday, August 12, 1997, Drudge e-mailed the retraction to AOL which posted it on the AOL service. [...][5] Defendant Drudge later publicly apologized to the Blumenthals. [...]

23   II. AOL's MOTION FOR SUMMARY JUDGMENT

24   [...]

28   **B.** *Communications Decency Act of 1996, Section 230*

30   In February of 1996, Congress made an effort to deal with some of these challenges in enacting the Communications Decency Act of 1996. While various policy options were open to the Congress, it chose to "promote the continued development of the Internet and other interactive computer services and other interactive media" and "to preserve the vibrant and competitive free market" for such services, largely "unfettered by Federal or State regulation...." 47 U.S.C. § 230(b)(1) and (2). Whether wisely or not, it made the legislative

judgment to effectively immunize providers of interactive computer services from civil liability in tort with respect to material disseminated by them but created by others. In recognition of the speed with which information may be disseminated and the near impossibility of regulating information content, Congress decided not to treat providers of interactive computer services like other information providers such as newspapers, magazines or television and radio stations, all of which may be held liable for publishing or distributing obscene or defamatory material written or prepared by others. While Congress could have made a different policy choice, it opted not to hold interactive computer services liable for their failure to edit, withhold or restrict access to offensive material disseminated through their medium.

31   Section 230(c) of the Communications Decency Act of 1996 provides:

32   No provider or user of an interactive computer service shall be treated as the publisher or speaker of any information provided
              by another information content provider.

33   47 U.S.C. § 230(c)(1). The statute goes on to define the term "information content provider" as "any person or entity that is responsible,
      in whole or in part, for the creation or development of information provided through the Internet or any other interactive computer
      service." 47 U.S.C. § 230(e)(3). In view of this statutory language, plaintiffs' argument that the *Washington Post* would be liable if it had
      done what AOL did here — "publish Drudge's story without doing anything whatsoever to edit, verify, or even read it (despite knowing
      what Drudge did for a living and how he did it)," [...] — has been rendered irrelevant by Congress.

34   Plaintiffs concede that AOL is a "provider … of an interactive computer service" [...] for purposes of Section 230, [...] and that if AOL
      acted exclusively as a provider of an interactive computer service it may not be held liable for making the Drudge Report available to AOL
      subscribers. *See* 47 U.S.C. § 230(c)(1). They also concede that Drudge is an "information content provider" because he wrote the alleged
      defamatory material about the Blumenthals contained in the Drudge Report. Pls.' Mem. at 4. While plaintiffs suggest that AOL is
      responsible along with Drudge because it had some role in writing or editing the material in the Drudge Report, they have provided no
      factual support for that assertion. Indeed, plaintiffs affirmatively state that "no person, other than Drudge himself, edited, checked,
      verified, or supervised the information that Drudge published in the Drudge Report." [...] It also is apparent to the Court that there is no
      evidence to support the view originally taken by plaintiffs that Drudge is or was an employee or agent of AOL, and plaintiffs seem to have
      all but abandoned that argument. [...]

35   AOL acknowledges both that Section 230(c)(1) would not immunize AOL with respect to any information AOL developed or created
      entirely by itself and that there are situations in which there may be two or more information content providers responsible for material
      disseminated on the Internet — joint authors, a lyricist and a composer, for example. [...] While Section 230 does not preclude joint
      liability for the joint development of content, AOL maintains that there simply is no evidence here that AOL had any role in creating or
      developing any of the information in the Drudge Report. The Court agrees. It is undisputed that the Blumenthal story was written by
      Drudge without any substantive or editorial involvement by AOL. [...] AOL was nothing more than a provider of an interactive computer
      service on which the Drudge Report was carried, and Congress has said quite clearly that such a provider shall not be treated as a
      "publisher or speaker" and therefore may not be held liable in tort. [...]

36   As Chief Judge Wilkinson recently wrote for the Fourth Circuit:

37   [...]

              Congress made a policy choice, however, not to deter harmful online speech through the separate route of imposing tort
              liability on companies that serve as intermediaries for other parties' potentially injurious messages.

38   *Zeran v. America Online, Inc.,* 129 F.3d 327, 330-31 (4th Cir.1997). The court in *Zeran* has provided a complete answer to plaintiffs'
      primary argument, an answer grounded in the statutory language and intent of Section 230. [...]

39   Plaintiffs make the additional argument, however, that Section 230 of the Communications Decency Act does not provide immunity to

AOL in this case because Drudge was not just an anonymous person who sent a message over the Internet through AOL. He is a person with whom AOL contracted, whom AOL paid $3,000 a month — $36,000 a year, Drudge's sole, consistent source of income — and whom AOL promoted to its subscribers and potential subscribers as a reason to subscribe to AOL. [...] Furthermore, the license agreement between AOL and Drudge by its terms contemplates more than a passive role for AOL; in it, AOL reserves the "right to remove, or direct [Drudge] to remove, any content which, as reasonably determined by AOL ... violates AOL's then-standard Terms of Service...." [...] By the terms of the agreement, AOL also is "entitled to require reasonable changes to ... content, to the extent such content will, in AOL's good faith judgment, adversely affect operations of the AOL network." [...]

40   In addition, shortly after it entered into the licensing agreement with Drudge, AOL issued a press release making clear the kind of material Drudge would provide to AOL subscribers — gossip and rumor — and urged potential subscribers to sign onto AOL in order to get the benefit of the Drudge Report. The press release was captioned: "AOL Hires Runaway Gossip Success Matt Drudge." [...] It noted that "[m]averick gossip columnist Matt Drudge has teamed up with America Online," and stated: "Giving the Drudge Report a home on America Online (keyword: Drudge) opens up the floodgates to an audience ripe for Drudge's brand of reporting.... AOL has made Matt Drudge instantly accessible to members who crave instant gossip and news breaks." [...] Why is this different, the Blumenthals suggest, from AOL advertising and promoting a new purveyor of child pornography or other offensive material? Why should AOL be permitted to tout someone as a gossip columnist or rumor monger who will make such rumors and gossip "instantly accessible" to AOL subscribers, and then claim immunity when that person, as might be anticipated, defames another?

41   If it were writing on a clean slate, this Court would agree with plaintiffs. AOL has certain editorial rights with respect to the content provided by Drudge and disseminated by AOL, including the right to require changes in content and to remove it; and it has affirmatively promoted Drudge as a new source of unverified instant gossip on AOL. Yet it takes no responsibility for any damage he may cause. AOL is not a passive conduit like the telephone company, a common carrier with no control and therefore no responsibility for what is said over the telephone wires. [...] Because it has the fight to exercise editorial control over those with whom it contracts and whose words it disseminates, it would seem only fair to hold AOL to the liability standards applied to a publisher or, at least, like a book store owner or library, to the liability standards applied to a distributor. [...] But Congress has made a different policy choice by providing immunity even where the interactive service provider has an active, even aggressive role in making available content prepared by others. In some sort of tacit *quid pro quo* arrangement with the service provider community, Congress has conferred immunity from tort liability as an incentive to Internet service providers to self-police the Internet for obscenity and other offensive material, even where the self-policing is unsuccessful or not even attempted.

42   In Section 230(c)(2) of the Communications Decency Act, Congress provided:

43   No provider or user of an interactive computer service shall be held liable on account of —

            (A) Any action voluntarily taken in good faith to restrict access to or availability of material that the provider or user considers to be obscene, lewd, lascivious, filthy, excessively violent, harassing, or otherwise objectionable, whether or not such material is constitutionally protected; or

            (B) any action taken to enable or make available to information content providers or others the technical means to restrict access to material described in paragraph (1).

44   47 U.S.C. § 230(c)(2).[13] As the Fourth Circuit stated in *Zeran*: "Congress enacted § 230 to remove ... disincentives to self-regulation.... Fearing that the specter of liability would ... deter service providers from blocking and screening offensive material .... § 230 forbids the imposition of publisher liability on a service provider for the exercise of its editorial and selfregulatory functions." [...]

45   Any attempt to distinguish between "publisher" liability and notice-based "distributor" liability and to argue that Section 230 was only intended to immunize the former would be unavailing. Congress made no distinction between publishers and distributors in providing immunity from liability. As the Fourth Circuit has noted: "[I]f computer service providers were subject to distributor liability, they would face potential liability each time they receive notice of a potentially defamatory statement — from any party, concerning any message," and such notice-based liability "would deter service providers from regulating the dissemination of offensive material over their own

services" by confronting them with "ceaseless choices of suppressing controversial speech or sustaining prohibitive liability" — exactly what Congress intended to insulate them from in Section 230. *[...]* While it appears to this Court that AOL in this case has taken advantage of all [...] the benefits conferred by Congress in the Communications Decency Act, and then some, without accepting any of the burdens that Congress intended, the statutory language is clear: AOL is immune from suit, and the Court therefore must grant its motion for summary judgment. [...]

70   SO ORDERED.

71   [...]

73   [3] According to AOL, it operates "the world's largest interactive computer service. AOL's more than nine million subscribers use the AOL service as a conduit to receive and disseminate vast quantities of information by means of modern connections to AOL's computer network." [...]

75   [5] AOL later removed the August 10 edition of the Drudge Report from the electronic archive of previous editions of the Drudge Report available to AOL subscribers. [...]

89   [13] While this provision of the statute primarily addresses obscenity and violent material, it also references material that is "otherwise objectionable," a broad enough category to cover defamatory statements as well. Indeed, the legislative history makes clear that one of the primary purposes of Section 230 was to overrule the *Stratton Oakmont* decision of a New York State court that was itself a defamation case in which Prodigy Services, an Internet computer service like AOL, was held liable as a publisher of defamatory material. [

Barrett v. Rosenthal

July 17, 2014 by mrisch

This case explores the limits of Section 230 immunity

1

[...]
40 Cal.4th 33
[...]

2

Stephen J. BARRETT et al., Plaintiffs and Appellants,
v.
Ilena ROSENTHAL, Defendant and Respondent.

3

[...]

4

Supreme Court of California.

5

November 20, 2006.

6

[...]

13

[...] CORRIGAN, J.

14

In the Communications Decency Act of 1996, Congress declared: "No provider or user of an interactive computer service shall be treated as the publisher or speaker of any information provided by another information content provider." (47 U.S.C. § 230(c)(1).)[...] "No cause of action may be brought and no liability may be imposed under any State or local law that is inconsistent with this section." (§ 230(e)(3).)

15

These provisions have been widely and consistently interpreted to confer broad immunity against defamation liability for those who use the Internet to publish information that originated from another source. The immunity has been applied regardless of the traditional distinction between "publishers" and "distributors." Under the common law, "distributors" like newspaper vendors and book sellers are liable only if they had notice of a defamatory statement in their merchandise. The publisher of the newspaper or book where the statement originally appeared, however, may be held liable even without notice.

16

[...]

17

We conclude that section 230 prohibits "distributor" liability for Internet publications. We further hold that section 230(c)(1) immunizes individual "users" of interactive computer services, and that no practical or principled distinction can be drawn between active and passive use. Accordingly, we reverse the Court of Appeal's judgment.

18

We acknowledge that recognizing broad immunity for defamatory republications on the Internet has some troubling consequences. Until Congress chooses to revise the settled law in this area, however, plaintiffs who contend they were defamed in an Internet posting may only seek recovery from the original source of the statement.

19   [...]

20   Plaintiffs, Dr. Stephen J. Barrett and Dr. Terry Polevoy, operated Web sites [59] devoted to exposing health frauds. Defendant Ilena Rosenthal directed the Humantics Foundation for Women and operated an Internet discussion group. Plaintiffs alleged that Rosenthal and others committed libel by maliciously distributing defamatory statements in e-mails and Internet postings, impugning plaintiffs' character and competence and disparaging their efforts to combat fraud.[2] They alleged that Rosenthal republished various messages even after Dr. Barrett warned her they contained false and defamatory information.

21   [...]

II. DISCUSSION

24

25   [...] Recognizing "distributor" liability would have a dramatic impact on Internet service providers. We agree with the *Zeran* court that Congress did not intend to create such an exception to section 230 immunity.[...]

26   Rosenthal, however, is not a service provider, at least with respect to the newsgroups where she posted the Bolen article. This appears to be the first published case in which section 230 immunity has been invoked by an individual who had no supervisory role in the operation of the Internet site where allegedly defamatory material appeared, and who thus was clearly not a provider of an "interactive computer service" under the broad definition provided in the CDA. (§ 230(f)(2); see fn. 7, *ante*.) Accordingly, we asked the parties to brief the meaning of the term "user" in section 230, and whether any distinction might be drawn between active and passive use under the statute. In part C of our discussion, we conclude that Congress employed the term "user" to refer simply to anyone using an interactive computer service, without distinguishing between active and passive use.

27   [...]

60   The Court of Appeal gave insufficient consideration to the burden its rule would impose on Internet speech. It is inaccurate to suggest that Congress was indifferent to free speech protection when it enacted section 230. The statute includes findings welcoming the "extraordinary advance in the availability of educational and informational resources" on the Internet, and applauding the Internet as a "forum for a true diversity of political discourse" that offers "myriad avenues for intellectual activity" and provides "a variety of political, educational, cultural, and entertainment services." (§ 230(a)(1), (3), & (5).) Congress sought to "promote the continued development of the Internet and other interactive computer services." (§ 230(b)(1).) The provisions of section 230(c)(1), conferring broad immunity on Internet intermediaries, are themselves a strong demonstration of legislative commitment to the value of maintaining a free market for online expression.

67   [...]

68   We agree with the *Zeran* court, and others considering the question, that subjecting Internet service providers and users to defamation liability would tend to chill online speech. [...] Certainly, that conclusion is no more speculative than the surmise that market forces might deter providers from removing postings without investigating their defamatory character.

69   We reject the argument that the difficulty of prevailing on a defamation claim mitigates the deterrent effect of potential liability. Defamation law is complex, requiring consideration of multiple factors. These include whether the statement at issue is true or false, factual or figurative, privileged or unprivileged, whether the matter is of public or private concern, and whether the plaintiff is a public or private figure. [...] Any investigation of a potentially defamatory Internet posting is thus a daunting and expensive challenge. For that reason, we have observed that even when a defamation claim [...] is "clearly nonmeritorious," the threat of liability "ultimately chills the free exercise of expression." [...]

72   The great variety of Internet publications, and the different levels of content control that may be exercised by service providers and users, do not undermine the conclusion that Congress intended to create a blanket immunity from tort liability for online republication of third party content. Requiring providers, users, and courts to account for the nuances of common law defamation, and all the various ways they might play out in the Internet environment, is a Herculean assignment that we are reluctant to impose. We conclude the *Zeran* court accurately diagnosed the problems that would attend notice-based liability for service providers.

73   [...]

74   **C.** *"User" Liability*

75   The "distributor" liability theory endorsed by the Court of Appeal recognizes no distinction between Internet service providers and individuals. Individual Internet "users" like Rosenthal, however, are situated differently from institutional service providers with regard to some of the principal policy considerations discussed by the *Zeran* court and reflected in the Congressional Record. In particular, individuals do not face the massive volume of third-party postings that providers encounter. Self-regulation is a far less challenging enterprise for them. Furthermore, service providers, no matter how active or passive a role they take in screening the content posted by users of their services, typically bear less responsibility for that content than do the users. Users are more likely than service providers to actively engage in malicious propagation of defamatory or other offensive material. These considerations bring into question the scope of the term "user" in section 230, and whether it matters if a user is engaged in active or passive conduct for purposes of the statutory immunity.

76   "User" is not defined in the statute, and the limited legislative record does not indicate why Congress included users as well as service providers under the umbrella of immunity granted by section 230(c)(1). The standard rules of statutory construction, however, yield an unambiguous result. We must begin with the language employed by Congress and the assumption that its ordinary meaning expresses the legislative purpose. [...] "User" plainly refers to someone who uses something, and the statutory context makes it clear that Congress simply meant someone who uses an interactive computer service.

77   Section 230(c)(1) refers directly to the "user of an interactive computer service." Section 230(f)(2) defines "interactive computer service" as "any information service, system, or access software provider that provides or enables computer access by multiple users to a computer server, including specifically a service or system that provides access to the Internet...." Section 230(a)(2) notes that such services "offer users a great degree of control over the information that they receive," and section 230(b)(3) expresses Congress's intent "to encourage the development of technologies which maximize user control over what information is received by individuals, families, and schools who use the Internet and other interactive computer services." Thus, Congress consistently referred to "users" of interactive computer services, specifically including "individuals" in section 230(b)(3).

78   There is no reason to suppose that Congress attached a different meaning to the term "user" in section 230(c)(1). [...] Rosenthal used the Internet to gain access to newsgroups where she posted Bolen's article about Polevoy. She was therefore a "user" under [...] the CDA, as the parties conceded below. Nor is there any basis for concluding that Congress intended to treat service providers and users differently when it declared that "[n]o provider or user of an interactive computer service shall be treated as [a] publisher or speaker ...." [. We note that in cases where an individual's role as operator of a Web site raised a question as to whether he was a "service provider" or a "user," the courts found it unnecessary to resolve the issue because the statute confers immunity on both. [...]

79   Polevoy urges us to distinguish between "active" and "passive" Internet use, and to restrict the statutory term "user" to those who engage in passive use. [...] He argues that those who actively post or republish information on the Internet are "information content providers" unprotected by the statutory immunity. "Information content provider" is defined as "any person or entity that is responsible, in whole or in part, for the creation or development of information provided through the Internet or any other interactive computer service ...."(§ 230(f)(3).)

80   Polevoy's view fails to account for the statutory provision at the center of our inquiry: the prohibition in section 230(c)(1) against treating any "user" as "the publisher or speaker of any information provided by another information content provider." A user who merely receives information on a computer without making it available to anyone else would be neither a "publisher" nor a "speaker." Congress obviously had a broader meaning in mind. Nor is it clear how a user who removes a posting may be deemed "passive" while one who merely allows a posting to remain online is "active." Furthermore, Congress plainly did not intend to deprive all "information content providers" of immunity, because the reference to "another" such provider in section 230(c)(1) presumes that the immunized publisher or speaker is also an information content provider. [...]

81   [76] The distinction between "active" and "passive" use was explored in *Batzel v. Smith, supra,* 333 F.3d 1018. Smith sent an e-mail to the operator of a Web site devoted to museum security and stolen art, accusing Batzel of possessing paintings that may have been stolen by the Nazis during World War II. The operator posted the message on the Web site, with some changes, and distributed it to the subscribers of his e-mail newsletter. Batzel sued Smith and the operator for defamation. [...]

82   The court of appeals vacated the order denying the motion, remanded, and directed the trial court to determine whether the operator should reasonably have known Smith intended his e-mail to be published on the Internet. If not, the court reasoned the message was not "provided" by another "information content provider" under section 230, and the operator would not be immune from liability.[[...]]

83   The *Batzel* dissent criticized the majority for adopting a rule that provides Internet intermediaries with immunity to spread information intended for republication, "licens[ing] professional rumor-mongers and gossip-hounds to spread false and hurtful information with impunity." [...] The dissent proposed a rule based on the defendant's actions instead of the author's intent. It would "hold that the CDA immunizes a defendant only when the defendant took no active role in selecting the questionable information for publication. If the defendant took an active role in selecting information for publication, the information is no longer `information provided by another' within the meaning of § 230." [...]

84   The dissent reasoned that information actively selected for republication has been "transformed ... bolstered, [and] strengthened to do more harm if it is wrongful." [...] It acknowledged that service providers cannot be expected to screen the millions of messages sent over their networks for offensive content. However, it argued that a person who does actively screen communications to select some for republication is able to detect defamatory content and should not be immunized. The dissent would grant immunity to bulletin board moderators and the like if they did not actively select among messages for publication, but would expose them to liability if they made a conscious decision to disseminate a particular defamatory communication. Congress's goal of encouraging self-regulation would be furthered, according to the dissent, because those who remove all or part of an offensive message would be immune. The dissenting justice did not believe Congress intended to immunize those who select defamatory information for distribution on the Internet. [...]

85   The *Batzel* majority responded that no logical distinction can be drawn between a defendant who actively selects information for publication and one who screens submitted material, removing offensive content. "The scope of the immunity cannot turn on whether the publisher approaches the selection process as one of inclusion or removal, as the difference is one of method or degree, not substance." [We agree with this reasoning. Furthermore, we reject the dissent's view that actively selected and republished information is no longer "information provided by another information content provider" under section 230(c)(1). All republications involve a "transformation" in some sense. A user who actively selects and posts material based on its content fits well within the traditional role of "publisher." Congress has exempted that role from liability.

86   As Rosenthal points out, the congressional purpose of fostering free speech on the Internet supports the extension of section 230 immunity to active individual "users." It is they who provide much of the "diversity of political discourse," the pursuit of "opportunities for cultural development," and the exploration of "myriad avenues for intellectual activity" that the statute was meant to protect. (§ 230(a) (3).) The approach taken by the *Batzel* dissent would tend to chill the free exercise of Internet expression, and could frustrate the goal of providing an incentive for self-regulation. A user who removed some offensive content might face liability for "actively selecting" the remaining material. Users in this position, no less than the service providers discussed by the *Zeran* court, would be motivated to delete marginally offensive material, restricting the scope of online discussion. Some users, at least those like Rosenthal who engage in high-

volume Internet posting, might be discouraged from screening third party content. Although individual users may face the threat of liability less frequently than institutional service providers, their lack of comparable financial and legal resources makes that threat no less intimidating.

87   We conclude there is no basis for deriving a special meaning for the term "user" in section 230(c)(1), or any operative distinction between "active" and "passive" Internet use. By declaring that no "user" may be treated as a "publisher" of third party content, Congress has comprehensively immunized republication by individual Internet users.

88   **D.** *Conclusion*

89   We share the concerns of those who have expressed reservations about the *Zeran* court's broad interpretation of section 230 immunity. The prospect of blanket immunity for those who intentionally redistribute defamatory statements on the Internet has disturbing implications. Nevertheless, by its terms section 230 exempts Internet intermediaries from defamation liability for republication. The statutory immunity serves to protect online freedom of expression and to encourage self-regulation, as Congress intended. Section 230 has been interpreted literally. It does not permit Internet service providers or users to be sued as "distributors," nor does it expose "active users" to liability.

90   Plaintiffs are free under section 230 to pursue the originator of a defamatory Internet publication. Any further expansion [...] of liability must await Congressional action.

91   [...]

95   ## CONCURRING OPINION BY MORENO, J.

96   I concur in the majority opinion. Although there may be a considerable gap between the specific wrongs Congress was intending to right in enacting the immunity at issue here and the broad statutory language of that immunity, that gap is ultimately for Congress, rather than the courts, to bridge. I write separately to express the view that publishers that conspire with original content providers to defame would not be covered by the immunity provided by title 47 United States Code section 230(c)(1) and (e)(3) (hereafter section 230). I further explain why there is no prima facie showing of conspiracy in the present case.

97   [...]

100   Unlike the Internet service provider, or even the typical user of an interactive computer service, one engaged in a tortious conspiracy with the original information content provider is hardly one of the neutral "intermediaries" that Congress intended to absolve of liability. Imposing liability on such conspirators would not cause service providers to curtail the robust Internet communication they facilitate nor inhibit them from engaging in self-regulation of offensive material. Rather, imposition of liability on those who conspire to defame on the Internet supports Congress's intent to impose liability on "original posters of defamatory speech" *Do later cases support this?* [...] discouraging collusive arrangements that are designed to maximize the original poster's impact and/or minimize his or her liability.

101   [...]

115   [...]

116   [...]

Fair Housing Council of San Fernando Valley v. Roommates.com LLC - note

July 19, 2014 by mrisch

This short excerpt highlights one of the few circumstances in which 230 does not provide immunity

1   521 F.3d 1157 (2008)

2   **FAIR HOUSING COUNCIL OF SAN FERNANDO VALLEY**[...]

v.

ROOMMATES.COM, LLC[...]

4   United States Court of Appeals, Ninth Circuit.

5   [...]

Filed April 3, 2008.

6   [...]

12   **KOZINSKI, Chief Judge:**

13   We plumb the depths of the immunity provided by section 230 of the Communications Decency Act of 1996 ("CDA").

14   [...]

15   Defendant Roommate.com, LLC ("Roommate") operates a website designed to match people renting out spare rooms with people looking for a place to live.[...]

16   Before subscribers can search listings or post[...] housing opportunities on Roommate's website, they must create profiles, a process that requires them to answer a series of questions. In addition to requesting basic information — such as name, location and email address — Roommate requires each subscriber to disclose his sex, sexual orientation and whether he would bring children to a household. Each subscriber must also describe his preferences in roommates with respect to the same three criteria: sex, sexual orientation and whether they will bring children to the household. The site also encourages subscribers to provide "Additional Comments" describing themselves and their desired roommate in an open-ended essay. After a new subscriber completes the application, Roommate assembles his answers into a "profile page." [...]

18   The Fair Housing Councils of the San Fernando Valley and San Diego ("Councils") sued Roommate in federal court, alleging that Roommate's business violates the federal Fair Housing Act [...] Councils claim that Roommate is effectively a housing broker doing online what it may not lawfully do off-line. The district court held that Roommate is immune under section 230 of the CDA, 47 U.S.C. § 230(c), and dismissed the federal claims without considering whether Roommate's actions violated the FHA. [...]

730

24   A website operator can be both a service provider and a content provider: If it passively displays content that is created entirely by third parties, then it is only a service provider with respect to that content. But as to content that it creates itself, or is "responsible, in whole or in part" for creating or developing, the website is also a content provider. Thus, a website may be immune from liability for [...] some of the content it displays to the public but be subject to liability for other content.[...]

25   1. Councils first argue that the questions Roommate poses to prospective subscribers during the registration process violate the Fair Housing Act and the analogous California law. Councils allege that requiring subscribers to disclose their sex, family status and sexual orientation "indicates" an intent to discriminate against them, and thus runs afoul of both the FHA and state law.[...]

26   Roommate created the questions and choice of answers, and designed its website registration process around them. Therefore, Roommate is undoubtedly the "information content provider" as to the questions and can claim no immunity for posting them on its website, or for forcing subscribers to answer them as a condition of using its services.

27   [...] we examine the scope of plaintiffs' substantive claims only insofar as necessary to determine whether section 230 immunity applies. However, we note that asking questions certainly *can* violate the Fair Housing Act and analogous laws in the physical world.[...] For example, a real estate broker may not inquire as to the race of a prospective buyer, and an employer may not inquire as to the religion of a prospective employee. If such questions are unlawful when posed face-to-face or by telephone, they don't magically become lawful when asked electronically online. The Communications Decency Act was not meant to create a lawless noman's-land on the Internet.[...]

28   Councils also claim that requiring subscribers to answer the questions as a condition of using Roommate's services unlawfully "cause[s]" subscribers to make a "statement . . . with respect to the sale or rental of a dwelling that indicates [a] preference, limitation, or discrimination," in violation of 42 U.S.C. § 3604(c). The CDA does not grant immunity for inducing third parties to express illegal preferences. Roommate's own acts — posting the questionnaire and requiring answers to it — are entirely its doing and thus section 230 of the CDA does not apply to them. Roommate is entitled to no immunity.[...]

29   Councils also charge that Roommate's development and display of subscribers' discriminatory preferences is unlawful. Roommate publishes a "profile page" for each subscriber on its website. The page describes the client's personal information — such as his sex, sexual orientation and whether he has children — as well as the attributes of the housing situation he seeks. The content of these pages is drawn directly from the registration process: For example, Roommate requires subscribers to specify, using a drop-down menu[...] provided by Roommate, whether they are "Male" or "Female" and then displays that information on the profile page. Roommate also requires subscribers who are listing available housing to disclose whether there are currently "Straight male(s)," "Gay male(s)," "Straight female(s)" or "Lesbian(s)" living in the dwelling. Subscribers who are seeking housing must make a selection from a drop-down menu, again provided by Roommate, to indicate whether they are willing to live with "Straight or gay" males, only with "Straight" males, only with "Gay" males or, with "No males." Similarly, Roommate requires subscribers listing housing to disclose whether there are "Children present" or "Children not present" and requires housing seekers to say "I will live with children" or "I will not live with children." Roommate then displays these answers, along with other information, on the subscriber's profile page. [...]

30   The dissent tilts at windmills when it shows, quite convincingly, that Roommate's *subscribers* are information content providers who create the profiles by picking among options and providing their own answers. [...] There is no disagreement on this point. But, the fact that users are information content providers does not preclude Roommate from *also* being an information content provider by helping "develop" at least "in part" the information in the profiles. [...]

31   Here, the part of the profile that is alleged to offend the Fair Housing Act and state housing discrimination laws — the information about sex, family status and sexual orientation — is provided by subscribers in response to Roommate's questions, which they cannot refuse to answer if they want to use defendant's services. By requiring subscribers to provide the information as a condition of accessing its service, and by providing a limited set of pre-populated answers, Roommate becomes much more than a passive transmitter of information provided by others; it becomes the developer, at least in part, of that information. And section 230 provides immunity only if

the interactive computer service does not "creat[e] or develop[]" the information "in whole or in part." *See* 47 U.S.C. § 230(f)(3).

32   [...]

41   In an abundance of caution, and to avoid the kind of misunderstanding the dissent seems to encourage, we offer a few examples to elucidate what does and does not amount to "development" under section 230 of the Communications Decency Act: If an individual uses an ordinary search engine to query for a "white roommate," the search engine has not contributed to i any alleged unlawfulness in the individual's conduct; providing *neutral* tools to carry out what may be unlawful or illicit searches does not amount to "development" for purposes of the immunity exception. A dating website that requires users to enter their sex, race, religion and marital status through drop-down menus, and that provides means for users to search along the same lines, retains its CDA immunity insofar as it does not contribute to any alleged illegality;[23] this immunity is retained even if the website is sued for libel based on these characteristics because the website would not have contributed materially to any alleged defamation. Similarly, a housing website that allows users to specify whether they will or will not receive emails by means of *user-defined* criteria might help some users exclude email from other users of a particular race or sex. However, that website would be immune, so long as it does not require the use of discriminatory criteria. A website operator who edits user-created content — such as by correcting spelling, removing obscenity or trimming for length — retains his "immunity for any illegality in the user-created content, provided that the edits are unrelated to the illegality. However, a website operator who edits in a manner that contributes to the alleged illegality — such as by removing the word "not" from a user's message reading "[Name] did *not* steal the artwork" in order to transform an innocent message into a libelous one — is directly involved in the alleged illegality and thus not immune.[...]

589

Barnes v. Yahoo!, Inc. - note

July 20, 2014 by mrisch

This short excerpt illustrates another potential exception to CDA Section 230 – promissory estoppel

1

570 F.3d 1096

Cecilia L. BARNES, Plaintiff-Appellant,

v.

YAHOO!, INC., a Delaware Corp., Defendant-Appellee.

No. 05-36189.

United States Court of Appeals, Ninth Circuit.

[...]

Amended June 22, 2009.

[...]

2

Before: DIARMUID F. O'SCANNLAIN, SUSAN P. GRABER, and CONSUELO M. CALLAHAN, Circuit Judges.

[...]

OPINION

O'SCANNLAIN, Circuit Judge:

We must decide whether the Communications Decency Act of 1996 protects an internet service provider from suit where it undertook to remove from its website material harmful to the plaintiff but failed to do so.

I

This case stems from a dangerous, cruel, and highly indecent use of the internet for the apparent purpose of revenge.[1]

In late 2004, Cecilia Barnes broke off a lengthy relationship with her boyfriend. For reasons that are unclear, he responded by posting profiles of Barnes on a website run by Yahoo!, Inc. ("Yahoo"). According to Yahoo's Member Directory, "[a] public profile is a page with information about you that other Yahoo! members can view. You[r] profile allows you to publicly post information about yourself that you want to share with the world. Many people post their age, pictures, location, and hobbies on their profiles." Through Yahoo's online service, computer users all over the country and the world can view such profiles.

Barnes did not authorize her now former boyfriend to post the profiles, which is hardly surprising considering their content. The profiles contained nude photographs of Barnes and her boyfriend, taken without her knowledge, and some kind of open solicitation, whether express or implied is unclear, to engage in sexual intercourse. The ex-boyfriend then conducted discussions in Yahoo's online "chat rooms," posing as Barnes and directing male correspondents to the fraudulent profiles he had created. The profiles also included the addresses, real and electronic, and telephone number at Barnes' place of employment. Before long, men whom Barnes did not know were peppering her office with emails, phone calls, and personal visits, all in the expectation of sex.

In accordance with Yahoo policy, Barnes mailed Yahoo a copy of her photo ID and a signed statement denying her involvement with the profiles and requesting their removal. One month later, Yahoo had not responded but the undesired advances from unknown men continued; Barnes again asked Yahoo by mail to remove the profiles. Nothing happened. The following month, Barnes sent Yahoo two more mailings. During the same period, a local news program was preparing to broadcast a report on the incident. A day before the [...] initial air date of the broadcast, Yahoo broke its silence; its Director of Communications, a Ms. Osako, called Barnes and asked her to fax directly the previous statements she had mailed. Ms. Osako told Barnes that she would "personally walk the statements over to the division responsible for stopping unauthorized profiles and they would take care of it." Barnes claims to have relied on this statement and took no further action regarding the profiles and the trouble they had caused. Approximately two months passed without word from Yahoo, at which point Barnes filed this lawsuit against Yahoo in Oregon state court. Shortly thereafter, the profiles disappeared from Yahoo's website, apparently never to return.

Barnes' complaint against Yahoo is somewhat unclear, but it appears to allege two causes of action under Oregon law. First, the complaint suggests a tort for the negligent provision or non-provision of services which Yahoo undertook to provide. [...] For the sake of brevity, we refer to this tort, which is really a species of negligence, as a "negligent undertaking." Barnes also refers in her complaint and in her briefs to Yahoo's "promise" to remove the indecent profiles and her reliance thereon to her detriment. We construe such references to allege a cause of action under section 90 of the Restatement (Second) of Contracts (1981).

After Yahoo removed the action to federal court, it moved to dismiss the complaint under Federal Rule of Civil Procedure 12(b)(6). Yahoo contended that section 230(c)(1) of the Communications Decency Act ("the Act") renders it immune from liability in this case. See 47 U.S.C. § 230(c)(1). The district court granted the motion to dismiss, finding that the Act did in fact protect Yahoo from liability as a matter of law. Barnes timely appealed, claiming that, in the first place, the so-called immunity under section 230(c) did not apply to the cause of action she has brought and that, even if it did, Yahoo did not fit under the terms of such immunity.

II

The district court dismissed Barnes' claim on the ground that section 230(c)(1) makes Yahoo "immune" against any liability for the content that Barnes' former boyfriend had posted. We begin by analyzing the structure and reach of the statute itself.

A

Section 230 of the Act, also known as the Cox-Wyden Amendment ("the Amendment"), protects certain internet-based actors from certain kinds of lawsuits. [...]

Section 230(c) has two parts. Yahoo relies exclusively on the first part, which bars courts from treating certain internet service providers as publishers or speakers. Looking at the text, it appears clear that neither this subsection nor any other declares a general immunity from liability deriving from third-party content, as Yahoo argues it does. "Subsection (c)(1) does not mention `immunity' or any synonym." Our recent en banc decision in Fair Housing Council of San Fernando Valley v. Roommates.Com, LLC, rested not on broad statements of immunity but rather on a careful exegesis of the statutory language. [...]

[...] it appears that subsection (c)(1) only protects from liability (1) a provider or user of an interactive computer service (2) whom a plaintiff seeks to treat, under a state law cause of action,[4] as a publisher or speaker [...] (3) of information provided by another information content provider.

Barnes did not contest in the district court that Yahoo is a provider of an interactive computer service, and we have no trouble concluding that it qualifies as one.[5] Nor is there any dispute that the "information content"—such as it is—at issue in this case was provided by another "information content provider."[6] The flashpoint in this case is the meaning of the "publisher or speaker" part of subsection (c)(1), and that is where we train our sights.

B

By its terms, then, section (c)(1) only ensures that in certain cases an internet service provider[7] will not be "treated" as the "publisher or speaker" of third-party content for the purposes of another cause of action. The question before us is how to determine when, for purposes of this statute, a plaintiff's theory of liability would treat a defendant as a publisher or speaker of third-party content.

[...]

III

Which leads us to whether Barnes, in her negligent undertaking claim, seeks to treat Yahoo as a "publisher or speaker" of the indecent profiles in order to hold Yahoo liable.

A

The Oregon law tort that Barnes claims Yahoo committed derives from section 323[...] of the Restatement (Second) of Torts, which states: One who undertakes, gratuitously or for consideration, to render services to another which he should recognize as necessary for the protection of the other's person or things, is subject to liability to the other for physical harm resulting from his failure to exercise reasonable care to perform his undertaking, if

(a) his failure to exercise such care increases the risk of such harm, or

(b) the harm is suffered because of the other's reliance upon the undertaking.

Barnes argues that this tort claim would not treat Yahoo as a publisher. She points to her complaint, which acknowledges that although Yahoo "may have had no initial responsibility to act, once [Yahoo,] through its agent, undertook to act, [it] must do so reasonably." According to Barnes, this makes the undertaking, not the publishing or failure to withdraw from publication, the source of liability. […]

We are not persuaded. As we implied above, a plaintiff cannot sue someone for publishing third-party content simply by changing the name of the theory from defamation to negligence. Nor can he or […] she escape section 230(c) by labeling as a "negligent undertaking" an action that is quintessentially that of a publisher. […]

[…]

IV

As we indicated above, Barnes' complaint could also be read to base liability on section 90 of the Restatement (Second) of Contracts, which describes a theory of recovery often known as promissory estoppel. At oral argument, counsel for Barnes acknowledged that its tort claim might be "recast" in terms of promissory estoppel. We think it might, and in analyzing it as such now we add that liability for breach of promise is different from, and not merely a rephrasing of, liability for negligent undertaking.

A

Oregon has accepted promissory estoppel as a theory of recovery. […] The "principal criteria" that determine "when action renders a promise enforceable" under this doctrine are: "(1) a promise[;] (2) which the promisor, as a reasonable person, could foresee would induce conduct of the kind which occurred[;] (3) actual reliance on the promise[;] (4) resulting in a substantial change in position." […]

In most states, including Oregon, "'[p]romissory estoppel' is not a 'cause of action' in itself; rather it is a subset of a theory of recovery based on a breach of contract and serves as a substitute for consideration."[…]

Thus, aside from consideration, ordinary contract principles usually apply.[…] […]

It is no small thing for courts to enforce private bargains. The law justifies such intervention only because the parties manifest, ex ante, their mutual desire that each be able to call upon a judicial remedy if the other should breach. [...]

Such, then, is the promise that promissory estoppel requires: one that the promissor intends, actually or constructively, to induce reliance on the part of the promisee. From such intention courts infer the intention that the promise be legally enforceable. Thus, when A sues B for breach of contract, A is alleging that B violated an obligation that B intended to be legally enforceable. In promissory estoppel cases, courts simply infer that intention not from consideration but from a promise that B could have foreseen would induce A's reliance.

B

Against this background, we inquire whether Barnes' theory of recovery under promissory estoppel would treat Yahoo as a "publisher or speaker" under the Act.

As we explained above, subsection 230(c)(1) precludes liability when the duty the plaintiff alleges the defendant violated derives from the defendant's status or conduct as a publisher or speaker. In a promissory estoppel case, as in any other contract case, the duty the defendant allegedly violated springs from a contract— an enforceable promise—not from any non-contractual conduct or capacity of the defendant. See GTE Corp., 347 F.3d at 662 ("Maybe [the] plaintiffs would have a better argument that, by its contracts ..., [the defendant] assumed a duty to protect them."). Barnes does not seek to hold Yahoo liable as a publisher or speaker of third-party content, but rather as the counter-party to a contract, as a promisor who has breached.

How does this analysis differ from our discussion of liability for the tort of negligent undertaking? [...] After all, even if Yahoo did make a promise, it promised to take down third-party content from its website, which is quintessential publisher conduct, just as what Yahoo allegedly undertook to do consisted in publishing activity. The difference is that the various torts we referred to above each derive liability from behavior that is identical to publishing or speaking: publishing defamatory material; publishing material that inflicts emotional distress; or indeed attempting to de-publish hurtful material but doing it badly. To undertake a thing, within the meaning of the tort, is to do it.

Promising is different because it is not synonymous with the performance of the action promised. That is, whereas one cannot undertake to do something without simultaneously doing it, one can, and often does, promise to do something without actually doing it at the same time. Contract liability here would come not from Yahoo's publishing conduct, but from Yahoo's manifest intention to be legally obligated to do something, which happens to be removal of material from publication. Contract law treats the outwardly manifested intention to create an expectation on the part of another as a legally significant event. That event generates a legal duty distinct from the conduct at hand, be it the conduct of a publisher, of a doctor, or of an overzealous uncle. [...]

[...] a general monitoring policy, or even an attempt to help a particular person, on the part of an interactive computer service such as Yahoo does not suffice for contract liability. This makes it easy for Yahoo to avoid liability: it need only disclaim any intention to be bound. |

One might also approach this question from the perspective of waiver.[15] The objective intention to be bound by a promise—which, again, promissory estoppel derives from a promise that induces reasonably foreseeable, detrimental reliance—also signifies the waiver of certain defenses. A putative promisor might defend on grounds that show that the contract was never formed (the lack of acceptance or a meeting of the minds, for example) or that he could not have intended as the evidence at first suggests he did (unconscionability, duress, or incapacity, for example). Such defenses go to the integrity of the promise and the intention it signifies; they usually cannot be waived by the agreement they purport to undermine. But once a court concludes a promise is legally enforceable according to contract law, it has implicitly concluded that the promisor has manifestly intended that the court enforce his promise. By so intending, he has agreed to depart from the baseline rules (usually derived from tort or statute) that govern the mine-run of relationships between strangers. Subsection 230(c)(1) creates a baseline rule: no liability for publishing or speaking the content of other information service providers. Insofar as Yahoo made a promise with the constructive intent that it be enforceable, it has implicitly [...] agreed to an alteration in such baseline.

Therefore, we conclude that, insofar as Barnes alleges a breach of contract claim under the theory of promissory estoppel, subsection 230(c)(1) of the Act does not preclude her cause of action. Because we have only reviewed the affirmative defense that Yahoo raised in this appeal, we do not reach the question whether Barnes has a viable contract claim or whether Yahoo has an affirmative defense under subsection 230(c)(2) of the Act.

V

For the foregoing reasons, we AFFIRM IN PART, REVERSE IN PART, and REMAND for further proceedings. Each party shall bear its own costs.

[...]

Jones v. Dirty World Entertainment Recordings LLC - note

July 30, 2014 by mrisch

This case explores what it means to "develop" content

1

SARAH JONES, Plaintiff-Appellee,

v.

[...]

DIRTY WORLD, LLC, dba thedirty.com, Defendants-Appellants.

2

[...]

3

United States Court of Appeals, Sixth Circuit.

4

[...]
Decided and Filed: June 16, 2014.

5

[...]

13 This case presents the issue of whether the Communications Decency Act of 1996 (CDA), 47 U.S.C. § 230, bars the state-law defamation claims of plaintiff-appellee Sarah Jones. Jones was the unwelcome subject of several posts anonymously uploaded to www.TheDirty.com, a popular website operated by defendants-appellants Nik Lamas-Richie and DIRTY WORLD, LLC ("Dirty World"), and of remarks Richie posted on the site. The website enables users to anonymously upload comments, photographs, and video, which Richie then selects and publishes along with his own distinct, editorial comments. In short, the website is a user-generated tabloid primarily targeting non-public figures.

14 [...]

15 We now consider when a website is not an "information content provider" under 47 U.S.C. § 230(f)(3) with respect to information it publishes such that § 230(c)(1) bars state-law tort claims predicated on that information.

16 [...]

18 Richie is currently employed as the manager of DIRTY WORLD, LLC ("Dirty World"), which owns and operates the website www.TheDirty.com. [...]

19 In the beginning, Richie created nearly all the content on the site, and users could not directly upload content. This is no longer true. For the past several years and currently, users of the site, who colloquially refer to themselves as "The Dirty Army," may submit "dirt"—*i.e.,* content that may include text, photographs, or video about any subject. Users may also post comments about the content submitted by others. The vast majority of the content appearing on www.TheDirty.com is comprised of submissions uploaded directly by third-party users.

20   The content submission form instructs users to "Tell us what's happening. Remember to tell us who, what, when, where, why." The content submission form requires users to submit a title and category for their submission as well as their city or college for indexing. Submissions appear on the website as though they were authored by a single, anonymous author—"THE DIRTY ARMY." This eponymous introduction is automatically added to every post that Richie receives from a third-party user. Many, but not all, of the submissions and commentaries appearing on the website relate to stories, news, and gossip about local individuals who are not public figures. The site receives thousands of new submissions each day. Richie or his staff selects and edits approximately 150 to 200 submissions for publication each day. The editing done to published submissions only consists of deletion. Richie or his staff briefly reviews each submission selected for publication to ensure that nudity, obscenity, threats of violence, profanity, and racial slurs are removed. Richie typically adds a short, one-line comment about the post with "some sort of humorous or satirical observation." Richie, however, does not materially change, create, or modify any part of the user-generated submission, nor does he fact-check submissions for accuracy. Apart from his clearly denoted comments appended at the end of each submission, which appear in bold-face text and are signed "-nik," Richie does not create any of the posts that appear on www.TheDirty.com. The bold-face text and signature are designed to distinguish editorial remarks from third-party submissions. Comments that appear in bold face and are signed "-nik" are only written and published by Richie.

21   Sarah Jones is a resident of northern Kentucky. Jones was a teacher at Dixie Heights High School in Edgewood, Kentucky, and a member of the Cincinnati BenGals, the cheerleading squad for the Cincinnati Bengals professional football team. From October 2009 to January 2010, Jones was the subject of several submissions posted by anonymous users on www.TheDirty.com and of editorial remarks posted by Richie.

22   First, on October 27, 2009, a visitor to www.TheDirty.com submitted two photographs of Jones and a male companion and the following post:

23   THE DIRTY ARMY: Nik, this is Sara J, Cincinnati Bengal Cheerleader. She's been spotted around town lately with the infamous Shayne Graham. She has also slept with every other Bengal Football player. This girl is a teacher too!! You would think with Graham's paycheck he could attract something a little easier on the eyes Nik!

24   Appearing directly beneath this post, Richie added: Everyone in Cincinnati knows this kicker is a Sex Addict. It is no secret . . . he can't even keep relationships because his Red Rocket has freckles that need to be touched constantly. -nik   *Note that these comments are about Graham, not Jones. This will be important later.*

25   [...]

26   Second, on December 7, 2009, a visitor submitted a photograph of Jones and the following post:

27   THE DIRTY ARMY: Nik, here we have Sarah J, captain cheerleader of the playoff bound cinci bengals. . Most ppl see Sarah has [sic] a gorgeous cheerleader AND highschool teacher. . yes she's also a teacher. . but what most of you don't know is. . Her ex Nate. . cheated on her with over 50 girls in 4 yrs. . in that time he tested positive for Chlamydia Infection and Gonorrhea. . so im sure Sarah also has both. . whats worse is he brags about doing sarah in the gym. . football field. . her class room at the school she teaches at DIXIE Heights.

28   Appearing directly after this post, Richie remarked: "Why are all high school teachers freaks in the sack? -nik"

29   Third, on December 9, 2009, a visitor submitted another photograph of Jones and a male companion and the following post:

30   THE DIRTY ARMY: Nik, ok you all seen the past posting of the dirty Bengals cheerleader/teacher . . . well here is her main man Nate. Posted a few pics of the infected couple. Oh an for everyone saying sarah is so gorgeous check her out in these non photoshopped pics.

31   Appearing directly after this post, Richie added:

32   Cool tribal tat man. For a second yesterday I was jealous of those high school kids for having a cheerleader teacher, but not
          anymore. -nik

33   Jones sent Richie over twenty-seven emails, pleading for Richie to remove these posts from the website, to no avail. Jones's father
      similarly wrote to Richie, also to no avail. [...]

63   This case turns on how narrowly or capaciously the statutory term "development" in § 230(f)(3) is read. [...]

64   limited circuit precedent suggests the proper interpretation of "*development* of information provided through the Internet," § 230(f)(3),
      means something more involved than merely displaying or allowing access to content created by a third party; otherwise § 230(c)(1)
      would be meaningless. And instances of development *may* include some functions a website operator may conduct with respect to
      content originating from a third party. *[...]*

66   A material contribution to the alleged illegality of the content does not mean merely taking action that is necessary to the display of
      allegedly illegal content. Rather, it means being responsible for what makes the displayed content allegedly unlawful. *[...]*

68   Consistent with our sister circuits, we adopt the material contribution test to determine whether a website operator is "responsible, in
      whole or in part, for the creation or development of [allegedly tortious] information." 47 U.S.C. § 230(f)(3). *[...]*

84   We do not adopt the district court's encouragement test of immunity under the CDA. The district court misapprehended how other
      circuits, particularly the Ninth Circuit in *Roommates,* have separated what constitutes "development" in § 230(f)(3) from what does not.
      The district court elided the crucial distinction between, on the one hand, taking actions (traditional to publishers) that are necessary to
      the display of unwelcome and actionable content and, on the other hand, responsibility for what makes the displayed content illegal or
      actionable. *[...]*

85   an encouragement test would inflate the meaning of "development" to the point of eclipsing the immunity from publisher-liability that
      Congress established. Many websites not only allow but also actively invite and encourage users to post particular types of content.
      Some of this content will be unwelcome to others—*e.g.,* unfavorable reviews of consumer products and services, allegations of price
      gouging, complaints of fraud on consumers, reports of bed bugs, collections of cease-and-desist notices relating to online speech. And
      much of this content is commented upon by the website operators who make the forum available. Indeed, much of it is "adopted" by
      website operators, gathered into reports, and republished online. Under an encouragement test of development, these websites would
      lose the immunity under the CDA and be subject to hecklers' suits aimed at the publisher. [...]

88   Because Dirty World and Richie did not materially contribute to the illegality of those statements, the CDA bars Jones's claims. *[...]*

89   Dirty World and Richie did not author the statements at issue; however, they did select the statements for publication. But Richie and
      Dirty World cannot be found to have materially contributed to the defamatory content of the statements posted on October 27 and
      December 7, 2009, simply because those posts were selected for publication. *[...]*

91   Further, Richie's comment on the December 7 post—*viz.,* "Why are all high school teachers freaks in the sack?"—although absurd, did not
      materially contribute to the defamatory content of the statements uploaded on October 27 and December 7, 2009. Richie's remark was
      made after each of the defamatory postings had already been displayed. It would break the concepts of responsibility and material
      contribution to hold Richie responsible for the defamatory content of speech because he later commented on that speech. Although

ludicrous, Richie's remarks did not materially contribute to the defamatory content of the posts appearing on the website. More importantly, the CDA bars claims lodged against website operators for their editorial functions, such as the posting of comments concerning third-party posts, so long as those comments are not themselves actionable. *Should this be the rule? Post whatever you want if a user sends it, and then say what you want because you are not adding to what the user sent? How can this be gamed? [...]*

92   Jones did not allege that *Richie's* comments were defamatory. And the district court did not hold that Richie's comments were themselves tortious. Rather, the court concluded that those comments "effectively ratified and adopted the defamatory third-party post" and thereby developed the defamatory statements, thus ruling that the CDA did not bar Jones's claims. *[...]* The district court's adoption or ratification test, however, is inconsistent with the material contribution standard of "development" and, if established, would undermine the CDA. Therefore, Dirty World and Richie did not develop the statements forming the basis of Jones's tort claims and accordingly are not information content providers as to them.

93   *[...]*

94

Multi-Class Unit: <u>OIL Casebook Topic VIII: Unauthorized Access</u>

Class 19: 8.1 <u>OIL Casebook: Trespass to Chattels</u>

CompuServe v. Cyber Promotions

September 04, 2014 by mrisch

1 962 F.Supp. 1015

2 ## COMPUSERVE INCORPORATED, Plaintiff,

v.

CYBER PROMOTIONS, INC. and Sanford Wallace, Defendants.

3 [...]

4 United States District Court, S.D. Ohio, Eastern Division.

5 February 3, 1997.

6 [...]

8 ## MEMORANDUM OPINION AND ORDER

9 ## GRAHAM, District Judge.

10 This case presents novel issues regarding the commercial use of the Internet, specifically the right of an online computer service to prevent a commercial enterprise from sending unsolicited electronic mail advertising to its subscribers.

11 Plaintiff CompuServe Incorporated ("CompuServe") is one of the major national commercial online computer services. It operates a computer communication service through a proprietary nationwide computer network. In addition to allowing access to the extensive content available within its own proprietary network, CompuServe also provides its subscribers with a link to the much larger resources of the Internet. This allows its subscribers to send and receive electronic messages, known as "e-mail," by the Internet. Defendants Cyber Promotions, Inc. and its president Sanford Wallace are in the business of sending unsolicited e-mail advertisements on behalf of themselves and their clients to hundreds of thousands of Internet users, many of whom are CompuServe subscribers. CompuServe has notified defendants that they are prohibited from using its computer equipment to process and store the unsolicited e-mail and has requested that they terminate the practice. Instead, defendants have sent an increasing volume of e-mail solicitations to CompuServe subscribers. CompuServe has attempted to employ technological means to block the flow of defendants' e-mail transmissions to its computer equipment, but to no avail.

12 [...]

13 For the reasons which follow, this Court holds that where defendants engaged in a course of conduct of transmitting a substantial volume of electronic data in the form of unsolicited e-mail to plaintiff's proprietary computer equipment, where defendants continued such practice after repeated demands to cease and desist, and where defendants deliberately evaded plaintiff's affirmative efforts to protect its computer equipment from such use, plaintiff has a viable claim for trespass to personal property and is entitled to injunctive relief to protect its property.

14 **I.**

745

15   [...]

18   Internet users often pay a fee for Internet access. However, there is no per-message charge to send electronic messages over the Internet and such messages usually reach their destination within minutes. _Within minutes!_ Thus electronic mail provides an opportunity to reach a wide audience quickly and at almost no cost to the sender. It is not surprising therefore that some companies, like defendant Cyber Promotions, Inc., have begun using the Internet to distribute advertisements by sending the same unsolicited commercial message to hundreds of thousands of Internet users at once. Defendants refer to this as "bulk e-mail," while plaintiff refers to it as "junk e-mail." In the vernacular of the Internet, unsolicited e-mail advertising is sometimes referred to pejoratively as "spam."[1]

19   CompuServe subscribers use CompuServe's domain name "CompuServe.com" together with their own unique alpha-numeric identifier to form a distinctive e-mail mailing address. That address may be used by the subscriber to exchange electronic mail with any one of tens of millions of other Internet users who have electronic mail capability. E-mail sent to CompuServe subscribers is processed and stored on CompuServe's proprietary computer equipment. Thereafter, it becomes accessible to CompuServe's subscribers, who can access CompuServe's equipment and electronically retrieve those messages.

20   [...] Over the past several months, CompuServe has received many complaints from subscribers threatening to discontinue their subscription unless CompuServe prohibits electronic mass mailers from using its equipment to send unsolicited advertisements. CompuServe asserts that the volume of messages generated by such mass mailings places a significant burden on its equipment which has finite processing and storage capacity. CompuServe receives no payment from the mass mailers for processing their unsolicited advertising. However, CompuServe's subscribers pay for their access to CompuServe's services in increments of time and thus the process of accessing, reviewing and discarding unsolicited e-mail costs them money, which is one of the reasons for their complaints. CompuServe has notified defendants that they are prohibited from using its proprietary computer equipment to process and store unsolicited e-mail and has requested them to cease and desist from sending unsolicited e-mail to its subscribers. Nonetheless, defendants have sent an increasing volume of e-mail solicitations to CompuServe subscribers.

21   In an effort to shield its equipment from defendants' bulk e-mail, CompuServe has implemented software programs designed to screen out the messages and block their receipt. In response, defendants have modified their equipment and the messages they send in such a fashion as to circumvent CompuServe's screening software. Allegedly, defendants have been able to conceal the true origin of their messages by falsifying the point-of-origin information contained in the header of the electronic messages. Defendants have removed the "sender" information in the header of their messages and replaced it with another address. Also, defendants have developed the capability of configuring their computer servers to conceal their true domain name and appear on the Internet as another computer, further concealing the true origin of the messages. By manipulating this data, defendants have been able to continue sending messages to CompuServe's equipment in spite of CompuServe's protests and protective efforts.

22   Defendants assert that they possess the right to continue to send these communications to CompuServe subscribers. CompuServe contends that, in doing so, the defendants are trespassing upon its personal property.

23   **II.**

24   [...] In determining whether a motion for preliminary injunction should be granted, a court must consider and balance four factors: (1) the likelihood that the party seeking the preliminary injunction will succeed on the merits of the claim; [...]

32   **IV.**

33   This Court will now address the second aspect of plaintiff's motion in which it seeks to enjoin defendants Cyber Promotions, Inc. and its president Sanford Wallace from sending any unsolicited advertisements to any electronic mail address maintained by CompuServe.

34   CompuServe predicates this aspect of its motion for a preliminary injunction on the common law theory of trespass to personal property or to chattels, asserting that defendants' continued transmission of electronic messages to its computer equipment constitutes an actionable tort.

35   Trespass to chattels has evolved from its original common law application, concerning primarily the asportation of another's tangible
      property, to include the unauthorized use of personal property:

36   Its chief importance now, is that there may be recovery ... for interferences with the possession of chattels which are not
          sufficiently important to be classed as conversion, and so to compel the defendant to pay the full value of the thing with which
          he has interfered. Trespass to chattels survives today, in other words, largely as a little brother of conversion.

37   Prosser & Keeton, *Prosser and Keeton on Torts,* § 14, 85-86 (1984).

38   The scope of an action for conversion recognized in Ohio may embrace the facts in the instant case. The Supreme Court of Ohio
      established the definition of conversion under Ohio law in *Baltimore & O.R. Co. v. O'Donnell,* 49 Ohio St. 489, 32 N.E. 476, 478 (1892) by
      stating that:

39   [I]n order to constitute a conversion, it was not necessary that there should have been an actual appropriation of the property
          by the defendant to its own use and benefit. It might arise from the exercise of a dominion over it in exclusion of the rights of
          the owner, or withholding it from his possession under a claim inconsistent with his rights. If one take the property of another,
          for a temporary purpose only, in disregard of the owner's right, it is a conversion. Either a wrongful taking, an assumption of
          ownership, an illegal use or [...] misuse, or a wrongful detention of chattels will constitute a conversion.

40   [...]

41   Both plaintiff and defendants cite the Restatement (Second) of Torts to support their respective positions. In determining a question
      unanswered by state law, it is appropriate for this Court to consider such sources as the restatement of the law and decisions of other juris

42   The Restatement § 217(b) states that a trespass to chattel may be committed by intentionally using or intermeddling with the chattel in
      possession of another. Restatement § 217, Comment e defines physical "intermeddling" as follows:

43   ... intentionally bringing about a physical contact with the chattel. The actor may commit a trespass by an act which brings him
          into an intended physical contact with a chattel in the possession of another[.]

44   Electronic signals generated and sent by computer have been held to be sufficiently physically tangible to support a trespass cause of acti
      It is undisputed that plaintiff has a possessory interest in its computer systems. Further, defendants' contact with plaintiff's computers is
      clearly intentional. Although electronic messages may travel through the Internet over various routes, the messages are affirmatively
      directed to their destination.

45   Defendants, citing Restatement (Second) of Torts § 221, which defines "dispossession", assert that not every interference with the
      personal property of another is actionable and that physical dispossession or substantial interference with the chattel is required.
      Defendants then argue that they did not, in this case, physically dispossess plaintiff of its equipment or substantially interfere with it.
      However, the Restatement (Second) of Torts § 218 defines the circumstances under which a trespass to chattels may be actionable:

46   One who commits a trespass to a chattel is subject to liability to the possessor of the chattel if, but only if,

          (a) he dispossesses the other of the chattel, or

          (b) the chattel is impaired as to its condition, quality, or value, or

          (c) the possessor is deprived of the use of the chattel for a substantial time, or

          (d) bodily harm is caused to the possessor, or harm is caused to some person or thing [...] in which the possessor has a legally
          protected interest.

47   Therefore, an interference resulting in physical dispossession is just one circumstance under which a defendant can be found liable. Defendants suggest that "[u]nless an alleged trespasser actually takes physical custody of the property or physically damages it, courts will not find the `substantial interference' required to maintain a trespass to chattel claim." [...] In *Glidden v. Szybiak,* 95 N.H. 318, 63 A.2d 233 (1949), the court simply indicated that an action for trespass to chattels could not be maintained in the absence of some form of damage. The court held that where plaintiff did not contend that defendant's pulling on her pet dog's ears caused any injury, an action in tort could not be maintained. *Id.* 63 A.2d at 235. In contrast, plaintiff in the present action has alleged that it has suffered several types if injury as a result of defendants' conduct. [...]

48   A plaintiff can sustain an action for trespass to chattels, as opposed to an action for conversion, without showing a substantial interference with its right to possession of that chattel. *[...]* Harm to the personal property or diminution of its quality, condition, or value as a result of defendants' use can also be the predicate for liability. Restatement § 218(b).

49   An unprivileged use or other intermeddling with a chattel which results in actual impairment of its physical condition, quality or value to the possessor makes the actor liable for the loss thus caused. In the great majority of cases, the actor's intermeddling with the chattel impairs the value of it to the possessor, as distinguished from the mere affront to his dignity as possessor, only by some impairment of the physical condition of the chattel. There may, however, be situations in which the value to the owner of a particular type of chattel may be impaired by dealing with it in a manner that does not affect its physical condition.... In such a case, the intermeddling is actionable even though the physical condition of the chattel is not impaired.

50   [...] In the present case, any value CompuServe realizes from its computer equipment is wholly derived from the extent to which that equipment can serve its subscriber base. Michael Mangino, a software developer for CompuServe who monitors its mail processing computer equipment, states by affidavit that handling the enormous volume of mass mailings that CompuServe receives places a tremendous burden on its equipment. [...] Defendants' more recent practice of evading CompuServe's filters by disguising the origin of their messages commandeers even more computer resources because CompuServe's computers are forced to store undeliverable e-mail messages and labor in vain to return the messages to an address that does not exist. [...] To the extent that defendants' multitudinous electronic mailings demand the disk space and drain the processing power of plaintiff's computer equipment, those resources are not available to serve CompuServe subscribers. Therefore, the value of that equipment to CompuServe is diminished even though it is not physically damaged by defendants' conduct.

51   Next, plaintiff asserts that it has suffered injury aside from the physical impact of defendants' messages on its equipment. Restatement § 218(d) also indicates that recovery may be had for a trespass that causes [...] harm to something in which the possessor has a legally protected interest. Plaintiff asserts that defendants' messages are largely unwanted by its subscribers, who pay incrementally to access their e-mail, read it, and discard it. Also, the receipt of a bundle of unsolicited messages at once can require the subscriber to sift through, at his expense, all of the messages in order to find the ones he wanted or expected to receive. These inconveniences decrease the utility of CompuServe's e-mail service and are the foremost subject in recent complaints from CompuServe subscribers. Patrick Hole, a customer service manager for plaintiff, states by affidavit that in November 1996 CompuServe received approximately 9,970 e-mail complaints from subscribers about junk e-mail, a figure up from approximately two hundred complaints the previous year. [...] Approximately fifty such complaints per day specifically reference defendants. [...] Defendants contend that CompuServe subscribers are provided with a simple procedure to remove themselves from the mailing list. However, the removal procedure must be performed by the e-mail recipient at his expense, and some CompuServe subscribers complain that the procedure is inadequate and ineffectual. [...]

52   Many subscribers have terminated their accounts specifically because of the unwanted receipt of bulk e-mail messages. [...] Defendants' intrusions into CompuServe's computer systems, insofar as they harm plaintiff's business reputation and goodwill with its customers, are actionable under Restatement § 218(d).

53   [...]

58   Plaintiff CompuServe has attempted to exercise this privilege to protect its computer systems. However, defendants' persistent

affirmative efforts to evade plaintiff's security measures have circumvented any protection those self-help measures might have provided. In this case CompuServe has alleged and supported by affidavit that it has suffered several types of injury as a result of defendants' conduct. The foregoing discussion simply underscores that the damage sustained by plaintiff is sufficient to sustain an action for trespass to chattels. However, this Court also notes that the implementation of technological means of self-help, to the extent that reasonable measures are effective, is particularly appropriate in this type of situation and should be exhausted before legal action is proper.

56   Under Restatement § 252, the owner of personal property can create a privilege in the would-be trespasser by granting consent to use the property. A great portion of the utility of CompuServe's e-mail service is that it allows subscribers to receive messages from individuals and entities located anywhere on the Internet. Certainly, then, there is at least a tacit invitation for anyone on the Internet to utilize plaintiff's computer [...] equipment to send e-mail to its subscribers.[...] However, in or around October 1995, CompuServe employee Jon Schmidt specifically told Mr. Wallace that he was "prohibited from using CompuServe's equipment to send his junk e-mail messages." [...] There is apparently some factual dispute as to this point, but it is clear from the record that Mr. Wallace became aware at about this time that plaintiff did not want to receive messages from Cyber Promotions and that plaintiff was taking steps to block receipt of those messages. [...]

57   Defendants argue that plaintiff made the business decision to connect to the Internet and that therefore it cannot now successfully maintain an action for trespass to chattels. Their argument is analogous to the argument that because an establishment invites the public to enter its property for business purposes, it cannot later restrict or revoke access to that property, a proposition which is erroneous under Ohio law. *See, e.g., State v. Carriker*, 5 Ohio App.2d 255, 214 N.E.2d 809 (1964) (the law in Ohio is that a business invitee's privilege to remain on the premises of another may be revoked upon the reasonable notification to leave by the owner or his agents) [...] On or around October 1995, CompuServe notified defendants that it no longer consented to the use of its proprietary computer equipment. Defendants' continued use thereafter was a trespass. [...]

58   Further, CompuServe expressly limits the consent it grants to Internet users to send e-mail to its proprietary computer systems by denying unauthorized parties the use of CompuServe equipment to send unsolicited electronic mail messages. [...] This policy statement, posted by CompuServe online, states as follows:

59   Compuserve is a private online and communications services company. CompuServe does not permit its facilities to be used by unauthorized parties to process and store unsolicited e-mail. If an unauthorized party attempts to send unsolicited messages to e-mail addresses on a CompuServe service, Compuserve will take appropriate action to attempt to prevent those messages from being processed by CompuServe. Violations of CompuServe's policy prohibiting unsolicited e-mail should be reported to....

60   [...] Defendants Cyber Promotions, Inc. and its president Sanford Wallace have used plaintiff's equipment in a fashion that exceeds that consent. The use of personal property exceeding consent is a trespass. [...] It is arguable that CompuServe's policy statement, insofar as it may serve as a limitation upon the scope of its consent to the use of its computer equipment, may be insufficiently communicated to potential third-party users when it is merely posted at some location on the network. However, in the present case the record indicates that defendants were actually notified that they were using CompuServe's equipment in an unacceptable manner. To prove that a would-be trespasser acted with the intent required to support liability in tort it is crucial that defendant be placed on notice that he is trespassing.

61   [...]

68   Defendants assert that CompuServe has assumed the role of a postmaster, to whom all of the strictures of the First Amendment apply, and that to allow it to enjoy a legally protected interest in its computer equipment in this context is to license a form of censorship which violates the First Amendment. However, such an assertion must be accompanied by a showing that CompuServe is a state actor. As earlier mentioned, defendants have neither specifically argued this point nor provided any evidence to support it. CompuServe is entitled to restrict access to its private property.

69   [...]

83   **V.**

84   Based on the foregoing, plaintiff's motion for a preliminary injunction is GRANTED. The temporary restraining order filed on October 24, 1996 by this Court is hereby extended in duration until final judgment is entered in this case. Further, defendants Cyber Promotions, Inc. and its president Sanford Wallace are enjoined from sending any unsolicited advertisements to any electronic mail address maintained by plaintiff CompuServe during the pendency of this action.

85   [...]

86   [1] This term is derived from a skit performed on the British television show Monty Python's Flying Circus, in which the word "spam" is repeated to the point of absurdity in a restaurant menu.

87   [...]

eBay, Inc. v. Bidder's Edge, Inc.

September 02, 2014 by mrisch

1   100 F.Supp.2d 1058 (2000)

2   **EBAY, INC., Plaintiff,**

v.

BIDDER'S EDGE, INC., Defendant.

3   [...]

4   United States District Court, N.D. California.

5   May 24, 2000.

6   [...]

8   **ORDER GRANTING PRELIMINARY INJUNCTION**

9   **WHYTE, District Judge.**

10   [...]

11   **I. BACKGROUND**

12   eBay is an Internet-based, person-to-person trading site. (Jordan Decl. ¶ 3.) eBay offers sellers the ability to list items for sale and prospective buyers the ability to search those listings and bid on items. (*Id.*) The seller can set the terms and conditions of the auction. (*Id.*) The item is sold to the highest bidder. (*Id.*) The transaction is consummated directly between the buyer and seller without eBay's involvement. (*Id.*) A potential purchaser looking for a particular item can access the eBay site and perform a key word search for relevant auctions and bidding status. (*Id.*) eBay has also created category listings that identify items in over 2500 categories, such as antiques, computers, and dolls. (*Id.*) Users may browse these category listing pages to identify items of interest. (*Id.*)

13   Users of the eBay site must register and agree to the eBay User Agreement. (*Id.* ¶ 4.) Users agree to the seven page User Agreement by clicking on an "I Accept" button located at the end of the User Agreement. (*Id.* Ex. D.) The current version of the User Agreement prohibits the use of "any robot, spider, other automatic device, or manual process to monitor or copy our web pages or the content contained herein without our prior expressed written permission." (*Id.*) It is not clear that the version of the User Agreement in effect at the time BE began searching the eBay site prohibited such activity, or that BE ever agreed to comply with the User Agreement.

14   eBay currently has over 7 million registered users. (Jordan Decl. ¶ 4.) Over 400,000 new items are added to the site every day. (*Id.*) Every minute, 600 bids are placed on almost 3 million items. (*Id.*) Users currently perform, on average, 10 million searches per day on eBay's database. Bidding for and sales of items are continuously ongoing in millions of separate auctions. (*Id.*)

15   A software robot is a computer program which operates across the Internet to perform searching, copying and retrieving functions on

751

the web sites of others.[2] [...] A software robot is capable of executing [...] thousands of instructions per minute, far in excess of what a human can accomplish. [...]) Robots consume the processing and storage resources of a system, making that portion of the system's capacity unavailable to the system owner or other users. (*Id.*) Consumption of sufficient system resources will slow the processing of the overall system and can overload the system such that it will malfunction or "crash." (*Id.*) A severe malfunction can cause a loss of data and an interruption in services. (*Id.*)

16   The eBay site employs "robot exclusion headers." (*Id.* ¶ 5.) A robot exclusion header is a message, sent to computers programmed to detect and respond to such headers, that eBay does not permit unauthorized robotic activity. (*Id.*) Programmers who wish to comply with the Robot Exclusion Standard design their robots to read a particular data file, "robots.txt," and to comply with the control directives it contains. [...]

17   To enable computers to communicate with each other over the Internet, each is assigned a unique Internet Protocol ("IP") address. [...] When a computer requests information from another computer over the Internet, the requesting computer must offer its IP address to the responding computer in order to allow a response to be sent. (*Id.*) These IP addresses allow the identification of the source of incoming requests. (*Id.*) eBay identifies robotic activity on its site by monitoring the number of incoming requests from each particular IP address. (*Id.* ¶ 7.) Once eBay identifies an IP address believed to be involved in robotic activity, an investigation into the identity, origin and owner of the IP address may be made in order to determine if the activity is legitimate or authorized. (*Id.* ¶ 8.) If an investigation reveals unauthorized robotic activity, eBay may attempt to ignore ("block") any further requests from that IP address. (*Id.*) Attempts to block requests from particular IP addresses are not always successful. [...]

19   BE is a company with 22 employees that was founded in 1997. (Carney Decl. ¶ 2.) The BE web site debuted in November 1998. (*Id.* ¶ 3.) BE does not host auctions. (*Id.* ¶ 2.) BE is an auction aggregation site designed to offer on-line auction buyers the ability to search for items across numerous on-line auctions without having to search each host site individually. (*Id.*) As of March 2000, the BE web site contained information on more that five million items being auctioned on more than one hundred auction sites. (*Id.* ¶ 3.) BE also provides its users with additional auction-related services and information. (*Id.* ¶ 2.) The [1062] information available on the BE site is contained in a database of information that BE compiles through access to various auction sites such as eBay. (*Id.* ¶ 4.) When a user enters a search for a particular item at BE, BE searches its database and generates a list of every item in the database responsive to the search, organized by auction closing date and time. (*Id.* ¶ 5.) Rather than going to each host auction site one at a time, a user who goes to BE may conduct a single search to obtain information about that item on every auction site tracked by BE. (*Id.* ¶ 6.) It is important to include information regarding eBay auctions on the BE site because eBay is by far the biggest consumer to consumer on-line auction site. (*Id.*)

20   [...]

21   In early 1998, eBay gave BE permission to include information regarding eBay-hosted auctions for Beanie Babies and Furbies in the BE database. (*Id.* ¶ 7.) In early 1999, BE added to the number of person-to-person auction sites it covered and started covering a broader range of items hosted by those sites, including eBay. (*Id.* ¶ 8.) On April 24, 1999, eBay verbally approved BE crawling the eBay web site for a period of 90 days. (*Id.*) The parties contemplated that during this period they would reach a formal licensing agreement. (*Id.*) They were unable to do so.

22   It appears that the primary dispute was over the method BE uses to search the eBay database. eBay wanted BE to conduct a search of the eBay system only when the BE system was queried by a BE user. (Ploen Decl.Ex. 9.) This reduces the load on the eBay system and increases the accuracy of the BE data. (*Id.*) BE wanted to recursively crawl the eBay system to compile its own auction database. (Carney Decl. ¶ 18.) This increases the speed of BE searches and allows BE to track the auctions generally and automatically update its users when activity occurs in particular auctions, categories of auctions, or when new items are added. (*Id.*)

23   In late August or early September 1999, eBay requested by telephone that BE cease posting eBay auction listings on its site. [...] BE agreed to do so. (Rock Decl. ¶ 5.) In October 1999, BE learned that other auction aggregations sites were including information regarding eBay auctions. (Carney Decl. ¶ 12.) On November 2, 1999, BE issued a press release indicating that it had resumed including

eBay auction listings on its site. (Rock Decl.Ex. H.) On November 9, 1999, eBay sent BE a letter reasserting that BE's activities were unauthorized, insisting that BE cease accessing the eBay site, alleging that BE's activities constituted a civil trespass and offering to license BE's activities. (*Id.* Ex. I.) eBay and BE were again unable to agree on licensing terms. As a result, eBay attempted to block BE from accessing the eBay site; by the end of November, 1999, eBay had blocked a total of 169 IP addresses it believed BE was using to query eBay's system. (Maynor Decl. ¶ 12.) BE elected to continue crawling eBay's site by using [...] proxy servers to evade eBay's IP blocks. [...]

24 Approximately 69% of the auction items contained in the BE database are from auctions hosted on eBay. [...] BE estimates that it would lose one-third of its users if it ceased to cover the eBay auctions. [...]

25 The parties agree that BE accessed the eBay site approximate 100,000 times a day. (Felton Decl. ¶ 33.) eBay alleges that BE activity constituted up to 1.53% of the number of requests received by eBay, and up to 1.10% of the total data transferred by eBay during certain periods in October and November of 1999. [...] BE alleges that BE activity constituted no more than 1.11% of the requests received by eBay, and no more than 0.70% of the data transferred by eBay. [...] eBay alleges that BE activity had fallen 27%, to 0.74% of requests and 0.61% of data, by February 20, 2000. [...] eBay has not alleged any specific incremental damages due to BE activity. [...] [4]

26 It appears that major Internet search engines, such as Yahoo!, Google, Excite and AltaVista, respect the Robot Exclusion Standard. [...]

27 eBay now moves for preliminary injunctive relief preventing BE from accessing the eBay computer system [...]

28 ## II. LEGAL STANDARD

29 To obtain preliminary injunctive relief, a movant must demonstrate "either a likelihood of success on the merits and the possibility of irreparable injury, or that serious questions going to the merits were raised and the balance of hardships tips [...] sharply in its favor." [...]

30 ## III. ANALYSIS

31 ### A. Balance of Harm

32 [...]

33 As noted above, eBay does not seek an injunction that is tailored to independently address the manner in which BE uses the information it obtains from eBay.[8] [...]

34 According to eBay, the load on its servers resulting from BE's web crawlers represents between 1.11% and 1.53% of the total load on eBay's listing servers. eBay alleges both economic loss from BE's current activities and potential harm resulting [...] from the total crawling of BE and others. In alleging economic harm, eBay's argument is that eBay has expended considerable time, effort and money to create its computer system, and that BE should have to pay for the portion of eBay's system BE uses. eBay attributes a pro rata portion of the costs of maintaining its entire system to the BE activity. However, eBay does not indicate that these expenses are incrementally incurred because of BE's activities, nor that any particular service disruption can be attributed to BE's activities.[10] eBay provides no support for the proposition that the pro rata costs of obtaining an item represent the appropriate measure of damages for unauthorized use. In contrast, California law appears settled that the appropriate measure of damages is the actual harm inflicted by the conduct:

35   Where the conduct complained of does not amount to a substantial interference with possession or the right thereto, but consists of intermeddling with or use of or damages to the personal property, the owner has a cause of action for trespass or case, and may recover only the actual damages suffered by reason of the impairment of the property or the loss of its use.

36   *[...]*Moreover, even if BE is inflicting incremental maintenance costs on eBay, potentially calculable monetary damages are not generally a proper foundation for a preliminary injunction. *[...]* Nor does eBay appear to have made the required showing that this is the type of extraordinary case in which monetary damages may support equitable relief. *[...]*

37   eBay's allegations of harm are based, in part, on the argument that BE's activities should be thought of as equivalent to sending in an army of 100,000 robots a day to check the prices in a competitor's store. This analogy, while graphic, appears inappropriate. Although an admittedly formalistic distinction, unauthorized robot intruders into a "brick and mortar"[11] store would be committing a trespass to real property. There does not appear to be any doubt that the appropriate remedy for an ongoing trespass to business premises would be a preliminary injunction. *See e.g., State v. Carriker,* 5 Ohio App.2d 255, 214 N.E.2d 809, 811-12 (1964) (interpreting Ohio criminal trespass law to cover a business invitee who, with no intention of *[...]* making a purchase, uses the business premises of another for his own gain after his invitation has been revoked); *[...]* More importantly, for the analogy to be accurate, the robots would have to make up less than two out of every one-hundred customers in the store, the robots would not interfere with the customers' shopping experience, nor would the robots even be seen by the customers. Under such circumstances, there is a legitimate claim that the robots would not pose any threat of irreparable harm. However, eBay's right to injunctive relief is also based upon a much stronger argument.

38   If BE's activity is allowed to continue unchecked, it would encourage other auction aggregators to engage in similar recursive searching of the eBay system such that eBay would suffer irreparable harm from reduced system performance, system unavailability, or data losses.) BE does not appear to seriously contest that reduced system performance, system unavailability or data loss would inflict irreparable harm on eBay consisting of lost profits and lost customer goodwill. Harm resulting from lost profits and lost customer goodwill is irreparable because it is neither easily calculable, nor easily compensable and is therefore an appropriate basis for injunctive relief. *[...]* Where, as here, the denial of preliminary injunctive relief would encourage an increase in the complained of activity, and such an increase would present a strong likelihood of irreparable harm, the plaintiff has at least established a possibility of irreparable harm.[15]

39   *[...]*

41   BE argues that even if eBay is entitled to a presumption of irreparable harm, the presumption may be rebutted. The presumption may be rebutted by evidence that a party has engaged in a pattern of granting licenses to engage in the complained of activity such that it may be reasonable to expect that invasion of the right can be recompensed with a royalty rather than with an injunction, or by evidence that a party has unduly delayed in bringing suit, thereby negating the idea of irreparability. *[...]* BE alleges that eBay has both engaged in a pattern of licensing aggregators to crawl its site as well as delayed in seeking relief. For the reasons set forth below, the court finds that neither eBay's limited licensing activities nor its delay in seeking injunctive relief while it attempted to resolve the matter without judicial intervention are sufficient to rebut the possibility of irreparable harm.

42   If eBay's irreparable harm claim were premised solely on the potential harm caused by BE's current crawling activities, evidence that eBay had licensed others to crawl the eBay site would suggest that BE's activity would not result in irreparable harm to eBay. However, the gravamen of the alleged irreparable harm is that if BE is allowed to continue to crawl the eBay site, it may encourage frequent and unregulated crawling to the point that eBay's system will be irreparably harmed. There is no evidence that eBay has indiscriminately licensed all comers. Rather, it appears that eBay has carefully chosen to permit crawling by a limited number of aggregation sites that agree to abide by the terms of eBay's licensing agreement. "The existence of such a [limited] license, unlike a general license offered to all comers, does not demonstrate a decision to relinquish all control over the distribution of the product [1068] in exchange for a readily computable fee." *[...]*

47   **B. Likelihood of Success**

48   As noted above, eBay moves for a preliminary injunction on all nine of its causes of action. These nine causes of action correspond to eight legal theories: (1) trespass to chattels, *[...]*

50   Trespass to chattels "lies where an intentional interference with the possession of personal property has proximately cause injury." *Thrifty-Tel v. Bezenek,* 46 Cal.App.4th 1559, 1566, 54 Cal.Rptr.2d 468 (1996). Trespass to chattels "although seldom employed as a tort theory in California" was recently applied to cover the unauthorized use of long distance telephone lines. *Id.* Specifically, the court noted "the electronic signals generated by the [defendants'] activities were sufficiently tangible to support a trespass cause of action." *[...]* Thus, it appears likely that the electronic signals sent by BE to retrieve information from eBay's computer system are also sufficiently tangible to support a trespass cause of action.

51   In order to prevail on a claim for trespass based on accessing a computer system, the plaintiff must establish: (1) defendant intentionally and without authorization *[...]* interfered with plaintiff's possessory interest in the computer system; and (2) defendant's unauthorized use proximately resulted in damage to plaintiff. *[...]* Here, eBay has presented evidence sufficient to establish a strong likelihood of proving both prongs and ultimately prevailing on the merits of its trespass claim.

52   ***a. BE's Unauthorized Interference***

53   eBay argues that BE's use was unauthorized and intentional. eBay is correct. BE does not dispute that it employed an automated computer program to connect with and search eBay's electronic database. BE admits that, because other auction aggregators were including eBay's auctions in their listing, it continued to "crawl" eBay's web site even after eBay demanded BE terminate such activity.

54   BE argues that it cannot trespass eBay's web site because the site is publicly accessible. BE's argument is unconvincing. eBay's servers are private property, conditional access to which eBay grants the public. eBay does not generally permit the type of automated access made by BE. In fact, eBay explicitly notifies automated visitors that their access is not permitted. "In general, California does recognize a trespass claim where the defendant exceeds the scope of the consent." *[...]*

55   Even if BE's web crawlers were authorized to make individual queries of eBay's system, BE's web crawlers exceeded the scope of any such consent when they began acting like robots by making repeated queries. *[...]* Moreover, eBay repeatedly and explicitly notified BE that its use of eBay's computer system was unauthorized. The entire reason BE directed its queries through proxy servers was to evade eBay's attempts to stop this unauthorized access. The court concludes that BE's activity is sufficiently outside of the scope of the use permitted by eBay that it is unauthorized for the purposes of establishing a trespass. *[...]*

56   eBay argues that BE interfered with eBay's possessory interest in its computer system. Although eBay appears unlikely to be able to show a substantial interference at this time, such a showing is not required. Conduct that does not amount to a substantial interference with possession, but which consists of intermeddling with or use of another's personal property, is sufficient to establish a cause of action for trespass to chattel. *[...]* Although the court admits some uncertainty as to the precise level of possessory interference required to constitute an intermeddling, there does not appear to be any dispute that eBay can show that BE's conduct amounts to use of eBay's computer systems. Accordingly, eBay has made a strong showing that it is likely to prevail on the merits of its assertion that BE's use of eBay's computer system was an unauthorized *[...]* and intentional interference with eBay's possessory interest.

57   ***b. Damage to eBay's Computer System***

58   A trespasser is liable when the trespass diminishes the condition, quality or value of personal property. *[...]* The quality or value of personal property may be "diminished even though it is not physically damaged by defendant's conduct." *[...]* The Restatement offers the following explanation for the harm requirement:

59   The interest of a possessor of a chattel in its inviolability, unlike the similar interest of a possessor of land, is not given legal protection by an action for nominal damages for harmless intermeddlings with the chattel. In order that an actor who interferes with another's chattel may be liable, his conduct must affect some other and more important interest of the possessor. Therefore, one who intentionally intermeddles with another's chattel is subject to liability only if his intermeddling is harmful to

the possessor's materially valuable interest in the physical condition, quality, or value of the chattel, or if the possessor is deprived of the use of the chattel for a substantial time, or some other legally protected interest of the possessor is affected.... Sufficient legal protection of the possessor's interest in the mere inviolability of his chattel is afforded by his privilege to use reasonable force to protect his possession against even harmless interference.

60   Restatement (Second) of Torts § 218 cmt. e (1977).

61   eBay is likely to be able to demonstrate that BE's activities have diminished the quality or value of eBay's computer systems. BE's activities consume at least a portion of plaintiff's bandwidth and server capacity. Although there is some dispute as to the percentage of queries on eBay's site for which BE is responsible, BE admits that it sends some 80,000 to 100,000 requests to plaintiff's computer systems per day. [...] Although eBay does not claim that this consumption has led to any physical damage to eBay's computer system, nor does eBay provide any evidence to support the claim that it may have lost revenues or customers based on this use,[18] eBay's claim is that BE's use is appropriating eBay's personal property by using valuable bandwidth and capacity, and necessarily compromising eBay's ability to use that capacity for its own purposes. See CompuServe, 962 F.Supp. at 1022 ("any value [plaintiff] realizes from its computer equipment is wholly derived from the extent to which that equipment can serve its subscriber base.").

62   BE argues that its searches represent a negligible load on plaintiff's computer systems, and do not rise to the level of impairment to the condition or value of eBay's computer system required to constitute a trespass. However, it is undisputed that eBay's server and its capacity are personal property, and that BE's searches use a portion of this property. Even if, as BE argues, its searches use only a small amount of eBay's computer system capacity, BE has nonetheless deprived eBay of the ability to use that portion of its personal property for its own purposes. The law recognizes no such right to use another's personal property. Accordingly, BE's actions appear to have caused injury to eBay and appear likely to continue to cause injury to eBay. If the court were to hold otherwise, it would likely encourage other auction aggregators to crawl the eBay site, potentially to the point of denying effective access to eBay's customers. If preliminary [1072] injunctive relief were denied, and other aggregators began to crawl the eBay site, there appears to be little doubt that the load on eBay's computer system would qualify as a substantial impairment of condition or value. California law does not require eBay to wait for such a disaster before applying to this court for relief. The court concludes that eBay has made a strong showing that it is likely to prevail on the merits of its trespass claim, and that there is at least a possibility that it will suffer irreparable harm if preliminary injunctive relief is not granted. eBay is therefore entitled to preliminary injunctive relief.

63   *[...]*

68   **IV. ORDER**

70   Bidder's Edge, its officers, agents, servants, employees [...] are hereby enjoined pending the trial of this matter, from using any automated query program, robot, web crawler or other similar device, without written authorization, to access eBay's computer systems or networks, for the purpose of copying any part of eBay's auction database. [...]

71   Nothing in this order precludes BE from utilizing information obtained from eBay's site other than by automated query program, robot, web crawler or similar device. The court denies eBay's request for a preliminary injunction barring access to its site [...]

73   [2] Programs that recursively query other computers over the Internet in order to obtain a significant amount of information are referred to in the pleadings by various names, including software robots, robots, spiders and web crawlers.

74   [...]

75   [4] Q: Are you aware of any complaints from eBay users about slowdowns that were caused by aggregators?

76   A: No.

77   [...]

80   [8] Although, as a practical matter, enjoining BE from accessing eBay's computers or searching eBay's auction database may result in
        BE's inability to make effective use of information from eBay's auction site.

81   [...]

87   [15] As discussed below, eBay has a established a strong likelihood of success on the merits of the trespass claim, and is therefore
        entitled to preliminary injunctive relief because it has established the possibility of irreparable harm. Accordingly, the court does not reach
        the issue of whether the threat of increased activity would be sufficient to support preliminary injunctive relief where the plaintiff has not
        made as strong of a showing of likelihood of success on the merits.

88   [...]

Intel Corp. v. Hamidi

June 24, 2014 by mrisch

1   1 Cal.Rptr.3d 32

2   30 Cal.4th 1342

3   [...]

4   INTEL CORPORATION, Plaintiff and Respondent,
         v.
         Kourosh Kenneth HAMIDI, Defendant and Appellant.

5   [...]

6   Supreme Court of California.

7   June 30, 2003.

8   [...]

10   Philip H. Weber, Placerville; Dechert, William M. McSwain, Richard L. Berkman, F. Gregory Lastowka   *Greg Lastowka later became a professor at Rutgers. He passed away from cancer in early 2015* ; Levy, Ram & Olson, Karl Olson, San Francisco, and Erica L. Craven for Defendant and Appellant.

11   [...]

24   WERDEGAR, J.

25   Intel Corporation (Intel) maintains an electronic mail system, connected to the Internet, through which messages between employees and those outside the company can be sent and received, and permits its employees to make reasonable nonbusiness use of this system. On six occasions over almost two years, Kourosh Kenneth Hamidi, a former Intel employee, sent e-mails criticizing Intel's employment practices to numerous current employees on Intel's electronic mail system. Hamidi breached no computer security barriers in order to communicate with Intel employees. He offered to, and did, remove from his mailing list any recipient who so wished. Hamidi's communications to individual Intel employees caused neither physical damage nor functional disruption to the company's computers, nor did they at any time deprive Intel of the use of its computers. The contents of the messages, however, caused discussion among employees and managers.

26   On these facts, Intel brought suit, claiming that by communicating with its employees over the company's e-mail system Hamidi committed the tort of

758

27   [...]

28   trespass to chattels. The trial court granted Intel's motion for summary judgment and enjoined Hamidi from any further mailings. A divided
        Court of Appeal affirmed.

29   After reviewing the decisions analyzing unauthorized electronic contact with computer systems as potential trespasses to chattels,
        we conclude that under California law the tort does not encompass, and should not be extended to encompass, an electronic
        communication that neither damages the recipient computer system nor impairs its functioning. Such an electronic communication does
        not constitute an actionable trespass to personal property, i.e., the computer system, because it does not interfere with the possessor's
        use or possession of, or any other legally protected interest in, the personal property itself. [...] The consequential economic damage
        Intel claims to have suffered, i.e., loss of productivity caused by employees reading and reacting to Hamidi's messages and company
        efforts to block the messages, is not an injury to the company's interest in its computers— which worked as intended and were unharmed
        by the communications—any more than the personal distress caused by reading an unpleasant letter would be an injury to the recipient's
        mailbox, or the loss of privacy caused by an intrusive telephone call would be an injury to the recipient's telephone equipment.

30   Our conclusion does not rest on any special immunity for communications by electronic mail; we do not hold that

31   [...]

32   messages transmitted through the Internet are exempt from the ordinary rules of tort liability. To the contrary, e-mail, like other forms of
        communication, may in some circumstances cause legally cognizable injury to the recipient or to third parties and may be actionable
        under various common law or statutory theories. Indeed, on facts somewhat similar to those here, a company or its employees might be
        able to plead causes of action for interference with prospective economic relations ([...] or intentional infliction of emotional distress [...]
        And, of course, as with any other means of publication, third party subjects of e-mail communications may under appropriate facts make
        claims for

33   [...]

34   defamation, publication of private facts, or other speechbased torts. [...] Intel's claim fails not because e-mail transmitted through the
        Internet enjoys unique immunity, but because the trespass to chattels tort—unlike the causes of action just mentioned—may not, in
        California, be proved without evidence of an injury to the plaintiffs personal property or legal interest therein.

35   Nor does our holding affect the legal remedies of Internet service providers (ISP's) against senders of unsolicited commercial bulk e-
        mail (UCE), also known as "spam." [...] A series of federal district court decisions, beginning with CompuServe, Inc. v. Cyber Promotions,
        Inc. (1997),962 F.Supp. 1015, has approved the use of trespass to chattels as a theory of spammers' liability to ISP's, based upon
        evidence that the vast quantities of mail sent by spammers both overburdened the ISP's own computers and made the entire computer
        system harder to use for recipients, the ISP's customers. [...] In those cases, discussed in greater detail below, the underlying complaint
        was that the extraordinary quantity of UCE impaired the computer system's functioning. In the present case, the claimed injury is located
        in the disruption or distraction caused to recipients by the contents of the e-mail messages, an injury entirely separate from, and not
        directly affecting, the possession or value of personal property.

36   [...]

38   Hamidi, a former Intel engineer, together with others, formed an organization named Former and Current Employees of

39   […]

40   Intel (FACE-Intel) to disseminate information and views critical of Intel's employment and personnel policies and practices. FACE-Intel maintained a Web site (which identified Hamidi as Webmaster and as the organization's spokesperson) containing such material. In addition, over a 21-month period Hamidi, on

41   […]

42   behalf of FACE-Intel, sent six mass e-mails to employee addresses on Intel's electronic mail system. The messages criticized Intel's employment practices, warned employees of the dangers those practices posed to their careers, suggested employees consider moving to other companies, solicited employees' participation in FACE-Intel, and urged employees to inform themselves further by visiting FACE-Intel's Web site. The messages stated that recipients could, by notifying the sender of their wishes, be removed from FACE-Intel's mailing list; Hamidi did not subsequently send messages to anyone who requested removal.

43   Each message was sent to thousands of addresses (as many as 35,000 according to FACE-Intel's Web site), though some messages were blocked by Intel before reaching employees. Intel's attempt to block internal transmission of the messages succeeded only in part; Hamidi later admitted he evaded blocking efforts by using different sending computers. When Intel, in March 1998, demanded in writing that Hamidi and FACE-Intel stop sending e-mails to Intel's computer system, Hamidi asserted the organization had a right to communicate with willing Intel employees; he sent a new mass mailing in September 1998.

44   […] Intel did present uncontradicted evidence, however, that many employee recipients asked a company official to stop the messages and that staff time was consumed in attempts to block further messages from FACE-Intel. According to the FAC-Intel Web site, moreover, the messages had prompted discussions between "[e]xcited and nervous managers" and the company's human resources department.

45   Intel sued Hamidi and FACE-Intel, pleading causes of action for trespass to chattels and nuisance, and seeking both actual damages and an injunction

46   […]

47   against further e-mail messages. […] The court then granted Intel's motion for summary judgment, permanently enjoining Hamidi, FACE-Intel, and their agents "from sending unsolicited e-mail to addresses on Intel's computer systems." Hamidi appealed; FACE-Intel did not.[2]

48   […]

51   Discussion
52   I. Current California Tort Law

53   Dubbed by Prosser the "little brother of conversion," the tort of trespass to chattels allows recovery for interferences with possession of personal property "not sufficiently important to be classed as conversion, and so to compel the defendant to pay the full value of the thing with which he has interfered." (Prosser & Keeton, Torts (5th ed.1984) § 14, pp. 85-86.)

54   Though not amounting to conversion, the defendant's interference must, to be actionable, have caused some injury to the chattel or

760

to the plaintiffs rights in it. Under California law, trespass to chattels "lies where an intentional interference with the possession of personal property has proximately

55   [...]

56   caused injury." [...] In cases of interference with possession of personal property not amounting to conversion, "the owner has a cause of action for trespass or case, and may recover only the actual damages suffered by reason of the impairment of the property or the loss of its use." [...] In modern American law generally, "[t]respass remains as an occasional remedy for minor interferences, resulting in some damage, but not sufficiently serious or sufficiently important to amount to the greater tort" of conversion. ([...]

57   The Restatement, too, makes clear that some actual injury must have occurred in order for a trespass to chattels to be actionable. Under section 218 of the Restatement Second of Torts, dispossession alone, without further damages, is actionable [...], but other forms of interference require some additional harm to the personal property or the possessor's interests

58   [...]

59   in it. [...] "The interest of a possessor of a chattel in its inviolability, unlike the similar interest of a possessor of land, is not given legal protection by an action for nominal damages for harmless intermeddlings with the chattel. In order that an actor who interferes with another's chattel may be liable, his conduct must affect some other and more important interest of the possessor. Therefore, one who intentionally intermeddles with another's chattel is subject to liability only if his intermeddling is harmful to the possessor's materially valuable interest in the physical condition, quality, or value of the chattel, or if the possessor is deprived of the use of the chattel for a substantial time, or some other legally protected interest of the possessor is affected as stated in Clause (c). Sufficient legal protection of the possessor's interest in the mere inviolability of his chattel is afforded by his privilege to use reasonable force to protect his possession against even harmless interference." [...]

60   The Court of Appeal [...] referred to "`a number of very early cases [showing that] any unlawful interference, however slight, with the enjoyment by another of his personal property, is a trespass.'" But while a harmless use or touching of personal property may be a technical trespass (see Rest.2d Torts, § 217), an interference (not amounting to dispossession) is not actionable, under modern California and broader American law, without a showing of harm. As already discussed, this is the rule embodied in the Restatement (Rest.2d Torts, § 218) and adopted by California law

61   [...]

63   In this respect, as Prosser explains, modern day trespass to chattels differs both from the original English writ and from the action for trespass to land: "Another departure from the original rule of the old writ of trespass concerns the necessity of some actual damage to the chattel before the action can be maintained. Where the defendant merely interferes without doing any harm—as where, for example, he merely lays hands upon the plaintiffs horse, or sits in his car—there has been a division of opinion among the writers, and a surprising dearth of authority. By analogy to trespass to land there might be a technical tort in such a case .... Such scanty authority as there is, however, has considered that the dignitary interest in the inviolability of chattels, unlike that as to land, is not sufficiently important to require any greater defense than the privilege of using reasonable force when necessary to protect them. Accordingly it has been held that nominal damages will not be awarded, and that in the absence of any actual damage the action will not lie." [...]

64   Intel suggests that the requirement of actual harm does not apply here because it sought only injunctive relief, as protection from future injuries. But as Justice Kolkey, dissenting below, observed, "[t]he fact the relief sought is injunctive does not excuse a showing of injury, whether actual or threatened." Indeed, in order to obtain injunctive relief the plaintiff must ordinarily show that the defendant's

wrongful acts threaten to cause irreparable injuries, ones that cannot be adequately compensated in damages. $\left[...\right]$ Even in an action for trespass to real property, in which damage to the property is not an

65      $\left[...\right]$

66   element of the cause of action, "the extraordinary remedy of injunction" cannot be invoked without showing the likelihood of irreparable harm. $\left[...\right]$ A fortiori, to issue an injunction without a showing of likely irreparable injury in an action for trespass to chattels, in which injury to the personal property or the possessor's interest in it is an element of the action, would make little legal sense.

67   The dispositive issue in this case, therefore, is whether the undisputed facts demonstrate Hamidi's actions caused or threatened to cause damage to Intel's computer system, or injury to its rights in that personal property, such as to entitle Intel to judgment as a matter of law. To review, the undisputed

68      $\left[...\right]$

69   evidence revealed no actual or threatened damage to Intel's computer hardware or software and no interference with its ordinary and intended operation. Intel was not dispossessed of its computers, nor did Hamidi's messages prevent Intel from using its computers for any measurable length of time. Intel presented no evidence its system was slowed or otherwise impaired by the burden of delivering Hamidi's electronic messages. Nor was there any evidence transmission of the messages imposed any marginal cost on the operation of Intel's computers. In sum, no evidence suggested that in sending messages through Intel's Internet connections and internal computer system Hamidi used the system in any manner in which it was not intended to function or impaired the system in any way. Nor does the evidence show the request of any employee to be removed from FACE-Intel's mailing list was not honored. The evidence did show, however, that some employees who found the messages unwelcome asked management to stop them and that Intel technical staff spent time and effort attempting to block the messages. A statement on the FACE-Intel Web site, moreover, could be taken as an admission that the messages had caused "[e]xcited and nervous managers" to discuss the matter with Intel's human resources department.

70   Relying on a line of decisions, most from federal district courts, applying the tort of trespass to chattels to various types of unwanted electronic contact between computers, Intel contends that, while its computers were not damaged by receiving Hamidi's messages, its interest in the "physical condition, quality or value" $\left[...\right]$ of the computers was harmed. We disagree. The cited line of decisions does not persuade us that the mere sending of electronic communications that assertedly cause injury only because of their contents constitutes an actionable trespass to a computer system through which the messages are transmitted. Rather, the decisions finding electronic contact to be a trespass to computer systems have generally involved some actual or threatened interference with the computers' functioning.

71   In Thrifty-Tel, Inc. v. Bezenek, supra, 46 Cal.App.4th at pages 1566-1567, 54 Cal. Rptr.2d 468 (Thrifty-Tel), the California Court of Appeal held that evidence of automated searching of a telephone carrier's system for authorization codes supported a cause of action for trespass to chattels. The defendant's automated dialing program "overburdened the [plaintiffs] system, denying some subscribers access to

72      $\left[...\right]$

73   phone lines" $\left[...\right]$, showing the requisite injury.

74      $\left[...\right]$

76   by Hotmail Corp. v. Van$ Money Pie, Inc. [...], America Online, Inc. v. IMS [...], and America Online, Inc. v. LCGM, Inc. [...]

77   In each of these spamming cases, the plaintiff showed, or was prepared to show, some interference with the efficient functioning of its computer system. In CompuServe, the plaintiff ISP's mail equipment monitor stated that mass UCE mailings, especially from nonexistent addresses such as those used by the defendant, placed "a tremendous burden" on the ISP's equipment, using "disk space and draining] the processing power," making those resources unavailable to serve subscribers. [...]

78   Building on the spamming cases, in particular CompuServe, three even more recent district court decisions addressed whether unauthorized robotic data collection

79   [...]

80   In the leading case, eBay, the defendant Bidder's Edge (BE), operating an auction aggregation site, accessed the eBay Web site about 100,000 times

81   [...]

82   per day, accounting for between 1 and 2 percent of the information requests received by eBay

83   [...]

84   and a slightly smaller percentage of the data transferred by eBay. ([...] The district court rejected eBay's claim that it was entitled to injunctive relief because of the defendant's unauthorized presence alone, or because of the incremental cost the defendant had imposed on operation of the eBay site [...], but found sufficient proof of threatened harm in the potential for others to imitate the defendant's activity: "If BE's activity is allowed to continue unchecked, it would encourage other auction aggregators to engage in similar recursive searching of the eBay system such that eBay would suffer irreparable harm from reduced system performance, system unavailability, or data losses." [...] Again, in addressing the likelihood of eBay's success on its trespass to chattels cause of action, the court held the evidence of injury to eBay's computer system sufficient to support a preliminary injunction: "If the court were to hold otherwise, it would likely encourage other auction aggregators to crawl the eBay site, potentially to the point of denying effective access to eBay's customers. If preliminary injunctive relief were denied, and other aggregators began to crawl the eBay site, there appears to be little doubt that the load on eBay's computer system would qualify as a substantial impairment of condition or value." [...]

85   Another district court followed eBay on similar facts—a domain name registrar's claim against a Web hosting and development site that robotically searched the registrar's database of newly registered domain names in search of business leads—in Register.com, Inc. v. Verio, Inc., [...] Although the plaintiff was unable to measure the burden the defendant's searching had placed on its system [...] the district court, quoting the declaration of one of the plaintiffs officers, found sufficient evidence of threatened harm to the system in the possibility the defendant's activities would be copied by others: "'I believe that if Verio's searching of Register.com's WHOIS database were determined to be lawful, then every purveyor of Internet-based services would engage in similar conduct.'" [...] Like eBay, the court observed, Register.com had a legitimate fear "that its servers will be flooded by search robots." [...]

86   In the third decision discussing robotic data collection as a trespass, Ticketmaster Corp. v. Tickets.com, Inc., [...] the court, distinguishing eBay, found insufficient evidence of harm to the chattel to constitute an actionable trespass: "A basic element of trespass to chattels must be physical harm to the chattel (not present here) or some obstruction of its basic function (in the court's opinion not sufficiently

87   […]

88   shown here).... The comparative use [by the defendant of the plaintiffs computer system] appears very small and there is no showing that
       the use interferes to any extent with the regular business of [the plaintiff].... Nor here is the specter of dozens or more parasites joining
       the fray, the cumulative total of which could affect the operation of [the plaintiffs] business." […]

89   In the decisions so far reviewed, the defendant's use of the plaintiffs computer system was held sufficient to support an action for
       trespass when it actually did, or threatened to, interfere with the intended functioning of the system, as by significantly reducing its
       available memory and processing power. In Ticketmaster, […] the one case where no such effect, actual or threatened, had been
       demonstrated, the court found insufficient evidence of harm to support a trespass

90   […]

91   action. These decisions do not persuade us to Intel's position here, for Intel has demonstrated neither any appreciable effect on the
       operation of its computer system from Hamidi's messages, nor any likelihood that Hamidi's actions will be replicated by others if found
       not to constitute a trespass.

92   That Intel does not claim the type of functional impact that spammers and robots have been alleged to cause is not surprising in light
       of the differences between Hamidi's activities and those of a commercial enterprise that uses sheer quantity of messages as its
       communications strategy. Though Hamidi sent thousands of copies of the same message on six occasions over 21 months, that number
       is minuscule compared to the amounts of mail sent by commercial operations. The individual advertisers sued in America Online, Inc. v.
       IMS, […] and America Online, Inc. v. LCGM, Inc., […] were alleged to have sent more than 60 million messages over 10 months and
       more than 92 million messages over seven months, respectively. Collectively, UCE has reportedly come to constitute about 45 percent of
       all e-mail. […] The functional burden on Intel's computers, or the cost in time to individual recipients, of receiving Hamidi's occasional
       advocacy messages cannot be compared to the burdens and costs caused ISP's and their customers by the ever-rising deluge of
       commercial e-mail.

93   Intel relies on language in the eBay decision suggesting that unauthorized use of another's chattel is actionable even without any
       showing of injury: "Even if, as [defendant] BE argues, its searches use only a small amount of eBay's computer system capacity, BE has
       nonetheless deprived eBay of the ability to use that portion of its personal property for its own purposes. The law recognizes no such
       right to use another's personal property." […]

95   But as the eBay court went on immediately to find that the defendant's conduct, if widely replicated, would likely impair the functioning of
       the plaintiffs system […], we do not read the quoted remarks as expressing the court's complete view of the issue. In isolation, moreover,
       they would not be a correct statement of California or general American law on this point. While one may have no right temporarily to use
       another's personal property, such use is actionable as a trespass only if it "has proximately caused injury." […] "[I]n the absence of any
       actual damage the action will not lie." […] Short of dispossession, personal injury, or physical damage (not present here), intermeddling is
       actionable only if "the chattel is impaired as to its condition, quality, or value, or [¶] ... the possessor is deprived of the use of the chattel
       for a substantial time." […] In particular, an actionable deprivation of use "must be for a time so substantial that it is possible to estimate
       the loss caused thereby. A mere momentary or theoretical deprivation of use is not sufficient unless there is a dispossession...." […] That
       Hamidi's messages temporarily used some portion of the Intel computers' processors or storage is, therefore, not enough; Intel must, but
       does not, demonstrate some measurable loss from the use of its computer system.[5]

96   […]

97   In addition to impairment of system functionality, CompuServe and its progeny also refer to the ISP's loss of business reputation and customer goodwill, resulting from the inconvenience and cost that spam causes to its members, as harm to the ISP's legally protected interests in its personal property. [...] Intel argues that its own interest in employee productivity, assertedly disrupted by Hamidi's messages, is a comparable protected interest in its computer system. We disagree.

98   [...]

99   Whether the economic injuries identified in CompuServe were properly considered injuries to the ISP's possessory interest in its personal property, the type of property interest the tort is primarily intended to protect [...] has been questioned.[6] "[T]he court broke the chain between the trespass and the harm, allowing indirect harms to CompuServe's business interests—reputation, customer goodwill, and employee time—to count as harms to the chattel (the server)." [...] "[T]his move cuts trespass to chattels free from its moorings of dispossession or the equivalent, allowing the court free reign [sic] to hunt for `impairment.'" [...] But even if the loss of goodwill identified in CompuServe were the type of injury that would give rise to a trespass to chattels claim under California law, Intel's position would not follow, for Intel's claimed injury has even less connection to its personal property than did CompuServe's.

100   CompuServe's customers were annoyed because the system was inundated with unsolicited commercial messages, making its use for personal communication more difficult and costly. [...] Their complaint, which allegedly led some to cancel their

101   [...]

102   CompuServe service, was about the functioning of CompuServe's electronic mail service. Intel's workers, in contrast, were allegedly distracted from their work not because of the frequency or quantity of Hamidi's messages, but because of assertions and opinions the messages conveyed. Intel's complaint is thus about the contents of the messages rather than the functioning of the company's e-mail system. Even accepting CompuServe's economic injury rationale, therefore, Intel's position represents a further extension of the trespass to chattels tort, fictionally recharacterizing the allegedly injurious effect of a communication's contents on recipients as an impairment to the device which transmitted the message.

103   This theory of "impairment by content" (Burk, The Trouble with Trespass, supra, 4 J. Small & Emerging Bus.L. at p. 37) threatens to stretch trespass

104   [...]

105   law to cover injuries far afield from the harms to possession the tort evolved to protect. Intel's theory would expand the tort of trespass to chattels to cover virtually any unconsented—to communication that, solely because of its content, is unwelcome to the recipient or intermediate transmitter. As the dissenting justice below explained, "'Damage' of this nature—the distraction of reading or listening to an unsolicited communication—is not within the scope of the injury against which the trespass-to-chattel tort protects, and indeed trivializes it. After all, `[t]he property interest protected by the old action of trespass was that of possession; and this has continued to affect the character of the action.' [...] Reading an e-mail transmitted to equipment designed to receive it, in and of itself, does not affect the possessory interest in the equipment. [...] Indeed, if a chattel's receipt of an electronic communication constitutes a trespass to that chattel, then not only are unsolicited telephone calls and faxes trespasses to chattel, but unwelcome radio waves and television signals also constitute a trespass to chattel every time the viewer inadvertently sees or hears the unwanted program." We agree. While unwelcome communications, electronic or otherwise, can cause a variety of injuries to economic relations, reputation and emotions, those interests are protected by other branches of tort law; in order to address them, we need not create a fiction of injury to the communication system.

106   Nor may Intel appropriately assert a property interest in its employees' time. "The Restatement test clearly speaks in the first instance to the impairment of the chattel.... But employees are not chattels (at least not in the legal sense of the term)." (Burk, The Trouble with Trespass, supra, 4 J. Small & Emerging Bus.L. at p. 36.) Whatever interest Intel may have in preventing its employees from receiving disruptive communications, it is not an interest in personal property, and trespass to chattels is therefore not an action that will lie to protect it. Nor, finally, can the fact Intel staff spent time attempting to block Hamidi's messages be bootstrapped into an injury to Intel's possessory interest in its computers. To quote, again, from the dissenting opinion in the Court of Appeal: "[I]t is circular to premise the damage element of a tort solely upon the steps taken to prevent the damage. Injury can only be established by the completed tort's consequences, not by the cost of the steps taken to avoid the injury and prevent the tort; otherwise, we can create injury for every supposed tort."

107   Intel connected its e-mail system to the Internet and permitted its employees to make use of this connection both for business and, to a reasonable extent, for their own purposes. In doing so, the company

108   [...]

109   necessarily contemplated the employees' receipt of unsolicited as well as solicited communications from other companies and individuals. That some communications

110   [...]

111   would, because of their contents, be unwelcome to Intel management was virtually inevitable. Hamidi did nothing but use the e-mail system for its intended purpose—to communicate with employees. The system worked as designed, delivering the messages without any physical or functional harm or disruption. These occasional transmissions cannot reasonably be viewed as impairing the quality or value of Intel's computer system. We conclude, therefore, that Intel has not presented undisputed facts demonstrating an injury to its personal property, or to its legal interest in that property, that support, under California tort law, an action for trespass to chattels.

112   [...]

136

145   DISPOSITION
146   The judgment of the Court of Appeal is reversed.

147   [...]

149

157   7. The tort law discussion in Justice Brown's dissenting opinion similarly suffers from an overreliance on metaphor and analogy.

Attempting to find an actionable trespass, Justice Brown analyzes Intel's e-mail system as comparable to the exterior of an automobile [...
, the interior of an automobile [...], a toothbrush [...] a head of livestock [...], and a mooring buoy [...] while Hamidi is characterized as a
vandal damaging a school building [...] or a prankster unplugging and moving employees' computers [...] These colorful analogies tend
to obscure the plain fact that this case involves communications equipment, used by defendant to communicate. Intel's e-mail system
was equipment designed for speedy communication between employees and the outside world; Hamidi communicated with Intel
employees over that system in a manner entirely consistent with its design; and Intel objected not because of an offense against the
integrity or dignity of its computers, but because the communications themselves affected employee-recipients in a manner Intel found
undesirable. The proposal that we extend trespass to chattels to cover any communication that the owner of the communications
equipment considers annoying or distracting raises, moreover, concerns about control over the flow of information and views that would
not be presented by, for example, an injunction against chasing another's cattle or sleeping in her car.

158   [...]

219

303

327

364

373

383

Ticketmaster Corp. v. Tickets.Com, Inc. - trespass to chattels

September 01, 2014 by mrisch

This brief note considers the trespass to chattels in ticket price scraping

1
TICKETMASTER CORP. et al., Plaintiff
v.
TICKETS.COM, INC. et al., Defendants.

2
[...]

3
United States District Court, C.D. California.

4
March 7, 2003.

5
[...]

7
TICKETS.COM'S NOTICE OF MOTION AND MOTION FOR SUMMARY JUDGMENT ON [...] TRESPASS

8
HUPP, J.

9
ORDER

10
[...]

14
Starting in 1998 and continuing to July 2001, when it stopped the practice, TX employed an electronic program called a "spider" or "crawler" to review the internal web pages (available to the public) of TM. The "spider" "crawled" through the internal web pages to TM and electronically extracted the electronic information from which the web page is shown on the user's computer. The spider temporarily loaded this electronic information into the Random Access Memory ("RAM") of TX's computers for a period of from 10–15 seconds. TX then extracted the factual information (event, date, time, tickets prices, and URL) and discarded the rest (which consisted of TM identification, logos, ads, and other information which TX did not intend to use; much of this discarded material was protected by copyright). The factual information was then organized in the TX format to be displayed on the TX internal web page. The TX internal web page carried no TM identification and had only the factual information about the event on it which was taken from TM's interior web page but rearranged in TX format plus any information or advertisement added by TX. From March 1998, to early 2000, the TX user was provided the deep linking option described above to go directly from the TX web site to the relevant TM interior web page. [...]

16
The trespass to chattels issue requires adapting the ancient common law action to the modern age. No cases seem to have reached the appellate courts although there appears to be a number of district court cases. One case (*Intel v. Hamadi* '01 94 CA4th 325, 114 CR 244) is pending in the California Supreme Court since it granted a hearing which has the effect of vacating the state Court of Appeal opinion (and which has no precedent value once the hearing was granted). The court is informed that the *eBay*NDCA'00 100 FSupp2d 1058 preliminary injunction was not appealed. At the time of the preliminary injunction motion, only the *eBay*case was before the court. Since then, there have been a number of district court cases discussing the chattel theory (some published and some not). These cases tend to support the proposition that mere invasion or use of a portion of the web site by a spider is a trespass (leading at least to nominal damages), and that there need not be an independent showing of direct harm either to the chattel (unlikely in the case of a spider) or tangible interference with the use of the computer being invaded. However, scholars and practitioners alike have criticized the extension

of the trespass to chattels doctrine to the internet context, noting that this doctrinal expansion threatens basic internet functions (*i.e.,* search engines) and exposes the flaws inherent in applying doctrines based in real and tangible property to cyberspace. *[…]* Pending appellate guidance, this court comes down on the side of requiring some tangible interference with the use or operation of the computer being invaded by the spider. Restatement (Second) of Torts § 219 requires a showing that "the chattel is impaired as to its condition, quality, or value." Therefore, unless there is actual dispossession of the chattel for a substantial time (not present here), the elements of the tort have not been made out. Since the spider does not cause physical injury to the chattel, there must be some evidence that the use or utility of the computer (or computer network) being "spiderized" is adversely affected by the use of the spider. No such evidence is presented here. This court respectfully disagrees with other district courts' finding that mere use of a spider to enter a publically available web site to gather information, without more, is sufficient to fulfill the harm requirement for trespass to chattels.

17   TM complains that the information obtained by the use of the spider was valuable (and even that it was sold by TX), and that it spent time and money attempting to frustrate the spider, but neither of these items shows damage to the computers or their operation. One must keep in mind that we are talking about the common law tort of trespass, not damage from breach of contract or copyright infringement. The tort claim may not succeed without proof of tort-type damage. Plaintiff TM has the burden to show such damage. None is shown here. The motion for summary judgment is granted to eliminate the claim for trespass to chattels. This minute order is the order eliminating that claim. This approach to the tort of trespass to chattels should hurt no one's policy feelings; after all, what is being attempted is to apply a medieval common law concept in an entirely new situation which should be disposed of by modern law designed to protect intellectual property interests.

18   [...]

Class 20: 8.2 <u>OIL Casebook: Computer Fraud & Abuse Act I</u>

Computer Fraud and Abuse Act: 18 U.S. Code § 1030 - Fraud and related activity in connection with computers

September 04, 2014 by mrisch

1   **(a)** Whoever—

(1) having knowingly accessed a computer without authorization or exceeding authorized access, and by means of such conduct having obtained information that has been determined by the United States Government pursuant to an Executive order or statute to require protection against unauthorized disclosure for reasons of national defense or foreign relations, or any restricted data, as defined in paragraph y. of section 11 of the Atomic Energy Act of 1954, with reason to believe that such information so obtained could be used to the injury of the United States, or to the advantage of any foreign nation willfully communicates, delivers, transmits, or causes to be communicated, delivered, or transmitted, or attempts to communicate, deliver, transmit or cause to be communicated, delivered, or transmitted the same to any person not entitled to receive it, or willfully retains the same and fails to deliver it to the officer or employee of the United States entitled to receive it;

(2) intentionally accesses a computer without authorization or exceeds authorized access, and thereby obtains—

(A) information contained in a financial record of a financial institution, or of a card issuer as defined in section 1602 (n) [1] of title 15, or contained in a file of a consumer reporting agency on a consumer, as such terms are defined in the Fair Credit Reporting Act (15 U.S.C. 1681 et seq.);

(B) information from any department or agency of the United States; or

(C) information from any protected computer;

(3) intentionally, without authorization to access any nonpublic computer of a department or agency of the United States, accesses such a computer of that department or agency that is exclusively for the use of the Government of the United States or, in the case of a computer not exclusively for such use, is used by or for the Government of the United States and such conduct affects that use by or for the Government of the United States;

(4) knowingly and with intent to defraud, accesses a protected computer without authorization, or exceeds authorized access, and by means of such conduct furthers the intended fraud and obtains anything of value, unless the object of the fraud and the thing obtained consists only of the use of the computer and the value of such use is not more than $5,000 in any 1-year period;

(5)

(A) knowingly causes the transmission of a program, information, code, or command, and as a result of such conduct, intentionally causes damage without authorization, to a protected computer;

(B) intentionally accesses a protected computer without authorization, and as a result of such conduct, recklessly causes damage; or

(C) intentionally accesses a protected computer without authorization, and as a result of such conduct, causes damage and loss. [2]

(6) knowingly and with intent to defraud traffics (as defined in section 1029) in any password or similar information through which a computer may be accessed without authorization, if—

(A) such trafficking affects interstate or foreign commerce; or

(B) such computer is used by or for the Government of the United States;   *"traffic" means to transfer to another or to obtain with the intent of transferring to another* [3]

(7) with intent to extort from any person any money or other thing of value, transmits in interstate or foreign commerce any communication containing any—

(A) threat to cause damage to a protected computer;

(B) threat to obtain information from a protected computer without authorization or in excess of authorization or to impair the confidentiality of information obtained from a protected computer without authorization or by exceeding authorized access; or

(C) demand or request for money or other thing of value in relation to damage to a protected computer, where such damage was caused to facilitate the extortion;

shall be punished as provided in subsection (c) of this section.

2 **(b)** Whoever conspires to commit or attempts to commit an offense under subsection (a) of this section shall be punished as provided in subsection (c) of this section.

3 **(c)** The punishment for an offense under subsection (a) or (b) of this section is—

(1)

(A) a fine under this title or imprisonment for not more than ten years, or both, in the case of an offense under subsection (a)(1) of this section which does not occur after a conviction for another offense under this section, or an attempt to commit an offense punishable under this subparagraph; and

(B) a fine under this title or imprisonment for not more than twenty years, or both, in the case of an offense under subsection (a)(1) of this section which occurs after a conviction for another offense under this section, or an attempt to commit an offense punishable under this subparagraph;

(2)

(A) except as provided in subparagraph (B), a fine under this title or imprisonment for not more than one year, or both, in the case of an offense under subsection (a)(2), (a)(3), or (a)(6) of this section which does not occur after a conviction for another offense under this section, or an attempt to commit an offense punishable under this subparagraph;

(B) a fine under this title or imprisonment for not more than 5 years, or both, in the case of an offense under subsection (a)(2), or an attempt to commit an offense punishable under this subparagraph, if—

(i) the offense was committed for purposes of commercial advantage or private financial gain;

(ii) the offense was committed in furtherance of any criminal or tortious act in violation of the Constitution or laws of the United States or of any State; or

(iii) the value of the information obtained exceeds $5,000; and

(C) a fine under this title or imprisonment for not more than ten years, or both, in the case of an offense under subsection (a)(2), (a)(3) or (a)(6) of this section which occurs after a conviction for another offense under this section, or an attempt to commit an offense punishable under this subparagraph;

(3)

(A) a fine under this title or imprisonment for not more than five years, or both, in the case of an offense under subsection (a)(4) or (a)(7) of this section which does not occur after a conviction for another offense under this section, or an attempt to commit an offense punishable under this subparagraph; and

(B) a fine under this title or imprisonment for not more than ten years, or both, in the case of an offense under subsection (a)(4), [4] or (a)(7) of this section which occurs after a conviction for another offense under this section, or an attempt to commit an offense punishable under this subparagraph;

(4)

(A) except as provided in subparagraphs (E) and (F), a fine under this title, imprisonment for not more than 5 years, or both, in the case of—

(i) an offense under subsection (a)(5)(B), which does not occur after a conviction for another offense under this section, if the offense caused (or, in the case of an attempted offense, would, if completed, have caused)—

(I) loss to 1 or more persons during any 1-year period (and, for purposes of an investigation, prosecution, or other proceeding brought by the United States only, loss resulting from a related course of conduct affecting 1 or more other protected computers) aggregating at least $5,000 in value;

(II) the modification or impairment, or potential modification or impairment, of the medical examination, diagnosis, treatment, or care of 1 or more individuals;

(III) physical injury to any person;

(IV) a threat to public health or safety;

(V) damage affecting a computer used by or for an entity of the United States Government in furtherance of the administration of justice, national defense, or national security; or

(VI) damage affecting 10 or more protected computers during any 1-year period; or

(ii) an attempt to commit an offense punishable under this subparagraph;

(B) except as provided in subparagraphs (E) and (F), a fine under this title, imprisonment for not more than 10 years, or both, in the case of—

(i) an offense under subsection (a)(5)(A), which does not occur after a conviction for another offense under this section, if the offense caused (or, in the case of an attempted offense, would, if completed, have caused) a harm provided in subclauses (I) through (VI) of subparagraph (A)(i); or

(ii) an attempt to commit an offense punishable under this subparagraph;

(C) except as provided in subparagraphs (E) and (F), a fine under this title, imprisonment for not more than 20 years, or both, in the case of—

(i) an offense or an attempt to commit an offense under subparagraphs (A) or (B) of subsection (a)(5) that occurs after a conviction for another offense under this section; or

(ii) an attempt to commit an offense punishable under this subparagraph;

(D) a fine under this title, imprisonment for not more than 10 years, or both, in the case of—

(i) an offense or an attempt to commit an offense under subsection (a)(5)(C) that occurs after a conviction for another offense under this section; or

(ii) an attempt to commit an offense punishable under this subparagraph;

(E) if the offender attempts to cause or knowingly or recklessly causes serious bodily injury from conduct in violation of subsection (a)(5)(A), a fine under this title, imprisonment for not more than 20 years, or both;

(F) if the offender attempts to cause or knowingly or recklessly causes death from conduct in violation of subsection (a)(5)(A), a fine under this title, imprisonment for any term of years or for life, or both; or

(G) a fine under this title, imprisonment for not more than 1 year, or both, for—

(i) any other offense under subsection (a)(5); or

(ii) an attempt to commit an offense punishable under this subparagraph.

4   (d)

(1) The United States Secret Service shall, in addition to any other agency having such authority, have the authority to investigate offenses under this section.

(2) The Federal Bureau of Investigation shall have primary authority to investigate offenses under subsection (a)(1) for any cases involving espionage, foreign counterintelligence, information protected against unauthorized disclosure for reasons of national defense or foreign relations, or Restricted Data (as that term is defined in section 11y of the Atomic Energy Act of 1954 (42 U.S.C. 2014 (y)),

except for offenses affecting the duties of the United States Secret Service pursuant to section 3056 (a) of this title.

(3) Such authority shall be exercised in accordance with an agreement which shall be entered into by the Secretary of the Treasury and the Attorney General.

(e) As used in this section—

(1) the term "computer" means an electronic, magnetic, optical, electrochemical, or other high speed data processing device performing logical, arithmetic, or storage functions, and includes any data storage facility or communications facility directly related to or operating in conjunction with such device, but such term does not include an automated typewriter or typesetter, a portable hand held calculator, or other similar device;

(2) the term "protected computer" means a computer—

(A) exclusively for the use of a financial institution or the United States Government, or, in the case of a computer not exclusively for such use, used by or for a financial institution or the United States Government and the conduct constituting the offense affects that use by or for the financial institution or the Government; or

(B) which is used in or affecting interstate or foreign commerce or communication, including a computer located outside the United States that is used in a manner that affects interstate or foreign commerce or communication of the United States;

(3) the term "State" includes the District of Columbia, the Commonwealth of Puerto Rico, and any other commonwealth, possession or territory of the United States;

(4) the term "financial institution" means—

(A) an institution, with deposits insured by the Federal Deposit Insurance Corporation;

(B) the Federal Reserve or a member of the Federal Reserve including any Federal Reserve Bank;

(C) a credit union with accounts insured by the National Credit Union Administration;

(D) a member of the Federal home loan bank system and any home loan bank;

(E) any institution of the Farm Credit System under the Farm Credit Act of 1971;

(F) a broker-dealer registered with the Securities and Exchange Commission pursuant to section 15 of the Securities Exchange Act of 1934;

(G) the Securities Investor Protection Corporation;

(H) a branch or agency of a foreign bank (as such terms are defined in paragraphs (1) and (3) of section 1(b) of the International Banking Act of 1978); and

(I) an organization operating under section 25 orsection 25(a) [1] of the Federal Reserve Act;

(5) the term "financial record" means information derived from any record held by a financial institution pertaining to a customer's relationship with the financial institution;

(6) the term "exceeds authorized access" means to access a computer with authorization and to use such access to obtain or alter information in the computer that the accesser is not entitled so to obtain or alter;

(7) the term "department of the United States" means the legislative or judicial branch of the Government or one of the executive departments enumerated in section 101 of title 5;

(8) the term "damage" means any impairment to the integrity or availability of data, a program, a system, or information;

(9) the term "government entity" includes the Government of the United States, any State or political subdivision of the United States, any foreign country, and any state, province, municipality, or other political subdivision of a foreign country;

(10) the term "conviction" shall include a conviction under the law of any State for a crime punishable by imprisonment for more than 1 year, an element of which is unauthorized access, or exceeding authorized access, to a computer;

(11) the term "loss" means any reasonable cost to any victim, including the cost of responding to an offense, conducting a damage assessment, and restoring the data, program, system, or information to its condition prior to the offense, and any revenue lost, cost incurred, or other consequential damages incurred because of interruption of service; and

(12) the term "person" means any individual, firm, corporation, educational institution, financial institution, governmental entity, or legal or other entity.

6   **(f)** This section does not prohibit any lawfully authorized investigative, protective, or intelligence activity of a law enforcement agency of the United States, a State, or a political subdivision of a State, or of an intelligence agency of the United States.

7   **(g)** Any person who suffers damage or loss by reason of a violation of this section may maintain a civil action against the violator to obtain compensatory damages and injunctive relief or other equitable relief. A civil action for a violation of this section may be brought only if the conduct involves 1 of the factors set forth in subclauses [5] (I), (II), (III), (IV), or (V) of subsection (c)(4)(A)(i). Damages for a violation involving only conduct described in subsection (c)(4)(A)(i)(I) are limited to economic damages. *The primary category of interest is loss more than $5,000, but also includes physical injury, etc.* No action may be brought under this subsection unless such action is begun within 2 years of the date of the act complained of or the date of the discovery of the damage. No action may be brought under this subsection for the negligent design or manufacture of computer hardware, computer software, or firmware.

8   **(h)** The Attorney General and the Secretary of the Treasury shall report to the Congress annually, during the first 3 years following the date of the enactment of this subsection, concerning investigations and prosecutions under subsection (a)(5).

9   **(i)**

(1) The court, in imposing sentence on any person convicted of a violation of this section, or convicted of conspiracy to violate this section, shall order, in addition to any other sentence imposed and irrespective of any provision of State law, that such person forfeit to the United States—

(A) such person's interest in any personal property that was used or intended to be used to commit or to facilitate the commission of such violation; and

(B) any property, real or personal, constituting or derived from, any proceeds that such person obtained, directly or indirectly, as a result of such violation.

(2) The criminal forfeiture of property under this subsection, any seizure and disposition thereof, and any judicial proceeding in relation thereto, shall be governed by the provisions of section 413 of the Comprehensive Drug Abuse Prevention and Control Act of 1970 (21 U.S.C. 853), except subsection (d) of that section.

10   **(j)** For purposes of subsection (i), the following shall be subject to forfeiture to the United States and no property right shall exist in them:

(1) Any personal property used or intended to be used to commit or to facilitate the commission of any violation of this section, or a conspiracy to violate this section.

(2) Any property, real or personal, which constitutes or is derived from proceeds traceable to any violation of this section, or a conspiracy to violate this section [6]

11

[1] See References in Text note below.

[2] So in original. The period probably should be a semicolon.

[3] So in original. Probably should be followed by "or".

[4] So in original. The comma probably should not appear.

[5] So in original. Probably should be "subclause".

[6] So in original. Probably should be followed by a period.

U.S. v. Morris

September 05, 2014 by mrisch

1   928 F.2d 504 (1991)

2   **UNITED STATES of America, Appellee,**

                                                                      v.

                                          Robert Tappan MORRIS, Defendant-Appellant.

3   [...]

4   United States Court of Appeals, Second Circuit.

5   [...]

                                                            Decided March 7, 1991.

6   [...]

9   **JON O. NEWMAN, Circuit Judge:**

10   This appeal presents two narrow issues of statutory construction concerning a provision Congress recently adopted to strengthen
       protection against computer crimes. Section 2(d) of the Computer Fraud and Abuse Act of 1986, 18 U.S.C. § 1030(a)(5)(A) (1988),
       punishes anyone who intentionally accesses without authorization a category of computers known as "[f]ederal interest computers" and
       damages or prevents authorized use of information in such computers, causing loss of $1,000 or more. The issues raised are (1) whether
       the Government must prove not only that the defendant intended to access a federal interest computer, but also that the defendant
       intended to prevent authorized use of the computer's information and thereby cause loss; and (2) what satisfies the statutory
       requirement of "access without authorization."

11   These questions are raised on an appeal by Robert Tappan Morris from the May 16, 1990, judgment of the District Court for the Northern
       District of New York (Howard G. Munson, Judge) convicting him, after a jury trial, of violating 18 U.S.C. § 1030(a)(5)(A). Morris released
       into INTERNET, a national computer network, a computer program known as a "worm"[2] that spread and multiplied, eventually causing
       computers at various educational institutions and military sites to "crash" or cease functioning.

12   We conclude that section 1030(a)(5)(A) does not require the Government to demonstrate that the defendant intentionally prevented
       authorized use and thereby caused loss. We also find that there was sufficient evidence for the jury to conclude that Morris acted
       "without authorization" within the meaning of section 1030(a)(5)(A). We therefore affirm.

13   **FACTS**

14   In the fall of 1988, Morris was a first-year graduate student in Cornell University's computer science Ph.D. program. Through
       undergraduate work at Harvard and in various jobs he had acquired significant computer experience and expertise. When Morris entered
       Cornell, he was given an account on the computer at the Computer Science Division. This account gave him explicit authorization to use
       computers at Cornell. Morris engaged in various discussions with fellow graduate students about the security of computer networks and

his ability to penetrate it.

15   In October 1988, Morris began work on a computer program, later known as the INTERNET "worm" or "virus." The goal of this program was to demonstrate the inadequacies of current security measures on computer networks by exploiting the security defects that Morris had discovered. The tactic he selected was release of a worm into network computers. Morris designed the program to spread across a national network of computers after being inserted at one computer location connected to the network. Morris released the worm into INTERNET, which is a group of national networks that connect university, governmental, and military computers around the country. The network permits communication and transfer of information between computers on the network.

16   Morris sought to program the INTERNET worm to spread widely without drawing attention to itself. The worm was supposed to occupy little computer operation time, and thus not interfere with normal use of the computers. Morris programmed the worm to make it difficult to detect and read, so that other programmers would not be able to "kill" the worm easily.

17   [...] Morris also wanted to ensure that the worm did not copy itself onto a computer that already had a copy. Multiple copies of the worm on a computer would make the worm easier to detect and would bog down the system and ultimately cause the computer to crash. Therefore, Morris designed the worm to "ask" each computer whether it already had a copy of the worm. If it responded "no," then the worm would copy onto the computer; if it responded "yes," the worm would not duplicate. However, Morris was concerned that other programmers could kill the worm by programming their own computers to falsely respond "yes" to the question. To circumvent this protection, Morris programmed the worm to duplicate itself every seventh time it received a "yes" response. As it turned out, Morris underestimated the number of times a computer would be asked the question, and his one-out-of-seven ratio resulted in far more copying than he had anticipated. The worm was also designed so that it would be killed when a computer was shut down, an event that typically occurs once every week or two. This would have prevented the worm from accumulating on one computer, had Morris correctly estimated the likely rate of reinfection.

18   Morris identified four ways in which the worm could break into computers on the network:

19   (1) through a "hole" or "bug" (an error) in SEND MAIL, a computer program that transfers and receives electronic mail on a computer;

        (2) through a bug in the "finger demon" program, a program that permits a person to obtain limited information about the users of another computer;

        (3) through the "trusted hosts" feature, which permits a user with certain privileges on one computer to have equivalent privileges on another computer without using a password; and

        (4) through a program of password guessing, whereby various combinations of letters are tried out in rapid sequence in the hope that one will be an authorized user's password, which is entered to permit whatever level of activity that user is authorized to perform.

20   On November 2, 1988, Morris released the worm from a computer at the Massachusetts Institute of Technology. MIT was selected to disguise the fact that the worm came from Morris at Cornell. Morris soon discovered that the worm was replicating and reinfecting machines at a much faster rate than he had anticipated. Ultimately, many machines at locations around the country either crashed or became "catatonic." When Morris realized what was happening, he contacted a friend at Harvard to discuss a solution. Eventually, they sent an anonymous message from Harvard over the network, instructing programmers how to kill the worm and prevent reinfection. However, because the network route was clogged, this message did not get through until it was too late. Computers were affected at numerous installations, including leading universities, military sites, and medical research facilities. The estimated cost of dealing with the worm at each installation ranged from $200 to more than $53,000.

21   Morris was found guilty, following a jury trial, of violating 18 U.S.C. § 1030(a)(5)(A). He was sentenced to three years of probation, 400 hours of community service, a fine of $10,050, and the costs of his supervision.

22   **DISCUSSION**

23   **I. The intent requirement in section 1030(a)(5)(A)**

24   Section 1030(a)(5)(A), covers anyone who

25   (5) *intentionally accesses* a Federal interest computer without authorization, *and* by means of one or more instances of such conduct alters, damages, or destroys information in any such Federal interest computer, or *prevents authorized use* of any such computer or information, *and thereby*

     (A) *causes loss* to one or more others of a value aggregating $1,000 or more during any one year period; ... [emphasis added]. *1030(A)(5)(A) is obviously different now, but intentionality and authorization remain in the statute: "(A) knowingly causes the transmission of a program, information, code, or command, and as a result of such conduct, intentionally causes damage without authorization, to a protected computer:"*

26   The District Court concluded that the intent requirement applied only to the accessing and not to the resulting damage. *The statute has been modified since this time, and is now clear that one must intend damage with respect to transmission of a program.* […]

36   **II. The unauthorized access requirement in section 1030(a)(5)(A)**

46   Section 1030(a)(5)(A) penalizes the conduct of an individual who "intentionally accesses a Federal interest computer without authorization." Morris contends that his conduct constituted, at most, "exceeding authorized access" rather than the "unauthorized access" that the subsection punishes. Morris argues that there was insufficient evidence to convict him of "unauthorized access," and that even if the evidence sufficed, he was entitled to have the jury instructed on his "theory of defense." *Note this difference between (a)(2) and (a)(5). Later cases will consider "exceeds authorized access"*

47   We assess the sufficiency of the evidence under the traditional standard. Morris was authorized to use computers at Cornell, Harvard, and Berkeley, all of which were on INTERNET. As a result, Morris was authorized to communicate with other computers on the network to send electronic mail (SEND MAIL), and to find out certain information about the users of other computers [510] (finger demon). The question is whether Morris's transmission of his worm constituted exceeding authorized access or accessing without authorization.

48   The Senate Report stated that section 1030(a)(5)(A), like the new section 1030(a)(3), would "be aimed at 'outsiders,' *i.e.*, those lacking authorization to access any Federal interest computer." […] But the Report also stated, in concluding its discussion on the scope of section 1030(a)(3), that it applies "where the offender is completely outside the Government, ... *or where the offender's act of trespass is interdepartmental in nature.*" […]

49   Morris relies on the first quoted portion to argue that his actions can be characterized only as exceeding authorized access, since he had authorized access to a federal interest computer. However, the second quoted portion reveals that Congress was not drawing a bright line between those who have some access to any federal interest computer and those who have none. Congress contemplated that individuals with access to some federal interest computers would be subject to liability under the computer fraud provisions for gaining unauthorized access to other federal interest computers. *See, e.g., id.* (stating that a Labor Department employee who uses Labor's computers to access without authorization an FBI computer can be criminally prosecuted).

50   The evidence permitted the jury to conclude that Morris's use of the SEND MAIL and finger demon features constituted access without authorization. While a case might arise where the use of SEND MAIL or finger demon falls within a nebulous area in which the line between accessing without authorization and exceeding authorized access may not be clear, Morris's conduct here falls well within the area of unauthorized access. Morris did not use either of those features in any way related to their intended function. He did not send or read mail nor discover information about other users; instead he found holes in both programs that permitted him a special and

unauthorized access route into other computers.

51   Moreover, the jury verdict need not be upheld solely on Morris's use of SEND MAIL and finger demon. As the District Court noted, in denying Morris' motion for acquittal,

52   Although the evidence may have shown that defendant's initial insertion of the worm simply exceeded his authorized access, the evidence also demonstrated that the worm was designed to spread to other computers at which he had no account and no authority, express or implied, to unleash the worm program. Moreover, there was also evidence that the worm was designed to gain access to computers at which he had no account by guessing their passwords. Accordingly, the evidence did support the jury's conclusion that defendant accessed without authority as opposed to merely exceeding the scope of his authority.

53   In light of the reasonable conclusions that the jury could draw from Morris's use of SEND MAIL and finger demon, and from his use of the trusted hosts feature and password guessing, his challenge to the sufficiency of the evidence fails.

54   Morris endeavors to bolster his sufficiency argument by contending that his conduct was not punishable under subsection (a)(5) but was punishable under subsection (a)(3). That concession belies the validity of his claim that he only exceeded authorization rather than made unauthorized access. Neither subsection (a)(3) nor (a)(5) punishes conduct that exceeds authorization. Both punish a person who "accesses" "without authorization" certain computers. Subsection (a)(3) covers the computers of a department or agency of the United States; subsection (a)(5) more broadly covers any federal interest computers, defined to include, among other computers, those used exclusively by the United States, 18 U.S.C. § 1030(e)(2)(A), and adds the element of causing damage or loss [...] If Morris violated subsection (a)(3), as he concedes, then his conduct in inserting the worm into the INTERNET [...] must have constituted "unauthorized access" under subsection (a)(5) to the computers of the federal departments the worm reached, for example, those of NASA and military bases.

55   To extricate himself from the consequence of conceding that he made "unauthorized access" within the meaning of subsection (a)(3), Morris subtly shifts his argument and contends that he is not within the reach of subsection (a)(5) at all. He argues that subsection (a)(5) covers only those who, unlike himself, lack access to *any* federal interest computer. It is true that a primary concern of Congress in drafting subsection (a)(5) was to reach those unauthorized to access any federal interest computer. The Senate Report stated, "[T]his subsection [(a)(5)] will be aimed at `outsiders,' *i.e.,* those lacking authorization to access any Federal interest computer." [...] But the fact that the subsection is "aimed" at such "outsiders" does not mean that its coverage is limited to them. Congress understandably thought that the group most likely to damage federal interest computers would be those who lack authorization to use any of them. But it surely did not mean to insulate from liability the person authorized to use computers at the State Department who causes damage to computers at the Defense Department. Congress created the misdemeanor offense of subsection (a)(3) to punish intentional trespasses into computers for which one lacks authorized access; it added the felony offense of subsection (a)(5) to punish such a trespasser who also causes damage or loss in excess of $1,000, not only to computers of the United States but to any computer within the definition of federal interest computers. With both provisions, Congress was punishing those, like Morris, who, with access to some computers that enable them to communicate on a network linking other computers, gain access to other computers to which they lack authorization [...]

59   ## CONCLUSION

60   For the foregoing reasons, the judgment of the District Court is affirmed.

61   [...]

62   [2] In the colorful argot of computers, a "worm" is a program that travels from one computer to another but does not attach itself to the operating system of the computer it "infects." It differs from a "virus," which is also a migrating program, but one that attaches itself to the operating system of any computer it enters and can infect any other computer that uses files from the infected computer.

Register.com, Inc. v. Verio, Inc.

September 04, 2014 by mrisch

1   126 F.Supp.2d 238 (2000)

2   **REGISTER.COM, INC., Plaintiff,**

v.

VERIO, INC., Defendant.

3   [...]

4   United States District Court, S.D. New York.

5   December 8, 2000.

6   [...]

8   *Order*

9   **JONES, District Judge.**

10   *Introduction*

11   Plaintiff Register.com, a registrar of Internet domain names, moves for a preliminary injunction against the defendant, Verio, Inc. ("Verio"),
       a provider of Internet services. [...] In essence Register.com seeks an injunction barring Verio from using automated software processes
       to access and collect the registrant contact information contained in its WHOIS database and from using any of that information,
       however accessed, for mass marketing purposes.

12   ## I. Findings of Fact

13   *The Parties*

14   Plaintiff Register.com is one of over fifty domain name registrars for customers who wish to register a name in the .com, .net, and .org
       top-level domains. As a registrar it contracts with these second-level domain ("SLD") name holders and a registry, collecting registration
       data about the SLD holder and submitting zone file information for entry in the registry database. In addition to its domain name
       registration services, Register.com offers to its customers, both directly and through its more than 450 co-branded and private label
       partners, a variety of other related services, such as (i) web site creation tools; (ii) web site hosting; (iii) electronic mail; (iv) domain name
       hosting; (v) domain name forwarding, and (vi) real-time domain name management. Register .com has invested over $15 million dollars in
       equipment, software, service fees, and human resources in designing, developing, and maintaining its website and the computer systems
       necessary to host Register.com's Internet-based services. [...] It has also spent in excess of $25 million on advertising and brand
       promotion in the year 2000 alone, including through print, radio, and television media. [...]

16   Defendant Verio is one of the largest operators of web sites for businesses and a leading provider of comprehensive Internet services.
       Although not a registrar of domain names, Verio directly competes with Register.com and its partners to provide registration services and

783

a variety of other Internet services including website hosting and development. Verio recently made a multimillion dollar investment in its computer system and facilities for its expanded force of telephone sales associates in its efforts to "provide recent domain name registration customers with the services they need, at the time they need them." [...]

17   **The WHOIS database**

18   To become an accredited domain name registrar for the .com, .net, and .org domains, all registrars, including Register.com are required to enter into a registrar Accreditation Agreement ("Agreement") with the Internet Corporation for Assigned Names and Numbers [...] ("ICANN").[1] Under that Agreement, Register.com, as well as all other registrars, is required to provide an on-line, interactive WHOIS database. This database contains the names and contact information — postal address, telephone number, electronic mail address and in some cases facsimile number — for customers who register domain names through the registrar. The Agreement also requires Register.com to make the database freely accessible to the public via its web page and through an independent access port called port 43. These query-based channels of access to the WHOIS database allow the user to collect registrant contact information for one domain name at a time by entering the domain name into the provided search engine.[2]

19   The primary purpose of the WHOIS database is to provide necessary information in the event of domain name disputes, such as those arising from cybersquatting or trademark infringement. [...] The parties also agree that the WHOIS data may be used for market research.

20   Specifically, section II.F.5 of Register.com's Accreditation Agreement with ICANN requires that:

21   In providing query-based public access to registration data as required by Sections II.F.1 and II.F.4, Registrar shall not impose terms and conditions on use of the data provided except as permitted by ICANN-adopted policy. Unless and until ICANN adopts a different policy, Registrar shall permit use of data it provides in response to queries *for any lawful purposes except to:* (a) *allow, enable, or otherwise support the transmission of mass unsolicited, commercial advertising or solicitations via e-mail (spam);* or (b) *enable high volume, automated, electronic processes that apply to Registrar (or its systems).*

22   [...]

23   Originally Register.com's terms and conditions for users of its WHOIS database were substantially the same. In April 2000, however, Register.com implemented the following more restrictive terms of use governing its WHOIS database:

24   By submitting a WHOIS query, you agree that you will use this data *only for lawful purposes* and that, *under no circumstances will you use this data to:* (1) *allow, enable, or otherwise support the transmission of mass unsolicited, commercial advertising or solicitations via direct mail, electronic mail, or by telephone;* or (2) *enable high volume, automated, electronic processes that apply to Register.com (or its systems).* The compilation, repackaging, dissemination or other use of this data is expressly prohibited without the prior [...] written consent of Register.com. Register.com reserves the right to modify these terms at any time. By submitting this query, you agree to abide by these terms.

25   [...]

26   **Verio's Project Henhouse**

27   In late 1999, to better target their marketing and sales efforts toward customers in need of web hosting services and to reach those customers more quickly, Verio developed an automated software program or "robot."[4] With its search robot, Verio accessed the WHOIS database maintained by the accredited registrars, including Register.com, and collected the contact information of customers who had recently registered a domain name. Then, despite the marketing prohibitions in Register.com's terms of use, Verio utilized this data in a marketing initiative known as Project Henhouse and began to contact and solicit Register.com's customers, within the first several days

after their registration, by e-mail, regular mail, and telephone.

28   *Verio's Search Robots*

29   In general, the process worked as follows: First, each day Verio downloaded, in compressed format, a list of all currently registered domain names, of all registrars, ending in .com, .net, and .org. That list or database is maintained by Network Solutions, Inc. ("NSI") and is published on 13 different "root zone" servers. The registry list is updated twice daily and provides the domain name, the sponsoring registrar, and the nameservers for all registered names. Using a computer program, Verio then compared the newly downloaded NSI registry with the NSI registry it downloaded a day earlier in order to isolate the domain names that had been registered in the last day and the names that had been removed. After downloading the list of new domain names, only then was a search robot used to query the NSI database to extract the name of the accredited registrar of each new name.[5] That search robot then automatically made successive queries to the various registrars' WHOIS databases, via the port 43 access channels, to harvest the relevant contact information for each new domain name registered. [...] Once retrieved, the WHOIS data was deposited into an information database maintained by Verio. The resulting database of sales leads was then provided to Verio's telemarketing staff.

30   *Marketing History*

31   Beginning in January, 2000, Register.com learned that Verio was e-mailing its customers to solicit business. Register.com through its Director of Strategic Initiatives Lauren Gaviser complained to Eric Eden, Director of Sales and Channel Operations of Verio, citing an e-mail received by a customer which identified Verio as the sender but stated "[b]y now you [...] should have received an email from us confirming the registration of your domain name(s) ... you have taken the first step towards having your own website ... the next step is to set up a hosting account ..." [...]

32   Register.com continued to get complaints about e-mail and telephone solicitations by Verio from its customers and co-brand partners through January. In March 2000 Gaviser again contacted Eden to complain that Register.com was still receiving numerous complaints, including that a number of telephone messages similar to the following were left with Register.com customers: "This is [name of telemarketer] calling from Verio regarding the registration of [customer's domain name]. Please contact me at your earliest convenience." [...]

33   On May 5, 2000 Register.com's lawyers wrote to Verio's General Counsel requesting that Verio immediately cease and desist from this marketing conduct. Register.com complained generally that the use of its mark as well as the timing of the solicitations was harming its good will and specifically warned Verio that it was violating the terms of use it had agreed to in submitting its WHOIS queries by sending "mass unsolicited, commercial advertising or solicitations via e-mail (spam)." [...]

34   On May 9, 2000 Verio, through an Associate Counsel, communicated that it had stopped using the Register.com mark or any other similar mark or phrase which would lead to confusion and had ceased accessing the WHOIS database for the purpose of marketing through e-mail. [...] In an effort to confirm settlement of the dispute, Register.com's lawyers sent Verio a terms letter for it to sign and acknowledge. In that letter Register.com specifically required Verio to cease use of the WHOIS database for not just e-mail marketing, but also direct mail and telemarketing. Verio refused to sign and although it ceased e-mail solicitation, it continued to use the WHOIS contact information for telemarketing purposes into July 2000. [...]

35   Accordingly, Register.com commenced this lawsuit and moved for a temporary restraining order and preliminary injunction on August 3, 2000. [...]

36   ## II. Discussion

37   This dispute centers on both Verio's end use of the WHOIS data and its use of the automated search robot. While Register.com

acknowledges its obligation to provide public access to its customers' contact information, it has developed "terms of use" which prohibit third parties, such as Verio, from using the contact information for any mass marketing purpose — whether by e-mail, regular mail or telephone. Register.com also argues that the use of automated software to access the WHOIS database violates its terms of use and harms its computer systems.

38   [...] Verio admits both the use of the WHOIS data for marketing purposes and the use of the search robot. Verio also concedes that its end use of the information violates the marketing restriction imposed by Register.com, but argues that this restriction should not be enforced because — at a minimum — direct mail and telephone marketing are permissible uses under the terms of the Accreditation Agreement Register.com signed with ICAAN.[6] Verio argues that by imposing these impermissible anti-marketing restrictions Register.com is in breach of that Agreement. Verio also argues that the use of the robot is not prohibited by Register.com's terms of use and claims that Register.com has not proven that the robot causes any harm, let alone irreparable harm, to Register.com's computer systems.

39   ## III. Standard For Injunctive Relief

40   In order to obtain a preliminary injunction, a plaintiff must demonstrate both (1) that it will suffer irreparable harm if the motion is not granted and (2) either (a) a likelihood that it will succeed on the merits of the action [...]

42   ## IV. Register.com's Claims

43   [...]

60   ### B. *Trespass To Chattels*

66   Register.com argues that Verio's use of an automated software robot to search the "WHOIS" database constitutes trespass to chattels. Register.com states that it has made its computer system available on the Internet, and that "Verio has used `software automation' to flood that computer [...] system with traffic in order to retrieve the contact information of Register.com customers for the purpose of solicitation in knowing violation of Register.com's posted policies and terms of use." [...]

67   The standard for trespass to chattels in New York is based upon the standard set forth in the Restatement of Torts:

68   One who uses a chattel with the consent of another is subject to liability in trespass for any harm to the chattel which is caused by or occurs in the course of any use exceeding the consent, even though such use is not a conversion.

69   *[...]*

70   As an initial matter, the Court does not believe that Register.com's terms of use forbid the particular use of the search robot at issue here. Register.com's posted policies and terms of use require a party who seeks access to its WHOIS database to agree that it will not "use this data to ... enable high volume, automated, electronic processes that apply to Register.com (or its systems)." Register.com argues that use of a search robot is prohibited by that term of use. The Court disagrees.

71   The terms state that under no circumstances may one "use this data [the WHOIS data] to ... *enable* high volume, automated, electronic processes that apply to Register.com." The temporal aspect of this term is important because it only bars future automated processes. Although Verio uses an automated process to *collect* the WHOIS data, it does not then use the collected data to enable an automated process that applies to Register.com's systems. Once Verio's software robot secures the WHOIS information from Register.com's systems, it has completed its automated process with respect to Register.com's systems. The robot does not then use that WHOIS data to "enable high volume, automated, electronic processes that apply to Register.com (or its systems)," it simply deposits the data into a database.

72   However, despite the fact that Register.com's terms of use may not specifically forbid this use of a search robot by Verio and such use
      does not therefore constitute a breach of contract, it is clear since at least the date this lawsuit was filed that Register.com does not
      consent to Verio's use of a search robot, and Verio is on notice that its search robot is unwelcome. [...]

73   Accordingly, Verio's future use of a search robot to access the database exceeds the scope of Register.com's consent, and Verio is liable
      for any harm to the chattel (Register.com's computer systems) caused by that unauthorized access. *See CompuServe,* 962 F.Supp. at
      1024 (holding that defendants' continued use after CompuServe notified defendants that it no longer consented to the use of its
      proprietary computer equipment was a trespass) [...]

74   Having established that Verio's access to its WHOIS database by robot is unauthorized, Register.com must next demonstrate that Verio's
      unauthorized access caused harm to its chattels, namely its computer system. To that end, Robert Gardos, Register.com's Vice President
      for Technology, submitted a declaration estimating that Verio's searching of Register.com's WHOIS database has resulted in a
      diminishment of 2.3% of Register.com's system resources. [...] However, during discovery, the basis for Gardos' estimations of the
      impact Verio's search robot had on Register.com's computer systems was thoroughly undercut. Gardos admitted in his deposition that he
      had taken measurements of neither the capacity of Register.com's computer systems nor the portion of that capacity which was
      consumed by Verio's search robots. Furthermore, when describing how he arrived [...] at his conclusion that Verio's search robots
      occupied a certain percentage of Register.com's systems capacity, Mr. Gardos testified that the numbers he used were "all rough
      estimates." [...]

75   Although Register.com's evidence of any burden or harm to its computer system caused by the successive queries performed by search
      robots is imprecise, evidence of mere possessory interference is sufficient to demonstrate the quantum of harm necessary to establish a
      claim for trespass to chattels. "A trespasser is liable when the trespass diminishes the condition, quality, or value of personal property."
      EBay, Inc. v. Bidder's Edge, Inc. [...] "The quality or value of personal property may be `diminished even though it is not physically damaged
      by defendant's conduct.'" *Id.* Though it does correctly dispute the trustworthiness and accuracy of Mr. Gardos' calculations, Verio does
      not dispute that its search robot occupies some of Register.com's systems capacity.

76   Although Register.com was unable to directly measure the amount by which its systems capacity was reduced, the record evidence is
      sufficient to establish the possessory interference necessary to establish a trespass to chattels claim. [...]

79   Furthermore, Gardos also noted in his declaration "if the strain on Register.com's resources generated by Verio's searches becomes large
      enough, it could cause Register.com's computer systems to malfunction or crash" and "I believe that if Verio's searching of Register.com's
      WHOIS database were determined to be lawful, then every purveryor of Internet-based services would engage in similar conduct." [...]
      Gardos' concerns are supported by Verio's testimony that it sees no need to place a limit on the number of other companies that should
      be allowed to harvest data from Register.com's computers. [...] Furthermore, Verio's own internal documents reveal that Verio was aware
      that its robotic queries could slow the response times of the registrars' databases and even overload them. [...]

80   Accordingly, Register.com's evidence that Verio's search robots have presented and will continue to present an unwelcome interference
      with, and a risk of interruption to, its computer system and servers is sufficient to demonstrate a likelihood of success on the merits of its
      trespass to chattels claim.

81   There is no adequate remedy at law for an ongoing trespass and without an injunction the victim of such a trespass will be irreparably
      harmed. The *eBay* court specifically held that eBay was entitled to preliminary injunctive relief based on the claim that if such relief were
      denied, other companies would be encouraged to deploy search robots against eBay's servers and would further diminish eBay's server
      capacity [251] to the point of denying effective access to eBay's customers. [...]

82   The same reasoning applies here. Register.com, through Mr. Gardos, has expressed the fear that its servers will be flooded by search robots deployed by competitors in the absence of injunctive relief. Register.com has therefore demonstrated both a likelihood of success on the merits of its trespass to chattels claim and the existence of irreparable harm, and is entitled to a preliminary injunction against Verio based upon that claim.

83   **C.** *Computer Fraud And Abuse Act §§ 1030(a)(2)(C) and (a)(5)(C)*

84   The issue of the scope of Verio's authorization to access the WHOIS database is also central to the Court's analysis of Register.com's claims that Verio is violating two discrete provisions of the Computer Fraud and Abuse Act ("CFAA"), 18 U.S.C. § 1030 *et seq.*[10]

85   Register.com claims both that the use of software robots to harvest customer information from its WHOIS database in violation of its terms of use violates 18 U.S.C. §§ 1030(a)(2)(C) and (a)(5)(C), and that using the harvested information in violation of Register.com's policy forbidding the use of WHOIS data for marketing also violates those sections. That is, that both Verio's method of accessing the WHOIS data and Verio's end uses of the data violate the CFAA.

86   **1.** *Verio's Use of Search Robots*

87   Both §§ 1030(a)(2)(C) and (a)(5)(C) require that the plaintiff prove that the defendant's access to its computer system was unauthorized, or in the case of § 1030(a)(2)(C) that it was unauthorized or exceeded authorized access. However, although each section requires proof of some degree of unauthorized access, each addresses a different type of harm. Section 1030(a)(2)(C) requires Register.com to prove that Verio intentionally accessed its computers without authorization *and thereby obtained information.* Section 1030(a)(5)(C) requires Register.com to show that Verio intentionally accessed its computer without authorization *and thereby caused damage.*

88   As discussed more fully in the context of the trespass to chattels claim, because Register.com objects to Verio's use of search robots they represent an unauthorized access to the WHOIS database.

89   The type of harm that Register.com alleges is caused by the search robots, including diminished server capacity and potential system shutdowns, is better analyzed under § 1030(a)(5)(C), which specifically addresses damages to the computer system. Pursuant to the pertinent part[11] of § 1030(e)(8), "the term `damage' means any impairment to the integrity or availability of data, a program, a system, or information that (A) causes loss aggregating at least $5000 in value during any 1-year period to one or more individuals."

90   On this record Register.com has demonstrated that Verio's unauthorized use of search robots to harvest registrant contact information from Register.com' WHOIS database has diminished server capacity, however slightly, and could diminish response time, which could impair the availability of data to clients trying to get registrant contact information. Moreover, Register.com has raised the possibility that if Verio's robotic queries of Register.com's WHOIS database were determined [...] to be lawful, then other vendors of Internet services would engage in similar conduct. This Court finds that it is highly probable that other Internet service vendors would also use robots to obtain this potential customer information were it to be permitted. [...]

91   If the strain on Register.com's resources generated by robotic searches becomes large enough, it could cause Register.com's computer systems to malfunction or crash. Such a crash would satisfy § 1030(a)(5)(C)'s threshold requirement that a plaintiff demonstrate $5000 in economic damages[12] resulting from the violation, both because of costs relating to repair and lost data and also because of lost good will based on adverse customer reactions.

92   A potential harm which cannot be addressed by a legal or equitable remedy following a trial, such as the loss of customers that might result from a system shutdown or slowed response times complained of here, constitutes an irreparable injury. [...]

93   Because Register.com has demonstrated that Verio's access to its WHOIS database by means of an automated search robot is unauthorized and caused or could cause $5000 in damages by impairing the availability of data or the availability of its computer systems, Register.com has established both irreparable harm and a likelihood of success on the merits of its claim that Verio's use of the search robot violated § 1030(a)(5)(C) of the Computer Fraud And Abuse Act. Register.com is therefore entitled to injunctive relief based upon this claim.

94   **2. *Verio's Use of WHOIS Data For Marketing Purposes***

95   With respect to its use of Register.com's WHOIS data for e-mail, direct mail and telephone marketing, Verio argues that such an act can only be analyzed under § 1030(a)(2)(C)'s provision assessing liability where a party exceeds authorized access and obtains information it is not entitled to obtain. Verio argues that because it is authorized to access the WHOIS database for some purposes its access was authorized. Verio then argues that its conduct must meet the Act's specific definition of conduct that "exceeds authorized [...] access." Pursuant to the definition contained in § 1030(e)(6) of the CFAA, "the term `exceeds authorized access' means to access a computer with authorization and to use such access to obtain or alter information in the computer *that the accessor is not entitled to obtain* or alter." 18 U.S.C. § 1030(e)(6) (emphasis added). Verio then argues that this definition does not contemplate a violation of end use restrictions placed on data as "exceeding authorized access," and therefore that Verio has not violated § 1030(a)(2)(C).

96   Again, neither party disputes that Verio is not authorized under Register.com's terms of use to use the data for mass marketing purposes, and neither party disputes that Verio is authorized to obtain the data for some purposes. However, Verio's distinctions between authorized access and an unauthorized end use of information strike the Court as too fine. First, the means of access Verio employs, namely the automated search robot, is unauthorized. Second, even if Verio's means of access to the WHOIS database would otherwise be authorized, that access would be rendered unauthorized *ab initio* by virtue of the fact that prior to entry Verio knows that the data obtained will be later used for an unauthorized purpose.

97   Accordingly, the Court finds that Verio's access to the WHOIS database was unauthorized and that Verio violated § 1030(a)(2)(C) by using that unauthorized access to obtain data for mass marketing purposes. As discussed above, the harvesting and subsequent use of that data has caused and will cause Register.com irreparable harm. Therefore, because Register.com has demonstrated a likelihood of success on the merits of its claim that Verio's use of its WHOIS data for mass marketing purposes violates § 1030(a)(2)(C) of the Computer Fraud And Abuse Act and has demonstrated irreparable harm stemming from that violation, Register.com is entitled to injunctive relief based on that claim.

98   [...]

100 **V. Injunction**

111 For the foregoing reasons and pursuant to Fed.R.Civ.P. 65, it is hereby ORDERED, that pending a final decision on the merits of plaintiff's claims, defendant Verio Inc., its officers, agents, servants, employees, [...] are enjoined from engaging in the following activities:

112 [...]

114 3. Accessing Register.com's computers and computer networks in any manner, including, but not limited to, by software programs performing multiple, automated, successive queries, provided that nothing in this Order shall prohibit Verio from accessing Register.com's WHOIS database in accordance with the terms and conditions thereof; and

115 4. Using any data currently in Verio's possession, custody or control, that using its best efforts, Verio can identify as having been obtained from Register.com's computers and computer networks to enable the transmission of unsolicited commercial electronic mail, telephone calls, or direct mail to the individuals listed in said data [...]

110   [1] ICANN was created in 1998 to assume the U.S. Government's responsibilities for the management of the Internet Domain Name System ("DNS"). It is a private, not-for-profit corporation initiated by the Department of Commerce to privatize the Domain Name System in a manner that increases competition and facilitates international participation in its management. [...] Network Solutions, Inc. ("NSI") formerly enjoyed a monopoly as the only domain name registrar. NSI still operates and maintains the top-level domain name servers and zone files which enable the other registrars to access the DNS and to transmit domain name registration information for the .com, .net, and .org top level domain names to the System.

120   [2] The Agreement also obligates Register.com to provide third parties with bulk access to the same WHOIS data pursuant to a license agreement. The bulk access license entitles the licensee to receive weekly — in one transmission — an electronic copy of the same WHOIS information that is provided continuously through Register.com's web page and its access port 43. The Agreement allows Register.com to charge a $10,000 yearly fee for the license. Register.com has imposed the same mass marketing prohibition on the use the bulk license data. [...]

126   [6] Verio contests Register.com's assertion that its particular use of e-mail to solicit Register.com's customers constitutes the "spamming" that is prohibited by the ICANN agreement. The Court need not determine whether Verio' e-mails constitute "spam" because it is Register.com's terms of use, rather than ICANN's, that are at issue here. Register.com's terms do not specifically prohibit "spam", but rather simply prohibit the use of WHOIS data for mass, unsolicited e-mail. Verio's e-mails clearly violate Register.com's terms of use. Verio's unsolicited e-mail solicitations are "mass" by any definition of the term. Even though the e-mails are not sent simultaneously with one mouse click, as Verio argues, they are sent in massive quantities over a short period of time, and thus fit the definition of "mass" e-mails.

127   [...]

132   [12] Register.com relies upon lost revenue from Verio's exploitation of the WHOIS data for marketing purposes to constitute the damages required under § 1030(a)(5)(C). Although lost good will or business could provide the loss figure required under § 1030(a)(5) (C), it could only do so if it resulted from the impairment or unavailability of data or systems. The good will losses cited by Register.com are not the result of the harm addressed by § 1030(a)(5)(C). How Verio uses the WHOIS data, once extracted, has no bearing on whether Verio has impaired the availability or integrity of Register.com's data or computer systems in extracting it. Accordingly, because violating an anti-marketing restriction on the end use of data harms neither the data nor the computer and therefore does not cause the type of harm that § 1030(a)(5)(C) addresses, the specific good will damages cited by Register.com cannot satisfy its burden under § 1030(a)(5)(C).

EF Cultural Travel BV v. Explorica, Inc.

September 05, 2014 by mrisch

This case considers website "scraping." Be sure to read the footnotes – they include a lot of important facts and limitations of the holding.

1   274 F.3d 577 (2001)

2   **EF CULTURAL TRAVEL BV**[...]

                                v.

                      EXPLORICA, INC. [...]

4   United States Court of Appeals, First Circuit.

5   [...]
                    Decided December 17, 2001.

6   [...]

8   Before BOUDIN, Chief Judge, COFFIN, Senior Circuit Judge, and LYNCH, Circuit Judge.

9   ## COFFIN, Senior Circuit Judge.

10   Appellant Explorica, Inc. ("Explorica") and several of its employees challenge a preliminary injunction issued against them for alleged violations of the Computer Fraud and Abuse Act ("CFAA"), 18 U.S.C. § 1030.[1] We affirm the district court's [579] conclusion that appellees will likely succeed on the merits of their CFAA claim, but rest on a narrower basis than the court below.

11   *I. Background*

12   Explorica was formed in 2000 to compete in the field of global tours for high school students. Several of Explorica's employees formerly were employed by appellee EF, which has been in business for more than thirty-five years. EF and its partners and subsidiaries make up the world's largest private student travel organization.

13   Shortly after the individual defendants left EF in the beginning of 2000, Explorica began competing in the teenage tour market. The company's vice president (and former vice president of information strategy at EF), Philip Gormley, envisioned that Explorica could gain a substantial advantage over all other student tour companies, and especially EF, by undercutting EF's already competitive prices on student tours. Gormley considered several ways to obtain and utilize EF's prices: by manually keying in the information from EF's brochures and other printed materials; by using a scanner to record that same information; or, by manually searching for each tour offered through EF's website. Ultimately, however, Gormley engaged Zefer, Explorica's Internet consultant, to design a computer program called a "scraper" to glean all of the necessary information from EF's website. Zefer designed the program in three days.

14   The scraper has been likened to a "robot," a tool that is extensively used on the Internet. Robots are used to gather information for countless purposes, ranging from compiling results for search engines such as Yahoo! to filtering for inappropriate content. The

widespread deployment of robots enables global Internet users to find comprehensive information quickly and almost effortlessly.

15   Like a robot, the scraper sought information through the Internet. Unlike other robots, however, the scraper focused solely on EF's website, using information that other robots would not have. Specifically, Zefer utilized tour codes whose significance was not readily understandable to the public. With the tour codes, the scraper accessed EF's website repeatedly and easily obtained pricing information for those specific tours. The scraper sent more than 30,000 inquiries to EF's website and recorded the pricing information into a spreadsheet.[2]

16   [580] Zefer ran the scraper program twice, first to retrieve the 2000 tour prices and then the 2001 prices. All told, the scraper downloaded 60,000 lines of data, the equivalent of eight telephone directories of information.[3] Once Zefer "scraped" all of the prices, it sent a spreadsheet containing EF's pricing information to Explorica, which then systematically undercut EF's prices.[4] Explorica thereafter printed its own brochures and began competing in EF's tour market.

17   [...]

18   On May 30, 2001, the district court granted a preliminary injunction against Explorica based on the CFAA, which criminally and civilly prohibits certain access to computers. See 18 U.S.C. § 1030(a)(4). The court found that EF would likely prove that Explorica violated the CFAA when it used EF's website in a manner outside the "reasonable expectations" of both EF and its ordinary users. The court also concluded that EF could show that it suffered a loss, as required by the statute, consisting of reduced business, harm to its goodwill, and the cost of diagnostic measures it incurred to evaluate possible harm to EF's systems, although it could not show that Explorica's actions physically damaged its computers. In a supplemental opinion[5] the district court further articulated its "reasonable expectations" standard and explained that copyright, contractual and technical restraints sufficiently notified Explorica that its use of a scraper would be unauthorized and thus would violate the CFAA.

19   The district court first relied on EF's use of a copyright symbol on one of the pages of its website and a link directing users with questions to contact the company,[6] finding that "such a clear statement should have dispelled any notion a reasonable person may have had that the `presumption of open access' applied to information on EF's website." The court next found that the manner by which Explorica accessed EF's website likely violated a confidentiality agreement between appellant Gormley and EF, because Gormley provided to Zefer technical instructions concerning the creation of the scraper. Finally, the district court noted without elaboration that the scraper bypassed technical restrictions embedded in the [...] website to acquire the information. [...]

20   *[...]*

22   ***III. The Computer Fraud and Abuse Act***

23   Although appellees alleged violations of three provisions of the CFAA, the district court found that they were likely to succeed only under section 1030(a)(4).[7] That section provides

24   [Whoever] knowingly and with intent to defraud, accesses a protected computer without authorization, or exceeds authorized access, and by means of such conduct furthers the intended fraud and obtains anything of value ... shall be punished.

25   18 U.S.C. § 1030(a)(4).[8]

26   Appellees allege that the appellants knowingly and with intent to defraud accessed the server hosting EF's website more than 30,000 times to obtain proprietary pricing and tour information, and confidential information about appellees' technical abilities. At the heart of the parties' dispute is whether appellants' actions either were "without authorization" or "exceed[ed] authorized access" as defined by the CFAA.[9] We conclude that because of the broad confidentiality agreement appellants' actions "exceed[ed] authorized access," and

so we do not reach the more general arguments made about statutory [...] meaning, including whether use of a scraper alone renders access unauthorized.[10]

27   **A. *"Exceeds authorized access"***

28   Congress defined "exceeds authorized access," as accessing "a computer with authorization and [using] such access to obtain or alter information in the computer that the accesser is not entitled so to obtain or alter." 18 U.S.C. § 1030(e)(6). EF is likely to prove such excessive access based on the confidentiality agreement between Gormley and EF. Pertinently, that agreement provides:

29   Employee agrees to maintain in strict confidence and not to disclose to any third party, either orally or in writing, any Confidential or Proprietary information ... and never to at any time (i) directly or indirectly publish, disseminate or otherwise disclose, deliver or make available to anybody any Confidential or Proprietary Information or (ii) use such Confidential or [P]roprietary Information for Employee's own benefit or for the benefit of any other person or business entity other than EF.

            * * *

            As used in this Agreement, the term "Confidential or Proprietary Information" means (a) any trade or business secrets or confidential information of EF, whether or not reduced to writing ...; (b) any technical, business, or financial information, the use or disclosure of which might reasonably be construed to be contrary to the interests of EF.

            ...

30   The record contains at least two communications from Gormley to Zefer seeming to rely on information about EF to which he was privy only because of his employment there. First, in an email to Zefer employee Joseph Alt exploring the use of a scraper, Gormley wrote: " [m]ight one of the team be able to write a program to automatically extract prices ... ? I could work with him/her on the specification." Gormley also sent the following email to Zefer employee John Hawley:

31   Here is a link to the page where you can grab EF's prices. There are two important drop down menus on the right.... With the lowest one you select one of about 150 tours. * * * You then select your origin gateway from a list of about 100 domestic gateways (middle drop down menu). When you select your origin gateway a page with a couple of tables comes up. One table has 1999-2000 prices and the other has 2000-2001 prices. * * * On a high speed connection it is possible to move quickly from one price table to the next by hitting backspace and then the down arrow.

32   This documentary evidence points to Gormley's heavy involvement in the conception of the scraper program. Furthermore, the voluminous spreadsheet containing all of the scraped information includes the tour codes, which EF claims are proprietary [583] information. Each page of the spreadsheet produced by Zefer includes the tour and gateway codes, the date of travel, and the price for the tour. An uninformed reader would regard the tour codes as nothing but gibberish.[11] Although the codes can be correlated to the actual tours and destination points, the codes standing alone need to be "translated" to be meaningful.

33   Explorica argues that none of the information Gormley provided Zefer was confidential and that the confidentiality agreement therefore is irrelevant.[12] [...]

34   there is ample evidence that Gormley provided Explorica proprietary information about the structure of the website and the tour codes. To be sure, gathering manually the various codes through repeated searching and deciphering of the URLs[13] theoretically may be possible. Practically speaking, however, if proven, Explorica's wholesale use of EF's travel codes to facilitate gathering EF's prices from its website reeks of use — and, indeed, abuse — of proprietary information that goes beyond any authorized use of EF's website.[14]

35   Gormley voluntarily entered a broad confidentiality agreement prohibiting his disclosure of any information "which might reasonably be construed to be contrary to the interests of EF."[15] Appellants would face an uphill battle trying to argue that it was not against EF's

interests for appellants to use the tour codes to mine EF's pricing data. *[...]* If EF's allegations are proven, it will likely prove that whatever authorization Explorica had to navigate around EF's site (even in a competitive vein), it exceeded that authorization by providing proprietary information and know-how to Zefer to create the scraper.[16] Accordingly, the district *[...]* court's finding that Explorica likely violated the CFAA was not clearly erroneous.

36   **B.** *Damage or Loss under section 1030(g)*

37   Appellants also challenge the district court's finding that the appellees would likely prove they met the CFAA's "damage or loss" requirements. Under the CFAA, EF may maintain a private cause of action if it suffered "damage or loss." 18 U.S.C. § 1030(g). "Damage" is defined as "any impairment to the integrity or availability of data, a program, a system, or information that ... causes loss aggregating at least $5,000 in value during any 1-year period to one or more individuals...." 18 U.S.C. § 1030(e)(8). "Loss" is not defined.

38   The district court held that although EF could not show any "damage" it would likely be able to show "loss" under the statute. It reasoned that a general understanding of the word "loss" would fairly encompass a loss of business, goodwill, and the cost of diagnostic measures that EF took after it learned of Explorica's access to its website.[17] Appellants respond that such diagnostic measures cannot be included in the $5,000 threshold because their actions neither caused any physical damage nor placed any stress on EF's website.

39   *[...]* In *Shurgard Storage Centers v. Safeguard Self Storage, Inc.,* 119 F.Supp.2d 1121 (W.D.Wa.2000), the district court found that the need to assess whether a defendant's actions compromised the plaintiff's computers was compensable under the CFAA because the computer's integrity was called into question. The court based its finding on the legislative history of the 1996 amendments to the CFAA:

40   The 1994 Amendment required both "damage" and "loss," but it is not always clear what constitutes "damage." For example, intruders often alter existing log-on programs so that user passwords are copied to a file which the hackers can retrieve later. After retrieving the newly created password file, the intruder restores the altered log-on file to its original condition. Arguably, in such a situation, neither the computer nor its information is damaged. Nonetheless, this conduct allows the intruder to accumulate valid user passwords to the system, requires all system users to change their passwords, and requires the system administrator to devote resources to re-securing the system. Thus, although there is arguably no "damage," the victim does suffer "loss." If the loss to the victim meets the required monetary threshold, the conduct should be criminal, and the victim should be entitled to relief. *[...]* Another district court held that this legislative history makes "clear that Congress intended the term `loss' to target remedial expenses borne by victims that could not properly be considered direct damage caused by a computer hacker." *[...]*

41   We agree with this construction of the CFAA. In the absence of a statutory definition for "loss," we apply the well-known rule of assigning undefined words their normal, everyday meaning. *[...]* The word "loss" means "detriment, disadvantage, or deprivation from failure to keep, have or get." *[...]* Appellees unquestionably suffered a detriment and a disadvantage by having to expend substantial sums to assess the extent, if any, of the physical damage to their website caused by appellants' intrusion. That the physical components were not damaged is fortunate, but it does not lessen the loss represented by consultant fees. Congress's use of the disjunctive, "damage or loss," confirms that it anticipated recovery in cases involving other than purely physical damage. *But see In re Intuit Privacy Litig.,* 138 F.Supp.2d 1272, 1281 (C.D.Ca.2001) (loss means "irreparable damage" and any other interpretation "would render the term `damage' superfluous"); *Register.com, Inc. v. Verio, Inc.,* 126 F.Supp.2d 238, 252 n. 12 (S.D.N.Y. 2000) (lost business or goodwill could not constitute loss absent the impairment or unavailability of data or systems). To parse the words in any other way would not only impair Congress's intended scope of the Act, but would also serve to reward sophisticated intruders. As we move into an increasingly electronic world, the instances of physical damage will likely be fewer while the value to the victim of what has been stolen and the victim's costs in shoring up its security features undoubtedly will loom ever-larger. If we were to restrict the statute as appellants urge, we would flout Congress's intent by effectively permitting the CFAA to languish in the twentieth century, as violators of the Act move into the twenty-first century and beyond.

42   We do not hold, however, that any loss is compensable. The CFAA provides recovery for "damage" only if it results in a loss of at least

$5,000. We agree with the court in *In re DoubleClick Inc. Privacy Litigation,* 154 F.Supp.2d 497 (S.D.N.Y. 2001), that Congress could not have intended other types of loss to support recovery unless that threshold were met. Indeed, the Senate Report explicitly states that "if the loss to the victim meets the required monetary threshold," the victim is entitled to relief under the CFAA. S. Rep. 104-357, at 11. We therefore conclude that expenses of at least $5,000 resulting from a party's intrusion are "losses" for purposes of the "damage or loss" requirement of the CFAA.

43   *IV. Conclusion*

44   For the foregoing reasons, we agree with the district court that appellees will likely succeed on the merits of their CFAA claim under 18 U.S.C. § 1030(a)(4). Accordingly, the preliminary injunction was properly ordered.

45   *Affirmed.*

46   [...]

48   [2] John Hawley, one of Zefer's senior technical associates, explained the technical progression of the scraper in an affidavit:

49   [a.] Open an Excel spreadsheet. The initially contains EFTours gateway and destination city codes, which are available on the EFTours web site.

         [b.] Identify the first gateway and destination city codes [on the] Excel spreadsheet.

         [c.] Create a [website address] request for the EFTours tour prices page based on a combination of gateway and destination city. Example: show me all the prices for a London trip leaving JFK.

         [d.] View the requested web page which is retained in the random access memory of the requesting computer in the form of HTML [computer language] code. * * *

         [e.] Search the HTML for the tour prices for each season, year, etc.

         [f.] Store the prices into the Excel spreadsheet.

         [g.] Identify the next gateway and city codes in the spreadsheet.

         [8.] Repeat steps 3-7 for all gateway and destination city combinations.

50   [3] Appellants dispute the relevance of the size of the printed data, arguing that 60,000 printed lines, while voluminous on paper, is not a large amount of data for a computer to store. This is a distinction without a difference. The fact is that appellants utilized the scraper program to download EF's pricing data. In June 2000, EF's website listed 154,293 prices for various tours.

51   [4] Explorica later varied its prices slightly to mask its across-the-board discount of EF's prices.

52   [...]

55   [7] Appellees have not challenged the district court's finding that they were unlikely to succeed on claims brought under 18 U.S.C. §§ 1030(5)(C) and(6)(A).

56   [8] Although the CFAA is primarily a criminal statute, under § 1030(g), "any person who suffers damage or loss ... may maintain a civil action ... for compensatory damages and injunctive relief or other equitable relief."

57   [9] At oral argument, appellants contended that they had no "intent to defraud" as defined by the CFAA. That argument was not raised in the briefs and thus has been waived. *[...]*

58   [10] Congress did not define the phrase "without authorization," perhaps assuming that the words speak for themselves. The meaning, however, has proven to be elusive. The district court applied what it termed the "default rule" that conduct is without authorization only if it is not "in line with the reasonable expectations" of the website owner and its users. Appellants argue that this is an overly broad reading that restricts access and is at odds with the Internet's intended purpose of providing the "open and free exchange of information." They urge us to adopt instead the Second Circuit's reasoning that computer use is "without authorization" only if the use is not "in any way related to [its] intended function," *[...]* Appellees contend that the result would be the same under either test, but we need not resolve this dispute because we affirm the court's ruling based on the "exceeds authorized access" prong of § 1030(a)(4).

59   [11] An example of the website address including the tour information is *http://www.eftours. com/tours/PriceResult.asp? Gate=GTF & TourID=LPM.* In this address, the proprietary codes are "GTF" and "LPM."

60   [...]

61   [13] URL is the acronym for "uniform resource locator," the technical name for the web address typed in by an Internet user. For example, EF's URL is http://www.eftours.com.

62   [14] Among the several emails in the record is one from Zefer employee Joseph Alt to the Explorica "team" at Zefer:

63   Below is the information needed to log into EF's site as a tour leader. Please use this to gather competitor information from both a business and experience design perspective. We may also be able to glean knowledge of their technical abilities. As with all of our information, this is extremely confidential. Please do not share it with anyone.

64   [...]

65   [16] EF also claims that Explorica skirted the website's technical restraints. To learn about a specific tour, a user must navigate through several different web pages by "clicking" on various drop-down menus and choosing the desired departure location, date, tour destination, tour length, and price range. The district court found that the scraper circumvented the technical restraints by operating at a warp speed that the website was not normally intended to accommodate. We need not reach the argument that this alone was a violation of the CFAA, however, because the apparent transfer of information in violation of the Confidentiality Agreement furnishes a sufficient basis for injunctive relief.

66   Likewise, we express no opinion on the district court's ruling that EF's copyright notice served as a "clear statement [that] should have dispelled any notion a reasonable person may have had the `presumption of open access'" to EF's website.

67   [17] It is undisputed that appellees paid $20,944.92 to assess whether their website had been compromised. Appellees also claim costs exceeding $40,000 that they will incur to "remedy and secure their website and computer." We need not consider whether these expenses constitute loss because the initial $20,944.92 greatly exceeds the threshold.

Academics Go To Jail - CFAA Edition

Michael Risch

April 9, 2013

http://madisonian.net/2013/04/09/academics-go-to-jail-cfaa-edition/

Though the Aaron Swartz tragedy has brought some much needed attention to the CFAA, I want to focus on a more recent CFAA event—one that has received much less attention but might actually touch many more people than the case against Swartz.

Andrew "Weev" Auernheimer (whom I will call AA for short) was recently convicted under the CFAA and sentenced to 41 months and $73K restitution. Orin Kerr is representing him before the Third Circuit. I am seriously considering filing an amicus brief on behalf of all academics. In short, this case scares me in a much more personal way than prior discussed in my prior CFAA posts.

Here's the basic story, as described by Orin Kerr:

> When iPads were first released, iPad owners could sign up for Internet access using AT&T. When they signed up, they gave AT&T their e-mail addresses. AT&T decided to configure their webservers to "pre load" those e-mail addresses when it recognized the registered iPads that visited its website. When an iPad owner would visit the AT&T website, the browser would automatically visit a specific URL associated with its own ID number; when that URL was visited, the webserver would open a pop-up window that was preloaded with the e-mail address associated with that iPad. The basic idea was to make it easier for users to log in to AT&T's website: The user's e-mail address would automatically appear in the pop-up window, so users only needed to enter in their passwords to access their account. But this practice effectively published the e-mail addresses on the web. You just needed to visit the right publicly-available URL to see a particular user's e-mail address. Spitler [AA's alleged co-conspirator] realized this, and he wrote a script to visit AT&T's website with the different URLs and thereby collect lots of different e-mail addresses of iPad owners. And they ended up collecting a lot of e-mail addresses — around 114,000 different addresses — that they then disclosed to a reporter. Importantly, however, only e-mail addresses were obtained. No names or passwords were obtained, and no accounts were actually accessed.

Let me paraphrase this: AA went to a publicly accessible website, using publicly accessible URLs, and saved the results that AT&T sent back in response to that URL. In other words, AA did what you do every time you load up a web page. The only difference is that AA did it for multiple URLs, using sequential guesses at what those URLs would be. There was no robot.txt file that I'm aware of (this file tells search engines which URLs should not be searched by spiders). There was no user notice or agreement that barred use of the web page in this manner. Note that I'm not saying such things should make the conduct illegal, but only that such things didn't even exist here. It was just two people loading data from a website. Note also that a commenter on my prior post asked this exact same question--whether "link guessing" was illegal--and I was noncommital. I guess now we have our answer.

The government's indictment makes the activity sound far more nefarious, of course. It claims that AA "impersonated" an iPad. This allegation is a bit odd: the script impersonated an iPad in the same way that you might impersonate a cell phone by loading http://m.facebook.com to load the mobile version of Facebook. Go ahead, try it and you'll see – Facebook will think you are a cell phone. Should you go to jail?

So, readers might say, what's the problem here? AA should not have done what he did – he should have known that AT&T did not want

797

him downloading those emails. Yeah, he probably did know that. But consider this: AA did not share the information with the world, as he could have. I am reasonably certain that if his intent was to harm users, we would never know that he did this – he would have obtained the addresses over an encrypted VPN and absconded. Instead, AA shared this flaw with the world. AT&T set up this ridiculously insecure system that allowed random web users to tie Apple IDs to email addresses through ignorance at best or hubris at worst. I don't know if AA attempted to inform AT&T of the issue, but consider how far you got last time you contacted tech support with a problem on an ISP website. AA got AT&T's attention, and the problem got fixed with no (known) divulgence of the records.

Before I get to academia, let me add one more point. To the extent that AA should have known AT&T didn't desire this particular access, the issue is one of degree not of kind. And that is the real problem with the statute. There is nothing in the statute, absolutely nothing, that would help AA know whether he violated the law by testing this URL with one, five, ten, or ten thousand IDs. Here's one to try: click here for a link to a concert web page deep link using a URL with a numerical code. Surely Ticketmaster can't object to such deep linking, right? Well, it did, and sued Tickets.com over such behavior. Itclaimed, among other things, that each and every URL was copyrighted and thus infringed if linked to by another. It lost that argument, but today it could just say that such access was unwanted. For example, maybe Tickemaster doesn't like me pointing out its ridiculous argument in the tickets.com case, making my link unauthorized. Or maybe I should have known because the Ticketmaster terms of service says that an express condition of my authorization to view the site is that I will not "Link to any portion of the Site other than the URL assigned to the home page of our site." That's right, TicketMaster still thinks deep linking is unauthorized, and I suppose that means I risk criminal prosecution for linking it. Imagine if I actually saved some of the data!

This is where academics come in. Many, many academics scrape. (Don't stop reading here – I'll get to non-scrapers below.) First, scraping is a key way to get data from online databases that are not easily downloadable. This includes, for example, scraping of the US Patent & Trademark Office site; although data is now available for mass download, that data is cumbersome, and scraper use is still common. That the PTO is public data does not help matters. In fact, it might make it worse, since "unauthorized" access to government servers might receive enhanced penalties!

Academics (and non-academics) in other disciplines scrape websites for research as well. How are these academics to know that such scraping is disallowed? What if there is no agreement barring them from doing so? What if there is a web-wrap notice as broad as Ticketmaster's, purporting to bar such activities but with no consent by the user? The CFAA could send any academic to jail for ignoring such warnings—or worse—not seeing them in the first place. Such a prosecution would be preposterous, skeptics might say. I hope the skeptics are right, but I'm not hopeful. Though I can't find the original source, I recall Orin Kerr recounting how his prosecutor colleagues said the same thing 10 years ago when he argued the CFAA might apply to those who breach contracts, and now such prosecutions are commonplace.

Finally, non-scrapers are surely safe, right? Maybe it depends on if they use Zotero. Thousands of people use it. How does Zotero get information about publications when the web site does not provide standardized citation data? You guessed it: a scraper. Indeed, a primary reason I don't use Zotero is that the Lexis and Westlaw scrapers don't work. But the PubMed importer scrapes. What if PubMed decide that it considered scraping of information unauthorized? Surely people should know this, right? If it wanted people to have this data, they would provide it in Zotero readable format. The fact that the information on those pages is publicly available is irrelevant; the statute makes no distinction. And if one does a lot of research, for example, checking 20 documents, downloading each, and scraping each page, the difference from AA is in degree only, not in kind.

The irony of this case is that the core conviction is only tangentially a problem with the statute (there are some ancillary issues that are a problem with the statute). "Unauthorized access" and even "exceeds authorized access" should never have been interpreted to apply to publicly accessible data on publicly accessible web sites. Since they have, then I am convinced that the statute is impermissibly broad, and must be struck down. At the very least it must be rewritten.

Class 21: 8.3 <u>OIL Casebook: Computer Fraud & Abuse Act II</u>

U.S. v. Drew

September 05, 2014 by mrisch

This case considers CFAA violations for breach of terms of service

1   259 F.R.D. 449

2   **UNITED STATES of America, Plaintiff,**

v.

Lori DREW, Defendant.

3   [...]

4

5

8   **GEORGE H. WU, District Judge.**

10   **I. *INTRODUCTION***

11   This case raises the issue of whether (and/or when will) violations of an Internet website's[1] terms of service constitute a crime under the Computer Fraud and Abuse Act ("CFAA"), 18 U.S.C. § 1030. Originally, the question arose in the context of Defendant Lori Drew's motions to dismiss the Indictment on grounds of vagueness, failure to state an offense, and unconstitutional delegation of prosecutorial power. *[...]* At that time, this Court found that the presence of the scienter element (*i.e.* the requirement that the intentional accessing of a computer without authorization or in excess of authorization be in furtherance of the commission of a criminal or tortious act) within the CFAA felony provision as delineated in 18 U.S.C. § 1030(c)(2)(B)(ii) overcame Defendant's constitutional challenges and arguments against the criminalization of breaches of contract involving the use of computers. *[...]* However, Drew was subsequently acquitted by a jury of the felony CFAA counts but convicted of misdemeanor CFAA violations. Hence, the question in the present motion under Federal Rule of Criminal Procedure ("F.R.Crim.P.") 29(c) is whether an intentional breach of an Internet website's terms of service, without more, is sufficient to constitute a misdemeanor violation of the CFAA; and, if so, would the statute, as so interpreted, survive constitutional challenges on the grounds of vagueness and related doctrines.[...]

12   **II. *BACKGROUND***

13   **A. *Indictment***

14   In the Indictment, Drew was charged with one count of conspiracy in violation of 18 U.S.C. § 371 and three counts of violating a felony portion of the CFAA, *i.e.,* 18 U.S.C. §§ 1030(a)(2)(C) and 1030(c)(2)(B)(ii), which prohibit accessing a computer without authorization or in excess of authorization and obtaining information from a protected computer where the conduct involves an interstate or foreign communication and the offense is committed in furtherance of a crime or tortious act. *See* [...]

15   The Indictment included, *inter alia,* the following allegations (not all of which were established by the evidence at trial). Drew, a resident of O'Fallon, Missouri, entered into a conspiracy in which its members agreed to intentionally access a computer used in interstate commerce without (and/or in excess of) authorization in order to obtain information for the purpose of committing the tortious act of intentional infliction of emotional distress[3] upon "M.T.M.," subsequently identified as Megan Meier ("Megan"). Megan was a 13 year old

girl living in O'Fallon who had been a classmate of Drew's daughter Sarah. *[...]* Pursuant to the conspiracy, on or about September 20, 2006, the conspirators registered and set up a profile for a fictitious 16 year old male juvenile named "Josh Evans" on the www.My Space.com website ("MySpace"), and posted a photograph of a boy without that boy's knowledge or consent. *[...]* Such conduct violated My Space's terms of service. The conspirators contacted Megan through the MySpace network (on which she had her own profile) using the Josh Evans pseudonym and began to flirt with her over a number of days. *[...]* On or about October 7, 2006, the conspirators had "Josh" inform Megan that he was moving away. *[...]* On or about October 16, 2006, the conspirators had "Josh" tell Megan that he no longer liked her and that "the world would be a better place without her in it." *[...]* Later on that same day, after learning that Megan had killed herself, Drew caused the Josh Evans MySpace account to be deleted. *[...]*

16   **B. *Verdict***

17   At the trial, after consultation between counsel and the Court, the jury was instructed that, if they unanimously decided that they were not convinced beyond a reasonable doubt as to the Defendant's guilt as to the felony CFAA violations of 18 U.S.C. §§ 1030(a)(2)(C) and 1030(c)(2)(B)(ii), they could then consider whether the Defendant was guilty of the "lesser included"[4]misdemeanor [453] CFAA violation of 18 U.S.C. §§ 1030(a)(2)(C) and 1030(c)(2)(A).[5]

18   *[...]* As to Counts 2 through 4, the jury unanimously found the Defendant "not guilty" "of [on the dates specified in the Indictment] accessing a computer involved in interstate or foreign communication without authorization or in excess of authorization to obtain information in furtherance of the tort of intentional infliction of emotional distress in violation of Title 18, United States Code, Section 1030(a)(2)(C) and (c)(2)(B)(ii)...." *Id.* The jury did find Defendant "guilty" "of [on the dates specified in the Indictment] accessing a computer involved in interstate or foreign communication without authorization or in excess of authorization to obtain information in violation of Title 18, United States Code, Section 1030(a)(2)(C) and (c)(2)(A), a misdemeanor." *Id.*

19   ## C. MySpace.com

20   As Jae Sung (Vice President of Customer Care at MySpace) ("Sung") testified at trial, MySpace is a "social networking" website where members can create "profiles" and interact with other members. *[...]* Anyone with Internet access can go onto the MySpace website and view content which is open to the general public such as a music area, video section, and members' profiles which are not set as "private." *[...]* However, to create a profile, upload and display photographs, communicate with persons on the site, write "blogs," and/or utilize other services or applications on the MySpace website, one must be a "member." *[...]* Anyone can become a member of MySpace at no charge so long as they meet a minimum age requirement and register. *[...]*

21   In 2006, to become a member, one had to go to the sign-up section of the MySpace website and register by filling in personal information (such as name, email address, date of birth, country/state/postal code, and gender) and creating a password. *[...]* In addition, the individual had to check on the box indicating that "You agree to the MySpace **Terms of Service** and **Privacy Policy**." *[...]* The terms of service did not appear on the same registration page that contained this "check box" for users to confirm their agreement to those provisions. *Id.* In order to find the terms of service, one had (or would have had) to proceed to the bottom of the page where there were several "hyperlinks" including one entitled "Terms." *[...]* Upon clicking the "Terms" hyperlink, the screen would display the terms of service section of the website. *Id.* A person could become a MySpace member without ever reading or otherwise becoming aware of the provisions and conditions of the MySpace terms of service by merely clicking on the "check box" and then the "Sign Up" button without first accessing the "Terms" section. *[...]*.[8]

22   *[...]* As used in its website, "terms of service" refers to the "MySpace.com Terms of Use Agreement" ("MSTOS"). *[...]* The MSTOS in 2006 stated, *inter alia:*

23   This Terms of Use Agreement ("Agreement") sets forth the legally binding terms for your use of the Services. By using the Services, you agree to be bound by this Agreement, whether you are a "Visitor" (which means that you simply browse the Website) or you are a "Member" (which means that you have registered with MySpace.com). The term "User" refers to a Visitor or a Member. You are only authorized to use the Services (regardless of whether your access or use is intended) if you agree to abide by all applicable laws and to this Agreement. Please read this Agreement carefully and save it. If you do not agree with it, you should leave the Website and discontinue use of the Services immediately. If you wish to become a Member, communicate with other Members and make use of the Services, you must read this Agreement and indicate your acceptance at the end of this document before proceeding.

By using the Services, you represent and warrant that (a) all registration information you submit is truthful and accurate; (b) you will maintain the accuracy of such information; (c) you are 14 years of age or older; and (d) your use of the Services does not violate any applicable law or regulation.

24   *[...]*

25   The MSTOS prohibited the posting of a wide range of content on the website including (but not limited to) material that: a) "is potentially offensive and promotes racism, bigotry, hatred or physical harm of any kind against any group or individual"; b) "harasses or advocates harassment of another person"; c) "solicits personal information from anyone under 18"; d) "provides information that you know is false or misleading or promotes illegal activities or conduct that is abusive, threatening, obscene, defamatory or libelous"; e) "includes a photograph of another person that you have posted without that person's consent"; f) "involves commercial activities and/or sales without our prior written consent"; g) "contains restricted or password only access pages or hidden pages or images"; or h) "provides any phone numbers, street addresses, last names, URLs or email addresses...." *[...]* MySpace also reserved the right to take appropriate legal action (including reporting the violating conduct to law enforcement authorities) against persons who engaged in "prohibited activity" which was defined as including, *inter alia:* a) "criminal or tortious activity", b) "attempting to impersonate another Member or person", c) "using any information obtained from the Services in order to harass, abuse, or harm another person", d) "using the Service in a manner inconsistent with any and all applicable laws and regulations", e) "advertising to, or solicitation of, any Member to buy or sell any products or services through the Services", f) "selling or otherwise transferring your profile", or g) "covering or obscuring the banner advertisements on your personal profile page...." *[...]* The MSTOS warned users that "information provided by other MySpace.com Members (for instance, in their Profile) may contain inaccurate, inappropriate, offensive or sexually explicit material, products or services, and MySpace.com assumes no responsibility or liability for this material."*[...]* Further, MySpace was allowed to unilaterally modify the terms of service, with such modifications taking effect upon the posting of notice on its website. *Id.* at 1. Thus, members would have to review the MSTOS each time they logged on to the website, to ensure that they were aware of any updates in order to avoid violating some new provision of the terms of service. *[...]*

26   "Generally speaking," MySpace would not monitor new accounts to determine if they complied with the terms of service except on a limited basis, mostly in regards to photographic content. *[...]* there is no way to determine how many of the 400 million existing MySpace accounts were created in a way that violated the MSTOS.*[...]* . MySpace attempts to maintain adherence to its terms of service. *Id.* at 60. It has different teams working in various areas such as "parent care" (responding to parents' questions about this site), handling "harassment/cyberbully cases, imposter profiles," removing inappropriate content, searching for underage users, *etc. [...]*. As to MySpace's response to reports of harassment:

27   It varies depending on the situation and what's being reported. It can range from ... letting the user know that if they feel threatened to contact law enforcement, to us removing the profile, and in rare circumstances we would actually contact law enforcement ourselves.

28   *[...]*

30   Members under 16 have a privacy setting for their profiles which cannot be altered to allow regular public access. *[...]* To communicate with a member whose profile has a privacy setting, one must initially send a "friend" request to that person who would have to accept the

request. *[...]* To become a "friend" of a person under 16, one must not only send a "friend" request but must also know his or her email address or last name. *[...]*

31   *[...]*

32   **III. *APPLICABLE LAW***

33   **[...]**

35   **B. *The CFAA***

36   In 2006, the CFAA (18 U.S.C. § 1030) provided in relevant part that:

> (a) Whoever—
>
> * * * *
>
> (2) intentionally accesses a computer without authorization or exceeds authorized access, and thereby obtains—
>
> *[...]*
>
> (C) information from any protected computer if the conduct involved an interstate or foreign communication;[11]
>
> *[...]*
>
> (c) The punishment for an offense under subsection (a) or (b) of this section is—
>
> *[...]*
>
> (2)(A) except as provided in subparagraph (B), a fine under this title or imprisonment for not more than one year, or both in the case of an offense under subsection (a)(2), (a)(3), (a)(5)(A)(iii), or (a)(6) of this section which does not occur after a conviction for another offense under this section or an attempt to commit an offense punishable under this subparagraph; ...
>
> (B) a fine under this title or imprisonment for not more than 5 years, or both, in the case of an offense under subsection (a)(2), or an attempt to commit an offense punishable under this subparagraph, if—
>
> *[...]*
>
> (ii) the offense was committed in furtherance of any criminal or tortious act in violation of the Constitution or laws of the United States or of any State; or
>
> (iii) the value of the information obtained exceeds $5,000....

38   As used in the CFAA, the term "computer" "includes any data storage facility or communication facility directly related to or operating in conjunction with such device...." 18 U.S.C. § 1030(e)(1). The term "protected computer" "means a computer—(A) exclusively for the use of a financial institution or the United States Government ...; or (B) which is used in interstate or foreign commerce or communication...." *Id.* § 1030(e)(2). The term "exceeds authorized access" means "to access a computer with authorization and to use such access to obtain or alter information in the computer that the accesser is not entitled so to obtain or alter ...." *Id.* § 1030(e)(6).

39   *[...]* Because of the availability of civil remedies, much of the law as to the meaning and scope of the *[...]* CFAA has been developed in the context of civil cases.

40   **IV.** *DISCUSSION*

41   **A.** *The Misdemeanor 18 U.S.C. § 1030(a)(2)(C) Crime Based on Violation of a Website's Terms of Service*

42   During the relevant time period herein,[12] the misdemeanor 18 U.S.C. § 1030(a)(2)(C) crime consisted of the following three elements:

43   First, the defendant intentionally [accessed without authorization] [exceeded authorized access of] a computer;

          Second, the defendant's access of the computer involved an interstate or foreign communication; and

          Third, by [accessing without authorization] [exceeding authorized access to] a computer, the defendant obtained information
          from a computer … [used in interstate or foreign commerce or communication]….   *The bracketed terms are now part of the*
          definition of "protected computer"

44   Ninth Circuit Model Criminal Jury Instruction 8.79 (2003 Ed.) (brackets in original).

45   In this case, a central question is whether a computer user's intentional violation of one or more provisions in an Internet website's terms
      of services (where those terms condition access to and/or use of the website's services upon agreement to and compliance with the
      terms) satisfies the first element of section 1030(a)(2)(C). If the answer to that question is "yes," then seemingly, any and every
      conscious violation of that website's terms of service will constitute a CFAA misdemeanor.

46   Initially, it is noted that the latter two elements of the section 1030(a)(2)(C) crime will always be met when an individual using a computer
      contacts or communicates with an Internet website. Addressing them in reverse order, the third element requires "obtain[ing]
      information" from a "protected computer"—which is defined in 18 U.S.C. § 1030(e)(2)(B) as a computer "which is used in interstate or
      foreign commerce or communication…." "Obtain [ing] information from a computer" has been described as " 'includ[ing] mere
      observation of the data. Actual aspiration … need not be proved in order to establish a violation….' […]

48   the third element is satisfied whenever a person using a computer contacts an Internet website and reads any response from that site.

49   As to the second element (*i.e.*, that the accessing of the computer involve an interstate or foreign communication),[14] an initial question
      arises as to whether the communication itself must be interstate or foreign (*i.e.*, it is transmitted across state lines or country borders) or
      whether it simply requires that the computer system, which is accessed for purposes of the communication, is interstate or foreign in
      nature (for example, akin to a national telephone system).[15]   *Note that this prong is no longer required. See the court's footnote 11 and the current statute.*   [
      It has been held that "[a]s a practical matter, a computer providing a 'web-based' application accessible through the internet would
      satisfy the 'interstate communication' requirement." *[…]*

50   As to the first element (*i.e.* intentionally accessing a computer without authorization or exceeding authorized access), the primary
      question here is whether any conscious violation of an Internet website's terms of service will cause an individual's contact with the
      website via computer to become "intentionally access[ing] … without authorization" or "exceeding authorization." Initially, it is noted that
      three of the key terms of the first element (*i.e.*, "intentionally," "access a computer," and "without authorization") are undefined, and there
      is a considerable amount of controversy as to the meaning of the latter two phrases. *See EF Cultural Travel BV v. Explorica, Inc. […]*

51   While "intentionally" is undefined, the legislative history of the CFAA clearly evinces Congress's purpose in its choice of that word. Prior to
      1986, 18 U.S.C. § 1030(a)(2) utilized the phrase "knowingly accesses." *See* United States Code 1982 Ed. Supp. III at 16–17. In the 1986
      amendments to the statute, the word "intentionally" was substituted for the word "knowingly." *[…]*In Senate Report No. 99–432 at 5–6,
      reprinted at 1986 U.S.C.C.A.N. 2479, 2483–84, it was stated that:

52   Section 2(a)(1) amends 18 U.S.C. 1030(a)(2) to change the scienter requirement from "knowingly" to "intentionally," for two

reasons. First, intentional acts of unauthorized access—rather than mistaken, inadvertent, or careless ones—are precisely what the Committee intends to proscribe. Second, the Committee is concerned that the "knowingly" standard in the existing statute might be inappropriate for cases involving computer technology.... The substitution of an "intentional" standard is designed to focus Federal criminal prosecutions on those whose conduct evinces a clear intent to enter, without proper authorization, computer files or data belonging to another. Again, this will comport with the Senate Report on the Criminal Code, which states that " 'intentional' means more than that one voluntarily engaged in conduct or caused a result. Such conduct or the causing of the result must have been the person's conscious objective." [Footnote omitted.]

53   Under § 1030(a)(2)(C), the "requisite intent" is "to obtain unauthorized access of a protected computer." *[...]*

54   As to the term "accesses a computer," one would think that the dictionary definition of verb transitive "access" would be sufficient. That definition is "to gain or have access to; to retrieve data from, or add data to, a database...." *Webster's New World Dictionary, Third College Edition,* 7 (1988) (henceforth "*Webster's New World Dictionary* "). Most courts that have actually considered the issue of the meaning of the word "access" in the CFAA have basically turned to the dictionary meaning. *[...]* However, academic commentators have generally argued for a different interpretation of the word. For example, as stated in Patricia L. Bellia, *Defending Cyberproperty,* *[...]*

55   A narrower understanding of "access" would focus not merely on the successful exchange of electronic signals, but rather on conduct by which one is in a position to obtain privileges or information not available to the general public. The choice between these two meanings of 'access' obviously affects what qualifies as unauthorized conduct. If we adopt the broader reading of access, and any successful interaction between computers qualifies, then breach of policies or contractual terms purporting to outline permissible uses of a system can constitute unauthorized access to the system. Under the narrower reading of access, however, *[...]* only breach of a code-based restriction on the system would qualify.

56   Professor Bellia goes on to conclude that "[c]ourts would better serve both the statutory intent of the CFAA and public policy by limiting its application to unwanted uses only in connection with code-based controls on access." *[...] But see* Kerr, *Cybercrime's Scope [...]* It is simply noted that, while defining "access" in terms of a code-based restriction might arguably be a preferable approach, no case has adopted it[17] and the CFAA legislative history does not support it.

57   As to the term "without authorization," the courts that have considered the phrase have taken a number of different approaches in their analysis. *[...]* for example, where a case arises in the context of employee misconduct, some courts have treated the issue as falling within an agency theory of authorization. *[...]* Likewise, the Ninth Circuit (in dealing with the issue of purported consent to access emails pursuant to a subpoena obtained in bad faith in the context of the Stored Communications Act, 18 U.S.C. § 2701 *et seq.,* and the CFAA) applied the law of trespass to determine whether a subpoenaed party had effectively authorized the defendants' access. *[...]* Further, where the relationship between the parties is contractual in nature or resembles such a relationship, access has been held to be unauthorized where there has been an ostensible breach of contract. *[...]*

58   Within the breach of contract approach, most courts that have considered the issue have held that a conscious violation of a website's terms of service/use will render the access unauthorized and/or cause it to exceed authorization. *[...] But see BoardFirst [...]* The court in *BoardFirst* further stated:

59   [It] is at least arguable here that BoardFirst's access of the Southwest website is not at odds with the site's intended function; after all, the site is designed to allow users to obtain boarding passes for Southwest flights via the computer. In no sense can BoardFirst be considered an "outside hacker[ ] who break[s] into a computer" given that southwest.com is a publicly available website that anyone can access and use. True, the Terms posted on southwest.com do not give sanction to the particular *manner* in which BoardFirst uses the site—to check in Southwest customers for financial gain. But then again § 1030(a)(2)(C) does not forbid the *use* of a protected computer for any prohibited *purpose;* instead it prohibits one from intentionally *accessing* a computer "without authorization". As previously explained, the term "access", while not defined by the CFAA, ordinarily means the "freedom or ability to ... make use of" something. Here BoardFirst or any other computer user obviously has the

ability to make use of southwest.com given the fact that it is a publicly available website the access to which is not protected by any sort of code or password. *[...]*

61   In this particular case, as conceded by the Government,[19] the only basis for finding that Drew intentionally accessed MySpace's computer/servers without authorization and/or in excess of authorization was her and/or her co-conspirator's violations of the MSTOS by deliberately creating the false Josh Evans profile, posting a photograph of a juvenile without his permission and pretending to be a sixteen year old O'Fallon resident for the purpose of communicating with Megan. Therefore, if conscious violations of the My Space terms of service were not sufficient to satisfy the first element of the CFAA misdemeanor violation as per 18 U.S.C. §§ 1030(a)(2)(C) and 1030(b)(2)(A), Drew's Rule 29(c) motion would have to be granted on that basis alone. However, this Court concludes that an intentional breach of the MSTOS can potentially constitute accessing the MySpace computer/server without authorization and/or in excess of authorization under the statute.

62   There is nothing in the way that the undefined words "authorization" and "authorized" are used in the CFAA (or from the CFAA's legislative history[20]) which indicates that Congress intended for them to have specialized meanings.[21] As delineated in *Webster's New World Dictionary* at 92, to "authorize" ordinarily means "to give official approval to or permission for...."

63   It cannot be considered a stretch of the law to hold that the owner of an Internet website has the right to establish the extent to (and the conditions under) which members of the public will be allowed access to information, services and/or applications which are available on the website. *[...]* Nor can it be doubted that the owner can relay and impose *[...]* those limitations/restrictions/conditions by means of written notice such as terms of service or use provisions placed on the home page of the website. *[...]* While issues might be raised in particular cases as to the sufficiency of the notice and/or sufficiency of the user's assent to the terms, *see generally Specht v. Netscape Communications Corp.* *[...]* and while public policy considerations might in turn limit enforcement of particular restrictions *[...]* the vast majority of the courts (that have considered the issue) have held that a website's terms of service/use can define what is (and/or is not) authorized access vis-a-vis that website.

64   Here, the MSTOS defined "services" as including "the MySpace.com Website ..., the MySpace.com instant messenger, and any other connection with the Website...." *[...]* It further notified the public that the MSTOS "sets forth the legally binding terms for your use of the services." *Id.* Visitors and members were informed that "you are only authorized to use the Services ... if you agree to abide by all applicable laws and to this Agreement." *Id.* Moreover, to become a MySpace member and thereby be allowed to communicate with other members and fully utilize the MySpace Services, one had to click on a box to confirm that the user had agreed to the MySpace Terms of Service. *[...]* Clearly, the MSTOS was capable of defining the scope of authorized access of visitors, members and/or users to the website.[22]

65   **B. *Contravention of the Void–for–Vagueness Doctrine***

66   # 1. Applicable Law

67   Justice Holmes observed that, as to criminal statutes, there is a "fair warning" requirement. *[...]*

68   The void-for-vagueness doctrine has two prongs: 1) a definitional/notice sufficiency requirement and, more importantly, 2) a guideline setting element to govern law enforcement. *[...]*

73   To avoid contraving the void-for-vagueness doctrine, the criminal statute must contain "relatively clear guidelines as to prohibited conduct" and provide "objective criteria" to evaluate whether a crime has been committed. *[...]*

78   However, a "difficulty in determining whether certain marginal offenses are within the meaning of the language under attack as *[...]*

vague does not automatically render a statute unconstitutional for indefiniteness.... Impossible standards of specificity are not required." ["What renders a statute vague is not the possibility that it will sometimes be difficult to determine whether the incriminating fact it establishes has been proved; but rather the indeterminacy of precisely what that fact is." [...] In this regard, the Supreme Court "has made clear that scienter requirements alleviate vagueness concerns." [...]

77 ## 2. Definitional/Actual Notice Deficiencies

78 The pivotal issue herein is whether basing a CFAA misdemeanor violation as per 18 U.S.C. §§ 1030(a)(2)(C) and 1030(c)(2)(A) upon the conscious violation of a website's terms of service runs afoul of the void-for-vagueness doctrine. This Court concludes that it does primarily because of the absence of minimal guidelines to govern law enforcement, but also because of actual notice deficiencies.

79 As discussed in Section IV(A) above, terms of service which are incorporated into a browsewrap or clickwrap agreement can, like any other type of contract, define the limits of authorized access as to a website and its concomitant computer/server(s). However, the question is whether individuals of "common intelligence" are on notice that a breach of a terms of service contract can become a crime under the CFAA. Arguably, they are not.

80 First, an initial inquiry is whether the statute, as it is written, provides sufficient notice. Here, the language of section 1030(a)(2)(C)does not explicitly state (nor does it implicitly suggest) that the CFAA has "criminalized breaches of contract" in the context of website terms of service. Normally, breaches of contract are not the subject of criminal prosecution. [...]Thus, while "ordinary people" might expect to be exposed to civil liabilities for violating a contractual provision, they would not expect criminal penalties.[23] *Id.* This would especially be the case where the services provided by MySpace are in essence offered at no cost to the users and, hence, there is no specter of the users "defrauding" MySpace in any monetary sense.[24]

81 Second, if a website's terms of service controls what is "authorized" and what is "exceeding authorization"—which in turn governs whether an individual's accessing information or services on the website is criminal or not, section 1030(a)(2)(C) would be unacceptably vague because it is unclear whether any or all violations of terms of service will render the access unauthorized, or whether only certain ones will. For example, in the present case, MySpace's terms of service prohibits a member from engaging in a multitude of activities on the website, including such conduct as "criminal or tortious [...] activity," "gambling," "advertising to ... any Member to buy or sell any products," "transmit[ting] any chain letters," "covering or obscuring the banner advertisements on your personal profile page," "disclosing your password to any third party," *etc.* [...]The MSTOS does not specify which precise terms of service, when breached, will result in a termination of MySpace's authorization for the visitor/member to access the website. If *any* violation of *any* term of service is held to make the access unauthorized, that strategy would probably resolve this particular vagueness issue; but it would, in turn, render the statute incredibly overbroad and contravene the second prong of the void-for-vagueness doctrine as to setting guidelines to govern law enforcement.[25]

82 Third, by utilizing violations of the terms of service as the basis for the section 1030(a)(2)(C) crime, that approach makes the website owner-in essence-the party who ultimately defines the criminal conduct. This will lead to further vagueness problems. The owner's description of a term of service might itself be so vague as to make the visitor or member reasonably unsure of what the term of service covers. For example, the MSTOS prohibits members from posting in "band and filmmaker profiles ... sexually suggestive imagery or any other unfair ... [c]ontent intended to draw traffic to the profile." [...] It is unclear what "sexually suggestive imagery" and "unfair content" [26] mean. Moreover, website owners can establish terms where either the scope or the application of the provision are to be decided by them *ad hoc* and/or pursuant to undelineated standards. For example, the MSTOS provides that what constitutes "prohibited content" on the website is determined "in the sole discretion of MySpace.com...." [...] Additionally, terms of service may allow the website owner to unilaterally amend and/or add to the terms with minimal notice to users. [...]

83 Fourth, because terms of service are essentially a contractual means for setting the scope of authorized access, a level of indefiniteness arises from the necessary application of contract law in general and/or other contractual requirements within the applicable terms of

service to any criminal prosecution. For example, the MSTOS has a provision wherein "any dispute" between MySpace and a visitor/member/user arising out of the terms of service is subject to arbitration upon the demand of either party. Before a breach of a term of service can be found and/or the effect of that breach upon MySpace's ability to terminate the visitor/member/user's access to the site can be determined, the issue would be subject to arbitration.[27] Thus, a question arises as to whether a finding of unauthorized access or in excess of authorized access can be made without arbitration.

84   Furthermore, under California law,[28] a material breach of the MSTOS by a user/member does not automatically discharge the contract, but merely "excuses the injured party's performance, and gives him or her the election [...] of certain remedies." [...] The MSTOS does provide that: "MySpace.com reserves the right, in its sole discretion ... to restrict, suspend, or terminate your access to all or part of the services at any time, for any or no reason, with or without prior notice, and without liability." [...] However, there is no provision which expressly states that a breach of the MSTOS automatically results in the termination of authorization to access the website. Indeed, the MSTOS cryptically states: "you are only authorized to use the Services ... if you *agree to* abide by all applicable laws and to this Agreement." *[...]*

85   ## 3. The Absence of Minimal Guidelines to Govern Law Enforcement

86   Treating a violation of a website's terms of service, without more, to be sufficient to constitute "intentionally access[ing] a computer without authorization or exceed[ing] authorized access" would result in transforming section 1030(a)(2)(C) into an overwhelmingly overbroad enactment that would convert a multitude of otherwise innocent Internet users into misdemeanant criminals. [...]

88   Given the incredibly broad sweep of 18 U.S.C. §§ 1030(a)(2)(C) and 1030(c)(2)(A), should conscious violations of a website's terms of service be deemed sufficient by themselves to constitute accessing without authorization or exceeding authorized access, the question arises as to whether Congress has "establish[ed] minimal guidelines to govern law enforcement." *[...]* Section 1030(a)(2)(C) does not set forth "clear guidelines" or "objective criteria" as to the prohibited conduct in the Internet/website or similar contexts. *[...]* For instance, section 1030(a)(2)(C) is not limited to instances where the website owner contacts law enforcement to complain about an individual's unauthorized access or exceeding permitted access on the site.[29] Nor is there any [...] requirement that there be any actual loss or damage suffered by the website or that there be a violation of privacy interests.

89   The Government argues that section 1030(a)(2)(C) has a scienter requirement which dispels any definitional vagueness and/or dearth of guidelines, [...]

90   The only scienter element in section 1030(a)(2)(C) is the requirement that the person must "intentionally" access a computer without authorization or "intentionally" exceed authorized access. It has been observed that the term "intentionally" itself can be vague in a particular statutory context. *[...]*

93   Here, the Government's position is that the "intentional" requirement is met simply by a conscious violation of a website's terms of service. The problem with that view is that it basically eliminates any limiting and/or guiding effect of the scienter element. It is unclear that every intentional breach of a website's terms of service would be or should be held to be equivalent to an intent to access the site without authorization or in excess of authorization. This is especially the case with MySpace and similar Internet venues which are publically available for access and use. *[...]* However, if every such breach does qualify, then there is absolutely no limitation or criteria as to which of the breaches should merit criminal prosecution. All manner of situations will be covered from the more serious (*e.g.* posting child pornography) to the more trivial (*e.g.* posting a picture of friends without their permission). All can be prosecuted. Given the "standardless sweep" that results, federal law enforcement entities would be improperly free "to pursue their personal predilections."[[...]

94   In sum, if any conscious breach of a website's terms of service is held to be sufficient by itself to constitute intentionally accessing a computer without authorization or in excess of authorization, the result will be that section 1030(a)(2)(C) becomes a law "that affords

too much discretion to the police and too little notice to citizens who wish to use the [Internet]." *[…]*

95 **[468] V.** *CONCLUSION*

96 For the reasons stated above, the Defendant's motion under F.R.Crim.P. 29(c) is GRANTED.

97 *[…]*

104 [5] Specifically, the jury was instructed that:

105 The crime of accessing a protected computer without authorization or in excess of authorization to obtain information, and to do so in furtherance of a tortious act in violation of the laws of any State, includes the lesser crime of accessing a protected computer without authorization or in excess of authorization. If (1) all of you are not convinced beyond a reasonable doubt that the defendant is guilty of accessing a protected computer without authorization or in excess of authorization to obtain information, and doing so in furtherance of a tortious act in violation of the laws of any State; and (2) all of you are convinced beyond a reasonable doubt that the defendant is guilty of the lesser crime of accessing a protected computer without authorization or in excess of authorization, you may find the defendant guilty of accessing a protected computer without authorization or in excess of authorization.

106 *S[…]*

109 [8] Certain websites endeavor to compel visitors to read their terms of service by requiring them to scroll down through such terms before being allowed to click on the sign-on box or by placing the box at the end of the "terms" section of the site. *Id.* at 93. MySpace did not have such provisions in 2006. *[…]*

115 [11] On September 26, 2008, the Identity Theft Enforcement and Restitution Act of 2008 was passed which amended 18 U.S.C. § 1030(a)(2)(C) by *inter alia* striking the words "if the conduct involved an interstate or foreign communication" after "protected computer." *[…]*

118 [14] It is noted that, with the 2008 amendment to section 1030(a)(2)(C) which struck the provision that "the conduct involved an interstate or foreign communication" (*see* footnote 11, *supra*), the second element is no longer a requirement for the CFAA 18 U.S.C. § 1030(a)(2)(C) crime, although the interstate/foreign nexus remains as part of the third element.

119 *[…]*

125 [20] For example, when Congress added the term "exceeds authorized access" to the CFAA in 1986 and defined it as meaning "to access a computer with authorization and to use such access to obtain or alter information in the computer that the accesser is not entitled so to obtain or alter", it was observed that the definition (which includes the concept of accessing a computer with authorization) was "self-explanatory." *See* S.Rep. No. 99–432 *[…]*

131 [24] Also, it is noted here that virtually all of the decisions which have found a breach of a website's terms of service to be a sufficient basis to establish a section 1030(a)(2)(C) violation have been in civil actions, not criminal cases.

132 [25] Another uncertainty is whether, once a user breaches a term of service, is every subsequent accessing of the website by him or her without authorization or in excess of authorization.

133   [...]

810

U.S. v. Lowson, Oct. 12, 2010 (D.N.J.)

September 05, 2014 by mrisch

This is another case that considers breach of contract. Does it reach the right outcome?

1   UNITED STATES of America

2   v.

3   Kenneth LOWSON, a/k/a "Money" [...]

4   United States District Court,

5   D. New Jersey.

6   [...] Oct. 12, 2010.

7   [...]

10

13

14   **I. Introduction**

15   Defendants are charged with violations of the Computer Fraud and Abuse Act and the wire fraud statute arising from an alleged scheme to circumvent security measures put in place by Online Ticket Vendors (OTVs) in order to buy large blocks of tickets meant for the general public and then to re-sell those tickets at great profit on the secondary market. Defendants argue that their conduct is not criminal, and that in fact the government seeks to criminalize what otherwise would be a breach of contract action for violating the terms of service for ticket sales on OTVs' websites. [...]

16

17   The yawning gap between the government's and the defendants' positions is not lost on the Court, and it highlights and echoes tensions in other courts' viewpoints on where the line falls between what is civilly actionable conduct, and what is criminal.

18

19   Defendants now move to dismiss the Superseding Indictment ("the indictment"). For the reasons to be discussed, the Court denies the defendants' motion.

20

21

22   **II. Legal Standard**

23   [...] "An indictment is generally deemed sufficient if it [ ](1) contains the elements of the offense intended to be charged, (2) sufficiently apprises the defendant of what he must be prepared to meet, and (3) allows the defendant to show with accuracy to what extent he may plead a former acquittal or conviction in the event of a subsequent prosecution." [...]

24

25   on occasion a defendant's legal contentions may be so bound up with those facts that a court cannot grant a motion to dismiss. $[...]$

26

27

30

32

34

36

38

40

42

44

46

48

49

50   **IV. The CFAA Counts:**

51   1. Counts 2 through 10: Obtaining Information from a Protected Computer, 18 U.S.C. §§ 1030(a)(2)(C) and (c)(2)(B)(i)

52   Counts 2 through 10 of the indictment charge that defendants Lowson, Kirsch and Stevenson knowingly and intentionally accessed computers without authorization and exceeded authorized access, and using an interstate communication, obtained information from protected computers used in and affecting interstate and foreign commerce and communication, for the purpose of commercial gain. In so doing, the Indictment charges a crime under CFAA § 1030(a)(2) (C), which prohibits intentionally accessing a computer without authorization or exceeding authorized access, and thereby obtaining information from any protected computer.

53

54   The crimes charged under the CFAA—including the two additional CFAA violations alleged in counts 11 to 26—center on the defendants' alleged unauthorized access of Ticketmaster's computer network. Throughout their briefs and at oral argument, both the government and the defendants have fiercely contested what constitutes "unauthorized access" for the purpose of a prosecution under the CFAA. The central and recurring question is whether the scheme and conduct alleged here is merely an egregious breach of contract based on violations of the terms of service on Ticketmaster's website, or something criminal. Defendants assert that the indictment "unambiguously depend[s] upon alleged breaches of contract to establish criminal liability." $[...]$ The government insists that defendants' conduct amounted to a crime.

55

56   The Court is satisfied that the indictment sufficiently alleges the elements of unauthorized access and exceeding authorized access under the CFAA, and sufficiently alleges conduct demonstrating defendants' knowledge and intent to gain unauthorized access.

57

58   The indictment alleges a number of actions taken by defendants to defeat code-based security restrictions on Ticketmaster's websites. (Although the government's briefs speak of unauthorized access of the websites of Online Ticket Vendors in general, the indictment's CFAA charges in counts 2 through 26 reference only the network belonging to Ticketmaster.) A non-exhaustive list of the steps defendants allegedly took to defeat Ticketmaster's code-based security measures includes: circumventing Proof of Work protections; writing automated software to defeat CAPTCHA (itself an extensive process which allegedly involved opening thousands of connections at once and using CAPTCHA Bots to respond to CAPTCHA challenges in fractions of a second); employing optical character recognition to defeat CAPTCHA challenges; testing the vulnerability of security encryption to get directly to "Buy Pages"; and implementing "hacks" and using "backdoors" to enable automated programs to purchase tickets. The defendants also allegedly disregarded cease-and-desist letters and hired programmers, including "contract hackers," to defeat difficult security restrictions. $[...]$

59

61

62   The Court notes and must take seriously the arguments advanced by the defendants, as well as those made by Amici, regarding whether the unauthorized access alleged here amounts to contract-based violations of Ticketmaster's terms of service that are actionable under civil laws. The Court is aware, for example, that the investigation of Wiseguys, and ultimately these defendants, began after a civil case was successfully prosecuted by Ticketmaster. $\big[...\big]$ Courts have differed over what constitutes unauthorized access under the CFAA and where the line falls between a civil and criminal violation of the statute. Defendants point to *United States v. Drew*, in which a district court dismissed the indictment against a defendant who had been found guilty of a misdemeanor violation of the CFAA for unauthorized access based solely on the defendant's "conscious breach of a website's terms of service." *United States v. Drew*, 259 F.R.D. 449, 467 (C.D.Cal.2009). To hold otherwise, the *Drew* court stated, would be to transform § 1030(a)(2)(C) into a law that violates the void for vagueness doctrine by affording "too much discretion to the police and too little notice to citizens who wish to use the [Internet]." $\big[...\big]$ Defendants here go further and argue that, under the government's theory, a teenager hypothetically could be prosecuted under the CFAA for violating the age requirement restrictions in the terms of service when using a search engine like Google.

63

64   But, as the government goes to pains to stress, and as the indictment makes clear, the unauthorized access charges at the heart of this indictment involve allegations of breaches of both contract-and code-based restrictions. In *Drew,* the conduct charged did not involve allegations of circumvention of code-based restrictions. And significantly, the *Drew* court's decision to dismiss the indictment came *after* trial, which allowed for the full presentation of all the government's proofs and a development of the factual record in what admittedly is a technology-intensive and unsettled area of the law. This Court is satisfied that a full presentation of the government's proofs is required to determine if the defendants' arguments ring true that the "code-based restrictions ... are red herrings ... [and] are inextricably intertwined with the vendors' terms of use." $\big[...\big]$ For now, the indictment sufficiently alleges conduct supporting the government's theory of distinct code- and contract-based violations, and the government is entitled to the opportunity to fully offer its evidence, subject to cross-examination, as to why the conduct at issue here is criminal. In this case, the facts and the law are so closely related that further development of the record will shed light on crucial questions, such as what exactly the defendants did, how the alleged code-based restrictions worked, and whether the defeat of CAPTCHA challenges and circumvention of Ticketmaster's security measures is indeed distinct conduct from the terms of service violations described in *Drew.* It is only at that point that the Court can examine and rule on the defense theory that the CFAA and wire fraud counts are inextricably entwined, and so if the CFAA counts fall, so must the wire fraud counts.

65

66   Defendants also make a vagueness challenge. But as the Supreme Court has noted, "vagueness challenges to statutes which do not involve First Amendment freedoms must be examined in light of the facts of the case at hand." *Drew* $\big[...\big]$ Here, the factual record before the Court remains undeveloped.

67

68   In addition, defendants argue that the indictment fails to identify the "information" that defendants "obtained" under counts 2 through 10. They contend that the only things they obtained were tickets, that the "information" at issue was publicly available to "every other member of the public that uses the online vendors' public websites" $\big[...\big]$ and that "[c]omprehensive seating information was available from numerous other sources." (Def. Reply 10.) In effect, defendants argue, the government seeks to criminalize obtaining publicly available "information" and, in the process, the government will increase "exponentially" the universe of federal crimes. (Def. Moving Br. 18.) The government, however, argues that the information obtained included a detailed map of "available premium seats for each Event" that was unavailable to individual users and "confidential in the aggregate." $\big[...\big]$ These clashing characterizations of what exactly defendants saw and whether it constituted "obtaining information" within the meaning of the CFAA highlights yet again the need for further factual development of the record. Applying the analysis that is proper at this stage, the Court finds that the indictment does allege sufficient facts to satisfy the element of obtaining information.

69

70    $\big[...\big]\big[...\big]$

72

74

76

78

80

83

85

87

88

89 **V. Conclusion**

90 This case poses a good example of the complexity of criminal prosecutions under statutes written specifically about, for, and as a result of the Internet—and more, insofar as the parties are wrestling with the always perplexing issue of what constitutes criminal fraud. The challenge is to harmonize the CFAA and the government's charges of crime in the highly specialized marketplace the defendants operated in, with traditional and, indeed, sacrosanct tenets of the criminal law. The Court—and the parties as well—will be in a far better position to meet that challenge after the government presents its evidence. The motion to dismiss the Superseding Indictment is denied.

U.S. v. Nosal

September 05, 2014 by mrisch

This case considers a critical question: what does it mean to exceed authorized access? In this case, the contractual terms were much more clear and were affirmatively agreed to. Should this change things?

1   676 F.3d 854 (2012)

2   **UNITED STATES of America, Plaintiff-Appellant,**

                                                            v.

                              David NOSAL, Defendant-Appellee.

3   [...]

4   United States Court of Appeals, Ninth Circuit.

5   [...]
                                               Filed April 10, 2012.

6   [...]

14   **OPINION**

15   **KOZINSKI, Chief Judge:**

16   Computers have become an indispensable part of our daily lives. We use them for work; we use them for play. Sometimes we use them for play at work. Many employers have adopted policies prohibiting the use of work computers for nonbusiness purposes. Does an employee who violates such a policy commit a federal crime? How about someone who violates the terms of service of a social networking website? This depends on how broadly we read the Computer Fraud and Abuse Act (CFAA), 18 U.S.C. § 1030.

17   **FACTS**

18   David Nosal used to work for Korn/Ferry, an executive search firm. Shortly after he left the company, he convinced some of his former colleagues who were still working for Korn/Ferry to help him start a competing business. The employees used their log-in credentials to download source lists, names and contact information from a confidential database on the company's computer, and then transferred that information to Nosal. The employees were authorized to access the database, but Korn/Ferry had a policy that forbade disclosing confidential information.[1] The government indicted Nosal on twenty counts, including trade secret theft, mail fraud, conspiracy and violations of the CFAA. The CFAA counts charged Nosal with violations of 18 U.S.C. § 1030(a)(4), for aiding and abetting the Korn/Ferry employees in "exceed[ing their] authorized access" with intent to defraud.

19   Nosal filed a motion to dismiss the CFAA counts, arguing that the statute targets only hackers, not individuals who access a computer with authorization but then misuse information they obtain by means of such access. The district court initially rejected Nosal's argument, holding that when a person accesses a computer "knowingly and with the intent to defraud... [it] renders the access unauthorized or in excess of authorization." Shortly afterwards, however, we decided *LVRC Holdings LLC v. Brekka,* 581 F.3d 1127 (9th Cir.2009), which construed narrowly the phrases "without authorization" and "exceeds authorized access" in the CFAA. Nosal filed a motion for

815

reconsideration and a second motion to dismiss.

20   The district court reversed field and followed *Brekka's* guidance that "[t]here is simply no way to read [the definition of `exceeds authorized access'] to incorporate corporate policies governing use of information unless the word alter is interpreted to mean misappropriate," as "[s]uch an interpretation would defy the plain meaning of the word alter, as well as common sense." Accordingly, the district court dismissed counts 2 and 4-7 for failure to state an offense. The government appeals. [...]

21   ## DISCUSSION

22   The CFAA defines "exceeds authorized access" as "to access a computer with authorization and to use such access to obtain or alter information in the computer that the accesser is not entitled so to obtain or alter." 18 U.S.C. § 1030(e)(6). This language can be read either of two ways: First, as Nosal suggests and the district court held, it could refer to someone who's authorized to access only certain [data or files but accesses unauthorized data or files — what is colloquially known as "hacking." For example, assume an employee is permitted to access only product information on the company's computer but accesses customer data: He would "exceed[] authorized access" if he looks at the customer lists. Second, as the government proposes, the language could refer to someone who has unrestricted physical access to a computer, but is limited in the use to which he can put the information. For example, an employee may be authorized to access customer lists in order to do his job but not to send them to a competitor.

23   The government argues that the statutory text can support only the latter interpretation of "exceeds authorized access." In its opening brief, it focuses on the word "entitled" in the phrase an "accesser is not *entitled* so to obtain or alter." *Id.* § 1030(e)(6) (emphasis added). Pointing to one dictionary definition of "entitle" as "to furnish with a right," *Webster's New Riverside University Dictionary* 435, the government argues that Korn/Ferry's computer use policy gives employees certain rights, and when the employees violated that policy, they "exceed[ed] authorized access." But "entitled" in the statutory text refers to how an accesser "obtain[s] or alter[s]" the information, whereas the computer use policy uses "entitled" to limit how the information is used after it is obtained. This is a poor fit with the statutory language. An equally or more sensible reading of "entitled" is as a synonym for "authorized."[2] So read, "exceeds authorized access" would refer to data or files on a computer that one is not authorized to access.

24   In its reply brief and at oral argument, the government focuses on the word "so" in the same phrase. *See* 18 U.S.C. § 1030(e)(6) ("accesser is not *so* to obtain or alter" (emphasis added)). The government reads "so" to mean "in that manner," which it claims must refer to use restrictions. In the government's view, reading the definition narrowly would render "so" superfluous.

25   The government's interpretation would transform the CFAA from an anti-hacking statute into an expansive misappropriation statute. This places a great deal of weight on a two-letter word that is essentially a conjunction. If Congress meant to expand the scope of criminal liability to everyone who uses a computer in violation of computer use restrictions — which may well include everyone who uses a computer — we would expect it to use language better suited to that purpose.[3] Under the presumption that Congress acts interstitially, we construe a statute as displacing a substantial portion of the common law only where Congress has clearly indicated its intent to do so.

26   In any event, the government's "so" argument doesn't work because the word has meaning even if it doesn't refer to use restrictions. Suppose an employer keeps certain information in a separate database that can be viewed on a computer screen, but not copied or downloaded. If an employee circumvents the security measures, copies the information to a thumb drive and walks out of the building with it in his pocket, he would then have obtained access to information in the computer that he is not "entitled *so* to obtain." Or, let's say an employee is given full access to the information, provided he logs in with his username and password. In an effort to cover his tracks, he uses another employee's login to copy information from the database. Once again, this would be an employee who is authorized to access the information but does so in a manner he was not authorized "so to obtain." Of course, this all assumes that "so" must have a substantive meaning to make sense of the statute. But Congress could just as well have included "so" as a connector or for emphasis.[4]

27   While the CFAA is susceptible to the government's broad interpretation, we find Nosal's narrower one more plausible. Congress enacted the CFAA in 1984 primarily to address the growing problem of computer hacking, recognizing that, "[i]n intentionally trespassing into someone else's computer files, the offender obtains at the very least information as to how to break into that computer system." S.Rep.

No. 99-432, at 9 (1986), 1986 U.S.C.C.A.N. 2479, 2487 (Conf. Rep.). The government agrees that the CFAA was concerned with hacking, which is why it also prohibits accessing a computer "without authorization." According to the government, *that* prohibition applies to hackers, so the "exceeds authorized access" prohibition must apply to people who are authorized to use the computer, but do so for an unauthorized purpose. But it is possible to read both prohibitions as applying to hackers: "[W]ithout authorization" would apply to *outside* hackers (individuals who have no authorized access to the computer at all) and "exceeds authorized access" would apply to *inside* hackers (individuals whose initial access to a computer is authorized but who access unauthorized information or files). This is a perfectly plausible construction of the statutory language that maintains the CFAA's focus on hacking rather than turning it into a sweeping Internet-policing mandate.[5]

28   [...] The government's construction of the statute would expand its scope far beyond computer hacking to criminalize any unauthorized use of information obtained from a computer. This would make criminals of large groups of people who would have little reason to suspect they are committing a federal crime. While ignorance of the law is no excuse, we can properly be skeptical as to whether Congress, in 1984, meant to criminalize conduct beyond that which is inherently wrongful, such as breaking into a computer.

29   The government argues that defendants here did have notice that their conduct was wrongful by the fraud and materiality requirements in subsection 1030(a)(4), which punishes whoever:

30   knowingly and with intent to defraud, accesses a protected computer without authorization, or exceeds authorized access, and by means of such conduct furthers the intended fraud and obtains anything of value, unless the object of the fraud and the thing obtained consists only of the use of the computer and the value of such use is not more than $5,000 in any 1-year period.

31   18 U.S.C. § 1030(a)(4). But "exceeds authorized access" is used elsewhere in the CFAA as a basis for criminal culpability without intent to defraud. Subsection 1030(a)(2)(C) requires only that the person who "exceeds authorized access" have "obtain[ed]... information from any protected computer." Because "protected computer" is defined as a computer affected by or involved in interstate commerce — effectively all computers with Internet access — the government's interpretation of "exceeds authorized access" makes every violation of a private computer use policy a federal crime. *See id.* § 1030(e)(2)(B).

32   The government argues that our ruling today would construe "exceeds authorized access" only in subsection 1030(a)(4), and we could give the phrase a narrower meaning when we construe other subsections. This is just not so: Once we define the phrase for the purpose of subsection 1030(a)(4), that definition must apply equally to the rest of the statute pursuant to the "standard principle of statutory construction ... that identical words and phrases within the same statute should normally be given the same meaning." *[...]* The phrase appears five times in the first seven subsections of the statute, including subsection 1030(a)(2)(C). *See* 18 U.S.C. § 1030(a)(1), (2), (4) and (7). Giving a different interpretation to each is impossible because Congress provided a *single* definition of "exceeds authorized access" for all iterations of the statutory phrase. *See id.* § 1030(e)(6). Congress obviously meant "exceeds authorized access" to have the same meaning throughout section 1030. We must therefore consider how the interpretation we adopt will operate wherever in that section the phrase appears.

33   In the case of the CFAA, the broadest provision is subsection 1030(a)(2)(C), which makes it a crime to exceed authorized access of a computer connected to the Internet *without* any culpable intent. Were we to adopt the government's proposed interpretation, millions of unsuspecting individuals would find that they are engaging in criminal conduct.

34   [...] Minds have wandered since the beginning of time and the computer gives employees new ways to procrastinate, by gchatting with friends, playing games, shopping or watching sports highlights. Such activities are routinely prohibited by many computer-use policies, although employees are seldom disciplined for occasional use of work computers for personal purposes. Nevertheless, under the broad interpretation of the CFAA, such minor dalliances would become federal crimes. While it's unlikely that you'll be prosecuted for watching Reason.TV on your work computer, you *could* be. Employers wanting to rid themselves of troublesome employees without following proper procedures could threaten to report them to the FBI unless they quit.[6] Ubiquitous, seldom-prosecuted crimes invite arbitrary and discriminatory enforcement.[7]

35   Employer-employee and company-consumer relationships are traditionally governed by tort and contract law; the government's proposed interpretation of the CFAA allows private parties to manipulate their computer-use and personnel policies so as to turn these relationships into ones policed by the criminal law. Significant notice problems arise if we allow criminal liability to turn on the vagaries of private polices that are lengthy, opaque, subject to change and seldom read. Consider the typical corporate policy that computers can be used only for business purposes. What exactly is a "nonbusiness purpose"? If you use the computer to check the weather report for a business trip? For the company softball game? For your vacation to Hawaii? And if minor personal uses are tolerated, how can an employee be on notice of what constitutes a violation sufficient to trigger criminal liability?

36   Basing criminal liability on violations of private computer use polices can transform whole categories of otherwise innocuous behavior into federal crimes simply because a computer is involved. Employees who call family members from their work phones will become criminals if they send an email instead. Employees can sneak in the sports section of the *New York Times* to read at work, but they'd better not visit ESPN.com. And sudoku enthusiasts should stick to the printed puzzles, because visiting www.dailysudoku.com from their work computers might give them more than enough time to hone their sudoku skills behind bars.

37   The effect this broad construction of the CFAA has on workplace conduct pales by [...] comparison with its effect on everyone else who uses a computer, smart-phone, iPad, Kindle, Nook, X-box, Blu-Ray player or any other Internet-enabled device. The Internet is a means for communicating via computers: Whenever we access a web page, commence a download, post a message on somebody's Facebook wall, shop on Amazon, bid on eBay, publish a blog, rate a movie on IMDb, read www.NYT.com, watch YouTube and do the thousands of other things we routinely do online, we are using one computer to send commands to other computers at remote locations. Our access to those remote computers is governed by a series of private agreements and policies that most people are only dimly aware of and virtually no one reads or understands.[8]

38   For example, it's not widely known that, up until very recently, Google forbade minors from using its services. *See* Google Terms of Service, effective April 16, 2007 — March 1, 2012, § 2.3, http://www.google.com/intl/en/policies/terms/archive/20070416 ("You may not use the Services and may not accept the Terms if ... you are not of legal age to form a binding contract with Google....") (last visited Mar. 4, 2012).[9] Adopting the government's interpretation would turn vast numbers of teens and pre-teens into juvenile delinquents — and their parents and teachers into delinquency contributors. Similarly, Facebook makes it a violation of the terms of service to let anyone log into your account. *See* Facebook Statement of Rights and Responsibilities § 4.8 http://www.facebook.com/legal/terms ("You will not share your password, ... let anyone else access your account, or do anything else that might jeopardize the security of your account.") (last visited Mar. 4, 2012). Yet it's very common for people to let close friends and relatives check their email or access their online accounts. Some may be aware that, if discovered, they may suffer a rebuke from the ISP or a loss of access, but few imagine they might be marched off to federal prison for doing so.

39   Or consider the numerous dating websites whose terms of use prohibit inaccurate or misleading information. *See, e.g.,* eHarmony Terms of Service § 2(I), http://www.eharmony.com/about/terms ("You will not provide inaccurate, misleading or false information to eHarmony or to any other user.") (last visited Mar. 4, 2012). Or eBay and Craigslist, where it's a violation of the terms of use to post items in an [...] inappropriate category. *See, e.g.,* eBay User Agreement, http://pages.ebay.com/help/policies/user-agreement.html ("While using eBay sites, services and tools, you will not: post content or items in an inappropriate category or areas on our sites and services ....") (last visited Mar. 4, 2012). Under the government's proposed interpretation of the CFAA, posting for sale an item prohibited by Craigslist's policy, or describing yourself as "tall, dark and handsome," when you're actually short and homely, will earn you a handsome orange jumpsuit.

40   Not only are the terms of service vague and generally unknown — unless you look real hard at the small print at the bottom of a webpage — but website owners retain the right to change the terms at any time and without notice. *See, e.g.,* YouTube Terms of Service § 1.B, http://www.youtube.com/t/terms ("YouTube may, in its sole discretion, modify or revise these Terms of Service and policies at any time, and you agree to be bound by such modifications or revisions.") (last visited Mar. 4, 2012). Accordingly, behavior that wasn't criminal yesterday can become criminal today without an act of Congress, and without any notice whatsoever.

41   The government assures us that, whatever the scope of the CFAA, it won't prosecute minor violations. But we shouldn't have to live at the

mercy of our local prosecutor. *Cf. United States v. Stevens*, ___ U.S. ___, 130 S.Ct. 1577, 1591, 176 L.Ed.2d 435 (2010) ("We would not uphold an unconstitutional statute merely because the Government promised to use it responsibly."). And it's not clear we *can* trust the government when a tempting target comes along. Take the case of the mom who posed as a 17-year-old boy and cyber-bullied her daughter's classmate. The Justice Department prosecuted her under 18 U.S.C. § 1030(a)(2)(C) for violating MySpace's terms of service, which prohibited lying about identifying information, including age. *See United States v. Drew*, 259 F.R.D. 449 (C.D.Cal.2009). Lying on social media websites is common: People shave years off their age, add inches to their height and drop pounds from their weight. The difference between puffery and prosecution may depend on whether you happen to be someone an AUSA has reason to go after.

42   In *United States v. Kozminski*, 487 U.S. 931, 108 S.Ct. 2751, 101 L.Ed.2d 788 (1988), the Supreme Court refused to adopt the government's broad interpretation of a statute because it would "criminalize a broad range of day-to-day activity." *Id.* at 949, 108 S.Ct. 2751. Applying the rule of lenity, the Court warned that the broader statutory interpretation would "delegate to prosecutors and juries the inherently legislative task of determining what type of ... activities are so morally reprehensible that they should be punished as crimes" and would "subject individuals to the risk of arbitrary or discriminatory prosecution and conviction." *Id.* By giving that much power to prosecutors, we're inviting discriminatory and arbitrary enforcement.

43   We remain unpersuaded by the decisions of our sister circuits that interpret the CFAA broadly to cover violations of corporate computer use restrictions or violations of a duty of loyalty. *[...]* These courts looked only at the culpable behavior of the defendants before them, and failed to consider the effect on millions of ordinary citizens caused by the statute's unitary definition of "exceeds authorized access." They therefore failed to apply the long-standing principle that we must *[...]* construe ambiguous criminal statutes narrowly so as to avoid "making criminal law in Congress's stead." *[...]*

44   We therefore respectfully decline to follow our sister circuits and urge them to reconsider instead. For our part, we continue to follow in the path blazed by *Brekka*, 581 F.3d 1127, and the growing number of courts that have reached the same conclusion. These courts recognize that the plain language of the CFAA "target[s] the unauthorized procurement or alteration of information, not its misuse or misappropriation." *[...]*

45   ## CONCLUSION

46   We need not decide today whether Congress *could* base criminal liability on violations of a company or website's computer use restrictions. Instead, we hold that the phrase "exceeds authorized access" in the CFAA does not extend to violations of use restrictions. If Congress wants to incorporate misappropriation liability into the CFAA, it must speak more clearly. The rule of lenity requires "penal laws ... to be construed strictly." *[...]*

47   The rule of lenity not only ensures that citizens will have fair notice of the criminal laws, but also that Congress will have fair notice of what conduct its laws criminalize. We construe criminal statutes narrowly so that Congress will not unintentionally turn ordinary citizens into criminals. *[...]* "If there is any doubt about whether Congress intended [the CFAA] to prohibit the conduct in which [Nosal] engaged, then `we must choose the interpretation least likely to impose penalties unintended by Congress.'" *[...]*

48   This narrower interpretation is also a more sensible reading of the text and legislative history of a statute whose general purpose is to punish hacking — the circumvention of technological access barriers — not misappropriation of trade secrets — a subject Congress has dealt with elsewhere. *See supra* note 3. Therefore, we hold that *[...]* "exceeds authorized access" in the CFAA is limited to violations of restrictions on *access* to information, and not restrictions on its *use*.

49   Because Nosal's accomplices had permission to access the company database and obtain the information contained within, the government's charges fail to meet the element of "without authorization, or exceeds authorized access" under 18 U.S.C. § 1030(a)(4). Accordingly, we affirm the judgment of the district court dismissing counts 2 and 4-7 for failure to state an offense. The government may, of course, prosecute Nosal on the remaining counts of the indictment. *Nosal was convicted on the other counts, which included violation of the federal trade secrets laws.*

50   AFFIRMED.

51   [...]

68   [1] The opening screen of the database also included the warning: "This product is intended to be used by Korn/Ferry employees for work on Korn/Ferry business only."

69   [...]

71   [4] The government fails to acknowledge that its own construction of "exceeds authorized access" suffers from the same flaw of superfluity by rendering an entire element of subsection 1030(a)(4) meaningless. Subsection 1030(a)(4) requires a person to (1) knowingly and (2) with intent to defraud (3) access a protected computer (4) without authorization or exceeding authorized access (5) in order to further the intended fraud. *See* 18 U.S.C. § 1030(a)(4). Using a computer to defraud the company necessarily contravenes company policy. Therefore, if someone accesses a computer with intent to defraud — satisfying elements (2) and (3) — he would invariably satisfy (4) under the government's definition.

72   [5] Although the legislative history of the CFAA discusses this anti-hacking purpose, and says nothing about exceeding authorized use of information, the government claims that the legislative history supports its interpretation. It points to an earlier version of the statute, which defined "exceeds authorized access" as "having accessed a computer with authorization, uses the opportunity such access provides for purposes to which such authorization does not extend." Pub. L. No. 99-474, § 2(c), 100 Stat. 1213 (1986). But *that* language was removed and replaced by the current phrase and definition. And Senators Mathias and Leahy — members of the Senate Judiciary Committee — explained that the purpose of replacing the original broader language was to "remove[] from the sweep of the statute one of the murkier grounds of liability, under which a[n] ... employee's access to computerized data might be legitimate in some circumstances, but criminal in other (not clearly distinguishable) circumstances." S.Rep. No. 99-432, at 21, 1986 U.S.C.C.A.N. 2479 at 2494. Were there any need to rely on legislative history, it would seem to support Nosal's position rather than the government's.

73   [6] Enforcement of the CFAA against minor workplace dalliances is not chimerical. Employers have invoked the CFAA against employees in civil cases. In a recent Florida case, after an employee sued her employer for wrongful termination, the company counterclaimed that plaintiff violated section 1030(a)(2)(C) by making personal use of the Internet at work — checking Facebook and sending personal email — in violation of company policy. *[...]*

74   [7] This concern persists even if intent to defraud is required. Suppose an employee spends six hours tending his FarmVille stable on his work computer. The employee has full access to his computer and the Internet, but the company has a policy that work computers may be used only for business purposes. The employer should be able to fire the employee, but that's quite different from having him arrested as a federal criminal. Yet, under the government's construction of the statute, the employee "exceeds authorized access" by using the computer for non-work activities. Given that the employee deprives his company of six hours of work a day, an aggressive prosecutor might claim that he's defrauding the company, and thereby violating section 1030(a)(4).

75   [8] *See, e.g.,* Craigslist Terms of Use (http://www.craigslist.org/about/terms.of.use), eBay User Agreement (http://pages.ebay.com/help/policies/user-agreement.html?rt=nc), eHarmony Terms of Service (http://www.eharmony.com/about/terms), Facebook Statement of Rights and Responsibilities (http://www.facebook.com/#!/legal/terms), Google Terms of Service (http://www.google.com/intl/en/policies/terms/), Hulu Terms of Use (http://www.hulu.com/terms), IMDb Conditions of Use (http://www.imdb.com/help/show_article?conditions), JDate Terms and Conditions of Service (http://www.jdate.com/Applications/Article/ArticleView.aspx?CategoryID=1948&ArticleID;=6498&HideNav;=True#service), LinkedIn User Agreement (http://www.linkedin.com/static?key=user_agreement), Match.com Terms of Use Agreement (http://www.match.com/registration/membagr.aspx?lid=4), MySpace.com Terms of Use Agreement (http://www.myspace.com/Help/Terms?pm_cmp=ed_footer), Netflix Terms of Use (https://signup.netflix.com/TermsOfUse), Pandora Terms of Use (http://www.pandora.com/legal), Spotify Terms and Conditions of Use

(http://www.spotify.com/us/legal/end-user-agreement/), Twitter Terms of Service (http://twitter.com/tos), Wikimedia Terms of Use (http://wikimediafoundation.org/wiki/Terms_of_use) and YouTube Terms of Service (http://www.youtube.com/t/terms).

76   [...]

Class 22: 8.4 <u>OIL Casebook: Digital Locks I</u>

Digital Millenium Copyright Act: 17 U.S. Code § 1201 - Circumvention of copyright protection systems

September 09, 2014 by mrisch

1

(a) Violations Regarding Circumvention of Technological Measures.—

(1)

(A) No person shall circumvent a technological measure that effectively controls access to a work protected under this title. The prohibition contained in the preceding sentence shall take effect at the end of the 2-year period beginning on the date of the enactment of this chapter.

(B) The prohibition contained in subparagraph (A) shall not apply to persons who are users of a copyrighted work which is in a particular class of works, if such persons are, or are likely to be in the succeeding 3-year period, adversely affected by virtue of such prohibition in their ability to make noninfringing uses of that particular class of works under this title, as determined under subparagraph (C).

(C) During the 2-year period described in subparagraph (A), and during each succeeding 3-year period, the Librarian of Congress, upon the recommendation of the Register of Copyrights, who shall consult with the Assistant Secretary for Communications and Information of the Department of Commerce and report and comment on his or her views in making such recommendation, shall make the determination in a rulemaking proceeding for purposes of subparagraph (B) of whether persons who are users of a copyrighted work are, or are likely to be in the succeeding 3-year period, adversely affected by the prohibition under subparagraph (A) in their ability to make noninfringing uses under this title of a particular class of copyrighted works. In conducting such rulemaking, the Librarian shall examine—

(i) the availability for use of copyrighted works;

(ii) the availability for use of works for nonprofit archival, preservation, and educational purposes;

(iii) the impact that the prohibition on the circumvention of technological measures applied to copyrighted works has on criticism, comment, news reporting, teaching, scholarship, or research;

(iv) the effect of circumvention of technological measures on the market for or value of copyrighted works; and

(v) such other factors as the Librarian considers appropriate.

(D) The Librarian shall publish any class of copyrighted works for which the Librarian has determined, pursuant to the rulemaking conducted under subparagraph (C), that noninfringing uses by persons who are users of a copyrighted work are, or are likely to be, adversely affected, and the prohibition contained in subparagraph (A) shall not apply to such users with respect to such class of works for the ensuing 3-year period.

(E) Neither the exception under subparagraph (B) from the applicability of the prohibition contained in subparagraph (A), nor any determination made in a rulemaking conducted under subparagraph (C), may be used as a defense in any action to enforce any provision of this title other than this paragraph.

(2) No person shall manufacture, import, offer to the public, provide, or otherwise traffic in any technology, product, service, device, component, or part thereof, that—

(A) is primarily designed or produced for the purpose of circumventing a technological measure that effectively controls access to a work protected under this title;

(B) has only limited commercially significant purpose or use other than to circumvent a technological measure that effectively

823

controls access to a work protected under this title; or

(C) is marketed by that person or another acting in concert with that person with that person's knowledge for use in circumventing a technological measure that effectively controls access to a work protected under this title.

(3) As used in this subsection—

(A) to "circumvent a technological measure" means to descramble a scrambled work, to decrypt an encrypted work, or otherwise to avoid, bypass, remove, deactivate, or impair a technological measure, without the authority of the copyright owner; and

(B) a technological measure "effectively controls access to a work" if the measure, in the ordinary course of its operation, requires the application of information, or a process or a treatment, with the authority of the copyright owner, to gain access to the work.

2   **(b) Additional Violations.—**

(1) No person shall manufacture, import, offer to the public, provide, or otherwise traffic in any technology, product, service, device, component, or part thereof, that—

(A) is primarily designed or produced for the purpose of circumventing protection afforded by a technological measure that effectively protects a right of a copyright owner under this title in a work or a portion thereof;

(B) has only limited commercially significant purpose or use other than to circumvent protection afforded by a technological measure that effectively protects a right of a copyright owner under this title in a work or a portion thereof; or

(C) is marketed by that person or another acting in concert with that person with that person's knowledge for use in circumventing protection afforded by a technological measure that effectively protects a right of a copyright owner under this title in a work or a portion thereof.

(2) As used in this subsection—

(A) to "circumvent protection afforded by a technological measure" means avoiding, bypassing, removing, deactivating, or otherwise impairing a technological measure; and

(B) a technological measure "effectively protects a right of a copyright owner under this title" if the measure, in the ordinary course of its operation, prevents, restricts, or otherwise limits the exercise of a right of a copyright owner under this title.

3   **(c)** Other Rights, Etc., Not Affected.—(1) Nothing in this section shall affect rights, remedies, limitations, or defenses to copyright infringement, including fair use, under this title.

(2) Nothing in this section shall enlarge or diminish vicarious or contributory liability for copyright infringement in connection with any technology, product, service, device, component, or part thereof.

(3) Nothing in this section shall require that the design of, or design and selection of parts and components for, a consumer electronics, telecommunications, or computing product provide for a response to any particular technological measure, so long as such part or component, or the product in which such part or component is integrated, does not otherwise fall within the prohibitions of subsection (a)(2) or (b)(1).

(4) Nothing in this section shall enlarge or diminish any rights of free speech or the press for activities using consumer electronics, telecommunications, or computing products.

4   **(d) Exemption for Nonprofit Libraries, Archives, and Educational Institutions.—**

(1) A nonprofit library, archives, or educational institution which gains access to a commercially exploited copyrighted work solely in order to make a good faith determination of whether to acquire a copy of that work for the sole purpose of engaging in conduct permitted under this title shall not be in violation of subsection (a)(1)(A). A copy of a work to which access has been gained under this paragraph—

(A) may not be retained longer than necessary to make such good faith determination; and

(B) may not be used for any other purpose.

(2) The exemption made available under paragraph (1) shall only apply with respect to a work when an identical copy of that work is not reasonably available in another form.

(3) A nonprofit library, archives, or educational institution that willfully for the purpose of commercial advantage or financial gain violates paragraph (1)—

  (A) shall, for the first offense, be subject to the civil remedies under section 1203; and

  (B) shall, for repeated or subsequent offenses, in addition to the civil remedies under section 1203, forfeit the exemption provided under paragraph (1).

(4) This subsection may not be used as a defense to a claim under subsection (a)(2) or (b), nor may this subsection permit a nonprofit library, archives, or educational institution to manufacture, import, offer to the public, provide, or otherwise traffic in any technology, product, service, component, or part thereof, which circumvents a technological measure.

(5) In order for a library or archives to qualify for the exemption under this subsection, the collections of that library or archives shall be —

  (A) open to the public; or

  (B) available not only to researchers affiliated with the library or archives or with the institution of which it is a part, but also to other persons doing research in a specialized field.

5 **(e) Law Enforcement, Intelligence, and Other Government Activities.—** This section does not prohibit any lawfully authorized investigative, protective, information security, or intelligence activity of an officer, agent, or employee of the United States, a State, or a political subdivision of a State, or a person acting pursuant to a contract with the United States, a State, or a political subdivision of a State. For purposes of this subsection, the term "information security" means activities carried out in order to identify and address the vulnerabilities of a government computer, computer system, or computer network.

6 **(f) Reverse Engineering.—**

  (1) Notwithstanding the provisions of subsection (a)(1)(A), a person who has lawfully obtained the right to use a copy of a computer program may circumvent a technological measure that effectively controls access to a particular portion of that program for the sole purpose of identifying and analyzing those elements of the program that are necessary to achieve interoperability of an independently created computer program with other programs, and that have not previously been readily available to the person engaging in the circumvention, to the extent any such acts of identification and analysis do not constitute infringement under this title.

  (2) Notwithstanding the provisions of subsections (a)(2) and (b), a person may develop and employ technological means to circumvent a technological measure, or to circumvent protection afforded by a technological measure, in order to enable the identification and analysis under paragraph (1), or for the purpose of enabling interoperability of an independently created computer program with other programs, if such means are necessary to achieve such interoperability, to the extent that doing so does not constitute infringement under this title.

  (3) The information acquired through the acts permitted under paragraph (1), and the means permitted under paragraph (2), may be made available to others if the person referred to in paragraph (1) or (2), as the case may be, provides such information or means solely for the purpose of enabling interoperability of an independently created computer program with other programs, and to the extent that doing so does not constitute infringement under this title or violate applicable law other than this section.

  (4) For purposes of this subsection, the term "interoperability" means the ability of computer programs to exchange information, and of such programs mutually to use the information which has been exchanged.

7 **(g) Encryption Research.—**

  (1) Definitions.— For purposes of this subsection—

  (A) the term "encryption research" means activities necessary to identify and analyze flaws and vulnerabilities of encryption technologies applied to copyrighted works, if these activities are conducted to advance the state of knowledge in the field of encryption technology or to assist in the development of encryption products; and

(B) the term "encryption technology" means the scrambling and descrambling of information using mathematical formulas or algorithms.

(2) Permissible acts of encryption research.— Notwithstanding the provisions of subsection (a)(1)(A), it is not a violation of that subsection for a person to circumvent a technological measure as applied to a copy, phonorecord, performance, or display of a published work in the course of an act of good faith encryption research if—

(A) the person lawfully obtained the encrypted copy, phonorecord, performance, or display of the published work;

(B) such act is necessary to conduct such encryption research;

(C) the person made a good faith effort to obtain authorization before the circumvention; and

(D) such act does not constitute infringement under this title or a violation of applicable law other than this section, including section 1030 of title 18 and those provisions of title 18 amended by the Computer Fraud and Abuse Act of 1986.

(3) Factors in determining exemption.— In determining whether a person qualifies for the exemption under paragraph (2), the factors to be considered shall include—

(A) whether the information derived from the encryption research was disseminated, and if so, whether it was disseminated in a manner reasonably calculated to advance the state of knowledge or development of encryption technology, versus whether it was disseminated in a manner that facilitates infringement under this title or a violation of applicable law other than this section, including a violation of privacy or breach of security;

(B) whether the person is engaged in a legitimate course of study, is employed, or is appropriately trained or experienced, in the field of encryption technology; and

(C) whether the person provides the copyright owner of the work to which the technological measure is applied with notice of the findings and documentation of the research, and the time when such notice is provided.

(4) Use of technological means for research activities.— Notwithstanding the provisions of subsection (a)(2), it is not a violation of that subsection for a person to—

(A) develop and employ technological means to circumvent a technological measure for the sole purpose of that person performing the acts of good faith encryption research described in paragraph (2); and

(B) provide the technological means to another person with whom he or she is working collaboratively for the purpose of conducting the acts of good faith encryption research described in paragraph (2) or for the purpose of having that other person verify his or her acts of good faith encryption research described in paragraph (2).

(5) Report to congress.— Not later than 1 year after the date of the enactment of this chapter, the Register of Copyrights and the Assistant Secretary for Communications and Information of the Department of Commerce shall jointly report to the Congress on the effect this subsection has had on—

(A) encryption research and the development of encryption technology;

(B) the adequacy and effectiveness of technological measures designed to protect copyrighted works; and

(C) protection of copyright owners against the unauthorized access to their encrypted copyrighted works.

The report shall include legislative recommendations, if any.

8 **(h) Exceptions Regarding Minors.—** In applying subsection (a) to a component or part, the court may consider the necessity for its intended and actual incorporation in a technology, product, service, or device, which—

(1) does not itself violate the provisions of this title; and

(2) has the sole purpose to prevent the access of minors to material on the Internet.

9 **(i) Protection of Personally Identifying Information.—**

(1) Circumvention permitted.— Notwithstanding the provisions of subsection (a)(1)(A), it is not a violation of that subsection for a person to circumvent a technological measure that effectively controls access to a work protected under this title, if—

(A) the technological measure, or the work it protects, contains the capability of collecting or disseminating personally identifying information reflecting the online activities of a natural person who seeks to gain access to the work protected;

(B) in the normal course of its operation, the technological measure, or the work it protects, collects or disseminates personally identifying information about the person who seeks to gain access to the work protected, without providing conspicuous notice of such collection or dissemination to such person, and without providing such person with the capability to prevent or restrict such collection or dissemination;

(C) the act of circumvention has the sole effect of identifying and disabling the capability described in subparagraph (A), and has no other effect on the ability of any person to gain access to any work; and

(D) the act of circumvention is carried out solely for the purpose of preventing the collection or dissemination of personally identifying information about a natural person who seeks to gain access to the work protected, and is not in violation of any other law.

(2) Inapplicability to certain technological measures.— This subsection does not apply to a technological measure, or a work it protects, that does not collect or disseminate personally identifying information and that is disclosed to a user as not having or using such capability.

10   **(j) Security Testing.—**

(1) Definition.— For purposes of this subsection, the term "security testing" means accessing a computer, computer system, or computer network, solely for the purpose of good faith testing, investigating, or correcting, a security flaw or vulnerability, with the authorization of the owner or operator of such computer, computer system, or computer network.

(2) Permissible acts of security testing.— Notwithstanding the provisions of subsection (a)(1)(A), it is not a violation of that subsection for a person to engage in an act of security testing, if such act does not constitute infringement under this title or a violation of applicable law other than this section, including section 1030 of title 18and those provisions of title 18 amended by the Computer Fraud and Abuse Act of 1986.

(3) Factors in determining exemption.— In determining whether a person qualifies for the exemption under paragraph (2), the factors to be considered shall include—

(A) whether the information derived from the security testing was used solely to promote the security of the owner or operator of such computer, computer system or computer network, or shared directly with the developer of such computer, computer system, or computer network; and

(B) whether the information derived from the security testing was used or maintained in a manner that does not facilitate infringement under this title or a violation of applicable law other than this section, including a violation of privacy or breach of security.

(4) Use of technological means for security testing.— Notwithstanding the provisions of subsection (a)(2), it is not a violation of that subsection for a person to develop, produce, distribute or employ technological means for the sole purpose of performing the acts of security testing described in subsection (2), [1] provided such technological means does not otherwise violate section [2] (a)(2).

11   **(k) Certain Analog Devices and Certain Technological Measures.—**

(1) Certain analog devices.—

(A) Effective 18 months after the date of the enactment of this chapter, no person shall manufacture, import, offer to the public, provide or otherwise traffic in any—

(i) VHS format analog video cassette recorder unless such recorder conforms to the automatic gain control copy control technology;

(ii) 8mm format analog video cassette camcorder unless such camcorder conforms to the automatic gain control technology;

(iii) Beta format analog video cassette recorder, unless such recorder conforms to the automatic gain control copy control technology, except that this requirement shall not apply until there are 1,000 Beta format analog video cassette recorders sold in the United States in any one calendar year after the date of the enactment of this chapter;

(iv) 8mm format analog video cassette recorder that is not an analog video cassette camcorder, unless such recorder conforms to the automatic gain control copy control technology, except that this requirement shall not apply until there are 20,000 such recorders sold in the United States in any one calendar year after the date of the enactment of this chapter; or

(v) analog video cassette recorder that records using an NTSC format video input and that is not otherwise covered under clauses (i) through (iv), unless such device conforms to the automatic gain control copy control technology.

(B) Effective on the date of the enactment of this chapter, no person shall manufacture, import, offer to the public, provide or otherwise traffic in—

(i) any VHS format analog video cassette recorder or any 8mm format analog video cassette recorder if the design of the model of such recorder has been modified after such date of enactment so that a model of recorder that previously conformed to the automatic gain control copy control technology no longer conforms to such technology; or

(ii) any VHS format analog video cassette recorder, or any 8mm format analog video cassette recorder that is not an 8mm analog video cassette camcorder, if the design of the model of such recorder has been modified after such date of enactment so that a model of recorder that previously conformed to the four-line colorstripe copy control technology no longer conforms to such technology.

Manufacturers that have not previously manufactured or sold a VHS format analog video cassette recorder, or an 8mm format analog cassette recorder, shall be required to conform to the four-line colorstripe copy control technology in the initial model of any such recorder manufactured after the date of the enactment of this chapter, and thereafter to continue conforming to the four-line colorstripe copy control technology. For purposes of this subparagraph, an analog video cassette recorder "conforms to" the four-line colorstripe copy control technology if it records a signal that, when played back by the playback function of that recorder in the normal viewing mode, exhibits, on a reference display device, a display containing distracting visible lines through portions of the viewable picture.

(2) Certain encoding restrictions.— No person shall apply the automatic gain control copy control technology or colorstripe copy control technology to prevent or limit consumer copying except such copying—

(A) of a single transmission, or specified group of transmissions, of live events or of audiovisual works for which a member of the public has exercised choice in selecting the transmissions, including the content of the transmissions or the time of receipt of such transmissions, or both, and as to which such member is charged a separate fee for each such transmission or specified group of transmissions;

(B) from a copy of a transmission of a live event or an audiovisual work if such transmission is provided by a channel or service where payment is made by a member of the public for such channel or service in the form of a subscription fee that entitles the member of the public to receive all of the programming contained in such channel or service;

(C) from a physical medium containing one or more prerecorded audiovisual works; or

(D) from a copy of a transmission described in subparagraph (A) or from a copy made from a physical medium described in subparagraph (C).

In the event that a transmission meets both the conditions set forth in subparagraph (A) and those set forth in subparagraph (B), the transmission shall be treated as a transmission described in subparagraph (A).

(3) Inapplicability.— This subsection shall not—

(A) require any analog video cassette camcorder to conform to the automatic gain control copy control technology with respect to any video signal received through a camera lens;

(B) apply to the manufacture, importation, offer for sale, provision of, or other trafficking in, any professional analog video cassette recorder; or

(C) apply to the offer for sale or provision of, or other trafficking in, any previously owned analog video cassette recorder, if such recorder was legally manufactured and sold when new and not subsequently modified in violation of paragraph (1)(B).

(4) Definitions.— For purposes of this subsection:

(A) An "analog video cassette recorder" means a device that records, or a device that includes a function that records, on electromagnetic tape in an analog format the electronic impulses produced by the video and audio portions of a television program, motion picture, or other form of audiovisual work.

(B) An "analog video cassette camcorder" means an analog video cassette recorder that contains a recording function that operates through a camera lens and through a video input that may be connected with a television or other video playback device.

(C) An analog video cassette recorder "conforms" to the automatic gain control copy control technology if it—

(i) detects one or more of the elements of such technology and does not record the motion picture or transmission protected by such technology; or

(ii) records a signal that, when played back, exhibits a meaningfully distorted or degraded display.

(D) The term "professional analog video cassette recorder" means an analog video cassette recorder that is designed, manufactured, marketed, and intended for use by a person who regularly employs such a device for a lawful business or industrial use, including making, performing, displaying, distributing, or transmitting copies of motion pictures on a commercial scale.

(E) The terms "VHS format", "8mm format", "Beta format", "automatic gain control copy control technology", "colorstripe copy control technology", "four-line version of the colorstripe copy control technology", and "NTSC" have the meanings that are commonly understood in the consumer electronics and motion picture industries as of the date of the enactment of this chapter.

(5) Violations.— Any violation of paragraph (1) of this subsection shall be treated as a violation of subsection (b)(1) of this section. Any violation of paragraph (2) of this subsection shall be deemed an "act of circumvention" for the purposes of section 1203(c)(3)(A) of this chapter.

12

[1] So in original. Probably should be subsection "(a)(2),".

[2] So in original. Probably should be "subsection".

Universal City Studios, Inc. v. Reimerdes

September 09, 2014 by mrisch

1   111 F.Supp.2d 294 (2000)

2   **UNIVERSAL CITY STUDIOS, INC., et al., Plaintiffs,**

v.

Shawn C. REIMERDES, et al., Defendants.

3   [...]

4   United States District Court, S.D. New York.

5   August 17, 2000.
As Amended September 6, 2000.

6   [...]

8   **OPINION**

9   **KAPLAN, District Judge.**

10   Plaintiffs, eight major United States motion picture studios, distribute many of their copyrighted motion pictures for home use on digital versatile disks ("DVDs"), which contain copies of the motion pictures in digital form. They protect those motion pictures from copying by using an encryption system called CSS. CSS-protected motion pictures on DVDs may be viewed only on players and computer drives equipped with licensed technology that permits the devices to decrypt and play — but not to copy — the films.

11   Late last year, computer hackers devised a computer program called DeCSS that circumvents the CSS protection system and allows CSS-protected motion pictures to be copied and played on devices that lack the licensed decryption technology. Defendants quickly posted DeCSS on their Internet web site, thus making it readily available to much of the world. Plaintiffs promptly brought this action under the Digital Millennium Copyright Act (the "DMCA")[1] to enjoin defendants from posting DeCSS and to prevent them from electronically "linking" their site to others that post DeCSS. Defendants responded with what they termed "electronic civil disobedience" — increasing their efforts to link their web site to a large number of [...] others that continue to make DeCSS available.

12   Defendants contend that their actions do not violate the DMCA and, in any case, that the DMCA, as applied to computer programs, or code, violates the First Amendment.[2] This is the Court's decision after trial, and the decision may be summarized in a nutshell.

13   Defendants argue first that the DMCA should not be construed to reach their conduct, principally because the DMCA, so applied, could prevent those who wish to gain access to technologically protected copyrighted works in order to make fair — that is, non-infringing — use of them from doing so. They argue that those who would make fair use of technologically protected copyrighted works need means, such as DeCSS, of circumventing access control measures not for piracy, but to make lawful use of those works.

14 Technological access control measures have the capacity to prevent fair uses of copyrighted works as well as foul. Hence, there is a potential tension between the use of such access control measures and fair use. Defendants are not the first to recognize that possibility. As the DMCA made its way through the legislative process, Congress was preoccupied with precisely this issue. Proponents of strong restrictions on circumvention of access control measures argued that they were essential if copyright holders were to make their works available in digital form because digital works otherwise could be pirated too easily. Opponents contended that strong anti-circumvention measures would extend the copyright monopoly inappropriately and prevent many fair uses of copyrighted material.

15 Congress struck a balance. The compromise it reached, depending upon future technological and commercial developments, may or may not prove ideal.[3] But the solution it enacted is clear. The potential tension to which defendants point does not absolve them of liability under the statute. There is no serious question that defendants' posting of DeCSS violates the DMCA.

16 [...]

19 *I. The Genesis of the Controversy*

20 As this case involves computers and technology with which many are unfamiliar, it is useful to begin by defining some of the vocabulary.

21 *A. The Vocabulary of this Case*

22 *1. Computers and Operating Systems*

23 A computer is "a digital information processing device .... consist[ing] of central processing components . . . and mass data storage .... certain peripheral input/output devices . . ., and an operating system." Personal computers ("PCs") are computers designed for use by one person at a time. "[M]ore powerful, more expensive computer systems known as `servers' . . . are designed to provide data, services, and functionality through a digital network to multiple users."[4]

24 An operating system is "a software program that controls the allocation and use of computer resources (such as central processing unit time, main memory space, disk space, and input/output channels). The operating system also supports the functions of software programs, called `applications,' that perform specific user-oriented tasks.... Because it supports applications while interacting more closely with the PC system's hardware, the operating system is said to serve as a `platform.'"[5]

25 Microsoft Windows ("Windows") is an operating system released by Microsoft Corp. It is the most widely used operating system for PCs in the United States, and its versions include Windows 95, Windows 98, Windows NT and Windows 2000.

26 Linux, which was and continues to be developed through the open source model of software development,[6] also is an operating system. [7] It can be run on a PC as an alternative to Windows, although the extent to which it is so used is limited.[8] Linux is more widely used on servers.[9]

27 *2. Computer Code*

28 "[C]omputers come down to one basic premise: They operate with a series of on and off switches, using two digits in the binary (base 2) number system — 0 (for off) and 1 (for on)."[10] All data and instructions input to or contained in computers therefore must be reduced the numerals 1 and 0.[11]

29 "The smallest unit of memory in a computer," a bit, "is a switch with a value of [306] 0(off) or 1(on)."[12] A group of eight bits is called a byte and represents a character — a letter or an integer.[13] A kilobyte ("K") is 1024 bytes, a megabyte ("MB") 1024 kilobytes, and a gigabyte ("GB") 1024 megabytes.[14]

30   Some highly skilled human beings can reduce data and instructions to strings of 1's and 0's and thus program computers to perform complex tasks by inputting commands and data in that form.[15] But it would be inconvenient, inefficient and, for most people, probably impossible to do so. In consequence, computer science has developed programming languages. These languages, like other written languages, employ symbols and syntax to convey meaning. The text of programs written in these languages is referred to as source code. [16] And whether directly or through the medium of another program,[17] the sets of instructions written in programming languages — the source code — ultimately are translated into machine "readable" strings of 1's and 0's, known in the computer world as object code, which typically are executable by the computer.[18]

31   The distinction between source and object code is not as crystal clear as first appears. Depending upon the programming language, source code may contain many 1's and 0's and look a lot like object code or may contain many instructions derived from spoken human language. Programming languages the source code for which approaches object code are referred to as low level source code while those that are more similar to spoken language are referred to as high level source code.

32   All code is human readable. As source code is closer to human language than is object code, it tends to be comprehended more easily by humans than object code.

33   **3. The Internet and the World Wide Web**

34   The Internet is "a global electronic network, consisting of smaller, interconnected networks, [...]

40   **4. Portable Storage Media**

41   Digital files may be stored on several different kinds of storage media, some of which are readily transportable. Perhaps the most familiar of these are so called floppy disks or "floppies," which now are 3½ inch magnetic disks upon which digital files may be recorded.[25] For present purposes, however, we are concerned principally with two more recent developments, CD-ROMs and digital versatile disks, or DVDs.

42   A CD-ROM is a five-inch wide optical disk capable of storing approximately 650 MB of data. To read the data on a CD-ROM, a computer must have a CD-ROM drive.

43   DVDs are five-inch wide disks capable of storing more than 4.7 GB of data. In the application relevant here, they are used to hold full-length motion pictures in digital form. They are the latest technology for private home viewing of recorded motion pictures and result in drastically improved audio and visual clarity and quality of motion pictures shown on televisions or computer screens.[26]

44   [...]**5. The Technology Here at Issue**

45   CSS, or Content Scramble System, is an access control and copy prevention system for DVDs developed by the motion picture companies, including plaintiffs.[27] It is an encryption-based system that requires the use of appropriately configured hardware such as a DVD player or a computer DVD drive to decrypt, unscramble and play back, but not copy, motion pictures on DVDs.[28] The technology necessary to configure DVD players and drives to play CSS-protected DVDs[29] has been licensed to hundreds of manufacturers in the United States and around the world.

46   DeCSS is a software utility, or computer program, that enables users to break the CSS copy protection system and hence to view DVDs on unlicensed players and make digital copies of DVD movies.[30] The quality of motion pictures decrypted by DeCSS is virtually identical to that of encrypted movies on DVD.[31]

47   DivX is a compression program available for download over the Internet.[32] It compresses video files in order to minimize required

storage space, often to facilitate transfer over The Internet or other networks.[33]

48   **B. Parties**

49   Plaintiffs are eight major motion picture studios. Each is in the business of producing and distributing copyrighted material including motion pictures. Each distributes, either directly or through affiliates, copyrighted motion pictures on DVDs.[34] Plaintiffs produce and distribute a large majority of the motion pictures on DVDs on the market today.[35]

50   Defendant Eric Corley is viewed as a leader of the computer hacker community and goes by the name Emmanuel Goldstein, after the leader of the underground in George Orwell's classic, *1984*.[36] He and his company, defendant 2600 Enterprises, Inc., together publish a magazine called *2600: The Hacker Quarterly,* which Corley founded in 1984,[37] and which is something of a bible to the hacker community.[38] The name "2600" was derived from the fact that hackers in the 1960's found that the transmission of a 2600 hertz tone over a long distance trunk connection gained access to "operator mode" and allowed the user to explore aspects of the telephone system that were not otherwise accessible.[39] Mr. Corley chose the name because he regarded it as a "mystical thing,"[40] commemorating something that he evidently admired. Not surprisingly, *2600: The Hacker Quarterly* has included articles on such topics as how to steal an Internet domain name,[41] access other people's e-mail,[42] intercept cellular phone calls,[43] and break into the computer systems [309] at Costco stores[44] and Federal Express.[45] One issue contains a guide to the federal criminal justice system for readers charged with computer hacking.[46] In addition, defendants operate a web site located at ("2600.com"), which is managed primarily by Mr. Corley and has been in existence since 1995.[47]

51   Prior to January 2000, when this action was commenced, defendants posted the source and object code for DeCSS on the 2600.com web site, from which they could be downloaded easily.[48] At that time, 2600.com contained also a list of links to other web sites purporting to post DeCSS.[49]

52   **C. The Development of DVD and CSS**

53   The major motion picture studios typically distribute films in a sequence of so-called windows, each window referring to a separate channel of distribution and thus to a separate source of revenue. The first window generally is theatrical release, distribution, and exhibition. Subsequently, films are distributed to airlines and hotels, then to the home market, then to pay television, cable and, eventually, free television broadcast. The home market is important to plaintiffs, as it represents a significant source of revenue.[50]

54   Motion pictures first were, and still are, distributed to the home market in the form of video cassette tapes. In the early 1990's, however, the major movie studios began to explore distribution to the home market in digital format, which offered substantially higher audio and visual quality and greater longevity than video cassette tapes.[51] This technology, which in 1995 became what is known today as DVD,[52] brought with it a new problem — increased risk of piracy by virtue of the fact that digital files, unlike the material on video cassettes, can be copied without degradation from generation to generation.[53] In consequence, the movie studios became concerned as the product neared market with the threat of DVD piracy.[54]

55   Discussions among the studios with the goal of organizing a unified response to the piracy threat began in earnest in late 1995 or early 1996.[55] They eventually came to include representatives of the consumer electronics and computer industries, as well as interested members of the public,[56] and focused on both legislative proposals and technological solutions.[57] In 1996, Matsushita Electric Industrial Co. ("MEI") and Toshiba Corp., presented — and the studios adopted — CSS.[58]

56   CSS involves encrypting, according to an encryption algorithm,[59] the digital [310] sound and graphics files on a DVD that together constitute a motion picture. A CSS-protected DVD can be decrypted by an appropriate decryption algorithm that employs a series of keys stored on the DVD and the DVD player. In consequence, only players and drives containing the appropriate keys are able to decrypt DVD files and thereby play movies stored on DVDs.

57   As the motion picture companies did not themselves develop CSS and, in any case, are not in the business of making DVD players and drives, the technology for making compliant devices, i.e., devices with CSS keys, had to be licensed to consumer electronics manufacturers.[60] In order to ensure that the decryption technology did not become generally available and that compliant devices could not be used to copy as well as merely to play CSS-protected movies, the technology is licensed subject to strict security requirements. [61] Moreover, manufacturers may not, consistent with their licenses, make equipment that would supply digital output that could be used in copying protected DVDs.[62] Licenses to manufacture compliant devices are granted on a royalty-free basis subject only to an administrative fee.[63] At the time of trial, licenses had been issued to numerous hardware and software manufacturers, including two companies that plan to release DVD players for computers running the Linux operating system.[64]

58   With CSS in place, the studios introduced DVDs on the consumer market in early 1997.[65] All or most of the motion pictures released on DVD were, and continue to be, encrypted with CSS technology.[66] [...]

59   DVDs have proven not only popular, but lucrative for the studios. Revenue from their sale and rental currently accounts for a substantial percentage of the movie studios' revenue from the home video market.[69] Revenue from the home market, in [311] turn, makes up a large percentage of the studios' total distribution revenue.[70]

60   **D. The Appearance of DeCSS**

61   In late September 1999, Jon Johansen, a Norwegian subject then fifteen years of age, and two individuals he "met" under pseudonyms over the Internet, reverse engineered a licensed DVD player and discovered the CSS encryption algorithm and keys.[71] They used this information to create DeCSS, a program capable of decrypting or "ripping" encrypted DVDs, thereby allowing playback on non-compliant computers as well as the copying of decrypted files to computer hard drives.[72] Mr. Johansen then posted the executable code on his personal Internet web site and informed members of an Internet mailing list that he had done so.[73] Neither Mr. Johansen nor his collaborators obtained a license from the DVD CCA.[74]

62   Although Mr. Johansen testified at trial that he created DeCSS in order to make a DVD player that would operate on a computer running the Linux operating system,[75] DeCSS is a Windows executable file; that is, it can be executed only on computers running the Windows operating system.[76] Mr. Johansen explained the fact that he created a Windows rather than a Linux program by asserting that Linux, at the time he created DeCSS, did not support the file system used on DVDs.[77] Hence, it was necessary, he said, to decrypt the DVD on a Windows computer in order subsequently to play the decrypted files on a Linux machine.[78] Assuming that to be true,[79] however, the fact remains that Mr. Johansen created DeCSS in the full knowledge that it could be used on computers running Windows rather than Linux. Moreover, he was well aware that the files, once decrypted, could be copied like any other computer files.

63   In January 1999, Norwegian prosecutors filed charges against Mr. Johansen stemming from the development of DeCSS.[80] The disposition of the Norwegian case does not appear of record.   *Johansen was acquitted after trial in Norway. Norway did not have a version of the DMCA at issue here at the time.*

64   **E. The Distribution of DeCSS**

65   In the months following its initial appearance on Mr. Johansen's web site, DeCSS has become widely available on the Internet, where hundreds of sites now purport to offer the software for download.[81] A few other applications said to decrypt CSS-encrypted DVDs also have appeared on the Internet.[82]

66   [...] In November 1999, defendants' web site began to offer DeCSS for download.[83] It established also a list of links to several web sites that purportedly "mirrored" or offered DeCSS for download.[84] The links on defendants' mirror list fall into one of three categories.

By clicking the mouse on one of these links, the user may be brought to a page on the linked-to site on which there appears a further link to the DeCSS software.[85] If the user then clicks on the DeCSS link, download of the software begins. This page may or may not contain content other than the DeCSS link.[86] Alternatively, the user may be brought to a page on the linked-to site that does not itself purport to link to DeCSS, but that links, either directly or via a series of other pages on the site, to another page on the site on which there appears a link to the DeCSS software.[87] Finally, the user may be brought directly to the DeCSS link on the linked-to site such that download of DeCSS begins immediately without further user intervention.[88]

67   *F. The Preliminary Injunction and Defendants' Response*

68   The movie studios, through the Internet investigations division of the Motion Picture Association of America ("MPAA"), became aware of the availability of DeCSS on the Internet in October 1999.[89] The industry responded by sending out a number of cease and desist letters to web site operators who posted the software, some of which removed it from their sites.[90] In January 2000, the studios filed this lawsuit against defendant Eric Corley and two others.[91]

69   After a hearing at which defendants presented no affidavits or evidentiary material, the Court granted plaintiffs' motion for a preliminary injunction barring defendants from posting DeCSS.[...]

70   Following the issuance of the preliminary injunction, defendants removed DeCSS from the 2600.com web site.[94] In what they termed an act of "electronic civil disobedience,"[95] however, they continued to support links to other web sites purporting to offer DeCSS for download, a list which had grown to nearly five hundred by July 2000.[96] Indeed, they carried a banner [...] saying "Stop the MPAA" and, in a reference to this lawsuit, proclaimed:

71   "We have to face the possibility that we could be forced into submission. For that reason it's especially important that as many of you as possible, all throughout the world, take a stand and mirror these files."[97]

72   Thus, defendants obviously hoped to frustrate plaintiffs' recourse to the judicial system by making effective relief difficult or impossible.

73   At least some of the links currently on defendants' mirror list lead the user to copies of DeCSS that, when downloaded and executed, successfully decrypt a motion picture on a CSS-encrypted DVD.[98]

74   *[...]*

81   At trial, defendants repeated, as if it were a mantra, the refrain that plaintiffs, as they stipulated,[120] have no direct evidence of a specific occasion on which any person decrypted a copyrighted motion picture with DeCSS and transmitted it over the Internet. But that is unpersuasive. Plaintiffs' expert expended very little effort to find someone in an IRC chat room who exchanged a compressed, decrypted copy of *The Matrix,* one of plaintiffs' copyrighted motion pictures, for a [...] copy of *Sleepless in Seattle.* [...]

82   The net of all this is reasonably plain. DeCSS is a free, effective and fast means of decrypting plaintiffs' DVDs and copying them to computer hard drives. [...]

83   These circumstances have two major implications for plaintiffs. First, the availability of DeCSS on the Internet effectively has compromised plaintiffs' system of copyright protection for DVDs, requiring them either to tolerate increased piracy or to expend resources to develop and implement a replacement system unless the availability of DeCSS is terminated.[126] It is analogous to the publication of a bank vault combination in a national newspaper. Even if no one uses the combination to open the vault, its mere publication has the effect of defeating the bank's security system, forcing the bank to reprogram the lock. Development and implementation of a new DVD copy protection system, however, is far more difficult and costly than reprogramming a combination lock and may carry with it the added problem of rendering the existing installed base of compliant DVD players obsolete.

84   Second, the application of DeCSS to copy and distribute motion pictures on DVD, both on CD-ROMs and via the Internet, threatens to reduce the studios' revenue from the sale and rental of DVDs. It threatens also to impede new, potentially lucrative initiatives for the distribution of motion pictures in digital form, such as video-on-demand via the Internet.[127]

85   [...]

86   **II. The Digital Millennium Copyright Act**

87   **A. Background and Structure of the Statute**

88   [...]

90   The DMCA contains two principal anti-circumvention provisions. The first, Section 1201(a)(1), governs "[t]he act of circumventing a technological protection measure put in place by a copyright owner to control access to a copyrighted work," an act described by Congress as "the electronic equivalent of breaking into a locked room in order to obtain a copy of a book."[131] The second, Section 1201(a)(2), which is the focus of this case, "supplements the prohibition against the act of circumvention in paragraph (a)(1) with prohibitions on creating and making available certain technologies ... developed or advertised to defeat technological protections against unauthorized access to a work."[132] As defendants are accused here only of posting and linking to other sites posting DeCSS, and not of using it themselves to bypass plaintiffs' access controls, it is principally the second of the anticircumvention provisions that is at issue in this case.[133]

91   **B. Posting of DeCSS**

92   **1. Violation of Anti-Trafficking Provision**

93   Section 1201(a)(2) of the Copyright Act, part of the DMCA, provides that:

94   "No person shall ... offer to the public, provide or otherwise traffic in any technology ... that —

           "(A) is primarily designed or produced for the purpose of circumventing a technological measure that effectively controls access to a work protected under [the Copyright Act];

           "(B) has only limited commercially significant purpose or use other than to circumvent a technological measure that effectively controls access to a work protected under [the Copyright Act]; or

           [...] (C) is marketed by that person or another acting in concert with that person with that person's knowledge for use in circumventing a technological measure that effectively controls access to a work protected under [the Copyright Act]."[134]

95   In this case, defendants concededly offered and provided and, absent a court order, would continue to offer and provide DeCSS to the public by making it available for download on the 2600.com web site. DeCSS, a computer program, unquestionably is "technology" within the meaning of the statute.[135] "[C]ircumvent a technological measure" is defined to mean descrambling a scrambled work, decrypting an encrypted work, or "otherwise to avoid, bypass, remove, deactivate, or impair a technological measure, without the authority of the copyright owner,"[136] so DeCSS clearly is a means of circumventing a technological access control measure.[137] In consequence, if CSS otherwise falls within paragraphs (A), (B) or (C) of Section 1201(a)(2), and if none of the statutory exceptions applies to their actions, defendants have violated and, unless enjoined, will continue to violate the DMCA by posting DeCSS.

96   **a. Section 1201(a)(2)(A)**

97   **(1) CSS Effectively Controls Access to Copyrighted Works**

98   During pretrial proceedings and at trial, defendants attacked plaintiffs' Section 1201(a)(2)(A) claim, arguing that CSS, which is based on a 40-bit encryption key, is a weak cipher that does not "effectively control" access to plaintiffs' copyrighted works. They reasoned from this premise that CSS is not protected under this branch of the statute at all. Their post-trial memorandum appears to have abandoned this argument. In any case, however, the contention is indefensible as a matter of law.

99   First, the statute expressly provides that "a technological measure `effectively controls access to a work' if the measure, in the ordinary course of its operation, requires the application of information or a process or a treatment, with the authority of the copyright owner, to gain access to a work."[138] One cannot gain access to a CSS-protected work on a DVD without application of the three keys that are required by the software. One cannot lawfully gain access to the keys except by entering into a license with the DVD CCA [...] under authority granted by the copyright owners or by purchasing a DVD player or drive containing the keys pursuant to such a license. In consequence, under the express terms of the statute, CSS "effectively controls access" to copyrighted DVD movies. It does so, within the meaning of the statute, whether or not it is a strong means of protection.[139]

100   This view is confirmed by the legislative history, which deals with precisely this point. The House Judiciary Committee section-by-section analysis of the House bill, which in this respect was enacted into law, makes clear that a technological measure "effectively controls access" to a copyrighted work if its *function* is to control access:

101   "The bill does define the *functions* of the technological measures that are covered — that is, what it means for a technological measure to `effectively control access to a work' ... and to `effectively protect a right of a copyright owner under this title' .... The practical, common-sense approach taken by H.R.2281 is that if, in the ordinary course of its operation, a technology actually works in the defined ways to control access to a work ... then the `effectiveness' test is met, and the prohibitions of the statute are applicable. This test, which focuses on the function performed by the technology, provides a sufficient basis for clear interpretation."[140]

102   Further, the House Commerce Committee made clear that measures based on encryption or scrambling "effectively control" access to copyrighted works,[141] although it is well known that what may be encrypted or scrambled often may be decrypted or unscrambled. As CSS, in the ordinary course of its operation — that is, when DeCSS or some other decryption program is not employed — "actually works" to prevent access to the protected work, it "effectively controls access" within the contemplation of the statute.

103   Finally, the interpretation of the phrase "effectively controls access" offered by defendants at trial — viz., that the use of the word "effectively" means that the statute protects only successful or efficacious technological means of controlling access — would gut the statute if it were adopted. If a technological means of access control is circumvented, it is, in common parlance, ineffective. Yet defendants' construction, if adopted, would limit the application of the statute to access control measures that thwart circumvention, but withhold protection for those measures that can be circumvented. In other words, defendants would have the Court construe the statute to offer protection where none is needed but to withhold protection precisely where protection is essential. The Court declines to do so. Accordingly, the Court holds that CSS effectively controls access to plaintiffs' copyrighted works.[142]

104   **(2) DeCSS Was Designed Primarily to Circumvent CSS**

105   As CSS effectively controls access to plaintiffs' copyrighted works, the only remaining question under Section 1201(a)(2)(A) is whether DeCSS was designed primarily to circumvent CSS. The [...] answer is perfectly obvious. By the admission of both Jon Johansen, the programmer who principally wrote DeCSS, and defendant Corley, DeCSS was created solely for the purpose of decrypting CSS — that is all it does.[143] Hence, absent satisfaction of a statutory exception, defendants clearly violated Section 1201(a)(2)(A) by posting DeCSS to their web site.

106   **b. Section 1201(a)(2)(B)**

107   As the only purpose or use of DeCSS is to circumvent CSS, the foregoing is sufficient to establish a *prima facie* violation of Section 1201(a)(2)(B) as well.

108   **c. The Linux Argument**

109   Perhaps the centerpiece of defendants' statutory position is the contention that DeCSS was not created for the purpose of pirating copyrighted motion pictures. Rather, they argue, it was written to further the development of a DVD player that would run under the Linux operating system, as there allegedly were no Linux compatible players on the market at the time.[144] The argument plays itself out in various ways as different elements of the DMCA come into focus. But it perhaps is useful to address the point at its most general level in order to place the preceding discussion in its fullest context.

110   As noted, Section 1201(a) of the DMCA contains two distinct prohibitions. Section 1201(a)(1), the so-called basic provision, "aims against those who engage in unauthorized circumvention of technological measures.... [It] focuses directly on wrongful conduct, rather than on those who facilitate wrongful conduct...."[145] Section 1201(a)(2), the anti-trafficking provision at issue in this case, on the other hand, separately bans offering or providing technology that may be used to circumvent technological means of controlling access to copyrighted works.[146] If the means in question meets any of the three prongs of the standard set out in Section 1201(a)(2)(A), (B), or (C), it may not be offered or disseminated.

111   As the earlier discussion demonstrates, the question whether the development of a Linux DVD player motivated those who wrote DeCSS is immaterial to the question whether the defendants now before the Court violated the anti-trafficking provision of the DMCA. The inescapable facts are that (1) CSS is a technological means that effectively controls access to plaintiffs' copyrighted works, (2) the one and only function of DeCSS is to circumvent CSS, and (3) defendants offered and provided DeCSS by posting it on their web site. Whether defendants did so in order to infringe, or to permit or encourage others to infringe, copyrighted works in violation of other provisions of the Copyright Act simply does not matter for purposes of Section 1201(a)(2). The offering or provision of the program is the prohibited conduct — and it is prohibited irrespective of why the program was written, except to whatever extent motive may be germane to determining whether their conduct falls within one of the statutory exceptions.

112   **2. Statutory Exceptions**

113   Earlier in the litigation, defendants contended that their activities came within several exceptions contained in the DMCA and the Copyright Act and constitute fair use under the Copyright Act. Their post-trial memorandum appears to confine their argument to the reverse engineering exception.[147] In any case, all of their assertions are entirely without merit.

114   **a. Reverse engineering**

115   Defendants claim to fall under Section 1201(f) of the statute, which provides [...] in substance that one may circumvent, or develop and employ technological means to circumvent, access control measures in order to achieve interoperability with another computer program provided that doing so does not infringe another's copyright[148] and, in addition, that one may make information acquired through such efforts "available to others, if the person [in question] ... provides such information solely for the purpose of enabling interoperability of an independently created computer program with other programs, and to the extent that doing so does not constitute infringement...."[149] They contend that DeCSS is necessary to achieve interoperability between computers running the Linux operating system and DVDs and that this exception therefore is satisfied.[150] This contention fails.

116   First, Section 1201(f)(3) permits information acquired through reverse engineering to be made available to others only by the person who acquired the information. But these defendants did not do any reverse engineering. They simply took DeCSS off someone else's web site and posted it on their own.

117   Defendants would be in no stronger position even if they had authored DeCSS. The right to make the information available extends only

to dissemination "solely for the purpose" of achieving interoperability as defined in the statute. It does not apply to public dissemination of means of circumvention, as the legislative history confirms.[151] These defendants, however, did not post DeCSS "solely" to achieve interoperability with Linux or anything else.

118 Finally, it is important to recognize that even the creators of DeCSS cannot credibly maintain that the "sole" purpose of DeCSS was to create a Linux DVD player. DeCSS concededly was developed on and runs under Windows — a far more widely used operating system. The developers of DeCSS therefore knew that DeCSS could be used to decrypt and play DVD movies on Windows as well as Linux machines. They knew also that the decrypted files could be copied like any other unprotected computer file. Moreover, the Court does not credit Mr. Johansen's testimony that he created DeCSS solely for the purpose of building a Linux player. Mr. Johansen is a very talented young man and a member of a well known hacker group who viewed "cracking" CSS as an end it itself and a means of demonstrating his talent and who fully expected that the use of DeCSS would not be confined to Linux machines. Hence, the Court finds that Mr. Johansen and the others who actually did develop DeCSS did not do so solely for the purpose of making a Linux DVD player if, indeed, developing a Linux-based DVD player was among their purposes.

119 Accordingly, the reverse engineering exception to the DMCA has no application here.

120 *[...]*

130 *d. Fair use*

131 Finally, defendants rely on the doctrine of fair use. Stated in its most general terms, the doctrine, now codified in Section 107 of the Copyright Act,[160] limits the exclusive rights of a copyright holder by permitting others to make limited use of portions of the copyrighted work, for appropriate purposes, free of liability for copyright infringement. For example, it is permissible for one other than the copyright owner to reprint or quote a suitable part of a copyrighted book or article in certain circumstances. The doctrine traditionally has facilitated literary and artistic criticism, teaching and scholarship, and other socially useful forms of expression. [...] It has been viewed by courts as a safety valve that accommodates the exclusive rights conferred by copyright with the freedom of expression guaranteed by the First Amendment.

132 The use of technological means of controlling access to a copyrighted work may affect the ability to make fair uses of the work.[161] Focusing specifically on the facts of this case, the application of CSS to encrypt a copyrighted motion picture requires the use of a compliant DVD player to view or listen to the movie. Perhaps more significantly, it prevents exact copying of either the video or the audio portion of all or any part of the film.[162] This latter point means that certain uses that might qualify as "fair" for purposes of copyright infringement — for example, the preparation by a film studies professor of a single CD-ROM or tape containing two scenes from different movies in order to illustrate a point in a lecture on cinematography, as opposed to showing relevant parts of two different DVDs — would be difficult or impossible absent circumvention of the CSS encryption. Defendants therefore argue that the DMCA cannot properly be construed to make it difficult or impossible to make any fair use of plaintiffs' copyrighted works and that the statute therefore does not reach their activities, which are simply a means to enable users of DeCSS to make such fair uses.

133 Defendants have focused on a significant point. Access control measures such as CSS do involve some risk of preventing lawful as well as unlawful uses of copyrighted material. Congress, however, clearly faced up to and dealt with this question in enacting the DMCA.

134 The Court begins its statutory analysis, as it must, with the language of the statute. Section 107 of the Copyright Act provides in critical part that certain uses of copyrighted works that otherwise would be wrongful are "not ... infringement[s] of copyright."[163] Defendants, however, are not here sued for copyright infringement. They are sued for offering and providing technology designed to circumvent technological measures that control access to copyrighted works and otherwise violating Section 1201(a)(2) of the Act. If Congress had meant the fair use defense to apply to such actions, it would have said so. Indeed, as the legislative history demonstrates, the decision not to make fair use a defense to a claim under Section 1201(a) was quite deliberate.

135   Congress was well aware during the consideration of the DMCA of the traditional role of the fair use defense in accommodating the exclusive rights of copyright owners with the legitimate interests of noninfringing users of portions of copyrighted works. It recognized the contention, voiced by a range of constituencies concerned with the legislation, that technological controls on access to copyrighted works might erode fair use by preventing access even for uses that would be deemed "fair" if only access might be gained.[164] And it struck a balance among the competing interests.

136   [...] The first element of the balance was the careful limitation of Section 1201(a)(1)'s prohibition of the act of circumvention to the act itself so as not to "apply to subsequent actions of a person once he or she has obtained authorized access to a copy of a [copyrighted] work...."[165] By doing so, it left "the traditional defenses to copyright infringement, including fair use, ... fully applicable" provided "the access is authorized."[166]

137   Second, Congress delayed the effective date of Section 1201(a)(1)'s prohibition of the act of circumvention for two years pending further investigation about how best to reconcile Section 1201(a)(1) with fair use concerns. Following that investigation, which is being carried out in the form of a rule-making by the Register of Copyright, the prohibition will not apply to users of particular classes of copyrighted works who demonstrate that their ability to make noninfringing uses of those classes of works would be affected adversely by Section 1201(a)(1).[167]

138   Third, it created a series of exceptions to aspects of Section 1201(a) for certain uses that Congress thought "fair," including reverse engineering, security testing, good faith encryption research, and certain uses by nonprofit libraries, archives and educational institutions. [168]

139   Defendants claim also that the possibility that DeCSS might be used for the purpose of gaining access to copyrighted works in order to make fair use of those works saves them under *Sony Corp. v. Universal City Studios, Inc.*[169] But they are mistaken. *Sony* does not apply to the activities with which defendants here are charged. Even if it did, it would not govern here. *Sony* involved a construction of the Copyright Act that has been overruled by the later enactment of the DMCA to the extent of any inconsistency between *Sony* and the new statute.

140   *Sony* was a suit for contributory infringement brought against manufacturers of video cassette recorders on the theory that the manufacturers were contributing to infringing home taping of copyrighted television broadcasts. The Supreme Court held that the manufacturers were not liable in view of the substantial numbers of copyright holders who either had authorized or did not object to such taping by viewers.[170] But *Sony* has no application here.

141   When *Sony* was decided, the only question was whether the manufacturers could be held liable for infringement by those who purchased equipment from them in circumstances in which there were many noninfringing uses for their equipment. But that is not the question now before this Court. The question here is whether the possibility of noninfringing fair use by someone who gains access to a protected copyrighted work through a circumvention technology distributed by the defendants saves the defendants from liability under Section 1201. But nothing in Section 1201 so suggests. By prohibiting the provision of circumvention technology, the DMCA fundamentally altered the landscape. A given device or piece of technology might have "a substantial noninfringing use, and hence be immune from attack under *Sony*'s construction of the Copyright Act — but nonetheless still be subject to suppression under Section 1201."[171] Indeed, [[...] Congress explicitly noted that Section 1201 does not incorporate *Sony*.[172]

142   The policy concerns raised by defendants were considered by Congress. Having considered them, Congress crafted a statute that, so far as the applicability of the fair use defense to Section 1201(a) claims is concerned, is crystal clear. In such circumstances, courts may not undo what Congress so plainly has done by "construing" the words of a statute to accomplish a result that Congress rejected. The fact that Congress elected to leave technologically unsophisticated persons who wish to make fair use of encrypted copyrighted works without the technical means of doing so is a matter for Congress unless Congress' decision contravenes the Constitution, a matter to which the Court turns below. Defendants' statutory fair use argument therefore is entirely without merit.

143 *C. Linking to Sites Offering DeCSS*

144 Plaintiffs seek also to enjoin defendants from "linking" their 2600.com web site to other sites that make DeCSS available to users. Their request obviously stems in no small part from what defendants themselves have termed their act of "electronic civil disobedience" — their attempt to defeat the purpose of the preliminary injunction by (a) offering the practical equivalent of making DeCSS available on their own web site by electronically linking users to other sites still offering DeCSS, and (b) encouraging other sites that had not been enjoined to offer the program. The dispositive question is whether linking to another web site containing DeCSS constitutes "offer[ing DeCSS] to the public" or "provid[ing] or otherwise traffic[king]" in it within the meaning of the DMCA.[173] Answering this question requires careful consideration of the nature and types of linking.

145 [...]

146 As noted earlier, the links that defendants established on their web site are of several types. Some transfer the user to a web page on an outside site that contains a good deal of information of various types, does not itself contain a link to DeCSS, but that links, either directly or via a series of other pages, to another page on the same site that posts the software. It then is up to the user to follow the link or series of links on the linked-to web site in order to arrive at the page with the DeCSS link and commence the download of the software. Others take the user to a page on an outside web site on which there appears a direct link to the DeCSS software and which may or may not contain text or links other than the DeCSS link. The user has only to click on the DeCSS link to commence the download. Still others may directly transfer the user to a file on the linked-to web site such that the download of DeCSS to the user's computer automatically [325] commences without further user intervention.

147 The statute makes it unlawful to offer, provide or otherwise traffic in described technology.[177] To "traffic" in something is to engage in dealings in it,[178] conduct that necessarily involves awareness of the nature of the subject of the trafficking. To "provide" something, in the sense used in the statute, is to make it available or furnish it.[179] To "offer" is to present or hold it out for consideration.[180] The phrase "or otherwise traffic in" modifies and gives meaning to the words "offer" and "provide."[181] In consequence, the anti-trafficking provision of the DMCA is implicated where one presents, holds out or makes a circumvention technology or device available, knowing its nature, for the purpose of allowing others to acquire it.

148 To the extent that defendants have linked to sites that automatically commence the process of downloading DeCSS upon a user being transferred by defendants' hyperlinks, there can be no serious question. Defendants are engaged in the functional equivalent of transferring the DeCSS code to the user themselves.

149 Substantially the same is true of defendants' hyperlinks to web pages that display nothing more than the DeCSS code or present the user only with the choice of commencing a download of DeCSS and no other content. The only distinction is that the entity extending to the user the option of downloading the program is the transferee site rather than defendants, a distinction without a difference.

150 Potentially more troublesome might be links to pages that offer a good deal of content other than DeCSS but that offer a hyperlink for downloading, or transferring to a page for downloading, DeCSS. If one assumed, for the purposes of argument, that the *Los Angeles Times* web site somewhere contained the DeCSS code, it would be wrong to say that anyone who linked to the *Los Angeles Times* web site, regardless of purpose or the manner in which the link was described, thereby offered, provided or otherwise trafficked in DeCSS merely because DeCSS happened to be available on a site to which one linked.[182] But that is not this case. Defendants urged others to post DeCSS in an effort to disseminate DeCSS and to inform defendants that they were doing so. Defendants then linked their site to those "mirror" sites, after first checking to ensure that the mirror sites in fact were posting DeCSS or something that looked like it, and proclaimed on their own site that DeCSS could be had by clicking on the hyperlinks on defendants' site. By doing so, they offered, provided or otherwise trafficked in DeCSS, and they continue to do so to this day.

151 *[...]*

238 *VI. Conclusion*

239   […]

242   clashes of competing interests like this are resolved by Congress. For now, at least, Congress has resolved this clash in the DMCA and in plaintiffs' favor. Given the peculiar characteristics of computer programs for circumventing encryption and other access control measures, the DMCA as applied to posting and linking here does not contravene the First Amendment. Accordingly, plaintiffs are entitled to appropriate injunctive and declaratory relief.

243   SO ORDERED.

244   […]

245   [2] Shortly after the commencement of the action, the Court granted plaintiffs' motion for a preliminary injunction barring defendants from posting DeCSS. *Universal City Studios, Inc. v. Reimerdes*, 82 F.Supp.2d 211 (S.D.N.Y. 2000). […]

315   [70] Distribution in the home video market accounts for approximately 40 percent of Warner Brothers' total income from movie distribution. *I*[…]

Universal City Studios, Inc. v. Corley

September 09, 2014 by mrisch

This opinion is an appeal of the Remeirdes case. This excerpt primarily considers the defenses.

1   273 F.3d 429 (2nd Cir. 2001)

2   **UNIVERSAL CITY STUDIOS, INC.** [...]

v.

ERIC CORLEY [...]

3

UNITED STATES COURT OF APPEALS FOR THE SECOND CIRCUIT.

[...]

Decided: November 28, 2001.

4   [...]

19   Before: Newman and Cabranes, Circuit Judges, and Thompson,[*] District Judge.

20   Jon O. Newman, Circuit Judge.

21   When the Framers of the First Amendment prohibited Congress from making any law "abridging the freedom of speech," they were not thinking about computers, computer programs, or the Internet. But neither were they thinking about radio, television, or movies. Just as the inventions at the beginning and middle of the 20th century presented new First Amendment issues, so does the cyber revolution at the end of that century. This appeal raises significant First Amendment issues concerning one aspect of computer technology—encryption to protect materials in digital form from unauthorized access. The appeal challenges the constitutionality of the Digital Millennium Copyright Act ("DMCA"), 17 U.S.C. § 1201 et seq. (Supp. V 1999) and the validity of an injunction entered to enforce the DMCA.

22   Defendant-Appellant Eric C. Corley and his company, 2600 Enterprises, Inc., (collectively "Corley," "the Defendants," or "the Appellants") appeal from the amended final judgment of the United States District Court for the Southern District of New York (Lewis A. Kaplan, District Judge), entered August 23, 2000, enjoining them from various actions concerning a decryption program known as "DeCSS." [...]

23   ## Introduction

24   [...]

29   Corley renews his constitutional challenges on appeal. Specifically, he argues primarily that: (1) the DMCA oversteps limits in the Copyright Clause on the duration of copyright protection; (2) the DMCA as applied to his dissemination of DeCSS violates the First Amendment because computer code is "speech" entitled to full First Amendment protection and the DMCA fails to survive the exacting scrutiny accorded statutes that regulate "speech"; and (3) the DMCA violates the First Amendment and the Copyright Clause by unduly

843

obstructing the "fair use" of copyrighted materials. Corley also argues that the statute is susceptible to, and should therefore be given, a narrow interpretation that avoids alleged constitutional objections.

30   [...]

Discussion

I. Narrow Construction to Avoid Constitutional Doubt

66   The Appellants first argue that, because their constitutional arguments are at least substantial, we should interpret the statute narrowly so as to avoid constitutional problems. They identify three different instances of alleged ambiguity in the statute that they claim provide an opportunity for such a narrow interpretation.

67   First, they contend that subsection 1201(c)(1), which provides that "[n]othing in this section shall affect rights, remedies, limitations or defenses to copyright infringement, including fair use, under this title," can be read to allow the circumvention of encryption technology protecting copyrighted material when the material will be put to "fair uses" exempt from copyright liability.[12] We disagree that subsection 1201(c)(1) permits such a reading. Instead, it clearly and simply clarifies that the DMCA targets the circumvention of digital walls guarding copyrighted material (and trafficking in circumvention tools), but does not concern itself with the use of those materials after circumvention has occurred. Subsection 1201(c)(1) ensures that the DMCA is not read to prohibit the "fair use" of information just because that information was obtained in a manner made illegal by the DMCA. The Appellants' much more expansive interpretation of subsection 1201(c)(1) is not only outside the range of plausible readings of the provision, but is also clearly refuted by the statute's legislative history.[13] [...]

II. Constitutional Challenge Based on the Copyright Clause

72   In a footnote to their brief, the Appellants appear to contend that the DMCA, as construed by the District Court, exceeds the constitutional authority [...] of Congress to grant authors copyrights for a "limited time," U.S. Const. art. I, § 8, cl. 8, because it "empower[s] copyright owners to effectively secure perpetual protection by mixing public domain works with copyrighted materials, then locking both up with technological protection measures." [...] For two reasons, the argument provides no basis for disturbing the judgment of the District Court.

73   First, we have repeatedly ruled that arguments presented to us only in a footnote are not entitled to appellate consideration. [...] Although an amicus brief can be helpful in elaborating issues properly presented by the parties, it is normally not a method for injecting new issues into an appeal, at least in cases where the parties are competently represented by counsel. [...]

74   Second, to whatever extent the argument might have merit at some future time in a case with a properly developed record, the argument is entirely premature and speculative at this time on this record. There is not even a claim, much less evidence, that any Plaintiff has sought to prevent copying of public domain works, or that the injunction prevents the Defendants from copying such works. As Judge Kaplan noted, the possibility that encryption would preclude access to public domain works "does not yet appear to be a problem, although it may emerge as one in the future." [...]

III. Constitutional Challenges Based on the First Amendment

A. Applicable Principles

77   Last year, in one of our Court's first forays into First Amendment law in the digital age, we took an "evolutionary" approach to the task of tailoring familiar constitutional rules to novel technological circumstances, favoring "narrow" holdings that would permit the law to mature on a "case-by-case" basis. [...] In that spirit, we proceed, with appropriate caution, to consider the Appellants' First Amendment challenges by analyzing a series of preliminary issues the resolution of which provides a basis for adjudicating the specific objections to

the DMCA and its application to DeCSS. These issues, which we consider only to the extent necessary to resolve the pending appeal, are whether computer code is speech, whether computer programs are speech, the scope of First Amendment protection for computer code, and the scope of First Amendment protection for decryption code. Based on our analysis of these issues, we then consider the Appellants' challenge to the injunction's provisions concerning posting and linking.

78   ## 1. Code as Speech

79   Communication does not lose constitutional protection as "speech" simply because it is expressed in the language of computer code. Mathematical formulae and musical scores are written in "code," i.e., symbolic notations not comprehensible to the uninitiated, and yet both are covered by the First Amendment. If someone [...] chose to write a novel entirely in computer object code by using strings of 1's and 0's for each letter of each word, the resulting work would be no different for constitutional purposes than if it had been written in English. The "object code" version would be incomprehensible to readers outside the programming community (and tedious to read even for most within the community), but it would be no more incomprehensible than a work written in Sanskrit for those unversed in that language. The undisputed evidence reveals that even pure object code can be, and often is, read and understood by experienced programmers. And source code (in any of its various levels of complexity) can be read by many more. [...] Ultimately, however, the ease with which a work is comprehended is irrelevant to the constitutional inquiry. If computer code is distinguishable from conventional speech for First Amendment purposes, it is not because it is written in an obscure language. [...]

80   ## 2. Computer Programs as Speech

81   Of course, computer code is not likely to be the language in which a work of literature is written. Instead, it is primarily the language for programs executable by a computer. These programs are essentially instructions to a computer. In general, programs may give instructions either to perform a task or series of tasks when initiated by a single (or double) click of a mouse or, once a program is operational ("launched"), to manipulate data that the user enters into the computer.[16] Whether computer code that gives a computer instructions is "speech" within the meaning of the First Amendment requires consideration of the scope of the Constitution's protection of speech.

82   The First Amendment provides that "Congress shall make no law . . . abridging the freedom of speech. . . ." U.S. Const. amend. I. "Speech" is an elusive term, and judges and scholars have debated its bounds for two centuries. Some would confine First Amendment protection to political speech. [...] Others would extend it further to artistic expression. [...]

83   Whatever might be the merits of these and other approaches, the law has not been so limited. Even dry information, devoid of advocacy, political relevance, or artistic expression, has been accorded First Amendment protection. [...]

84   Thus, for example, courts have subjected to First Amendment scrutiny restrictions on the dissemination of technical scientific information and scientific research [...] and attempts to regulate the publication of instructions,[17] see, e.g., United States v. Raymond, 228 F.3d 804, 815 (7th Cir. 2000) (First Amendment does not protect instructions for violating the tax laws) [...]

85   Computer programs are not exempted from the category of First Amendment speech simply because their instructions require use of a computer. A recipe is no less "speech" because it calls for the use of an oven, and a musical score is no less "speech" because it specifies performance on an electric guitar. Arguably distinguishing computer programs from conventional language instructions is the fact that programs are executable on a computer. But the fact that a program has the capacity to direct the functioning of a computer does not mean that it lacks the additional capacity to convey information, and it is the conveying of information that renders instructions "speech" for purposes of the First Amendment.[19] The information [...] conveyed by most "instructions" is how to perform a task.

86   Instructions such as computer code, which are intended to be executable by a computer, will often convey information capable of comprehension and assessment by a human being.[20] A programmer reading a program learns information about instructing a computer,

and might use this information to improve personal programming skills and perhaps the craft of programming. Moreover, programmers communicating ideas to one another almost inevitably communicate in code, much as musicians use notes.[21] Limiting First Amendment protection of programmers to descriptions of computer code (but not the code itself) would impede discourse among computer scholars, [22] just as limiting protection for musicians to descriptions of musical scores (but not sequences of notes) would impede their exchange of ideas and expression. Instructions that communicate information comprehensible to a human qualify as speech whether the instructions are designed for execution by a computer or a human (or both).

87   [...]

90   For all of these reasons, we join the other courts that have concluded that computer code, and computer programs constructed from code can merit First Amendment protection [...] although the scope of such protection remains to be determined.

91   **3. The Scope of First Amendment Protection for Computer Code**

92   Having concluded that computer code conveying information is "speech" [...] within the meaning of the First Amendment, we next consider, to a limited extent, the scope of the protection that code enjoys. As the District Court recognized [...] the scope of protection for speech generally depends on whether the restriction is imposed because of the content of the speech. Content-based restrictions are permissible only if they serve compelling state interests and do so by the least restrictive means available. [...] A content-neutral restriction is permissible if it serves a substantial governmental interest, the interest is unrelated to the suppression of free expression, and the regulation is narrowly tailored, which "in this context requires . . . that the means chosen do not 'burden substantially more speech than is necessary to further the government's legitimate interests.'" [...]

93   "[G]overnment regulation of expressive activity is 'content neutral' if it is justified without reference to the content of regulated speech." ["The government's purpose is the controlling consideration. A regulation that serves purposes unrelated to the content of expression is deemed neutral, even if it has an incidental effect on some speakers or messages but not others." [...] The Supreme Court's approach to determining content-neutrality appears to be applicable whether what is regulated is expression [...] or any "activity" that can be said to combine speech and non-speech elements [...]

94   To determine whether regulation of computer code is content-neutral, the initial inquiry must be whether the regulated activity is "sufficiently imbued with elements of communication to fall within the scope of the First . . . Amendment[]." [...] Computer code, as we have noted, often conveys information comprehensible to human beings, even as it also directs a computer to perform various functions. Once a speech component [...] is identified, the inquiry then proceeds to whether the regulation is "justified without reference to the content of regulated speech." [...]

95   The Appellants vigorously reject the idea that computer code can be regulated according to any different standard than that applicable to pure speech, i.e., speech that lacks a nonspeech component. Although recognizing that code is a series of instructions to a computer, they argue that code is no different, for First Amendment purposes, than blueprints that instruct an engineer or recipes that instruct a cook. [...] We disagree. Unlike a blueprint or a recipe, which cannot yield any functional result without human comprehension of its content, human decision-making, and human action, computer code can instantly cause a computer to accomplish tasks and instantly render the results of those tasks available throughout the world via the Internet. The only human action required to achieve these results can be as limited and instantaneous as a single click of a mouse. These realities of what code is and what its normal functions are require a First Amendment analysis that treats code as combining nonspeech and speech elements, i.e., functional and expressive elements. [...]

96   We recognize, as did Judge Kaplan, that the functional capability of computer code cannot yield a result until a human being decides to insert the disk containing the code into a computer and causes it to perform its function (or programs a computer to cause the code to

perform its function). Nevertheless, this momentary intercession of human action does not diminish the nonspeech component of code, nor render code entirely speech, like a blueprint or a recipe. […]

98   The functionality of computer code properly affects the scope of its First Amendment protection.

99   ### 4. The Scope of First Amendment Protection for Decryption Code

100   In considering the scope of First Amendment protection for a decryption program like DeCSS, we must recognize that the essential purpose of encryption code is to prevent unauthorized access. Owners of all property rights are entitled to prohibit access to their property by unauthorized persons. Homeowners can install locks on the doors of their houses. Custodians of valuables can place them in safes. Stores can attach to products security devices that will activate alarms if the products are taken away without purchase. These and similar security devices can be circumvented. Burglars can use skeleton keys to open door locks. Thieves can obtain the combinations to safes. Product security devices can be neutralized.

101   Our case concerns a security device, CSS computer code, that prevents access by unauthorized persons to DVD movies. The CSS code is embedded in the DVD movie. Access to the movie cannot be obtained unless a person has a device, a licensed DVD player, equipped with computer code capable of decrypting the CSS encryption code. In its basic function, […] CSS is like a lock on a homeowner's door, a combination of a safe, or a security device attached to a store's products.

102   DeCSS is computer code that can decrypt CSS. In its basic function, it is like a skeleton key that can open a locked door, a combination that can open a safe, or a device that can neutralize the security device attached to a store's products.[27] DeCSS enables anyone to gain access to a DVD movie without using a DVD player.

103   The initial use of DeCSS to gain access to a DVD movie creates no loss to movie producers because the initial user must purchase the DVD. However, once the DVD is purchased, DeCSS enables the initial user to copy the movie in digital form and transmit it instantly in virtually limitless quantity, thereby depriving the movie producer of sales. The advent of the Internet creates the potential for instantaneous worldwide distribution of the copied material.

104   At first glance, one might think that Congress has as much authority to regulate the distribution of computer code to decrypt DVD movies as it has to regulate distribution of skeleton keys, combinations to safes, or devices to neutralize store product security devices. However, despite the evident legitimacy of protection against unauthorized access to DVD movies, just like any other property, regulation of decryption code like DeCSS is challenged in this case because DeCSS differs from a skeleton key in one important respect: it not only is capable of performing the function of unlocking the encrypted DVD movie, it also is a form of communication, albeit written in a language not understood by the general public. As a communication, the DeCSS code has a claim to being "speech," and as "speech," it has a claim to being protected by the First Amendment. But just as the realities of what any computer code can accomplish must inform the scope of its constitutional protection, so the capacity of a decryption program like DeCSS to accomplish unauthorized—indeed, unlawful—access to materials in which the Plaintiffs have intellectual property rights must inform and limit the scope of its First Amendment protection. […]

105   With all of the foregoing considerations in mind, we next consider the Appellants' First Amendment challenge to the DMCA as applied in the specific prohibitions that have been imposed by the District Court's injunction.

106   ### B. First Amendment Challenge

107   The District Court's injunction applies the DMCA to the Defendants by imposing two types of prohibition, both grounded on the anti-trafficking provisions of the DMCA. The first prohibits posting DeCSS or any other technology for circumventing CSS on any Internet web site. […] The second prohibits knowingly linking any Internet web site to any other web site containing DeCSS. […] The validity of the posting and linking prohibitions must be considered separately.

108 **1. Posting**

109 The initial issue is whether the posting prohibition is content-neutral, since, as we have explained, this classification [...] determines the applicable constitutional standard. The Appellants contend that the anti-trafficking provisions of the DMCA and their application by means of the posting prohibition of the injunction are content-based. They argue that the provisions "specifically target ... scientific expression based on the particular topic addressed by that expression—namely, techniques for circumventing CSS." [...] We disagree. The Appellants' argument fails to recognize that the target of the posting provisions of the injunction—DeCSS—has both a nonspeech and a speech component, and that the DMCA, as applied to the Appellants, and the posting prohibition of the injunction target only the nonspeech component. Neither the DMCA nor the posting prohibition is concerned with whatever capacity DeCSS might have for conveying information to a human being, and that capacity, as previously explained, is what arguably creates a speech component of the decryption code. The DMCA and the posting prohibition are applied to DeCSS solely because of its capacity to instruct a computer to decrypt CSS. That functional capability is not speech within the meaning of the First Amendment. The Government seeks to "justif[y]," [... both the application of the DMCA and the posting prohibition to the Appellants solely on the basis of the functional capability of DeCSS to instruct a computer to decrypt CSS, i.e., "without reference to the content of the regulated speech," [...] This type of regulation is therefore content-neutral, just as would be a restriction on trafficking in skeleton keys identified because of their capacity to unlock jail cells, even though some of the keys happened to bear a slogan or other legend that qualified as a speech component.

110 As a content-neutral regulation with an incidental effect on a speech component, the regulation must serve a substantial governmental interest, the interest must be unrelated to the suppression of free expression, and the incidental restriction on speech must not burden substantially more speech than is necessary to further that interest. [...] he Government's interest in preventing unauthorized access to encrypted copyrighted material is unquestionably substantial, and the regulation of DeCSS by the posting prohibition plainly serves that interest. Moreover, that interest is unrelated to the suppression of free expression. The injunction regulates the posting of DeCSS, regardless of whether DeCSS code contains any information comprehensible by human beings that would qualify as speech. Whether the incidental regulation on speech burdens substantially more speech than is necessary to further the interest in preventing unauthorized access to copyrighted materials requires some elaboration.

111 Posting DeCSS on the Appellants' web site makes it instantly available at the click of a mouse to any person in the world with access to the Internet, and such person can then instantly transmit DeCSS to anyone else with Internet access. Although the prohibition on posting prevents the Appellants from conveying to others the speech component of DeCSS, the Appellants have not suggested, much less shown, any technique for barring them from making this instantaneous worldwide distribution of a decryption code that makes a lesser restriction on the code's speech component.[28] It is true that the [...] Government has alternative means of prohibiting unauthorized access to copyrighted materials. For example, it can create criminal and civil liability for those who gain unauthorized access, and thus it can be argued that the restriction on posting DeCSS is not absolutely necessary to preventing unauthorized access to copyrighted materials. But a content-neutral regulation need not employ the least restrictive means of accomplishing the governmental objective. Id. It need only avoid burdening "substantially more speech than is necessary to further the government's legitimate interests." Id. (internal quotation marks and citation omitted). The prohibition on the Defendants' posting of DeCSS satisfies that standard.[29]

112 **2. Linking**

113 In considering linking, we need to clarify the sense in which the injunction prohibits such activity. Although the injunction defines several terms, it does not define "linking." Nevertheless, it is evident from the District Court's opinion that it is concerned with "hyperlinks," [...] The code for the web page containing the hyperlink contains a computer instruction that associates the link with the URL of the web page to be accessed, such that clicking on the hyperlink instructs the computer to enter the URL of the desired web page and thereby access that page. With a hyperlink on a web page, the linked web site is just one click away.[31]

114 [...]

120 As they have throughout their arguments, the Appellants ignore the reality of the functional capacity of decryption computer code and

hyperlinks to facilitate instantaneous unauthorized access to copyrighted materials by anyone anywhere in the world. Under the circumstances amply shown by the record, the injunction's linking prohibition validly regulates the Appellants' opportunity instantly to enable anyone anywhere to gain unauthorized access to copyrighted movies on DVDs.[32]

121   At oral argument, we asked the Government whether its undoubted power to punish the distribution of obscene materials would permit an injunction prohibiting a newspaper from printing addresses of bookstore locations carrying such materials. In a properly cautious response, the Government stated that the answer would depend on the circumstances of the publication. The Appellants' supplemental papers enthusiastically embraced the arguable analogy between printing bookstore addresses and displaying on a web page links to web sites at which DeCSS may be accessed. Supplemental Brief for Appellants at 14. They confidently asserted that publication of bookstore locations carrying obscene material cannot be enjoined consistent with the First Amendment, and that a prohibition against linking to web sites containing DeCSS is similarly invalid. [...]

122   Like many analogies posited to illuminate legal issues, the bookstore analogy is helpful primarily in identifying characteristics that distinguish it from the context of the pending dispute. If a bookstore proprietor is knowingly selling obscene materials, the evil of distributing such materials can be prevented by injunctive relief against the unlawful distribution (and similar distribution by others can be deterred by punishment of the distributor). And if others publish the location of the bookstore, preventive relief against a distributor can be effective before any significant distribution of the prohibited materials has occurred. The digital world, however, creates a very different problem. If obscene materials are posted on one web site and other sites post hyperlinks to the first site, the materials are available for instantaneous worldwide distribution before any preventive measures can be effectively taken.

123   This reality obliges courts considering First Amendment claims in the context of the pending case to choose between two unattractive alternatives: either tolerate some impairment of communication in order [...] to permit Congress to prohibit decryption that may lawfully be prevented, or tolerate some decryption in order to avoid some impairment of communication. Although the parties dispute the extent of impairment of communication if the injunction is upheld and the extent of decryption if it is vacated, and differ on the availability and effectiveness of techniques for minimizing both consequences, the fundamental choice between impairing some communication and tolerating decryption cannot be entirely avoided.

124   In facing this choice, we are mindful that it is not for us to resolve the issues of public policy implicated by the choice we have identified. Those issues are for Congress. Our task is to determine whether the legislative solution adopted by Congress, as applied to the Appellants by the District Court's injunction, is consistent with the limitations of the First Amendment, and we are satisfied that it is.

125   ## IV. Constitutional Challenge Based on Claimed Restriction of Fair Use

126   Asserting that fair use "is rooted in and required by both the Copyright Clause and the First Amendment," [...] the Appellants contend that the DMCA, as applied by the District Court, unconstitutionally "eliminates fair use" of copyrighted materials [...] We reject this extravagant claim.

127   Preliminarily, we note that the Supreme Court has never held that fair use is constitutionally required, although some isolated statements in its opinions might arguably be enlisted for such a requirement. [...]

128   We need not explore the extent to which fair use might have constitutional protection, grounded on either the First Amendment or the Copyright Clause, because whatever validity a constitutional claim might have as to an application of the DMCA that impairs fair use of copyrighted materials, such matters are far beyond the [...] scope of this lawsuit for several reasons. In the first place, the Appellants do not claim to be making fair use of any copyrighted materials, and nothing in the injunction prohibits them from making such fair use. They are barred from trafficking in a decryption code that enables unauthorized access to copyrighted materials.

129   Second, as the District Court properly noted, to whatever extent the anti-trafficking provisions of the DMCA might prevent others from

copying portions of DVD movies in order to make fair use of them, "the evidence as to the impact of the anti-trafficking provision[s] of the DMCA on prospective fair users is scanty and fails adequately to address the issues." [...]

130   Third, the Appellants have provided no support for their premise that fair use of DVD movies is constitutionally required to be made by copying the original work in its original format.[34] Their examples of the fair uses that they believe others will be prevented from making all involve copying in a digital format those portions of a DVD movie amenable to fair use, a copying that would enable the fair user to manipulate the digitally copied portions. One example is that of a school child who wishes to copy images from a DVD movie to insert into the student's documentary film. We know of no authority for the proposition that fair use, as protected by the Copyright Act, much less the Constitution, guarantees copying by the optimum method or in the identical format of the original. Although the Appellants insisted at oral argument that they should not be relegated to a "horse and buggy" technique in making fair use of DVD movies,[35] the DMCA does not impose even an arguable limitation on the opportunity to make a variety of traditional fair uses of DVD movies, such as commenting on their content, quoting excerpts from their screenplays, and even recording portions of the video images and sounds on film or tape by pointing a camera, a camcorder, or a microphone at a monitor as it displays the DVD movie. The fact that the resulting copy will not be as perfect or as manipulable as a digital copy obtained by having direct access to the DVD movie in its digital form, provides no basis for a claim of unconstitutional limitation of fair use. A film critic making fair use of a movie by quoting selected lines of dialogue has no constitutionally valid claim that the review (in print or on television) would be technologically superior if the reviewer had not been prevented from using a movie camera in the theater, nor has an art student a valid constitutional claim to fair use of a painting by photographing it in a museum. Fair use has never been held to be a guarantee of access to copyrighted material in order to copy it by the fair user's preferred technique or in the format of the original.

131   ## Conclusion

132   We have considered all the other arguments of the Appellants and conclude that [...] they provide no basis for disturbing the District Court's judgment. Accordingly, the judgment is affirmed.

133   [...]

146   [13] The legislative history of the enacted bill makes quite clear that Congress intended to adopt a "balanced" approach to accommodating both piracy and fair use concerns, eschewing the quick fix of simply exempting from the statute all circumventions for fair use. H.R. Rep. No. 105-551, pt. 2, at 25 (1998). It sought to achieve this goal principally through the use of what it called a "fail-safe" provision in the statute, authorizing the Librarian of Congress to exempt certain users from the anti-circumvention provision when it becomes evident that in practice, the statute is adversely affecting certain kinds of fair use. [...]

150   [17] We note that instructions are of varied types. See Vartuli, 228 F.3d at 111. "Orders" from one member of a conspiracy to another member, or from a superior to a subordinate, might resemble instructions but nonetheless warrant less or even no constitutional protection because their capacity to inform is meager, and because it is unlikely that the recipient of the order will engage in the "intercession of . . . mind or . . . will" characteristic of the sort of communication between two parties protected by the Constitution, [...]

Class 23: 8.5 <u>OIL Casebook: Digital Locks II</u>

Digital Millennium Copyright Act: 37 CFR 201.40 - EXEMPTION TO PROHIBITION AGAINST CIRCUMVENTION.

September 09, 2014 by mrisch

Note that this list changes every two years, and is an example of some of the Copyright Office exceptions

1   [...]

2   **(a) *General.*** This section prescribes the classes of copyrighted works for which the Librarian of Congress has determined, pursuant to 17 U.S.C. 1201(a)(1)(C) and (D), that noninfringing uses by persons who are users of such works are, or are likely to be, adversely affected. The prohibition against circumvention of technological measures that control access to copyrighted works set forth in 17 U.S.C. 1201(a)(1)(A) shall not apply to such users of the prescribed classes of copyrighted works.

3   **(b) *Classes of copyrighted works.*** Pursuant to the authority set forth in 17 U.S.C. 1201(a)(1)(C) and (D), and upon the recommendation of the Register of Copyrights, the Librarian has determined that the prohibition against circumvention of technological measures that effectively control access to copyrighted works set forth in 17 U.S.C. 1201(a)(1)(A) shall not apply to persons who engage in noninfringing uses of the following classes of copyrighted works:

4   **(1)** Motion pictures on DVDs that are lawfully made and acquired and that are protected by the Content Scrambling System when circumvention is accomplished solely in order to accomplish the incorporation of short portions of motion pictures into new works for the purpose of criticism or comment, and where the person engaging in circumvention believes and has reasonable grounds for believing that circumvention is necessary to fulfill the purpose of the use in the following instances:

5   **(i)** Educational uses by college and university professors and by college and university film and media studies students;

6   **(ii)** Documentary filmmaking;

7   **(iii)** Noncommercial videos.

8   **(2)** Computer programs that enable wireless telephone handsets to execute software applications, where circumvention is accomplished for the sole purpose of enabling interoperability of such applications, when they have been lawfully obtained, with computer programs on the telephone handset.

9   **(3)** Computer programs, in the form of firmware or software, that enable used wireless telephone handsets to connect to a wireless telecommunications network, when circumvention is initiated by the owner of the copy of the computer program solely in order to connect to a wireless telecommunications network and access to the network is authorized by the operator of the network. *This exception was added, and then later withdrawn, but Congress recently passed a bill reinstating it.*

10   **(4)** Video games accessible on personal computers and protected by technological protection measures that control access to lawfully obtained works, when circumvention is accomplished solely for the purpose of good faith testing for, investigating, or correcting security flaws or vulnerabilities, if:

11   **(i)** The information derived from the security testing is used primarily to promote the security of the owner or operator of a computer, computer system, or computer network; and

12   **(ii)** The information derived from the security testing is used or maintained in a manner that does not facilitate copyright infringement or a violation of applicable law.

13   **(5)** Computer programs protected by dongles that prevent access due to malfunction or damage and which are obsolete. A dongle shall be considered obsolete if it is no longer manufactured or if a replacement or repair is no longer reasonably available in the commercial marketplace.

14   **(6)** Literary works distributed in ebook format when all existing ebook editions of the work (including digital text editions made available by authorized entities) contain access controls that prevent the enabling either of the book's read-aloud function or of

screen readers that render the text into a specialized format.

15   **(c) _Definition._** "Specialized format," "digital text" and "authorized entities" shall have the same meaning as in 17 U.S.C. 121.

16   [65 FR 64574, Oct. 27, 2000, as amended at 68 FR 62018, Oct. 31, 2003; 71 FR 68479, Nov. 27, 2006; 74 FR 55139, Oct. 27, 2009; 75 FR 43839, July 27, 2010; 75 FR 47465, Aug. 6, 2010]

Lexmark Int'l, Inc. v. Static Control Components, Inc.

September 09, 2014 by mrisch

1   387 F.3d 522 (2004)

2   **LEXMARK INTERNATIONAL, INC., Plaintiff-Appellee,**
                                          v.
           STATIC CONTROL COMPONENTS, INC., Defendant-Appellant.

3   [...]

4   United States Court of Appeals, Sixth Circuit.

5   [...]
                          Decided and Filed: October 26, 2004.

6   [...]

9   **OPINION**

10   **SUTTON, Circuit Judge.**

11   This copyright dispute involves two computer programs, two federal statutes and three theories of liability. The first computer program, known as the "Toner Loading Program," calculates toner level in printers manufactured by Lexmark International. The second computer program, known as the "Printer Engine Program," controls various printer functions on Lexmark printers.

12   [...] The second federal statute, the Digital Millenium Copyright Act (DMCA), 17 U.S.C. § 1201 *et seq.*, was enacted in 1998 and proscribes the sale of products that may be used to "circumvent a technological measure that effectively controls access to a work" protected by the copyright statute.

13   [...] These statutes became relevant to these computer programs when Lexmark began selling discount toner cartridges for its printers that only Lexmark could re-fill and that contained a microchip designed to prevent Lexmark printers from functioning with toner cartridges that Lexmark had not re-filled. In an effort to support the market for competing toner cartridges, Static Control Components (SCC) mimicked Lexmark's computer chip and sold it to companies interested in selling remanufactured toner cartridges.

14   Lexmark [...] claimed that SCC's chip violated the DMCA by circumventing a technological measure designed to control access to the Toner Loading Program. And it claimed that SCC's chip violated the DMCA by circumventing a technological measure designed to control access to the Printer Engine Program.

15   After an evidentiary hearing, the district court decided that Lexmark had shown a likelihood of success on each claim and entered a preliminary injunction against SCC. As we view Lexmark's prospects for success on each of these claims differently, we vacate the preliminary injunction and remand the case for further proceedings.

                                          854

Printed Lexmark Int'l, Inc. v. Static Control Components, Inc.

8/10/15, 1:14 AM

16   **I.**

17   **A.**

18   The Parties. Headquartered in Lexington, Kentucky, Lexmark is a leading manufacturer of laser and inkjet printers and has sold printers and toner cartridges for its printers since 1991. [...]

19   Static Control Components is a privately held company headquartered in Sanford, North Carolina. Started in 1987, it currently employs approximately 1,000 workers and makes a wide range of technology products, including microchips that it sells to third-party companies for use in remanufactured toner cartridges.

20   The Two Computer Programs. The first program at issue is Lexmark's "Toner Loading Program," which measures the amount of toner remaining in the cartridge based on the amount of torque (rotational force) sensed on the toner cartridge wheel. [...] The Toner Loading Program relies upon eight program commands — "add," "sub" (an abbreviation for subtract), "mul" (multiply), "pct" (take a percent), "jump," "if," "load," and "exit" — to execute one of several mathematical equations that convert the torque reading into an approximation of toner level. [...] To illustrate the modest size of this computer program, the phrase "Lexmark International, Inc. vs. Static Control Components, Inc." in ASCII format [...] would occupy more memory than either version of the Toner Loading Program. [...] The Toner Loading Program is located on a microchip contained in Lexmark's toner cartridges.

21   The second program is Lexmark's "Printer Engine Program." The Printer Engine Program occupies far more memory than the Toner Loading Program and translates into over 20 printed pages of program commands. The program controls a variety of functions on each printer — e.g., paper feed and movement, and printer motor control. [...] Unlike the Toner Loading Program, the Printer Engine Program is located within Lexmark's printers.

22   [...] Neither program is encrypted and each can be read (and copied) directly from its respective memory chip. [...]

23   Lexmark's Prebate and Non-Prebate Cartridges. Lexmark markets two types of toner cartridges for its laser printers: "Prebate" and "Non-Prebate." Prebate cartridges are sold to business consumers at an up-front discount. In exchange, consumers agree to use the cartridge just once, then return the empty unit to Lexmark; a "shrink-wrap" agreement on the top of each cartridge box spells out these restrictions and confirms that using the cartridge constitutes acceptance of these terms. [...] Non-Prebate cartridges are sold without any discount, are not subject to any restrictive agreements and may be re-filled with toner and reused by the consumer or a third-party remanufacturer. [...]

24   To ensure that consumers adhere to the Prebate agreement, Lexmark uses an "authentication sequence" that performs a "secret handshake" between each Lexmark printer and a microchip on each Lexmark toner cartridge. Both the printer and the chip employ a publicly available encryption algorithm known as "Secure Hash Algorigthm-1" or "SHA-1," which calculates a "Message Authentication Code" based on data in the microchip's memory. If the code calculated by the microchip matches the code calculated by the printer, the printer functions normally. If the two values do not match, the printer returns an error message and will not operate, blocking consumers from using toner cartridges that Lexmark has not authorized. [...]

25   SCC's Competing Microchip. SCC sells its own microchip — the "SMARTEK" chip — that permits consumers to satisfy Lexmark's authentication sequence each time it would otherwise be performed, i.e., when the printer is turned on or the printer door is opened and shut. SCC's advertising boasts that its chip breaks Lexmark's "secret code" (the authentication sequence), which "even on the fastest computer available today ... would take Years to run through all of the possible 8-byte combinations to break." [...] SCC sells these chips to third-party cartridge remanufacturers, permitting them to replace Lexmark's chip with the SMARTEK chip on refurbished Prebate

cartridges. These recycled cartridges are in turn sold to consumers as a low-cost alternative to new Lexmark toner cartridges.

26   [...]

27   The parties agree that Lexmark's printers perform a second calculation independent of the authentication sequence. After the authentication sequence concludes, the Printer Engine Program downloads a copy of the Toner Loading Program from the toner cartridge chip onto the printer in order to measure toner levels. Before the printer runs the Toner Loading Program, it performs a "checksum operation," a "commonly used technique" to ensure the "integrity" of the data downloaded from the toner cartridge microchip. [...] Under this operation, the printer compares the result of a calculation performed on the data bytes of the transferred copy of the Toner Loading Program with the "checksum value" located elsewhere on the toner cartridge microchip. If the two values do not match, the printer assumes that the data was corrupted in the program download, displays an error message and ceases functioning. If the two values do match, the printer continues to operate.

28   The Lawsuit. On December 30, 2002, Lexmark filed a complaint in the United States District Court for the Eastern District of Kentucky seeking to enjoin SCC (on a preliminary and permanent basis) from distributing the SMARTEK chips. [...]

29   **II.**

36   [...]

37   Four factors govern whether a district court should enter a preliminary injunction: (1) the plaintiff's likelihood of success on the merits; (2) the possibility of irreparable harm to the plaintiff in the absence of an injunction; (3) public interest considerations; and (4) potential harm to third parties. *[...]*

38   **III.**

39   **A.**   *Part A provides a nice summary of the copyright laws. It is worth looking at if you want further examples.*

40   [...]

56   **B.**   *In Part B, the court rules that the short Toner Loading Program is not copyrightable - at least for purposes of keeping others from using it on competing toner cartridges.*

57   [...]

84   **IV.**

85   **A.**

86   Enacted in 1998, the DMCA has three liability provisions. The statute first prohibits the circumvention of "a technological measure that effectively controls access to a work protected [by copyright]." 17 U.S.C. § 1201(a)(1). The statute then prohibits selling devices that circumvent access-control measures:

87   No person shall manufacture, import, offer to the public, provide, or otherwise traffic in any technology, product, service, device, component, or part thereof, that —

          (A) is primarily designed or produced for the purpose of circumventing a technological measure that effectively controls access to a [copyrighted work];

(B) has only limited commercially significant purpose or use other than to circumvent a technological measure that effectively controls access to a [copyrighted work]; or

(C) is marketed by that person or another acting in concert with that person with that person's knowledge for use in circumventing a technological measure that effectively controls access to a [copyrighted work].

88   *Id.* § 1201(a)(2). The statute finally bans devices that circumvent "technological measures" protecting "a right" of the copyright owner. *Id.* § 1201(b). The last provision prohibits devices aimed at circumventing technological measures that allow some forms of "access" but restrict other uses of the copyrighted work [...] such as streaming media, which permits users to view or watch a copyrighted work but prevents them from downloading a permanent copy of the work [...]

89   The statute also contains three "reverse engineering" defenses. A person may circumvent an access control measure "for the sole purpose of identifying and analyzing those elements of the program that are [...] necessary to achieve interoperability of an independently created computer program with other programs, and that have not previously been readily available to [that person]." 17 U.S.C. § 1201(f)(1). A person "may develop and employ technological means" that are "necessary" to enable interoperability. *Id.* § 1201(f)(2). And these technological means may be made available to others "solely for the purpose of enabling interoperability of an independently created computer program with other programs." *Id.* § 1201(f)(3). All three defenses apply only when traditional copyright infringement does not occur and only when the challenged actions (in the case of the third provision) would not violate other "applicable law[s]." *Id.*

90   In filing its complaint and in its motion for a preliminary injunction, Lexmark invoked the second liability provision — the ban on distributing devices that circumvent access-control measures placed on copyrighted works. *See id.* § 1201(a)(2). According to Lexmark, SCC's SMARTEK chip is a "device" marketed and sold by SCC that "circumvents" Lexmark's "technological measure" (the SHA-1 authentication sequence, not the checksum operation), which "effectively controls access" to its copyrighted works (the Toner Loading Program and Printer Engine Program). Lexmark claims that the SMARTEK chip meets all three tests for liability under § 1201(a)(2): (1) the chip "is primarily designed or produced for the purpose of circumventing" Lexmark's authentication sequence, 17 U.S.C. § 1201(a)(2)(A); (2) the chip "has only limited commercially significant purpose or use other than to circumvent" the authentication sequence, *id.* § 1201(a)(2)(B); and (3) SCC "market[s]" the chip "for use in circumventing" the authentication sequence, *id.* § 1201(a)(2)(C). The district court agreed and concluded that Lexmark had shown a likelihood of success under all three provisions.

91   **B.**

92   We initially consider Lexmark's DMCA claim concerning the Printer Engine Program, which (the parties agree) is protected by the general copyright statute. In deciding that Lexmark's authentication sequence "effectively controls access to a work protected under [the copyright provisions]," the district court relied on a definition in the DMCA saying that a measure "effectively controls access to a work" if, "in the ordinary course of operation," it "requires the application of information, or a process or treatment, with the authority of the copyright owner, to gain access to the work." 17 U.S.C. § 1201(a)(3). Because Congress did not explain what it means to "gain access to the work," the district court relied on the "ordinary, customary meaning" of "access": "the ability to enter, to obtain, or to make use of," [...] Based on this definition, the court concluded that "Lexmark's authentication sequence effectively `controls access' to the Printer Engine Program because it controls the consumer's ability to *make use of* these programs." [...]

93   We disagree. It is not Lexmark's authentication sequence that "controls access" to the Printer Engine Program. *See* 17 U.S.C. § 1201(a)(2). It is the purchase of a Lexmark printer that allows "access" to the program. Anyone who buys a Lexmark printer may read the literal code of the Printer Engine Program directly from the printer memory, with or without the benefit of the authentication sequence, and the data from the program may be translated into readable source code after which copies may be freely distributed. [...] No security device, in other words, protects access to the Printer Engine Program Code and no security device accordingly must be circumvented to obtain access to that program code.

94   The authentication sequence, it is true, may well block one form of "access" — the "ability to ... make use of" the Printer Engine Program by preventing the printer from functioning. But it does not block another relevant form of "access" — the "ability to [] obtain" a copy of the work or to "make use of" the literal elements of the program (its code). Because the statute refers to "control[ling] access to a work protected under this title," it does not naturally apply when the "work protected under this title" is otherwise accessible. Just as one would not say that a lock on the back door of a house "controls access" to a house whose front door does not contain a lock and just as one would not say that a lock on any door of a house "controls access" to the house after its purchaser receives the key to the lock, it does not make sense to say that this provision of the DMCA applies to otherwise-readily-accessible copyrighted works. Add to this the fact that the DMCA not only requires the technological measure to "control[] access" but also requires the measure to control that access "effectively," 17 U.S.C. § 1201(a)(2), and it seems clear that this provision does not naturally extend to a technological measure that restricts one form of access but leaves another route wide open. *See also id.* § 1201(a)(3) (technological measure must "*require* [] the application of information, or a process or a treatment ... to gain access to the work") $\lceil ... \rceil$

95   Nor are we aware of any cases that have applied this provision of the DMCA to a situation where the access-control measure left the literal code or text of the computer program or data freely readable. And several cases apply the provision in what seems to us its most natural sense. $\lceil ... \rceil$

97   Second, Lexmark counters that several cases have embraced a "to make use of" definition of "access" in applying the DMCA. While Lexmark is partially correct, these cases (and others as well) ultimately illustrate the liability line that the statute draws and in the end explain why access to the Printer Engine Program is not covered.

98   In the essential setting where the DMCA applies, the copyright protection operates on two planes: in the literal code governing the work and in the visual or audio manifestation generated by the code's execution. For example, the encoded data on CDs translates into music and on DVDs into motion pictures, while the program commands in software for video games or computers translate into some other visual and audio manifestation. In the cases upon which Lexmark relies, restricting "use" of the work means restricting consumers from making use of the copyrightable expression in the work. $\lceil ... \rceil$ As shown above, the DMCA applies in these settings when the product manufacturer prevents all access to the copyrightable material and the alleged infringer responds by marketing a device that circumvents the technological measure designed to guard access to the copyrightable material.

99   The copyrightable expression in the Printer Engine Program, by contrast, operates on only one plane: in the literal elements of the program, its source and object code. Unlike the code underlying video games or DVDs, "using" or executing the Printer Engine Program does not in turn create any protected expression. Instead, the program's output is purely functional: the Printer Engine Program "controls a number of operations" in the Lexmark printer such as "paper feed[,] paper movement[,] [and] motor control." $\lceil ... \rceil$ And unlike the code underlying video games or DVDs, no encryption or other technological measure prevents access to the Printer Engine Program. Presumably, it is precisely because the Printer Engine Program is not a conduit to protectable expression that explains why Lexmark (or any other printer company) would not block access to the computer software that makes the printer work. Because Lexmark's authentication sequence does not restrict access to this literal code, the DMCA does not apply.

100   Lexmark next argues that access-control measures may "effectively control access" to a copyrighted work within the meaning of the DMCA even though the measure may be evaded by an "`enterprising $\lceil ... \rceil$ end-user.'" $\lceil ... \rceil$ Doubtless, Lexmark is correct that a precondition for DMCA liability is not the creation of an impervious shield to the copyrighted work. $\lceil ... \rceil$ Otherwise, the DMCA would apply only when it is not needed.

101   But our reasoning does not turn on the *degree* to which a measure controls access to a work. It turns on the textual requirement that the challenged circumvention device must indeed circumvent *something,* which did not happen with the Printer Engine Program. Because Lexmark has not directed any of its security efforts, through its authentication sequence or otherwise, to ensuring that its copyrighted work (the Printer Engine Program) cannot be read and copied, it cannot lay claim to having put in place a "technological measure that effectively controls access to a work protected under [the copyright statute]." 17 U.S.C. § 1201(a)(2)(B).

102   Nor can Lexmark tenably claim that this reading of the statute fails to respect Congress's purpose in enacting it. Congress enacted the DMCA to implement the Copyright Treaty of the World Intellectual Property Organization, and in doing so expressed concerns about the threat of "massive piracy" of digital works due to "the ease with which [they] can be copied and distributed worldwide virtually instantaneously." [...] As Congress saw it, "copyrighted works will most likely be encrypted and made available to consumers once payment is made for access to a copy of the work. [People] will try to profit from the works of others by decoding the encrypted codes protecting copyrighted works, or engaging in the business of providing devices or services to enable others to do so." [...]

103   Nowhere in its deliberations over the DMCA did Congress express an interest in creating liability for the circumvention of technological measures designed to prevent consumers from using consumer goods while leaving the copyrightable content of a work unprotected. In fact, Congress added the interoperability provision in part to ensure that the DMCA would not diminish the benefit to consumers of interoperable devices "in the consumer electronics environment." [...]

104   **C.**

105   In view of our conclusion regarding the Printer Engine Program, we can dispose quickly of Lexmark's DMCA claim regarding the Toner Loading Program. The SCC chip does not provide [...] "access" to the Toner Loading Program but replaces the program. And to the extent a copy of the Toner Loading Program appears on the Printer Engine Program, Lexmark fails to overcome the same problem that undermines its DMCA claim with respect to the Printer Engine Program: Namely, it is not the SCC chip that permits access to the Printer Engine Program but the consumer's purchase of the printer. One other point deserves mention. All three liability provisions of this section of the DMCA require the claimant to show that the "technological measure" at issue "controls access to *a work protected under this title*," *see* 17 U.S.C. § 1201(a)(2)(A)-(C), which is to say a work protected under the general copyright statute, *id.* § 102(a). To the extent the Toner Loading Program is not a "work protected under [the copyright statute]," which the district court will consider on remand, the DMCA necessarily would not protect it.

106   **D.**

107   The district court also rejected SCC's interoperability defense — that its replication of the Toner Loading Program data is a "technological means" that SCC may make "available to others" "solely for the purpose of enabling interoperability of an independently created computer program with other programs." 17 U.S.C. § 1201(f)(3). In rejecting this defense, the district court said that "SCC's SMARTEK microchips cannot be considered independently created computer programs. [They] serve no legitimate purpose other than to circumvent Lexmark's authentication sequence and ... cannot qualify as independently created when they contain exact copies of Lexmark's Toner Loading Programs." [...]

108   Because the issue could become relevant at the permanent injunction stage of this dispute, we briefly explain our disagreement with this conclusion. In particular, the court did not explain why it rejected SCC's testimony that the SMARTEK chips do contain other functional computer programs beyond the copied Toner Loading Program data. The affidavit of Lynn Burchette, an SCC manager, states that "[the SMARTEK] chip has a microprocessor, with software routines we developed that control its operation and function. Our chip supports additional functionality performed by our software beyond that of [the chip on Lexmark's toner cartridges]." [...] And Dr. Goldberg testified that "Static Control has written a substantial amount of software for managing this chip; for not only providing the int[er]operability features, but also for managing the additional functionality that the [chip manufacturer] provides and which the remanufacturers may want." [...]

109   Because Lexmark has offered no reason why the testimony of SCC's experts is not "credible evidence" on this point and has offered no evidence of its own to dispute or even overcome the statements of Burchette and Goldberg, SCC also has satisfied the "independently created computer programs" requirement and may benefit from the interoperability defense, at least in the preliminary injunction context.

110   Lexmark argues alternatively that if independently created programs do exist, (1) they must have existed prior to the "reverse engineering" of Lexmark's Toner Loading Program, and (2) the technological [...] means must be "necessary or absolutely needed" to

enable interoperability of SCC's SMARTEK chip with Lexmark's Printer Engine Program. As to the first argument, nothing in the statute precludes simultaneous creation of an interoperability device and another computer program; it just must be "independently" created. As to the second argument, the statute is silent about the degree to which the "technological means" must be necessary, if indeed they must be necessary at all, for interoperability. The Toner Loading Program copy satisfies any such requirement, however, because without that program the checksum operation precludes operation of the printer (and, accordingly, operation of the Printer Engine Program), unless the checksum value located elsewhere on the chip is modified — which appears to be a computational impossibility without the contextual information that Lexmark does not disclose. *See supra.*

111   Also unavailing is Lexmark's final argument that the interoperability defense in § 1201(f)(3) does not apply because distributing the SMARTEK chip constitutes infringement and violates other "applicable law" (including tortious interference with prospective economic relations or contractual relations). Because the chip contains only a copy of the thus-far unprotected Toner Loading Program and does not contain a copy of the Printer Engine Program, infringement is not an issue. And Lexmark has offered no independent, let alone persuasive, reason why SCC's SMARTEK chip violates any state tort or other state law.

112   **V.**

113   Because Lexmark failed to establish a likelihood of success on any of its claims, whether under the general copyright statute or under the DMCA, we vacate the district court's preliminary injunction and remand the case for further proceedings consistent with this opinion.

114   [...]

100

MDY Industries, LLC v. Blizzard Entertainment, Inc.

September 09, 2014 by mrisch

1   629 F.3d 928 (2010)

2   **MDY INDUSTRIES, LLC** [...]

v.

BLIZZARD ENTERTAINMENT, INC [...]

4   United States Court of Appeals, Ninth Circuit.

5   [...]

6   Filed December 14, 2010.

7   [...]

14   **OPINION**

15   **CALLAHAN, Circuit Judge:**

16   Blizzard Entertainment, Inc. ("Blizzard") is the creator of World of Warcraft ("WoW"), a popular multiplayer online role-playing game in which players interact in a virtual world while advancing through the game's 70 levels. MDY Industries, LLC and its sole member Michael Donnelly ("Donnelly") (sometimes referred to collectively as "MDY") developed and sold Glider, a software program that automatically plays the early levels of WoW for players.

17   [935] MDY brought this action for a declaratory judgment to establish that its Glider sales do not infringe Blizzard's copyright or other rights, and Blizzard asserted counterclaims under the Digital Millennium Copyright Act ("DMCA"), 17 U.S.C. § 1201 *et seq.,* and for tortious interference with contract under Arizona law. The district court found MDY and Donnelly liable for secondary copyright infringement, violations of DMCA § 1201(a)(2) and (b)(1), and tortious interference with contract. We reverse the district court except as to MDY's liability for violation of DMCA § 1201(a)(2) and remand for trial on Blizzard's claim for tortious interference with contract.

18   **I.**

19   **A. World of Warcraft**

20   In November 2004, Blizzard created WoW, a "massively multiplayer online role-playing game" in which players interact in a virtual world.

861

WoW has ten million subscribers, of which two and a half million are in North America. The WoW software has two components: (1) the game client software that a player installs on the computer; and (2) the game server software, which the player accesses on a subscription basis by connecting to WoW's online servers. WoW does not have single-player or offline modes.

21 WoW players roleplay different characters, such as humans, elves, and dwarves. A player's central objective is to advance the character through the game's 70 levels by participating in quests and engaging in battles with monsters. As a player advances, the character collects rewards such as in-game currency, weapons, and armor. WoW's virtual world has its own economy, in which characters use their virtual currency to buy and sell items directly from each other, through vendors, or using auction houses. Some players also utilize WoW's chat capabilities to interact with others.

22 [...]

24 C. Development of Glider and Warden

25 Donnelly is a WoW player and software programmer. In March 2005, he developed Glider, a software "bot" (short for robot) that automates play of WoW's early levels, for his personal use. A user need not be at the computer while Glider is running. As explained in the Frequently Asked Questions ("FAQ") on MDY's website for Glider:

26 Glider . . . moves the mouse around and pushes keys on the keyboard. You tell it about your character, where you want to kill things, and when you want to kill. Then it kills for you, automatically. You can do something else, like eat dinner or go to a movie, and when you return, you'll have a lot more experience and loot.

27 Glider does not alter or copy WoW's game client software, does not allow a player to avoid paying monthly subscription dues to Blizzard, and has no commercial use independent of WoW. Glider was not initially designed to avoid detection by Blizzard.

28 [...]

30 In September 2005, Blizzard launched Warden, a technology that it developed to prevent its players who use unauthorized third-party software, including bots, from connecting to WoW's servers. Warden was able to detect Glider, and Blizzard immediately used Warden to ban most Glider users. MDY responded by modifying Glider to avoid detection and promoting its new anti-detection features on its website's FAQ. [...]

38 E. Pre-litigation contact between MDY and Blizzard

36 In August 2006, Blizzard sent MDY a cease-and-desist letter alleging that MDY's website hosted WoW screenshots and a Glider install file, all of which infringed Blizzard's copyrights. Donnelly removed the screenshots and requested Blizzard to clarify why the install file was infringing, but Blizzard did not respond. In October 2006, Blizzard's counsel visited Donnelly's home, threatening suit unless MDY immediately ceased selling Glider and remitted all profits to Blizzard. MDY immediately commenced this action.

37 [...] II.

38 On December 1, 2006, MDY filed an amended complaint seeking a declaration that Glider does not infringe Blizzard's copyright or other rights. In February 2007, Blizzard filed counterclaims and third-party claims against MDY and Donnelly for, *inter alia*, contributory and vicarious copyright infringement, violation of DMCA § 1201(a)(2) and (b)(1), and tortious interference with contract.

39 I[...]

40 After a January 2009 bench trial, the district court held MDY liable under DMCA § 1201(a)(2) and (b)(1). [...]

68 **V.**

70   After MDY began selling Glider, Blizzard launched Warden, its technology designed to prevent players who used bots from connecting to the WoW servers. Blizzard used Warden to ban most Glider users in September 2005. Blizzard claims that MDY is liable under DMCA § 1201(a)(2) and (b)(1) because it thereafter programmed Glider to avoid detection by Warden.

71   ## A. The Warden technology

72   Warden has two components. The first is a software module called "scan.dll," which scans a computer's RAM prior to allowing the player to connect to WoW's servers. If scan.dll detects that a bot is running, such as Glider, it will not allow the player to connect and play. After Blizzard launched Warden, MDY reconfigured Glider to circumvent scan.dll by not loading itself until after scan.dll completed its check. Warden's second component is a "resident" component that runs periodically in the background on a player's computer when it is connected to WoW's servers. It asks the computer to report portions of the WoW code running in RAM, and it looks for patterns of code associated with known bots or cheats. If it detects a bot or cheat, it boots the player from the game, which halts the computer's copying of copyrighted code into RAM.

73   ## B. The Digital Millennium Copyright Act

74   Congress enacted the DMCA in 1998 to conform United States copyright law to its obligations under two World Intellectual Property Organization ("WIPO") treaties, which require contracting parties to provide effective legal remedies against the circumvention of protective technological measures used by copyright owners. *[...]* In enacting the DMCA, Congress sought to mitigate the problems presented by copyright enforcement in the digital age. *Id.* The DMCA contains three provisions directed at the circumvention of copyright owners' technological measures. The Supreme Court has yet to construe these provisions, and they raise questions of first impression in this circuit.

75   The first provision, 17 U.S.C. § 1201(a)(1)(A), is a general prohibition against "circumventing a technological measure that effectively controls access to a work protected under [the Copyright Act]." The second prohibits trafficking in technology that circumvents a technological measure that "effectively controls access" to a copyrighted work. 17 U.S.C. § 1201(a)(2). The third prohibits trafficking in technology that circumvents a technological measure that "effectively protects" a copyright owner's right. 17 U.S.C. § 1201(b)(1).

76   ## C. The district court's decision

77   The district court assessed whether MDY violated DMCA § 1201(a)(2) and (b)(1) with respect to three WoW components. First, the district court considered the game client software's literal elements: the source code stored on players' hard drives. Second, the district court considered the game client software's individual non-literal elements: the 400,000+ discrete visual and audible components of the game, such as a visual image of a monster or its audible roar. Finally, it considered the game's dynamic non-literal [943] elements: that is, the "real-time experience of traveling through different worlds, hearing their sounds, viewing their structures, encountering their inhabitants and monsters, and encountering other players."

78   The district court granted MDY partial summary judgment as to Blizzard's § 1201(a)(2) claim with respect to WoW's literal elements. The district court reasoned that Warden does not effectively control access to the literal elements because WoW players can access the literal elements without connecting to a game server and encountering Warden; they need only install the game client software on their computers. The district court also ruled for MDY following trial as to Blizzard's § 1201(a)(2) claim with respect to WoW's individual non-literal elements, reasoning that these elements could also be accessed on a player's hard drive without encountering Warden.

79   The district court, however, ruled for Blizzard following trial as to its § 1201(a)(2) and (b)(1) claims with respect to WoW's dynamic non-literal elements, or the "real-time experience" of playing WoW. It reasoned that Warden effectively controlled access to these elements, which could not be accessed without connecting to Blizzard's servers. It also found that Glider allowed its users to circumvent Warden by avoiding or bypassing its detection features, and that MDY marketed Glider for use in circumventing Warden.

80   We turn to consider whether Glider violates DMCA § 1201(a)(2) and (b)(1) by allowing users to circumvent Warden to access WoW's various elements. MDY contends that Warden's scan.dll and resident components are separate, and only scan.dll should be considered as a potential access control measure under § 1201(a)(2). However, in our view, an access control measure can both (1) attempt to block initial access and (2) revoke access if a secondary check determines that access was unauthorized. Our analysis considers Warden's scan.dll and resident components together because the two components have the same purpose: to prevent players using detectable bots from continuing to access WoW software.

81   ## D. Construction of § 1201

82   One of the issues raised by this appeal is whether certain provisions of § 1201 prohibit circumvention of access controls when access does not constitute copyright infringement. To answer this question and others presented by this appeal, we address the nature and interrelationship of the various provisions of § 1201 in the overall context of the Copyright Act.

83   We begin by considering the scope of DMCA § 1201's three operative provisions, §§ 1201(a)(1), 1201(a)(2), and 1201(b)(1). We consider them side-by-side, because "[w]e do not ... construe statutory phrases in isolation; we read statutes as a whole. Thus, the [term to be construed] must be read in light of the immediately following phrase. ..." *[...]*

84   ### 1. *Text of the operative provisions*

85   "We begin, as always, with the text of the statute." *[...]* Section 1201(a)(1)(A) prohibits "circumvent[ing] [944] a technological measure that effectively controls access to a work protected under this title." *[...]*

88   ### 2. *Our harmonization of the DMCA's operative provisions*

89   For the reasons set forth below, we believe that § 1201 is best understood to create two distinct types of claims. First, § 1201(a) prohibits the circumvention of any technological measure that effectively controls access to a protected work and grants copyright owners the right to enforce that prohibition. *[...]* Second, and in contrast to § 1201(a), § 1201(b)(1) prohibits trafficking in technologies that circumvent technological measures that effectively protect "a right of a copyright owner." Section 1201(b)(1)'s prohibition is thus aimed at circumventions of measures that protect the copyright itself: it entitles copyright owners to protect their existing exclusive rights under the Copyright Act. Those exclusive rights are reproduction, distribution, public performance, public display, and creation of derivative works. 17 U.S.C. § 106. Historically speaking, preventing "access" to a protected work in itself has not been a right of a copyright owner arising from the Copyright Act.[...]

90   Our construction of § 1201 is compelled by the four significant textual differences between § 1201(a) and (b). First, § 1201(a)(2) prohibits the circumvention of *[...]* a measure that "effectively controls access to *a work protected under this title*," whereas § 1201(b)(1) concerns a measure that "effectively protects *a right of a copyright owner under this title in a work or portion thereof*." (emphasis added). We read § 1201(b)(1)'s language — "right of a copyright owner under this title" — to reinforce copyright owners' traditional exclusive rights under § 106 by granting them an additional cause of action against those who traffic in circumventing devices that facilitate infringement. Sections 1201(a)(1) and (a)(2), however, use the term "work protected under this title." Neither of these two subsections explicitly refers to traditional copyright infringement under § 106. Accordingly, we read this term as extending a new form of protection, i.e., the right to prevent circumvention of access controls, broadly to works protected under Title 17, i.e., copyrighted works.

91   Second, as used in § 1201(a), to "circumvent a technological measure" means "to descramble a scrambled work, to decrypt an encrypted work, or otherwise to avoid, bypass, remove, deactivate, or impair a technological measure, without the authority of the copyright owner." 17 U.S.C. § 1201(a)(3)(A). These two specific examples of unlawful circumvention under § 1201(a) — descrambling a scrambled work and decrypting an encrypted work — are acts that do not necessarily infringe or facilitate infringement of a copyright.[6] Descrambling or decrypting only enables someone to watch or listen to a work without authorization, which is not necessarily an infringement of a copyright owner's traditional exclusive rights under § 106. Put differently, descrambling and decrypting do not

necessarily result in someone's reproducing, distributing, publicly performing, or publicly displaying the copyrighted work, or creating derivative works based on the copyrighted work.

92   The third significant difference between the subsections is that § 1201(a)(1)(A) prohibits circumventing an effective access control measure, whereas § 1201(b) prohibits trafficking in circumventing devices, but does not prohibit circumvention itself because such conduct was already outlawed as copyright infringement. The Senate Judiciary Committee explained:

93   This . . . is the reason there is no prohibition on conduct in 1201(b) akin to the prohibition on circumvention conduct in 1201(a) (1). The prohibition in 1201(a)(1) is necessary because prior to this Act, the conduct of circumvention was never before made unlawful. The device limitation on 1201(a)(2) enforces this new prohibition on conduct. The copyright law has long forbidden copyright infringements, so no new prohibition was necessary.

94   S.Rep. No. 105-90, at 11 (1998). This difference reinforces our reading of § 1201(b) as strengthening copyright owners' traditional rights against copyright infringement and of § 1201(a) as granting copyright owners a new anti-circumvention right.

95   Fourth, in § 1201(a)(1)(B)-(D), Congress directs the Library of Congress ("Library") to identify classes of copyrighted works for which "noninfringing uses by persons who are users of a copyrighted work are, or are likely to be, adversely affected, and the [anti-circumvention] prohibition contained in [§ 1201(a)(1)(A)] shall not apply to such users with respect to such classes of works for the ensuing 3-year period." There is no analogous provision in § 1201(b). We impute this lack of symmetry to Congress' need to balance [...] copyright owners' new anti-circumvention right with the public's right to access the work. [...] Sections 1201(a)(1)(B)-(D) thus promote the public's right to access by allowing the Library to exempt circumvention of effective access control measures in particular situations where it concludes that the public's right to access outweighs the owner's interest in restricting access.[7] In limiting the owner's right to control access, the Library does not, and is not permitted to, authorize infringement of a copyright owner's traditional exclusive rights under the copyright. Rather, the Library is only entitled to moderate the new anti-circumvention right created by, and hence subject to the limitations in, DMCA § 1201(a)(1).[8]

96   Our reading of § 1201(a) and (b) ensures that neither section is rendered superfluous. A violation of § 1201(a)(1)(A), which prohibits circumvention itself, will not be a violation of § 1201(b), which does not contain an analogous prohibition on circumvention. A violation of § 1201(a)(2), which prohibits trafficking in devices that facilitate circumvention of *access* control measures, will not always be a violation of § 1201(b)(1), which prohibits trafficking in devices that facilitate circumvention of measures that protect against *copyright infringement*. Of course, if a copyright owner puts in place an effective measure that both (1) controls access and (2) protects against copyright infringement, a defendant who traffics in a device that circumvents that measure could be liable under both § 1201(a) and (b). Nonetheless, we read the differences in structure between § 1201(a) and (b) as reflecting Congress's intent to address distinct concerns by creating different rights with different elements.

97   [...]

10± **4.** *The Federal Circuit's decisions*

108   The Federal Circuit has adopted a different approach to the DMCA. In essence, it requires § 1201(a) plaintiffs to demonstrate that the circumventing technology infringes or facilitates infringement of the plaintiff's copyright (an "infringement nexus requirement"). *See Chamberlain Group, Inc. v. Skylink Techs., Inc.,* [...]

109   The seminal decision is *Chamberlain* [...] In *Chamberlain,* the plaintiff sold garage door openers ("GDOs") with a "rolling code" security system that purportedly reduced the risk of crime by constantly changing the transmitter signal necessary to open the door. [...] Customers used the GDOs' transmitters to send the changing signal, which in turn opened or closed their garage doors. *Id.*

110   Plaintiff sued the defendant, who sold "universal" GDO transmitters for use with plaintiff's GDOs, under § 1201(a)(2). *Id.* at 1185. The

plaintiff alleged that its GDOs and transmitters both contained copyrighted computer programs and that its rolling code security system was a technological measure that controlled access to those programs [...] Accordingly, plaintiff alleged that the defendant — by selling GDO transmitters that were compatible with plaintiff's GDOs — had trafficked in a technology that was primarily used for the circumvention of a technological measure (the rolling code security system) that effectively controlled access to plaintiff's copyrighted works. *Id.*

111   The Federal Circuit rejected the plaintiff's claim, holding that the defendant did not violate § 1201(a)(2) because, *inter alia,* the defendant's universal GDO transmitters did not infringe or facilitate infringement of the plaintiff's copyrighted computer programs. *I[...]* The linchpin of the *Chamberlain* court's analysis is its conclusion that DMCA coverage is limited to a copyright owner's rights under the Copyright Act as set forth in § 106 of the Copyright Act. *[...]* Thus, it held that § 1201(a) did not grant copyright owners a new anti-circumvention right, but instead, established new *[...]* causes of action for a defendant's unauthorized access of copyrighted material when it infringes upon a copyright owner's rights under § 106. *[...]* Accordingly, a § 1201(a)(2) plaintiff was required to demonstrate a nexus to infringement — i.e., that the defendant's trafficking in circumventing technology had a "reasonable relationship" to the protections that the Copyright Act affords copyright owners. *[...]* The Federal Circuit explained:

112   Defendants who traffic in devices that circumvent access controls in ways that facilitate infringement may be subject to liability under § 1201(a)(2). Defendants who use such devices may be subject to liability under § 1201(a)(1) whether they infringe or not. Because all defendants who traffic in devices that circumvent rights controls necessarily facilitate infringement, they may be subject to liability under § 1201(b). Defendants who use such devices may be subject to liability for copyright infringement. *And finally, defendants whose circumvention devices do not facilitate infringement are not subject to § 1201 liability.*

113   *[...]Chamberlain* concluded that § 1201(a) created a new cause of action linked to copyright infringement, rather than a new anti-circumvention right separate from copyright infringement, for six reasons.

114   First, *Chamberlain* reasoned that Congress enacted the DMCA to balance the interests of copyright owners and information users, and an infringement nexus requirement was necessary to create an anti-circumvention right that truly achieved that balance. *[...]* Second, *Chamberlain* feared that copyright owners could use an access control right to prohibit exclusively fair uses of their material even absent feared foul use. *[...]* Third, *Chamberlain* feared that § 1201(a) would allow companies to leverage their sales into aftermarket monopolies, in potential violation of antitrust law and the doctrine of copyright misuse. *[...]* Fourth, *Chamberlain* viewed an infringement nexus requirement as necessary to prevent "absurd and disastrous results," such as the existence of DMCA liability for disabling a burglary alarm to gain access to a home containing copyrighted materials. *[...]*

115   Fifth, *Chamberlain* stated that an infringement nexus requirement might be necessary to render Congress's exercise of its Copyright Clause authority rational. *Id.* at 1200. The Copyright Clause gives Congress "the task of defining the scope of the limited monopoly that should be granted to authors . . . in order to give the public appropriate access to their work product." *[...]* Without an infringement nexus requirement, Congress arguably would have allowed copyright owners in § 1201(a) to deny all access to the public by putting an effective access control measure in place that the public was not allowed to circumvent.

116   Finally, the *Chamberlain* court viewed an infringement nexus requirement as necessary for the Copyright Act to be internally consistent. It reasoned that § 1201(c)(1), enacted simultaneously, provides that "nothing in this section shall affect rights, remedies, limitations, or defenses to copyright infringement, including fair use, under this title." The *Chamberlain* court opined that if § 1201(a) creates liability for access without regard to the remainder of the Copyright Act, it "would *[...]* clearly affect rights and limitations, if not remedies and defenses." *Id.*

117   Accordingly, the Federal Circuit held that a DMCA § 1201(a)(2) action was foreclosed to the extent that the defendant trafficked in a

device that did not facilitate copyright infringement. *[...]*

118   **5.** *We decline to adopt an infringement nexus requirement*

119   While we appreciate the policy considerations expressed by the Federal Circuit in *Chamberlain,* we are unable to follow its approach because it is contrary to the plain language of the statute. In addition, the Federal Circuit failed to recognize the rationale for the statutory construction that we have proffered. Also, its approach is based on policy concerns that are best directed to Congress in the first instance, or for which there appear to be other reasons that do not require such a convoluted construction of the statute's language.

120   *i. Statutory inconsistencies*

121   Were we to follow *Chamberlain* in imposing an infringement nexus requirement, we would have to disregard the plain language of the statute. Moreover, there is significant textual evidence showing Congress's intent to create a new anticircumvention right in § 1201(a) distinct from infringement. As set forth *supra,* this evidence includes: (1) Congress's choice to link only § 1201(b)(1) explicitly to infringement; (2) Congress's provision in § 1201(a)(3)(A) that descrambling and decrypting devices can lead to § 1201(a) liability, even though descrambling and decrypting devices may only enable non-infringing access to a copyrighted work; and (3) Congress's creation of a mechanism in § 1201(a)(1)(B)-(D) to exempt certain non-infringing behavior from § 1201(a)(1) liability, a mechanism that would be unnecessary if an infringement nexus requirement existed.

122   Though unnecessary to our conclusion because of the clarity of the statute's text $[...]$ we also note that the legislative history supports the conclusion that Congress intended to prohibit even non-infringing circumvention and trafficking in circumventing devices. Moreover, in mandating a § 1201(a) nexus to infringement, we would deprive copyright owners of the important enforcement tool that Congress granted them to make sure that they are compensated for valuable non-infringing access — for instance, copyright owners who make movies or music available online, protected by an access control measure, in exchange for direct or indirect payment.

123   The *Chamberlain* court reasoned that if § 1201(a) creates liability for access without regard to the remainder of the Copyright Act, it "would clearly affect rights and limitations, if not remedies and defenses." $[...]$ This perceived tension is relieved by our recognition that § 1201(a) creates a new anti-circumvention right distinct from the traditional exclusive rights of a copyright owner. It follows that § 1201(a) does not limit the traditional framework of exclusive rights created by § 106, or defenses to those rights such as fair use.[12] We are thus unpersuaded by *Chamberlain's* reading of the DMCA's text and structure.

124   $[...]$

128   **E. Blizzard's § 1201(a)(2) claim**

129   **1.** *WoW's literal elements and individual non-literal elements*

130   We agree with the district court that MDY's Glider does not violate DMCA § 1201(a)(2) with respect to WoW's literal elements[15] and individual non-literal elements, because Warden does not effectively control access to these WoW elements. First, Warden does not control access to WoW's literal elements because these elements — the game client's software code — are available on a player's hard drive once the game client software is installed. Second, as the district court found:

131   [WoW's] individual nonliteral components may be accessed by a user without signing on to the server. As was demonstrated during trial, an owner of the game client software may use independently purchased computer programs to call up the visual images or the recorded sounds within the game client software. For instance, a user may call up and listen to the roar a particular monster makes within the game. Or the user may call up a virtual image of that monster.

132   Since a player need not encounter Warden to access WoW's individual non-literal elements, Warden does not effectively control access to those elements.

133   Our conclusion is in accord with the Sixth Circuit's decision in *Lexmark International v. Static Control Components[...]*

135   Here, a player's purchase of the WoW game client allows access to the game's literal elements and individual non-literal elements. Warden blocks one form of access to these elements: the ability to access them while connected to a WoW server. However, analogously to the situation in *Lexmark,* Warden leaves open the ability to access these elements directly via the user's computer. We conclude that Warden is not an effective access control measure with respect to WoW's literal elements and individual non-literal elements, and therefore, that MDY does not violate § 1201(a)(2) with respect to these elements.

138   **2. *WoW's dynamic non-literal elements***

139   We conclude that MDY meets each of the six textual elements for violating § 1201(a)(2) with respect to WoW's dynamic non-literal elements. That is, MDY (1) traffics in (2) a technology or part thereof (3) that is primarily designed, produced, or marketed for, or has limited commercially significant use other than (4) circumventing a technological measure (5) that effectively controls access (6) to a copyrighted work. *See* 17 U.S.C. § 1201(a)(2).

140   The first two elements are met because MDY "traffics in a technology or part thereof" — that is, it sells Glider. The third and fourth elements are met because Blizzard has established that MDY *markets* Glider for use in circumventing Warden, thus satisfying the requirement of § 1201(a)(2)(C).[16] Indeed, Glider has no function other than to facilitate the playing of WoW. The sixth element is met because, as the district court held, WoW's dynamic non-literal elements constitute a copyrighted work. *[...]*

141   The fifth element is met because Warden is an effective access control measure. To "effectively control access to a work," a technological measure must "in the ordinary course of its operation, require[ ] the application of information, or a process or a treatment, with the authority of the copyright owner, to gain access to the work." 17 U.S.C. § 1201(a)(3)(B). Both of Warden's two components "require[ ] the application of information, or a process or a treatment . . . to gain access to the work." For a player to connect to Blizzard's servers which provide access to WoW's dynamic non-literal elements, scan. dll must scan the player's computer RAM and confirm the absence of any bots or cheats. The resident component also requires a "process" in order for the user to continue accessing the work: the user's computer must report portions of WoW code running in RAM to the server. Moreover, Warden's provisions were put into place by Blizzard, and thus, function "with the authority of the copyright owner." Accordingly, Warden effectively controls access to WoW's dynamic non-literal elements.[17] We hold that MDY is liable under § 1201(a)(2) with respect to WoW's dynamic non-literal elements.[18] Accordingly, we affirm the district court's entry of a permanent injunction against MDY to prevent future § 1201(a)(2) violations.

142   ## F. Blizzard's § 1201(b)(1) claim

143   Blizzard may prevail under § 1201(b)(1) only if Warden "effectively protect[s] a right" of Blizzard under the Copyright Act. Blizzard contends that Warden protects its reproduction right against unauthorized copying. We disagree.

144   First, although WoW players copy the software code into RAM while playing the game, Blizzard's EULA and ToU authorize all licensed WoW players to do so. [...] Accordingly, MDY does not violate § 1201(b)(1) by enabling Glider users to avoid Warden's interruption of their *authorized* copying into RAM.

145   Second, although WoW players can theoretically record game play by taking screen shots, there is no evidence that Warden detects or prevents such allegedly infringing copying.[19] This is logical, because [...] Warden was designed to reduce the presence of cheats and bots, not to protect WoW's dynamic non-literal elements against copying. We conclude that Warden does not effectively protect any of Blizzard's rights under the Copyright Act, and MDY is not liable under § 1201(b)(1) for Glider's circumvention of Warden.[20]

146   [...]

158

163   **VII.**

164   [...] we determine that MDY [...] is liable under the DMCA only for violation of § 1201(a)(2) with respect to WoW's dynamic non-literal elements. [...]

171   [6] Perhaps for this reason, Congress did not list descrambling and decrypting as circumventing acts that would violate § 1201(b)(1). *See* 17 U.S.C. § 1201(b)(2)(A).

172   [...]

180   [15] We also agree with the district court that there are no genuine issues of material fact on Blizzard's § 1201(a)(2) claim regarding WoW's literal elements.

181   [...]

Multi-Class Unit: <u>OIL Casebook Topic IX: Contracts and Licensing</u>

Class 24: 9.1 <u>OIL Casebook: Contract Formation</u>

ProCD, Inc. v. Zeidenberg

September 13, 2014 by mrisch

1   86 F.3d 1447 (1996)

2   **ProCD, INCORPORATED** [...]

Matthew ZEIDENBERG [...]

4   United States Court of Appeals, Seventh Circuit.

5   [...]
               Decided June 20, 1996.

6   [...]

12   Before COFFEY, FLAUM, and EASTERBROOK, Circuit Judges.

13   **EASTERBROOK, Circuit Judge.**

14   Must buyers of computer software obey the terms of shrinkwrap licenses? The [...] district court held not, for two reasons: first, they are
not contracts because the licenses are inside the box rather than printed on the outside; second, federal law forbids enforcement even if
the licenses are contracts. [...] The parties and numerous amici curiae have briefed many other issues, but these are the only two that
matter — and we disagree with the district judge's conclusion on each. Shrinkwrap licenses are enforceable unless their terms are
objectionable on grounds applicable to contracts in general (for example, if they violate a rule of positive law, or if they are
unconscionable). Because no one argues that the terms of the license at issue here are troublesome, we remand with instructions to
enter judgment for the plaintiff.

15   I

16   ProCD, the plaintiff, has compiled information from more than 3,000 telephone directories into a computer database. We may assume
that this database cannot be copyrighted, although it is more complex, contains more information (nine-digit zip codes and census
industrial codes), is organized differently, and therefore is more original than the single alphabetical directory at issue in *Feist Publications,
Inc. v. Rural Telephone Service Co.* [...] ProCD sells a version of the database, called SelectPhone (trademark), on CD-ROM discs. (CD-
ROM means "compact disc — read only memory." The "shrinkwrap license" gets its name from the fact that retail software packages are
covered in plastic or cellophane "shrinkwrap," and some vendors, though not ProCD, have written licenses that become effective as soon
as the customer tears the wrapping from the package. Vendors prefer "end user license," but we use the more common term.) A
proprietary method of compressing the data serves as effective encryption too. Customers decrypt and use the data with the aid of an
application program that ProCD has written. This program, which is copyrighted, searches the database in response to users' criteria
(such as "find all people named Tatum in Tennessee, plus all firms with `Door Systems' in the corporate name"). The resulting lists (or, as
ProCD prefers, "listings") can be read and manipulated by other software, such as word processing programs.

17   The database in SelectPhone (trademark) cost more than $10 million to compile and is expensive to keep current. It is much more

valuable to some users than to others. The combination of names, addresses, and SIC codes enables manufacturers to compile lists of potential customers. Manufacturers and retailers pay high prices to specialized information intermediaries for such mailing lists; ProCD offers a potentially cheaper alternative. People with nothing to sell could use the database as a substitute for calling long distance information, or as a way to look up old friends who have moved to unknown towns, or just as an electronic substitute for the local phone book. ProCD decided to engage in price discrimination, selling its database to the general public for personal use at a low price (approximately $150 for the set of five discs) while selling information to the trade for a higher price. [...]

18   If ProCD had to recover all of its costs and make a profit by charging a single price — that is, if it could not charge more to commercial users than to the general public —it would have to raise the price substantially over $150. The ensuing reduction in sales would harm consumers who value the information at, say, $200. They get consumer surplus of $50 under the current arrangement but would cease to buy if the price rose substantially. If because of high elasticity of demand in the consumer segment of the market the only way to make a profit turned out to be a price attractive to commercial users alone, then all consumers would lose out — and so would the commercial clients, who would have to pay more for the listings because ProCD could not obtain any contribution toward costs from the consumer market.

19   [...] To make price discrimination work, however, the seller must be able to control arbitrage. An air carrier sells tickets for less to vacationers than to business travelers, using advance purchase and Saturday-night-stay requirements to distinguish the categories. A producer of movies segments the market by time, releasing first to theaters, then to pay-per-view services, next to the videotape and laserdisc market, and finally to cable and commercial tv. Vendors of computer software have a harder task. Anyone can walk into a retail store and buy a box. Customers do not wear tags saying "commercial user" or "consumer user." Anyway, even a commercial-user-detector at the door would not work, because a consumer could buy the software and resell to a commercial user. That arbitrage would break down the price discrimination and drive up the minimum price at which ProCD would sell to anyone.

20   Instead of tinkering with the product and letting users sort themselves — for example, furnishing current data at a high price that would be attractive only to commercial customers, and two-year-old data at a low price — ProCD turned to the institution of contract. Every box containing its consumer product declares that the software comes with restrictions stated in an enclosed license. This license, which is encoded on the CD-ROM disks as well as printed in the manual, and which appears on a user's screen every time the software runs, limits use of the application program and listings to non-commercial purposes.

21   Matthew Zeidenberg bought a consumer package of SelectPhone (trademark) in 1994 from a retail outlet in Madison, Wisconsin, but decided to ignore the license. He formed Silken Mountain Web Services, Inc., to resell the information in the SelectPhone (trademark) database. The corporation makes the database available on the Internet to anyone willing to pay its price — which, needless to say, is less than ProCD charges its commercial customers. [...]

22   **II**

23   Following the district court, we treat the licenses as ordinary contracts accompanying the sale of products, and therefore as governed by the common law of contracts and the Uniform Commercial Code. Whether there are legal differences between "contracts" and "licenses" (which may matter under the copyright doctrine of first sale) is a subject for another day. [...] Zeidenberg does argue, and the district court held, that placing the package of software on the shelf is an "offer," which the customer "accepts" by paying the asking price and leaving the store with the goods. [...] In Wisconsin, as elsewhere, a contract includes only the terms on which the parties have agreed. One cannot agree to hidden terms, the judge concluded. So far, so good — but one of the terms to which Zeidenberg agreed by purchasing the software is that the transaction was subject to a license. Zeidenberg's position therefore must be that the printed terms on the outside of a box are the parties' contract — except for printed terms that refer to or incorporate other terms. But why would Wisconsin fetter the parties' choice in this [...] way? Vendors can put the entire terms of a contract on the outside of a box only by using microscopic type, removing other information that buyers might find more useful (such as what the software does, and on which computers it works), or both. The "Read Me" file included with most software, describing system requirements and potential incompatibilities, may be equivalent to ten pages of type; warranties and license restrictions take still more space. Notice on the outside,

terms on the inside, and a right to return the software for a refund if the terms are unacceptable (a right that the license expressly extends), may be a means of doing business valuable to buyers and sellers alike. [...]

24   Transactions in which the exchange of money precedes the communication of detailed terms are common. Consider the purchase of insurance. The buyer goes to an agent, who explains the essentials (amount of coverage, number of years) and remits the premium to the home office, which sends back a policy. On the district judge's understanding, the terms of the policy are irrelevant because the insured paid before receiving them. Yet the device of payment, often with a "binder" (so that the insurance takes effect immediately even though the home office reserves the right to withdraw coverage later), in advance of the policy, serves buyers' interests by accelerating effectiveness and reducing transactions costs. Or consider the purchase of an airline ticket. The traveler calls the carrier or an agent, is quoted a price, reserves a seat, pays, and gets a ticket, in that order. The ticket contains elaborate terms, which the traveler can reject by canceling the reservation. To use the ticket is to accept the terms, even terms that in retrospect are disadvantageous. [...]

27   Our case has only one form; UCC § 2-207 is irrelevant. [...]

28   What then does the current version of the UCC have to say? We think that the place to start is § 2-204(1): "A contract for sale of goods may be made in any manner sufficient to show agreement, including conduct by both parties which recognizes the existence of such a contract." A vendor, as master of the offer, may invite acceptance by conduct, and may propose limitations on the kind of conduct that constitutes acceptance. A buyer may accept by performing the acts the vendor proposes to treat as acceptance. And that is what happened. ProCD proposed a contract that a buyer would accept by *using* the software after having an opportunity to read the license at leisure. This Zeidenberg did. He had no choice, because the software splashed the license on the screen and would not let him proceed without indicating acceptance. So although the district judge was right to say that a contract can be, and often is, formed simply by paying the price and walking out of the store, the UCC permits contracts to be formed in other ways. ProCD proposed such a different way, and without protest Zeidenberg agreed. Ours is not a case in which a consumer opens a package to find an insert saying "you owe us an extra $10,000" and the seller files suit to collect. Any buyer finding such a demand can prevent formation of the contract by returning the package, as can any consumer who concludes that the terms of the license make the software worth less than the purchase price. Nothing in the UCC requires a seller to maximize the buyer's net gains.

29   Section 2-606, which defines "acceptance of goods", reinforces this understanding. A buyer accepts goods under § 2-606(1)(b) when, after an opportunity to inspect, he fails to make an effective rejection under § 2-602(1). ProCD extended an opportunity to reject if a buyer should find the license terms [...] unsatisfactory; Zeidenberg inspected the package, tried out the software, learned of the license, and did not reject the goods. We refer to § 2-606 only to show that the opportunity to return goods can be important; acceptance of an offer differs from acceptance of goods after delivery, [...] but the UCC consistently permits the parties to structure their relations so that the buyer has a chance to make a final decision after a detailed review.

30   [...] Zeidenberg has not located any Wisconsin case — for that matter, any case in any state — holding that under the UCC the ordinary terms found in shrinkwrap licenses require any special prominence, or otherwise are to be undercut rather than enforced. In the end, the terms of the license are conceptually identical to the contents of the package. Just as no court would dream of saying that SelectPhone (trademark) must contain 3,100 phone books rather than 3,000, or must have data no more than 30 days old, or must sell for $100 rather than $150 — although any of these changes would be welcomed by the customer, if all other things were held constant — so, we believe, Wisconsin would not let the buyer pick and choose among terms. Terms of use are no less a part of "the product" than are the size of the database and the speed with which the software compiles listings. Competition among vendors, not judicial revision of a package's contents, is how consumers are protected in a market economy. [...]

38   REVERSED AND REMANDED.

Hill v. Gateway 2000, Inc.

September 14, 2014 by mrisch

1   105 F.3d 1147 (1997)

2   **Rich HILL** [...]
                                                              v.
                                                   GATEWAY 2000, INC. [...]

4   United States Court of Appeals, Seventh Circuit.

5   [...]
                                                    Decided January 6, 1997.
                                                              [...]

10   **EASTERBROOK, Circuit Judge.**

11   A customer picks up the phone, orders a computer, and gives a credit card number. Presently a box arrives, containing the computer and
     a list of terms, said to govern unless the customer returns the computer within 30 days. Are these terms effective as the parties' contract,
     or is the contract term-free because the order-taker did not read any terms over the phone and elicit the customer's assent?

12   One of the terms in the box containing a Gateway 2000 system was an arbitration clause. Rich and Enza Hill, the customers, kept the
     computer more than 30 days before complaining about its components and performance. They filed suit in federal court [...]

13   The Hills say that the arbitration clause did not stand out: they concede noticing the statement of terms but deny reading it closely
     enough to discover the agreement to arbitrate, and they ask us to conclude that they therefore may go to court. Yet an agreement to
     arbitrate must be enforced "save upon such grounds as exist at law or in equity for the revocation of any contract." [...] Terms inside
     Gateway's box stand or fall together. If they constitute the parties' contract because the Hills had an opportunity to return the computer
     after reading them, then all must be enforced.

14   *ProCD, Inc. v. Zeidenberg,* 86 F.3d 1447 (7th Cir.1996), holds that terms inside a box of software bind consumers who use the software
     after an opportunity to read the terms and to reject them by returning the product. Likewise, *Carnival Cruise Lines, Inc. v. Shute,* 499 U.S.
     585, 111 S.Ct. 1522, 113 L.Ed.2d 622 (1991), enforces a forum-selection clause that was included among three pages of terms
     attached to a cruise ship ticket. *ProCD* and *Carnival Cruise Lines* exemplify the many commercial transactions in which people pay for
     products with terms to follow; *ProCD* discusses others. [...] The district court concluded in *ProCD* that the contract is formed when the
     consumer pays for the software; as a result, the court held, only terms known to the consumer at that moment are part of the contract,
     and provisos inside the box do not count. Although this is one way a contract [...] could be formed, it is not the only way: "A vendor, as
     master of the offer, may invite acceptance by conduct, and may propose limitations on the kind of conduct that constitutes acceptance.
     A buyer may accept by performing the acts the vendor proposes to treat as acceptance." *[...]* Gateway shipped computers with the
     same sort of accept-or-return offer ProCD made to users of its software. *ProCD* relied on the Uniform Commercial Code rather than any
     peculiarities of Wisconsin law; both Illinois and South Dakota, the two states whose law might govern relations between Gateway and the
     Hills, have adopted the UCC; neither side has pointed us to any atypical doctrines in those states that might be pertinent; *ProCD*
     therefore applies to this dispute.

15   Plaintiffs ask us to limit *ProCD* to software, but where's the sense in that?   *One of my all time favorite lines in a judicial opinion.*   *ProCD* is about the law of contract, not the law of software. Payment preceding the revelation of full terms is common for air transportation, insurance, and many other endeavors. Practical considerations support allowing vendors to enclose the full legal terms with their products. Cashiers cannot be expected to read legal documents to customers before ringing up sales. If the staff at the other end of the phone for direct-sales operations such as Gateway's had to read the four-page statement of terms before taking the buyer's credit card number, the droning voice would anesthetize rather than enlighten many potential buyers. Others would hang up in a rage over the waste of their time. And oral recitation would not avoid customers' assertions (whether true or feigned) that the clerk did not read term X to them, or that they did not remember or understand it. Writing provides benefits for both sides of commercial transactions. Customers as a group are better off when vendors skip costly and ineffectual steps such as telephonic recitation, and use instead a simple approve-or-return device. Competent adults are bound by such documents, read or unread. For what little it is worth, we add that the box from Gateway was crammed with software. The computer came with an operating system, without which it was useful only as a boat anchor. [Gateway also included many application programs. So the Hills' effort to limit *ProCD* to software would not avail them factually, even if it were sound legally — which it is not.

16   [...]

17   Next the Hills insist that *ProCD* is irrelevant because Zeidenberg was a "merchant" and they are not. Section 2-207(2) of the UCC, the infamous battle-of-the-forms section, states that "additional terms [following acceptance of an offer] are to be construed as proposals for addition to a contract. Between merchants such terms become part of the contract unless ...". Plaintiffs tell us that *ProCD* came out as it did only because Zeidenberg was a "merchant" and the terms inside ProCD's box were not excluded by the "unless" clause. This argument pays scant attention to the opinion in *ProCD*, which concluded that, when there is only one form, "sec. 2-207 is irrelevant." [...] The question in *ProCD* was not whether terms were added to a contract after its formation, but how and when the contract was formed — in particular, whether a vendor may propose that a contract of sale be formed, not in the store (or over the phone) with the payment of money or a general "send me the product," but after the customer has had a chance to inspect both the item and the terms. *ProCD* answers "yes," for merchants and consumers alike. Yet again, for what little it is worth we observe that the Hills misunderstand the setting of *ProCD*. A "merchant" under the UCC "means a person who deals in goods of the kind or otherwise by his occupation holds himself out as having knowledge or skill peculiar to the practices or goods involved in the transaction", § 2-104(1). Zeidenberg bought the product at a retail store, an uncommon place for merchants to acquire inventory. His corporation put ProCD's database on the Internet for anyone to browse, which led to the litigation but did not make Zeidenberg a software merchant.

18   At oral, argument the Hills propounded still another distinction: the box containing ProCD's software displayed a notice that additional terms were within, while the box containing Gateway's computer did not. The difference is functional, not legal. Consumers browsing the aisles of a store can look at the box, and if they are unwilling to deal with the prospect of additional terms can leave the box alone, avoiding the transactions costs of returning the package after reviewing its contents. Gateway's box, by contrast, is just a shipping carton; it is not on display anywhere. Its function is to protect the product during transit, and the information on its sides is for the use of handlers

19   ("Fragile!" This Side Up!" ♻︎↑👕)

20   rather than would-be purchasers.

21   Perhaps the Hills would have had a better argument if they were first alerted to the bundling of hardware and legal-ware after opening the box and wanted to return the computer in order to avoid disagreeable terms, but were dissuaded by the expense of shipping. What the remedy would be in such a case — could it exceed the shipping charges? — is an interesting question, but one that need not detain us because the Hills knew before they ordered the computer that the carton would include *some* important terms, and they did not seek to discover these in advance. Gateway's ads state that their products come with limited warranties and lifetime support. How limited was the warranty — 30 days, with service contingent on shipping the computer back, or five years, with free onsite service? What sort of

support was offered? Shoppers have three principal ways to discover these things. First, they can ask the vendor to send a copy before deciding whether to buy. The Magnuson-Moss Warranty Act requires firms to distribute their warranty terms on request, 15 U.S.C. § 2302(b)(1)(A); the Hills do not contend that Gateway would have refused to enclose the remaining terms too. Concealment would be bad for business, scaring some customers away and leading to excess returns from others. Second, shoppers can consult public sources (computer magazines, the Web sites of vendors) that may contain this information. Third, they may inspect the documents after the product's delivery. Like Zeidenberg, the Hills took the third option. By keeping the computer beyond 30 days, the Hills accepted Gateway's offer, including the arbitration clause.

22   [...] The decision of the district court is vacated, and this case is remanded with instructions to compel the Hills to submit their dispute to arbitration.

Klocek v. Gateway, Inc.

September 14, 2014 by mrisch

1   104 F.Supp.2d 1332 (2000)

2   **William S. KLOCEK** [...]
                                                            v.
                                          GATEWAY, INC. [...]

3   [...]

4   United States District Court, D. Kansas.

5   June 15, 2000.

6   [...]

90   **VRATIL, District Judge.**

11   William S. Klocek brings suit against Gateway, Inc. and Hewlett-Packard, Inc. on claims arising from purchases of a Gateway computer
      and a Hewlett-Packard scanner. This matter comes before the Court on the *Motion to Dismiss* (Doc. # 6) which Gateway filed November
      22, 1999 [...] For reasons stated below, the Court overrules Gateway's motion to dismiss, [...]

12   **A. Gateway's Motion to Dismiss**

13   Plaintiff brings individual and class action claims against Gateway, alleging that it induced him and other consumers to purchase
      computers and special support packages by making false promises of technical support. *[...]* Individually, plaintiff also claims breach of
      contract and breach of warranty, in that Gateway breached certain warranties that its computer would be compatible with standard
      peripherals and standard internet services. *[...]*

14   Gateway asserts that plaintiff must arbitrate his claims under Gateway's Standard Terms and Conditions Agreement ("Standard Terms").
      Whenever it sells a computer, Gateway includes a copy of the Standard Terms in the box which contains the computer battery power
      cables and instruction manuals. At the top of the first page, the Standard Terms include the following notice:

15   NOTE TO THE CUSTOMER:

16   [...] This document contains Gateway 2000's Standard Terms and Conditions. By keeping your Gateway 2000 computer
           system beyond five (5) days after the date of delivery, you accept these Terms and Conditions.

17   The notice is in emphasized type and is located inside a printed box which sets it apart from other provisions of the document. The
      Standard Terms are four pages long and contain 16 numbered paragraphs. Paragraph 10 provides the following arbitration clause:

18   DISPUTE RESOLUTION. Any dispute or controversy arising out of or relating to this Agreement or its interpretation shall be settled exclusively and finally by arbitration. The arbitration shall be conducted in accordance with the Rules of Conciliation and Arbitration of the International Chamber of Commerce. The arbitration shall be conducted in Chicago, Illinois, U.S.A. before a sole arbitrator. Any award rendered in any such arbitration proceeding shall be final and binding on each of the parties, and judgment may be entered thereon in a court of competent jurisdiction.[1]

19   Gateway urges the Court to dismiss plaintiff's claims under the Federal Arbitration Act ("FAA"), 9 U.S.C. § 1 *et seq.* The FAA ensures that written arbitration agreements in maritime transactions and transactions involving interstate commerce are "valid, irrevocable, and enforceable." 9 U.S.C. § 2.[2] Federal policy favors arbitration agreements and requires that we "rigorously enforce" them. *[...]*

23   Gateway bears an initial summary-judgment-like burden of establishing that it is entitled to arbitration. *[...]* In this case, Gateway fails to present evidence establishing the most basic facts regarding the transaction. *[...]*

24   Before granting a stay or dismissing a case pending arbitration, the Court must determine that the parties have a written agreement to arbitrate. *[...]* When deciding whether the parties have agreed to arbitrate, the Court applies ordinary state law principles that govern the formation of contracts. *[...]* The existence of an arbitration agreement "is simply a matter of contract between the parties; [arbitration] is a way to resolve those disputes — but only those disputes — that the parties have agreed to submit to arbitration." *[...]*

25   Before evaluating whether the parties agreed to arbitrate, the Court must determine what state law controls the formation of the contract in this case. *[...]*

26   Depending on which factual version is correct, it appears that the parties may have performed the last act necessary to form the contract in Kansas (with plaintiff purchasing the computer in Kansas), Missouri (with Gateway shipping the computer to plaintiff in Missouri), or some unidentified other states (with Gateway agreeing to ship plaintiff's catalog order and/or Gateway actually shipping the order).[4]

27   The Court discerns no material difference between the applicable substantive law in Kansas and Missouri and — as to those two states — it perhaps would not need to resolve the choice of law issue at this time. *[...]*

28   The Uniform Commercial Code ("UCC") governs the parties' transaction under both Kansas and Missouri law. *[...]* Regardless whether plaintiff purchased the computer in person or placed an order and received shipment of the computer, the parties agree that plaintiff paid for and received a computer from Gateway. This conduct clearly demonstrates a contract for the sale of a computer. *[...]*

29   State courts in Kansas and Missouri apparently have not decided whether terms received with a product become part of the parties' agreement. Authority from other courts is split. *[...]* It appears that at least in part, the cases turn on whether the court finds that the parties formed their contract *before* or *after* the vendor communicated its terms to the purchaser. *[...]*

30   Gateway urges the Court to follow the Seventh Circuit decision in *Hill.* That case involved the shipment of a Gateway computer with terms similar to the Standard Terms in this case, except that Gateway gave the customer 30 days — instead of 5 days — to return the computer. In enforcing the arbitration clause, the Seventh Circuit relied on its decision in *ProCD,* where it enforced a software license which was contained inside a product box. *See Hill[...]* In *ProCD,* the Seventh Circuit noted that the exchange of money frequently precedes the communication of detailed terms in a commercial transaction. *See ProCD[...]* Citing UCC § 2-204, the court reasoned that by including the license with the software, the vendor proposed a contract that the buyer could accept by using the software after having an opportunity to read the license.[8] *ProCD,* 86 F.3d at 1452. Specifically, the court stated:

31   A vendor, as master of the offer, may invite acceptance by conduct, and may propose limitations on the kind of conduct [...] that constitutes acceptance. A buyer may accept by performing the acts the vendor proposes to treat as acceptance.

32   *ProCD*[...]The *Hill* court followed the *ProCD* analysis, noting that "[p]ractical considerations support allowing vendors to enclose the full legal terms with their products." [...]

33   The Court is not persuaded that Kansas or Missouri courts would follow the Seventh Circuit reasoning in *Hill* and *ProCD*. In each case the Seventh Circuit concluded without support that UCC § 2-207 was irrelevant because the cases involved only one written form. [...] This conclusion is not supported by the statute or by Kansas or Missouri law. Disputes under § 2-207 often arise in the context of a "battle of forms," [...] but nothing in its language precludes application in a case which involves only one form. The statute provides:

34   Additional terms in acceptance or confirmation.

      (1) A definite and seasonable expression of acceptance or a written confirmation which is sent within a reasonable time operates as an acceptance even though it states terms additional to or different from those offered or agreed upon, unless acceptance is expressly made conditional on assent to the additional or different terms.

      (2) The additional terms are to be construed as proposals for addition to the contract [if the contract is not between merchants]....

35   [...] By its terms, § 2-207 applies to an acceptance or written confirmation. It states nothing which requires another form before the provision becomes effective. In fact, the official comment to the section specifically provides that §§ 2-207(1) and (2) apply "where an agreement has been reached orally ... and is followed by one or both of the parties sending formal memoranda embodying the terms so far agreed and adding terms not discussed." Official Comment 1 of UCC § 2-207. Kansas and Missouri courts have followed this analysis. Thus, the Court concludes that Kansas and Missouri courts would apply § 2-207 to the facts in this case. [...]

36   In addition, the Seventh Circuit provided no explanation for its conclusion that "the vendor is the master of the offer." *See ProCD*[...] In typical consumer transactions, the purchaser is the offeror, and the vendor is the offeree. [...] While it is possible for the vendor to be the offeror, [...] Gateway provides no factual evidence which would support such a finding in this case. The Court therefore assumes for purposes of the motion to dismiss that plaintiff offered to purchase the computer (either in person or through catalog order) and that Gateway accepted plaintiff's offer (either by completing the sales transaction in person or by agreeing to ship and/or shipping the computer to plaintiff).[11] *Accord Arizona Retail,* 831 F.Supp. at 765 (vendor entered into contract by agreeing to ship goods, or at latest, by shipping goods).

37   Under § 2-207, the Standard Terms constitute either an expression of acceptance or written confirmation. As an expression of acceptance, the Standard Terms would constitute a counter-offer only if Gateway expressly made its acceptance conditional on plaintiff's assent to the additional or different terms. [...] "[T]he conditional nature of the acceptance must be clearly expressed in a manner sufficient to notify the offeror that the offeree is unwilling to proceed with the transaction unless the additional or different terms are included in the contract." [...] Gateway provides no evidence that at the time of the sales transaction, it informed plaintiff that the transaction was conditioned on plaintiff's acceptance of the Standard Terms. Moreover, the mere fact that Gateway shipped the goods with the terms attached did not communicate to plaintiff any unwillingness to proceed without plaintiff's agreement to the Standard Terms. [...]

38   Because plaintiff is not a merchant, additional or different terms contained in the Standard Terms did not become part of the parties' agreement unless plaintiff expressly agreed to them. *See* K.S.A. § 84-2-207 [...] Gateway argues that plaintiff demonstrated acceptance of the arbitration provision by keeping the computer more than five days after the date of delivery. Although the Standard Terms purport to work that result, Gateway has not presented evidence that plaintiff expressly agreed to those Standard Terms. Gateway states only

that it enclosed the Standard Terms inside the computer box for plaintiff to read afterwards. It provides no evidence that it informed plaintiff of the five-day review-and-return period as a condition of the sales transaction, or that the parties contemplated additional terms to the agreement.[14] [...] The Court finds that the act of keeping the computer past five days was not sufficient to demonstrate that plaintiff expressly agreed to the Standard Terms. *Accord Brown Machine*, 770 S.W.2d at 421 (express assent cannot be presumed by silence or mere failure to object). Thus, because Gateway has not provided evidence sufficient to support a finding under Kansas or Missouri law that plaintiff agreed to the arbitration provision contained in Gateway's Standard Terms, the Court overrules Gateway's motion to dismiss.

39   [...]

55   IT IS THEREFORE ORDERED that the *Motion to Dismiss* (Doc. # 6) which defendant Gateway filed November 22, 1999 be and hereby is OVERRULED. [...]

56   [1] Gateway states that after it sold plaintiff's computer, it mailed all existing customers in the United States a copy of its quarterly magazine, which contained notice of a change in the arbitration policy set forth in the Standard Terms. The new arbitration policy afforded customers the option of arbitrating before the International Chamber of Commerce ("ICC"), the American Arbitration Association ("AAA"), or the National Arbitration Forum ("NAF") in Chicago, Illinois, or any other location agreed upon by the parties. Plaintiff denies receiving notice of the amended arbitration policy. Neither party explains why — if the arbitration agreement was an enforceable contract — Gateway was entitled to unilaterally amend it by sending a magazine to computer customers.

57   [...]

59   [4] While Gateway may have shipped the computer to plaintiff in Missouri, the record contains no evidence regarding how plaintiff communicated his order to Gateway, where Gateway received plaintiff's order or where the shipment originated.

60   [...]

63   [8] Section 2-204 provides: "A contract for sale of goods may be made in any manner sufficient to show agreement, including conduct by both parties which recognizes the existence of such contract." [...]

66   [11] UCC § 2-206(b) provides that "an order or other offer to buy goods for prompt or current shipment shall be construed as inviting acceptance either by a prompt promise to ship or by the prompt or current shipment ..." The official comment states that "[e]ither shipment or a prompt promise to ship is made a proper means of acceptance of an offer looking to current shipment." UCC § 2-206, Official Comment 2.

67   [...]

69   [14] The Court is mindful of the practical considerations which are involved in commercial transactions, but it is not unreasonable for a vendor to clearly communicate to a buyer — at the time of sale — either the complete terms of the sale or the fact that the vendor will propose additional terms as a condition of sale, if that be the case.

70   [...]

Specht v. Netscape Communications Corp.

September 12, 2014 by mrisch

1   306 F.3d 17 (2002)

2   **Christopher SPECHT** [...]

                            v.

   NETSCAPE COMMUNICATIONS CORPORATION [...]

4   United States Court of Appeals, Second Circuit.

5   [...]

                   Decided: October 1, 2002.

6   [...]

8   Before McLAUGHLIN, LEVAL, and SOTOMAYOR, Circuit Judges.

9   **SOTOMAYOR, Circuit Judge.**

10   This is an appeal from a judgment of the Southern District of New York denying a motion by defendants-appellants Netscape Communications Corporation and its corporate parent, America Online, Inc. (collectively, "defendants" or "Netscape"), to compel arbitration and to stay court proceedings. In order to resolve the central question of arbitrability presented here, we must address issues of contract formation in cyberspace. Principally, we are asked to determine whether plaintiffs-appellees ("plaintiffs"), by acting upon defendants' invitation to download free software made available on defendants' webpage, agreed to be bound by the software's license terms (which included the arbitration clause at issue), even though plaintiffs could not have learned of the existence of those terms unless, prior to executing the download, they had scrolled down the webpage to a screen located below the download button. We agree with the district court that a reasonably prudent Internet user in circumstances such as these would not have known or learned of the existence of the license terms before responding to defendants' invitation to download the free software, and that defendants therefore did not provide reasonable notice of the license terms. In consequence, plaintiffs' bare act of downloading the software did not unambiguously manifest assent to the arbitration provision contained in the license terms.

11   We also agree with the district court that plaintiffs' claims relating to the software at issue — a "plug-in" program entitled SmartDownload ("SmartDownload" or "the plug-in program"), offered by Netscape to enhance the functioning of the separate browser program called Netscape Communicator ("Communicator" or "the browser program") — are not subject to an arbitration agreement contained in the license terms governing the use of Communicator. [...]

12   We therefore affirm the district court's denial of defendants' motion to compel arbitration and to stay court proceedings.

13   **BACKGROUND**

14   **I. Facts**

882

15　　In three related putative class actions,[1] plaintiffs alleged that, unknown to them, their use of SmartDownload transmitted to defendants private information about plaintiffs' downloading of files from the Internet, thereby effecting an electronic surveillance of their online activities in violation of two federal statutes, the Electronic Communications Privacy Act, 18 U.S.C. §§ 2510 *et seq.,* and the Computer Fraud and Abuse Act, 18 U.S.C. § 1030.

16　　[...]

17　　In the time period relevant to this litigation, Netscape offered on its website various software programs, including Communicator and SmartDownload, which visitors to the site were invited to obtain free of charge. It is undisputed that five of the six named plaintiffs — Michael Fagan, John Gibson, Mark Gruber, Sean Kelly, and Sherry Weindorf — downloaded Communicator from the Netscape website. These plaintiffs acknowledge that when they proceeded to initiate installation[3] of Communicator, [...] they were automatically shown a scrollable text of that program's license agreement and were not permitted to complete the installation until they had clicked on a "Yes" button to indicate that they accepted all the license terms.[4] If a user attempted to install Communicator without clicking "Yes," the installation would be aborted. All five named user plaintiffs[5] expressly agreed to Communicator's license terms by clicking "Yes." The Communicator license agreement that these plaintiffs saw made no mention of SmartDownload or other plug-in programs, and stated that "[t]hese terms apply to Netscape Communicator and Netscape Navigator"[6] and that "all disputes relating to this Agreement (excepting any dispute relating to intellectual property rights)" are subject to "binding arbitration in Santa Clara County, California."

18　　Although Communicator could be obtained independently of SmartDownload, all the named user plaintiffs, except Fagan, downloaded and installed Communicator in connection with downloading SmartDownload.[7] Each of these plaintiffs allegedly arrived at a Netscape webpage[8] captioned "SmartDownload Communicator" that urged them to "Download With Confidence Using SmartDownload!" At or near the bottom of the screen facing plaintiffs was the prompt "Start Download" and a tinted button labeled "Download." By clicking on the button, plaintiffs initiated the download of SmartDownload. [...] Once that process was complete, SmartDownload, as its first plug-in task, permitted plaintiffs to proceed with downloading and installing Communicator, an operation that was accompanied by the clickwrap display of Communicator's license terms described above.

19　　The signal difference between downloading Communicator and downloading SmartDownload was that no clickwrap presentation accompanied the latter operation. Instead, once plaintiffs Gibson, Gruber, Kelly, and Weindorf had clicked on the "Download" button located at or near the bottom of their screen, and the downloading of SmartDownload was complete, these plaintiffs encountered no further information about the plug-in program or the existence of license terms governing its use.[9] The sole reference to SmartDownload's license terms on the "SmartDownload Communicator" webpage was located in text that would have become visible to plaintiffs only if they had scrolled down to the next screen.

20　　Had plaintiffs scrolled down instead of acting on defendants' invitation to click on the "Download" button, they would have encountered the following invitation: "Please review and agree to the terms of the *Netscape SmartDownload software license agreement* before downloading and using the software." Plaintiffs Gibson, Gruber, Kelly, and Weindorf averred in their affidavits that they never saw this reference to the SmartDownload license agreement when they clicked on the "Download" button. They also testified during depositions that they saw no reference to license terms when they clicked to download SmartDownload, although under questioning by defendants' counsel, some plaintiffs added that they could not "remember" or be "sure" whether the screen shots of the SmartDownload page attached to their affidavits reflected precisely what they had seen on their computer screens when they downloaded SmartDownload.[10]

21　　In sum, plaintiffs Gibson, Gruber, Kelly, and Weindorf allege that the process of obtaining SmartDownload contrasted sharply with that of obtaining Communicator. Having selected SmartDownload, they were required neither to express unambiguous assent to that program's license agreement nor even to view the license terms or become aware of their existence before proceeding with the invited download of the free plug-in program. Moreover, once these plaintiffs had initiated the download, the existence of SmartDownload's license terms was not mentioned while the software was running or at any later point in plaintiffs' experience of the product.

22   Even for a user who, unlike plaintiffs, did happen to scroll down past the download button, SmartDownload's license terms would not have been immediately displayed in the manner of Communicator's clickwrapped terms. Instead, if such a user had seen the notice of SmartDownload's terms and then clicked on the underlined invitation to review and agree to [...] he terms, a hypertext link would have taken the user to a separate webpage entitled "License & Support Agreements." The first paragraph on this page read, in pertinent part:

23   The use of each Netscape software product is governed by a license agreement. You must read and agree to the license agreement terms BEFORE acquiring a product. Please click on the appropriate link below to review the current license agreement for the product of interest to you before acquisition. For products available for download, you must read and agree to the license agreement terms BEFORE you install the software. If you do not agree to the license terms, do not download, install or use the software.

24   Below this paragraph appeared a list of license agreements, the first of which was "*License Agreement for Netscape Navigator and Netscape Communicator Product Family* (Netscape Navigator, Netscape Communicator and Netscape SmartDownload)." If the user clicked on that link, he or she would be taken to yet another webpage that contained the full text of a license agreement that was identical in every respect to the Communicator license agreement except that it stated that its "terms apply to Netscape Communicator, Netscape Navigator, and Netscape SmartDownload." The license agreement granted the user a nonexclusive license to use and reproduce the software, subject to certain terms:

25   BY CLICKING THE ACCEPTANCE BUTTON OR INSTALLING OR USING NETSCAPE COMMUNICATOR, NETSCAPE NAVIGATOR, OR NETSCAPE SMARTDOWNLOAD SOFTWARE (THE "PRODUCT"), THE INDIVIDUAL OR ENTITY LICENSING THE PRODUCT ("LICENSEE") IS CONSENTING TO BE BOUND BY AND IS BECOMING A PARTY TO THIS AGREEMENT. IF LICENSEE DOES NOT AGREE TO ALL OF THE TERMS OF THIS AGREEMENT, THE BUTTON INDICATING NON-ACCEPTANCE MUST BE SELECTED, AND LICENSEE MUST NOT INSTALL OR USE THE SOFTWARE.

26   Among the license terms was a provision requiring virtually all disputes relating to the agreement to be submitted to arbitration:

27   Unless otherwise agreed in writing, all disputes relating to this Agreement (excepting any dispute relating to intellectual property rights) shall be subject to final and binding arbitration in Santa Clara County, California, under the auspices of JAMS/EndDispute, with the losing party paying all costs of arbitration.

28   Unlike the four named user plaintiffs who downloaded SmartDownload from the Netscape website, the fifth named plaintiff, Michael Fagan, claims to have downloaded the plug-in program from a "shareware" website operated by ZDNet, an entity unrelated to Netscape. Shareware sites are websites, maintained by companies or individuals, that contain libraries of free, publicly available software. The pages that a user would have seen while downloading SmartDownload from ZDNet differed from those that he or she would have encountered while downloading SmartDownload from the Netscape website. Notably, instead of any kind of notice of the SmartDownload license agreement, the ZDNet pages offered only a hypertext link to "more information" about SmartDownload, which, if clicked on, took the user to a Netscape webpage that, in turn, contained a link to the license agreement. Thus, a visitor to the ZDNet website could have obtained SmartDownload, as Fagan avers he did, without ever seeing a reference to that program's license terms, even if he or [...] she had scrolled through all of ZDNet's webpages.

29   [...]

DISCUSSION

I. Standard of Review and Applicable Law

36   A district court's denial of a motion to compel arbitration is reviewed *de novo*. [...]

39   The district court properly concluded that in deciding whether parties agreed to arbitrate a certain matter, a court should generally apply

state-law principles to the issue of contract formation. *[...]* Therefore, state law governs the question of whether the parties in the present case entered into an agreement to arbitrate disputes relating to the SmartDownload license agreement. The district court further held that California law governs the question of contract formation here; the parties do not appeal that determination.

40   *[...]*

45   ## III. Whether the User Plaintiffs Had Reasonable Notice of and Manifested Assent to the SmartDownload License Agreement

46   Whether governed by the common law or by Article 2 of the Uniform Commercial Code ("UCC"), a transaction, in order to be a contract, requires a manifestation of agreement between the parties. *[...]*.[13] Mutual manifestation of assent, whether by written or spoken word or by conduct, is the touchstone of contract. *[...]* Although an onlooker observing the disputed transactions in this case would have seen each of the user plaintiffs click on the SmartDownload "Download" button *[...]* a consumer's clicking on a download button does not communicate assent to contractual terms if the offer did not make clear to the consumer that clicking on the download button would signify assent *[...]* to those terms, *[...]* California's common law is clear that "an offeree, regardless of apparent manifestation of his consent, is not bound by inconspicuous contractual provisions of which he is unaware, contained in a document whose contractual nature is not obvious." *[...]*

47   Arbitration agreements are no exception to the requirement of manifestation of assent. "This principle of knowing consent applies with particular force to provisions for arbitration." *[...]* Clarity and conspicuousness of arbitration terms are important in securing informed assent. "If a party wishes to bind in writing another to an agreement to arbitrate future disputes, such purpose should be accomplished in a way that each party to the arrangement will fully and clearly comprehend that the agreement to arbitrate exists and binds the parties thereto." *[...]* Thus, California contract law measures assent by an objective standard that takes into account both what the offeree said, wrote, or did and the transactional context in which the offeree verbalized or acted.

48   ## A. The Reasonably Prudent Offeree of Downloadable Software

49   Defendants argue that plaintiffs must be held to a standard of reasonable prudence and that, because notice of the existence of SmartDownload license terms was on the next scrollable screen, plaintiffs were on "inquiry notice" of those terms.[14] We disagree with the proposition that a reasonably prudent offeree in plaintiffs' position would necessarily have known or learned of the existence of the SmartDownload license agreement prior to acting, so that plaintiffs may be held to have assented to that agreement with constructive notice of its terms. *[...]* It is true that "[a] party cannot avoid the terms of a contract on the ground that he or she failed to read it before signing." *[...]* But courts are quick to add: "An exception to this general rule exists when the writing does not appear to be a contract and the terms are not called to the attention of the recipient. In such a case, no contract is formed with respect to the undisclosed term." *[...]*

50   *[...]* Most of the cases cited by defendants in support of their inquiry-notice argument are drawn from the world of paper contracting. *[...]*

51   receipt of a physical document containing contract terms or notice thereof is frequently deemed, in the world of paper transactions, a sufficient circumstance to place the offeree on inquiry notice of those terms. "Every person who has actual notice of circumstances sufficient to put a prudent man upon inquiry as to a particular fact, has constructive notice of the fact itself in all cases in which, by prosecuting such inquiry, he might have learned such fact." Cal. Civ.Code § 19. These principles apply equally to the emergent world of online product delivery, pop-up screens, hyperlinked pages, clickwrap licensing, scrollable documents, and urgent admonitions to "Download Now!". What plaintiffs saw when they were being invited by defendants to download this fast, free plug-in called SmartDownload was a screen containing praise for the product and, at the very bottom of the screen, a "Download" button. Defendants argue that under the principles set forth in the cases cited above, a "fair and prudent person using ordinary care" would have been on inquiry notice of SmartDownload's license terms. *[...]*

52   We are not persuaded that a reasonably prudent offeree in these circumstances would have known of the existence of license terms. Plaintiffs were responding to an offer that did not carry an immediately visible notice of the existence of license terms or require unambiguous manifestation of assent to those terms. Thus, plaintiffs' "apparent manifestation of ... consent" was to terms "contained in a document whose contractual nature [was] not obvious." *[...]* Moreover, the fact that, given the position of the scroll bar on their computer screens, plaintiffs *[...]* may have been aware that an unexplored portion of the Netscape webpage remained below the download button does not mean that they reasonably should have concluded that this portion contained a notice of license terms. In their deposition testimony, plaintiffs variously stated that they used the scroll bar "[o]nly if there is something that I feel I need to see that is on — that is off the page," or that the elevated position of the scroll bar suggested the presence of "mere[ ] formalities, standard lower banner links" or "that the page is bigger than what I can see." Plaintiffs testified, and defendants did not refute, that plaintiffs were in fact unaware that defendants intended to attach license terms to the use of SmartDownload.

53   We conclude that in circumstances such as these, where consumers are urged to download free software at the immediate click of a button, a reference to the existence of license terms on a submerged screen is not sufficient to place consumers on inquiry or constructive notice of those terms.[15] The SmartDownload webpage screen was "printed in such a manner that it tended to conceal the fact that it was an express acceptance of [Netscape's] rules and regulations." *[...]*. Internet users may have, as defendants put it, "as much time as they need[ ]" to scroll through multiple screens on a webpage, but there is no reason to assume that viewers will scroll down to subsequent screens simply because screens are there. When products are "free" and users are invited to download them in the absence of reasonably conspicuous notice that they are about to bind themselves to contract terms, the transactional circumstances cannot be fully analogized to those in the paper world of arm's-length bargaining. In the next two sections, we discuss case law and other legal authorities that have addressed the circumstances of computer sales, software licensing, and online transacting. Those authorities tend strongly to support our conclusion that plaintiffs did not manifest assent to SmartDownload's license terms.

54   ## B. Shrinkwrap Licensing and Related Practices

55   Defendants cite certain well-known cases involving shrinkwrap licensing and related commercial practices in support of their contention that plaintiffs became bound by the SmartDownload license terms by virtue of inquiry notice. For example, in *Hill v. Gateway 2000, Inc. [...]* In *ProCD, Inc. v. Zeidenberg [...]*

56   These cases do not help defendants. To the extent that they hold that the purchaser of a computer or tangible software is contractually bound after failing to object to printed license terms provided with the product, *Hill* and *Brower* do not differ markedly from the cases involving traditional paper contracting discussed in the previous section. Insofar as the purchaser in *ProCD* was confronted with conspicuous, mandatory license terms every time he ran the software on his computer, that case actually undermines defendants' contention that downloading in the absence of conspicuous terms is an act that binds plaintiffs to those terms. In *Mortenson,* the full text of license terms was printed on each sealed diskette envelope inside the software box, printed again on the inside cover of the user manual, and notice of the terms appeared on the computer screen every time the purchaser executed the program. *[...]* In sum, the foregoing cases are clearly distinguishable from the facts of the present action.

57   ## C. Online Transactions

58   Cases in which courts have found contracts arising from Internet use do not assist defendants, because in those circumstances there was much clearer notice than in the present case that a user's act would manifest assent to contract terms.[16] *[...]*

59   After reviewing the California common law and other relevant legal authority, we conclude that under the circumstances here, plaintiffs' downloading of SmartDownload did not constitute acceptance of defendants' license terms. Reasonably conspicuous notice of the existence of contract terms and unambiguous manifestation of assent to those terms by consumers are essential if electronic bargaining is to have integrity and credibility. We hold that a reasonably prudent offeree in plaintiffs' position would not have known or learned, prior to acting on the invitation to download, of the reference to SmartDownload's license terms hidden below the "Download" button on the next screen. We affirm the district court's conclusion that the user plaintiffs, including Fagan, are not bound by the arbitration clause

contained in those terms. [...]

58 ## CONCLUSION

80   For the foregoing reasons, we affirm the district court's denial of defendants' motion to compel arbitration and to stay court proceedings.

81   [...]

93   [13] The district court concluded that the SmartDownload transactions here should be governed by "California law as it relates to the sale of goods, including the Uniform Commercial Code in effect in California." [...] It is not obvious, however, that UCC Article 2 ("sales of goods") applies to the licensing of software that is downloadable from the Internet. *Cf. Advent Sys. Ltd. v. Unisys Corp.,* 925 F.2d 670, 675 (3d Cir.1991) ("The increasing frequency of computer products as subjects of commercial litigation has led to controversy over whether software is a `good' or intellectual property. The [UCC] does not specifically mention software."); [...] Some courts have also applied Article 2, occasionally with misgivings, to sales of off-the-shelf software in tangible, packaged formats. *See, e.g., ProCD* [...]

96   [14] "Inquiry notice" is "actual notice of circumstances sufficient to put a prudent man upon inquiry." [...]

98   [16] Defendants place great importance on *Register.com, Inc. v. Verio, Inc.,* 126 F.Supp.2d 238 (S.D.N.Y.2000), which held that a user of the Internet domain-name database, Register.com, had "manifested its assent to be bound" by the database's terms of use when it electronically submitted queries to the database. *Id.* at 248. But *Verio* is not helpful to defendants. There, the plaintiff's terms of use of its information were well known to the defendant, which took the information daily with full awareness that it was using the information in a manner prohibited by the terms of the plaintiff's offer. The case is not closely analogous to ours.

99   [...]

100

Ticketmaster Corp. v. Tickets.Com, Inc. - contract

September 01, 2014 by mrisch

This short note considers the contract issues in Ticketmaster

1
TICKETMASTER CORP. et al., Plaintiff
v.
TICKETS.COM, INC. et al., Defendants.

2
[...]

3
United States District Court, C.D. California.

4
March 7, 2003.

5
[...]

7
TICKETS.COM'S NOTICE OF MOTION AND MOTION FOR SUMMARY JUDGMENT ON CONTRACT [...]

8
HUPP, J.

9
ORDER

10
[...]

14
Starting in 1998 and continuing to July 2001, when it stopped the practice, TX employed an electronic program called a "spider" or "crawler" to review the internal web pages (available to the public) of TM. The "spider" "crawled" through the internal web pages to TM and electronically extracted the electronic information from which the web page is shown on the user's computer. The spider temporarily loaded this electronic information into the Random Access Memory ("RAM") of TX's computers for a period of from 10–15 seconds. TX then extracted the factual information (event, date, time, tickets prices, and URL) and discarded the rest (which consisted of TM identification, logos, ads, and other information which TX did not intend to use; much of this discarded material was protected by copyright). The factual information was then organized in the TX format to be displayed on the TX internal web page. The TX internal web page carried no TM identification and had only the factual information about the event on it which was taken from TM's interior web page but rearranged in TX format plus any information or advertisement added by TX. From March 1998, to early 2000, the TX user was provided the deep linking option described above to go directly from the TX web site to the relevant TM interior web page. This option stopped (or was stopped by TM) in early 2000. For an unknown period afterward, the TX customer was given the option of linking to the TM home page, from which the customer could work his way to the interior web page in which he was interested. (The record does not reveal whether this practice still exists or whether TM objects to it.) Thus, the intellectual property issues in this case appear to be limited to events which occurred between November 1998, when spidering started, and July 2001, when it stopped. The "deep linking" aspect of the case is relevant only from March 1998, to early 2000, when it stopped.

15
The contract aspect of the case derives from a notice placed on the home page of the TM web site which states that anyone going beyond that point into the interior web pages of the web site accepts certain conditions, which include, relevant to this case, that all information obtained from the website is for the personal use of the user and may not be used for commercial purposes. Earlier in this

case (and at the time of the motion for preliminary injunction) the notice was placed at the bottom of the home page of the TM web site, so that a user without an especially large screen would have to scroll down the page to read the conditions of use. Since then, TM has placed in a prominent place on the home page the warning that proceeding further binds the user to the conditions of use. As one TX executive put it, it could not be missed. At the time of the preliminary injunction motion, the court commented that there was no evidence that the conditions of use were known to TX. Since then, there has been developed evidence that TX was fully familiar with the conditions TM claimed to impose on users, including a letter from TM to TX which quoted the conditions (and a reply by TX stating that it did not accept the conditions). Thus, there is sufficient evidence to defeat summary judgment on the contract theory if knowledge of the asserted conditions of use was had by TX, who nevertheless continued to send its spider into the TM interior web pages, and if it is legally concluded that doing so can lead to a binding contract. For reasons dealing with the desirability of clear unmistakable evidence of assent to the conditions on trial of such issues, the court would prefer a rule that required an unmistakable assent to the conditions easily provided by requiring clicking on an icon which says "I agree" or the equivalent. Such a rule would provide certainty in trial and make it clear that the user had called to his attention the conditions he or she accepted when using the web site. [...] However, the law has not developed this way. Use of a cruise ship ticket with a venue provision printed on the back commits one to the venue provided. (*Carnival Cruise Lines* '91 499 U.S. 585, 113 L.Ed.2d 622.) The Carriage of Goods by Sea Act, the Carmack Act, and the Warsaw Convention provide that limitations of liability on the bill of lading, air waybill, or airplane ticket are enforceable if the services are used by the customer. The "shrinkwrap" cases find the printed conditions plainly wrapped around the cassette or CD enforceable. Even the back of your parking lot ticket may be enforceable. The principle has been applied to cases similar to this. [...] The principle has long been established that no particular form of words is necessary to indicate assent–the offeror may specify that a certain action in connection with his offer is deemed acceptance, and ripens into a contract when the action is taken. [...] Thus, as relevant here, a contract can be formed by proceeding into the interior web pages after knowledge (or, in some cases, presumptive knowledge) of the conditions accepted when doing so. In *Specht* 2Cir'02 306 F.3d 17, the court found that there was no mutual assent when a notice of the existence of license terms governing the use of software was visible to internet users only if they scrolled down the screen. That case is distinguishable from the facts at hand on the grounds that in *Specht,* the plaintiff's terms of use were not plainly visible or known to defendants. [...] Moreover, *Specht* involved a different set of circumstances, that of consumers invited to download free software from an internet site that did not contain a plainly visible notice of license terms. [...] As a result, the TX motion for summary judgment on the contract issue is denied.

16   [...]

Nguyen v. Barnes & Noble Inc. - note

August 19, 2014 by mrisch

This short case note is a recent rejection of an unconsented to agreement. What could the seller have done differently?

1
--- F.3d ---- (2014)

2
Kevin Khoa NGUYEN, an individual, on behalf of himself and all others similarly situated, Plaintiff–Appellee,
v.
BARNES & NOBLE INC., Defendant–Appellant.

3
No. 12–56628.

4
United States Court of Appeals, Ninth Circuit.

5
Argued and Submitted May 16, 2014.
Filed Aug. 18, 2014.

6
[...]

10
OPINION

11
NOONAN, Circuit Judge:

12
[...] Barnes & Noble, Inc. ("Barnes & Noble") appeals the district court's denial of its motion to compel arbitration against Kevin Khoa Nguyen ("Nguyen") pursuant to the arbitration agreement contained in its website's Terms of Use. In order to resolve the issue of arbitrability, we must address whether Nguyen, by merely using Barnes & Noble's website, agreed to be bound by the Terms of Use, even though Nguyen was never prompted to assent to the Terms of Use and never in fact read them. We agree with the district court that Barnes & Noble did not provide reasonable notice of its Terms of Use, and that Nguyen therefore did not unambiguously manifest assent to the arbitration provision contained therein.

13
We also agree with the district court that Nguyen is not equitably estopped from avoiding arbitration because he relied on the Terms of Use's choice of law provision.

14
We therefore affirm the district court's denial of Barnes & Noble's motion to compel arbitration and to stay court proceedings.

15
I. Background

16
A.

17
The underlying facts are not in dispute. Barnes & Noble is a national bookseller that owns and operates hundreds of bookstores as well as the website . In August 2011, Barnes & Noble, along with other retailers across the country, liquidated its inventory of discontinued Hewlett–Packard Touchpads ("Touchpads"), an unsuccessful competitor to Apple's iPad, by advertising a "fire sale" of Touchpads at a

heavily discounted price. Acting quickly on the nationwide liquidation of Touchpads, Nguyen purchased two units on Barnes & Noble's website on August 21, 2011, and received an email confirming the transaction. The following day, Nguyen received another email informing him that his order had been cancelled due to unexpectedly high demand. Nguyen alleges that, as a result of "Barnes & Noble's representations, as well as the delay in informing him it would not honor the sale," he was "unable to obtain an HP Tablet during the liquidation period for the discounted price," and was "forced to rely on substitute tablet technology, which he subsequently purchased ... [at] considerable expense."

18   **B.**

19   In April 2012, Nguyen filed this lawsuit in California Superior Court on behalf of himself and a putative class of consumers whose Touchpad orders had been cancelled, alleging that Barnes & Noble had engaged in deceptive business practices and false advertising in violation of both California and New York law. Barnes & Noble removed the action to federal court and moved to compel arbitration under the Federal Arbitration Act ("FAA"), arguing that Nguyen was bound by the arbitration agreement in the website's Terms of Use.

20   The website's Terms of Use are available via a "Terms of Use" hyperlink located in the bottom left-hand corner of every page on the Barnes & Noble website, which appears alongside other hyperlinks labeled "NOOK Store Terms," "Copyright," and "Privacy Policy." These hyperlinks also appear underlined and set in green typeface in the lower lefthand corner of every page in the online checkout process.

21   [...] Nguyen neither clicked on the "Terms of Use" hyperlink nor actually read the Terms of Use. Had he clicked on the hyperlink, he would have been taken to a page containing the full text of Barnes & Noble's Terms of Use, which state, in relevant part: "By visiting any area in the Barnes & Noble.com Site, creating an account, [or] making a purchase via the Barnes & Noble.com Site ... a User is deemed to have accepted the Terms of Use."Nguyen also would have come across an arbitration provision[...]

23   Nguyen contends that he cannot be bound to the arbitration provision because he neither had notice of nor assented to the website's Terms of Use. Barnes & Noble, for its part, asserts that the placement of the "Terms of Use" hyperlink on its website put Nguyen on constructive notice of the arbitration agreement. Barnes & Noble contends that this notice, combined with Nguyen's subsequent use of the website, was enough to bind him to the Terms of Use. [...]

26   **III. Discussion**

27   [...]

33   "While new commerce on the Internet has exposed courts to many new situations, it has not fundamentally changed the principles of contract." [...]. One such principle is the requirement that "[m]utual manifestation of assent, whether by written or spoken word or by conduct, is the touchstone of contract."*Specht v. Netscape Commc'ns Corp.,* 306 F.3d 17, 29 (2d Cir.2002) (applying California law).

34   Contracts formed on the Internet come primarily in two flavors: "clickwrap" (or "click-through") agreements, in which website users are required to click on an "I agree" box after being presented with a list of terms and conditions of use; and "browsewrap" agreements, where a website's terms and conditions of use are generally posted on the website via a hyperlink at the bottom of the screen. [...]

35   "The defining feature of browsewrap agreements is that the user can continue to use the website or its services without visiting the page hosting the browsewrap agreement or even knowing that such a webpage exists." [...] "Because no affirmative action is required by the website user to agree to the terms of a contract other than his or her use of the website, the determination of the validity of the browsewrap contract depends on whether the user has actual or constructive knowledge of a website's terms and conditions." [...]

36   Were there any evidence in the record that Nguyen had actual notice of the Terms of Use or was required to affirmatively acknowledge the Terms of Use before completing his online purchase, the outcome of this case might be different. Indeed, courts have consistently

enforced browsewrap agreements where the user had actual notice of the agreement. $[...]$

37   But where, as here, there is no evidence that the website user had actual knowledge of the agreement, the validity of the browsewrap agreement turns on whether the website puts a reasonably prudent user on inquiry notice of the terms of the contract. $[...]$ Whether a user has inquiry notice of a browsewrap agreement, in turn, depends on the design and content of the website and the agreement's webpage. $[...]$ Where the link to a website's terms of use is buried at the bottom of the page or tucked away in obscure corners of the website where users are unlikely to see it, courts have refused to enforce the browsewrap agreement. $[...]$ On the other hand, where the website contains an explicit textual notice that continued use will act as a manifestation of the user's intent to be bound, courts have been more amenable to enforcing browsewrap agreements. $[...]$ In short, the conspicuousness and placement of the "Terms of Use" hyperlink, other notices given to users of the terms of use, and the website's general design all contribute to whether a reasonably prudent user would have inquiry notice of a browsewrap agreement.

38     $[...]$ Barnes & Noble argues that the placement of the "Terms of Use" hyperlink in the bottom left-hand corner of every page on the Barnes & Noble website, and its close proximity to the buttons a user must click on to complete an online purchase, is enough to place a reasonably prudent user on constructive notice. $[...]$

39   But the proximity or conspicuousness of the hyperlink alone is not enough to give rise to constructive notice, and Barnes & Noble directs us to no case law that supports this proposition.[...]

41     $[...]$ In light of the lack of controlling authority on point, and in keeping with courts' traditional reluctance to enforce browsewrap agreements against individual consumers,[2] we therefore hold that where a website makes its terms of use available via a conspicuous hyperlink on every page of the website but otherwise provides no notice to users nor prompts them to take any affirmative action to demonstrate assent, even close proximity of the hyperlink to relevant buttons users must click on—without more—is insufficient to give rise to constructive notice. While failure to read a contract before agreeing to its terms does not relieve a party of its obligations under the contract, $[...]$ the onus must be on website owners to put users on notice of the terms to which they wish to bind consumers. Given the breadth of the range of technological savvy of online purchasers, consumers cannot be expected to ferret out hyperlinks to terms and conditions to which they have no reason to suspect they will be bound.

42     $[...]$

49   We hold that Nguyen had insufficient notice of Barnes & Noble's Terms of Use, and thus did not enter into an agreement with Barnes & Noble to arbitrate his claims.

50   **AFFIRMED.**

51     $[...]$

Class 25: 9.2 <u>OIL Casebook: Licensing and Property</u>

Random House, Inc. v. Rosetta Books LLC

September 14, 2014 by mrisch

1   150 F.Supp.2d 613 (2001)

2   **RANDOM HOUSE, INC.** [...]

v.

ROSETTA BOOKS LLC [...]

4   United States District Court, S.D. New York.

5   July 11, 2001.

6   [...] *OPINION*

7   **STEIN, District Judge.**

8   In this copyright infringement action, Random House, Inc. seeks to enjoin Rosetta Books LLC and its Chief Executive Officer from selling in digital format eight specific works on the grounds that the authors of the works had previously granted Random House—not Rosetta Books— the right to "print, publish and sell the work[s] in book form." Rosetta Books, on the other hand, claims it is not infringing upon the rights those authors gave Random House because the licensing agreements between the publisher and the author do not include a grant of digital or electronic rights.[1] Relying on the language of the contracts and basic principles of contract interpretation, this Court finds that the right to "print, publish and sell the work[s] in book form" in the contracts at issue does not include the right to publish the works in the format that has come to be known as the "ebook." Accordingly, Random House's motion for a preliminary injunction is denied.

9   ## BACKGROUND

10   In the year 2000 and the beginning of 2001, Rosetta Books contracted with several authors to publish certain of their works—including *The Confessions of Nat Turner* and *Sophie's Choice* by William Styron; *Slaughterhouse-Five, Breakfast of Champions, The Sirens of Titan, Cat's Cradle,* and *Player Piano* by Kurt Vonnegut; and *Promised Land* by Robert B. Parker—in digital format over the internet. [...] On February 26, 2001 Rosetta Books launched its ebook business, offering those titles and others for sale in digital format. [...] The next day, Random House filed this complaint accusing Rosetta Books of committing copyright infringement and tortiously interfering with the contracts Random House had with Messrs. Parker, Styron and Vonnegut by selling its ebooks. It simultaneously moved for a preliminary injunction prohibiting Rosetta from infringing plaintiff's copyrights.

11   ## A. Ebooks

12   Ebooks are "digital book[s] that you can read on a computer screen or an electronic [...] device." [...] Ebooks are created by converting digitized text into a format readable by computer software. The text can be viewed on a desktop or laptop computer, personal digital assistant or handheld dedicated ebook reading device. [...]

13   Although the text of the ebook is exactly the same as the text of the original work, the ebook contains various features that take advantage of its digital format. For example, ebook users can search the work electronically to find specific words and phrases. They can electronically "highlight"[3] and "bookmark"[4] certain text, which can then be automatically indexed and accessed through hyperlinks.

894

They can use hyperlinks in the table of contents to jump to specific chapters.

14 Users can also type electronic notes which are stored with the related text. These notes can be automatically indexed, sorted and filed. Users can also change the font size and style of the text to accommodate personal preferences; thus, an electronic screen of text may contain more words, fewer words, or the same number of words as a page of the original published book. In addition, users can have displayed the definition of any word in the text. [...]

16 ## B. Random House's licensing agreements

17 While each agreement between the author and Random House differs in some respects, each uses the phrase "print, publish and sell the work in book form" to convey rights from the author to the publisher. [...]

18 ## 1. Styron Agreements

19 Forty years ago, in 1961, William Styron granted Random House the right to publish *The Confessions of Nat Turner.* Besides granting Random House an exclusive license to "print, publish and sell the work in book form," Styron also gave it the right to "license publication of the work by book clubs," "license publication of a reprint edition," "license after book publication the [...] publication of the work, in whole or in part, in anthologies, school books," and other shortened forms, "license without charge publication of the work in Braille, or photographing, recording, and microfilming the work for the physically handicapped," and "publish or permit others to publish or broadcast by radio or television ... selections from the work, for publicity purposes ...." [...] Styron demonstrated that he was not granting Random House the rights to license publication in the British Commonwealth or in foreign languages by crossing out these clauses on the form contract supplied by Random House. [...]

20 The contract also contains a non-compete clause that provides, in relevant part, that "[t]he Author agrees that during the term of this agreement he will not, without the written permission of the Publisher, publish or permit to be published any material in book or pamphlet form, based on the material in the work, or which is reasonably likely to injure its sale." [...]

21 ## 2. Vonnegut Agreements

22 Kurt Vonnegut's 1967 contract granting Random House's predecessor-in-interest Dell Publishing Co., Inc. the license to publish *Slaughterhouse-Five* and *Breakfast of Champions* follows a similar structure to the Styron agreements. Paragraph # 1 is captioned "grant of rights" and contains those rights the author is granting to the book publisher. Certain rights on the publisher's form contract are crossed out, indicating that the author reserved them for himself. ([...] One of the rights granted by the author includes the "[e]xclusive right to publish and to license the Work for publication, after book publication ... in anthologies, selections, digests, abridgements, magazine condensations, serialization, newspaper syndication, picture book versions, microfilming, Xerox and other forms of copying, either now in use or hereafter developed." [...]

23 Vonnegut specifically reserved for himself the "dramatic ... motion picture (silent and sound) ... radio broadcasting (including mechanical renditions and/or recordings of the text) ... [and] television" rights. [...] Unlike the Styron agreements, this contract does not contain a non-compete clause.

24 Vonnegut's 1970 contract granting Dell the license to publish *The Sirens of Titan, Cat's Cradle,* and *Player Piano* contains virtually identical grants and reservations of rights as his 1967 contract. However, it does contain a non-compete clause, which provides that "the Author... will not publish or permit to be published any edition, adaptation or abridgment of the Work by any party other than Dell without Dell's prior written consent." [...]

²⁵ **3. Parker Agreement**   *Parker's agreement is similar to Vonnegut's*

²⁶   [...]

²⁷ **DISCUSSION**

²⁸ **A. Preliminary Injunction Standard for Copyright Infringement**

²⁹ Random House seeks a preliminary injunction against Rosetta Book's alleged infringing activity pursuant to 17 U.S.C. § 502(a) of the Copyright Act. In order to obtain a preliminary injunction, Random House must demonstrate "(1) irreparable harm and (2) either (a) a likelihood of success on the merits or (b) sufficiently serious questions about the merits to make them a fair ground for litigation and a balance of hardships tipping decidedly toward the party requesting relief." [...]

³⁰ **B. Ownership of a Valid Copyright**

³¹ Two elements must be proven in order to establish a prima facie case of infringement: "(1) ownership of a valid copyright, and (2) copying of constituent elements of the work that are original." [...] In this case, only the first element—ownership of a valid copyright—is at issue, since all parties concede that the text of the ebook is identical to the text of the book published by Random House.

³² It is well settled that although the authors own the copyrights to their works, "[t]he legal or beneficial owner of an exclusive right under a copyright is entitled ... to institute an action for any infringement of that particular right committed while he or she is the owner of it." 17 U.S.C. § 501(b) [...] Melville B. Nimmer & David Nimmer, *Nimmer on Copyright* § 12.02[b] at 12-50-51 (May, 2000) ("[A]n exclusive licensee may not sue for infringement of rights as to which he is not licensed, even if the subject matter of the infringement is the work as to which he is a licensee."). The question for resolution, therefore, is whether Random House is the beneficial owner of the right to publish these works as ebooks.

³³ **1. Contract Interpretation of Licensing Agreements—Legal Standards**

³⁴ Random House claims to own the rights in question through its licensing agreements with the authors. Interpretation [...] of an agreement purporting to grant a copyright license is a matter of state contract law. [...]

³⁷ If the language of a contract is ambiguous, interpretation of the contract becomes a question of fact for the finder of fact and extrinsic evidence is admissible. [...]

³⁸ These principles are in accord with the approach the U.S. Court of Appeals for the Second Circuit uses in analyzing contractual language in disputes, such as this one, "about whether licensees may exploit licensed works through new marketing channels made possible by technologies developed after the licensing contract—often called `new use' problems." *Boosey & Hawkes Music Publishers, Ltd. v. Walt Disney Co.* [...] The two leading cases in this Circuit [...] on how to determine whether "new uses" come within prior grants of rights are *Boosey* and *Bartsch v. Metro-Goldwyn-Mayer, Inc.,* [...] decided three decades apart.

³⁹ In *Bartsch,* the author of the play "Maytime" granted Hans Bartsch in 1930 "the motion picture rights [to `Maytime'] throughout the world," including the right to "copyright, vend, license and exhibit such motion picture photoplays throughout the world; together with the further sole and exclusive rights by mechanical and/or electrical means to record, reproduce and transmit sound, including spoken words...." [...] He in turn assigned those rights to Warner Bros. Pictures, which transferred them to MGM. In 1958 MGM licensed its motion picture "Maytime" for viewing on television. Bartsch sued, claiming the right to transmit the play over television had not been given to MGM.

40   Judge Henry Friendly, for the Second Circuit, wrote in 1968 that "any effort to reconstruct what the parties actually intended nearly forty years ago is doomed to failure." [...] He added that the words of the grant by Bartsch "were well designed to give the assignee [i.e., MGM] the broadest rights with respect to its copyrighted property." [...] The words of the grant were broad enough to cover the new use —i.e. viewing on television —and Judge Friendly interpreted them to do so. This interpretation, he wrote, permitted the licensee to "properly pursue any uses which may reasonably be said to fall within the medium as described in the license." [...] That interpretation also avoided the risk "that a deadlock between the grantor and the grantee might prevent the work's being shown over the new medium at all." [...]

41   In *Boosey,* the plaintiff was the assignee of Igor Stravinsky's copyrights in the musical composition, "The Rite of Spring." In 1939, Stravinsky had licensed Disney's use of "The Rite of Spring" in the motion picture "Fantasia." Fifty-two years later, in 1991, Disney released "Fantasia" in video format and Boosey brought an action seeking, among other relief, a declaration that the grant of rights did not include the right to use the Stravinsky work in video format. In *Boosey,* just as in *Bartsch,* the language of the grant was broad, enabling the licensee "to record in any manner, medium or form, and to license the performance of, the musical composition [for use] in a motion picture." [...]

42   At the Second Circuit, a unanimous panel focused on "neutral principles of contract interpretation rather than solicitude for either party." [. "What governs," Judge Pierre Leval wrote, "is the language of the contract. If the contract is more reasonably read to convey one meaning, the party benefitted by that reading should be able to rely on it; the party seeking exception or deviation from the meaning reasonably conveyed by the words of the contract should bear the burden of negotiating for language that would express the limitation or deviation. This principle favors neither licensors nor licensees. It follows simply from the words of the contract." [...]

43   The Second Circuit's neutral approach was specifically influenced by policy considerations on both sides. On the one hand, the approach seeks to encourage licensees—here, the publishers—to develop new technologies that will enable all to enjoy the creative work in a new way. On the other hand, it seeks to fulfill the purpose underlying federal copyright law—to encourage authors to create literary works. [...]

44   ## 2. Application of Legal Standards

45   Relying on "the language of the license contract and basic principles of interpretation," B[...] as instructed to do so by *Boosey* and *Bartsch,* this Court finds that the most reasonable interpretation of the grant in the contracts at issue to "print, publish and sell the work in book form" does not include the right to publish the work as an ebook. At the outset, the phrase itself distinguishes between the pure content— i.e. "the work"—and the format of display —"in book form." The *Random House Webster's Unabridged Dictionary* defines a "book" as "a written or printed work of fiction or nonfiction, usually on sheets of paper fastened or bound together within covers" and defines "form" as "external appearance of a clearly defined area, as distinguished from color or material; the shape of a thing or person." [.

46   Manifestly, paragraph # 1 of each contract —entitled either "grant of rights" or "exclusive publication right"—conveys certain rights from the author to the publisher. ([...] In that paragraph, separate grant language is used to convey the rights to publish book club editions, reprint editions, abridged forms, and editions in Braille. This language would not be necessary if the phrase "in book form" encompassed all types of books. That paragraph specifies exactly which rights were being granted by the author to the publisher. Indeed, many of the rights set forth in the publisher's form contracts were in fact not granted to the publisher, but rather were reserved by the authors to themselves. For example, each of the authors specifically reserved certain rights for themselves by striking out phrases, sentences, and paragraphs of the publisher's form contract. This evidences an intent by these authors not to grant the publisher the broadest rights in their works.

47   Random House contends that the phrase "in book form" means to faithfully reproduce the author's text in its complete form as a reading experience and that, since ebooks concededly contain the complete text of the work, Rosetta cannot also possess those rights. [...] While Random House's definition distinguishes "book form" from other formats that require separate contractual language—such as audio books and serialization rights—it does not distinguish other formats specifically mentioned in paragraph # 1 of the contracts, such

as book club editions and reprint editions. Because the Court must, if possible, give effect to all contractual language in order to "safeguard against adopting an interpretation that would render any individual provision superfluous," *[...]* Random House's definition cannot be adopted.

48   Random House points specifically to the clause requiring it to "publish the work at its own expense and in such a style and manner and at such a price as [Random House] deems suitable" as support for its position. *[...]* However, plaintiff takes this clause out of context. It appears in paragraph # 2, captioned "Style, Price and Date of Publication," not paragraph # 1, which includes all the grants of rights. In context, the phrase simply means that Random House has control over the appearance of the formats granted to Random House in the first paragraph; i.e., control over the style of the book.

49   Random House also cites the non-compete clauses as evidence that the authors granted it broad, exclusive rights in their *[...]* work. Random House reasons that because the authors could not permit any material that would injure the sale of the work to be published without Random House's consent, the authors must have granted the right to publish ebooks to Random House. This reasoning turns the analysis on its head. First, the grant of rights follows from the grant language alone. *[...]* Second, non-compete clauses must be limited in scope in order to be enforceable in New York. *[...]* Third, even if the authors did violate this provision of their Random House agreements by contracting with Rosetta Books—a point on which this Court does not opine—the remedy is a breach of contract action against the authors, not a copyright infringement action against Rosetta Books. *[...]*

50   The photocopy clause—giving Random House the right to "Xerox and other forms of copying, either now in use or hereafter developed"— similarly does not bolster Random House's position. Although the clause does appear in the grant language paragraph, taken in context, it clearly refers only to new developments in xerography and other forms of photocopying. Stretching it to include new forms of publishing, such as ebooks, would make the rest of the contract superfluous because there would be no reason for authors to reserve rights to forms of publishing "now in use." This interpretation also comports with the publishing industry's trade usage of the phrase. *[...]*

51   Not only does the language of the contract itself lead almost ineluctably to the conclusion that Random House does not own the right to publish the works as ebooks, but also a reasonable person "cognizant of the customs, practices, usages and terminology as generally understood in the particular trade or business, *[...]* would conclude that the grant language does not include ebooks.[7] "To print, publish and sell the work in book form" is understood in the publishing industry to be a "limited" grant. *See Field v. True Comics,* 89 F.Supp. 611, 613-14 (S.D.N.Y.1950) *This is a pretty old case to rely on for what the publishing industry thinks, isn't it?* *[...]*

52   In fact, the publishing industry generally interprets the phrase "in book form" as granting the publisher "the exclusive right to publish a hardcover trade book in English for distribution in North America." 1 *Lindey on Entertainment, Publishing and the Arts* Form 1.01-1 (2d ed.2000) (using the Random House form contract to explain the meaning of each clause) *[...]*

53   ## 3. Comparison to Prior "New Use" Caselaw

54   The finding that the five licensing agreements at issue do not convey the right to publish the works as ebooks accords with Second Circuit and New York case law. Indeed, the two leading cases limned above that found that a particular new use was included within the grant language *[...]* can be distinguished from this case on four grounds.

55   First, the language conveying the rights in *Boosey* and *Bartsch* was far broader than here. *[...]* Second, the "new use" in those cases—i.e. display of a motion picture on television or videocassette —fell squarely within the same medium as the original grant. *See Boosey,* 145 F.3d at 486 (describing videocassettes and laser discs as "subsequently developed methods of distribution of a motion picture"); *Bourne,* 68 F.3d at 630 ("[T]he term `motion picture' reasonably can be understood to refer to `a broad genus whose fundamental characteristic is a series of related images that impart an impression of motion when shown in succession .... Under this concept the physical form in which the motion picture is fixed— film, tape, discs, and so forth—is irrelevant.'") *[...]*

56   In this case, the "new use"—electronic digital signals sent over the internet—is a separate medium from the original use— printed words on paper. Random House's own expert concludes that the media are distinct because information stored digitally can be manipulated in ways that analog information cannot. *[...]* Ebooks take advantage of the digital medium's ability to manipulate data by allowing ebook users to electronically search the text for specific words and phrases, change the font size and style, type notes into the text and electronically organize them, highlight and bookmark, hyperlink to specific parts of the text, and, in the future, to other sites on related topics as well, and access a dictionary that pronounces words in the ebook aloud. The need for a software program to interact with the data in order to make it usable, as well as the need for a piece of hardware to enable the reader to view the text, also distinguishes analog formats from digital formats. *[...]*

57   Therefore, *Boosey* and *Bartsch,* which apply to new uses within the same medium, do not control this case. *[...]*

58   The third significant difference between the licensee in the motion picture cases cited above and the book publisher in this action is that the licensees in the motion picture cases have actually created a new work based on the material from the licensor. Therefore, the right to display that new work—whether on television or video—is derivative of the right to create that work. In the book publishing context, the publishers, although they participate in the editorial process, display the words written by the author, not themselves. *Unclear how this helps differentiate*

59   Fourth, the courts in *Boosey* and *Bartsch* were concerned that any approach to new use problems that "tilts against licensees [here, Random House] gives rise to antiprogressive incentives" insofar as licensees "would be reluctant to explore and utilize innovative technologies." *[...]* However, in this action, the policy rationale of encouraging development in new technology is at least as well served by finding that the licensors —i.e., the authors—retain these rights to their works. In the 21st century, it cannot be said that licensees such as book publishers and movie producers are ipso facto more likely to make advances in digital technology than start-up companies.

60   *[...]*

CONCLUSION

66   Employing the most important tool in the armamentarium of contract interpretation —the language of the contract itself— this Court has concluded that Random House is not the beneficial owner of the right to publish the eight works at issue as ebooks. This is neither a victory for technophiles nor a defeat for Luddites. It is merely a determination, relying on neutral principles of contract interpretation, that because Random House is not likely to succeed on the merits of its copyright infringement claim and cannot demonstrate irreparable harm, its motion for a preliminary injunction should be denied. *On appeal from this order, the Second Circuit held that the court did not abuse its discretion in denying the preliminary injunction, but stated that a more developed record might well necessitate a ruling in favor of Random House.*

67   *[...]*

New York Times Co. v. Tasini

September 14, 2014 by mrisch

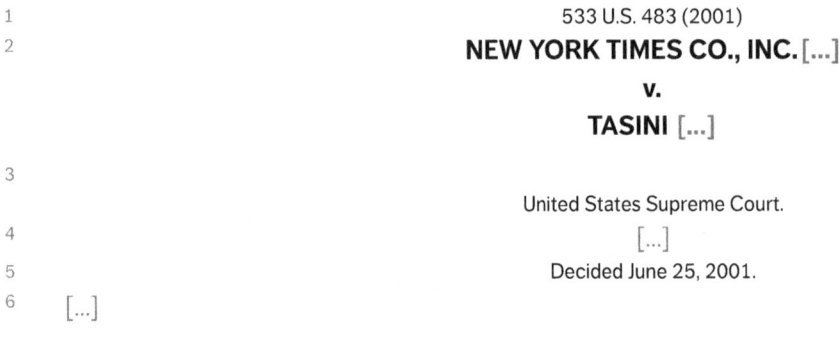

533 U.S. 483 (2001)

NEW YORK TIMES CO., INC. [...]

v.

TASINI [...]

United States Supreme Court.

[...]

Decided June 25, 2001.

[...]

10   Justice Ginsburg, delivered the opinion of the Court.

11   This copyright case concerns the rights of freelance authors and a presumptive privilege of their publishers. The litigation was initiated by six freelance authors and relates to articles they contributed to three print periodicals (two newspapers and one magazine). Under agreements with the periodicals' publishers, but without the freelancers' consent, two computer database companies placed copies of the freelancers' articles—along with all other articles from the periodicals in which the freelancers' work appeared—into three databases. Whether written by a freelancer or staff member, each article is presented to, and retrievable by, the user in isolation, clear of the context the original print publication presented.

12   The freelance authors' complaint alleged that their copyrights had been infringed by the inclusion of their articles in the databases. The publishers, in response, relied on the [...] privilege of reproduction and distribution accorded them by § 201(c) of the Copyright Act, which provides:

13   "Copyright in each separate contribution to a collective work is distinct from copyright in the collective work as a whole, and vests initially in the author of the contribution. In the absence of an express transfer of the copyright or of any rights under it, the owner of copyright in the collective work is presumed to have acquired only the privilege of reproducing and distributing the contribution as part of that particular collective work, any revision of that collective work, and any later collective work in the same series." 17 U. S. C. § 201(c).

14   Specifically, the publishers maintained that, as copyright owners of collective works, *i. e.,* the original print publications, they had merely exercised "the privilege" § 201(c) accords them to "reproduc[e] and distribut[e]" the author's discretely copyrighted contribution.

15   In agreement with the Second Circuit, we hold that § 201(c) does not authorize the copying at issue here. The publishers are not sheltered by § 201(c), we conclude, because the databases reproduce and distribute articles standing alone and not in context, not "as part of that particular collective work" to which the author contributed, "as part of . . . any revision" thereof, or "as part of . . . any later collective work in the same series." Both the print publishers and the electronic publishers, we rule, have infringed the copyrights of the freelance authors.

16   I

17   **A**

18   Respondents Jonathan Tasini, Mary Kay Blakely, Barbara Garson, Margot Mifflin, Sonia Jaffe Robbins, and David S. Whitford are authors (Authors). Between 1990 and 1993, they wrote the 21 articles (Articles) on which this dispute centers. Tasini, Mifflin, and Blakely contributed 12 Articles to The New York Times, the daily newspaper published by [489] petitioner The New York Times Company (Times). Tasini, Garson, Robbins, and Whitford wrote eight Articles for Newsday, another New York daily paper, published by petitioner Newsday, Inc. (Newsday). Whitford also contributed one Article to Sports Illustrated, a weekly magazine published by petitioner Time, Inc. (Time). The Authors registered copyrights in each of the Articles. The Times, Newsday, and Time (Print Publishers) registered collective work copyrights in each periodical edition in which an Article originally appeared. The Print Publishers engaged the Authors as independent contractors (freelancers) under contracts that in no instance secured consent from an Author to placement of an Article in an electronic database.[1]

19   At the time the Articles were published, all three Print Publishers had agreements with petitioner LEXIS/NEXIS (formerly Mead Data Central Corp.), owner and operator of NEXIS, a computerized database that stores information in a text-only format. NEXIS contains articles from hundreds of journals (newspapers and periodicals) spanning many years. The Print Publishers have licensed to LEXIS/NEXIS the text of articles appearing in the three periodicals. The licenses authorize LEXIS/NEXIS to copy and sell any portion of those texts.

20   Pursuant to the licensing agreements, the Print Publishers regularly provide LEXIS/NEXIS with a batch of all the articles published in each periodical edition. The Print Publisher codes each article to facilitate computerized retrieval, then transmits it in a separate file. After further coding, LEXIS/NEXIS places the article in the central discs of its database.

21   [...]

31   **II**

32   Under the Copyright Act, as amended in 1976, "[c]opyright protection subsists . . . in original works of authorship fixed in any tangible medium of expression ... from which they can be perceived, reproduced, or otherwise communicated." 17 U. S. C. § 102(a). When, as in this case, a freelance author has contributed an article to a "collective work" such as a newspaper or magazine, see § 101 (defining "collective work"), the statute recognizes two distinct copyrighted works: "Copyright in *each separate contribution to a collec*[...] *tive work* is distinct from copyright in *the collective work as a whole* . . . ." § 201(c) (emphasis added). Copyright in the separate contribution "vests initially in the author of the contribution" (here, the freelancer). *Ibid.* Copyright in the collective work vests in the collective author (here, the newspaper or magazine publisher) and extends only to the creative material contributed by that author, not to "the preexisting material employed in the work," § 103(b). [...]

34   The 1976 Act rejected the doctrine of indivisibility, recasting the copyright as a bundle of discrete "exclusive rights," 17 U. S. C. § 106 (1994 ed. and Supp. V),[4] each of which "may be transferred [...] . . . and owned separately," § 201(d)(2).[...] Congress also provided, in § 404(a), that "a single notice applicable to the collective work as a whole is sufficient" to protect the rights of freelance contributors. And in § 201(c), Congress codified the discrete domains of "[c]opyright in each separate contribution to a collective work" and "copyright in the collective work as a whole." Together, § 404(a) and § 201(c) "preserve the author's copyright in a contribution even if the contribution does not bear a separate notice in the author's name, and without requiring any unqualified transfer of rights to the owner of the collective work." [...]

35   Section 201(c) both describes and circumscribes the "privilege" a publisher acquires regarding an author's contribution to a collective work:

36   "In the absence of an express transfer of the copyright or of any rights under it, the owner of copyright in the collective work is presumed to have acquired *only* the privilege of reproducing and distributing the contribution as part of that particular

collective work, any revision of that collective work, and any later collective work in the same series." (Emphasis added.)

37   A newspaper or magazine publisher is thus privileged to reproduce or distribute an article contributed by a freelance author, absent a contract otherwise providing, only "as part of" any (or all) of three categories of collective works: (a) "that collective work" to which the author contributed her work, (b) "any revision of that collective work," or (c) "any later collective work in the same series." […]

38   If there is demand for a freelance article standing alone or in a new collection, the Copyright Act allows the freelancer to benefit from that demand; after authorizing initial publication, the freelancer may also sell the article to others. […]

39   **III**

40   In the instant case, the Authors wrote several Articles and gave the Print Publishers permission to publish the Articles in certain newspapers and magazines. It is undisputed that the Authors hold copyrights and, therefore, exclusive rights in the Articles.[7] […]

41   […] Against the Authors' charge of infringement, the Publishers do not here contend the Authors entered into an agreement authorizing reproduction of the Articles in the Databases. […] Instead, the Publishers rest entirely on the privilege described in § 201(c). Each discrete edition of the periodicals in which the Articles appeared is a "collective work," the Publishers agree. They contend, however, that reproduction and distribution of each Article by the Databases lie within the "privilege of reproducing and distributing the [Articles] as part of . . . [a] revision of that collective work," § 201(c). The Publishers' encompassing construction of the § 201(c) privilege is unacceptable, we conclude, for it would diminish the Authors' exclusive rights in the Articles.

42   […]

49   The Publishers claim the protection of § 201(c) because users can manipulate the Databases to generate search results consisting entirely of articles from a particular periodical edition. By this logic, § 201(c) would cover the hypothetical library if, in response to a request, that library's expert staff assembled all of the articles from a particular periodical edition. However, the fact that a third party can manipulate a database to produce a noninfringing document does not mean the database is not infringing. Under § 201(c), the question is not whether a user can generate a revision of a collective work from a database, but whether the database itself perceptibly presents the author's contribution as part of a revision of the collective work. That result is not accomplished by these Databases. *Query: What about online versions of newspapers, where articles are also viewed one by one, but under the newspaper's masthead?*

50   […]

55   We conclude that the Electronic Publishers infringed the Authors' copyrights by reproducing and distributing the Articles in a manner not authorized by the Authors and not privileged by § 201(c). We further conclude that the Print Publishers infringed the Authors' copyrights by authorizing the Electronic Publishers to place the Articles in the Databases and by aiding the Electronic Publishers in that endeavor. We therefore affirm the judgment of the Court of Appeals.

56   *It is so ordered.*

57   [...]

105   [7] The Publishers do not claim that the Articles are "work[s] made for hire." 17 U. S. C. § 201(b). As to such works, the employer or person for whom a work was prepared is treated as the author. *Ibid.* The Print Publishers, however, neither engaged the Authors to write the Articles as "employee[s]" nor "commissioned" the Articles through "a written instrument signed by [both parties]" indicating that the Articles shall be considered "work[s] made for hire." […]

125

903

MDY Industries, LLC v. Blizzard Entertainment, Inc. - contract/copyright

September 11, 2014 by mrisch

A common licensing tactic is to use the threat of copyright infringement to force compliance with license terms. This is how open source software works, for example. This excerpt of the Glider case considers the copyright implications associated with the Worl of Warcraft EULA, and whether use of a bot constitutes copyright infringement.

1   629 F.3d 928 (2010)

2   # MDY INDUSTRIES, LLC[...]
            ## v.
            # BLIZZARD ENTERTAINMENT, INC[...]

4   United States Court of Appeals, Ninth Circuit.

5   [...]

6   Filed December 14, 2010.

7   [...]

14   **OPINION**

15   **CALLAHAN, Circuit Judge:**

16   Blizzard Entertainment, Inc. ("Blizzard") is the creator of World of Warcraft ("WoW"), a popular multiplayer online role-playing game in which players interact in a virtual world while advancing through the game's 70 levels. MDY Industries, LLC and its sole member Michael Donnelly ("Donnelly") (sometimes referred to collectively as "MDY") developed and sold Glider, a software program that automatically plays the early levels of WoW for players.

17   [...] MDY brought this action for a declaratory judgment to establish that its Glider sales do not infringe Blizzard's copyright or other rights, and Blizzard asserted counterclaims under the Digital Millennium Copyright Act ("DMCA"), 17 U.S.C. § 1201 *et seq.*, and for tortious interference with contract under Arizona law. The district court found MDY and Donnelly liable for secondary copyright infringement, violations of DMCA § 1201(a)(2) and (b)(1), and tortious interference with contract. We reverse the district court except as to MDY's liability for violation of DMCA § 1201(a)(2) and remand for trial on Blizzard's claim for tortious interference with contract.

904

18   I.

19   **A. World of Warcraft**

20   In November 2004, Blizzard created WoW, a "massively multiplayer online role-playing game" in which players interact in a virtual world. WoW has ten million subscribers, of which two and a half million are in North America. The WoW software has two components: (1) the game client software that a player installs on the computer; and (2) the game server software, which the player accesses on a subscription basis by connecting to WoW's online servers. WoW does not have single-player or offline modes.

21   WoW players roleplay different characters, such as humans, elves, and dwarves. A player's central objective is to advance the character through the game's 70 levels by participating in quests and engaging in battles with monsters. As a player advances, the character collects rewards such as in-game currency, weapons, and armor. WoW's virtual world has its own economy, in which characters use their virtual currency to buy and sell items directly from each other, through vendors, or using auction houses. Some players also utilize WoW's chat capabilities to interact with others.

22   **B. Blizzard's use agreements**

23   Each WoW player must read and accept Blizzard's End User License Agreement ("EULA") and Terms of Use ("ToU") on multiple occasions. The EULA pertains to the game client, so a player agrees to it both before installing the game client and upon first running it. The ToU pertains to the online service, so a player agrees to it both when creating an account and upon first connecting to the online service. Players who do not accept both the EULA and the ToU may return the game client for a refund.

24   **C. Development of Glider and Warden**

25   Donnelly is a WoW player and software programmer. In March 2005, he developed Glider, a software "bot" (short for robot) that automates play of WoW's early levels, for his personal use. A user need not be at the computer while Glider is running. As explained in the Frequently Asked Questions ("FAQ") on MDY's website for Glider:

26   Glider . . . moves the mouse around and pushes keys on the keyboard. You tell it about your character, where you want to kill things, and when you want to kill. Then it kills for you, automatically. You can do something else, like eat dinner or go to a movie, and when you return, you'll have a lot more experience and loot.

27   Glider does not alter or copy WoW's game client software, does not allow a player to avoid paying monthly subscription dues to Blizzard, and has no commercial use independent of WoW. Glider was not initially designed to avoid detection by Blizzard.

28   The parties dispute Glider's impact on the WoW experience. Blizzard contends that Glider disrupts WoW's environment [...] for non-Glider players by enabling Glider users to advance quickly and unfairly through the game and to amass additional game assets. MDY contends that Glider has a minimal effect on non-Glider players, enhances the WoW experience for Glider users, and facilitates disabled players' access to WoW by auto-playing the game for them.

29   In summer 2005, Donnelly began selling Glider through MDY's website for fifteen to twenty-five dollars per license. Prior to marketing Glider, Donnelly reviewed Blizzard's EULA and client-server manipulation policy. He reached the conclusion that Blizzard had not prohibited bots in those documents.

30   In September 2005, Blizzard launched Warden, a technology that it developed to prevent its players who use unauthorized third-party software, including bots, from connecting to WoW's servers. Warden was able to detect Glider, and Blizzard immediately used Warden to ban most Glider users. MDY responded by modifying Glider to avoid detection and promoting its new anti-detection features on its website's FAQ. [...]

905

31   Thus, by late 2005, MDY was aware that Blizzard was prohibiting bots. MDY modified its website to indicate that using Glider violated Blizzard's ToU. In November 2005, Donnelly wrote in an email interview, "Avoiding detection is rather exciting, to be sure. Since Blizzard does not want bots running at all, it's a violation to use them." Following MDY's anti-detection modifications, Warden only occasionally detected Glider. As of September 2008, MDY had gross revenues of $3.5 million based on 120,000 Glider license sales.

32   [...]

35   **E. Pre-litigation contact between MDY and Blizzard**

36   In August 2006, Blizzard sent MDY a cease-and-desist letter alleging that MDY's website hosted WoW screenshots and a Glider install file, all of which infringed Blizzard's copyrights. Donnelly removed the screenshots and requested Blizzard to clarify why the install file was infringing, but Blizzard did not respond. In October 2006, Blizzard's counsel visited Donnelly's home, threatening suit unless MDY immediately ceased selling Glider and remitted all profits to Blizzard. MDY immediately commenced this action.

37   [...] **II.**

38   On December 1, 2006, MDY filed an amended complaint seeking a declaration that Glider does not infringe Blizzard's copyright or other rights. In February 2007, Blizzard filed counterclaims and third-party claims against MDY and Donnelly for, *inter alia*, contributory and vicarious copyright infringement, violation of DMCA § 1201(a)(2) and (b)(1), and tortious interference with contract.

39   In July 2008, the district court granted Blizzard partial summary judgment, finding that MDY's Glider sales contributorily and vicariously infringed Blizzard's copyrights [...]

40   In September 2008, the parties stipulated to entry of a $6 million judgment against MDY for the copyright infringement [...] After a January 2009 bench trial, the district court [...] held Donnelly personally liable for MDY's copyright infringement [...]

45   We first consider whether MDY committed contributory or vicarious infringement (collectively, "secondary infringement") of Blizzard's copyright by selling Glider to WoW players.[1] [...] To establish secondary infringement, Blizzard must first demonstrate direct infringement. [...] To establish direct infringement, Blizzard must demonstrate copyright ownership and violation of one of its exclusive rights by Glider users. [...] MDY is liable for contributory infringement if it has "intentionally induc[ed] or encourag[ed] direct infringement" by [...] Glider users. [...] MDY is liable for vicarious infringement if it (1) has the right and ability to control Glider users' putatively infringing activity and (2) derives a direct financial benefit from their activity. *Id.* If Glider users directly infringe, MDY does not dispute that it satisfies the other elements of contributory and vicarious infringement.

46   As a copyright owner, Blizzard possesses the exclusive right to reproduce its work. 17 U.S.C. § 106(1). The parties agree that when playing WoW, a player's computer creates a copy of the game's software in the computer's random access memory ("RAM"), a form of temporary memory used by computers to run software programs. This copy potentially infringes unless the player (1) is a licensee whose use of the software is within the scope of the license or (2) owns the copy of the software. [...] As to the scope of the license, ToU § 4(B), "Limitations on Your Use of the Service," provides:

47   You agree that you will not . . . (ii) create or use cheats, bots, "mods," and/or hacks, or any other third-party software designed to modify the World of Warcraft experience; or (iii) use any third-party software that intercepts, "mines," or otherwise collects information from or through the Program or Service.

48   By contrast, if the player owns the copy of the software, the "essential step" defense provides that the player does not infringe by making a copy of the computer program where the copy is created and used solely "as an essential step in the utilization of the computer program in conjunction with a machine." 17 U.S.C. § 117(a)(1).

49   ## A. Essential step defense

50   We consider whether WoW players, including Glider users, are owners or licensees of their copies of WoW software. If WoW players own their copies, as MDY contends, then Glider users do not infringe by reproducing WoW software in RAM while playing, and MDY is not secondarily liable for copyright infringement.

51   In *Vernor v. Autodesk, Inc.,* we recently distinguished between "owners" and "licensees" of copies for purposes of the essential step defense. *[...]* In *Vernor,* we held "that a software user is a licensee rather than an owner of a copy where the copyright owner (1) specifies that the user is granted a license; (2) significantly restricts the user's ability to transfer the software; and (3) imposes notable use" restrictions. *[...]*

52   Applying *Vernor,* we hold that WoW players are licensees of WoW's game client software. Blizzard reserves title in the software and grants players a non-exclusive, limited license. Blizzard also imposes transfer restrictions if a player seeks to transfer the license: the player must (1) transfer all original packaging and documentation; (2) permanently delete all of the copies and installation of the game client; and (3) transfer only to a recipient who accepts the EULA. A player may not sell or give away the account.

53   Blizzard also imposes a variety of use restrictions. The game must be used only for non-commercial entertainment purposes and may not be used in cyber cafes and computer gaming centers without Blizzard's *[...]* permission. Players may not concurrently use unauthorized third-party programs. Also, Blizzard may alter the game client itself remotely without a player's knowledge or permission, and may terminate the EULA and ToU if players violate their terms. Termination ends a player's license to access and play WoW. Following termination, players must immediately destroy their copies of the game and uninstall the game client from their computers, but need not return the software to Blizzard.

54   Since WoW players, including Glider users, do not own their copies of the software, Glider users may not claim the essential step defense. 17 U.S.C. § 117(a)(1). Thus, when their computers copy WoW software into RAM, the players may infringe unless their usage is within the scope of Blizzard's limited license.

55   ## B. Contractual covenants vs. license conditions

56   "A copyright owner who grants a nonexclusive, limited license ordinarily waives the right to sue licensees for copyright infringement, and it may sue only for breach of contract." *[...]* However, if the licensee acts outside the scope of the license, the licensor may sue for copyright infringement. *[...]* Enforcing a copyright license "raises issues that lie at the intersection of copyright and contract law." *Id.* *[...]*

57   We refer to contractual terms that limit a license's scope as "conditions," the breach of which constitute copyright infringement. *[...]* We refer to all other license terms as "covenants," the breach of which is actionable only under contract law. *Id.* We distinguish between conditions and covenants according to state contract law, to the extent consistent with federal copyright law and policy. *[...]*

58   A Glider user commits copyright infringement by playing WoW while violating a ToU term that is a license condition. To establish copyright infringement, then, Blizzard must demonstrate that the violated term — ToU § 4(B) — is a condition rather than a covenant. *[...]* Blizzard's EULAs and ToUs provide that they are to be interpreted according to Delaware law. Accordingly, we first construe them under Delaware law, and then evaluate whether that construction is consistent with federal copyright law and policy.

59   A covenant is a contractual promise, i.e., a manifestation of intention to act or refrain from acting in a particular way, such that the promisee is justified in understanding that the promisor has made a commitment. *[...]* A condition precedent is an act or event that must occur before a duty to perform a promise arises. *[...]* Conditions precedent are disfavored because they tend to work forfeitures. *[...]* Wherever possible, equity construes ambiguous contract provisions as covenants rather than conditions. *[...]* However, if the contract is

unambiguous, the court construes it according to its terms. *[...]*

60   Applying these principles, ToU § 4(B)(ii) and (iii)'s prohibitions against *[...]* bots and unauthorized third-party software are covenants rather than copyright-enforceable conditions. *[...]* Although ToU § 4 is titled, "Limitations on Your Use of the Service," nothing in that section conditions Blizzard's grant of a limited license on players' compliance with ToU § 4's restrictions. To the extent that the title introduces any ambiguity, under Delaware law, ToU § 4(B) is not a condition, but is a contractual covenant. *Cf. Sun Microsystems, Inc. v. Microsoft Corp.,* 81 F.Supp.2d 1026, 1031-32 (N.D.Cal.2000) ("*Sun II*") (where Sun licensed Microsoft to create only derivative works compatible with other Sun software, Microsoft's "compatibility obligations" were covenants because the license was not specifically conditioned on their fulfillment).

61   To recover for copyright infringement based on breach of a license agreement, (1) the copying must exceed the scope of the defendant's license and (2) the copyright owner's complaint must be grounded in an exclusive right of copyright (e.g., unlawful reproduction or distribution). *[...]* Contractual rights, however, can be much broader:

62   [C]onsider a license in which the copyright owner grants a person the right to make one and only one copy of a book with the caveat that the licensee may not read the last ten pages. Obviously, a licensee who made a hundred copies of the book would be liable for copyright infringement because the copying would violate the Copyright Act's prohibition on reproduction and would exceed the scope of the license. Alternatively, if the licensee made a single copy of the book, but read the last ten pages, the only cause of action would be for breach of contract, because reading a book does not violate any right protected by copyright law.

63   *[...]* Consistent with this approach, we have held that the potential for infringement exists only where the licensee's action (1) exceeds the license's scope (2) in a manner that implicates one of the licensor's exclusive statutory rights. *[...]*

64   Here, ToU § 4 contains certain restrictions that are grounded in Blizzard's exclusive rights of copyright and other restrictions that are not. For instance, ToU § 4(D) forbids creation of derivative works based on WoW without Blizzard's consent. A player who violates this prohibition [941] would exceed the scope of her license and violate one of Blizzard's exclusive rights under the Copyright Act. In contrast, ToU § 4(C)(ii) prohibits a player's disruption of another player's game experience. *Id.* A player might violate this prohibition while playing the game by harassing another player with unsolicited instant messages. Although this conduct may violate the contractual covenants with Blizzard, it would not violate any of Blizzard's exclusive rights of copyright. The antibot provisions at issue in this case, ToU § 4(B)(ii) and (iii), are similarly covenants rather than conditions. A Glider user violates the covenants with Blizzard, but does not thereby commit copyright infringement because Glider does not infringe any of Blizzard's exclusive rights. For instance, the use does not alter or copy WoW software.

65   Were we to hold otherwise, Blizzard — or any software copyright holder — could designate any disfavored conduct during software use as copyright infringement, by purporting to condition the license on the player's abstention from the disfavored conduct. The rationale would be that because the conduct occurs while the player's computer is copying the software code into RAM in order for it to run, the violation is copyright infringement. This would allow software copyright owners far greater rights than Congress has generally conferred on copyright owners.[3]

66   We conclude that for a licensee's violation of a contract to constitute copyright infringement, there must be a nexus between the condition and the licensor's exclusive rights of copyright.[4] Here, WoW players do not commit copyright infringement by using Glider in violation of the ToU. MDY is thus not liable for secondary copyright infringement, which requires the existence of direct copyright infringement. *[...]*

68   We thus reverse the district court's grant of summary judgment to Blizzard on its secondary copyright infringement *[...]* claims. *[...]*

▓▓▓   [1] Alternatively, MDY asks that we determine whether there are any genuine issues of material fact that warrant a remand for trial on Blizzard's secondary copyright infringement claims. We find none.

167   [...]

168   [3] A copyright holder may wish to enforce violations of license agreements as copyright infringements for several reasons. First, breach of contract damages are generally limited to the value of the actual loss caused by the breach. *[...]* In contrast, copyright damages include the copyright owner's actual damages and the infringer's actual profits, or statutory damages of up to $150,000 per work. [...] Second, copyright law offers injunctive relief, seizure of infringing articles, and awards of costs and attorneys' fees. 17 U.S.C. §§ 502-03, 505. Third, as amicus Software & Information Industry Association highlights, copyright law allows copyright owners a remedy against "downstream" infringers with whom they are not in privity of contract. *[...]*

169   [4] A licensee arguably may commit copyright infringement by continuing to use the licensed work while failing to make required payments, even though a failure to make payments otherwise lacks a nexus to the licensor's exclusive statutory rights. We view payment as *sui generis,* however, because of the distinct nexus between payment and all commercial copyright licenses, not just those concerning software.

170   [...]

Jacobsen v. Katzer and Kamind Assoc.

September 13, 2014 by mrisch

This note considers the use of copyright to enforce contracts in open source software

1   535 F.3d 1373 (2008)

2   **Robert JACOBSEN**[...]

v.

Matthew KATZER[...]

3   United States Court of Appeals, Federal Circuit.

5   August 13, 2008.

6   [...]

9   Before MICHEL, Chief Judge, PROST, Circuit Judge, and HOCHBERG,[*] District Judge.

10   **HOCHBERG, District Judge.**

11   We consider here the ability of a copyright holder to dedicate certain work to free public use and yet enforce an "open source" copyright license to control the future distribution and modification of that work. [...] Jacobsen holds a copyright to computer programming [...] code. He makes that code available for public download from a website without a financial fee pursuant to the Artistic License, an "open source" or public license. Appellees Matthew Katzer and Kamind Associates, Inc. (collectively "Katzer/Kamind") develop commercial software products for the model train industry and hobbyists. Jacobsen accused Katzer/Kamind of copying certain materials from Jacobsen's website and incorporating them into one of Katzer/Kamind's software packages without following the terms of the Artistic License. Jacobsen brought an action for copyright infringement and moved for a preliminary injunction.

12   [...]

16   **I.**

17   Jacobsen manages an open source software group called Java Model Railroad Interface ("JMRI"). Through the collective work of many participants, JMRI created a computer programming application called DecoderPro, which allows model railroad enthusiasts to use their computers to program the decoder chips that control model trains. DecoderPro files are available for download and use by the public free of charge from an open source incubator website called SourceForge; Jacobsen maintains the JMRI site on SourceForge. The downloadable files contain copyright notices and refer the user to a "COPYING" file, which clearly sets forth the terms of the Artistic License.

18   Katzer/Kamind offers a competing software product, Decoder Commander, which is also used to program decoder chips. During development of Decoder Commander, one of Katzer/Kamind's predecessors or employees is alleged to have downloaded the decoder definition files from DecoderPro and used portions of these files as part of the Decoder Commander software. The Decoder Commander software files that used DecoderPro definition files did not comply with the terms of the Artistic License. Specifically, the Decoder Commander software did not include (1) the author' names, (2) JMRI copyright notices, (3) references to the COPYING file, (4) an identification of SourceForge or JMRI as the original source of the definition files, and (5) a description of how the files or computer code

910

had been changed from the original source code. The Decoder Commander software also changed [...] various computer file names of Decoder-Pro files without providing a reference to the original JMRI files or information on where to get the Standard Version.[...]

19   Jacobsen moved for a preliminary injunction, arguing that the violation of the terms of the Artistic License constituted copyright infringement and that, under Ninth Circuit law, irreparable harm could be presumed in a copyright infringement case. The District Court reviewed the Artistic License and determined that "Defendants' alleged violation of the conditions of the license may have constituted a breach of the nonexclusive license, but does not create liability for copyright infringement where it would not otherwise exist." [...] The District Court found that Jacobsen had a cause of action only for breach of contract, rather than an action for copyright infringement based on a breach of the conditions of the Artistic License. Because a breach of contract creates no presumption of irreparable harm, the District Court denied the motion for a preliminary injunction.

20   [...]

21   **II.**

22   [...]

24   **A.**

25   Public licenses, often referred to as "open source" licenses, are used by artists, authors, educators, software developers, and scientists who wish to create collaborative projects and to dedicate certain works to the public. Several types of public licenses have been designed to provide creators of copyrighted materials a means to protect and control their copyrights. Creative Commons, one of the amici curiae, provides free copyright licenses to allow parties to dedicate their works to the public or to license certain uses of their works while keeping some rights reserved.

26   Open source licensing has become a widely used method of creative collaboration that serves to advance the arts and sciences in a manner and at a pace that few could have imagined just a few decades ago. For example, the Massachusetts Institute of Technology ("MIT") uses a Creative Commons public license for an OpenCourseWare project that licenses all 1800 MIT courses. Other public licenses support the GNU/Linux operating system, the Perl programming language, the Apache web server programs, the Firefox web browser, and a collaborative web-based encyclopedia called Wikipedia. Creative Commons notes that, by some estimates, there are close to 100,000,000 works licensed under various Creative Commons licenses. The Wikimedia Foundation, another of the amici curiae, estimates that the Wikipedia website has more than 75,000 active contributors working on some 9,000,000 articles in more than 250 languages.

27   Open Source software projects invite computer programmers from around the [...] world to view software code and make changes and improvements to it. Through such collaboration, software programs can often be written and debugged faster and at lower cost than if the copyright holder were required to do all of the work independently. In exchange and in consideration for this collaborative work, the copyright holder permits users to copy, modify and distribute the software code subject to conditions that serve to protect downstream users and to keep the code accessible.[2] By requiring that users copy and restate the license and attribution information, a copyright holder can ensure that recipients of the redistributed computer code know the identity of the owner as well as the scope of the license granted by the original owner. The Artistic License in this case also requires that changes to the computer code be tracked so that downstream users know what part of the computer code is the original code created by the copyright holder and what part has been newly added or altered by another collaborator.

28   Traditionally, copyright owners sold their copyrighted material in exchange for money. The lack of money changing hands in open source licensing should not be presumed to mean that there is no economic consideration, however. There are substantial benefits, including economic benefits, to the creation and distribution of copyrighted works under public licenses that range far beyond traditional license royalties. For example, program creators may generate market share for their programs by providing certain components free of charge.

Similarly, a programmer or company may increase its national or international reputation by incubating open source projects. Improvement to a product can come rapidly and free of charge from an expert not even known to the copyright holder. The Eleventh Circuit has recognized the economic motives inherent in public licenses, even where profit is not immediate. *[...]*

29   **B.**

30   The parties do not dispute that Jacobsen is the holder of a copyright for certain materials distributed through his website.[3] Katzer/Kamind also admits that portions of the DecoderPro software were copied, modified, and distributed as part of the Decoder Commander software. Accordingly, Jacobsen has made out a prima facie case of copyright infringement. Katzer/Kamind argues that they cannot be liable for copyright infringement because they had a license to use the material. Thus, the Court must evaluate whether the use by Katzer/Kamind was outside the scope of the license. *[...]* The copyrighted materials in this case are downloadable by any user and are labeled to include a copyright notification and a COPYING file that includes the text of the Artistic License. *[...]* The Artistic License grants users the right to copy, modify, and distribute the software:

31   provided that [the user] insert a prominent notice in each changed file stating how and when [the user] changed that file, and provided that [the user] do at least ONE of the following:

32   a) place [the user's] modifications in the Public Domain or otherwise make them Freely Available, such as by posting said modifications to Usenet or an equivalent medium, or placing the modifications on a major archive site such as ftp.uu.net, or by allowing the Copyright Holder to include [the user's] modifications in the Standard Version of the Package.

                    b) use the modified Package only within [the user's] corporation or organization.

                    c) rename any non-standard executables so the names do not conflict with the standard executables, which must also be provided, and provide a separate manual page for each nonstandard executable that clearly documents how it differs from the Standard Version, or

                    d) make other distribution arrangements with the Copyright Holder.

33   The heart of the argument on appeal concerns whether the terms of the Artistic License are conditions of, or merely covenants to, the copyright license. Generally, a "copyright owner who grants a nonexclusive license to use his copyrighted material waives his right to sue the licensee for copyright infringement" and can sue only for breach of contract. *[...]*

34   Thus, if the terms of the Artistic License allegedly violated are both covenants and conditions, they may serve to limit the scope of the license and are governed by copyright law. If they are merely covenants, by contrast, they are governed by contract law. *[...]* The District Court did not expressly state whether the limitations in the Artistic License are independent covenants or, rather, conditions to the scope; its analysis, however, clearly treated the license limitations as contractual covenants rather than conditions of the copyright license.[4]

35   *[...]*

36   **III.**

37   The Artistic License states on its face that the document creates conditions: "The intent of this document is to state the *conditions* under which a Package may be copied." (Emphasis added.) The Artistic License also uses the traditional language of conditions by noting that the rights to copy, modify, and distribute are granted "*provided that*" the conditions are met. Under California contract law, "provided that" typically denotes a condition. *[...]*

38   The conditions set forth in the Artistic License are vital to enable the copyright holder to retain the ability to benefit from the work of downstream users. By requiring that users who modify or distribute the copyrighted material retain the reference to the original source

files, downstream users are directed to Jacobsen's website. Thus, downstream users know about the collaborative effort to improve and expand the SourceForge project once they learn of the "upstream" project from a "downstream" distribution, and they may join in that effort.

39   The District Court interpreted the Artistic License to permit a user to "modify the material in any way" and did not find that any of the "provided that" limitations in the Artistic License served to limit this grant. The District Court's interpretation of the conditions of the Artistic License does not credit the explicit restrictions in the license that govern a downloader's right to modify and distribute the copyrighted work. The copyright holder here expressly stated the terms upon which the right to modify and distribute the material depended and invited direct contact if a downloader wished to negotiate other terms. These restrictions were both clear and necessary to accomplish the objectives of the open source licensing collaboration, including economic benefit. Moreover, the District Court did not address the other restrictions of the license, such as the requirement that all modification from the original be clearly shown with a new name and a separate page for any such modification that shows how it differs from the original.

40   Copyright holders who engage in open source licensing have the right to control the modification and distribution of copyrighted material. As the Second Circuit explained in *Gilliam v. ABC,* 538 F.2d 14, 21 (2d Cir.1976), the "unauthorized editing of the underlying work, if proven, would constitute an infringement of the copyright in that work similar to any other use of a work that exceeded the license granted by the proprietor of the copyright." Copyright licenses are designed to support the right to exclude; money damages [...] alone do not support or enforce that right. The choice to exact consideration in the form of compliance with the open source requirements of disclosure and explanation of changes, rather than as a dollar-denominated fee, is entitled to no less legal recognition. Indeed, because a calculation of damages is inherently speculative, these types of license restrictions might well be rendered meaningless absent the ability to enforce through injunctive relief.

41   In this case, a user who downloads the JMRI copyrighted materials is authorized to make modifications and to distribute the materials "provided that" the user follows the restrictive terms of the Artistic License. A copyright holder can grant the right to make certain modifications, yet retain his right to prevent other modifications. Indeed, such a goal is exactly the purpose of adding conditions to a license grant.[5] The Artistic License, like many other common copyright licenses, requires that any copies that are distributed contain the copyright notices and the COPYING file. *[...]*

42   It is outside the scope of the Artistic License to modify and distribute the copyrighted materials without copyright notices and a tracking of modifications from the original computer files. If a down loader does not assent to these conditions stated in the COPYING file, he is instructed to "make other arrangements with the Copyright Holder." Katzer/Kamind did not make any such "other arrangements." The clear language of the Artistic License creates conditions to protect the economic rights at issue in the granting of a public license. These conditions govern the rights to modify and distribute the computer programs and files included in the downloadable software package. The attribution and modification transparency requirements directly serve to drive traffic to the open source incubation page and to inform downstream users of the project, which is a significant economic goal of the copyright holder that the law will enforce. Through this controlled spread of information, the copyright holder gains creative collaborators to the open source project; by requiring that changes made by downstream users be visible to the copyright holder and others, the copyright holder learns about the uses for his software and gains others' knowledge that can be used to advance future software releases.

43   **IV.**

44   For the aforementioned reasons, we vacate and remand. While Katzer/Kamind appears to have conceded that they did not comply with the aforedescribed conditions of the Artistic License, the District Court did not make factual findings on the likelihood of success on the merits in proving that Katzer/Kamind violated the conditions of the Artistic License. [...]

46   *VACATED* and *REMANDED*

47   [...]

49   [2] For example, the GNU General Public License, which is used for the Linux operating system, prohibits downstream users from charging for a license to the software. *[...]*

52   [5] Open source licensing restrictions are easily distinguished from mere "author attribution" cases. Copyright law does not automatically protect the rights of authors to credit for copyrighted materials. *[...]*

Bragg v. Linden Research, Inc.

September 12, 2014 by mrisch

This case illustrates the convergence of contract, intellectual property licensing, and property – in the form of virtual worlds

1   487 F.Supp.2d 593 (2007)

2   **Marc BRAGG**[...]

                                           v.

                                           LINDEN RESEARCH, INC. [...]

4   United States District Court, E.D. Pennsylvania.

5   May 30, 2007.

6   [...]

8   [...] **MEMORANDUM**

9   **EDUARDO C. ROBRENO, District Judge.**

10   This case is about virtual property maintained on a virtual world on the Internet. Plaintiff, March Bragg, Esq., claims an ownership interest in such virtual property. Bragg contends that Defendants, the operators of the virtual world, unlawfully confiscated his virtual property and denied him access to their virtual world. Ultimately at issue in this case are the novel questions of what rights and obligations grow out of the relationship between the owner and creator of a virtual world and its resident-customers. While the property and the world where it is found are "virtual," the dispute is real.

11   Presently before the Court are Defendants' Motion to Dismiss for Lack of Personal Jurisdiction (doc. no. 2) and Motion to Compel Arbitration (doc. no. 3). For the reasons set forth below, the motions will be denied.

12   **I. BACKGROUND**

13   **A.** *Second Life*

14   The defendants in this case, Linden Research Inc. ("Linden") and its Chief Executive Officer, Philip Rosedale, operate a multiplayer role-playing game set in the virtual world[1] known as "Second Life."[2] Participants create avatars[3] to represent themselves, and Second Life is populated by hundreds of thousands of avatars, whose interactions with one another are limited only by the human imagination.[4] According to Plaintiff, many people "are now living large portions of their lives, forming friendships with others, building and acquiring virtual property, forming contracts, substantial business relationships and forming social organizations" in virtual worlds such as Second Life. [...] Owning property in and having access to this virtual world is, moreover, apparently important to the plaintiff in this case.

15   **B.** *Recognition of Property Rights*

16   In November 2003, Linden announced that it would recognize participants' full intellectual property protection for the digital content they created or otherwise owned in Second Life. As a result, Second Life avatars may now buy, own, and sell virtual goods ranging "from cars

to homes to slot machines." [...][5] Most significantly [...] for this case, avatars may purchase "virtual land," make improvements to that land, exclude other avatars from entering onto the land, rent the land, or sell the land to other avatars for a profit. Assertedly, by recognizing virtual property rights, Linden would distinguish itself from other virtual worlds available on the Internet and thus increase participation in Second Life.

17   Defendant Rosedale personally joined in efforts to publicize Linden's recognition of rights to virtual property. For example, in 2003, Rosedale stated in a press release made available on Second Life's website that:

18   Until now, any content created by users for persistent state worlds, such as Everquest® or Star Wars Galaxies™, has essentially become the property of the company developing and hosting the world. . . . We believe our new policy recognizes the fact that persistent world users are making significant contributions to building these worlds and should be able to both own the content they create and share in the value that is created. The preservation of users' property rights is a necessary step toward the emergence of genuinely real online worlds.

19   Press Release, Linden Lab, *Linden Lab Preserves Real World Intellectual Property Rights of Users of its Second Life Online Services* (Nov. 14, 2003). After this initial announcement, Rosedale continued to personally hype the ownership of virtual property on Second Life. In an interview in 2004, for example, Rosedale stated: "The idea of land ownership and the ease with which you can own land and do something with it . . . is intoxicating. . . . Land ownership feels important and tangible. It's a real piece of the future." Michael Learmonth, *Virtual Real Estate Boom Draws Real Dollars,* USA Today, June 3, 2004. Rosedale recently gave an extended interview for Inc. magazine, where he appeared on the cover stating, "What you have in Second Life is real and it is yours. It doesn't belong to us. You can make money." Michael Fitzgerald, *How Philip Rosedale Created Second Life,* Inc., Feb. 2007.[6]

20   Rosedale even created his own avatar and held virtual town hall meetings on Second Life where he made representations about the purchase of virtual land. [...] Bragg "attended" such meetings and relied on the representations that Rosedale made therein. [...]

21   **C.** *Plaintiffs' Participation in Second Life*

22   In 2005, Plaintiff Marc Bragg, Esq., signed up and paid Linden to participate in Second Life. Bragg claims that he was induced into "investing" in virtual land by representations made by Linden and Rosedale in press releases, interviews, and through the Second Life website. [...] Bragg also paid Linden [...] real money as `tax" on his land.[7] By April 2006, Bragg had not only purchased numerous parcels of land in his Second Life, he had also digitally crafted "fireworks" that he was able to sell to other avatars for a profit. Bragg also acquired other virtual items from other avatars.

23   The dispute ultimately at issue in this case arose on April 30, 2006, when Bragg acquired a parcel of virtual land named "Taessot" for $300. Linden sent Bragg an email advising him that Taessot had been improperly purchased through an "exploit." Linden took Taesot away. It then froze Bragg's account, effectively confiscating all of the virtual property and currency that he maintained on his account with Second Life.

24   Bragg brought suit against Linden and Rosedale in the Court of Common Pleas of Chester County, Pennsylvania, on October 3, 2006.[8] Linden and Rosedale removed the case to this Court (doc, no. 1) and then, within a week, moved to compel arbitration (doe. no. 3).

25   [...]

III. MOTION TO COMPEL ARBITRATION

59   Defendants have also filed a motion to compel arbitration that seeks to dismiss this action and compel Bragg to submit his claims to arbitration according to the Rules of the International Chamber of Commerce ("ICC") in San Francisco.

60   **A.** *Relevant Facts*

61   Before a person is permitted to participate in Second Life, she must accept the Terms of Service of Second Life (the "TOS") by clicking a button indicating acceptance of the TOS. Bragg concedes that he clicked the "accept" button before accessing Second Life. [...] Included in the TOS are a California choice of law provision, an arbitration provision, and forum selection clause. Specifically, located in the fourteenth line of the thirteenth paragraph under the heading "GENERAL PROVISIONS," and following provisions regarding the applicability [...] of export and import laws to Second Life, the following language appears:

62   Any dispute or claim arising out of or in connection with this Agreement or the performance, breach or termination thereof, shall be finally settled by binding arbitration in San Francisco, California under the Rules of Arbitration of the International Chamber of Commerce by three arbitrators appointed in accordance with said rules. . . . Notwithstanding the foregoing, either party may apply to any court of competent jurisdiction for injunctive relief or enforcement of this arbitration provision without breach of this arbitration provision.

63   [...]

64   **B.** *Legal Standards*

65   **1.** *Federal law applies*

66   The Federal Arbitration Act ("FAA") requires that the Court apply federal substantive law here because the arbitration agreement is connected to a transaction involving interstate commerce. [...]

68   **2.** *The Legal Standard Under the FAA*

69   Under the FAA, on the motion of a party, a court must stay proceedings and order the parties to arbitrate the dispute if the court finds that the parties have agreed in writing to do so. [...] A party seeking to compel arbitration must show (1) that a valid agreement to arbitrate exists between the parties and (2) that the specific dispute falls within the scope of the agreement. [...]

70   In determining whether a valid agreement to arbitrate exists between the parties, the Third Circuit has instructed district courts to give the party opposing arbitration "the benefit of all reasonable doubts and inferences that may arise," or, in other words, to apply the familiar Federal Rule of Civil Procedure 56(c) summary judgment standard. [...] While there is a presumption that a particular dispute is within the *scope* of an arbitration agreement, [...] there is no such "presumption" or "policy" that favors the *existence* of a valid agreement to arbitrate. [...]

71   **C.** *Application*

72   **1.** *Unconscionabilty of the Arbitration Agreement*

73   Bragg resists enforcement of the. TOS's arbitration provision on the basis that it is "both procedurally and substantively unconscionable and is itself evidence of defendants' scheme to deprive Plaintiff (and others) of both their money and their day in court." [...] [15]

74   Section 2 of the FAA provides that written arbitration agreements "shall be valid, irrevocable, and enforceable, save upon such grounds as exist at law or in equity for the revocation of any contract." [...] Thus, "generally applicable contract defenses, such as fraud, duress, or unconscionability, may be applied to invalidate arbitration agreements without contravening § 2." [...] When determining whether such defenses might apply to any purported agreement to arbitrate the dispute in question, "courts generally . . . should apply ordinary state-law principles that govern the formation of contracts." [...] Thus, the Court will apply California state law to determine whether the arbitration provision is unconscionable.[16]

75   Under California law, unconscionability has both procedural and substantive components. *[...]* The procedural component can be satisfied by showing (1) oppression through the existence of unequal bargaining positions or (2) surprise through hidden terms common in the context of adhesion contracts. *[...]* The substantive component can be satisfied by showing overly harsh or one-sided results that "shock the conscience." *[...]* The two elements operate on a sliding scale such that the more significant one is, the less significant the other need be. *[...]* However, a claim of unconscionability cannot be determined merely by examining the face of the contract; there must be an inquiry into the circumstances under which the contract was executed, and the contract's purpose, and effect. *[...]*

76   **(a)** *Procedural Unconscionability*

77   A contract or clause is procedurally unconscionable if it is a contract of adhesion. *[...]* A contract of adhesion, in *[...]* turn, is a "standardized contract, which, imposed and drafted by the party of superior bargaining strength, relegates to the subscribing party only the opportunity to adhere to the contract or reject it." *[...]* Under California law, "the critical factor in procedural unconscionability analysis is the manner in which the contract or the disputed clause was presented and negotiated." *[...]* "When the weaker party is presented the clause and told to `take it or leave it' without the opportunity for meaningful negotiation, oppression, and therefore procedural unconscionability, are present." *[...]*

78   The TOS are a contract of adhesion. Linden presents the TOS on a takeit-or-leave-it basis. A potential participant can either click "assent" to the TOS, and then gain entrance to Second Life's virtual world, or refuse assent and be denied access. Linden also clearly has superior bargaining strength over Bragg. Although Bragg is an experienced attorney, who believes he is expert enough to comment on numerous industry standards and the "rights" or participants in virtual worlds, *[...]* he was never presented with an opportunity to use his experience and lawyering skills to negotiate terms different from the TOS that Linden offered.

79   Moreover, there was no "reasonably available market alternatives [to defeat] a claim of adhesiveness." *[...]* Although it is not the only virtual world on the Internet, Second Life was the first and only virtual world to specifically grant its participants property rights in virtual land.

80   The procedural element of unconscionability also "focuses on . . . surprise." *[...]* In determining whether surprise exists, California courts focus not on the plaintiff's subjective reading of the contract, but rather, more objectively, on "the extent to which the supposedly agreed-upon terms of the bargain are hidden in the prolix printed form drafted by the party seeking to enforce the disputed terms." *Id.* In *Gutierrez,* the court found such surprise where an arbitration clause was "particularly inconspicuous, printed in eight-point typeface on the opposite side of the signature page of the lease." *Id.*

81   Here, although the TOS are ubiquitous throughout Second Life,[17] Linden buried the TOS's arbitration provision in a lengthy paragraph under the benign heading "GENERAL PROVISIONS." *[...]* Linden also failed to make available the costs and rules of arbitration in the ICC by either setting them forth in the TOS or by providing a hyper-link to another page or website where they are available. *[...]*

82   *Comb* is most instructive. In that case, the plaintiffs challenged an arbitration provision that was part of an agreement to which they had assented, in circumstances similar to this case, by clicking their assent on an online application page. *[...]* The defendant, PayPal, was a large company with millions of individual online customers. *[...]* The plaintiffs, with one exception, were all individual customers of PayPal. Given the small amount of the average transaction with PayPal, the fact that most PayPal customers were private individuals, and that there was a "dispute as to whether PayPal's competitors offer their services without requiring customers to enter into arbitration agreements," the court concluded that the user agreement at issue "satisfie[d] the criteria for procedural unconscionability under California law." *[...]* Here, as in *Comb,* procedural unconscionability is satisfied.

83   **(b)** *Substantive Unconscionability*

84   Even if an agreement is procedurally unconscionable, "it may nonetheless be enforceable if the substantive terms are reasonable." *[...]* Substantive unconscionability focuses on the one-sidedness of the contract terms. *Armendariz,* *[...]* Here, a number of the TOS's elements lead the Court to conclude that Bragg has demonstrated that the TOS are substantively unconscionable.

85   **(i)** *Mutuality*

86   Under California law, substantive unconscionability has been found where an arbitration provision forces the weaker party to arbitrate claims but permits a choice of forums for the stronger party. *[...]*. In other words, the arbitration remedy must contain a "modicum of bilaterality." *[...]* This principle has been extended to arbitration provisions that allow the stronger party a range of remedies before arbitrating a dispute, such as self-help, while relegating to the weaker party the sole remedy of arbitration.[18]

87   *[[...]* In *Comb,* for example, the court found a lack of mutuality where the user agreement allowed PayPal "at its sole discretion" to restrict accounts, withhold funds, undertake its own investigation of a customer's financial records, close accounts, and procure ownership of all funds in dispute unless and until the customer is "later determined to be entitled to the funds in dispute." *[...]* Also significant was the fact that the user agreement was "subject to change by PayPal without prior notice (unless prior notice is required by law), by posting of the revised Agreement on the PayPal website." *[...]*

88   Here, the TOS contain many of the same elements that made the PayPal user agreement substantively unconscionable for lack of mutuality. The TOS proclaim that "Linden has the right at any time for any reason or no reason to suspend or terminate your Account, terminate this Agreement, and/or refuse any and all current or future use of the Service without notice or liability to you." TOS ¶ 7.1. Whether or not a customer has breached the Agreement is "determined in Linden's sole discretion." *Id.* Linden also reserves the right to return no money at all based on mere "suspicions of fraud" or other violations of law. *Id.* Finally, the TOS state that "Linden may amend this Agreement . . . at any time in its sole discretion by posting the amended Agreement [on its website]." TOS ¶ 1.2.

89   In effect, the TOS provide Linden with a variety of one-sided remedies to resolve disputes, while forcing its customers to arbitrate any disputes with Linden. This is precisely what occurred here. When a dispute arose, Linden exercised its option to use self-help by freezing Bragg's, account, retaining funds that Linden alone determined were subject to dispute, and then telling Bragg that he could resolve the dispute by initiating a costly arbitration process. The TOS expressly authorized Linden to engage in such unilateral conduct. As in *Comb,* "[f]or all practical purposes, a customer may resolve disputes only after [Linden] has had control of the disputed funds for an indefinite period of time," and may only resolve those disputes by initiating arbitration. *[...]*

90   Linden's right to modify the arbitration clause is also significant. "The effect of [Linden's] unilateral right to modify the arbitration clause is that it could . . . craft precisely the sort of asymmetrical arbitration agreement that is prohibited under California law as unconscionable." *[* This lack of mutuality supports a finding of substantive unconscionability.

91   **(ii)** *Costs of Arbitration and Fee-Sharing*

92   Bragg claims that the cost of an individual arbitration under the TOS is likely to exceed $13,540, with an estimated initiation cost of at least $10,000. *[...]* He has also submitted a Declaration of Personal Financial Information stating that such arbitration would be cost-prohibitive for him (doc. no. 41). Linden disputes Bragg's calculations, estimating that the costs associated with arbitration *[...]* would total $7,500, with Bragg advancing $3,750 at the outset of arbitration. *S[...]*

93   At oral argument, the parties were unable to resolve this dispute, even after referencing numerous provisions and charts contained within the ICC Rules. *[...]* The Court's own calculations, however, indicate that, the costs of arbitration, excluding arbitration, would total

$17,250. With a recovery of $75,000,[19] the ICC's administrative expenses would be $2,625 (3.5% of $75,000). [...] In addition, arbitrator's fees could be set between 2.0% ($1,500) and 11.0% ($8,250) of the amount at issue per arbitrator. *Id.* If the ICC set the arbitrator's fees at the midpoint of this range, the arbitrator's fees would be $4,875 per arbitrator. *Id.* Here, however, the TOS requires that three arbitrators be used to resolve a dispute. TOS ¶ 13. Thus, the Court estimates the costs of arbitration with the ICC to be $17,250 ($2,625 + (3 × $4,875)), although they could reach as high as $27,375 ($2,625 + (3 × $8,250)).[20]

94   These costs might not, on their own, support a finding of substantive unconscionability. However, the ICC Rules also provide that the costs and fees must be shared among the parties, and an estimate of those costs and fees must be advanced at the initiation of arbitration. [...] California law has often been applied to declare arbitration fee-sharing schemes unenforceable. *See Ting v. AT&T,* 319 F.3d 1126, 1151 (9th Cir.2003). Such schemes are unconscionable where they "impose[] on some consumers costs greater than those a complainant would bear if he or she would file the same complaint in court." *Id.* In *Ting,* for example, the Ninth Circuit held that a scheme requiring AT & T customers to split arbitration costs with AT & T rendered an arbitration provision unconscionable. *Id.See also Circuit City Stores v. Adams,* 279 F.3d 889, 894 (9th Cir.2002) ("This fee allocation scheme alone would render an arbitration agreement unenforceable."); *Armendariz,* 99 Cal.Rptr.2d 745, 6 P.3d at 687 ("[T]he arbitration process cannot generally require the employee to bear any *type* of expenses that the employee would not be required to bear if he or she were free to bring the action in court.") [...]

95   Here, even taking Defendants characterization of the fees to be accurate, the total estimate of costs and fees would be $7,500, which would result in Bragg having to advance $3,750 at the outset of arbitration. [...] The court's own estimates place the amount that Bragg would likely have to advance at $8,625, but they could reach as high as $13,687.50. Any of these figures are significantly greater than the costs that Bragg bears by [...] filing his action in a state or federal court. Accordingly, the arbitration costs and fee-splitting scheme together also support a finding of unconscionability.

96   **(iii)** *Venue*

97   The TOS also require that any arbitration take place in San Francisco, California. [...] In *Comb,* the Court found that a similar forum selection clause supported a finding of substantive unconscionability, because the place in which arbitration was to occur was unreasonable, taking into account "the respective circumstances of the parties." [...] As in *Comb,* the record in this case shows that Linden serves millions of customers across the United States and that the average transaction through or with Second Life involves a relatively small amount. [...] In such circumstances, California law dictates that it is not "reasonable for individual consumers from throughout the country to travel to one locale to arbitrate claims involving such minimal sums." *Id.* Indeed, "[l]imiting venue to [Linden's] backyard appears to be yet one more means by which the arbitration clause serves to shield [Linden] from liability instead of providing a neutral forum in which to arbitrate disputes." *Id.*

98   **(iv)** *Confidentiality Provision*

99   Arbitration before the ICC, pursuant to the TOS, must be kept confidential pursuant to the ICC rules. [...] Applying California law to an arbitration provision, the Ninth Circuit held that such confidentiality supports a finding that an arbitration clause was substantively unconscionable. [...] The Ninth Circuit reasoned that if the company succeeds in imposing a gag order on arbitration proceedings, it places itself in a far superior legal posture by ensuring that none of its potential opponents have access to precedent while, at the same time, the company accumulates a wealth of knowledge on how to negotiate the terms of its own unilaterally crafted contract. [...] The unavailability of arbitral decisions could also prevent potential plaintiffs from obtaining the information needed to build a case of intentional misconduct against a company. [...]

100 This does not mean that confidentiality provisions in an arbitration scheme or agreement are, in every instance, per se unconscionable under California law. [...] Here, however, taken together with other provisions of the TOS, the confidentiality provision gives rise for concern of the conscionability of the arbitration clause. [...]

101   Thus, the confidentiality of the arbitration scheme that Linden imposed also supports a finding that the arbitration clause is unconscionable.

102   **(v)** *Legitimate Business Realities*

103   Under California law, a contract may provide a "margin of safety" that provides the party with superior bargaining strength protection for which it has a legitimate commercial need. "However, unless the `business realities' that create the special need for such an advantage are explained in the contract itself, . . . it must be factually established." *[...]* When a contract *[...]* is alleged to be unconscionable, "the parties shall be afforded a reasonable opportunity to present evidence as to its commercial setting, purpose, and effect to aid the court in making the determination." *[...]* The statutory scheme reflects "legislative recognition that a claim of unconscionability often cannot be determined merely by examining the, face of the contract, but will require inquiry into its setting, purpose, and effect." *[...]*

104   Here, neither in its briefing nor at oral argument did Linden even attempt to offer evidence that "business realities" justify the one-sidedness of the dispute resolution scheme that the TOS constructs in Linden's favor.

105   **(c)** *Conclusion*

106   When a dispute arises in Second Life, Linden is not obligated to initiate arbitration. Rather, the TOS expressly allow Linden, at its "sole discretion" and based on mere "suspicion," to unilaterally freeze a participant's account, refuse access to the virtual and real currency contained within that account, and then confiscate the participant's virtual property and real estate. A participant wishing to resolve any dispute, on the other hand, after having forfeited its interest in Second Life, must then initiate arbitration in Linden's place of business. To initiate arbitration involves advancing fees to pay for no less than three arbitrators at a cost far greater than would be involved in litigating in the state or federal court system. Moreover, under these circumstances, the confidentiality of the proceedings helps ensure that arbitration itself is fought on an uneven field by ensuring that, through the accumulation of experience, Linden becomes an expert in litigating the terms of the TOS, while plaintiffs remain novices without the benefit of learning from past precedent.

107   Taken together, the lack of mutuality, the costs of arbitration, the forum selection clause, and the confidentiality provision that Linden unilaterally imposes through the TOS demonstrate that the arbitration clause is not designed to provide Second Life participants an effective means of resolving disputes with Linden. Rather, it is a one-sided means which tilts unfairly, in almost all situations, in Linden's favor. As in *Comb,* through the use of an arbitration clause, Linden "appears to be attempting to insulate itself contractually from any meaningful challenge to its alleged practices." *[...]*

108   The Court notes that the concerns with procedural unconscionability are somewhat mitigated by Bragg's being an experienced attorney. However, "because the unilateral modification clause renders the arbitration provision severely one-sided in the substantive dimension, even moderate procedural unconscionability renders the arbitration agreement unenforceable." *[...] [...]*

109   Finding that the arbitration clause is procedurally and substantively unconscionable, the Court will refuse to enforce it.[21]

110   [...]

115   **IV. CONCLUSION**

116   [...] The Court will also deny Defendants' motion to compel [...] arbitration. [...]

123   [5] Although participants purchase virtual property using the virtual currency of "lindens," lindens themselves are bought and sold for real U.S. dollars. Linden maintains a currency exchange that sets an exchange rate between lindens and U.S. dollars. Third parties, including ebay.com, also provide additional currency exchanges.

126   [...]

127   [7] Linden taxes virtual land. In fact, according to Bragg, by June 2004, Linden reported that its "real estate tax revenue on land sold to the participants exceeded the amount the company was generating in subscriptions." [...]

136   [15] This challenge must be determined by the Court, not an arbitrator. [...] Bragg does not challenge enforceability by claiming that a provision of the arbitration agreement will deny him a statutory right, a question of interpretation of the arbitration agreement which an arbitrator is "well situated to answer." I[...] Rather, Bragg claims that the arbitration agreement itself would effectively deny him access to an arbitrator, because the costs would be prohibitively expensive, a question that is more appropriately reserved for the Court to answer. [...]

137   [...]

139   [18] The Court notes that the Third Circuit has found that "parties to an arbitration agreement need not equally bind each other with respect to an arbitration agreement if they have provided each other with consideration beyond the promise to arbitrate." [...] however, the Third Circuit was applying Pennsylvania law, not California law. [...] In any event, Pennsylvania courts have criticized this aspect of *Green Tree*'s holding. [...]

Class 26: 9.3 <u>OIL Casebook: Contract Preemption</u>

17 U.S.C. § 301.—Preemption with respect to other laws

September 14, 2014 by mrisch

1   (a) On and after January 1, 1978, all legal or equitable rights that are equivalent to any of the exclusive rights within the general scope of copyright as specified by section 106 in works of authorship that are fixed in a tangible medium of expression and come within the subject matter of copyright as specified by sections 102 and 103, whether created before or after that date and whether published or unpublished, are governed exclusively by this title. Thereafter, no person is entitled to any such right or equivalent right in any such work under the common law or statutes of any State.

2   [...]

ProCD, Inc. v. Zeidenberg -preemption note

September 13, 2014 by mrisch

recall that ProCD involved a shrinkwrap license relating to phonebook software

1   86 F.3d 1447 (1996)

2   **ProCD, INCORPORATED** [...]

                            v.

              Matthew ZEIDENBERG [...]

4   United States Court of Appeals, Seventh Circuit.

5   [...]

                   Decided June 20, 1996.

6   [...]

13   **EASTERBROOK, Circuit Judge.**

14   Must buyers of computer software obey the terms of shrinkwrap licenses? [...]

15   **I**

16   ProCD, the plaintiff, has compiled information from more than 3,000 telephone directories into a computer database. [...]

20   Instead of tinkering with the product and letting users sort themselves — for example, furnishing current data at a high price that would be attractive only to commercial customers, and two-year-old data at a low price — ProCD turned to the institution of contract. Every box containing its consumer product declares that the software comes with restrictions stated in an enclosed license. This license, which is encoded on the CD-ROM disks as well as printed in the manual, and which appears on a user's screen every time the software runs, limits use of the application program and listings to non-commercial purposes.

21   [...]

32   **III**

32   The district court held that, even if Wisconsin treats shrinkwrap licenses as contracts, § 301(a) of the Copyright Act, 17 U.S.C. § 301(a), prevents their enforcement. [...] The relevant part of § 301(a) preempts any "legal or equitable rights [under state law] that are equivalent to any of the exclusive rights within the general scope of copyright as specified by section 106 in works of authorship that are fixed in a tangible medium of expression and come within the subject matter of copyright as specified by sections 102 and 103". ProCD's software and data are "fixed in a tangible medium of expression", and the district judge held that they are "within the subject matter of copyright". The latter conclusion is plainly right for the copyrighted application program, and the judge thought that the data likewise are

"within the subject matter of copyright" even if, after Feist, they are not sufficiently original to be copyrighted. [...] One function of §
301(a) is to prevent states from giving special protection to works of authorship that Congress has decided should be in the public
domain, which it can accomplish only if "subject matter of copyright" includes all works of a *type* covered by sections 102 and 103, even
if federal law does not afford protection to them. [...]

33   But are rights created by contract "equivalent to any of the exclusive rights within the general scope of copyright"? Three courts of
       appeals have answered "no." [...] Rights "equivalent to any of the exclusive rights within the general scope of copyright" are rights
       established *by law* — rights that restrict the options of persons who are strangers to the author. Copyright law forbids duplication, public
       performance, and so on, unless the person wishing to copy or perform the work gets permission; silence means a ban on copying. A
       copyright is a right against the world. Contracts, by contrast, generally affect only their parties; strangers may do as they please, so
       contracts do not create "exclusive rights." Someone who found a copy of SelectPhone (trademark) on the street would not be affected
       by the shrinkwrap license — though the federal copyright laws of their own force would limit the finder's ability to copy or transmit the
       application program.

34   [...] Think, too, about everyday transactions in intellectual property. A customer visits a video store and rents a copy of *Night of the Lepus*.
       The customer's contract with the store limits use of the tape to home viewing and requires its return in two days. May the customer keep
       the tape, on the ground that § 301(a) makes the promise unenforceable?

35   A law student uses the LEXIS database, containing public-domain documents, under a contract limiting the results to educational
       endeavors; may the student resell his access to this database to a law firm from which LEXIS seeks to collect a much higher hourly rate?
       Suppose ProCD hires a firm to scour the nation for telephone directories, promising to pay $100 for each that ProCD does not already
       have. The firm locates 100 new directories, which it sends to ProCD with an invoice for $10,000. ProCD incorporates the directories into
       its database; does it have to pay the bill? Surely yes; *Aronson v. Quick Point Pencil Co.* [...] holds that promises to pay for intellectual
       property may be enforced even though federal law (in *Aronson*, the patent law) offers no protection against third-party uses of that
       property. [...] But these illustrations are what our case is about. ProCD offers software and data for two prices: one for personal use, a
       higher price for commercial use. Zeidenberg wants to use the data without paying the seller's price; if the law student and Quick Point
       Pencil Co. could not do that, neither can Zeidenberg.

36   Although Congress possesses power to preempt even the enforcement of contracts about intellectual property — or railroads, [...] —
       courts usually read preemption clauses to leave private contracts unaffected. [...] Just as § 301(a) does not itself interfere with private
       transactions in intellectual property, so it does not prevent states from respecting those transactions. Like the Supreme Court in *Wolens*,
       we think it prudent to refrain from adopting a rule that anything with the label "contract" is necessarily outside the preemption clause: the
       variations and possibilities are too numerous to foresee. *National Car Rental* likewise recognizes the possibility that some applications of
       the law of contract could interfere with the attainment of national objectives and therefore come within the domain of § 301(a). But
       general enforcement of shrinkwrap licenses of the kind before us does not create such interference.

37   *Aronson* emphasized that enforcement of the contract between Aronson and Quick Point Pencil Company would not withdraw any
       information from the public domain. That is equally true of the contract between ProCD and Zeidenberg. Everyone remains free to copy
       and disseminate all 3,000 telephone books that have been incorporated into ProCD's database. Anyone can add SIC codes and zip
       codes. ProCD's rivals have done so. Enforcement of the shrinkwrap license may even make information more readily available, by
       reducing the price ProCD charges to consumer buyers. To the extent licenses facilitate distribution of object code while concealing the
       source code (the point of a clause forbidding disassembly), they serve the same procompetitive functions as does the law of trade
       secrets. R[...] Licenses may have other benefits for consumers: many licenses permit users to make extra copies, to use the software on
       multiple computers, even to incorporate the software into the user's products. But whether a particular license is generous or restrictive,
       a simple two-party contract is not "equivalent to any of the exclusive rights within the general scope of copyright" and therefore may be
       enforced.

38   REVERSED AND REMANDED.

Bowers v. Baystate Technologies, Inc.

September 14, 2014 by mrisch

1   320 F.3d 1317 (2003)

2   **Harold L. BOWERS [...]**

v.

BAYSTATE TECHNOLOGIES, INC. [...]

4   United States Court of Appeals, Federal Circuit.

5   January 29, 2003.

6   [...]

11   **RADER, Circuit Judge.**

12   Following trial in the United States District Court for the District of Massachusetts, the jury returned a verdict for Harold L. Bowers on his patent infringement, copyright infringement, and breach of contract claims, while rejecting Baystate Technologies, Inc.'s claim for patent invalidity. The jury awarded Mr. Bowers separate damages on each of his claims. The district court, however, omitted the copyright damages as duplicative of the contract damages. Because substantial evidence supports the jury's verdict that Baystate breached the contract, this court affirms that verdict. [...]

13   **I.**

14   Harold L. Bowers (Bowers) created a template to improve computer aided design (CAD) software, such as the CADKEY [...] tool of Cadkey, Inc. Mr. Bowers filed a patent application for his template on February 27, 1989. On June 12, 1990, United States Patent No. 4,933,514 ('514 patent) issued from that application.

15   [...]

17   Mr. Bowers commercialized the '514 patent template as Cadjet for use with CADKEY.

18   [...]

19   Since the early 1980s, CAD programs have assisted engineers to draft and design on a computer screen. George W. Ford, III, a development engineer and supervisor of quality control at Heinemann Electric, envisioned a way to improve Mr. Bowers' template and CAD software. Specifically, Mr. Ford designed Geodraft, a DOS-based add-on program to operate with CAD. Geodraft allows an engineer to insert technical tolerances for features of the computer-generated design. These [1322] tolerances comply with the geometric dimensioning and tolerancing (GD & T) requirements in ANSI Y14.5M, a standard promulgated by the American National Standards Institute (ANSI). Geodraft works in conjunction with the CAD system to ensure that the design complies with ANSI Y14.5M-a task previously error-prone due to the standard's complexity. Geodraft automatically includes symbols specifying the correct GD & T

parameters. Mr. Ford obtained a registered copyright, TX 2-939-672, covering Geodraft.

20   In 1989, Mr. Ford offered Mr. Bowers an exclusive license to his Geodraft software. Mr. Bowers accepted that offer and bundled Geodraft and Cadjet together as the Designer's Toolkit. Mr. Bowers sold the Designer's Toolkit with a shrink-wrap license that, *inter alia,* prohibited any reverse engineering.

21   In 1989, Baystate also developed and marketed other tools for CADKEY. One of those tools, Draft-Pak version 1 and 2, featured a template and GD & T software. In 1988 and 1989, Mr. Bowers offered to establish a formal relationship with Baystate, including bundling his template with Draft-Pak. Baystate rejected that offer, however, telling Mr. Bowers that it believed it had "the in-house capability to develop the type of products you have proposed."

22   In 1990, Mr. Bowers released Designer's Toolkit. By January 1991, Baystate had obtained copies of that product. Three months later, Baystate introduced the substantially revised Draft-Pak version 3, incorporating many of the features of Designer's Toolkit. Although Draft-Pak version 3 operated in the DOS environment, Baystate later upgraded it to operate with Microsoft Windows ®.

23   Baystate's introduction of Draft-Pak version 3 induced intense price competition between Mr. Bowers and Baystate. To gain market share over Baystate, Mr. Bowers negotiated with Cadkey, Inc., to provide the Designer's Toolkit free with CADKEY. Mr. Bowers planned to recoup his profits by selling software upgrades to the users that he hoped to lure to his products. Following pressure from Baystate, however, Cadkey, Inc., repudiated its distribution agreement with Mr. Bowers. Eventually, Baystate purchased Cadkey, Inc., and eliminated Mr. Bowers from the CADKEY network — effectively preventing him from developing and marketing the Designer's Toolkit for that program.

24   [...] Mr. Bowers filed counterclaims for copyright infringement, patent infringement, and breach of contract.

25   Following trial, the jury found for Mr. Bowers and awarded $1,948,869 for copyright infringement, $3,831,025 for breach of contract [...] The district court, however, set aside the copyright damages as duplicative of the contract damages and entered judgment [...]

26   **II.**

27   [...]

30   **A.**

31   Baystate contends that the Copyright Act preempts the prohibition of reverse engineering embodied in Mr. Bowers' shrink-wrap license agreements. Swayed by this argument, the district court considered Mr. Bowers' contract and copyright claims coextensive. The district court instructed the jury that "reverse engineering violates the license agreement only if Baystate's product that resulted from reverse engineering infringes Bowers' copyright because it copies protectable expression." Mr. Bowers lodged a timely objection to this instruction. This court holds that, under First Circuit law, the Copyright Act does not preempt or narrow the scope of Mr. Bowers' contract claim.

32   Courts respect freedom of contract and do not lightly set aside freely-entered agreements. [...] Nevertheless, at times, federal regulation may [[...]] preempt private contract. [...] The Copyright Act provides that "all legal or equitable rights that are equivalent to any of the exclusive rights within the general scope of copyright ... are governed exclusively by this title." 17 U.S.C. § 301(a) (2000). The First Circuit does not interpret this language to require preemption as long as "a state cause of action requires an extra element, beyond mere copying, preparation of derivative works, performance, distribution or display." [...] Nevertheless, "[n]ot every `extra element' of a state law claim will establish a qualitative variance between the rights protected by federal copyright law and those protected by state law." [...

33   In *Data General,* Data General alleged that Grumman misappropriated its trade secret software. [...] Grumman obtained that software from Data General's customers and former employees who were bound by confidentiality agreements to refrain from disclosing the software. [...] In defense, Grumman argued that the Copyright Act preempted Data General's trade secret claim. I[...] The First Circuit held that the Copyright Act did not preempt the state law trade secret claim. [...] Beyond mere copying, that state law claim required proof of a trade secret and breach of a duty of confidentiality. *Id.* These additional elements of proof, according to the First Circuit, made the trade secret claim qualitatively different from a copyright claim. *Id.* In contrast, the First Circuit noted that claims might be preempted whose extra elements are illusory, being "mere label[s] attached to the same odious business conduct." [...] For example, the First Circuit observed that "a state law misappropriation claim will not escape preemption ... simply because a plaintiff must prove that copying was not only unauthorized but also commercially immoral." [...]

34   The First Circuit has not addressed expressly whether the Copyright Act preempts a state law contract claim that restrains copying. This court perceives, however, that *Data General's* rationale would lead to a judgment that the Copyright Act does not preempt the state contract action in this case. Indeed, most courts to examine this issue have found that the Copyright Act does not preempt contractual constraints on copyrighted articles. *See, e.g., ProCD, Inc. v. Zeidenberg* [...]

35   Consistent with *Data General's* reliance on a contract element, the court in *ProCD* reasoned: "A copyright is a right against the world. Contracts, by contrast, generally affect only their parties; strangers may do as they please, so contracts do not create `exclusive rights.'" *Id.* Indeed, the Supreme Court recently noted "[i]t goes without saying that a contract cannot bind a nonparty." [...] This court believes that the First Circuit would follow the reasoning of *ProCD* and the majority of other courts to consider this issue. This court, therefore, holds that the Copyright Act does not preempt Mr. Bowers' contract claims.

36   In making this determination, this court has left untouched the conclusions reached in *Atari Games v. Nintendo* regarding reverse engineering as a statutory fair use exception to copyright infringement. [...] In *Atari,* this court stated that, with respect to 17 U.S.C. § 107 (fair use section of the Copyright Act), "[t]he legislative history of section 107 suggests that courts should adapt the fair use exception to accommodate new technological innovations." [...] This court noted "[a] prohibition on all copying whatsoever would stifle the free flow of ideas without serving any legitimate interest of the copyright holder." *Id.* Therefore, this court held "reverse engineering object code to discern the unprotectable ideas in a computer program is a fair use." *Id.* Application of the First Circuit's view distinguishing a state law contract claim having additional elements of proof from a copyright claim does not alter the findings of *Atari.* Likewise, this claim distinction does not conflict with the expressly defined circumstances in which reverse engineering is not copyright infringement under 17 U.S.C. § 1201(f) (section of the Digital Millennium Copyright Act) [...]

37   Moreover, while the Fifth Circuit has held a state law prohibiting all copying of a computer program is preempted by the federal Copyright Act, *Vault Corp. v. Quaid Software, Ltd.* [...] no evidence suggests the First Circuit would extend this concept to include private contractual agreements supported by mutual assent and consideration. The First Circuit recognizes contractual waiver of affirmative defenses and statutory rights. [...] Thus, case law indicates the First Circuit would find that private parties [...] are free to contractually forego the limited ability to reverse engineer a software product under the exemptions of the Copyright Act. Of course, a party bound by such a contract may elect to efficiently breach the agreement in order to ascertain ideas in a computer program unprotected by copyright law. Under such circumstances, the breaching party must weigh the benefits of breach against the arguably de minimus damages arising from merely discerning non-protected code.

38   This court now considers the scope of Mr. Bowers' contract protection. [...]

39   In this case, the contract unambiguously prohibits "reverse engineering." That term means ordinarily "to study or analyze (a device, as a microchip for computers) in order to learn details of design, construction, and operation, perhaps to produce a copy or an improved version." [...] Thus, the contract in this case broadly prohibits any "reverse engineering" of the subject matter covered by the shrink-wrap

agreement.

40   The record amply supports the jury's finding of a breach of that agreement. [...]

41   The record indicates, for example, that Baystate scheduled two weeks in Draft-Pak's development schedule to analyze the Designer's Toolkit. Indeed, Robert Bean, Baystate's president and CEO, testified that Baystate generally analyzed competitor's products to duplicate their functionality.

42   The record also contains evidence of extensive and unusual similarities between Geodraft and the accused Draft-Pak — further evidence of reverse engineering. James Spencer, head of mechanical engineering and integration at the Space and Naval Warfare Systems Center, testified that he examined the relevant software programs to determine "the overall structure of the operating program" such as "how the operating programs actually executed the task of walking a user through [...] creating a [GD&T;] symbol." Mr. Spencer concluded: "In the process of taking the [ANSI Y14.5M] standard and breaking it down into its component parts to actually create a step-by-step process for a user using the software, both Geodraft and Draft-Pak [for DOS] use almost the identical process of breaking down that task into its individual pieces, and it's organized essentially identically." This evidence supports the jury's verdict of a contract breach based on reverse engineering.

43   Mr. Ford also testified that he had compared Geodraft and Draft-Pak. When asked to describe the Draft-Pak interface, Mr. Ford responded: "It looked like I was looking at my own program [i.e., Geodraft]." Both Mr. Spencer and Mr. Ford explained in detail similarities between Geodraft and the accused Draft-Pak. Those similarities included the interrelationships between program screens, the manner in which parameter selection causes program branching, and the manner in which the GD&T; symbols are drawn.

44   Both witnesses also testified that those similarities extended beyond structure and design to include many idiosyncratic design choices and inadvertent design flaws. For example, both Geodraft and Draft-Pak offer "straightness tolerance" menu choices of "flat" and "cylindric," unusual in view of the use by ANSI Y14.5M of the terms "linear" and "circular," respectively. As another example, neither program requires the user to provide "angularity tolerance" secondary datum to create a feature control frame — a technical oversight that causes creation of an incomplete symbol. In sum, Mr. Spencer testified: "Based on my summary analysis of how the programs function, their errors from the standard and their similar nomenclatures reflecting nonstandard items, I would say that the Draft-Pak [for DOS] is a derivative copy of a Geodraft product."

45   Mr. Ford and others also demonstrated to the jury the operation of Geodraft and both the DOS and Windows versions of the accused Draft-Pak. Those software demonstrations undoubtedly conveyed information to the jury that the paper record on appeal cannot easily replicate. This court, therefore, is especially reluctant to substitute its judgment for that of the jury on the sufficiency and interpretation of that evidence. In any event, the record fully supports the jury's verdict that Baystate breached its contract with Mr. Bowers.

46   Baystate does not contest the contract damages amount on appeal. Thus, this court sustains the district court's award of contract damages. Mr. Bowers, however, argues that the district court abused its discretion by dropping copyright damages from the combined damage award. To the contrary, this court perceives no abuse of discretion.

47   The shrink-wrap license agreement prohibited, *inter alia*, all reverse engineering of Mr. Bowers' software, protection encompassing but more extensive than copyright protection, which prohibits only certain copying. Mr. Bowers' copyright and contract claims both rest on Baystate's copying of Mr. Bowers' software. Following the district court's instructions, the jury considered and awarded damages on each separately. This was entirely appropriate. The law is clear that the jury may award separate damages for each claim, "leaving it to the judge to make appropriate adjustments to avoid double recovery." [...] In this case, the breach of contract damages arose from the same copying and included the same lost sales that form the basis for the copyright damages. The district court, therefore, did not abuse its discretion by omitting from the final damage award the duplicative copyright damages. Because this court affirms the district court's omission of the copyright damages, this court need not reach the merits of Mr. Bowers' copyright infringement claim.

48   [...]

51

88